ORIENTALISM: EARLY SOURCES

ORIENTALISM: EARLY SOURCES
Edited by Bryan S. Turner

VOLUME I: READINGS IN ORIENTALISM
Edited by Bryan S. Turner

VOLUME II: THE MOHAMMADAN DYNASTIES
Stanley Lane-Poole

VOLUME III: THE CALIPHATE
Sir William Muir

VOLUME IV: THE RELIGIOUS ORDERS OF ISLAM
Edward Sell

VOLUME V: MODERN EGYPT – PART 1
Evelyn Baring (Earl of Cromer)

VOLUME VI: MODERN EGYPT – PART 2
Evelyn Baring (Earl of Cromer)

VOLUME VII: THE ARAB KINGDOM AND ITS FALL
J. Wellhausen

VOLUME VIII: THE MYSTICS OF ISLAM
Reynold A. Nicholson

VOLUME IX: WHITHER ISLAM?
H.A.R. Gibb

VOLUME X: ISLAM AND MODERNISM IN EGYPT
Charles C. Adams

VOLUME XI: HISTORY OF THE ISLAMIC PEOPLES
Carl Brockelmann

VOLUME XII: THE SOCIAL STRUCTURE OF ISLAM
Reuben Levy

ORIENTALISM: EARLY SOURCES

Volume I

Readings in Orientalism

Edited and with an introduction
by Bryan S. Turner

London and New York

First published 2000
by Routledge
2 Park Square, Milton Park, Abingdon, Oxfordshire OX14 4RN

Simultaneously published in the USA and Canada
by Routledge
711 Third Avenue, New York, NY 10017

Routledge is an imprint of the Taylor & Francis Group

First issued in paperback 2011

Typeset in Times by The Florence Group, Stoodleigh, Devon

British Library Cataloguing in Publication Data
A catalogue record for this book is available from the British Library

Library of Congress Cataloging in Publication Data
A catalogue record for this book has been requested

ISBN 978-0-415-20899-4 (hbk)
ISBN 978-0-415-51064-6 (pbk)
ISBN 978-0-415-20898-7 (set)
ISBN 978-0-415-20899-8 (volume I)

Publisher's note

The publisher has gone to great lengths to ensure the quality of this reprint but points out that some imperfections in the original book may be apparent.

CONTENTS

ACKNOWLEDGEMENTS

The publishers would like to thank the following for permission to reprint their material:

Revue des Études Islamiques for permission to reprint Poliak, A.N., 'Les révoltes populaires en Égypte à l'époque des Mamelouks et leurs causes économiques', *Revue des Études Islamiques*, part 3, 1934, pp. 251–73; Poliak, A.N., 'Le caractère colonial de l'état Mamelouk dans ses rapports avec la Horde d'Or, *Revue des Études Islamiques*, 1935, vol. 22, pp. 231–48.

Islamic Culture for permission to reprint Lewis, B., 'An epistle on manual crafts', *Islamic Culture*, 1943, vol. 17, pp. 142–51.

Cambridge University Press for permission to reprint Ivanov, V., 'The organization of the Fatimid Propaganda', *Journal of the Royal Asiatic Society*, (Bombay Branch), 1939, vol. 15, pp. 1–35.

University of Calcutta for permission to reprint Wellhausen, J., *The Arab Kingdom and Its Fall*, 1927 (volume VI in this series).

Quelle & Meyer for permission to reprint Becker, C.H., *Das Erbe der Antike im Orient und Okzident*, 1931 (volume VIII in this series). Copyright 1964 by Quelle & Meyer Verlag, Heidelberg.

Victor Gollancz Ltd for permission to reprint Gibb, H.A.R., *Whither Islam? A Survey of Modern Movements in the Moslem World*, 1932 (volume IX in this series).

Oxford University Press for permission to reprint Adams, Charles C., *Islam and Modernism in Egypt*, 1933 (volume X in this series).

ACKNOWLEDGEMENTS

The publishers have made every effort to contact authors/copyright holders of works reprinted in ***Orientalism: Early Sources***. This has not been possible in every case, however, and we would welcome correspondence from those individuals/companies we have been unable to trace.

1

OUTLINE OF A THEORY OF ORIENTALISM

Bryan S. Turner

INTRODUCTION: ORIENTALISM AND OTHERNESS

While the modern discussion about western views of the Orient is a product of postwar global conflicts, the controversy about 'other cultures' can be traced back historically to the ancient encounter between the Abrahamic religions. The fundamental issue is that Islam, Christianity and Judaism are variations of a generic religion (of Abraham), but they have been differentiated in order for the West to be categorically distinguished from the East. In historical and cultural terms, the Abrahamic faiths cannot be neatly and definitely assigned to specific geographical locations and destinations, but for political reasons such a designation has to take place. These religions share the tradition of a high god, a sacred book, a religious teleology, and a lineage of charismatic prophets. While the modern equation of Christendom and Europe may be unproblematic, Christianity is a religion whose theological roots are in the prophetic tradition of Jewish radical monotheism and whose geographical origins are Near Eastern. In this respect, Orientalism is a family feud and hence the otherness of the other religions is both inevitable and curious. The East appears in western imagination as the forbidden Other, which is simultaneously repulsive, seductive and attractive. Like the veil, the East is both secluded and inviting. From the eighteenth century, the Orient has existed within a literary and visual tradition which is both romantic and fantastic.

In this study of Orientalism, I shall restrict my attention to one section of the debate, namely western attitudes towards Islam, the Arabic homelands and the Middle East. The larger and more comprehensive problem of Orientalism with respect to Asia and its complex cultures lies outside the scope of this study. The renaissance of European interest in Asia has been studied comprehensively by Raymond Schwab (1950). More specifically, my attention is drawn to the issue of relationships between Islam and Christian cultures in the Middle East, especially since the seventeenth century. As I shall indicate shortly, Christian–Muslim relationships have become emotionally charged in the late twentieth century, because a secular process of decolonisation, the collapse of communism and the spread of fundamentalist values have sharpened the political competition between Europe and the Middle East. Inevitably these secular and political changes have augmented the ancient tensions between Christianity and Islam.

In this collection, I am concerned to show that these contemporary tensions have a long history beginning with the foundation of Islam as a 'household of faith' in the seventh century (Christian Era), that these relationships are complex and diverse rather than simple and narrow, and that the religious connections between Islam and Christianity are overshadowed by inter-regional conflicts over economic and political resources. I am also concerned in the conclusion of this discussion to consider, somewhat along the lines suggested by William Montgomery Watt (1991) in *Muslim–Christian Encounters*, the nature of religious ecumenicalism as a model for secular cosmopolitanism and the opportunities for inter-civilisational co-operation and understanding. I am less interested in the political economy of inter-religious conflict and co-operation, and more concerned to understand the texts which shaped Orientalist discourse itself. The aim here is to grasp the principal components of Orientalism as a special type of ideology through an exploration of the writings of a number of influential authors. The textual qualities of this oriental exchange have a special prominence in this overview. Finally, this introductory essay may be regarded as an extended discussion of the literary and cultural theories of Edward W. Said, whose intellectual contribution over the last twenty years has shaped the current debate. Said's analysis of Orientalism has touched upon a range of issues which are fundamental to the possibility of cross-cultural understanding and this chapter can be read as an attempt to answer the following question:

> The net positive effect of such encroachments [on western hegemony] is that for the first time Orientalism is being

> asked critically to examine not only the truth or falseness of its methodology and its investigative results, but its relationship both to the culture from which it is derived and the historical period in which its main ideas were advanced. And this leads to the question: How capable is Orientalism of asking itself these critical questions, given the constitution of Orientalism as a field with a recognizable domain, traditions and praxis?
>
> (Said, 1984a: 274–5)

PRINCIPAL ELEMENTS OF THE ORIENTALIST PARADIGM

The recent philosophical and literary preoccupation with texts, textuality and intertextuality is a testimony to the contemporary assumption that any adequate knowledge of social reality must take into account the field of power which constitutes and makes possible such knowledge (Said, 1984a). We have to understand the self-referencing of texts as an interplay of power, and thus all hermeneutics are an effect of power relations and power struggles. This principle of power/knowledge, which was central to the philosophy of Michel Foucault (1972), is clearly illustrated by the history of western understanding of the Orient. While the modern debate about western views of the Orient was (re-)established by Said's *Orientalism* (1978), the controversy about the character of other cultures can be traced back through the European encounter between Christianity and its antagonists. Said's controversial paradigm established the notion of 'Orientalism' as a distinctive and pervasive ideology about Islamic Otherness. This critique has laid the foundation for an extensive inquiry into the problematic relationships between political power, sexual desire, religious identity and intellectual dominance (McClintock, 1995; Young, 1995).

Said's thesis and its criticisms are well known and I shall merely summarise the major components (Turner, 1994). 'The Orient' is constructed in western ideology as a permanent and enduring object of knowledge in opposition to the Occident as its negative and alternative pole. Orientalism creates a stationary East through the essentialisation of the divergent cultural phenomena of oriental societies into a unitary, integrated and coherent object for the scrutiny of western literary and scientific discourse. The Orient is reiterated, represented and reproduced over time and space by these ideological forces; the Orient is both called up and called to account as an object of western scholarship. While the Occident is seen to develop through history in terms of a series of modernising, violent revolutions, the unhistorical and stationary Orient exists outside of history. Karl Marx in the so-called 'Asiatic mode of production' contended that India and China had no real history, that is no historical revolutions which brought about significant changes in the social order, for example through the introduction of private property (Turner, 1978). The Orient is, in Said's perspective, conceptualised through Michel Foucault's analysis of the necessary combination of power/knowledge, and the lineage of oriental concepts is mapped out by the historical formation of power between Occident and Orient, namely through the history of imperialism and colonial expansion. For Foucault, the conventional separation of power and knowledge in liberal theory obscures the fact that the Orient is an effect of imperial powers, and cannot be known independently of that knowledge/power combination.

The Foucauldian argument is that discursive formations are constructed around both positive and negative contrasts or dichotomies. These polarities constitute knowledge of an object; for example, we understand Islam through a series of contrasts. As a result, Orientalism produces a balance sheet or an audit of negativities between West and East in which the Orient is defined by a series of lacunae: the absence of revolutionary change, the missing middle class, the erosion or denial of active citizenship, the failure of participatory democracy, the absence of autonomous cities, the lack of ascetic disciplines and the limitations of instrumental rationality as the critical culture of natural science, industrial capitalism and rational government. In the social sciences, this negative accounting sheet found its classical expression in the concept of 'oriental despotism', Karl Marx's Asiatic mode of production and Max Weber's analysis of patrimonialism (Turner, 1996). The absolutist tradition of oriental polities placed decisive limitations on the capacity for such systems to adapt and evolve. Weber sought the cultural origins of capitalism in asceticism, means–ends rationalism and secularism in *The Protestant Ethic and the Spirit of Capitalism* (Weber, 1930). The Orient lacked the dynamic impact of autonomous cities, rational law, work discipline and rational administration. Weber's sociology then was organised around a comparative project that involved the analysis of the economic ethics of religious traditions and their impact on the social capacity for transformation. The questions and assumptions behind classical Orientalism – the nature of oriental despotism, the rise and fall of Arab dynasties, the history of the Assassins, the mystical nature of Sufism, the traditional constraints on Islamic philosophy, the conservative force of Islamic law and the conservative nature of Islamic guilds – have often been preserved and continued in contemporary Orientalism, but within a new vocabulary and with less strident values. These sociological questions have nevertheless remained fundamental to Orientalism: does Islam have an elective affinity with authoritarian political regimes? Has the egalitarian message of the Qur'ān failed to prevent the existence of hierarchical social orders? Does the *shari'a* or Holy Law in fact regulate, patterns of banking, investment and exchange?

In the geography of the imagination, the Orient is that part of the intellectual map by which the West has historically and negatively oriented itself. The noun 'Orient', which defines a geographical arena is also a verb 'to orient', that is Orientalism offers a political and psychological positioning which constitutes social identities in a condition of antagonism. Orientalism as a textual practice divided the world into friends and strangers whose endless struggles define 'the political'. The Orient has been the negative Other which defines the edges and boundaries of the civilised world, and thus patrols the transgressive possibilities of culture. The Occident was part of the ethical cartography of the West; it celebrated the Puritan consciousness in terms of a set of principles about moral responsibility and probity.

It is this geographic Otherness which at the same time defines our subjective inwardness; our being is articulated in a terrain of negativities which are oppositional and, according to Said, permanent and ineluctable. In *Culture and Imperialism*, Said (1993) claims that the modern identity of the West has been defined by its colonies, but these colonies are not merely physical places in a political geography: they also organise the boundaries and borders of our consciousness by defining our attitudes towards, for example, sexuality and race. Within the paradigm of the Protestant Ethic thesis, the aboriginal is defined as somebody who is not only poor and traditional, but licentious and lazy. Colonial policy and ideology produced a wide range of national types based on the myth of the lazy native (Alatas, 1977). For example, in the evolution of Orientalism, the plays of Shakespeare present a valuable insight into the characterology of such oriental figures. *The*

Tempest, written in 1611, was based on naval records describing shipwrecks from the period. Caliban, who is probably modelled on early encounters with the indigenous peoples of the West Indies and North America, is treacherous and dangerous, contrasting as a negative mirror image of Miranda, who is perfect, naive and beautiful. Caliban's sexual desire for 'admir'd Miranda' forms part of the moral struggle of the play under the careful scrutiny of the island's patriarch. It is Prospero's rational interventions which master both storms and characters (Tillyard, 1958). It is in this respect the foundation of the literary analysis of modern colonialism, because the magical island offered Shakespeare an ideal context for representing the struggles between European reason and its colonial subjects as a confrontation between magic and anarchy on the one hand and reason and statecraft on the other. It was Prospero's neglect of statesmanship which resulted in his original downfall and his careful management of the sexuality of his island subjects which eventually restores peace and good order to the land. While Prospero's original neglect of his princely responsibilities resulted in political despotism, his island kingdom is a model of patriarchal control.

THE CRITICAL DEBATE WITH EDWARD W. SAID

Having briefly described the principal features of Said's argument in *Orientalism*, I can now indicate some of the major criticisms of Said's perspective (Turner, 1994). Although Said recognised important differences between French and English Orientalism (Said, 1984a: 9), he nevertheless exaggerates the degree of coherence in the western academic discourse on Islam and he also neglects the range of heterogeneous views which characterised different disciplines within the Orientalist sciences. In the twentieth century, it is difficult to classify neatly and unambiguously such diverse figures as Gustave von Grunebaum, Louis Massignon, Wilfred Cantwell Smith, Maxime Rodinson, Montgomery Watt and Marshall G.S. Hodgson in Said's paradigm as occupying the same location within the Orientalist field. In any case, Said concentrates primarily on literary figures and not on historians and social scientists. Furthermore, Said's analysis is primarily a history of French Orientalism and his approach is overtly dependent on Schwab's monumental *La Renaissance orientale* of 1950 (Said, 1984a). French Orientalism dominated European perspectives on the Orient, mainly as a consequence of the influence of Silvestre de Sacy (1755–1838), who was called by his disciples 'the patriarch of the orientalists'. Students of Sacy filled the chairs of oriental languages in universities throughout Europe and guaranteed the continuity of French Orientalist studies. Sacy and his students prepared the way for the New Philology that dominated intellectual developments in nineteenth-century Europe. While philological studies laid the basis for humanities research in France with Renan (1823–92), in Denmark with Rask (1787–1832) and in Germany with Bopp (1791–1867), in England philology was marginalised. With the exception of Edward William Lane's *The Manners and Customs of the Modern Egyptians* (1836) the Orient surfaced principally in English fictional writing rather than in mainstream scientific publications. By contrast, French Orientalism, especially in the figures of Ernest Renan and Louis Massignon (1883–1962), was central to French culture as such, precisely because the French elite, unlike the British, assumed both a mission and a responsibility for Islamic culture (Said, 1984a: 268–89).

The western image of the Orient has not been invariably negative. In the seventeenth and early eighteenth centuries, authors in order to protect themselves from religious prosecution felt obliged to condemn the Prophet and to reject Islam. In the nineteenth century, Islam was no longer seen as a threat, and western attitudes became more complex. Employing the Orient as a mirror of the Occident, many radical writers have often used either 'Asia' or 'Islam' as a device to attack or to question western culture. Both Nietzsche and Foucault, who are obviously crucial in Said's own theoretical evolution, looked towards Islam as means of critically attacking aspects of western culture of which they disapproved. Nietzsche's attitude may itself be Orientalist, but nevertheless he praised Islam in *The Anti-Christ* as a strong heroic or manly religion in contrast to Christianity which he treated as a form of sickness and weakness. Islam is 'noble' because it 'owed its origins to manly instincts, because it said Yes to life' (Nietzsche, 1968: 183). He argued that 'In Christianity neither morality nor religion come into contact with reality at any point' (Nietzsche, 1968: 125). All of its main theological concepts are imaginary. By contrast, Nietzsche praised Buddhism for its realism, its philosophical objectivity and rationalism; Buddhism had already dispensed with the concept of God long before Christianity appeared on the historical horizon. Nietzsche was also influenced by the German oriental renaissance in his composition of *Thus Spake Zarathustra* and in his later life became indebted to Paul Deussen's research on the Vedanta system, which formed the basis of his concept of the deification of the critical philosopher.

Nietzsche's studies in comparative religions are ironic comments on the problems of religious truth in an epoch of relativism and perspectivism. Nietzsche's comparative critique of religion as sickness provided a foundational ethic for the analysis of the moral value of modern cultures. The German sociologist Max Weber was decisively influenced by Nietzsche, especially in his comparative sociology of religion. In Weber's sociological studies, this Nietzschean critique was re-directed towards an analysis of the religious bases of utilitarian economics (Stauth and Turner, 1988). In a similar fashion, Foucault, in his journalistic writing on Iran in *Corriere della Sera*, treated the Iranian revolution as a significant 'spiritual revolution'. The Iranian revolution provided Foucault with an occasion to express his emotional commitment to the idea of a spiritual revolution as a way of life, which contrasted with the mundane and routine reality of the everyday world. The religious revolution was a triumph of values over the profane world of materialist activity.

If Orientalism expresses a particular combination of power and knowledge, then it must vary and change over time and between different national configurations and traditions. While there is good reason to believe that classical Orientalism created 'Islam' as a changeless essence, oriental discourse itself changes over time. In the early seventeenth century, Muslim culture ('the Turk') was threatening and dominant, because the Ottoman Empire exercised extensive commercial and military control over the Mediterranean. These attitudes changed profoundly with the growth of European power through the eighteenth and nineteenth centuries. One can distinguish between classical Orientalism that was dominant in academic circles until the 1930s, and weaker, less strident and more uncertain forms of Orientalism since 1945. It is important to recognise that there have been significant changes in Orientalism in the second half of the century which reflect changes in state relations with globalisation, the changing status of intellectuals in modern society and political changes following the collapse of communism. In short, globalisation has brought about a sense of confusion in the world map, a sense of confusion which has produced a degree of (dis)orientation in contemporary scholarship.

A series of events have challenged classical Orientalism, resulting in a more reflexive and less strident view of cultural differences. Political globalisation and the limited erosion of the constitutional sovereignty of nation states have disrupted the old Westphalian pattern of separate and autonomous states. Economic globalisation has created rapid and voluminous flows of labour, goods and services. Of course, it is important not to exaggerate these global processes. With the increasing dominance of transnational corporations, there are newly emergent patterns of politics and cultural structures between states. There has been, alongside these changes in the international system, a period of decolonisation which started shortly after the Second World War. Classical Orientalism was the confident expression of a dominant mood of imperialism. Decolonisation and the collapse of an English literary canon have produced a weaker and more uncertain pattern of Orientalist assumptions. However, it is important to recognise that despite the growth of a borderless world, there are still strong patterns of economic dominance. In this context, military imperialism has been replaced by more covert and indirect structures of economic colonialism (Miyoshi, 1996).

Said's perspective on Orientalism has been dominated, in particular, by his concern for the relationships between French culture, North Africa and the Middle East. Within a broader context, we also need to consider the growing power of many Asian economies (regardless of the specific economic difficulties of 1998). For example, Said's theory of what one might call 'one-way Orientalism' neglected the importance of Japanese economic power in the postwar period. With the growth of the Asian Tiger Economies, the notion of the lazy native could not be easily sustained. In addition, Said's thesis understates the strength of racial images which have been generated against western intrusion. Orientalism is in fact relational and dialogic. The issue of 'the yellow cab women' and general dislike of white foreigners or *Gaijin* give a clear expression of Japanese ambiguity towards contact with the outside world (Kelsky, 1996). Yellow cab women, in the sexual imaginary of racial stereotypes against male outsiders, are defined as rich, sexually aggressive women who travel to exotic locations in search of sexual conquests. They challenge the image of the Japanese woman in *Madame Butterfly*. These 'yellow' women can, like the Yellow Taxi Cab, be ridden at any time. In this discourse good *Gaijin* (white men) are often compared with cruel Japanese men. Japan can be taken as an illustration of what we might call 'reverse orientalism'. International racial stereotypes force us to consider a dialogue of Oriental positions that are mutually negative.

Said's original theory did not consider the responses to these colonial changes, namely the growth of fundamentalism in many of the 'world religions' as a defensive protest against incorporation and dilution into western consumerism and western life-styles. With the failure of communism, Islamic fundamentalism becomes one of the few remaining political options in the Third World as a protest against secularisation and consumerism. One could also see the movement for the Islamisation of science in the same light, namely as an attempt to check secularisation and incorporation into a western model of scientific knowledge (Stenberg, 1996). Islamic fundamentalism challenges the universalistic claims of western natural and social sciences, and offers an alternative model of understanding and significance (Tibi, 1995). Other cultural movements have also questioned the dominance of western literature and arts resulting in a widespread debate on decolonisation, subaltern studies and hybridity. These social and cultural movements can all be seen as an erosion of the authority and legitimacy of the English literary canon as the principal criterion of value.

Said's approach to Orientalism also raises important questions about the role of intellectuals in relation to the modern state. In contemporary societies, the state no longer assumes responsibility for the protection and promotion of high culture and instead relies upon the market to determine what constitutes cultural taste and distinction. Intellectuals no longer have the authority of the state and the elite institutions behind them when they come to pronounce on culture. They have as a result stopped being cultural legislators and are now merely cultural interpreters (Bauman, 1987). Intellectuals have become increasingly separated from the state. With the rise of nationalism, intellectuals had been important in defining national cultures – hence, for example, the importance of ethnographic studies in defining and shaping core values and standards. The commercialisation of culture, the growth of mass culture, the integration of high and low culture in postmodernity, and the transformation of universities by economic rationalism have undermined the traditional role of the public intellectual. The growing popularity of cultural studies and the decline of traditional departments of English literature in many British and Commonwealth universities are indicative of these changes in the modern university. Intellectuals no longer have the authority and state support which characterised the intellectuals of nineteenth-century Europe in the heyday of classical Orientalism.

We can also understand this decline of the public intellectual as an example of postmodernisation in a culture that is increasingly dominated by information technology. If we define postmodernism as scepticism towards 'grand narratives' (Lyotard, 1984), then in the contemporary world intellectuals are unwilling or unable to defend grand narratives since academic intellectuals no longer have the authority to pronounce on such matters. This uncertainty about what Richard Rorty (1989) calls our 'final vocabularies' means that the assurance to pronounce confidently on other cultures is less characteristic of contemporary intellectuals. Anthropological relativism and postmodern uncertainty are dominant moods of the academy – at least in the humanities and the social sciences. Hence classical Orientalism in its strong form has been disoriented, leaving behind weak, fragmented and contradictory versions. There are obviously exceptions to this scepticism towards grand narratives in writers like Francis Fukuyama's triumphalist liberalism (1992), but generally the mood of academics appears to be more inclined to uncertainty, self doubt or guilt. Reflexive modernity is less certain of universal truths and more inclined to recognise local and particularistic visions of contingent and incomplete realities.

Said (1984a: 10–16) has discussed these changes in intellectual climate through an analysis of Matthew Arnold's *Culture and Anarchy* (1869). Writing of culture as the best that can be thought in a society, Arnold was able to assume the moral authority of English high culture and the role of intellectual as its defender. Arnold could also assume that a strong national culture required a powerful state to impose its hegemonic force at home and abroad. The fragmentation of modern cultures and the growing hybridity of national traditions have reinforced the feeling among public intellectuals, not only that there are no final vocabularies, but that multiculturalism imposes a certain detachment from one's own culture. The intellectual context of Orientalism has changed radically since the publication of *Culture and Anarchy* in 1869.

Because Said's analysis was driven to a large measure by his commitment to the Palestinian movement in general and by the contradictory status of the Palestinian intellectual in the United States in particular, his attention was oriented outwards to the question of imperialism and postcolonialism. Said somewhat neglected the issue of Occidentalism, that is Orientalism has to create a perspective on internal colonialism. Imperialism generates internal images of the West which we may call 'Occidentalism' (Carrier, 1995). While Orientalism created a series of stereotypes towards outsiders and strangers who inhabited the new colonies of world capitalism, it also set up a collection of negative pictures of subordinate or marginal populations through a process of internal colonialism. In Britain in particular, the so-called Celtic Fringe represented a challenge to the Englishness of the Anglican Establishment in the formation of the nation state (Hechter, 1975). The Irish were a suppressed 'black' interior which had to be managed and controlled in order to protect England as 'a green and pleasant land' (Lebow, 1976).

The study of Orientalism must also include an analysis of anti-Semitism. The negative view of Islam is part of a larger hostility towards Semitic cultures in the West. If Caliban represents one formative figure in the evolution of European notions of Otherness, Shylock presents another. *The Merchant of Venice* that was written in 1596, has some parallel with Marlowe's *Jew of Malta* and expresses the anti-Semitism of Elizabethan England. There is a general anti-Semitism in Europe, in which antagonism to Jews has often accompanied hostility to Muslims. Generally speaking, the critique of Orientalism has not noticed the ironic connection between two forms of racism, namely against Arabs and against Jews. In his Introduction to *Orientalism*, Said writes that:

> in addition, and by an almost inescapable logic, I have found myself writing the history of a strange, secret sharer of Western anti-Semitism. That anti-Semitism and, as I have discussed it in its Islamic branch, Orientalism resemble each other very closely, is a historical, cultural and political truth that needs only be mentioned to an Arab Palestinian for its irony to be perfectly understood.
> (Said, 1978: 27–8)

In a reply to his critics, Said also noted the parallels between what he calls 'Islamophobia' and anti-Semitism. There are in fact two discourses of Orientalism for Semites, one relating to Islam and the other to Judaism. Within Orientalism, there are two related discourses for Semites, namely 'the Islamic discourse of gaps and the Judaic discourse of contradictions' (Turner, 1983: 29). While

Islam had been defined by its absences (of rationality, cities, asceticism and so forth), Judaism had been defined by the contradictory nature of its religious injunctions where, for example, its dietary laws transferred the quest for personal salvation into a set of ritualistic prescriptions which inhibited the full expression of its monotheistic rationalism according to Weber's analysis in *Ancient Judaism* (Weber, 1952). For Weber, the rationality of Jewish monotheistic prophecy was undermined by a ritualistic dietary scheme.

The West oriented its identity between two poles – the lazy, sensual Arab and the untrustworthy, greedy Jew. While Weber criticised the Islamic paradise as merely a sensual reward for warriors, he controversially described Jewish communities as a 'pariah status group', because their social and geographical migrations were seen to be politically dangerous. Throughout the medieval and modern periods, Jews disturbed the consciousness of the Christian West. In the Protestant Reformation, there emerged a millenarian heresy that the Jews, in being restored to Palestine, would fight the Turks and thereby assist Christianity in its struggle against Islam. Restorationists believed that the Jews would undertake a crusade against the Muslims and, in the seventeenth century, British Puritans enthusiastically received the news of a messianic Jewish leader Sabbatai Sevi who had inflicted significant military defeats on the Turks. Their eschatological hopes were of course disappointed and in 1666 news of Sevi's conversion to Islam was circulating in London (Scholem, 1973). He was subsequently denounced as an impostor who had misled his followers.

The experience of Diaspora and ethnic hatred meant that displaced Jews were seen to be cosmopolitan and strange; the notion of the 'wandering Jew' pinpoints the idea that their commitment to the national polity could not be taken for granted. In the twentieth century, Hitler's hatred of Viennese Jews arose from the encounter with what he took to be a seething mass of unfriendly and strange faces (Oxaal, 1990). While Jews were strange, they were also guilty, according to New Testament theology, of religious treachery. These anti-Semitic stereotypes have been culturally crucial, because Christianity as the foundation of western values has traditionally attempted to maintain its difference from other Abrahamic faiths. Precisely because Judaism and Islam shared so much in common (monotheism, prophetic and charismatic revelation, the religion of the Book, and a radical eschatology), they had to be separated culturally by a discourse of ethnic and moral difference from the Christian tradition. Jewish separate identity raised significant questions about the character of civilisation processes in Europe (Russell, 1996: 83).

We can now summarise this introduction by showing that Orientalism can be described in terms of two dimensions. First, there is internal and external Orientalism in which attention is focused inwards on ethnic subcommunities or outwards towards an externalised Otherness. Second, there is a dimension which is divided into positive and negative evaluations. Classical Orientalism involved a negative, external framework of critical rejection of the Other as alien and dangerous. The stereotypes of the 'lazy Arab' and the 'wandering Jew' perfectly express this interpretative option. In the opposite direction, positive, internal Occidentalism identified some communities within the nation state as a positive expression of identity and consciousness. For example, in late Victorian England, there emerged a romantic view of Scottishness in which the heroic Scotsman could safely enter the English consciousness. Queen Victoria did much in the long run to legitimise this image of the brave Scottish soldier as the corner-stone of British colonial power. This position contrasts with internal, negative Occidentalism that treated the Irish as a dangerous, but ultimately pathetic, adversary within the evolving British polity. Finally, there is positive, external Orientalism which converted the native peoples of North America into 'the Noble Savage'.

This typology helps us to realise that Orientalism also produced Occidentalism, and that racial stereotypes can be both positive and negative. For Islam, there was a positive view of the manly ethic of Arabic nomadism that was embraced by writers like T. E. Lawrence. There was a strong movement of Orientalism that assumed a romantic view of the East as a land of promise, sensuality and pleasure which contrasted with the drab reality of bourgeois asceticism. This mood was closely associated with the aristocratic tradition of the Grand Tour (Tregaskis, 1979) and with the sensuality of Gérard de Nerval's *Voyage en Orient* (Nerval, 1980). The Qur'ān also had a considerable impact on the English romantic tradition. In 1801 Robert Southey's *Thalaba* set out to discover the common ethical foundations of Islam and Christianity; his understanding of Islam rested heavily on George Sale's translation of the Qur'ān, especially on Sale's 'Preliminary

Discourse'. Both Southey and Walter Savage Landor employed koranic themes to illustrate the idea that imperial pride and tyranny are transitory (Sharafuddin, 1994: 55).

TRADITIONAL ORIENTALISM

Classical Orientalism addressed a number of specific issues that in various ways questioned the authenticity and authority of Islam as a religion. For example, there was a tendency falsely to equate Islam with the Prophet, and thus to refer to the religion as 'Mohammedanism' or even to suggest that Islam was a sectarian movement, namely 'Muhammed's sect'. The term 'Mohammedism' was used contemptuously by George Sale in 1734 in the 'Preliminary discourse' to his translation of the Qur'ān. We find as late as 1911 D.S. Margoliouth, Professor of Arabic in the University of Oxford, opting for 'Mohammedanism' rather than 'Islam' as the title of his book. He was followed by Sir Hamilton Gibb who, on the advice of his publishers, kept the title 'Mohammedanism' in *An Historical Survey* (Gibb, 1949).

The notion behind these labels was that the Prophet was in fact an impostor. There was a predisposition as a result to probe the claims of the Qur'ān to be a transcendental revelation of Allah through the vehicle of His Messenger. Translations of the Qur'ān were enormously significant therefore in mediating inter-cultural exchanges. Then there are questions raised about the ability of Islam to foster and promote rationalism and scientific investigation. This polemical issue was crucial in the work of Ernest Renan, especially in *L'avenir de la science* (Renan, 1890). By contrast, the fascination with the mystical tradition of Islam, and in particular with the role and teaching of the 'dervishes', preoccupied Edward Sell and R.A. Nicholson (Arberry, 1960: 197–232). Finally, there was a persistent interest in the theme of the rise and fall of empires in the writings of Stanley Lane Poole, William Muir, Julius Wellhausen and Carl H. Becker. We need to understand these themes in the context of long-term transformations in international political and economic conflicts.

Attitudes towards Islam changed radically in the sixteenth and seventeenth centuries as Nabil Matar's *Islam in Britain 1558–1685* so clearly illustrates (Matar, 1998). Fear of and apprehension towards Islam grew in Britain under pressure from Islamic expansion in the Mediterranean. In particular, the Church feared and condemned the conversion of Christians either by force or by persuasion in this period, and converts to Islam were referred to as 'renegades'. Converts or renegades were regarded as cowards who had rejected Christianty to avoid slavery or punishment. They were unheroic characters who had 'turned Turk' through threats or allurements. Renegades were also regarded as people from the lower social ranks, and thus their conversions were the product of poverty and ignorance. The categorical condemnation of these converts also indicates a certain nervousness on the part of ecclesiastical and political authorities. England, in the throes of civil war and religious conflict, appeared unstable. Conversion to Islam suggested that the Ottoman Empire was more coherent and better governed than England. Furthermore, because many slaves within Islam actually rose to high office as Janissary leaders, it was assumed correctly that there was an egalitarianism of social mobility and opportunity in the Islamic empires. These anxieties about the appeal of Islam were well illustrated by western attitudes towards the translation of the Qur'ān.

In 1649 the first English translation of the Qur'ān appeared by Alexander Ross (1592–1654) with the title *The Alcoran of Mahomet*; it was taken from a French version of the Qur'ān by André du Ryer, the French consul in Egypt, which had been published in 1647. Ross had no knowledge of Arabic and translated from the French with no reference to the original Arabic. When Ross's translation was announced, there was a petition to the Council of State of the Commonwealth to suppress the publication and to prevent any further printing. With the failure of the petition, Ross's translation was safely published. Ross, who was a Royalist and Anglican, assumed correctly that part of the opposition to the Qur'ān came from Puritan anxieties about religious schism. In fact the unity of the Ottoman Empire contrasted clearly with the political divisions within English civil society. George Sale's translation is clearly a major improvement on both du Ryer and Alexander Ross; Sale's own attitude towards 'the Mohammedan system' was highly critical as were his views on Roman Catholicism and previous translations of the Qur'ān. Sale's highly negative commentary on Islam reflects the continuing anxiety by translators that their work would be condemned by the Church or by nervous governments.

European fears about Ottoman expansion began to decline towards the end of the seventeenth century. In 1683, the Ottoman army was defeated outside Vienna and the Treaty of Karlowitz in

1699 recognised at least implicity the military decline of the Ottoman Empire through ceding territory in Austria, Poland and Venice. The reform of the English navy was an important foundation for the growth of trade and the ability of English governments to impose treaties and trading arrangements. Dutch control over the East Indies was matched by British expansion in the Malayan peninsula, Australia and New Zealand. More significantly, the European nations began to look towards the New World as a market for goods and resources. Western technological supremacy, military dominance and the expansion of trade were obvious consequences of the growth of industrial capitalism. Islam ceased being a real threat to the economic and political dominance of Europe and became instead an object of scholarly curiosity. The growth of interest in Islam from around the middle of the eighteenth century was fuelled by an academic interest in (dead) languages, translations and the creation of catalogues and oriental libraries. With the decline of military power, Islam, along with Rome and the classical world, entered into the European story of the rise and fall of empires. In the eighteenth and nineteenth centuries, the Islamic lands became appropriate sites for European travel tales and exotic fiction.

From Napoleon's Egyptian expedition, European control over the Middle East grew continuously. France occupied Algeria in 1830 and Italy occupied Libya in 1912. England occupied Egypt and Sudan in 1882, and Lord Cromer's account of administrative control of Egypt has become a major document of English Oriental attitudes (Baring, 1908). Lord Cromer automatically assumed that 'the Oriental' was incapable of self-government and rational argument. Confidence in English superiority over foreign cultures was perhaps nowhere better illustrated than in Lord Macaulay's Minute of 1835 with respect to the future of education in India in which he announced that a shelf of European literature was worth the whole literary culture of India and Arabia.

MODERN ORIENTALISM AND THE SOCIAL SCIENCES

The collapse of the Soviet Union and the erosion of Marxism as an intellectual force changed the nature of Orientalism in the social sciences where it had been inevitably connected with Marxist views of capitalism and development. These conflicting views were also connected with intellectual conflicts between 'bourgeois sociology' and 'scientific Marxism'. Whereas in classical political theory Russia had often been connected with oriental despotism, in communist theory it was the Soviet Union which was the progressive historical force. The question of oriental despotism had been a legacy initially of liberal political philosophy which contrasted the individual freedoms of European constitutionalism with the 'general slavery' of the East. These attitudes shaped late nineteenth- and early twentieth-century political analysis of the Orient, which was influenced by a general interest in the rise and fall of empires. Weber's commentary on Islam is a classic illustration (Turner, 1974).

It is possible to identify two separate Weberian arguments. First, there is Weber's view of Islam as a warrior religion that had produced values and cultural standards which were inimical to the emergence of liberal capitalism. In Weber's sociology of religion, the social carriers of the various world religions were held to have contributed a lasting impression on their entire cultural outlook. The early social carriers of Buddhism (mendicant monks) and Confucianism (the literati) were clearly contrasted, in terms of long-term consequences, with the nomadic warriors whom Weber identified as the original carriers of triumphant Islam. However, Weber appeared to have been simply wrong about the carriers of Islam who were in fact not tribal warriors but trading groups. Merchants rather than warriors seem to have been crucial in the spread of Islam as a world religion, and koranic morality, with its concern for balances and accounting, reflects this trading culture rather than the values of a feudalistic warrior class. However, Weber had a second argument that was about the consequences of patrimonial bureaucracy on the development of Islam. In this argument, which considered the role of state structures rather than foundational cultures, the absence of autonomous cities, the underdevelopment of institutions of private property, the absence of an individualistic culture, the insecurity of social life under patrimonialism from centralised power and the absence of a bourgeois class were regarded as consequences of a particular pattern of state formation. These social features were crucial to the underdevelopment of civil society in Islamic history. This particular type of state was closely associated in Weber's historical sociology with differences in military organisation namely the contrasting importance of infantry and cavalry in decentralised political systems. In short, it was not the religious values of Islam which constrained the development of capitalism but social stationariness resulting from the dead weight of oriental bureaucracy. It was the burden of bureaucracy that limited entrepreneurial activity and restricted the emergence of an urban, ascetic, bourgeois class.

Both Marx and Weber could be criticised for their Orientalist reconstruction of Islam as a historical problem, namely as a deviation from the radical character of Abrahamic prophetic religions. In characterising oriental societies as stationary and incapable of achieving internal reform, Marx and Weber have implicitly provided a historical legitimation of western cultural and economic dominance (Turner, 1978). In the case of Marx, it was obvious that the only way in which Chinese and Indian social stagnation could be undermined was through the destructive importation of western commodities, transport systems, army discipline and newspapers In addition, both Weber and Marx recognised the radical consequences of science and technology on capitalist means of economic production and thus assumed that Islam had been and would remain incapable of internal change and transformation. As a result, they underestimated the importance of scientific cultures within Islam itself, treated Islamic philosophy as merely a derivation from Greek sources, and regarded Islamic religion as parasitic on Judaeo-Christian monotheism. Contemporary history of science has periodically attempted to change the conventional view of the absence of any genuine scientific culture in Islam (Watt, 1972).

In retrospect, sociological analysis of oriental society and Islam in the 1970s neglected the earlier work of Karl Wittfogel, whose *Oriental Despotism* had provided a powerful critique of political authoritarianism within both oriental cultures and contemporary communism (Wittfogel, 1957). In Wittfogel's treatment of Russian history, Stalinist authoritarianism was merely the contemporary manifestation of an age-old Asiatic power system. The critical reception of Wittfogel's work was shaped by the cold-war ideologies of the period. Wittfogel's analysis of oriental despotism is one of the classic texts of political science and yet his 'comparative study of total power' was a popular target of left-wing criticism during the cold war. The problem with Wittfogel's thesis about absolute power was not so much his attempt to demonstrate that there were pre-industrial forms of totalitarian social control, but rather his historical study of the rise and fall of the concept of the Asiatic mode of production in Soviet communist theory. In short, Wittfogel had argued that the Marxist concept of Asiatic society had been suppressed by Stalin and others, because it was an embarrassment to Soviet power. For Wittfogel, Stalinism was merely the restoration of Asiatic authoritarianism, since the Soviet state reproduced precisely the centralised regulation of pre-modern hydraulic society. Wittfogel's concern with the history of the Asiatic mode of production in the Soviet Union was seen as an example of his 'obsessive anti-communism and anti-Sovietism' (Hindess and Hirst, 1975: 207) and at a theoretical level his thesis was criticised as a functionalist explanation which involved an unacceptable circularity: large-scale irrigation for agriculture required the existence of the powerful state, while the existence of the state presupposed an irrigation agriculture as its foundation.

In retrospect, much of this criticism now appears somewhat implausible, formalistic or irrelevant. Wittfogel, who had himself spent time in a concentration camp where he had, as it were, studied totalitarianism at close quarters, was deeply influenced by the intellectual legacy of Weber, especially in terms of theory of bureaucracy and the state. Wittfogel's main intention was to produce a critique of state power based upon a monopoly of public utilities. In particular, he was critical of bureaucratic state power in the Soviet Union from 1917 onwards, and this critique of state power was the real origin of his treatment of the Asiatic mode of production. He rejected any unilinear view of history, but hydraulic government within what he called an agro-managerial bureaucracy was a distinctive pattern of power, quite separate from the more differentiated and localised feudal system. He did not really approve of the concept of 'oriental despotism', preferring to talk instead about hydraulic societies and conditions. Hydraulic power was seen to be an issue in Hawaii as much as in China. Wittfogel's basic interest was the consequences for political life of the interaction between environment (nature) and culture, and clearly continues to be a central issue in modern political theory.

In contemporary discussions of Islam, this question about democracy and egalitarianism continues to shape anthropological and sociological approaches. Sociological understanding of the contours and dynamic of Islamic social structures has in the second half of the twentieth century been significantly influenced, at least in the Anglo-Saxon academic world, by the political anthropology of the late Ernest Gellner. This intellectual influence was often covert and grudging, but nevertheless real and widespread.

Building on his fieldwork in the Atlas Mountains of central Morocco, his central ideas were 'plainly stolen' (Gellner, 1981: vii) from Ibn Khaldun, David Hume, Robert Montagne and Edward Evans-Pritchard. On the basis of these stolen ideas, he created a brilliant, if frequently flawed, view of Islamic structures in *Saints of the Atlas* (1969), *Muslim Society* (1981), and *Postmodernism, Reason and Religion* (1992). Within the framework of the historical sociology of Ibn Khaldun, his work continued to raise issues that were part of the legacy of Islamic Orientalism: egalitarianism versus hierarchy, imperial authoritarianism versus cultural openness, and stagnation versus change.

His basic theory was that tribal Islam was egalitarian and nomadic. Whereas it was held together by an intense sense of social solidarity (*asabiyya*) drawing its strength from a loyalty and commitment to religious values, in the urban centres, commercial interactions in marketplaces represented a weaker form of social cohesion, creating its social norms from individualism and exchange. Periodically, fundamentalist tribesmen conquer the cities, impose a new social order in the name of Allah and remove the old corrupt elite. Although there is hostility between towns- and tribes-men, they also depend upon each other for crucial economic services. Tribal warriors required guns and grain; merchants required luxury goods and safe trading routes. Alongside this social division of labour, there is also a religious one. In the rural hinterland, Sufi saints practise a deviant, folk religiosity based on personal charisma; in the towns, the puritanical religious leaders follow the ascetic religion of the Book. In the modern world, fundamentalist Islam has asserted the authority of the urban over the tribal model and the only challenge to militant and ascetic Islam is from postmodern cultures and rampant commercialism. After communism, radical Islam emerges in the Orientalist paradigm as the only force that can challenge the hegemony of western capitalism.

Some of the issues in Gellner's political anthropology can be illustrated by considering Louise Marlow's *Hierarchy and Egalitarianism in Islamic Thought* (1997), where she takes up a perennial issue in Islam, namely that Islamic doctrine is radically egalitarian, because its strict monotheism proscribes any ontological hierarchy in either human society or nature. Its basic theological premise is the affirmation in the Surah of Unity (Surah cxii): He is God alone, God the Eternal. Although Muhammad is the Messenger of God, it was a fundamental misrepresentation of traditional

Orientalism to refer to Islam as 'Muhammadanism'. All beings are subordinated to Allah, because koranic orthodoxy precludes any divine associates. This theological notion of Unity establishes the foundation for a belief in the radical equality of human beings.

However, actual Islamic societies have been profoundly hierarchical. The sociological argument is that in its inception Islam was an egalitarian brotherhood which assumed the equality of free male believers, developing neither specific ecclesiastical institutions nor a sacerdotal priesthood. This prophetic egalitarianism was initially reinforced by patriarchal tribalism that also had a fraternal ethic for sharing resources. With the growth of imperial power, these doctrines were compromised by the success of Islamic military expansion, which encouraged the growth of a more status-conscious and hierarchical social order. The prominent religious role played by women in early Islamic communities was eventually overshadowed by the patriarchical cultures of imperial Islamic systems, when these tendencies were increasingly legitimised by the Islamic incorporation of Greek political thought, which conceptualised the city as a hierarchical political formation. In the polis, social order requires the harmony that is produced by a wise but despotic leader. In Iraq and Iran in the Sassanian period, social inequality became progressively hereditary, and the dominant class was a landed nobility.

The pre-Islamic Iranian priestly model of despotism was imitated by later Islamic regimes, whose aristocratic power was legitimised by the religious leaders (*ulama*). The model was both functional and hierarchical. In response to these despotic institutions, political conflict in Islam has been subsequently organised around utopian criticism of urban hierarchy, a utopian opposition which often appeals nostalgically to the egalitarian solidarity (*asabiyya*) of the foundation community. For example, in the Iranian Revolution of 1977–9 Ayatollah Khomeini mobilised the oppressed and the innocent against the urban elite, who were the principal agents of the Shah's authoritarian programme of economic modernisation, in the name of a radical Islamic state. The revolution involved a successful alliance between the clergy behind Khomeini, sections of urban working class, and the dispossessed, who were typically landless rural migrants. In radical Islam, the voice of the people became an expression of divine will against the inequalities of the secular state. It was this aspect of the Islamic revolution that attracted the attention of Michel Foucault as an example of a spiritual protest against western powers.

As we have seen, Gellner's model assumes a significant religious split between the rural saints and the urban clergy. While the saints embody charisma (*baraka*) in their ritual performance, the urban clergy preach a rational and orthodox religious worldview which is grounded in the Qur'ān and the *hadith* (orthodox traditions). The rural saints maintain their lay disciples by providing them with (magical) cures for their misfortune and sickness, and in return the laity offer them material support. In this respect, we could argue that Gellner's view of the split between populist and orthodox religiosity reproduced the debate between Renan and Al-Afghani in which it was assumed that there was a significant division between Muslim society and its intellectual leaders. The traditional anthropological picture of popular religious deviance has been challenged by contemporary anthropological fieldwork. For example, Nadia Abu-Zahra (1997), whose fieldwork describes the popular rituals of Egypt and Tunisia, is concerned to identify the channels of communication between the common people and the *ulama*, and to establish the view that the common laity and the educated clergy in fact share a set of common Islamic beliefs and practices.

Her ethnographic work, which is designed to 'refute Gellner's claim that the Islamic text is outside society' (1997: xii), demonstrates that the common people understand their religion, know large sections of the Qur'ān by heart and attempt to follow orthodox precepts, often consulting with the local shaykh for guidance on their religious duties. Her ethnographic study of the ritualistic practices and festivals, which celebrate al-Sayyida Zaynab, the granddaughter of the Prophet Muhammad, the epitome of purity and motherhood, shows that many educated people share the same beliefs and practices which honour her memory. There is, therefore, a constant traffic of belief and practice between the people and the elite, from which she derives the conclusion that Islam is a common religion, which embraces the whole of society. Against Gellner, Sufi practices do not constitute a separate tradition, because the common people typically follow *shari'a* law and adhere to Sufi rituals, while some *ulama* will also use Sufi sayings in their preaching to the common people. Finally, her study sets out to refute the widely held view of classical Orientalism that women do not know much about Islam. The ethnographic data reject the Orientalist view that mainstream Islam is orthoprax not orthodox, namely based on common practices rather than a common belief; they also throw doubt on the anthropological division between a little tradition of the village and the great tradition of the urban mosque. In conclusion, the circulation of elites, which was described in Gellner's study of the Atlas Mountains, is not necessarily valid for Islamic societies in Asia and the argument that there is an inevitable bifurcation of rural and urban Islam obscures the integration of the great and little traditions.

However, Gellner's view that Islam has replaced communism as the principal alternative in the developing world to the liberal ideology of western capitalism has considerable credibility. With the collapse of organised communism and the end of the cold war in 1989–91, there has been an identification of Islam in the popular press as the principal threat to the West. The Gulf War resulted in a further demonisation of the Arab as the main antagonist in the international system (Halliday, 1997). Increasing conflict in Israel between right-wing religious groups and Hizbullah Shi'ite forces has reinforced the negative view of Arab fanaticism. Television coverage of Israeli civilians blown to bits by suicide bomb attacks has resurrected the image of the dangerous and irrational Arab. Islam is of course also perceived as an internal European threat. The Rushdie Affair (Asad, 1993) has many dimensions but one centred on the feeling that Iran's radical Shi'ite leadership could strike at any location in Europe and North America; Islam had become a major threat to civil liberties and individual freedoms in Europe.

COSMOPOLITANISM VERSUS ORIENTALISM

The history of Orientalism is in large measure the depressing history of inter-civilisational misunderstanding, antagonism and racial bigotry. However, Said (1984a) has also been concerned to identify a number of scholars whose work attempted to transcend the narrow limitations of the Orientalist tradition of which they were members. In this respect his observations on Louis Massignon and Raymond Schwab are instructive, because they provide us with a model of what we might call cosmopolitan scholarship. Massignon's principal work was *The Passion of al-Hallaj* (Massignon, 1962–3), which provides a theological and historical analysis of the religious significance of the mystic Mansur al-Hallaj who became a martyr for peace in Baghdad in 922. For Massignon, al-Hallaj provides a religious figure through whom one can apprehend the mystical truths of both Christianity and Islam. It is through suffering that one can learn compassion, and through compassion a scholar might sympathetically approach and value other cultures. Massignon was, following a shattering religious experience in Iraq in May 1908, converted to Christianity through the witness of Islam. Many of his colleagues regarded him as a Muslim, although in his later life he also practised as a Melkite priest. A withdrawn scholar, Massignon became publicly involved in the protests against the Algerian War and in 1961 struggled with friends to drag the bodies of murdered Algerians from the Seine (Mason, 1989). In Massignon's theology of mysticism, the religious experiences of the divine presence in different traditions provides a common experience of man's alienation and humanity's need for reconciliation.

Raymond Schwab plays an equally important role in Said's vision of intellectual responsibility towards other cultures. While Schwab's intellectual world was quite remote from the Catholicism of Massignon's work, Schwab's task was to understand the impact of the Orient on the West in the period 1770–1850, roughly, that is, from the French Revolution to the high tide of western imperialism in the Middle East. In this period, Orientalism became a great adventure of human consciousness in which the polarities between East and West generated a new range of humanistic possibilities, namely a renaissance. This movement is opened up by translation for example in the work of Abraham Anquetil-Duperron about whom Schwab (1934) wrote an engaging intellectual biography. While the first Renaissance asserted the similarities and commonalities of European cultures, the second renaissance constructed a culture of differences through its comparative philology, historical studies and sociology. Orientalism expressed the European need to assimilate and absorb the Other through a set of linguistic strategies, but Schwab's own position was driven by an implicit notion of 'integral humanism', of the need for a dynamic humanism which could transcend these differences (Rousseaux, 1956).

Said's analysis of these writers prepares the groundwork for a defence of cosmopolitanism as the ethical world-view of scholars in a global context, where cultural hybridity and multiculturalism are beginning to re-write the traditional Orientalist agenda. Cosmopolitanism can be defended morally, because exclusive national loyalties and ethnic solidarities are more likely to be points of conflict and violence in culturally diverse societies. We need an ideology of membership, therefore, which will celebrate the uncertainty of belonging, where our 'final vocabularies' are never final. One can suggest that the components of cosmopolitan virtue are as follows: irony both as a method and as a mentality; emotional distance and reflexivity with respect to our own cultural values; scepticism towards grand narratives of modern ideologies; transcultural sympathies and interests; care for other cultures arising from an awareness of their precarious condition and acceptance of cultural hybridisation; support for positive programmes of multiculturalism; and an ecumenical appreciation of other religions. Intercultural sensitivities and the need to interact constantly with strangers promote irony as the most prized norm of wit and principle of taste. For Said (1984a: 29), irony is a useful word to use alongside 'oppositional' and 'critical'.

Perhaps it is not too fanciful to believe that, precisely because of their exposure to global concerns and global issues, the cosmopolitan intellectual might, in recognising the ubiquity of hybridisation, reject claims to cultural superiority and cultural dominance. Precisely because we are exposed to global forces of postmodernisation, the cosmopolitan ironist should welcome a stance which supports post-colonial cultures and celebrates the teeming diversity of human cultures. In their awareness of the tensions between local cultures and global processes, cosmopolitan virtue might come to recognise a stewardship over, and for, cultures which are precarious. The cosmopolitan ironist, being convinced of the evolutionary importance of bio-diversity, would be equally careful in his or her support of cultural heterogeneity.

CONCLUSION: NATIONALISM AND ORIENTALISM

The creation of nation states in Europe from the seventeenth century necessarily involved the creation of nationalistic 'imagined communities' (Benedict, 1983), which asserted and partly created homogeneous populations which were held together, against the pressures of class and community, by nationalistic ideologies. If we identify the Treaty of Westphalia in 1648 as the origin of the modern world system of nation states, then state formation throughout Europe involved the creation of nationalist identities on the basis of a double colonisation, both internal and external. Here again 'the wandering Jew' provided the pretext in many European states for 'ethnic cleansing' in order to create a homogeneous population, but in a less violent form one can find various political and social pressures to create civil societies on the basis of common languages, a shared religious culture and a single ethnic identity.

What produced this process of cultural standardisation? One argument is that the rise of the system of nation states coincided with the rise of national forms of competitive capitalism. It was the capitalist economy which undermined the conventional patterns of rural communities based on traditional forms of agrarianism. Industrial capitalism saw the emergence, through urbanisation and the demographic revolutions of the late eighteenth and early nineteenth century, of a large urban proletariat which was a potential threat to the new order of nation states. Nationalism was created by nation states either as a substitute for, or in combination with, religion as the social glue of an urban society, which was organised around conflicting class structures.

The political and cultural processes of nation formation involved various forms of internal colonialism whereby minority or subordinate cultures and traditions were destroyed or excluded. However, these violent forms of exclusion were also accompanied by what one might regard as more positive modes of inclusion and incorporation, namely the building of modern patterns of social citizenship (James, 1996). The history of social citizenship and the welfare state was a history of 'ruling class strategies' to include and co-opt the working class into capitalist society through the construction of reformist policies of social security (Mann, 1988). National citizenship confers not only economic and political rights, but socio-cultural identities, loyalties and commitments. Citizenship thus establishes exclusionary boundaries and borders which define insiders and outsiders. Thus the nature and extent of the processes of incorporation into citizenship by various combinations of descent and residence are highly instructive comparative indicators of national identity; for example, migration policies which determine the opportunities of naturalisation by residence are strong indications of the openness of social communities. Migration policy is thus a clear and definite statement of the state's claim to sovereignty over both people and territory. One of the primary functions of (rich) nation states is to keep (poor) foreigners out. Although this exclusionary thrust is primarily based on economic and military interests, it is also deeply cultural and symbolic.

The imagined communities that were constituted by the growth of literacy and nationalist strategies formed the social basis of the nation states in the Westphalian world system. These imaginary communities then constituted themselves by a double enmity – outwards as Orientalism and inwards as Occidentalism. The enemies of these states were constructed around racist parameters and were seen to be communities that existed at the borders of society. The wandering Jew represented a dangerous cosmopolitanism and therefore the loyalties of Jews were seen to be suspect. Gypsies had the same qualities, because their quasi-nomadic existence and 'oriental' origins set them apart. Muslim Arabs occupied another borderland, which separated reason and asceticism from luxury and lasciviousness. The paintings of Jean-Léon Gérôme, whose painting of the youthful snake charmer adorns the cover of Said's *Orientalism*, are a perfect illustration of the genre of French Orientalism which depicted the East as a place of magical sexuality and sensuality. Again, Shakespeare's figure of the Moor in *Othello* was possibly inspired by the story of Leo Africanus who, having converted to Christianity in Rome, reconverts to Islam on his return to North Africa. The unpredictable and untrustworthy character of the Moor captures the sense of sexual danger to the stability of Christian society.

Orientalism in its strong, classical form was a necessary product of rising nationalism which created the solidaristic basis of the western polity from the middle of the seventeenth century. Jews and Muslims were special targets of this discourse because their relationship to Christianity was paradoxically too close. A robust form of identification with the state was required because the economic market in capitalism has a corrosive effect on religion and community, the traditional binding forces of pre-capitalist societies. Classical Orientalism was a product of strong identification in terms of citizens who enjoyed social solidarity in a nationalist civil society and who were expected to display strong loyalties in their adherence to and service of the state, against a background of international uncertainty and imperialist struggles. Orientalism and Occidentalism in their strong forms followed the emergence of nationalism as the appropriate culture of the Westphalian state system. At the end of the twentieth century, the force of the nationalistic dimension of the conflict between Christians and Muslims has been tragically illustrated by the bloody conflict between Muslims, Orthodox Serbs and Croatians in former Yugoslavia. Clearly, the political forces that produced classical Orientalism are potent elements in racial conflicts in contemporary Europe and the need to understand and transcend its cultural limitations has never been more important.

BIBLIOGRAPHY

Abu-Zahra, N. (1997) *The Pure and the Powerful: Studies in Contemporary Muslim Society*. Reading: Ithaca Press.

Alatas, S.H. (1977) *The Myth of the Lazy Native*. London: Frank Cass.

Arberry, A.J. (1960) *Oriental Essays: Portraits of Seven Scholars*. London: George Allen & Unwin.

Asad, T. (1993) *Genealogies of Religion: Discipline and Reasons of Power in Christianity and Islam*. Baltimore and London: Johns Hopkins University Press.

Auerbach, E. (1953) *Mimesis: The Representation of Reality in Western Literature*. Princeton: Princeton University Press.

Baring, E. (1908) *Modern Egypt*. London: Macmillan.

Bauman, Z. (1987) *Legislators and Interpreters: On Modernity, Post-modernity and Intellectuals*. Cambridge: Polity Press.

Benedict, A. (1983) *Imagined Communities: Reflections on the Origin and Spread of Nationalism*. London: Verso.

Carrier, J.G. (ed) (1995) *Occidentalism: Images of the West*. Oxford: Clarendon Press.

Foucault, M. (1972) *The Archaeology of Knowledge*. London: Tavistock.

Fukuyama, F. (1992) *The End of History and the Last Man*. New York: Free Press.

Gellner, E. (1969) *Saints of the Atlas*. London: Weidenfeld & Nicolson.

Gellner, E. (1981) *Muslim Society*. Cambridge: Cambridge University Press.

Gellner, E. (1992) *Postmodernism, Reason and Religion*. London: Routledge.

Gibb, H.A.R. (1949) *Mohammedanism: An Historical Survey*. New York: Henry Holt.

Halliday, F. (1997) 'Neither Treason nor Conspiracy: Reflections on Media Coverage of the Gulf War 1990–1991', *Citizenship Studies*, Vol. 1(2): 157–72.

Hechter, M. (1975) *Internal Colonialism: The Celtic Fringe in British National Development 1536–1966*. London: Routledge & Kegan Paul.

Hindess, B. And Hirst, P.Q. (1975) *Pre-Capitalist Modes of Production* London: Routledge & Kegan Paul.

James, P. (1996) *Nation Formation: Towards a Theory of Abstract Community*. London: Sage.

Kelsky, K. (1996) 'Flirting with the Foreign: Interracial Sex in Japan's "International" Age' in R. Wilson and W. Dissanayake (eds) *Global/Local: Cultural Production and the Transnational Imaginary*. Durham and London: Duke University Press, pp. 179–92.

Lane, E.W. (1836) *The Manners and Customs of the Modern Egyptians*. London: Charles Knight.
Lebow, R. (1976) *White Britain, Black Ireland: The Influence of Stereotypes on Colonial Policy*. Philadelphia: Institute for the Study of Human Issues.
Lyotard, J.-F. (1984) *The Postmodern Condition: A Report on Knowledge*. Manchester: Manchester University Press.
McClintock, A. (1995) *Imperial Leather: Race, Gender and Sexuality in the Colonial Contest*. London and New York: Routledge.
Mann, M. (1988) *States, War and Capitalism: Studies in Political Sociology*. Oxford: Basil Blackwell.
Margoliouth, D.S. (1911) *Mohammedanism*. London: Williams and Norgate.
Marlow, L. (1977) *Hierarchy and Egalitarianism in Islamic Thought*. Cambridge: Cambridge University Press.
Massignon, L. (1962–3) *Opera Minora*. Beirut: Dar el-Maaref, 3 vols.
Massignon, L. (1989) *Testimonies and Reflections: Essays*. Ed. by H. Mason. Notre Dame, Indiana: University of Notre Dame.
Matar, N. (1998) *Islam in Britain 1558–1685*. Cambridge: Cambridge University Press.
Miyoshi, M. (1996) 'A Borderless World? From Colonialism to Transnationalism and the Decline of the Nation-State', in R. Wilson and W. Dissanayake (eds) *Global/Local: Cultural Production and the Transnational Imaginary*. Durham and London: Duke University Press, pp. 78–107.
Nerval, Gérard de (1980) *Voyage en Orient*. Paris: Flammarion, 2 vols.
Nietzsche, F. (1968) *Twilight of the Idols: The Anti-Christ*. Harmondsworth: Penguin Books.
Oxaal, I. (1990) 'Die Juden im Wien des jungen Hitler: Historische und soziologische Aspekte', in G. Boltz, I. Oxaal and M. Pollak (eds) *Eine zerstoerte Kultur: Juedisches Leben und Antisemitismus in Wien seit dem 19 Jahrhundert*. Buchloe: Druck und Verlag Obermayer, pp. 29–60.
Renan, E. (1890) *L'avenir de la science*. Paris: Calmann-Lévy.
Rorty, R. (1989) *Contingency, Irony and Solidarity*. Cambridge: Cambridge University Press.
Rousseaux, A. (1956) 'Raymond Schwab et l'humanisme intégrale', *Mercure de France* 1120, 663–71.
Russell, S. (1996) *Jewish Identity and Civilizing Processes*. London: Macmillan.
Said, E.W. (1978) *Orientalism*. Harmondsworth: Penguin.
Said, E.W. (1984a) *The World, the Text and the Critic*. London: Faber & Faber.
Said, E.W. (1984b) 'Foreword', in R. Schwab, *The Oriental Renaissance: Europe's Rediscovery of India and the East 1680–1880*. New York: Columbia University Press, pp. vii–xx.
Said, E.W. (1985) 'Orientalism Reconsidered', *Race and Class*, 27(2): 1–15.
Said, E.W. (1993) *Culture and Imperialism*. New York: Alfred A. Knopf.
Scholem, G. (1973) *Sabbatai Sevi, the Mystical Messiah*. Princeton, NJ: Princeton University Press.

Schwab, R. (1934) *Vie d'Anquetil-Duperron, suivie des usages civils et religieux des Parses par Anquetil-Duperron*. Paris: Leroux.
Schwab, R. (1950) *La Renaissance orientale*. Paris: Payot.
Sharafuddin, M. (1994) *Islam and Romantic Orientalism: Literary Encounters with the Orient*. London and New York: I.B. Tauris.
Stauth, G. and Turner, B.S. (1988) *Nietzsche's Dance: Resentment, Reciprocity and Resistance in Social Life*. Oxford: Blackwell.
Stenberg, L (1996) *The Islamization of Science: Four Muslim Positions Developing an Islamic Modernity*. Lund: Novapress.
Tibi, B. (1995) 'Culture and Knowledge. The Politics of Islamization of Knowledge as a Postmodern Project? The Fundamentalist Claim to De-Westernization', *Theory Culture & Society*, 12(1): 1–24.
Tillyard, E.M.W. (1958) *Shakespeare's Last Plays*. London: Chatto and Windus.
Tregaskis, H. (1979) *Beyond the Grand Tour*. London: Ascent Books.
Turner, B.S. (1974) *Weber and Islam: A Critical Study*. London: Routledge & Kegan Paul.
Turner, B.S. (1978) *Marx and the End of Orientalism*. London: Allen & Unwin.
Turner, B.S. (1983) *Religion and Social Theory*. London: Heinemann.
Turner, B.S. (1994) *Orientalism, Postmodernism and Globalism*. London: Routledge.
Watt, W.M. (1972) *The Influence of Islam on Medieval Europe*. Edinburgh: Edinburgh University Press.
Watt, W.M. (1991) *Muslim–Christian Encounters: Perceptions and Misperceptions*. London and New York: Routledge.
Weber, M. (1930) *The Protestant Ethic and the Spirit of Capitalism*. London: George Allen & Unwin.
Weber, M. (1952) *Ancient Judaism* Glencoe, IL: Free Press.
Wittfogel, K. (1957) *Oriental Despotism: A Comparative Study of Total Power*. New Haven: Yale University Press.
Young, R.J.C. (1995) *Colonial Desire: Hybridity in Theory, Culture and Race*. London and New York: Routledge.

2

THE KORAN: PRELIMINARY DISCOURSE

George Sale

Mohammed came into the world under some disadvantages, which he soon surmounted. His father Abd'allah was a younger son of Abd'almotalleb, and dying very young and in his father's lifetime, left his widow and infant son in very mean circumstances; his whole substance consisting but of five camels and one Ethiopian she-slave. Abd'almotalleb was therefore obliged to take care of his grand-child Mohammed, which he not only did during his life, but at his death enjoined his eldest son Abu Tâleb, who was brother to Abd'allah by the same mother, to provide for him for the future; which he very affectionately did, and instructed him in the business of a merchant, which he followed; and to that end he took him with him into Syria when he was but thirteen, and afterward recommended him to Khadîjah, a noble and rich widow, for her factor, in whose service he behaved himself so well, that by making him her husband she soon raised him to an equality with the richest in Mecca.

After he began by this advantageous match to live at his ease it was that he formed the scheme of establishing a new religion, or, as he expressed it, of replanting the only true and ancient one, professed by Adam, Noah, Abraham, Moses, Jesus, and all the prophets, by destroying the gross idolatry into which the generality of his countrymen had fallen, and weeding out the corruptions and superstitions which the latter Jews and Christians had, as he

Source: G. Sale *The Koran or, Alcoran of Mohammed*, n.d., London and New York, Frederick Warne and Co., pp. 27–94.

thought, introduced into their religion, and reducing it to its original purity, which consisted chiefly in the worship of one only God.

Whether this was the effect of enthusiasm, or only a design to raise himself to the supreme government of his country, I will not pretend to determine. The latter is the general opinion of Christian writers, who agree that ambition and the desire of satisfying his sensuality were the motives of his undertaking. His original design of bringing the pagan Arabs to the knowledge of the true God was certainly noble, and highly to be commended; for I cannot possibly subscribe to the assertion of a late learned writer, that he made that nation exchange their idolatry for another religion altogether as bad. Mohammed was no doubt fully satisfied in his conscience of the truth of his grand point, the unity of God, which was what he chiefly attended to; all his other doctrines and institutions being rather accidental and unavoidable, than premeditated and designed.

Since then Mohammed was certainly himself persuaded of his grand article of faith, which, in his opinion, was violated by all the rest of the world; not only by the idolaters, but by the Christians, as well those who rightly worshipped Jesus as God, as those who superstitiously adored the Virgin Mary, saints, and images; and also by the Jews, who are accused in the Korân of taking Ezra for the Son of God; it is easy to conceive that he might think it a meritorious work to rescue the world from such ignorance and superstition; and by degrees, with the help of a warm imagination, which an Arab seldom wants, to suppose himself destined by Providence for the effecting that great reformation. And this fancy of his might take still deeper root in his mind during the solitude he thereupon affected, usually retiring for a month in the year to a cave in Mount Hara near Mecca. One thing which may be probably urged against the enthusiasm of this prophet of the Arabs, is the wise conduct and great prudence he all along showed in pursuing his design, which seem inconsistent with the wild notions of a hot-brained religionist. But, though all enthusiasts or madmen do not behave with the same gravity and circumspection that he did, yet he will not be the first instance, by several, of a person who has been out of the way only *quoad hoc*, and in all other respects acted with the greatest decency and precaution.

The terrible destruction of the eastern churches, once so glorious and flourishing, by the sudden spreading of Mohammedism, and the great successes of its professors against the Christians, necessarily inspire a horror of that religion in those to whom it has been so fatal; and no wonder if they endeavour to set the character of its founder, and its doctrines, in the most infamous light. But the damage done by Mohammed to Christianity seems to have been rather owing to his ignorance than malice; for his great misfortune was, his not having competent knowledge of the real and pure doctrines of the Christian religion, which was in his time so abominably corrupted that it is not surprising if he went too far, and resolved to abolish what he might think incapable of reformation.

It is scarce to be doubted but that Mohammed had a violent desire of being reckoned an extraordinary person, which he could attain to by no means more effectually than by pretending to be a messenger sent from God, to inform mankind of his will. This might be at first his utmost ambition, and had his fellow citizens treated him less injuriously, and not obliged him by their persecutions to seek refuge elsewhere, and to take up arms against them in his own defence, he had perhaps continued a private person, and contented himself with the veneration and respect due to his prophetical office; but being once got at the head of a little army, and encouraged by success, it is no wonder if he raised his thoughts to attempt what had never before entered into his imagination.

That Mohammed was, as the Arabs are by complexion, a great lover of women, we are assured by his own confessions; and he is constantly upbraided with it by the controversial writers, who fail not to urge the number of women with whom he had to do as a demonstrative argument of his sensuality, which they think sufficiently proves him to have been a wicked man, and consequently an impostor. But, it must be considered that polygamy, though it be forbidden by the Christian religion, was, in Mohammed's time, frequently practised in Arabia and other parts of the east, and was not counted an immorality, nor was a man the worse esteemed on that account; for which reason Mohammed permitted the plurality of wives, with certain limitations, among his own followers, who argue for the lawfulness of it from several reasons, and particularly from the examples of persons allowed on all hands to have been good men; some of whom have been honoured with the divine correspondence. The several laws relating to marriages and divorces, and the peculiar privileges granted to Mohammed in his Korân, were almost all taken by him from the Jewish decisions, as will appear hereafter; and therefore he might think those institutions the more just and reasonable, as he found them practised or approved by the professors of a religion which was confessedly of divine origin.

But whatever were his motives, Mohammed had certainly the personal qualifications which were necessary to accomplish his undertaking. The Mohammedan authors are excessive in their commendations of him, and speak much of his religious and moral virtues; as his piety, veracity, justice, liberality, clemency, humility, and abstinence. His charity in particular, they say, was so conspicuous, that he had seldom any money in his house, keeping no more for his own use than was just sufficient to maintain his family; and he frequently spared even some part of his own provisions to supply the necessities of the poor; so that before the year's end he had generally little or nothing left. "God," says al Bokhâri, "offered him the keys of the treasures of the earth, but he would not accept them." Though the eulogies of these writers are justly to be suspected of partiality, yet thus much, I think, may be inferred from thence, that for an Arab who had been educated in paganism, and had but a very imperfect knowledge of his duty, he was a man of at least tolerable morals, and not such a monster of wickedness as he is usually represented. And indeed it is scarce possible to conceive that a wretch of so profligate a character should ever have succeeded in an enterprise of this nature; a little hypocrisy and saving of appearances, at least, must have been absolutely necessary; and the sincerity of his intentions is what I pretend not to inquire into.

He had indisputably a very piercing and sagacious wit, and was thoroughly versed in all the arts of insinuation. The eastern historians describe him to have been a man of an excellent judgment, and a happy memory; and these natural parts were improved by a great experience and knowledge of men, and the observations he had made in his travels. They say he was person of few words, of an equal, cheerful temper, pleasant and familiar in conversation, of inoffensive behaviour towards his friends, and of great condescension towards his inferiors. To all which were joined a comely, agreeable person, and a polite address; accomplishments of no small service in preventing those in his favour whom he attempted to persuade.

As to acquired learning, it is confessed he had none at all; having had no other education than what was customary in his tribe, who neglected, and perhaps despised, what we call literature; esteeming no language in comparison with their own, their skill in which they gained by use and not by books, and contenting themselves with improving their private experience, by committing to memory such passages of their poets as they judged might be of use to them in life. This defect was so far from being prejudicial or putting a stop to his design, that he made the greatest use of it; insisting that the writing which he produced as revelations from God, could not possibly be a forgery of his own; because it was not conceivable that a person who could neither write nor read should be able to compose a book of such excellent doctrine, and in so elegant a style; and thereby obviating an objection that might have carried a great deal of weight. And for this reason his followers, instead of being ashamed of their master's ignorance, glory in it as an evident proof of his divine mission, and scruple not to call him (as he is indeed called in the Korân itself) the illiterate prophet.

The scheme of religion which Mohammed framed, and the design and artful contrivance of those written revelations (as he pretended them to be) which compose his Korân, shall be the subject of the following sections: I shall, therefore, in the remainder of this relate, as briefly as possible, the steps he took towards the effecting of his enterprise, and the accidents which concurred to his success therein.

Before he made any attempt abroad, he rightly judged that it was necessary for him to begin by the conversion of his own household. Having therefore retired with his family, as he had done several times before, to the above-mentioned cave in Mount Hara, he there opened the secret of his mission to his wife Khadîjah: and acquainted her that the angel Gabriel had just before appeared to him, and told him that he was appointed the apostle of God: he also repeated to her a passage which he pretended had been revealed to him by the ministry of the angel, with those other circumstances of his first appearance which are related by the Mohammedan writers. Khadîjah received the news with great joy; swearing by him in whose hands her soul was, that she trusted he would be the prophet of his nation: and immediately communicated what she had heard to her cousin Warakah Ebn Nowfal, who, being a Christian, could write in the Hebrew character, and was tolerably well versed in the Scriptures; and he as readily came into her opinion, assuring her that the same angel who had formerly appeared unto Moses was now sent to Mohammed. This first overture the prophet made in the month of Ramadân, in the fortieth year of his age, which is therefore usually called the year of his mission.

Encouraged by so good a beginning, he resolved to proceed, and try for some time what he could do by private persuasion, not daring to hazard the whole affair by exposing it too suddenly to the public. He soon made proselytes of those under his own roof, viz. his wife Khadîjah, his servant Zeid Ebn Hâretha (to whom he gave his freedom on that occasion, which afterwards became a rule to his followers), and his cousin and pupil Ali, the son of Abu Tâleb, though then very young: but his last, making no account of the other two, used to style himself the first of believers. The next person Mohammed applied to was Abdallah Ebn Abi Kohâfa, surnamed Abu Becr, a man of great authority among the Koreish, and one whose interest he well knew would be of great service to him, as it soon appeared; for Abu Becr being gained over, prevailed also on Othmân Ebn Affân, Abd'alrahmân Ebn Awf, Saad Ebn Abi Wakkâs, al Zobeir Ebn al Awâm, and Telha Ebn Obeid'allah, all principal men in Mecca, to follow his example. These men were the six chief companions, who, with a few more, were converted in the space of three years; at the end of which Mohammed having, as he hoped, a sufficient interest to support him, made his mission no longer a secret, but gave out that God had commanded him to admonish his near relations, and in order to do it with more convenience and prospect of success, he directed Ali to prepare an entertainment, and invite the sons and descendants of Abd'almotalleb, intending then to open his mind to them; this was done, and about forty of them came, but Abu Laheb, one of his uncles, making the company break up before Mohammed had an opportunity of speaking, obliged him to give them a second invitation the next day; and when they were come, he made them the following speech: "I know no man in all Arabia who can offer his kindred a more excellent thing than I now do you; I offer you happiness both in this life, and in that which is to come: God Almighty hath commanded me to call you unto him; who, therefore, among you will be assisting to me herein, and become my brother, and my vicegerent?" All of them hesitating, and declining the matter, Ali at length rose up, and declared that he would be his assistant; and vehemently threatened those who should oppose him. Mohammed upon this embraced Ali with great demonstrations of affection, and desired all who were presented to hearken to and obey him as his deputy; at which the company broke out into great laughter, telling Abu Tâleb that he must now pay obedience to his son.

This repulse, however, was so far from discouraging Mohammed, that he began to preach in public to the people, who heard him with some patience, till he came to upbraid them with the idolatry, obstinacy, and perverseness of themselves and their fathers; which so highly provoked them, that they declared themselves his enemies, and would soon have procured his ruin, had he not been protected by Abyu Tâleb. The chief of the Koreish warmly solicited this person to desert his nephew, making frequent remonstrances against the innovations he was attempting; which proving ineffectual, they at length threatened him with an open rupture if he did not prevail on Mohammed to desist. At this Abu Tâleb was so far moved that he earnestly dissuaded his nephew from pursuing the affair any further, representing the great danger he and his friends must otherwise run. But Mohammed was not to be intimidated, telling his uncle plainly, that if they set the sun against him on his right hand, and the moon on his left, he would not leave his enterprise: and Abu Tâleb, seeing him so firmly resolved to proceed, used no further arguments, but promised to stand by him against all his enemies.

The Koreish, finding they could prevail neither by fair words nor menaces, tried what they could do by force and ill treatment; using Mohammed's followers so very injuriously that it was not safe for them to continue at Mecca any longer; whereupon Mohammed gave leave to such of them as had not friends to protect them to seek for refuge elsewhere. And accordingly in the fifth year of the prophet's mission, sixteen of them, four of whom were women, fled into Ethiopia: and among them Othmân Ebn Affân and his wife Rakîah, Mohammed's daughter. This was the first flight; but afterwards several others followed them, retiring one after another, to the number of eighty-three men and eighteen women, besides children. These refugees were kindly received by the Najáshi, or king of Ethiopia, who refused to deliver them up to those whom the Koreish sent to demand them, and as the Arab writers unanimously attest, even professed the Mohammedan religion.

In the sixth year of his mission Mohammed had the pleasure of seeing his party strengthened by the conversion of his uncle Hamza, a man of great valour and merit, and of Omar Ebn al Khattâb, a person highly esteemed, and once a violent opposer of the prophet. As persecution generally advances rather than obstructs the spreading of a religion, Islamism made so great a progress among the Arab tribes, that the Koreish, to suppress it effectually, if possible, in the seventh year of Mohammed's mission, made a solemn league or covenant against the Hashemites and the family of Al Motalleb, engaging themselves to contract no marriages with any of them, and to have no communication with them; and, to give it the greater sanction, reduced it into writing, and laid it up in the Caaba. Upon this the tribe became divided into two factions; and the family of Hashem all repaired to Abu Tâleb, as their head, except only Abd'al Uzza, surnamed Abu Laheb, who, out of his inveterate hatred to his nephew and his doctrine, went over to the opposite party, whose chief was Abu Sofiân Ebn Harb, of the family of Ommeya.

The families continued thus at variance for three years; but in the tenth year of his mission, Mohammed told his uncle Abu Tâleb, that God had manifestly showed his disapprobation of the league which the Koreish had made against them, by sending a worm to eat out every word of the instrument except the name of God. Of this accident Mohammed had probably some private notice, for Abu Tâleb, went immediately to the Koreish and acquainted them with it; offering, if it proved false, to deliver his nephew up to them; but in case it were true, he insisted that they ought to lay aside their animosity, and annul the league they had made against the Hashemies. To this they acquiesced, and, going to inspect the writing, to their great astonishment found it to be as Abu Tâleb had said; and the league was thereupon declared void.

In the same year Abu Tâleb died, at the age of above fourscore; and it is the general opinion that he died an infidel, though others say, that when he was at the point of death he embraced Mohammedism, and produced some passages out of his poetical compositions to confirm their assertion. About a month, or, as some write, three days after the death of this great benefactor and patron, Mohammed had the additional mortification to lose his wife Khadîjah, who had so generously made his fortune. For which reason this year is called the year of mourning.

On the death of these two persons, the Koreish began to be more troublesome than ever to their prophet, and especially some who had formerly been his intimate friends; insomuch that he found himself obliged to seek for shelter elsewhere, and first pitched upon Tâyef, about sixty miles east from Mecca, for the place of his retreat. Thither therefore he went, accompanied by his servant Zeid, and applied himself to two of the chief of the tribe of Thakîf, who were the inhabitants of that place, but they received him very coldly. However, he stayed there a month; and some of the more considerate and better sort of men treated him with a little respect: but the slaves and inferior people at length rose against him, and bringing him to the wall of the city, obliged him to depart, and return to Mecca, where he put himself under the protection of al Motáam Ebn Adi.

This repulse greatly discouraged his followers: however, Mohammed was not wanting to himself, but boldly continued to preach to the public assemblies at the pilgrimage, and gained several proselytes, and among them six of the inhabitants of Yathreb of the Jewish tribe of Khazraj, who, on their return home, failed not to speak much in commendation of their new religion, and exhorted their fellow-citizens to embrace the same.

In the twelfth year of his mission it was that Mohammed gave out that he had made his night journey from Mecca to Jerusalem, and thence to heaven, so much spoken of by all that write of him. Dr Prideaux thinks he intended it either to answer the expectations of those who demanded some miracle as a proof of his mission; or else, by pretending to have conversed with God, to establish the authority of whatever he should think fit to leave behind by way of oral tradition, and make his sayings to serve the same purpose as the oral law of the Jews. But I do not find that Mohammed himself ever expected so great a regard should be paid to his sayings as his followers have since done: and seeing he all along disclaimed any power of performing miracles, it seems rather to have been a fetch of policy to raise his reputation, by pretending to have actually conversed with God in heaven, as Moses had heretofore done on the mount, and to have received several institutions immediately from him, whereas before he contented himself with persuading them that he had all by the ministry of Gabriel.

However, this story seemed so absurd and incredible that several of his followers left him upon it, and it had probably ruined his whole design, had not Abu Becr vouched for its veracity, and declared that if Mohammed affirmed it to be true, he verily believed the whole. Which happy incident not only retrieved the prophet's credit, but increased it to such a degree, that he was secure of being able to make his disciples swallow whatever he pleased to impose on them for the future. And I am apt to think this fiction, notwithstanding its extravagance, was one of the most artful contrivances Mohammed ever put in practice, and what chiefly contributed to the raising of his reputation to that great height to which it afterwards arrived.

In this year, called by Mohammedans the accepted year, twelve men of Yathreb or Medina, of whom ten were of the tribe of Khazraj, and the other two of that of Aws, came to Mecca, and took an oath of fidelity to Mohammed at al Akaba, a hill on the north of that city. This oath was called the woman's oath; not that any women were present at this time, but because a man was not thereby obliged to take up arms in defence of Mohammed or his religion; it being the same oath that was afterwards exacted of the women, the form of which we have in the Korân, and is to this effect, viz. – "That they should renounce all idolatry; that they should not steal, nor commit fornication, nor kill their children (as the pagan Arabs used to do when they apprehended they should not be able to maintain them), nor forge calumnies; and that they should obey the prophet in all things that were reasonable." When they had solemnly engaged to do all this, Mohammed sent one of his disciples, named Masáb Ebn Omair, home with them, to instruct them more fully in the grounds and ceremonies of his new religion.

Masáb, being arrived at Medina, by the assistance of those who had been formerly converted, gained several proselytes, particularly Osaid Ebn Hodeira, a chief man of the city, and Saad Ebn Moâdh, prince of the tribe of Aws; Mohammedism spreading so fast that there was scarce a house wherein there were not some who had embraced it.

The next year, being the thirteenth of Mohammed's mission, Masáb returned to Mecca, accompanied by seventy-three men and two women of Medina who had professed Islamism, besides some others who were as yet unbelievers. On their arrival, they immediately sent to Mohammed, and offered him their assistance, of which he was now in great need, for his adversaries were by this time grown so powerful in Mecca, that he could not stay there much longer without imminent danger. Wherefore he accepted their proposal, and met them one night, by appointment, at al Akaba above mentioned, attended by his uncle al Abbas, who, though he was not then a believer, wished his nephew well, and made a speech to those of Medina, wherein he told them, that, as Mohammed was obliged to quit his native city and seek an asylum elsewhere, and they had offered him their protection, they would do well not to deceive him; and that, if they were not firmly resolved to defend and not betray him, they had better declare their minds, and let him provide for his safety in some other manner. Upon their protesting their sincerity, Mohammed swore to be faithful to them; on condition that they should protect him against all insults, as heartily as they would their own wives and families. They then asked him what recompense they were to expect if they should happen to be killed in his quarrel; he answered paradise. Whereupon they pledged their faith to him, and so returned home, after Mohammed had chosen twelve out of their number, who were to have the same authority among them as the twelve apostles of Christ had among his disciples.

Hitherto Mohammed had propagated his religion by fair means, so that the whole success of his enterprise before his flight to Medina must be attributed to persuasion only, and not to compulsion. For before this second oath of fealty or inauguration at al Akaba, he had no permission to use any force at all; and in several places of the Korân, which he pretended were revealed during his stay at Mecca, he declares his business was only to preach and admonish, that he had no authority to compel any person to embrace his religion; and that whether people believed, or not, was none of his concern, but belonged solely unto God. And he was so far from allowing his followers to use force, that he exhorted them to bear patiently those injuries which were offered them on account of their faith; and when persecuted himself, chose rather to quit the place of his birth and retire to Medina, than to make any resistance. But this great passiveness and moderation seems entirely owing to his want of power, and the great superiority of his opposers for the first twelve years of his mission; for no sooner was he enabled, by the assistance of those of Medina, to make head against his enemies, than he gave out that God had allowed him and his followers to defend themselves against the infidels; and at length, as his forces increased, he pretended to have the divine leave even to attack them and to destroy idolatry, and set up the true faith by the sword; finding, by experience, that his designs would otherwise proceed very slowly, if they were not utterly overthrown; and knowing on the other hand that innovators, when they depend solely on their own strength, and can compel, seldom run any risk; from whence the politician observes, it follows, that all the armed prophets have succeeded, and the unarmed ones have failed. Moses, Cyrus, Theseus, and Romulus would not have been able to establish the observance of their institutions for any length of time, had they not been armed. The first passage of the Korân which gave Mohammed the permission of defending himself by arms is said to have been that in the twenty-second chapter; after which a great number to the same purpose were revealed.

That Mohammed had a right to take up arms for his own defence against his unjust persecutors, may perhaps be allowed; but whether he ought afterwards to have made use of that means for the establishing of his religion is a question I will not here determine. How far the secular power may or ought to interpose in affairs of this nature mankind are not agreed. The method of converting by the sword gives no very favourable idea of the faith which is so propagated, and is disallowed by every body in those of another religion, though the same persons are willing to admit of it for the advancement of their own; supposing that though a false religion ought not to be established by authority, yet a true one may; and accordingly force is almost as constantly employed in these cases by those who have the power in their hands, as it is constantly complained of by those who suffer the violence. It is certainly one of the most convincing proofs that Mohammedism was no other than a human invention, that it owed it progress and establishment almost entirely to the sword; and it is one of the strongest demonstrations of the divine original of Christianity, that it prevailed against all the force and powers of the world by the mere dint of its own truth, after having stood the assaults of all manner of persecutions, as well as other oppositions, for three hundred years together, and at length made the Roman emperors themselves submit thereto, after which time indeed this proof seems to fail, Christianity being then established and paganism abolished by public authority, which has had great influence in the propagation of the one and destruction of the other ever since. But to return.

Mohammed having provided for the security of his companions as well as his own, by the league offensive and defensive which he had now concluded with those of Medina, directed them to repair thither, which they accordingly did; but himself with Abu Becr and Ali stayed behind, having not yet received the divine permission, as he pretended, to leave Mecca. The Koreish, fearing the consequence of this new alliance, began to think it absolutely necessary to prevent Mohammed's escape to Medina, and having held a council thereon, after several milder expedients had been rejected, they came to a resolution that he should be killed; and agreed that a man should be chosen out of every tribe for the execution of this design, and that each man should have a blow at him with his sword, that the guilt of his blood might fall equally on all the tribes, to whose united power the Hashemites were much inferior, and therefore durst not attempt to revenge their kinsman's death.

This conspiracy was scarce formed when by some means or other it came to Mohammed's knowledge, and he gave out that it was revealed to him by the angel Gabriel, who had now ordered him to retire to Medina. Whereupon, to amuse his enemies, he directed Ali to lie down in his place and wrap himself up in his green cloak, which he did, and Mohammed escaped miraculously as they pretend, to Abu Becr's house, unperceived by the conspirators, who had already assembled at the prophet's door. They in the mean time, looking through a crevice and seeing Ali, whom they took to be Mohammed himself, asleep, continued watching there till morning, when Ali arose and they found themselves deceived.

From Abu Becr's house Mohammed and he went to a cave in Mount Thûr, to the south-east of Mecca, accompanied only by Amer Ebn Foheirah, Abu Becr's servant, and Abd'allah Ebn Oreikat, an idolater, whom they had hired for a guide. In this cave they lay hid three days to avoid the search of their enemies, which they very narrowly escaped, and not without the assistance of more miracles than one; for some say that the Koreish were struck with blindness, so that they could not find the cave; others, that after Mohammed and his companions were got in, two pigeons laid their eggs at the entrance, and a spider covered the mouth of the cave with her web, which made them look no farther. Abu Becr seeing the prophet in such imminent danger became very sorrowful, whereupon Mohammed comforted him with these words, recorded in the Korân – "Be not grieved, for God is with us." Their enemies being retired, they left the cave and set out for Medina, by a by-road, and having fortunately, or as the Mohammedans tell us, miraculously escaped some who were sent to pursue them, arrived safely in the city; whither Ali followed them in three days, after he had settled some affairs at Mecca.

The first thing Mohammed did after his arrival in Medina was to build a temple for his religious worship; and a house for himself, which he did on a parcel of ground which had before served to put camels in, or as others tell us, for a burying ground, and belonged to Sahal and Soheil the sons of Amru, who were orphans. This action Dr Prideaux exclaims against, representing it as a flagrant instance of injustice, for that, says he, he violently dispossessed these poor orphans, the sons of an inferior artificer (whom the author he quotes calls a carpenter) of this ground, and so founded the first fabric of his worship with the like wickedness as he did his religion. But to say nothing of the improbability that Mohammed should act in so impolitic a manner at his first coming, the Mohammedan writers set this affair in a quite different light; one tells us that he treated with the lads about the price of the ground, but they desired he would accept it as a present; however, as historians of good credit assure us, he actually bought it, and the money was paid by Abu Becr. Besides, had Mohammed accepted it as a present, the orphans were in circumstances sufficient to have afforded it; for they were of a very good family, of the tribe Najjâr, one of the most illustrious among the Arabs, and not the sons of a carpenter, as Dr Prideaux's author writes, who took the word Najjâr, which signifies a carpenter, for an appellative, whereas it is a proper name.

Mohammed being securely settled at Medina, and able not only to defend himself against the insults of his enemies, but to attack them, began to send out small parties to make reprisals on the Koreish; the first party consisting of no more than nine men, who intercepted and plundered a caravan belonging to that tribe, and in the action took two prisoners. But what established his affairs very much, and was the foundation on which he built all his succeeding greatness, was the gaining of the battle of Bedr, which was fought in the second year of the Hejra, and is so famous in the Mohammedan history. As my design is not to write the life of Mohammed, but only to describe the manner in which he carried on his enterprise, I shall not enter into any detail of his subsequent battles and expeditions, which amounted to a considerable number. Some reckon no fewer than twenty-seven expeditions wherein Mohammed was personally present, in nine of which he gave battle, besides several other expeditions in which he was not present. Some of them however will be necessarily taken notice of in explaining several passages of the Korân. His forces he maintained partly by the contributions of his followers for this purpose, which he called by the name of zacât or alms, and the paying of which he very artfully made one main article of his religion; and partly by ordering a fifth part of the plunder to be brought into the public treasury for that purpose, in which matter he likewise pretended to act by the divine direction.

In a few years, by the success of his arms (notwithstanding he sometimes came off the worst), he considerably raised his credit and power. In the sixth year of the Hejra he set out with 1400 men to visit the temple of Mecca, not with any intent of committing hostilities, but in a peaceable manner. However when he came to al Hodeibiya, which is situated partly within and partly without the sacred territory, the Koreish sent to let him know that they would not permit him to enter Mecca, unless he forced his way; whereupon he called his troops about him, and they all took a solemn oath of fealty or homage to him, and he resolved to attack the city; but those of Mecca sending Arwa Ebn Masúd, prince of the tribe of Thakîf, as their ambassador to desire peace, a truce was concluded between them for ten years, by which any person was allowed to enter into league either with Mohammed or the Koreish as he thought fit.

It may not be improper, to show the inconceivable veneration and respect the Mohammedans by this time had for their prophet, to mention the account which the above-mentioned ambassador gave the Koreish, at his return, of their behaviour. He said he had been at the courts both of the Roman emperor and of the king of Persia, and never saw any prince so highly respected by his subjects as Mohammed was by his companions; for whenever he made the ablution, in order to say his prayers, they ran and catched the water that he had used; and whenever he spit, they immediately licked it up, and gathered every hair that fell from him with great superstition.

In the seventh year of the Hejra, Mohammed began to think of propagating his religion beyond the bounds of Arabia, and sent messengers to the neighbouring princes with letters to invite them to Mohammedism. Nor was this project without some success. Khosrû Parviz, then king of Persia, received his letter with great disdain, and tore it in a passion, sending away the messenger very abruptly; which, when Mohammed heard, he said, God shall tear his kingdom. And soon after a messenger came to Mohammed from Badhân king of Yaman, who was a dependant on the Persians, to acquaint him that he had received orders to send him to Khosrû. Mohammed put off his answer till the next morning, and then told the messenger it had been revealed to him that night, that Khosrû was slain by his son Shirûyeh; adding that he was well assured his new religion and empire should rise to as great a height as that of Khosrû; and therefore bid him advise his master to embrace Mohammedism. The messenger being returned, Badhân in a few days received a letter from Shirûyeh informing him of his father's death, and ordering him to give the prophet no further disturbance. Whereupon Badhân and the Persians with him turned Mohammedans.

The emperor Heraclius, as the Arabian historians assure us, received Mohammed's letter with great respect, laying it on his pillow, and dismissed the bearer honourably. And some pretend that he would have professed this new faith, had he not been afraid of losing his crown.

Mohammed wrote to the same effect to the king of Ethiopia, though he had been converted before, according to the Arab writers; and to Mokawkas, governor of Egypt, who gave the messenger a very favourable reception, and sent several valuable presents to Mohammed, and among the rest two girls, one of which, named Mary, became a great favourite with him. He also sent letters of the like purport to several Arab princes, particularly one to al Hareth Ebn Abi Shamer king of Ghassân, who returning for answer that he would go to Mohammed himself, the prophet said, May his kingdom perish; another to Hawdha Ebu Ali, king of Yamâma, who was a Christian, and having some time before professed Islamism, had lately returned to his former faith; this prince sent back a very rough answer, upon which, Mohammed cursing him, he died soon after; a third to al Mondar Ebn Sâwa, king of Bahrein, who embraced Mohammedism, and all the Arabs of that country followed his example.

The eighth year of the Hejra was a very fortunate year to Mohammed. In the beginning of it Khâled Ebn al Walîd and Amru Ebn al As, both excellent soldiers, the first of whom afterwards conquered Syria and other countries, and the latter Egypt, became proselytes of Mohammedism. And soon after the prophet sent 3000 men against the Grecian forces, to revenge the death of one of his ambassadors, who being sent to the governor of Bosra, on the same errand as those who went to the above-mentioned princes, was slain by an Arab of the tribe of Ghassân at Mûta, a town in the territory of Balkâ in Syria, about three days' journey eastward from Jerusalem, near which town they encountered. The Grecians being vastly superior in number (for, including the auxiliary Arabs, they had an army of 100,000 men), the Mohammedans were repulsed in the first attack, and lost successively three of their generals, viz. Zeid Ebn Hâretha, Mohammed's freedman, Jaafar the son of Abu Tâleb, and Abdâllah Ebn Rawâha; but Khâled Ebn al Walîd, succeeding to the command, overthrew the Greeks with a great slaughter, and brought away abundance of rich spoil, on occasion of which action Mohammed gave him the honourable title of Seif min soyûf Allah, one of the swords of God.

In this year also Mohammed took the city of Mecca, the inhabitants whereof had broken the truce concluded on two years before. For the tribe of Becr, who were confederates of the Koreish, attacking those of Khozâah, who were allies of Mohammed, killed several of them, being supported in the action by a party of the Koreish themselves. The consequence of this violation was soon apprehended; and Abu Sofiân himself made a journey to Medina on purpose to heal the breach and renew the truce; but in vain; for Mohammed, glad of this opportunity, refused to see him; whereupon he applied to Abu Becr and Ali, but they giving him no answer, he was obliged to return to Mecca as he came.

Mohammed immediately gave orders for preparations to be made, that he might surprise the Meccans while they were unprovided to receive him: in a little time he began his march thither, and by the time he came near the city his forces were increased to 10,000 men. Those of Mecca being not in a condition to defend themselves against so formidable an army, surrendered at discretion; and Abu Sofiân saved his life by turning Mohammedan. About twenty-eight of the idolaters were killed by a party under the command of Khâled; but this happened contrary to Mohammed's orders, who, when he entered the town, pardoned all the Koreish on their submission, except only six men and four women, who were more obnoxious than ordinary (some of them having apostatized), and were solemnly proscribed by the prophet himself; but of these no more than three men and one woman were put to death, the rest obtaining pardon on their embracing Mohammedism, and one of the women making her escape.

The remainder of this year Mohammed employed in destroying the idols in and round about Mecca, sending several of his generals on expeditions for that purpose, and to invite the Arabs to Islamism; wherein it is no wonder if they now met with success.

The next year, being the ninth of the Hejra, the Mohammedans call the year of embassies: for the Arabs had been hitherto expecting the issue of the war between Mohammed and the Koreish; but so soon as the tribe, the principal of the whole nation, and the genuine descendants of Ishmael, whose prerogatives none offered to dispute, had submitted, they were satisfied that it was not in their power to oppose Mohammed, and therefore began to come in to him in great numbers, and to send embassies to make their submissions to him, both to Mecca while he staid there, and also to Medina whither he returned this year. Among the rest, five kings of the tribe of Hamyar professed Mohammedism, and sent ambassadors to notify the same.

In the tenth year Ali was sent into Yaman to propagate the Mohammedan faith there, and, as it is said, converted the whole tribe of Hamdân in one day. Their example was quickly followed by all the inhabitants of that province, except only those of Najrân, who, being Christians, chose rather to pay tribute.

Thus was Mohammedism established, and idolatry rooted out, even in Mohammed's life time (for he died the next year) throughout all Arabia, except only Yamama; where Moseilama, who set up also for a prophet as Mohammed's competitor, had a great party, and was not reduced till the Khalîfat of Abu Becr. And the Arabs being then united in one faith under one prince, found themselves in a condition of making those conquests which extended the Mohammedan faith over so great a part of the world.

OF THE KORAN ITSELF, THE PECULIARITIES OF THAT BOOK; THE MANNER OF ITS BEING WRITTEN AND PUBLISHED, AND THE GENERAL DESIGN OF IT

The word Korân, derived from the verb karaa, to read, signifies properly in Arabic, the reading, or rather, that which ought to be read; by which name the Mohammedans denote not only the entire book or volume of the Korân, but also any particular chapter or section of it; just as the Jews call either the whole scripture, or any part of it by the name of Karâh, or Mikra, words of the same origin and import. Which observation seems to overthrow the opinion of some learned Arabians, who would have the Korân so named, because it is a collection of the loose chapters or sheets which compose it; the verb karaa signifying also to gather or collect: and may also, by the way, serve as an answer to those who object that the Korân must be a book forged at once, and could not possibly be revealed by parcels at different times, during the course of several years, as the Mohammedans affirm; because the Korân is often mentioned, and called by the name, in the very book itself. It may not be amiss to observe, that the syllable Al in the word Alkoran is only the Arabic article, signifying *the*; and therefore ought to be omitted when the English article is prefixed.

Beside this peculiar name, the Korân is also honoured with several appellations common to other books of scripture: as al Forkân, from the verb faraka, to divide or distinguish; not as the Mohammedan doctors say, because those books are divided into chapters or sections, or distinguish between good and evil, but in the same notion that the Jews use the word Perek, or Pirka, from the same root, to denote a section or portion of Scripture. It is also called al Moshâf, the volume, and al Kitâb, the book, by way of eminence, which answers to the Biblia of the Greeks; and al Dhikr, the admonition, which name is also given to the Pentateuch and Gospel.

The Korân is divided into one hundred and fourteen larger portions of very unequal length, which we call chapters, but the Arabians Sowar, in the singular Sûra, a word rarely used on any other occasion, and properly signifying a row, order, or regular series; as a course of bricks in building, or a rank of soldiers in an army; and is the same in use and import with the Sûra, or Tora of the Jews, who also call the fifty-three sections of the Pentateuch Sedârim, a word of the same signification.

These chapters are not in the manuscript copies distinguished by their numerical order, though, for the reader's ease, they are numbered in this edition, but by particular titles, which (except that of the first, which is the initial chapter, or introduction to the rest, and by the old Latin translator not numbered among the chapters) are taken sometimes from a particular matter treated of, or person mentioned therein; but usually from the first word of note, exactly in the same manner as the Jews have named their Sedârim; though the word from which some chapters are denominated be very far distant, towards the middle, or perhaps the end of the chapter, which seems ridiculous. But the occasion of this seems to have been, that the verse or passage wherein such word occurs was, in point of time, revealed and committed to writing before the other verses of the same chapter which precede it in order; and the title being given to the chapter before it was completed, or the passages reduced to their present order, the verse from whence such title was taken did not always happen to begin the chapter. Some chapters have two or more titles, occasioned by the difference of the copies.

Some of the chapters having been revealed at Mecca, and others at Medina, the noting this difference makes a part of the title: but the reader will observe that several of the chapters are said to have been revealed partly at Mecca, and partly at Medina; and as to others, it is yet a dispute among the commentators to which place of the two they belong.

Every chapter is subdivided into smaller portions, of very unequal length also, which we customarily call verses; but the Arabic word is Ayât, the same with the Hebrew Ototh, and signifies signs, or wonders; such as are the secrets of God, his attributes, works, judgments, and ordinances, delivered in those verses; many of which have their particular titles also, imposed in the same manner as those of the chapters.

Notwithstanding this subdivision is common, and well known, yet I have never yet seen any manuscript wherein the verses are actually numbered; though in some copies the number of verses in each chapter is set down after the title, which we have therefore added in the table of the chapters. And the Mohammedans seem to have some scruple in making an actual distinction in their copies, because the chief disagreement between their several editions of the Korân consists in the division and number of the verses; and for this reason I have not taken upon me to make any such division.

Having mentioned the different editions of the Korân, it may not be amiss here to acquaint the reader, that there are seven principal editions, if I may so call them, or ancient copies of that book; two of which were published and used at Medina, a third at Mecca, a fourth at Cufa, a fifth at Basra, a sixth in Syria, and a seventh called the common or vulgar edition. Of these editions, the first of Medina makes the whole number of the verses six thousand; the second and fifth, six thousand two hundred and fourteen; the third, six thousand two hundred and nineteen; the fourth, six thousand two hundred and thirty-six; the sixth, six thousand two hundred and twenty-six; and the last, six thousand two hundred and twenty-five. But they are all said to contain the same number of words, namely seventy-seven thousand six hundred and thirty-nine, and the same number of letters, viz., three hundred and twenty-three thousand and fifteen: for the Mohammedans have in this also imitated the Jews, that they have superstitiously numbered the very words and letters of their law; nay, they have taken the pains to compute (how exactly I know not) the number of times each particular letter of the alphabet is contained in the Korân.

Besides these unequal divisions of chapter and verse, the Mohammedans have also divided their Korân into sixty equal portions, which they call Ahzâb, in the singular Hizb, each subdivided into four equal parts; which is also an imitation of the Jews, who have an ancient division of their Mishna into sixty portions called Massictoth: but the Korân is more usually divided into thirty sections only, named Ajzâ, from the singular Joz, each of twice the length of the former, and in the like manner subdivided into four parts. These divisions are for the use of the readers of the

Korân in the royal temples, or in the adjoining chapels where the emperors and great men are interred. There are thirty of these readers belonging to every chapel, and each reads his section every day, so that the whole Korân is read over once a day. I have seen several copies divided in this manner, and bound up in as many volumes; and have thought it proper to mark these divisions in the margin of this translation by numeral letters.

Next after the title, at the head of every chapter except only the ninth, is prefixed the following solemn form, by the Mohammedans called the Bismillah, "In the name of the most merciful God"; which form they constantly place at the beginning of all their books and writings in general, as a peculiar mark or distinguishing characteristic of their religion, it being counted a sort of impiety to omit it. The Jews for the same purpose make use of the form, In the name of the Lord, or, in the name of the great God: and the eastern Christians that of, In the name of the Father, and of the Son, and of the Holy Ghost. But I am apt to believe Mohammed really took this form, as he did many other things, from the Persian Magi, who used to begin their books in these words, Benâm Yezdân bakhshaïshgher dâdâr, that is, In the name of the most merciful, just God.

This auspicatory form, and also the titles of the chapters, are, by the generality of the doctors and commentators, believed to be of divine original, no less than the text itself; but the more moderate are of opinion they are only human additions, and not the very word of God.

There are twenty-nine chapters of the Korân, which have this peculiarity, that they begin with certain letters of the alphabet, some with a single one, others with more. These letters the Mohammedans believe to be the peculiar marks of the Korân, and to conceal several profound mysteries, the certain understanding of which, the more intelligent confess has not been communicated to any mortal, their prophet only excepted. Notwithstanding which, some will take the liberty of guessing at their meaning by that species of Cabbala called by the Jews Notarikon, and suppose the letters to stand for as many words expressing the names and attributes of God, his works, ordinances, and decrees; and therefore these mysterious letters, as well as the verses themselves, seem in the Korân to be called signs. Others explain the intent of these letters from the nature or organ, or else from their value in numbers, according to another species of the Jewish Cabbala called Gematria; the uncertainty of which conjectures sufficiently appears from their disagreement. Thus, for example, five chapters, one of which is the second, begin with these letters, A. L. M. which some imagine to stand for Allah latîf magîd; God is gracious and to be glorified; or, Ana li minni, to me and from me, viz. belongs all perfection, and proceeds all good: or else for Ana Allah âlam, I am the most wise God, taking the first letter to mark the beginning of the first word, the second the middle of the second word, and the third the last of the third word; or for Allah, Gabriel, Mohammed, the author, revealer, and preacher of the Korân. Others say, that as the letter A belongs to the lower part of the throat, the first of the organs of speech; L to the palate, the middle organ; and M to the lips, which are the last organ; so these letters signify that God is the beginning, middle, and end, or ought to be praised in the beginning, middle, and end, of all our words and actions: or, as the total value of those three letters in numbers is seventy-one, they signify that in the space of so many years, the religion preached in the Korân should be fully established. The conjecture of a learned Christian is at least as certain as any of the former, who supposes these letters were set there by the amanuensis, for Amar li Mohammed, i.e. At the command of Mohammed, as the five letters prefixed to the nineteenth chapter seem to be there written by a Jewish scribe, Cob Yaas, i.e. Thus he commanded.

The Korân is universally allowed to be written with the utmost elegance and purity of language, in the dialect of the tribe of Koreish, the most noble and polite of all the Arabians, but with some mixture, though very rarely, of other dialects. It is confessedly the standard of the Arabic tongue, and as the more orthodox believe, and are taught by the book itself, inimitable by any human pen (though some sectaries have been of another opinion) and therefore insisted on as a permanent miracle, greater than that of raising the dead, and alone sufficient to convince the world of its divine original.

And to this miracle did Mohammed himself chiefly appeal for the confirmation of his mission, publicly challenging the most eloquent men in Arabia, which was at this time stocked with thousands whose sole study and ambition it was to excel in elegance of style and composition, to produce even a single chapter that might be compared with it. I will mention but one instance out of several, to show that this book was really admired for the beauty of its composure by those who must be allowed to have been competent judges. A poem of Labîd Ebn Rabîa, one of the greatest wits in Arabia in Mohammed's time, being fixed up on the gate of the temple of Mecca, an honour allowed to none but the most esteemed performances, none of the other poets durst offer any of their own in competition with it. But the second chapter of the Korân being fixed up by it soon after, Labîd himself (then an idolater) on reading the first verses only, was struck with admiration, and immediately professed the religion taught thereby, declaring that such words could proceed from an inspired person only. This Labîd was afterwards of great service to Mohammed, in writing answers to the satires and invectives that were make on him and his religion by the infidels, and particularly by Amri al Kais, prince of the tribe of Asad, and author of one of those seven famous poems called al Moallakat.

The style of the Korân is generally beautiful and fluent, especially where it imitates the prophetic manner, and scripture phrases. It is concise, and often obscure, adorned with bold figures after the eastern taste, enlivened with florid and sententious expressions, and in many places, especially where the majesty and attributes of God are described, sublime and magnificent; of which the reader cannot but observe several instances, though he must not imagine the translation comes up to the original, notwithstanding my endeavours to do it justice.

Though it be written in prose, yet the sentences generally conclude in a long continued rhyme, for the sake of which the sense is often interrupted, and unnecessary repetitions too frequently made, which appear still more ridiculous in a translation, where the ornament, such as it is, for whose sake they were made, cannot be perceived. However, the Arabians are so mightily delighted with this jingling that they employ it in their most elaborate compositions, which they also embellish with frequent passages of and allusions to the Korân, so that it is next to impossible to understand them without being well versed in this book.

It is probable the harmony of expression which the Arabians find in the Korân might contribute not a little to make them relish the doctrine therein taught, and give an efficacy to arguments, which, had they been nakedly proposed without this rhetorical dress, might not have so easily prevailed. Very extraordinary effects are related of the power of words well chosen and artfully placed, which are no less powerful either to ravish or amaze than music itself; wherefore as much has been ascribed by the best orators to this part of rhetoric as to any other. He must have a very bad ear, who is not uncommonly moved with the very cadence of a well-turned sentence; and Mohammed seems not to have been ignorant of the enthusiastic operation of rhetoric on the minds of men; for which reason he has not only employed his utmost skill in these his pretended revelations, to preserve that dignity and sublimity of style, which might seem not unworthy of the majesty of that Being, whom he gave out to be the author of them; and to imitate the prophetic manner of the Old Testament; but he has not neglected even the other arts of oratory; wherein he succeeded so well, and so strangely captivated the minds of his audience, that several of his opponents thought it the effect of witchcraft and enchantment, as he sometimes complains.

"The general design of the Korân" (to use the words of a very learned person), "seems to be this. To unite the professors of the three different religions then followed in the populous country of Arabia, who, for the most part, lived promiscuously, and wandered without guides, the far greater number being idolators, and the rest Jews and Christians mostly of erroneous and heterodox belief, in the knowledge and worship of one eternal, invisible God, by whose power all things were made, and those which are not, may be, the supreme Governor, Judge, and absolute Lord of the creation; established under the sanction of certain laws, and the outward signs of certain ceremonies, partly of ancient and partly of novel institution, and enforced by setting before them rewards and punishments, both temporal and eternal: and to bring them all to the obedience of Mohammed, as the prophet and ambassador of God, who after the repeated admonitions, promises, and threats of former ages, was at last to establish and propagate God's religion on earth by force of arms, and to be acknowledged chief pontiff in spiritual matters, as well as supreme prince in temporal."

The great doctrine then of the Korân is the unity of God; to restore which point Mohammed pretended was the chief end of his mission; it being laid down by him as a fundamental truth, that there never was nor ever can be more than one true orthodox religion. For though the particular laws or ceremonies are only temporary, and subject to alteration according to the divine direction, yet the substance of it being eternal truth, is not liable to change, but continues immutably the same. And he taught that whenever this religion became neglected, or corrupted in essentials, God had the goodness to reinform and readmonish mankind thereof, by several prophets, of whom Moses and Jesus were the most distinguished, till the appearance of Mohammed, who is their seal, no other being to be expected after him. And the more effectually to engage people to hearken to him, great part of the Korân is employed in relating examples of dreadful punishments formerly inflicted by God on those who rejected and abused his messengers; several of which stories or some circumstances of them are taken from the Old and New Testament, but many more from the apocryphal books and traditions of the Jews and Christians of those ages, set up in the Korân as truths in opposition to the scriptures, which the Jews and Christians are charged with having altered; and I am apt to believe that few or none of the relations or circumstances in the Korân were invented by Mohammed, as is generally supposed, it being easy to trace the greatest part of them much higher, as the rest might be, were more of those books extant, and it was worth while to make the inquiry.

The other part of the Korân is taken up in giving necessary laws and directions, in frequent admonitions to moral and divine virtues, and above all to the worshipping and reverencing of the only true God, and resignation to his will; among which are many excellent things intermixed, not unworthy even a Christian's perusal.

But, besides these, there are a great number of passages which are occasional, and relate to particular emergencies. For whenever any thing happened which perplexed and gravelled Mohammed, and which he could not otherwise get over, he had constant recourse to a new revelation, as an infallible expedient in all nice cases; and he found the success of this method answered his expectation. It was certainly an admirable and politic contrivance of his to bring down the whole Korân at once to the lowest heaven only, and not to the earth, as a bungling prophet would have done; for if the whole had been published at once, innumerable objections might have been made which it would have been very hard, if not impossible for him to solve: but as he pretended to have received it by parcels, as God saw proper that they should be published for the conversion and instruction of the people, he had a sure way to answer all emergencies, and to extricate himself with honour from any difficulty which might occur. If any objection be hence made to that eternity of the Korân, which the Mohammedans are taught to believe, they easily answer it by their doctrine of absolute predestination; according to which all the accidents for the sake of which these occasional passages were revealed were predetermined by God from all eternity.

That Mohammed was really the author and chief contriver of the Korân, is beyond dispute; though it is highly probable that he had no small assistance in his design from others, as his countrymen failed not to object to him; however they differed so much in their conjectures as to the particular persons who gave him such assistance, that they were not able, it seems, to prove the charge; Mohammed, it is to be presumed, having taken his measures too well to be discovered. Dr Prideaux has given the most probable account of this matter, though chiefly from Christian writers, who generally mix such ridiculous fables with what they deliver, that they deserve not much credit.

However it be, the Mohammedans absolutely deny the Korân was composed by their prophet himself, or any other for him; it being their general and orthodox belief that it is of divine origin, nay that it is eternal and uncreated, remaining, as some express it, in the very essence of God; that the first transcript has been from everlasting by God's throne, written on a table of vast bigness, called the preserved table, in which are also recorded the divine decrees past and future, that a copy from this table, in one volume on paper, was, by the ministry of the angel Gabriel, sent down to the lowest heaven, in the month of Ramadân, on the night of power: from whence Gabriel revealed it to Mohammed by parcels, some at Mecca and some at Medina, at different times, during the space of twenty-three years, as the exigency of affairs required: giving him however the consolation to show him the whole (which they tell us was bound in silk, and adorned with gold and precious stones of paradise) once a year: but in the last year of his life he had the favour to see it twice. They say that few chapters were delivered entire, the most part being revealed piecemeal, and written down from time to time by the prophet's amanuensis in such or such a part of such or such a chapter till they were completed, according to the directions of the angel. The first parcel that was revealed is generally agreed to have been the first five verses of the ninety-sixth chapter.

After the new revealed passages had been from the prophet's mouth taken down in writing by his scribe, they were published to his followers, several of whom took copies for their private use, but the far greater number got them by heart. The originals, when returned, were put promiscuously into a chest, observing no order of time, for which reason it is uncertain when many passages were revealed

When Mohammed died, he left his revelations in the same disorder I have mentioned, and not digested into the method, such as it is, which we now find them in. This was the work of his successor Abu Becr, who, considering that a great number of passages were committed to the memory of Mohammed's followers, many of whom were slain in their wars, ordered the whole to be collected, not only from the palm-leaves and skins on which they had been written, and which were kept between two boards or covers but also from the mouths of such as had gotten them by heart. And this transcript, when completed, he committed to the custody of Hafsa the daughter of Omar, one of the prophet's widows.

From this relation it is generally imagined, that Abu Becr was really the compiler of the Korân; though for aught appears to the contrary, Mohammed left the chapters complete as we now have them, excepting such passages as his successor might add or correct from those who had gotten them by heart; what Abu Becr did else being perhaps no more than to range the chapters in their present order, which he seems to have done without any regard to time, having generally placed the longest first.

However, in the thirtieth year of the Hejra, Othmân being then Khalîf, and observing the great disagreement in the copies of the Korân in the several provinces of the empire, those of Irak, for example, following the reading of Abu Musa al Ashari, and the Syrians that of Macdâd Ebn Aswad, he, by advice of the companions, ordered a great number of copies to be transcribed from that of Abu Becr, in Hafsa's care, under the inspection of Zeid Ebn Thabet, Abd'allah Ebn Zobair, Saïd Ebn al As, and Abd'alrahamân Ebn al Hâreth the Makhzumite; whom he directed that wherever they disagreed about any word, they should write it in the dialect of the Koreish, in which it was at first delivered. These copies when made were dispersed in the several provinces of the empire, and the old ones burnt and suppressed. Though many things in Hafsa's copy were corrected by the above-mentioned supervisors, yet some few various readings still occur; the most material of which will be taken notice of in their proper places.

The want of vowels in the Arabic character made Mokrîs, or readers, whose peculiar study and profession it was to read the Korân with its proper vowels, absolutely necessary. But these differing in their manner of reading, occasioned still further variations in the copies of the Korân, as they are now written with the vowels; and herein consist much the greater part of the various readings throughout the book. The readers whose authority the commentators chiefly allege, in admitting these various readings, are seven in number.

There being some passages in the Korân which are contradictory, the Mohammedan doctors obviate any objection from thence, by the doctrine of abrogation; for they say, that God in the Korân commanded several things which were, for good reasons, afterward revoked and abrogated.

Passages abrogated are distinguished into three kinds: the first, where the letter and sense are both abrogated; the second, where the letter only is abrogated, but the sense remains; and the third were the sense is abrogated, though the letter remains.

Of the first kind were several verses, which, by the tradition of Malec Ebn Ans, were in the prophet's lifetime read in the chapter of repentance, but are not now extant; one of which, being all he remembered of them, was the following, "If a son of Adam had two rivers of gold, he would covet yet a third; and if he had three, he would covet yet a fourth (to be added) unto them; neither shall the belly of a son of Adam be filled, but with dust. God will turn unto him who shall repent." Another instance of this kind we have from the tradition of Abd'allah Ebn Masûd, who reported that the prophet gave him a verse to read which he wrote down; but the next morning looking in his book, he found it was vanished, and the leaf blank: this he acquainted Mohammed with, who assured him the verse was revoked the same night.

Of the second kind is a verse called the verse of stoning, which, according to the tradition of Omar, afterwards Khalîf, was extant while Mohammed was living, though it be not now to be found. The words are these, "Abhor not your parents, for this would be ingratitude in you. If a man and woman of reputation commit adultery, ye shall stone them both; it is a punishment ordained by God; for God is mighty and wise."

Of the last kind are observed several verses in sixty-three different chapters, to the number of two hundred and twenty-five. Such as the precepts of turning in prayer to Jerusalem; fasting after the old custom; forbearance towards idolaters; avoiding the ignorant and the like. The passages of this sort have been carefully selected by several writers, and are most of them remarked in their proper places.

Though it is the belief of the Sonnites or orthodox that the Korân is uncreated and eternal, subsisting in the very essence of God, and Mohammed himself is said to have pronounced him an infidel who asserted the contrary, yet several have been of a different opinion; particularly the sect of the Mótazalites, and the followers of Isa Ebn Sobeih Abu Musa, surnamed al Mozdâr, who stuck not to accuse those who held the Korân to be uncreated of infidelity, as asserters of two eternal beings.

This point was controverted with so much heat that it occasioned many calamities under some of the Khalîfs of the family of Abbâs, al Mamûn making a public edict declaring the Korân to be created which was confirmed by his successors al Mótasem and al Wâthek, who whipt, imprisoned, and put to death those of the contrary opinion. But at length al Motawakkel, who succeeded al Wâthek, put an end to these persecutions, by revoking the former edicts, releasing those that were imprisoned on that account, and leaving every man at liberty as to his belief in this point.

Al Ghazâli seems to have tolerably reconciled both opinions, saying, that the Korân is read and pronounced with the tongue, written in books, and kept in memory; and is yet eternal, subsisting in God's essence, and not possible to be separated thence by any transmission into men's memories or the leaves of books; by which he seems to mean no more than that the original idea of the Korân only is really in God, and consequently co-essential and co-eternal with him, but that the copies are created, and the work of man.

The opinion of al Jahedh, chief of a sect bearing his name, touching the Korân, is too remarkable to be omitted: he used to say it was a body, which might sometimes be turned into a man, and sometimes into a beast; which seems to agree with the notion of those who assert the Korân to have two faces, one of a man, the other of beast: thereby, as I conceive, intimating the double interpretation it will admit of, according to the letter or the spirit.

As some have held the Korân to be created, so there have not been wanting those who have asserted that there is nothing miraculous in that book in respect to style or composition, excepting only the prophetical relations of things past, and predictions of things to come; and that had God left men to their natural liberty, and not restrained them in that particular, the Arabians could have composed something not only equal, but superior to the Korân in eloquence, method, and purity of language. This was another opinion of the Mótazalites, and in particular of al Mozdâr above mentioned and al Nodhâm.

The Korân being the Mohammedans' rule of faith and practice, it is no wonder its expositors and commentators are so very numerous. And it may not be amiss to take notice of the rules they observe in expounding it.

One of the most learned commentators distinguishes the contents of the Korân, into allegorical and literal. The former comprehends the more obscure, parabolical, and enigmatical passages, and such as are repealed or abrogated; the latter those which are plain, perspicuous, liable to no doubt, and in full force.

To explain these severally in a right manner, it is necessary from tradition and study to know the time when each passage was revealed, its circumstances, state, and history, and the reasons or particular emergencies for the sake of which it was revealed. Or more explicitly, whether the passage was revealed at Mecca, or at Medina; whether it be abrogated, or does itself abrogate any other passage; whether it be anticipated in order of time, or postponed; whether it be distinct from the context, or depends thereon; whether it be particular or general; and lastly whether it be implicit by intention, or explicit in words.

By what has been said the reader may easily believe this book is in the greatest reverence and esteem among the Mohammedans. They dare not so much as touch it without being first washed or legally purified, which lest they should do by inadvertence, they write these words on the cover or label, "Let none touch it, but they who are clean." They read it with great care and respect, never holding it below their girdles. They swear by it, consult it in their weighty occasions, carry it with them to war, write sentences of it on their banners, adorn it with gold and precious stones, and knowingly suffer it not to be in the possession of any of a different persuasion.

The Mohammedans, far from thinking the Korân to be profaned by a translation, as some authors have written, have taken care to have their scriptures translated not only into the Persian tongue, but into several others, particularly the Javan and Malayan, though out of respect to the original Arabic, these versions are generally (if not always) interlineary.

OF THE DOCTRINES AND POSITIVE PRECEPTS OF THE KORAN, WHICH RELATE TO FAITH AND RELIGIOUS DUTIES

It has been already observed, more than once, that the fundamental position on which Mohammed erected the superstructure of his religion was, that from the beginning to the end of the world there has been, and for ever will be, but one true orthodox belief; consisting, as to matter of faith, in the acknowledging of the only true God, and the believing in and obeying such messengers or prophets as he should from time to time send, with proper credentials, to reveal his will to mankind; and as to matter of practice, in the observance of the immutable and eternal laws of right and wrong, together with such other precepts and ceremonies as God should think fit to order for the time being, according to the different dispensations in different ages of the world: for these last he allowed were things indifferent in their own nature, and became obligatory by God's positive precept only; and were therefore temporary and subject to alteration according to his will and pleasure. And to this religion he gives the name of Islâm, which word signifies *resignation*, or *submission* to the service and commands of God; and is used as the proper name of the Mohammedan religion, which they will also have to be the same at bottom with that of all the prophets from Adam. Under pretext that this eternal religion was in his time corrupted, and professed in its purity by no one sect of men, Mohammed pretended to be a prophet sent by God, to reform those abuses which had crept into it, and to reduce it to its primitive simplicity; with the addition however of peculiar laws and ceremonies, some of which had been used in former times, and others were now first instituted. And he comprehended the whole substance of his doctrine under these two propositions, or articles of faith; viz. That there is but one God, and that himself was the apostle of God; in consequence of which latter article, all such ordinances and institutions as he thought fit to establish must be received as obligatory and of divine authority.

The Mohammedans divide their religion, which as I just now said they call *Islâm*, into two distinct parts: *Imân*, i.e. *faith* or theory, and *Dîn*, i.e. *religion*, or practice; and teach that it is built on five fundamental points, one belonging to faith, and the other four to practice.

The first is that confession of faith which I have already mentioned; that "there is no god but the true God; and that Mohammed is his apostle." Under which they comprehend six distinct branches; viz. (1) Belief in God; (2) In his angels; (3) In his scriptures; (4) In his prophets; (5) In the resurrection and day of judgment; and, (6) In God's absolute decree and predetermination both of good and evil.

The four points relating to practice are: (1) Prayer, under which are comprehended those washings or purifications which are necessary preparations required before prayer; (2) Alms; (3) Fasting; and (4) The pilgrimage to Mecca. Of each of these I shall speak in their order.

That both Mohammed and those among his followers who are reckoned orthodox had, and continue to have, just and true notions of God and his attributes (always excepting their obstinate and impious rejecting of the Trinity), appears so plain from the Korân itself, and all the Mohammedan divines, that it would be loss of time to refute those who suppose the God of Mohammed to be different from the true God, and only a fictitious deity or idol of his own creation. Nor shall I here enter into any of the Mohammedan controversies concerning the divine nature and attributes because I shall have a more proper opportunity of doing it elsewhere.

The existence of angels and their purity are absolutely required to be believed in the Korân; and he is reckoned an infidel who denies there are such beings, or hates any of them, or asserts any distinction of sexes among them. They believe them to have pure and subtle bodies, created of fire; that they neither eat nor drink, nor propagate their species; that they have various forms and offices; some adoring God in different postures, others singing praises to him, or interceding for mankind. They hold that some of them are employed in writing down the actions of men; others in carrying the throne of God and other services.

The four angels whom they look on as more eminently in God's favour, and often mention on account of the offices assigned them, are Gabriel, to whom they give several titles, particularly those of the *holy spirit*, and the *angel of revelations*, supposing him to be honoured by God with a greater confidence than any other, and to be employed in writing down the divine decrees; Michael, the friend and protector of the Jews; Azraël, the *angel of death*, who separates men's souls from their bodies; and Israfîl, whose office it will be to sound the trumpet at the resurrection. The Mohammedans also believe that two guardian angels attend on every man, to observe and write down his actions, being changed every day, and therefore called al Moakkibât, or the angels who continually *succeed* one another.

This whole doctrine concerning angels Mohammed and his disciples have borrowed from the Jews, who learned the names and offices of those beings from the Persians, as themselves confess. The ancient Persians firmly believed the ministry of angels, and the superintendence over the affairs of this world (as the Magians still do), and therefore assigned them distinct charges and provinces, giving their names to their months and the days of their months. Gabriel they called Sorûsh and Revân bakhsh, or *the giver of souls*, in opposition to the contrary office of the angel of death, to whom, among other names, they gave that of Mordâd, or, *the giver of death*, Michael they called Beshter, who, according to them, provides sustenance for mankind. The Jews teach that the angels were created of fire: that they have several offices; that they intercede for men, and attend them. The angel of death they name Dûma, and say he calls dying persons by their respective names at their last hour.

The devil, whom Mohammed names Eblîs, from his *despair*, was once one of those angels who are nearest to God's presence, called Azazîl, and fell, according to the doctrine of the Korân, for refusing to pay homage to Adam at the command of God.

Besides angels and devils, the Mohammedans are taught by the Korân to believe the existence of an intermediate order of creatures, which they call Jin or Genii, created also of fire, but of a grosser fabric than angels: since they eat and drink, and propagate their species, and are subject to death. Some of these are supposed to be good, and others bad, and capable of future salvation or damnation, as men are; whence Mohammed pretended to be sent for the conversion of Genii as well as men. The Orientals pretend that these Genii inhabited the world for many ages before Adam was created, under the government of several successive princes, who all bore the common name of Solomon; but falling at length into an almost general corruption, Eblîs was sent to drive them into a remote part of the earth, there to be confined; that some of that generation still remaining, were by Tahmûrath, one of the ancient kings of Persia, who waged war against them, forced to retreat into the famous mountains of Kâf. Of which successions and wars they have many fabulous and romantic stories. They also make different ranks and degrees among these beings (if they be not rather supposed to be of a different species), some being called absolutely Jin, some Peri or fairies, some Div or giants, other Tacwîns or fates.

The Mohammedan notions concerning these Genii agree almost exactly with what the Jews write of a sort of demons, called Shedim, whom some fancy to have been begotten by two angels name Azar and Azaël, on Maamah the daughter of Lamech, before the flood. However the Shedim, they tell us, agree in three things with the ministering angels; for that, like them, they have wings, and fly from one end of the world to the other, and have some knowledge of futurity; and in three things they agree with men, like whom they eat and drink, are propagated, and die. They also say that some believe in the law of Moses, and are consequently good, and that others of them are infidels and reprobates.

As to the Scriptures, the Mohammedans are taught by the Korân that God, in divers ages of the world, gave revelations of his will in writing to several prophets, the whole and every word of which it is absolutely necessary for a good Moslem to believe. The number of these sacred books was, according to the, 104. Of which ten were given to Adam, fifty to Seth, thirty to Edrîs or Enoch, ten to Abraham; and the other four, being the Pentateuch, the Psalms, the Gospel, and the Korân, were successively delivered to Moses, David, Jesus, and Mohammed; which last being the seal of the prophets, those revelations are now closed, and no more are to be expected. All these divine books, except the four last, they agree to be now entirely lost, and their contents unknown; though the Sabians have several books which they attribute to some of the antediluvian prophets. And of those four, the Pentateuch, Psalms, and Gospel, they say, have undergone so many alterations and corruptions, that though there may possibly be some part of the true word of God therein, yet no credit is to be given to the present copies in the hands of the Jews and Christians. The Jews in particular are frequently reflected on in the Korân for falsifying and corrupting their copies of their law; and some instances of such pretended corruptions, both in the book and the two others, are produced by Mohammedan writers; wherein they merely follow their own prejudices, and the fabulous accounts of spurious legends. Whether they have any copy of the Pentateuch among them different from that of the Jews or not, I am not entirely satisfied, since a person who travelled into the east was told, that they had the books of Moses, though very much corrupted; but I know nobody that has ever seen them. However they certainly have and privately read a book which they call the Psalms of David, in Arabic and Persian, to which are added some prayers of Moses, Jonas, and others. This Mr Reland supposes to be a translation from our copies (though no doubt falsified in more places than one); but M. D'Herbelot says it contains not the same Psalms which are in our Psalter, being no more than an extract from thence mixed with other very different pieces. The easiest way to reconcile these two learned gentlemen is to presume that they speak of different copies. The Mohammedans have also a Gospel in Arabic, attributed to St Barnabas, wherein the history of Jesus Christ is related in a manner very different from what we find in the true Gospels, and correspondent to those traditions which Mohammed has followed in his Korân. Of this Gospel the Moriscoes in Africa have a translation in Spanish; and there is in the library of prince Eugene of Savoy a manuscript of some antiquity, containing an Italian translation of the same Gospel, made, it is to be supposed, for the use of renegades. This book appears to be no original forgery of the Mohammedans, though they have no doubt interpolated and altered it since, the better to serve their purpose; and in particular, instead of the Paraclete or Comforter, they have in this apocryphal gospel inserted the word Periclyte, that is, the famous or illustrious, by which they pretend their prophet was foretold by name, that being the signification of Mohammed in Arabic: and this they say to justify that passage of the Korân, where Jesus Christ is formally asserted to have foretold his coming, under his other name of Ahmed; which is derived from the same root as Mohammed, and of the same import. From these or some other forgeries of the same stamp it is that the Mohammedans quote several passages of which there are not the least footsteps in the New Testament. But after all we must not hence infer that the Mohammedans, much less all of them, hold these copies of theirs to be the ancient and genuine Scriptures themselves. If any argue, from the corruption which they insist has happened to the Pentateuch and Gospel, that the Korân may possibly be corrupted also; they answer, that God has promised that he will take care of the latter, and preserve it from any addition or diminution; but that he left the two others to the care of men. However, they confess there are some various readings in the Korân, as has been observed.

Besides the books above mentioned, the Mohammedans also take notice of the writings of Daniel and several other prophets, and even make quotations thence: but these they do not believe to be divine scripture, or of any authority in matters of religion.

The number of prophets, which have been from time to time sent by God into the world, amounts to no fewer than 224,000, according to one Mohammedan tradition, or to 134,000, according to another; among whom 313 were apostles, sent with special commission to reclaim mankind from infidelity and superstition; and six of them brought new laws or dispensations, which successively abrogated the preceding: these were Adam, Noah, Abraham, Moses, Jesus, and Mohammed. All the prophets in general the Mohammedans believe to have been free from great sins, and errors of consequence, and professors of one and the same religion, that is Islâm, notwithstanding the different laws and institutions which they observed. They allow of degrees among them, and hold some of them to be more excellent and honourable than others. The first place they give to the revealers and establishers of new dispensations, and the next to the apostles.

In this great number of prophets, they not only reckon divers patriarchs and persons named in Scripture, but not recorded to have been prophets (wherein the Jewish and Christian writers have sometimes led the way), as Adam, Seth, Lot, Ismael, Nun, Joshua, &c., and introduce some of them under different names, as Enoch, Heber, and Jethro, who are called in the Korân, Edrîs, Hûd, and Shoaib; but several others, whose very names do not appear in the Scripture (though they endeavour to find some persons there to fix them on), as Saleh, Khedr, Dhu'lkefl, &c. Several of their fabulous traditions concerning these prophets we shall occasionally mention in the notes on the Korân.

As Mohammed acknowledged the divine authority of the Pentateuch, Psalms, and the Gospel, he often appeals to the consonancy of the Korân with those writings, and to the prophecies which he pretended were therein concerning himself, as proofs of his mission; and he frequently charges the Jews and Christians with stifling the passages which bear witness to him. His followers also fail not to produce several texts even from our present copies of the Old and New Testament, to support their master's cause.

The next article of faith required by the Korân is the belief of a general resurrection and a future judgment. But before we consider the Mohammedan tenets in those points, it will be proper to mention what they are taught to believe concerning the intermediate state, both of the body and of the soul, after death.

When a corpse is laid in the grave, they say he is received by an angel, who gives him notice of the coming of the two Examiners; who are two black livid angels, of a terrible appearance, named Monker and Nakîr. These order the dead person to sit upright, and examine him concerning his faith, as to the unity of God, and the mission of Mohammed: if he answers rightly, they suffer the body to rest in peace, and it is refreshed by the air of paradise; but if not, they beat him on the temples with iron maces, till he roars out for anguish so loud, that he is heard by all from east to west, except men and genii. Then they press the earth on the corpse, which is gnawed and stung till the resurrection by ninety-nine dragons with seven heads each: or, as others say, their sins will become venomous beasts, the grievous ones stinging like dragons, the smaller like scorpions, and the others like serpents: circumstances which some understand in a figurative sense.

This examination of the sepulchre is not only founded on an express tradition of Mohammed, but it also plainly hinted at, though not directly taught, in the Korân, as the commentators agree. It is therefore believed by the orthodox Mohammedans in general, who take care to have their graves made hollow, that they may sit up with more ease while they are examined by the angels; but is utterly rejected by the sect of the Motázalites, and perhaps by some others.

These notions Mohammed certainly borrowed from the Jews, among whom they were very anciently received. They say that the angel of death coming and sitting on the grave, the soul immediately enters the body and raises it on its feet; that he then examines the departed person, and strikes him with a chain half of iron and half of fire; at the first blow all his limbs are loosened, at the second the bones are scattered, which are gathered together again by angels, and the third stroke reduces the body to dust and ashes, and it returns into the grave. This rack or torture they call Hibbût hakkeber, or the beating of the sepulchre, and pretend that all men in general must undergo it, except only those who die on the evening of the Sabbath, or have dwelt in the land of Israel.

If it be objected to the Mohammedans that the cry of the persons under such examination has been never heard; or if they be asked how those can undergo it whose bodies are burnt or devoured by beasts or birds, or otherwise consumed without burial; they answer, that it is very possible notwithstanding, since men are not able to perceive what is transacted on the other side the grave; and that it is sufficient to restore to life any part of the body which is capable of understanding the questions put by the angels.

As to the soul, they hold that when it is separated from the body by the angel of death, who performs his office with ease and gentleness towards the good, and with violence towards the wicked, it enters into that state which they call al Berzakh, or the interval between death and the resurrection. If the departed person was a believer, they say two angels meet it, who convey it to heaven, that its place there may be assigned, according to its merit and degree. For they distinguish the souls of the faithful into three classes: the first of prophets, whose souls are admitted into paradise immediately; the second of martyrs, whose spirits, according to a tradition of Mohammed, rest in the crops of green birds which eat of the fruits and drink of the river of paradise;

and the third of other believers, concerning the state of whose souls before the resurrection there are various opinions. For (1) Some say they stay near the sepulchres, with liberty however of going wherever they please; which they confirm from Mohammed's manner of saluting them at their graves, and his affirming that the dead heard those salutations as well as the living, though they could not answer. Whence perhaps proceeded the custom of visiting the tombs of relations, so common among the Mohammedans. (2) Others imagine they are with Adam, in the lowest heaven; and also support their opinion by the authority of their prophet, who gave out that in his return from the upper heavens in his pretended night journey, he saw there the souls of those who were destined to paradise on the right hand of Adam, and of those who were condemned to hell on his left. (3) Others fancy the souls of believers remain in the well Zemzem, and those of infidels in a certain well in the province of Hadramaut, called Borbût; but this opinion is branded as heretical. (4) Others say they stay near the graves for seven days; but that whither they go afterwards is uncertain. (5) Others, that they are all in the trumpet whose sound is to raise the dead. And, (6) Others, that the souls of the good dwell in the forms of white birds, under the throne of God. As to the condition of the souls of the wicked, besides the opinions that have been already mentioned, the more orthodox hold that they are offered by the angels to heaven, from whence being repulsed as stinking and filthy, they are offered to the earth, and being also refused a place there, are carried down to the seventh earth, and thrown into a dungeon, which they call Sajîn, under a green rock, or according to a tradition of Mohammed, under the devil's jaw, to be there tormented, till they are called up to be joined again to their bodies.

Though some among the Mohammedans have thought that the resurrection will be merely spiritual, and no more than the returning of the soul to the place whence it first came (an opinion defended by Ebn Sina, and called by some the opinion of the philosophers); and others, who allow man to consist of body only, that it will be merely corporeal; the received opinion is, that both body and soul will be raised, and their doctors argue strenuously for the possibility of the resurrection of the body, and dispute with great subtlety concerning the manner of it. But Mohammed has taken care to preserve one part of the body, whatever becomes of the rest, to serve for a basis of the future edifice, or rather a leaven for the mass which is to be joined to it. For he taught, that a man's body was entirely consumed by the earth, except only the bone called Ajb, which we name the os coccygis, or rump-bone; and that as it was the first formed in the human body, it will also remain uncorrupted till the last day, as a seed from whence the whole is to be renewed: and this he said will be effected by a forty days' rain which God should send, and which would cover the earth to the height of twelve cubits, and cause the bodies to sprout forth like plants. Herein also is Mohammed beholden to the Jews; who say the same things of the bone Luz, excepting that what he attributes to a great rain will be effected according to them by a dew, impregnating the dust of the earth.

The time of the resurrection the Mohammedans allow to be a perfect secret to all but God alone; the angel Gabriel himself acknowledging his ignorance in this point when Mohammed asked him about it. However they say the approach of that day may be known from certain signs which are to precede it. These signs they distinguish into two sorts, the lesser, and the greater; which I shall briefly enumerate after Dr Pocock.

The lesser signs are (1) The decay of faith among men. (2) The advancing of the meanest persons to eminent dignity. (3) That a maid servant shall become the mother of her mistress (or master); by which is meant either that towards the end of the world men shall be much given to sensuality, or that the Mohammedans shall then take many captives. (4) Tumults and seditions. (5) A war with the Turks. (6) Great distress in the world, so that a man when he passes by another's grave shall say, Would to God I were in his place! (7) That the provinces of Irâk and Syria shall refuse to pay their tribute. And (8) That the buildings of Medina shall reach to Ahâb, or Yahâb.

The greater signs are:

1. The sun's rising in the west. Which some have imagined it originally did.
2. The appearance of the beast, which shall rise out of the earth, in the temple of Mecca, or on mount Safâ, or in the territory of Tâyef, or some other place. This beast they say is to be sixty cubits high; though others, not satisfied with so small a size, will have her reach to the clouds and to heaven, when her head only is out; and that she will appear for three days, but show only a third of her body. They describe this monster, as to her form, to be a compound of various species; having the head of a bull, the eyes of a hog, the ears of an elephant,

the horns of a stag, the neck of an ostrich, the breast of a lion, the colour of a tiger, the back of a cat, the tail of a ram, the legs of a camel, and the voice of an ass. Some say this beast is to appear three times in several places, and that she will bring with her the rod of Moses, and the seal of Solomon; and being so swift that none can overtake or escape her, will with the first strike all the believers on the face, and mark them with the word Mûmen, i.e. *believer*; and with the latter will mark the unbelievers on the face likewise, with the word Câfer i.e. *infidel*, that every person may be known for what he really is. They add that the same beast is to demonstrate the vanity of all religions except Islâm, and to speak Arabic. All this stuff seems to be the result of a confused idea of the beast in the Revelations.

3. War with the Greeks, and the taking of Constantinople by seventy thousand of the posterity of Isaac, who shall not win that city by force of arms, but the walls shall fall down while they cry out, *There is no god but* God: God *is most great!* As they are dividing the spoil, news will come to them of the appearance of Antichrist; whereupon they shall leave all, and return back,
4. The coming of Antichrist, whom the Mohammedans call al Masîh al Dajjâl, i.e. the *false or lying Christ*, and simply al Dajjâl. He is to be one-eyed, and marked on the forehead with the letters C. F. R. Signifying Câfer, or *infidel*. They say that the Jews give him the name of messiah Ben David, and pretend he is to come in the last days, and to be lord both of land and sea, and that he will restore the kingdom to them. According to the traditions of Mohammed, he is to appear first between Irâk and Syria, or according to others, in the province of Khorasân; they add that he is to ride on an ass; that he will be followed by seventy thousand Jews of Ispahân, and continue on earth forty days, of which one will be equal in length to a year, another to a month, another to a week, and the rest will be common days; that he is to lay waste all places, but will not enter Mecca or Medina, which are to be guarded by angels; and that at length he will be slain by Jesus, who is to encounter him at the gate of Lud. It is said that Mohammed foretold several Antichrists, to the number of about thirty; but one of greater note than the rest.
5. The descent of Jesus on earth. They pretend that he is to descend near the white tower to the east of Damascus, when

the people are returned from the taking of Constantinople; that he is to embrace the Mohammedan religion, marry a wife, get children, kill Antichrist, and at length die after forty years', or according to others twenty-four years' continuance on earth. Under him they say there will be great security and plenty in the world, all hatred and malice being laid aside; when lions and camels, bears and sheep, shall live in peace, and a child shall play with serpents unhurt.

6. War with the Jews; of whom the Mohammedans are to make a prodigious slaughter, the very trees and stones discovering such of them as hide themselves, except only the tree called Gharkad, which is the tree of the Jews.
7. The eruption of Gog and Magog, or, as they are called in the east, Yâjûj and Mâjûj; of whom many things are related in the Korân, and the traditions of Mohammed. These barbarians, they tell us, having passed the lake of Tiberias, which the vanguard of their vast army will drink dry, will come to Jerusalem, and there greatly distress Jesus and his companions; till at his request God will destroy them, and fill the earth with their carcasses, which after some time God will send birds to carry away, at the prayers of Jesus and his followers. Their bows, arrows, and quivers the Moslems will burn for seven years together; and at last God will send a rain to cleanse the earth, and to make it fertile.
8. A smoke, which shall fill the whole earth.
9. An eclipse of the moon. Mohammed is reported to have said, that there would be three eclipses before the last hour; one to be seen in the east, another in the west, and the third in Arabia.
10. The returning of the Arabs to the worship of Allât and al Uzza, and the rest of their ancient idols; after the decease of every one in whose heart there was faith equal to a grain of mustard seed, none but the very worst of men being left alive. For God, they say, will send a cold odoriferous wind, blowing from Syria Damascena, which shall sweep away the souls of all the faithful, and the Korân itself, so that men will remain in the grossest ignorance for a hundred years.
11. The discovery of a vast heap of gold and silver by the retreating of the Euphrates, which will be the destruction of many.
12. The demolition of the Caaba, or temple of Mecca, by the Ethiopians.

13. The speaking of beasts and inanimate things.
14. The breaking out of fire in the province of Hejâz; or, according to others, in Yaman.
15. The appearance of a man of the descendants of Kahtân, who shall drive men before him with his staff.
16. The coming of the Mohdi, or *director*; concerning whom Mohammed prophesied, that the world should not have an end till one of his own family should govern the Arabians, whose name should be the same with his own name, and whose father's name should also be the same with his father's name; and who should fill the earth with righteousness. This person the Shiites believe to be now alive, and concealed in some secret place, till the time of his manifestation; for they suppose him to be no other than the last of the twelve Imâms, named Mohammed Abu'lkasem, as their prophet was, and the son of Hassan al Askeri, the eleventh of that succession. He was born at Sermanrai in the two hundred and fifty-fifth year of the Hejra. From this tradition, it is to be presumed an opinion pretty current among the Christians took its rise, that the Mohammedans are in expectation of their prophet's return.
17. A wind which shall sweep away the souls of all who have but a grain of faith in their hearts, as has been mentioned under the tenth sign.

These are the greater signs which, according to their doctrine, are to precede the resurrection, but still leave the hour of it uncertain: for the immediate sign of its being come will be the first blast of the trumpet; which they believe will be sounded three times. The first they call the *blast of consternation*; at the hearing of which all creatures in heaven and earth shall be struck with terror, except those whom God shall please to exempt from it. The effects attributed to this first sound of the trumpet are very wonderful: for they say, the earth will be shaken, and not only all buildings, but the very mountains, levelled; that the heavens shall melt, the sun be darkened, the stars fall on the death of the angels, who, as some imagine, hold them suspended between heaven and earth, and the sea shall be troubled and dried up, or, according to others, turned into flames, the sun, moon, and stars being thrown into it: the Korân, to express the greatness of the terror of that day, adds that women who give suck shall abandon the care of their infants, and even the she-camels which have gone ten months with young (a most valuable part of the substance of that nation) shall be utterly neglected. A farther effect of this blast will be that concourse of beasts mentioned in the Korân, though some doubt whether it be to precede the resurrection or not. They who suppose it will precede, think that all kinds of animals, forgetting their respective natural fierceness and timidity, will run together into one place, being terrified by the sound of the trumpet and the sudden shock of nature.

The Mohammedans believe that this first blast will be followed by a second, which they call the *blast of exanimation*; when all creatures both in heaven and earth shall die or be annihilated, except those which God shall please to exempt from the common fate; and this, they say, shall happen in the twinkling of an eye, nay in an instant; nothing surviving except God alone, with paradise and hell, and the inhabitants of those two places, and the throne of glory. The last who shall die will be the angel of death.

Forty years after this will be heard the *blast of resurrection*, when the trumpet shall be sounded the third time by Israfîl, who, together with Gabriel and Michael, will be previously restored to life, and standing on the rock of the temple of Jerusalem, shall at God's command call together all the dry and rotten bones, and other dispersed parts of the bodies, and the very hairs, to judgment. This angel having, by the divine order, set the trumpet to his mouth, and called together all the souls from all parts, will throw them into his trumpet, from whence, on his giving the last sound, at the command of God, they shall fly forth like bees, and fill the whole space between heaven and earth, and then repair to their respective bodies, which the opening earth will suffer to arise; and the first who shall so arise, according to a tradition of Mohammed, will be himself. For this birth the earth will be prepared by the rain above mentioned, which is to fall continually for forty years, and will resemble the seed of a man, and be supplied from the water under the throne of God, which is called *living water*; by the efficacy and virtue of which the dead bodies shall spring forth from their graves, as they did in their mother's womb, or as corn sprouts forth by common rain, till they become perfect; after which, breath will be breathed into them, and they will sleep in their sepulchres till they are raised to life at the last trump.

As to the length of the day of judgment, the Korân in one place tells us that it will last one thousand years, and in another fifty thousand. To reconcile this apparent contradiction, the commentators use several shifts: some saying, they know not what measure of time

God intends in those passages; others, that these forms of speaking are figurative, and not to be strictly taken, and were designed only to express the terribleness of that day, it being usual for the Arabs to describe what they dislike as of long continuance, and what they like as the contrary; and others suppose them spoken only in reference to the difficulty of the business of the day, which if God should commit to any of his creatures, they would not be able to go through it in so many thousand years; to omit some other opinions which we may take notice of elsewhere.

Having said so much in relation to the time of the resurrection, let us now see who are to be raised from the dead, in what manner and form they shall be raised, in what place they shall be assembled, and to what end; according to the doctrine of the Mohammedans.

That the resurrection will be general, and extend to all creatures, both angels, genii, men, and animals, is the received opinion, which they support by the authority of the Korân; though that passage which is produced to prove the resurrection of brutes be otherwise interpreted by some.

The manner of their resurrection will be very different. Those who are destined to be partakers of eternal happiness will arise in honour and security; and those who are doomed to misery, in disgrace and under dismal apprehensions. As to mankind, they say, that they will be raised perfect in all their parts and members, and in the same state as they came out of their mother's wombs, that is, barefooted, naked, and uncircumcised; which circumstances when Mohammed was telling his wife Ayesha, she, fearing the rules of modesty might be thereby violated, objected that it would be very indecent for men and women to look upon one another in that condition: but he answered her, that the business of the day would be too weighty and serious to allow them the making use of that liberty. Others, however, allege the authority of the prophet for a contrary opinion as to their nakedness, and pretend he asserted that the dead should arise dressed in the same clothes in which they died; unless we interpret these words, as some do, not so much of the outward dress of the body, as the inward clothing of the mind; and understand thereby that every person will rise again in the same state as to his faith or infidelity, knowledge or ignorance, his good or bad works. Mohammed is also said to have farther taught, by another tradition, that mankind shall be assembled at the last day, distinguished into three classes. The first, of those who go on foot; the second, of those who ride; and the third, of those who creep grovelling with their faces on the ground. The first class is to consist of those believers whose good works have been few; the second of those who are in greater honour with God, and more acceptable to him; whence Ali affirmed that the pious, when they come forth from the sepulchres, shall find ready prepared for them white winged camels, with saddles of gold; wherein are to be observed some footsteps of the doctrine of the ancient Arabians; and the third class, they say, will be composed of the infidels, whom God shall cause to make their appearance with their faces on the earth, blind, dumb, and deaf. But the ungodly will not be thus only distinguished; for, according to a tradition of the prophet, there will be ten sorts of wicked men on whom God shall on the day fix certain discretory marks. The first will appear in the form of apes; these are the professors of Zendicism: the second in that of swine; these they who have been greedy of filthy lucre, and enriched themselves by public oppression: the third will be brought with their heads reversed, and their feet distorted; these are the usurers: the fourth will wander about blind; these are unjust judges: the fifth will be deaf, dumb, and blind, understanding nothing; these are they who glory in their works: the sixth will gnaw their tongues, which will hang down upon their breasts, corrupted blood flowing from their mouths like spittle, so that every body shall detest them; these are the learned men and doctors, whose actions contradict their sayings: the seventh will have their hands and feet cut off; these are they who have injured their neighbours; the eighth will be fixed to the trunks of palm-trees or stakes of wood; these are the false accusers and informers: the ninth will stink worse than a corrupted corpse; these are they who have indulged their passions and voluptuous appetites, but refused God such part of their wealth as was due to him: the tenth will be clothed with garments daubed with pitch; and these are the proud, the vainglorious, and the arrogant.

As to the place where they are to be assembled to judgment, the Korân and the traditions of Mohammed agree that it will be on the earth, but in what part of the earth it is not agreed. Some say their prophet mentioned Syria for the place; others, a white and even tract of land, without inhabitants or any signs of buildings. Al Ghazâli imagines it will be a second earth, which he supposes to be of silver; and others an earth which has nothing in common with ours, but the name; having, it is possible, heard something of the new heavens and new earth mentioned in

Scripture: whence the Korân has this expression, "on the day wherein the earth shall be changed into another earth."

The end of the resurrection the Mohammedans declare to be, that they who are so raised may give an account of their actions, and receive the reward thereof. And they believe that not only mankind, but the genii and irrational animals also shall take vengeance on the horned, till entire satisfaction shall be given to the injured.

As to mankind, they hold that when they are all assembled together, they will not be immediately brought to judgment, but the angels will keep them in their ranks and order while they attend for that purpose: and this attendance some say is to last forty years, others seventy, others three hundred; nay, some say no less than fifty thousand years, each of them vouching their prophet's authority. During this space they will stand looking up to heaven, but without receiving any information or orders thence, and are to suffer grievous torments, both the just and the unjust, though with manifest difference. For the limbs of the former, particularly those parts which they used to wash in making the ceremonial ablution before prayer, shall shine gloriously, and their sufferings shall be light in comparison, and shall last no longer than the time necessary to say the appointed prayers; but the latter will have their faces obscured with blackness, and disfigured with all the marks of sorrow and deformity. What will then occasion not the least of their pain, is a wonderful and incredible sweat, which will even stop their mouths, and in which they will be immersed in various degrees according to their demerits, some to the ankles only and some to the knees, some to the middle, some so high as their mouth, and others as their ears. And this sweat, they say, will be provoked not only by that vast concourse of all sorts of creatures mutually pressing and treading on one another's feet, but by the near and unusual approach of the sun, which will be then no farther from them than the distance of a mile, or (as some translate the word, the signification of which is ambiguous) than the length of a bodkin. So that their skulls will boil like a pot, and they will be all bathed in sweat. From this inconvenience, however, the good will be protected by the shade of God's throne; but the wicked will be so miserably tormented with it, and also with hunger and thirst, and a stifling air, that they will cry out *Lord, deliver us from this anguish, though thou send us into hell-fire.* What they fable of the extraordinary heat of the sun on this occasion, the Mohammedans certainly borrowed from the Jews, who say that, for the punishment of the wicked on the last day, that planet shall be drawn forth from its *sheath*, in which it is now put up, lest it should destroy all things by its excessive heat.

When those who have risen shall have waited the limited time, the Mohammedans believe God will at length appear to judge them, Mohammed undertaking the office of intercessor, after it shall have been declined by Adam, Noah, Abraham, and Jesus, who shall beg deliverance only for their own souls. They say that on this solemn occasion God will come in the clouds, surrounded by angels, and will produce the books wherein the actions of every person are recorded by their guardian angels, and will command the prophets to bear witness against those to whom they have been respectively sent. Then every one will be examined concerning all his words and actions, uttered and done by him in this life; not as if God needed any information in those respects, but to oblige the person to make public confession and acknowledgement of God's justice. The particulars of which they shall give an account, as Mohammed himself enumerated them, are: of their time, how they spent it; of their wealth, by what means they acquired it, and how they employed it; of their bodies, wherein they exercised them; of their knowledge and learning, what use they made of them. It is said, however, that Mohammed has affirmed that no less than seventy thousand of his followers should be permitted to enter paradise without any previous examination; which seems to be contradictory to what is said above. To the questions it is said each person shall answer, and make his defence in the best manner he can, endeavouring to excuse himself by casting the blame of his evil deeds on others; so that a dispute shall arise even between the soul and the body, to which of them their guilt ought to be imputed: the soul saying, "O Lord, my body I received from thee; for thou createdst me without a hand to lay hold with, a foot to walk with, an eye to see with, or an understanding to apprehend with, till I came and entered into this body; therefore punish it eternally, but deliver me." The body on the other side will make this apology, "O Lord, thou createdst me like a stock of wood, having neither hand that I could lay hold with, nor foot that I could walk with, till this soul, like a ray of light, entered into me, and my tongue began to speak, my eye to see, and my foot to walk; therefore punish it eternally, but deliver me." But God will propound to them the following parable of the blind man and the lame man, which, as well as the preceding dispute, was borrowed by the Mohammedans from the Jews. A certain king having a pleasant garden, in which were ripe fruits, set two persons to keep it, one of whom was blind, and the other lame, the former not being able to see the fruit, nor the latter to gather it; the lame man, however, seeing the fruit, persuaded the blind man to take him upon his shoulders; and by that means he easily gathered the fruit, which they divided between them. The lord of the garden coming some time after, and inquiring after his fruit, each began to excuse himself; the blind man said he had no eyes to see with; and the lame man that he had no feet to approach the trees. But the king, ordering the lame man to be set on the blind, passed sentence on and punished them both. And in the same manner will God deal with the body and the soul. As these apologies will not avail on the day, so will it also be in vain for any one to deny his evil actions, since men and angels and his own members, nay, the very earth itself, will be ready to bear witness against him.

Though the Mohammedans assign so long a space for the attendance of the resuscitated before their trial, yet they tell us the trial itself will be over in much less time, and, according to an expression of Mohammed, familiar enough to the Arabs, will last no longer than while one may milk an ewe, or than the space between two milkings of a she-camel. Some, explaining those words so frequently used in the Korân, "God will be swift in taking an account," say that he will judge all creatures in the space of half a day, and others that it will be done in less time than the twinkling of an eye.

At this examination they also believe that each person will have the book wherein all the actions of his life are written delivered to him; which books the righteous will receive in their right hand, and read with great pleasure and satisfaction; but the ungodly will be obliged to take them against their wills in their left, which will be bound behind their backs, their right hand being tied up to their necks.

To show the exact justice which will be observed on this great day of trial, the next thing they describe is the *balance*, wherein all things shall be weighed. They say it will be held by Gabriel, and that it is of so vast a size, that its two scales, one of which hangs over paradise, and the other over hell, are capacious enough to contain both heaven and earth. Though some are willing to understand what is said in the Korân concerning this balance allegorically, and only as a figurative representation of God's equity, yet the more ancient and orthodox opinion is that it is to be taken literally; and since words and actions, being mere accidents, are not capable of being themselves weighed, they say that the books wherein they are written will be thrown into the scales, and according as those wherein the good or the evil actions are recorded shall preponderate, sentence will be given; those whose balances laden with their good works shall be heavy will be saved, but those whose balances are light will be condemned. Nor will any one have cause to complain that God suffers any good action to pass unrewarded, because the wicked for the good they do have their reward in this life, and therefore can expect no favour in the next.

The old Jewish writers make mention as well of the books to be produced at the last day, wherein men's actions are registered, as of the balance wherein they shall be weighed, and the Scripture itself seems to have given the first notion of both. But what the Persian Magi believe of the balance comes nearest to the Mohammedan opinion. They hold that on the day of judgment two angels, named Mihr and Sorûsh, will stand on the bridge we shall describe by and by, to examine every person as he passes; that the former, who represents the divine mercy, will hold a balance in his hand, to weigh the actions of men; that according to the report he shall make thereof to God, sentence will be pronounced, and those whose good works are found more ponderous, if they turn the scale but by the weight of a hair, will be permitted to pass forward to paradise; but those whose good works shall be found light will be, by the other angel, who represents God's justice, precipitated from the bridge into hell.

This examination being past, and every one's works weighed in a just balance, that mutual retaliation will follow, according to which every creature will take vengeance one of another, or have satisfaction made them for the injuries which they have suffered. And since there will then be no other way of returning like for like, the manner of giving this satisfaction will be, by taking away a proportionable part of the good works of him who offered the injury, and adding it to those of him who suffered it. Which being done, if the angels (by whose ministry this is to be performed) say, "Lord, we have given to every one his due; and there remaineth of this person's good works so much as equalleth the weight of an ant," God will of his mercy cause it to be doubled unto him, that he may be admitted into paradise; but if, on the contrary, his good works be exhausted, and there remain evil works only, and there be any who have not yet received satisfaction from him, God will order that an equal weight of their sins be added unto his, that he may be punished for them in their stead, and he will be sent to hell laden with both. This will be the method of God's dealing with mankind. As to brutes, after they shall have likewise taken vengeance of one another, as we have mentioned above, he will command them to be changed into dust; wicked men being reserved to more grievous punishment: so that they shall cry out, on hearing this sentence pronounced on the brutes, "Would to God that we were dust also!" As to the genii, many Mohammedans are of opinion that such of them as are true believers will undergo the same fate as the irrational animals, and have no other reward than the favour of being converted into dust; and for this they quote the authority of their prophet. But this, however, is judged not so very reasonable, since the genii, being capable of putting themselves in the state of believers as well as men, must consequently deserve, as it seems, to be rewarded for their faith, as well as to be punished for their infidelity. Wherefore some entertain a more favourable opinion, and assign the believing genii a place near the confines of paradise, where they will enjoy sufficient felicity, though they be not admitted into that delightful mansion. But the unbelieving genii, it is universally agreed, will be punished eternally, and be thrown into hell with the infidels of mortal race. It may not be improper to observe, that under the denomination of unbelieving genii, the Mohammedans comprehend also the devil and his companions.

The trials being over and the assembly dissolved, the Mohammedans hold, that those who are to be admitted into paradise will take the right hand way, and those who are destined to hell-fire will take the left, but both of them must first pass the bridge, called in Arabic, al Sirât, which they say is laid over the midst of hell, and described to be finer than a hair, and sharper than the edge of a sword; so that it seems very difficult to conceive how any one shall be able to stand upon it: for which reason most of the sect of the Mótazalites reject it as a fable, though the orthodox think it a sufficient proof of the truth of this article, that it was seriously affirmed by him who never asserted a falsehood, meaning their prophet; who, to add to the difficulty of the passage, has likewise declared that this bridge is beset on each side with briars and hooked thorns; which will however be no impediment to the good, for they shall pass with wonderful ease and swiftness, like lightning, or the wind, Mohammed and his Moslems leading the way; whereas the wicked, what with the slipperiness and extreme narrowness of the path, the entangling of the thorns, and the extinction of the light which directed the former to paradise, will soon miss their footing, and fall down headlong into hell, which is gaping beneath them.

This circumstance Mohammed seems also to have borrowed from the Magians, who teach that on the last day all mankind will be obliged to pass a bridge which they call Pûl Chînavad, or Chînavar, that is, *the strait bridge*, leading directly into the other world; on the midst of which they suppose the angels, appointed by God to perform that office, will stand, who will require of every one a strict account of his actions, and weigh them in the manner we have already mentioned. It is true the Jews speak likewise of the bridge of hell, which they say is no broader than a thread; but then they do not tell us that any shall be obliged to pass it, except the idolaters, who will fall thence into perdition.

As to the punishment of the wicked, the Mohammedans are taught that hell is divided into seven stories, or apartments, one below another, designed for the reception of as many distinct classes of the damned. The first, which they call Jehennam, they say will be the receptacle of those who acknowledged one God, that is, the wicked Mohammedans, who, after having there been punished according to their demerits, will at length be released. The second, named Ladhâ, they assign to the Jews; the third, named al Hotama, to the Christians; the fourth, named al Säîr, to the Sabians; the fifth, named Sakar, to the Magians; the sixth, named al Jahîm, to the idolaters; and the seventh, which is the lowest and worst of all, and is called al Hâwiyat, to the hypocrites, or those who outwardly professed some religion, but in their hearts were of none. Over each of these apartments they believe there will be set a guard of angels, nineteen in number, to whom the damned will confess the just judgment of God, and beg them to intercede with him for some alleviation of their pain, or that they may be delivered by being annihilated.

Mohammed has, in his Korân and traditions, been very exact in describing the various torments of hell, which, according to him, the wicked will suffer both from intense heat and excessive cold. We shall however enter into no detail of them here, but only observe that the degrees of these pains will also vary, in proportion to the crimes of the sufferer, and the apartment he is condemned to; and that he who is punished most lightly of all will be shod with shoes of fire, the fervour of which will cause his skull to boil like a cauldron. The condition of these unhappy wretches, as the same prophet teaches, cannot be properly called either life or death; and their misery will be greatly increased by their despair of being delivered from that place, since according to that frequent expression in the Korân, "they must remain therein for ever." It must be remarked, however, that the infidels alone will be liable to eternity of damnation, for the Moslems, or those who have embraced the true religion, and have been guilty of heinous sins, will be delivered thence after they shall have expiated their crimes by their sufferings. The contrary of either of these opinions is reckoned heretical; for it is the constant orthodox doctrine of the Mohammedans that no unbeliever or idolater will ever be released, nor any person who in his lifetime professed and believed the unity of God be condemned to eternal punishment. As to the time and manner of the deliverance of those believers whose evil actions shall outweigh their good, there is a tradition of Mohammed that they shall be released after they shall have been scorched and their skins burnt black, and shall afterwards be admitted into paradise; and when the inhabitants of that place shall in contempt call them *infernals*, God will, on their prayers, take from them that opprobrious appellation. Others say he taught, that while they continue in hell they shall be deprived of life, or (as his words are otherwise interpreted) be cast into a most profound sleep, that they may be the less sensible of their torments; and that they shall afterwards be received into paradise, and there revive on their being washed with the *water of life*; though some suppose they will be restored to life before they come forth from their place of punishment, that at their bidding farewell to their pains, they may have some little taste of them. The time which these believers shall be detained there, according to a tradition handed down from their prophet, will not be less than nine hundred years, nor more than seven thousand. And as to the manner of their delivery, they say that they shall be distinguished by the marks of prostration on those parts of their bodies with which they used to touch the ground in prayer, and over which the fire will therefore have no power; and that being known by this characteristic, they will be released by the mercy of God, at the intercession of Mohammed and the blessed; whereupon those who shall have been dead will be restored to life, as has been said; and those whose bodies shall have contracted any sootiness or filth from the flames and smoke of hell will be immersed in one of the rivers of paradise, called the *river of life*, which will wash them whiter than pearls.

For most of these circumstances relating to hell and the state of the damned, Mohammed was likewise in all probability indebted to the Jews and in part to the Magians; both of whom agree in making seven distinct apartments in hell, though they vary in other particulars. The former place an angel as a guard over each of these infernal apartments, and suppose he will intercede for the miserable wretches there imprisoned, who will openly acknowledge the justice of God in their condemnation. They also teach that the wicked will suffer a diversity of punishments, and that by intolerable cold as well as heat, and that their faces shall become black; and believe those of their own religion shall also be punished in hell hereafter, according to their crimes (for they hold that few or none will be found so exactly righteous as to deserve no punishment at all), but will soon be delivered thence, when they shall be sufficiently purged from their sins, by their father Abraham, or at the intercession of him or some other of the prophets. The Magians allow but one angel to preside over all the seven hells, who is named by them Vanánd Yezád, and, as they teach, assigns punishments proportionate to each person's crimes, restraining also the tyranny and excessive cruelty of the devil, who would, if left to himself, torment the damned beyond their sentence. Those of this religion do also mention and describe various kinds of torments, wherewith the wicked will be punished in the next life; among which though they reckon extreme cold to be one, yet they do not admit fire, out of respect, as it seems, to that element, which they take to be the representation of the divine nature; and therefore they rather choose to describe the damned souls as suffering by other kinds of punishment: such as an intolerable stink, the stinging and biting of serpents and wild beasts, the cutting and tearing of the flesh by the devils, excessive hunger and thirst, and the like.

Before we proceed to a description of the Mohammedan paradise, we must not forget to say something of the wall or partition which they imagine to be between that place and hell, and seems to be copied from the great gulf of separation mentioned in Scripture. They call it al Orf, and more frequently in the plural, al Arâf, a word derived from the verb *arafa*, which signifies to *distinguish* between things, or to *part* them; though some commentators give another reason for the imposition of this name, because, say they, those who stand on this partition will *know* and *distinguish* the blessed from the damned, by their respective marks or characteristics: and others say the word properly intends any thing that is *high raised* or *elevated*, as such a wall of separation must be supposed to be. The Mohammedan writers greatly differ as to the persons who are to be found on al Arâf. Some imagine it to be a sort of *limbo*, for the patriarchs and prophets, or for the martyrs and those who have been most eminent for sanctity, among whom they say there will be also angels in the form of men. Others place here such whose good and evil works are so equal that they exactly counterpoise each other, and therefore deserve neither reward nor punishment; and these, they say, will on the last day be admitted into paradise, after they shall have performed an act of adoration, which will be imputed to them as a merit, and will make the scale of their good works to over-balance. Others suppose this intermediate space will be a receptacle for those who have gone to war, without their parents' leave, and therein suffered martyrdom; being excluded paradise for their disobedience, and escaping hell because they are martyrs. The breadth of this partition wall cannot be supposed to be exceeding great, since not only those who shall stand thereon will hold conference with the inhabitants both of paradise and of hell, but the blessed and the damned themselves will also be able to talk to one another.

If Mohammed did not take his notions of the partition we have been describing from Scripture, he must at least have borrowed it at second-hand from the Jews, who mention a thin wall dividing paradise from hell.

The righteous, as the Mohammedans are taught to believe, having surmounted the difficulties, and passed the sharp bridge above mentioned, before they enter paradise will be refreshed by drinking at the *pond* of their prophet, who describes it to be an exact square, of a month's journey in compass; its water, which is supplied by two pipes from al Cawthar, one of the rivers of paradise, being whiter than milk or silver, and more odoriferous than musk, with as many cups set around it as there are stars in the firmament; of which water whoever drinks will thirst no more for ever. This is the first taste which the blessed will have of their future and now near approaching felicity.

Though paradise be so very frequently mentioned in the Korân, yet it is a dispute among the Mohammedans whether it be already created, or to be created hereafter; the Mótazalites and some other sectaries asserting that there is not at present any such place in nature, and that the paradise which the righteous will inhabit in the next life will be different from that from which Adam was expelled. However the orthodox profess the contrary, maintaining that it was created even before the world, and describe it, from their prophet's traditions, in the following manner:

They say it is situate above the seven heavens (or in the seventh heaven), and next under the throne of God; and to express the amenity of the place tell us, that the earth of it is of the finest wheat flour, or of the purest musk; or, as others will have it, of saffron; that its stones are pearls and jacinths, the walls of its buildings enriched with gold and silver, and that the trunks of all its trees are of gold; among which the most remarkable is the tree called Tûba, or the tree of *happiness.* Concerning this tree they fable that it stands in the palace of Mohammed, though a branch of it will reach to the house of every true believer; that it will be loaded with pomegranates, grapes, dates, and other fruits of surprising bigness, and of tastes unknown to mortals. So that if a man desire to eat of any particular kind of fruit, it will immediately be presented to him, or if he choose flesh, birds ready dressed will be set before him, according to his wish. They add, that the boughs of this tree will spontaneously bend down to the hand of the person who would gather of its fruits, and that it will supply the blessed not only with food, but also with silken garments, and beasts to ride on ready saddled and bridled, and adorned with rich trappings, which will burst forth from its fruits; and that this tree is so large that a person mounted on the fleetest horse would not be able to gallop from one end of its shade to the other in a hundred years.

As plenty of water is one of the greatest additions to the pleasantness of any place, the Korân often speaks of the rivers of paradise as a principal ornament thereof: some of these rivers they say, flow with water, some with milk, some with wine, and others with honey; all taking their rise from the root of the tree Tûba, two of which rivers, named al Cawthar and the *river of life*, we have already mentioned. And, lest these should not be sufficient, we are told this garden is also watered by a great number of lesser springs and fountains, whose pebbles are rubies and emeralds, their earth of camphire, their beds of musk, and their sides of saffron; the most remarkable among them being Salsabîl and Tasnîm.

But all these glories will be eclipsed by the resplendent and ravishing girls of paradise, called, from their large black eyes. Hûr al oyûn, the enjoyment of whose company will be a principal felicity of the faithful. These, they say, are created, not of clay, as mortal women are, but of pure musk; being, as their prophet often affirms in his Korân, free from all natural impurities, defects, and inconveniences incident to the sex, of the strictest modesty, and secluded from public view in pavilions of hollow pearls, so large that, as some traditions have it, one of them will be no less than four parasangs (or as others say, sixty miles) long, and as many broad.

The name which the Mohammedans usually give to this happy mansion is al Jannat, or *the garden*; and sometimes they call it, with an addition, Jannat al Ferdaws, *the garden of paradise*, Jannat Aden, *the garden of Eden* (though they generally interpret the word Eden, not according to its acceptation in Hebrew, but according to its meaning in their own tongue, wherein it signifies a *settled or perpetual habitation*), Jannat al Máwa, *the garden of abode*, Jannat al Naïm, *the garden of pleasure*, and the like; by which several appellations some understand so many different gardens, or at least places of different degrees of felicity (for they reckon no less than a hundred such in all), the very meanest whereof will afford its inhabitants so many pleasures and delights, that one would conclude they must even sink under them, had not Mohammed declared, that, in order to qualify the blessed for a full enjoyment of them, God will give to every one the abilities of a hundred men.

We have already described Mohammed's pond, whereof the righteous are to drink before their admission into this delicious seat; besides which some authors mention two fountains, springing from under a certain tree near the gate of paradise, and say that the blessed will also drink of one of them, to purge their bodies and carry off all excrementitious dregs, and will wash themselves in the other. When they are arrived at the gate itself, each person will there be met and saluted by the beautiful youths appointed to serve and wait upon him, one of them running before, to carry the news of his arrival to the wives destined for him; and also by two angels, bearing the presents sent him by God, one of whom will invest him with a garment of paradise, and the other will put a ring on each of his fingers, with inscriptions on them alluding to the happiness of his condition. By which of the eight gates (for so many they suppose paradise to have) they are respectively to enter, is not worth inquiry; but it must be observed that Mohammed has declared that no person's good works will gain him admittance and that even himself shall be saved, not by his merits, but merely by the mercy of God. It is, however, the constant doctrine of the Korân, that the felicity of each person will be proportioned to his desserts, and that there will be abodes of different degrees of happiness; the most eminent degree being reserved for the prophets, the second for the doctors and teachers of God's worship, the next for the martyrs, and the lower for the rest of the righteous, according to their several merits. There will also some distinction be made in respect to the time of their admission; Mohammed (to whom, if you will believe him, the gates will first be opened) having affirmed, that the poor will enter paradise five hundred years before the rich; nor is this the only privilege which they will enjoy in the next life; since the same prophet has also declared, that when he took a view of paradise, he saw the majority of its inhabitants to be the poor, and when he looked down into hell, he saw the greater part of the wretches confined there to be women.

For the first entertainment of the blessed on their admission, they fable that the whole earth will then be as one loaf of bread, which God will reach to them with his hand, holding it like a cake; and that for meat that will have the ox Balâm, and the fish Nûn, the lobes of whose livers wil suffice seventy thousand men, being, as some imagine, to be set before the principal guests, viz. those who, to that number, will be admitted into paradise without examination, though others suppose that a definite number is here put for an indefinite, and that nothing more is meant thereby than to express a great multitude of people.

From this feast every one will be dismissed to the mansion designed for him, where (as has been said) he will enjoy such a share of felicity as will be proportioned to his merits, but vastly exceed comprehension or expectation; since the very meanest in paradise (as he who, it is pretended, must know best, has declared) will have eighty thousand servants, seventy-two wives of the girls of paradise, besides the wives he had in his world, and a tent erected for him of pearls, jacinths, and emeralds, of a very large extent; and, according to another tradition, will be waited on by three hundred attendants while he eats, will be served in dishes of gold, whereof three hundred shall be set before him at once, containing each a different kind of food, the last morsel of which will be as grateful as the first; and will also be supplied with as many sorts of liquors in vessels of the same metal; and, to complete the entertainment, there will be no want of wine, which, though forbidden in this life, will yet be freely allowed to be drunk in the next, and without danger, since the wine of paradise will not inebriate, as that we drink here. The flavour of this wine we may conceive to be delicious without a description, since the water of Tasnîm and the other fountains which will be used to dilute it, is said to be wonderfully sweet and fragrant. If any object to these pleasures, as an impudent Jew did to Mohammed, that so much eating and drinking must necessarily require proper evacuations, we answer, as the prophet did, that the inhabitants of paradise will not need to ease themselves, nor even to blow their nose, for that all superfluities will be discharged and carried off by perspiration, or a sweat as odoriferous as musk, after which their appetite shall return afresh.

The magnificence of the garments and furniture promised by the Korân to the godly in the next life is answerable to the delicacy of their diet: for they are to be clothed in the richest silks and brocades, chiefly of green, which will burst forth from the fruits of paradise, and will also be supplied by the leaves of the tree Tûba; they will be adorned with bracelets of gold and silver, and crowns set with pearls of incomparable lustre; and will make use of silken carpets, litters of a prodigious size, couches, pillows, and other rich furniture embroidered with gold and precious stones.

That we may the more readily believe what has been mentioned of the extraordinary abilities of the inhabitants of paradise to taste these pleasures in their height, it is said they will enjoy a perpetual youth; that in whatever age they happen to die, they will be raised in their prime and vigour, that is, of about thirty years of age, which age they will never exceed (and the same they say of the damned), and that when they enter paradise they will be of the same stature with Adam, who, as they fable, was no less than sixty cubits high. And to this age and stature their children, if they shall desire any (for otherwise their wives will not conceive), shall immediately attain; according to that saying of their prophet, "If any of the faithful in paradise be desirous of issue, it shall be conceived, born, and grown up, within the space of an hour. And in the same manner, if any one shall have a fancy to employ himself in agriculture (which rustic pleasure may suit the wanton fancy of some), what he shall sow will spring up and come to maturity in a moment.

Lest any of the senses should want their proper delight, we are told the ear will there be entertained, not only with the ravishing songs of the angel Israfîl, who has the most melodious voice of all God's creatures, and of the daughters of paradise; but even the trees themselves will celebrate the divine praises with a harmony exceeding whatever mortals have heard; to which will be joined the sound of the bells hanging on the trees, which will be put in motion by the wind proceeding from the throne of God, so often as the blessed wish for music: nay, the very clashing of the golden-bodied trees, whose fruits are pearls and emeralds, will surpass human imagination; so that the pleasures of this sense will not be the least of the enjoyments of paradise.

The delights we have hitherto taken a view of, it is said, will be common to all the inhabitants of paradise, even those of the lowest order. What then, think we, must they enjoy who shall obtain a superior degree of honour and felicity? To these they say, there are prepared, besides all this, "such things as eye hath not seen, nor hath ear heard, nor hath it entered into the heart of man to conceive"; an expression most certainly borrowed from Scripture. That we may know wherein the felicity of those who shall attain the highest degree will consist, Mohammed is reported to have said, that the meanest of the inhabitants of paradise will see his gardens, wives, servants, furniture, and other possessions, take up the space of a thousand years' journey (for so far and farther will the blessed see in the next life); but that he will be in the highest honour with God, who shall behold his face morning and evening: and this favour al Ghazâli supposes to be that *additional* or *superabundant recompense*, promised in the Korân, which will give such exquisite delight that, in respect thereof, all the other pleasures of paradise will be forgotten and lightly esteemed; and not without reason, since, as the author says, every other enjoyment is equally tasted by the very brute beast who is turned loose into luxuriant pasture. The reader will observe, by the way, that this is a full confutation of those who pretend the Mohammedans admit of no spiritual pleasure in the next life, but make the happiness of the blessed to consist wholly in corporeal enjoyments.

Whence Mohammed took the greatest part of his paradise, it is easy to show. The Jews constantly describe the future mansion of the just as a delicious garden, and make it also reach to the seventh heaven, they also say it has three gates, or, as others will have it, two, and four rivers (which last circumstance they copied, to be sure, from those of the garden of Eden), flowing with milk, wine, balsam, and honey. Their Behemoth and Leviathan, which they pretend will be slain for the entertainment of the blessed, are so apparently the Balâm and Nûn of Mohammed that his followers themselves confess he is obliged to them for both. The Rabbins likewise mention seven different degrees of felicity, and say that the highest will be of those who perpetually contemplate the face of God. The Persian Magi had also an idea of the future happy estate of the good, very little different from that of Mohammed. Paradise they call Behisht, and Mînu which signifies *crystal*, where they believe the righteous shall enjoy all manner of delights, and particularly the company of the Hurâni behisht, or *black-eyed nymphs of paradise*, the care of whom they say is committed to the angel Zamiyâd; and hence Mohammed seems to have taken the first hint of his paradisiacal ladies.

It is not improbable, however, but that he might have been obliged, in some respect, to the Christian accounts of the felicity of the good in the next life. As it is scarce possible to convey, especially to the apprehensions of the generality of mankind, an idea of spiritual pleasures without introducing sensible objects, the Scriptures have been obliged to represent the celestial enjoyments by corporeal images; and to describe the mansion of the blessed as a glorious and magnificent city, built of gold and precious stones, with twelve gates; through the streets of which there runs a river of water of life, and having on either side the tree of life, which bears twelve sorts of fruits, and leaves of a healing virtue. Our Saviour likewise speaks of the future state of the blessed as of a kingdom, where they shall eat and drink at his table. But then these descriptions have none of those puerile imaginations which reign throughout that of Mohammed, much less any the most distant intimation of sensual delights, which he was so fond of; on the contrary, we are expressly assured, that "in the resurrection they will neither marry nor be given in marriage, but will be as the angels of God in heaven." Mohammed, however, to enhance the value of paradise with his Arabians, chose rather to imitate the indecency of the Magians than the modesty of the Christians in this particular, and lest his beatified Moslems should complain that any thing was wanting, bestows on them wives, as well as the other comforts of life; judging, it is to be presumed, from his own inclinations, that, like Panurgus's ass, they would think all other enjoyments not worth their acceptance if they were to be debarred from this.

Had Mohammed, after all, intimated to his followers that what he had told them of paradise was to be taken, not literally, but in a metaphorical sense (as it is said the Magians do the description of Zoroaster's), this might, perhaps, make some atonement; but the contrary is so evident from the whole tenor of the Korân, that although some Mohammedans, whose understandings are too refined to admit such gross conceptions, look on their prophet's descriptions as parabolical, and are willing to receive them in an allegorical or spiritual acceptation, yet the general and orthodox doctrine is, that the whole is to be strictly believed in the obvious and literal acceptation; to prove which I need only urge the oath they exact from Christians (who they know abhor such fancies), when they would bind them in the most strong and sacred manner; for in such a case they make them swear that if they falsify their engagement they will affirm that there will be black-eyed girls in the next world, and corporeal pleasures.

Before we quit this subject, it may not be improper to observe the falsehood of a vulgar imputation on the Mohammedans, who are by several writers reported to hold that women have no souls, or, if they have, that they will perish, like those of brute beasts, and will not be rewarded in the next life. But whatever may be the opinion of some ignorant people among them, it is certain that Mohammed had too great a respect for the fair sex to teach such a doctrine; and there are several passages in the Korân which affirm that women, in the next life, will not only be punished for their evil actions, but will also receive the rewards of their good deeds, as well as the men, and that in this case God will make no distinction of sexes. It is true, the general notion is, that they will not be admitted into the same abode as the men are, because their places will be supplied by the paradisiacal females (though some allow that a man will there also have the company of those who were his wives in this world, or at least such of them as he shall desire); but that good women will go into a separate place of happiness, where they will enjoy all sorts of delights; but whether one of those delights will be the enjoyment of agreeable paramours created for them, to complete the economy of the Mohammedan system, is what I have nowhere found decided. One circumstance relating to these beatified females, conformable to what he had asserted of the men, he acquainted his followers with in the answer he returned to an old woman, who desiring him to intercede with God that she might be admitted into paradise, he told her that no old woman would enter that place; which setting the poor old woman a crying, he explained himself by saying, that God would then make her young again.

The sixth great point of faith which the Mohammedans are taught by the Korân to believe, is God's absolute decree, and predestination both of good and evil. For the orthodox doctrine is, that whatever hath or shall come to pass in this world, whether it be good, or whether it be bad, proceedeth entirely from the divine will, and is irrevocably fixed and recorded from all eternity in the *preserved table*; God having secretly predetermined not only the adverse and prosperous fortune of every person in this world, in the most minute particulars, but also his faith or infidelity, his obedience or disobedience, and consequently his everlasting happiness or misery after death; which fate or predestination it is not possible, by any foresight or wisdom, to avoid.

Of this doctrine Mohammed makes great use in his Korân, for the advancement of his designs; encouraging his followers to fight without fear, and even desperately, for the propagation of their faith, by representing to them that all their caution could not avert their inevitable destiny, or prolong their lives for a moment; and deterring them from disobeying or rejecting him as an imposter, by setting before them the danger they might thereby incur of being, by the judgment of God, abandoned to seduction, hardness of heart, and a reprobate mind, as a punishment for their obstinacy.

As this doctrine of absolute election and reprobation has been thought by many of the Mohammedan divines to be derogatory to the goodness and justice of God, and to make God the author of evil; several subtle distinctions have been invented, and disputes raised, to explicate or soften it; and different sects have been formed, according to their several opinions, or methods of explaining this point: some of them going so far as even to hold the direct contrary position – of absolute free will in man, as we shall see hereafter.

Of the four fundamental points of religious practice required by the Korân, the first is *prayer*, under which, as has been said, are also comprehended those legal washings or purifications which are necessary preparations thereto.

Of these purifications there are two degrees, one called *Ghost*, being a total immersion or bathing of the body in water; and the other called *Wodû* (by the Persians, *abdest*), which is the washing of their faces, hands, and feet, after a certain manner. The first is required in some extraordinary cases only, as after having lain with a woman, or been polluted by emission of seed, or by approaching a dead body; women also being obliged to it after their courses or childbirth. The latter is the ordinary ablution in common cases, and before prayer, and must necessarily be used by every person before he can enter upon that duty. It is performed with certain formal ceremonies, which have been described by some writers, but are much easier apprehended by seeing them done than by the best description.

These purifications were perhaps borrowed by Mohammed of the Jews, at least they agree in a great measure with those used by that nation, who in process of time burdened the precepts of Moses in this point with so many traditionary ceremonies, that whole books have been written about them, and who were so exact and superstitious therein even in our Saviour's time, that they are often reproved by him for it. But as it is certain that the pagan Arabs used lustrations of this kind, long before the time of Mohammed, as most nations did, and still do in the east, where the warmth of the climate requires a greater nicety and degree of cleanliness than these colder parts; perhaps Mohammed only recalled his countrymen to a more strict observance of those purifying rites, which had been probably neglected by them, or at least performed in a careless and perfunctory manner. The Mohammedans, however, will have it that they are as ancient as Abraham, who, they say, was enjoined by God to observe them, and was showed the manner of making the ablution by the angel Gabriel, in the form of a beautiful youth. Nay, some deduce the matter higher, and imagine that these ceremonies were taught our first parents by the angels.

That his followers might be the more punctual in this duty, Mohammed is said to have declared, that *the practice of religion is founded on cleanliness*, which is the *one half of the faith, and the key of prayer*, without which it will not be heard by God. That these expressions may be the better understood, al Ghazâli reckons four degrees of purification; of which the first is, the cleansing of the body from all pollution, filth, and excrements; the second, the cleansing of the members of the body from all wickedness and unjust actions; the third, the cleansing of the heart from all blameable inclinations, and odious vices; and the fourth, the purging of a man's secret thoughts from all affections which may divert their attendance on God: adding that the body is but as the outward shell in respect to the heart, which is as the kernel. And for this reason he highly complains of those who are superstitiously solicitous in exterior purifications, avoiding those persons as unclean who are not so scrupulously nice as themselves, and at the same time have their minds lying waste, and overrun with pride, ignorance and hypocrisy. Whence it plainly appears with how little foundation the Mohammedans have been charged, by some writers, with teaching or imagining that these formal washings alone cleanse them from their sins.

Lest so necessary a preparation to their devotions should be omitted, either where water cannot be had, or when it may be of prejudice to a person's health, they are allowed in such cases to make use of fine sand or dust in lieu of it; and then they perform this duty by clapping their open hands on the sand, and passing them over the parts, in the same manner as if they were dipped in water. But for this expedient Mohammed was not so much indebted to his own cunning, as to the example of the Jews, or perhaps that of the Persian Magi, almost as scrupulous as the Jews themselves in their lustrations, who both of them prescribe the same method in cases of necessity; and there is a famous instance, in ecclesiastical history, of sand being used, for the same reason, instead of water, in the administration of the Christian sacrament of baptism, many years before Mohammed's time.

Neither are the Mohammedans contented with bare washing, but think themselves obliged to several other necessary points of cleanliness, which they make also parts of their duty; such as combing their hair, cutting the beard, paring the nails, pulling out the hairs of their arm-pits, shaving their private parts, and circumcision; of which last I will add a word or two, lest I should not find a more proper place.

Circumcision, though it be not so much as once mentioned in the Korân, is yet held by the Mohammedans to be an ancient divine institution, confirmed by the religion of Islâm, and though not so absolutely necessary but that it might be dispensed with in some cases, yet highly proper and expedient. The Arabs used this rite for many ages before Mohammed, having probably learned it from Ismael, though not only his descendants, but the Hamyarites, and other tribes, practised the same. The Ismaelites, we are told, used to circumcise their children, not on the eight day, as is the custom of the Jews, but when about twelve or thirteen years old, at which age their father underwent that operation: and the Mohammedans imitate them so far as not to circumcise children before they be able, at least, distinctly to pronounce that profession of their faith, *There is no* God *but* God, Mohammed *is the apostle of* God; but pitch on what age they please for the purpose between six and sixteen, or thereabouts. Though Moslem doctors are generally of opinion, conformably to the Scripture, that this precept was originally given to Abraham, yet some have imagined that Adam was taught it by the angel Gabriel, to satisfy an oath he had made to cut off that flesh which, after his fall, had rebelled against his spirit; whence an odd argument has been drawn for the universal obligation of circumcision. Though I cannot say the Jews led the Mohammedans the way here, yet they seem so unwilling to believe any of the principal patriarchs or prophets before Abraham were really uncircumcised, that they pretend several of them, as well as some holy men who lived after this time, were born ready circumcised, or without a foreskin, and that Adam, in particular, was so created; whence the Mohammedans affirm the same thing of their prophet.

Prayer was by Mohammed thought so necessary a duty, that he used to call it *the pillar of religion*, and *the key of paradise*; and when the Thakifites, who dwelt at Tâyef, sending in the ninth year of the Hejra to make their submission to that prophet, after the keeping of their favourite idol had been denied them, begged, at least, that they might be dispensed with as to their saying of the appointed prayers, he answered, *That there could be no good in that religion wherein was no prayer.*

That so important a duty, therefore, might not be neglected, Mohammed obliged his followers to pray five times every twenty-four hours, at certain stated times; viz. (1) In the morning, before sunrise; (2) When noon is past, and the sun begins to decline from the meridian; (3) In the afternoon, before sunset; (4) In the evening, after sunset, and before day be shut in; and (5) After the day is shut in, and before the first watch of the night. For this institution he pretended to have received the divine command from the throne of God himself, when he took his night journey to heaven: and the observing of the stated times of prayer is frequently insisted on in the Korân, though they be not particularly prescribed therein. Accordingly, at the aforesaid times, of which public notice is given by the Muedhdhins or Criers, from the steeples of their mosques (for they use no bell), every conscientious Moslem prepares himself for prayer, which he performs either in the mosque or any other place, provided it be clean, after a prescribed form, and with a certain number of phrases or ejaculations (which the more scrupulous count by a string of beads), and using certain postures of worship all which have been particularly set down and described, though with some few mistakes by other writers, and though not to be abridged, unless in some special cases; as on a journey, on preparing for battle, &c.

For the regular performance of the duty of prayer among the Mohammedans, besides the particulars above mentioned, it is also requisite that they turn their faces, while they pray, toward the temple of Mecca; the quarter where the same is situate being for that reason pointed out within their mosques by a niche, which they call al Mehrâb, and without, by the situation of the doors opening into the galleries of the steeples: there are also tables calculated for the ready finding out their Keblah, or part to which they ought to pray, in places where they have no other direction.

But what is principally to be regarded in the discharge of this duty, say the Moslem doctors is the inward disposition of the heart, which is the life and spirit of prayer; the most punctual observance of the external rites and ceremonies before mentioned being of little or no avail, if performed without due attention, reverence, devotion, and hope: so that we must not think the Mohammedans, or the considerate part of them at least, content themselves with the mere *opus operatum*, or imagine their whole religion to be placed therein.

I had like to have omitted two things which, in my mind, deserve mention on this head, and may, perhaps, be better defended than our contrary practice. One is, that the Mohammedans never address themselves to God in sumptuous apparel, though they are obliged to be decently clothed; but lay aside their costly habits and pompous ornaments, if they wear any, when they approach the divine presence, lest they should seem proud and arrogant. The other is, that they admit not their women to pray with them in public; that sex being obliged to perform their devotions at home, or if they visit the mosques, it must be at a time when the men are not there: for the Moslems are of opinion that their presence inspires a different kind of devotion from that which is requisite in a place dedicated to the worship of God.

The greater part of the particulars comprised in the Mohammedan institution of prayer their prophet seems to have copied from others, and especially the Jews; exceeding their institutions only in the number of daily prayers. The Jews are directed to pray three times a day, in the morning, in the evening, and within night; in imitation of Abraham, Isaac, and Jacob and the practice was as early, at least, as the time of Daniel. The several postures used by the Mohammedans in their prayers are also the same with those prescribed by the Jewish Rabbins, and particularly the most solemn act of adoration by prostrating themselves so as to touch the ground with their forehead; notwithstanding the latter pretend the practice of the former, in this respect, to be a relic of their ancient manner of paying their devotions to Baal-Peor. The Jews likewise constantly pray with their faces turned towards the temple of Jerusalem, which has been their Keblah from the time it was first dedicated by Solomon; for which reason Daniel, praying in Chaldea, had the windows of his chamber open towards that city;

and the same was the Keblah of Mohammed and his followers for six or seven months, and till he found himself obliged to change it for the Caaba. The Jews moreover are obliged by the precepts of their religion to be careful that the place they pray in, and the garments they have on when they perform their duty be clean; the men and women also among them pray apart (in which particular they are imitated by the eastern Christians); and several other conformities might be remarked between the Jewish public worship and that of the Mohammedans.

The next point of the Mohammedan religion is the giving of alms; which are of two sorts, *legal* and *voluntary*. The *legal alms* are of indispensable obligation, being commanded by the law, which directs and determines both the portion which is to be given, and of what things it ought to be given; but the *voluntary alms* are left to every one's liberty, to give more or less, as he shall see fit. The former kind of alms some think to be properly called Zacât, and the latter Sadakat; though this name be also frequently given to the legal alms. They are called Zacât, either because they *increase* a man's store, by drawing down a blessing thereon, and *produce* in his soul the virtue of liberality, or because they *purify* the remaining part of one's substance from pollution, and the soul from the filth of avarice; and Sadakat, because they are a proof of a man's *sincerity* in the worship of God. Some writers have called the legal alms *tythes*, but improperly, since in some cases they fall short, and in others exceed that proportion.

The giving of alms is frequently commanded in the Korân, and often recommended therein jointly with prayer; the former being held of great efficacy in causing the latter to be heard of God: for which reason the Khalif Omar Ebn Abd'alaziz used to say, "that prayer carries us half way to God, fasting brings us to the door of his palace, and alms procure us admission." The Mohammedans therefore esteem alms-deeds to be highly meritorious, and many of them have been illustrious for the exercise thereof. Hasan the son of Alî, and grandson of Mohammed, in particular, is related to have thrice in his life divided his substance equally between himself and the poor, and twice to have given away all he had: and the generality are so addicted to the doing of good, that they extend their charity even to brutes.

Alms, according to the prescriptions of the Mohammedan law, are to be given of five things: (1) Of cattle, that is to say, of camels, kine, and sheep; (2) Of money; (3) Of corn; (4) Of fruits, viz., dates and raisins; and (5) Of wares sold. Of each of these a certain portion is to be given in alms, being usually one part in forty, or two and a half per cent of the value. But no alms are due for them, unless they amount to a certain quantity or number; nor until a man has been in possession of them eleven months, he not being obliged to give alms thereout before the twelfth month is begun: nor are alms due for cattle employed in tilling the ground, or in carrying of burdens. In some cases a much larger portion than the before mentioned is reckoned due for alms: thus of what is gotten out of mines, or the sea, or by any art or profession over and above what is sufficient for the reasonable support of a man's family, and especially where there is a mixture or suspicion of unjust gain, a fifth part ought to given in alms. Moreover, at the end of the fast of Ramadân, every Moslem is obliged to give in alms for himself and for every one of his family, if he has any, measure of wheat, barley, dates, raisins, rice, or other provisions commonly eaten.

The legal alms were at first collected by Mohammed himself, who employed them as he thought fit, in the relief of his poor relations and followers, but chiefly applied them to the maintenance of those who served in his wars, and fought, as he termed it, in the way of God. His successors continued to do the same, till, in process of time, other taxes and tributes being imposed for the support of the government, they seem to have been weary of acting as almoners to their subjects, and to have left the paying them to their consciences.

In the foregoing rules concerning alms, we may observe also footsteps of what the Jews taught and practised in respect thereto. Alms, which they also call Sedaka, i.e. *justice*, or *righteousness*, are greatly recommended by their Rabbins, and preferred even to sacrifices; as a duty the frequent exercise whereof will effectually free a man from hell fire, and merit everlasting life: wherefore, besides the corners of the field, and the gleanings of their harvest and vineyard, commanded to be left for the poor and the stranger by the law of Moses, a certain portion of their corn and fruits is directed to be set apart for their relief, which portion is called the tithes of the poor. The Jews likewise were formerly very conspicuous for their charity. Zaccheus gave the half of his goods to the poor; and we are told that some gave their whole substance: so that their doctors, at length, decreed that no man should give above a fifth part of his goods in alms. There were also persons publicly appointed in every synagogue to collect and distribute the people's contributions.

The third point of religious practice is fasting; a duty of so great moment that Mohammed used to say it was "the gate of religion," and that "the odour of the mouth of him who fasteth is more grateful to God than that of musk"; and al Ghazâli reckons fasting "one fourth part of the faith." According to the Mohammedan divines, there are three degrees of fasting: (1) The restraining the belly and other parts of the body from satisfying their lusts; (2) The restraining the ears, eyes, tongue, hands, feet, and other members, from sin; and (3) The fasting of the heart from worldly cares, and refraining the thoughts from every thing besides God.

The Mohammedans are obliged, by the express command of the Korân, to fast the whole month of Ramadân, from the time the new moon first appears, till the appearance of the next new moon; during which time they must abstain from eating, drinking, and women, from daybreak till night, or sunset. And this injunction they observe so strictly, that while they fast they suffer nothing to enter their mouths, or other parts of their body, esteeming the fast broken and null if they smell perfumes, take a clyster or injection, bathe, or even purposely swallow their spittle; some being so cautious that they will not open their mouths to speak, lest they should breathe the air too freely: the fast is also deemed void if a man kiss or touch a woman, or if he vomit designedly. But after sunset they are allowed to refresh themselves and to eat and drink, and enjoy the company of their wives till daybreak; though the more rigid begin the fast again at midnight. This fast is extremely rigorous and mortifying when the month of Ramadân happens to fall in summer (for the Arabian year being lunar, each month runs through all the different seasons in the course of thirty-three years), the length and heat of the days making the observance of it much more difficult and uneasy then than in winter.

The reason given why the month of Ramadân was pitched on for this purpose is, that on that month the Korân was sent down from heaven. Some pretend that Abraham, Moses, and Jesus received their respective revelations in the same month.

From the fast of Ramadân none are excused, except only travellers and sick persons (under which last denomination the doctors comprehend all whose health would manifestly be injured by their keeping the fast; as women with child, and giving suck, ancient people and young children); but then they are obliged, as soon as the impediment is removed, to fast an equal number of other days; and the breaking the fast is ordered to be expiated by giving alms to the poor.

Mohammed seems to have followed the guidance of the Jews in his ordinances concerning fasting, no less than in the former particulars. That nation, when they fast, abstain not only from eating and drinking, but from women, and from anointing themselves, from daybreak until sunset, and the stars begin to appear; spending the night in taking what refreshments they please. And they allow women with child and giving suck, old persons and young children, to be exempted from keeping most of the public fasts.

Though my design here be briefly to treat of those points only which are of indispensable obligation on a Moslem, and expressly required by the Korân, without entering into their practice as to voluntary and supererogatory works; yet to show how closely Mohammed's institutions follow the Jewish, I shall add a word or two of the voluntary fasts of the Mohammedans. These are such as have been recommended either by the example of approbation of their prophet; and especially certain days of those months which they esteem sacred: there being a tradition that he used to say, That a fast of one day in a sacred month was better than a fast of thirty days in another month: and that the fast of one day in Ramadân was more meritorious than a fast of thirty days in a sacred month. Among the more commendable days is that of Ashûra, the tenth of Moharram; which, though some writers tell us it was observed by the Arabs, and particularly the tribe of Koreish, before Mohammed's time, yet, as others assure us, that prophet borrowed both the name and the fast from the Jews; it being, with them, the tenth of the seventh month, or Tisri, and the great day of expiation commanded to be kept by the law of Moses. Al Kazwîni relates, that when Mohammed came to Medina and found the Jews there fasted on the day of Ashûra, he asked them the reason of it; and they told him it was because on the day Pharaoh and his people were drowned, Moses, and those who were with him escaping: whereupon he said, that he bore a nearer relation to Moses than they; and ordered his followers to fast on that day. However, it seems, afterwards he was not so well pleased in having imitated the Jews herein; and therefore declared, that if he lived another year, he would alter the day, and fast on the ninth, abhorring so near an agreement with them.

The pilgrimage to Mecca is so necessary a point of practice, that according to a tradition of Mohammed, he who dies without performing it may as well die a Jew or a Christian; and the same is expressly commanded in the Korân. Before I speak of the time and manner of performing this pilgrimage, it may be proper to give a short account of the temple of Mecca, the chief scene of the Mohammedan worship; in doing which I need to be the less prolix, because that edifice has been already described by several writers, though they, following different relations, have been led into some mistakes, and agree not with one another in several particulars: nor, indeed, do the Arab authors agree in all things, one great reason whereof is their speaking of different times.

The temple of Mecca stands in the midst of the city, and is honoured with the title of Masjad al alharâm, i.e. *the sacred or inviolable temple*. What is principally reverenced in this place, and gives sanctity to the whole, is a square stone building, called the Caaba, as some fancy from its *height*, which surpasses that of the other buildings at Mecca, but more probably from its *quadrangular* form, and Beit Allah, i.e. the *house of* God, being peculiarly hallowed and set apart for his worship. The length of this edifice, from north to south, is twenty-four cubits, its breadth from east to west twenty-three cubits, and its height twenty-seven cubits: the door, which is on the east side, stands about four cubits from the ground; the floor being level with the bottom of the door. In the corner next this door is *the black stone*, of which I shall take notice by and by. On the north side of the Caaba, within a semicircular enclosure fifty cubits long, lies the *white stone*, said to be the sepulchre of Ismael, which receives the rain-water that falls off the Caaba by a spout, formerly of wood, but now of gold. The Caaba has a double roof, supported within by three octangular pillars of aloes wood: between which, on a bar of iron, hang some silver lamps. The outside is covered with rich black damask, adorned with an embroidered band of gold, which is changed every year, and was formerly sent by the Khalîfs, afterwards by the Soltâns of Egypt, and is now provided by the Turkish emperors. At a small distance from the Caaba, on the east side, is the station or place of Abraham, where is another stone much respected by the Mohammedans, of which something will be said hereafter.

The Caaba, at some distance, is surrounded, but not entirely, by a circular enclosure of pillars joined towards the bottom by a low balustrade, and towards the top by bars of silver. Just without this inner enclosure, on the south, north, and west sides of the Caaba, are three buildings, which are the oratories or places where three of the orthodox sects assemble to perform their devotions (the fourth sect, viz. that of al Shâfeï, making use of the station of Abraham for that purpose); and towards the south-east stands the edifice which covers the well Zemzem, the treasury and the cupola of al Abbas.

All these buildings are enclosed, at a considerable distance, by a magnificent piazza, or square colonnade, like that of the Royal Exchange in London, but much larger, covered with small domes or cupolas; from the four corners whereof rise as many minârets or steeples, with double galleries, and adorned with gilded spires and crescents, as are the cupolas which cover the piazza and the other buildings. Between the pillars of both enclosures hang a great number of lamps, which are constantly lighted at night. The first foundations of this outward enclosure were laid by Omar, the second Khalîf, who built no more than a low wall, to prevent the court of the Caaba, which before lay open, from being encroached on by private buildings; but the structure has been since raised, by the liberality of many succeeding princes and great men, to its present lustre.

This is properly all that is called the temple, but the whole territory of Mecca being also Harâm or sacred, there is a third enclosure, distinguished at certain distances by small turrets, some five, some seven, and others ten miles distant from the city. Within this compass of ground it is not lawful to attack an enemy, or even to hunt or fowl, or cut a branch from a tree; which is the true reason why the pigeons at Mecca are reckoned sacred, and not that they are supposed to be of the race of that imaginary pigeon which some authors, who should have known better, would persuade us Mohammed made pass for the Holy Ghost.

The temple of Mecca was a place of worship, and in singular veneration with the Arabs from great antiquity, and many centuries before Mohammed. Though it was most probably dedicated at first to an idolatrous use, yet the Mohammedans are generally persuaded that the Caaba is almost coeval with the world; for they say that Adam, after his expulsion from paradise, begged of God that he might erect a building like that he had seen there, called Beit al Mamûr, or the frequented house, and al Dorâh towards which he might direct his prayers, and which he might compass, as the angels do the celestial one. Whereupon God let down a representation of that house in curtains of light, and set it in Mecca, perpendicularly under its original, ordering the patriarch to turn towards it when he prayed, and to compass it by way of devotion. After Adam's death, his son Seth built a house in the same form, of stones and clay, which being destroyed by the deluge, was rebuilt by Abraham and Ishmael, at God's command, in the place where the former had stood, and after the same model, they being directed therein by revelation.

After this edifice had undergone several reparations, it was a few years after the birth of Mohammed rebuilt by the Koreish on the old foundation, and afterwards repaired by Abd'allah Ebn Zobeir, the Khalîf of Mecca, and at length again rebuilt by Yusof, surnamed al Hejâj Ebn Yûsuf; in the seventy-fourth year of the Hejra, with some alterations, in the form wherein it now remains. Some years after, however, the Khalîf Harûn al Rashîd (or, as others write, his father al Mohdi, or his grandfather al Mansur) intended again to change what had been altered by al Hejâj, and to reduce the Caaba to the old form in which it was left by Abd'allah; but was dissuaded from meddling with it, lest so holy a place should become the sport of princes, and being new-modelled after every one's fancy, should lose that reverence which was justly paid it. But notwithstanding the antiquity and holiness of this building, they have a prophecy, by tradition from Mohammed, that in the last times the Ethiopians shall come and utterly demolish it; after which it will not be rebuilt again for ever.

Before we leave the temple of Mecca, two or three particulars deserve further notice. One is the celebrated black stone, which is set in silver, and fixed in the south-east corner of the Caaba, being that which looks towards Basra, about two cubits and one-third, or which is the same thing, seven spans from the ground. This stone is exceedingly respected by the Mohammedans, and is kissed by the pilgrims with great devotion, being called by some the *right hand of God on earth*. They fable that it is one of the precious stones of paradise, and fell down to the earth with Adam, and being taken up again, or otherwise preserved at the deluge, the angel Gabriel afterwards brought it back to Abraham when he was building the Caaba. It was at first whiter than milk, but grew black long since by the touch of a menstruous woman, or, as others tell us, by the sins of mankind, or rather by the touches and kisses of so many people; the superficies only being black, and the inside still remaining white. When the Karmatians, among other profanations by them offered to the temple of Mecca, took away this stone, they could not be prevailed on for love or money to restore it, though those of Mecca offered no less than five thousand pieces of gold for it. However, after they had kept it twenty-two years, seeing they could not thereby draw the pilgrims from Mecca, they sent it back of their own accord; at the same time bantering its devotees by telling them it was not the true stone: but, as it is said, it was proved to be no counterfeit by its peculiar quality of swimming on water.

Another thing observable in this temple is the stone in Abraham's place, wherein they pretend to show his footsteps, telling us he stood on it when he built the Caaba, and that it served him for a scaffold, rising and falling of itself as he had occasion; though another tradition says he stood upon it while the wife of his son Ismael, whom he paid a visit to, washing his head. It is now enclosed in an iron chest, out of which the pilgrims drink the water of Zemzem, and are ordered to pray at it by the Korân. The officers of the temple took care to hide this stone when the Karmatians took the other.

The last thing I shall take notice of in the temple is the well Zemzem on the east side of the Caaba, and which is covered with a small building and cupola. The Mohammedans are persuaded it is the very spring which gushed out for the relief of Ismael, when Hagar his mother wandered with him in the desert; and some pretend it was so named from her calling to him, when she spied it, in the Egyptian tongue, Zem, zem, that is, Stay, stay, though it seems rather to have had the name from the murmuring of its waters. The water of this well is reckoned holy and is highly reverenced; being not only drunk with particular devotion by the pilgrims, but also sent in bottles, as a great rarity, to most parts of the Mohammedan dominions. Abd'allah, surnamed al Hâfedh, from his great memory particularly as to the traditions of Mohammed, gave out that he acquired that faculty by drinking large draughts of Zemzem water, to which I really believe it as efficacious as that of Helicon to the inspiring of a poet.

To this temple every Mohammedan, who has health and means sufficient, ought once at least in his life to go on pilgrimage; nor are women excused from the performance of this duty. The pilgrims meet at different places near Mecca, according to the different parts from whence they come during the months of Shawâl and Dhu'lkaada; being obliged to be there by the beginning of Dhu'lhajja; which month, as its name imports, is peculiarly set apart for the celebration of this solemnity.

At the places above mentioned the pilgrims properly commence such; when the men put on the Ihrâm or sacred habit, which consists only of two woollen wrappers, one wrapped about their middle to cover their privates, and the other thrown over their shoulders, having their heads bare, and a kind of slippers which cover neither heel nor the instep, and so enter the sacred territory in their way to Mecca. While they have this habit on they must neither hunt nor fowl (though they are allowed to fish), which precept is so punctually observed, that they will not kill even a louse or a flea, if they find them on their bodies; there are some noxious animals, however, which they have permission to kill during the pilgrimage, as kites, ravens, scorpions, mice, and dogs given to bite. During the pilgrimage it behoves a man to have a constant guard over his words and actions, and to avoid all quarrelling, or ill language, and all converse with women, and obscene discourse, and to apply his whole intention to the good work he is engaged in.

The pilgrims, arrived at Mecca, immediately visit the temple, and then enter on the performance of the prescribed ceremonies, which consist chiefly in going in procession round the Caaba, in running between the mounts Safâ and Merwâ, making the station on Mount Arafat, and slaying the victims, and shaving their heads in the valley of Mina. These ceremonies have been so particularly described by others, that I may be excused if I but just mention the most material circumstances thereof.

In compassing the Caaba, which they do seven times, beginning at the corner where the black stone is fixed, they use a short quick pace the three first times they go round it, and a grave ordinary pace the four last; which it is said was ordered by Mohammed, that his followers might show themselves strong and active, to cut off the hopes of the infidels, who gave out that the immoderate heats of Medina had rendered them weak. But the aforesaid quick pace they are not obliged to use every time they perform this piece of devotion, but only at some particular times. So often as they pass by the black stone they either kiss it, or touch it with their hand, and kiss that.

The running between Safâ and Merwâ is also performed seven times, partly with a slow pace, and partly running: for they walk gravely till they come to a place between two pillars; and there they run, and afterwards walk again; sometimes looking back, and sometime stopping, like one who has lost something, to represent Hagar seeking water for her son: for the ceremony is said to be as ancient as her time.

On the ninth of Dhul'hajja, after morning prayer, the pilgrims leave the valley of Mina, whither they come the day before, and proceed in a tumultuous and rushing manner to Mount Arafat, where they stay to perform their devotions till sunset: then they go to Mozdalifa, an oratory between Arafat and Mina, and there spend the night in prayer, and reading the Korân. The next morning by daybreak they visit al Mashêr al harâm, or the sacred monument, and departing thence before sunrise, haste by Batn Mohasser to the valley of Mina, where they throw seven stones at three marks or pillars, in imitation of Abraham, who meeting the devil in that place, and being by him disturbed in his devotions, or tempted to disobedience, when he was going to sacrifice his son, was commanded by God to drive him away by throwing stones at him; though others pretend this rite to be as old as Adam, who also put the devil to flight in the same place, and by the same means.

This ceremony being over, on the same day, the tenth of Dhul'hajja, the pilgrims slay their victims in the said valley of Mina; of which they and their friends eat part, and the rest is given to the poor. These victims must be either sheep, goats, kine, or camels; males, or either of the two former kinds, and females if of either of the latter, and of a fit age. The sacrifices being over, they shave their heads and cut their nails, burying them in the same place; after which the pilgrimage is looked on as completed: though they again visit the Caaba, to take their leave of that sacred building.

The above-mentioned ceremonies, by the confession of the Mohammedans themselves, were almost all of them observed by the Pagan Arabs many ages before their prophet's appearance; and particularly the compassing of the Caaba, the running between Safâ and Merwâ, and the throwing of the stones in Mina; and were confirmed by Mohammed, with some alterations in such points as seemed most exceptionable: thus, for example, he ordered that when they compassed the Caaba, they should be *clothed*; whereas before his time they performed that piece of devotion *naked*, throwing off their clothes as a mark that they had cast off their sins, or as signs of their disobedience towards God.

It is also acknowledged that the greater part of these rites are of no intrinsic worth, neither affecting the soul, nor agreeing with natural reason, but altogether arbitrary, and commanded merely to try the obedience of mankind, without any further view; and are therefore to be complied with, not that they are good in themselves, but because God has so appointed. Some, however, have endeavoured to find out some reasons for the arbitrary injunctions of this kind; and one writer, supposing men ought to imitate the heavenly bodies, not only in their purity but in their circular motion, seems to argue the procession round the Caaba to be therefore a rational practice. Reland has observed that the Romans had something like this in their worship, being ordered by Numa to use a circular motion in the adoration of the gods, either to represent the orbicular motion of the world, or the perfecting the whole office of prayer to that God who is maker of the universe, or else in allusion to the Egyptian wheels, which were hieroglyphics of the instability of human fortune.

The pilgrimage to Mecca, and the ceremonies prescribed to those who perform it, are, perhaps, liable to greater exception than any other of Mohammed's institutions; not only as silly and ridiculous in themselves, but as relics of idolatrous superstition. Yet whoever seriously considers how difficult it is to make people submit to the abolishing of ancient customs, how unreasonable soever, which they are fond of, especially where the interest of a considerable party is also concerned, and that a man may with less danger change many things than one great one, must excuse Mohammed's yielding some points of less moment, to gain the principal. The temple of Mecca was held in excessive veneration by all the Arabs in general (if we except only the tribes of Tay, and Khathâam, and some of the posterity of al Hareth Ebn Caab, who used not to go in pilgrimage thereto), and especially by those of Mecca, who had a particular interest to support that veneration; and as the most silly and insignificant things are generally the objects of the greatest superstition, Mohammed found it much easier to abolish idolatry itself than to eradicate the superstitious bigotry with which they were addicted to that temple, and the rites performed there: wherefore, after several fruitless trials to wean them therefrom, he thought it best to compromise the matter, and, rather than to frustrate his whole design, to allow them to go on pilgrimage thither, and to direct their prayers thereto: contenting himself with transferring the devotions there paid from their idols to the true God, and changing such circumstances therein as he judged might give scandal. And herein he followed the example of the most famous legislators, who instituted not such laws as were absolutely the best in themselves, but the best their people were capable of receiving: and we find God himself had the same condescendence for the Jews, whose hardness of heart he humoured in many things, giving them therefore *statutes that were not good, and judgments whereby they should not live.*

OF CERTAIN NEGATIVE PRECEPTS IN THE KORAN

Having in the preceding section spoken of the fundamental points of the Mohammedan religion, relating both to faith and to practice, I shall in this and the two following discourses, speak in the same brief method of some other precepts and institutions of the Korân, which deserve peculiar notice, and first of certain things which are thereby prohibited.

The drinking of wine, under which name all sorts of strong and inebriating liquors are comprehended, is forbidden in the Korân in more places than one. Some, indeed, have imagined that only excess therein is forbidden, and that the moderate use of wine is allowed by two passages in the same book: but the more received opinion is, that to drink any strong liquors, either in a lesser quantity or in a greater, is absolutely unlawful; and though libertines indulge themselves in the contrary practice, yet the more conscientious are so strict, especially if they have performed the pilgrimage to Mecca, that they hold it unlawful not only to taste wine, but to press grapes for the making of it, to buy or to sell it, or even to maintain themselves with the money arising by the sale of the liquor. The Persians, however, as well as the Turks, are very fond of wine; and if one asks them how it comes to pass that they venture to drink it, when it is so directly forbidden by their religion, they answer, that it is with them as with the Christians, whose religion prohibits drunkenness and whoredom as great sins, and who glory, notwithstanding, some in debauching girls and married women, and others in drinking to excess.

It has been a question whether coffee comes not under the above mentioned prohibition, because the fumes of it have some effect on the imagination. This drink, which was first publicly used at Aden, in Arabia Felix, about the middle of the ninth century of the Hejra, and thence gradually introduced into Mecca, Medina, Egypt, Syria, and other parts of the Levant, has been the occasion of great disputes and disorders, having been sometimes publicly condemned and forbidden, again declared lawful and allowed. At present the use of coffee is generally tolerated, if not granted, as is that of *tobacco*, though the more religious make a scruple of taking the latter, not only because it inebriates, but also out of respect to a traditional saying of their prophet (which, if it could be made out to be his, would prove him a prophet indeed), *That in the latter days there should be men who should bear the name of* Moslems, *but should not be really such; and that they should smoke a certain weed, which should be call* tobacco: however, the eastern nations are generally so addicted to both, that they say, *a dish of coffee and a pipe of tobacco are a complete entertainment*; and the Persians have a proverb, that *coffee without tobacco is meat without salt.*

Opium and beng (which latter is the leaves of hemp in pills or conserve) are also by the rigid Mohammedans esteemed unlawful, though not mentioned in the Korân, because they intoxicate and disturb the understanding as wine does, and in a more extraordinary manner: yet these drugs are now commonly taken in the east; but they who are addicted to them are generally looked upon as debauchees.

Several stories have been told as the occasion of Mohammed's prohibiting the drinking of wine: but the true reasons are given in the Korân, viz. Because the ill qualities of that liquor surpass its good ones, the common effects thereof being quarrels and disturbances in company, and neglect, or at least indecencies, in the performance of religious duties. For these reasons it was, that the priests were, by the Levitical law, forbidden to drink wine or strong drink when they entered the tabernacle, and that the Nazarites and Rechabites, and many pious persons among the Jews and primitive Christians, wholly abstained therefrom; nay, some of the latter went so far as to condemn the use of wine as sinful. But Mohammed is said to have had a nearer example than any of these, in the more devout persons of his own tribe.

Gaming is prohibited by the Korân in the same passages, and for the same reasons, as wine. The word *al Meisar*, which is there used, signifies a particular manner of casting lots by arrows, much practised by the pagan Arabs, and performed in the following manner. A young camel being bought and killed, and divided into ten, or twenty-eight parts, the persons who cast lots for them, to the number of seven, met for that purpose; and eleven arrows were provided, without heads of feathers, seven of which were marked, the first with one notch, and the second with two, and so on, and the other four had no mark at all; these arrows were put promiscuously into a bag, and then drawn by an indifferent person, who had another near him to receive them, and to see he acted fairly; those to whom the marked arrows fell won shares in proportion to their lot, and those to whom the blanks fell were entitled to no part of the camel at all, but were obliged to pay the full price of it. The winners, however, tasted not of the flesh, any more than the losers, but the whole was distributed among the poor; and this they did out of pride and ostentation, it being reckoned a shame for a man to stand out, and not venture his money on such an occasion. This custom, therefore, though it was of some use to the poor, and diversion to the rich, was forbidden by Mohammed, as the source of greater inconveniences, by occasioning quarrels and heartburnings, which arose from the winners' insulting of those who lost.

Under the name of *lots* the commentators agree that all other games whatsoever, which are subject to hazard or chance, are comprehended and forbidden; as dice, cards, tables, &c. And they are reckoned so ill in themselves, that the testimony of him who plays at them is, by the more rigid, judged to be of no validity in a court of justice. Chess is almost the only game which the Mohammedan doctors allow to be lawful (though it has been a doubt with some), because it depends wholly on skill and management, and not at all on chance: but then it is allowed under certain restrictions, viz. that it be no hindrance to the regular performance of their devotions, and that no money or other thing be played for or betted; which last the Turks and Sonnites religiously observe, but the Persians and Moguls do not. But what Mohammed is supposed chiefly to have disliked in the game of chess, was the carved pieces, or men, with which the pagan Arabs played, being little figures of men, elephants, horses, and dromedaries; and these are thought, by some commentators, to be truly meant by the *images* prohibited in one of the passages of the Korân quoted above. That the Arabs in Mohammed's time actually used such images for chessmen appears from what is related, in the Sonna, of Ali, who passing accidentally by some who were playing at chess, asked, *What images they were which they were so intent upon?* for they were perfectly new to him, that game having been but very lately introduced into Arabia, and not long before into Persia, whither it was first brought from India, in the reign of Kohsrû Nûshirwân. Hence the Mohammedan doctors infer that the game was disapproved only for the sake of the images: wherefore the Sonnites always play with plain pieces of wood or ivory; but the Persians and Indians, who are not so scrupulous, continue to make use of the carved ones.

The Mohammedans comply with the prohibition of gaming much better than they do with that of wine; for though the common people, among the Turks more frequently, and the Persians more rarely, are addicted to play, yet the better sort are seldom guilty of it.

Gaming, at least to excess, has been forbidden in all well-ordered states. Gaming-houses were reckoned scandalous places among the Greeks, and a gamester is declared by Aristotle to be no better than a *thief*: the Roman senate made very severe laws against playing at games of hazard, except only during the *Saturnalia*; though the people played often at other times, notwithstanding the prohibition: the civil law forbade all pernicious games: and though the laity were, in some cases, permitted to play for money, provided they kept within reasonable bounds, yet the clergy were forbidden to play at *tables* (which is a game hazard), or even to look on while others played. Accursius, indeed, is of opinion they may play at chess, notwithstanding that law, because it is a game not subject to chance, and being but newly invented in the time of Justinian, was not then known in the western parts. However the monks for some time were not allowed even chess.

As to the Jews, Mohammed's chief guides, they also highly disapprove gaming: gamesters being severely censured in the Talmud, and their testimony declared invalid.

Another practice of the idolatrous Arabs, forbidden also in one of the above-mentioned passages, was that of *divining* by *arrows*. The arrows used by them for this purpose were like those with which they cast lots, being without heads or feathers, and were kept in the temple of some idol, in whose presence they were consulted. Seven such arrows were kept at the temple of Mecca; but generally in divination they made use of three only, on one of which was written, *My Lord hath commanded me*: on another *My Lord hath forbidden me*; and the third was blank. If the first was drawn, they looked on it as an approbation of the enterprise in question; if the second, they made a contrary conclusion; but if the third happened to be drawn, they mixed them and drew over again, till a decisive answer was given by one of the others. These divining arrows were generally consulted before any thing of moment was undertaken; as when a man was about marry, or about to go a journey, or the like. This superstitious practice of divining by arrows was used by the ancient Greeks, and other nations; and is particularly mentioned in Scripture, where it is said, that "the king of Babylon stood at the parting of the way, at the head of the two ways, to use divination; he made his arrows bright" (or, according to the version of the vulgate, which seems preferable in this place, *he mixed together*, or shook *the arrows*), *he consulted with images*, &c.: the commentary of St Jerome on which passage wonderfully agrees with what we are told of the aforesaid custom of the old Arabs: "He shall stand," says he, "in the highway, and consult the oracle after the manner of his nation, that he may cast arrows into a quiver, and mix them together, being written upon or marked with the names of each people, that he may see whose arrow will come forth, and which city he ought first to attack.

A distinction of meats was so generally used by the eastern nations, that it is no wonder that Mohammed made some regulations in that matter. The Korân, therefore, prohibits the eating of blood, and swine's flesh, and whatever dies of itself, or is slain in the name or in honour of any idol, or is strangled, or killed by a blow, or a fall, or by any other beast. In which particulars Mohammed seems chiefly to have imitated the Jews, by whose law, as is well known, all those things are forbidden; but he allowed some things to be eaten which Moses did not, as camels' flesh in particular. In cases of necessity, however, where a man may be in danger of starving, he is allowed by the Mohammedan law to eat any of the said prohibited kinds of food; and the Jewish doctors grant the same liberty in the like case. Though the aversion to blood and what dies of itself may seem natural, yet some of the pagan Arabs used to eat both; of their eating of the latter some instances will be given hereafter: and as to the former, it is said they used to pour blood, which they sometimes drew from a live camel, into a gut, and then broiled it on the fire, or boiled it, and ate it: this food they called *moswadd*, from *aswad*, which signifies *black*; the same nearly resembling our *black-puddings* in name as well as composition.

The eating of meat offered to idols I take to be commonly practised by all idolaters, being looked on as a sort of communion in their worship, and for that reason esteemed by Christians, if not absolutely unlawful, yet as what may be the occasion of great scandal: but the Arabs were particularly superstitious in this matter, killing what they ate on stones erected on purpose round the Caaba, or near their own houses, and calling, at the same time, on the name of some idol. Swine's flesh, indeed, the old Arabs seem not to have eaten; and their prophet, in prohibiting the same, appears to have only confirmed the common aversion of the nation. Foreign writers tell us that the Arabs wholly abstained from swine's flesh, thinking it unlawful to feed thereon, and that very few, if any, of those animals are found in their country, because it produces not proper food for them; which has made one writer imagine that if a hog were carried thither, it would immediately die.

In the prohibition of usury I presume Mohammed also followed the Jews, who are strictly forbidden by their law to exercise it among one another, though they are so infamously guilty of it in their dealing with those of a different religion: but I do not find the prophet of the Arabs has made any distinction in this matter.

Several superstitious customs relating to cattle, which seem to have been peculiar to the pagan Arabs, were also abolished by Mohammed. The Korân mentions four names by them given to certain camels or sheep, which for some particular reasons were left at free liberty, and were not made use of as other cattle of the same kind. These names are Bahîra, Sâïba, Wasîla, and Hâmi: of each whereof in their order.

As to the first it is said that when a she-camel, or a sheep, had borne young ten times, they used to slit her ear, and turn her loose to feed at full liberty; and when she died, her flesh was eaten by the men only, the women being forbidden to eat thereof: and such a camel or sheep, from the *slitting of her ear*, they called Bahîra. Or the Bahîra was a she-camel, which was turned loose to feed, and whose fifth young one, if it proved a male, was killed and eaten by men and women promiscuously: but if it proved a female, had its ear slit, and was dismissed to free pasture, none being permitted to make use of its flesh or milk, or to ride on it; though the women were allowed to eat the flesh of it, when it died: or it was the female young of the Sâïba, which was used in the same manner as its dam; or else an ewe, which had yeaned five times. These, however, are not all the opinions concerning the Bahîra: for some suppose that name was given to a she-camel, which, after having brought forth young five times (if the last was a male), had her ear slit as a mark thereof, and was let go loose to feed, none driving her from pasture or water, nor using her for carriage; and others tell us, that when a camel had newly brought forth, they used to slit the ear of her young one, saying, "O God, if it live, it shall be for our use, but if it die, it shall be deemed rightly slain"; and when it died, they ate it.

Sâïba signifies a she-camel *turned loose* to go where she will. And this was done on various accounts: as when she had brought forth females ten times together; or in satisfaction of a vow; or when a man had recovered from sickness, or returned safe from a journey, or his camel had escaped some signal danger either in battle or otherwise. A camel so turned loose was declared to be Sâïba, and, as a mark of it, one of the *vertebræ* or bones was taken out of her back, after which none might drive her from pasture or water, or ride on her. Some say that the Sâïba, when she had ten times together brought forth females, was suffered to go at liberty, none being allowed to ride on her, and that her milk was not to be drunk by any but her young one, or a guest, till she died; and then her flesh was eaten by men as well as women, and her last female young one had her ear slit, and was called Bahîra, and turned loose as her dam had been.

This appellation, however, was not so strictly proper to female camels, but that it was given to the male when his young one had begotten another young one: nay a servant set at liberty and dismissed by his master was also called Sâïba: and some are of opinion that the word denotes any animal which the Arabs used to turn loose in honour of their idols, allowing none to make use of them thereafter, except women only.

Wasîla is, by one author, explained to signify a she-camel which had brought forth ten times, or an ewe which had yeaned seven times, and every time twins; and if the seventh time she brought forth a male and a female, they said, Wosilat akhâha, i.e. *She is joined* or *was brought forth with her brother*, after which none might drink the dam's milk, except men only; and she was used as the Sâïba. Or Wasîla was particularly meant of sheep; as when an ewe brought forth a female, they took it to themselves, but when she brought forth a male, they consecrated it to their gods, but if both a male and a female, they said, *She is joined to her brother*, and did not sacrifice that male to their gods: or Wasîla was an ewe which brought forth first a male, and then a female, on which account, or because *she followed her brother*, the male was not killed; but if she brought forth a male only, they said, *Let this be an offering to our gods*. Another writes, that if an ewe brought forth twins seven times together, and the eighth time a male, they sacrificed that male to their gods; but if the eighth time she brought forth a male and a female, they used to say, *She is joined to her brother*, and for the female's sake they spared the male, and permitted not the dam's milk to be drunk by women. A third writer tells us that Wasîla was an ewe, which having yeaned seven times, if that which she brought forth the seventh time was a male, they sacrificed it, but if a female, it was suffered to go loose, and was made use of by women only; and if the seventh time she brought forth both a male and a female, they held them both to be sacred, so that men only were allowed to make any use of them, or to drink the milk of the female: and a fourth describes it to be an ewe which brought forth ten females at five births one after another, i.e. every time twins and whatever she brought forth afterwards was allowed to men, and not to women, &c.

Hâmi was a male camel used for a stallion, which, if the females had conceived ten times by him, was afterwards *freed from labour*, and let go loose, none driving him from pasture or from water; nor was any allowed to receive the least benefit from him, not even to shear his hair.

These things were observed by the old Arabs in honour of their false gods, and as part of the worship which they paid them, and were ascribed to the divine institution; but are all condemned in the Korân, and declared to be impious superstitions.

The law of Mohammed also put a stop to the inhuman custom, which had been long practised by the pagan Arabs, of burying their daughters alive, lest they should be reduced to poverty by providing for them, or else to avoid the disgrace which would follow, if they should happen to be made captives, or to become scandalous by their behaviour; the birth of a daughter being, for these reasons, reckoned a great misfortune, and the death of one as great a happiness. The manner of their doing this is differently related; some say that when an Arab had a daughter born, if he intended to bring her up, he sent her, clothed in a garment of wool or hair, to keep camels or sheep in the desert; but if he designed to put her to death, he let her live till she became six years old, and then said to her mother, "Perfume her, and adorn her, that I may carry her to her mothers"; which being done, the father led her to a well or pit dug for that purpose, and having bid her to look down into it, pushed her in headlong, as he stood behind her, and then filling up the pit, levelled it with the rest of the ground: but others say, that when a woman was ready to fall in labour, they dug a pit, on the brink whereof she was to be delivered, and if the child happened to be a daughter, they threw it into the pit, but if a son, they saved it alive. This custom, though not observed by all the Arabs in general, was yet very common among several of their tribes, and particularly these of Koreish and Kendah; the former using to bury their daughters alive in mount Abu Dalâma, near Mecca. In the time of ignorance, while they used this method to get rid of their daughters, Sásaá, grandfather to the celebrated poet al Farazdak, frequently redeemed female children from death, giving for every one two she-camels big with young, and a he-camel; and hereto al Farazdak alluded when, vaunting himself before one of the Khalîfs of the family of Omeyya, he said, "I am the son of the giver of life to the dead; for which expression being censured, he excused himself by alleging the following words of the Korân: "He who saveth a soul alive shall be as if he had saved the lives of all mankind." The Arabs, in thus murdering of their children, were far from being singular; the practice of exposing infants and putting them to death being so common among the ancients, that it is remarked as a thing very extraordinary in the Egyptians, that they brought up *all* their children; and by the laws of Lycurgus no child was allowed to be brought up, without the approbation of public officers. At this day, it said, in China, the poorer sort of people frequently put their children, the females especially, to death, with impunity.

This wicked practice is condemned by the Korân in several passages; one of which, as some commentators judge, may also condemn another custom of the Arabians, altogether as wicked, and as common among other nations of old, viz., the sacrificing of their children to their idols; as was frequently done, in particular, in satisfaction of a vow they used to make, that if they had a certain number of sons born, they would offer one of them in sacrifice.

Several other superstitious customs were likewise abrogated by Mohammed; but the same being of less moment, and not particularly mentioned in the Korân, or having been occasionally taken notice of elsewhere, I shall say nothing of them in this place.

3

MÉMOIRE SUR LA DYNASTIE DES ASSASSINS ET SUR L'ÉTYMOLOGIE DE LEUR NOM

Antoine Silvestre de Sacy

Dans un travail que j'ai mis, il n'y a pas long-temps, sous les yeux de la Classe, j'ai fair connoître en détail les dogmes de la secte des Ismaéliens, et j'ai remonté, autant qu'il m'a été possible, à l'origine de cette secte et à celle du système religieux ou plutôt philosophique qui la caractérise spécialement. On a dû se convaincre que la doctrine secrète des Ismaéliens, à laquelle n'étoient initiés qu'un petit nombre d'adeptes, avoit pour but de substituer la philosophie à la relgion, la raison à la croyance la liberté indéfinie de penser à l'autorité de la révelation. Cette liberté, ou plutôt cette licence, ne sauroit demeurer long-temps une simple spéculation de l'esprit; elle passe au coeur, et son influence pernicieuse sur la morale ne tarde pas à se faire sentir. Aussie les Ismaéliens virent-ils naître parmi eux des partis qui réalisèrent toute l'immoralité dont leur doctrine avoit posé les bases, et qui secouèrent avec le joug de lay croyance et due culte public celui de la décence et des lois les plus sacrées de la nature. Ce qui se passoit dans les orgies des Karmates, ce que l'on a imputé plus d'une fois aux Druzes, ce que certaines sectes pratiquent encore aujourd'hui dans la Mésopotamie et dans quelques parties de la Syrie, eût peut-être fait rougir les premiers auteurs de cette doctrine, qui, sans doute, n'avoient pas prévu toutes les conséquences de leur système. Au

Source: *Mémoires de l'Institut Royal de France*, 1818, vol. 4, pp. 1–84.

surplus, ni la liberté indéfinie de penser, qui formoit essentiellement le dernier degré de l'enseignement des Ismaéliens, ni la licence qui caractérisa plusieurs branches de cette secte, n'étoient communes à tous ceux qui faisoient profession de la doctrine allégorique, et reconnoissoient la transmission de l'imamat à Ismaël, fils de Djafar Sadek. On ne precédoit même à l'admission des nouveaux prosélytes et à leur initiation que par degrés et avec beaucoup de réserve: car, comme la secte avoit en même temps un but politique et des vues ambitieuses, son intérêt étoit sur-tout d'avoir en tous lieux un grand nombre de partisans dans toutes les classes de la société. Il falloit donc s'accommoder au caractère, au tempérament, aux préjugés du plus grand nombre: ce que l'on révéloit aux uns auroit révolté et éloigné pour toujours des esprits moins hardis, des consciences plus faciles à alarmer. Pourvu que l'on pût insinuer, au moyen de la doctrine allégorique, la nécessité de reconnoître la succession légitime au khalifat dans la personne d'Ali et dans celle des imams sortis de son sang par Ismaël, fils de Djafar, et l'obligation de se soumettre aveuglément aux ordres des *dais* ou missionaires, comme ministres et interprètes des volontés de l'iman, qui se tenoit caché sous les voiles du mystère en attendant le moment favorable à sa manifestation, on s'embarrassoit peu d'introduire le prosélyte dans la connoissance des secrets ultérieurs. Il n'est pas étonnant, d'après cela, que les Ismaéliens se soient partagés en plusieurs sectes, dont la doctrine s'éloigne plus ou moins de celle de l'islamisme. Tels furent les Karmates, les Nosaïris, les Fatémites ou Baténiens d'Égypte, les Druzes, les Ismaéliens de Perse, connus sous le nom de *Molhed* ملحد (au pluriel ملاحدة *Malahida*) ou impies, et ceux de Syrie, auxquels s'applique spécialement le nom d'*Assassins*.

J'ai fait voir ailleurs que les Karmates étoient une branche des Ismaéliens, et que la doctrine allégorique étoit établie chez eux avec toutes ses conséquences. De là l'insurrections contre l'autorité, le pillage des caravanes de pélerins, les insultes aux lieux consacrés par l'islamisme, la profanation de la Mecque, l'enlèvement de la pierre noire, &c. Les Nosaïris, qui subsistent encore aujourd'hui dans les montagnes du Liban, sont, suivant toutes les apparences, un rameau de la faction des Karmates. Les Fatémites ou Baténiens d'Égypte se reconnoissoient eux-mêmes pour Ismaéliens. Leur dynastie avoit d'abord été fondée en Afrique, vers la fin du troisième siècle de l'hégire, par un daï des Karmates. Mais Mahdi et ses successeurs, parvenus au but politique de leurs vœux, eurent intérêt à changer un peu de langage; et, après avoir prêché la rebellion contre les khalifes Abbasides, ils durent prêcher la soumission à l'autorité. La doctrine allégorique dut aussi être restreinte; car, s'ils en eussent admis les conséquences, s'ils eussent aboli le culte public, supprimé la prière, le jeûne, le pélerinage, ils auroient révolté les esprits et renversé de leurs propres mains le trône où ils venoient de s'asseoir. Ils devinrent donc, par intérêt, tolérans, observateurs des pratiques extérieures, protecteurs de la hiérarchie; et ils se contentèrent d'introduire en Égypte, après leur conquête, quelques-uns des signes extérieurs qui caractérisent les Schiites ou sectateurs d'Ali, et que les histroiens Arabes nomment شعار التشيّع *les livrées du schiisme*. Mais si, à l'extérieur, ils se conformoient à la doctine et aux usages reçus parmi le commun des Musulmans et fondés sur la lettre de l'Alcoran et sur la tradition, ils conservoient néanmoins et ils propageoient secrètement leur doctrine allégorique. Ils avoient leurs daïs, à la tête desquels étoit le chef suprême de la secte, nommé *Daï-'ldoat* داعي الدعاة ou Daï des daïs, qui joignit souvent ces fonctions à celles de *kadhi-'lkodhat*, قاضي القضاة, ou juge suprême. Les assemblées de la secte se tenoient régulièrement dans le palais des khalifes, une ou deux fois par semaine. La secte se propageoit par l'admission des nouveaux initiés, hommes et femmes. Dans chaque séance, on lisoit des instructions mystiques, nommées *les Conférences de la sagesse* مجالس الحكمة; elles étoient composées exprès pour cet objet, lues et approuvées dans les réunions particulières des daïs, réunions qui se tenoient aussi dans le palais, et ensuite presèntées au khalife pour recevoir son approbation. Toutes ces pratiques appartenoient à la secte des Ismaéliens et à celle des Karmates. Divers faits prouvent d'ailleurs sans réplique que les Karmates et les Fatémites, sortis d'une source commune, avoient la même doctrine, le même but philosophique, et ne faisoient dans le vrai qu'une seule et même secte, quoique divisés par un intérêt politique.

Abou-Taher, chef des Karmates, avoit, en l'année 317 de l'hégire, inondé la Mecque et son temple sacré du sang des pélerins, et enlevé la pierre noire. II mourut en 332, ainsi que son frère Abou-Mansour Ahmed; mais ils avoient deux frères qui leur succédèrent, Abou'lkasem Saïd et Abou'labbas. Ce fut sous le gouvernement de ceux-ci que la pierre noire fut rapportée à la Mecque. Ce qui donna lieu à cette restitution, dit Nowaïri, ce fut une lettre d'Obaïd allah, premier khalife de la dynastie des Fatémites, qui écrivit au chef des Karmates pour lui reprocher la conduite qu'il avoit tenue en cette occasion. «Vous avez, lui disoit-il, justifié les reproches qu'on nous fait, vous avez révelé le secret et le véritable esprit de notre doctrine qui conduit a l'incredulité et à l'immoralité. Si vous ne restituez aux Mecquois ce que vous leur avez pris, si vous ne remettez la pierre noire à sa place, et si vous ne rendez l'étoffe qui couvroit la Caaba, je n'ai plus rien de commun avec vous, ni en ce monde ni en l'autre.»

Hamza Isfahani, cité par Reiske dans ses notes sur Abou'lféda, rapporte qu'Abou-Taher, de retour à Hadjar après le pillage de la Mecque, reconnut Obaïd-allah pour son souverain, fit faire les prières publiques en son nom, et l'en instruisit par une lettre, mais qu'ensuite il supprima ces marques d'obéissance, ayant reçu, au lieu des récompenses et des témoignages de reconnoissance qu'il espéroit, des reproches et des menaces.

Les Karmates s'étoient rendus tellement redoutables à l'empire des khalifes Abbasides par leurs incursions réitérées dans la Syrie, qu'il leur fut accordé, du temps des émirs Ikhschidites qui régnoient en Egypte et en Syrie sous le nom des khalifes, une composition annuelle de trois cent mille pièces d'or à prendre sur le trésor public de Damas. Lorsque Djewhar eut soumis l'Égypte aux Fatémites, et que la Syrie eut également été conquise pour eux par un autre général, Djafar ben-Fellah, les Karmates crurent ce moment favorable pour s'agrandir. Hasan, fils d'Abou-Mansour Ahmed, qui les gouvernoit alors, s'avança d'abord jusqu'à Coufa, dans le dessein d'entrer en Syrie. La haine contre les Fatémites détermina Bakhtiyar, prince de la famille de Bouwaih ou Bouya, qui remplissoit alors la place d'*emir-alomara* اميرالامرا à Bagdad, à favoriser son entreprise, en lui donnant toutes les armes de l'arsenal de Bagdad, et quatre cent mille pièces d'or à prendre sur Abou-Tagleb, fils de Naser-eddaula, de la famille de Hamdan. Abou-Tagleb, qui étoit bien aise de trouver une occasion de se venger du ton insultant et menaçant qu'avoit pris vis-à-vis de lui Djafar ben-Fellah, général des Fatémites en Syrie, paya les quatre cent mille pièces d'or au prince Karmate, et lui fournit en outre des approvisionnemens et des troupes. Son armée fut encore grossie de tous les soldats des Ikhschidites, qui, chassés de l'Égypte, avoient reflué dans la Syrie et dans la Palestine. Hasan le Karmate, se voyant ainsi à la tête d'une forte armée, s'avança jusqu'à Damas, dont il se rendit maître, et, après quelques autres conquêtes, il marcha vers l'Égypte. Djewhar, qui y commandoit, ne vit pas ce mouvement sans de très-vives alarmes, et il pressa fortement Moëzz, qui n'avoit point encore quitté Kaïrowan, de se rendre en Égypte. Moëzz y arriva en effet en 363, et il écrivit de là au prince Karmate, pour lui représenter qu'ils etoient l'un et l'autre de la même secte, et que c'étoit des Ismaéliens que les Karmates avoient reçu leur doctrine. Hasan, ajoute l'auteur duquel Nowaïri emprunte ce récit, savoit bien que les deux sectes n'en etoient qu'une seule; et, dans le fait, les Ismaéliens et les Karmates s'accordent à faire profession de l'athéisme et d'une licence entière relativement aux personnes et aux propriétés, et à nier la mission prophétique. Mais bien qu'ils soient d'accord sur la doctrine, quand un des deux partis a l'avantage sur l'autre, il ne respecte point la vie de ceux qui suivent le parti contraire, et ne leur fait aucune grâce.

Hasan n'eut point égard aux démarches de Moëzz; il entra en Égypte, vint jusqu'a Aïn-schems, assiégea le Caire, et se rendit maître du fossé. La perte de Moëzz étoit assurée, s'il n'eût gagné un des chefs de l'armée du Karmate, qui l'abandonna au plus fort de la mêlée. Hasan fut obligé de prendre la fuite: bientôt il perdit Damas. Après la mort de Hasan, arrivée en 366, les Karmates eurent encore quelques démêlés avec les princes voisins, jusqu'en l'année 375, où ils disparoissent en quelque sorte de l'histoire. Cependant j'ai appris par les livres des Druzes, qu'ils régnoient encore à Lahsa en 422.

Ce que je viens de dire des liaisons etroites qui existoient, du moins sous le point de vue de l'origine commune et de la doctrine, entre les Ismaéliens d'Égypte ou Fatémites et les Karmates, ne s'applique pas avec moins de certitude aux Ismaéliens de Perse et de Syrie, connus sous les noms de *Molheds* et d'*Assassins*. On a bien aperçu que les Assassins de Syrie, si fameux dans l'histoire des croisades, dependoient des Ismaéliens de Perse; mais on n'a pas assez connu les liaisons qui existoient entre ceux-ci et les Fatémites, et il est possible même qu'on ait été détourné de cette idée par ce qu'on lisoit du meurtre d'Amer-biahcam-allah, l'un de ces khalifes, tué par des Baténiens ou Ismaéliens.

M. de Guignes a cependant indiqué ce rapprochement, en disant que Hasan ben-Sabbah, fondateur de la dynastie des Ismaéliens de Perse, avoit demeuré pendant quelque temps auprès de Mostanser-billah, khalife d'Égypte, et que la religion qu'il fonda avoit quelque rapport avec la secte dont étoient les Fatémites. L'auteur du Tableau général de l'empire Othoman en parle aussi, quoique d'une manière peu exacte, en disant que Hasan Homaïri, fondateur de la secte des Ismaéliens de Perse, étoit un scheïkh séducteur, qui, après avoir prêché en Perse et en Syrie en faveur des Fatémites d'Égypte, contre les Abbasides de Bagdad, finit par débiter de faux commentaires sur l'Alcoran et par élever une nouvelle secte. M. l'abbé S. Assemani, de Padoue, dans une dissertation dont je parlerai plus loin, dit aussi, d'après l'auteur du Nighiaristan, que Hasan prêchoit en faveur des khalifes d'Égypte, contre les Abbasides. Mais ces légères indications ne suffisent pas pour prouver le rapport intime qui existoit entre les Fatémites d'Égypte et les Ismaéliens de Perse. Ce rapport est plus clairement indiqué par l'auteur du *Nizam altéwarikh,* abrégé chronologique de l'histoire des dynasties Orientales, dont j'ai donné l'extrait dans le tome IV des Notices et Extraits des manuscrits. Cet écrivain dit que Mostanser, khalife Fatémite d'Égypte, envoya à Hasan des patentes de gouverneur et de son lieutenant.

L'histoire de la dynastie fondée par Hasan, et qui subsista cent soixante-dix ans, est encore peu connue. D'Herbelot, et après lui Marigny dans ses *Révolutions des Arabes*, et M. de Guignes dans le premier volume de *l'Histoire des Huns*, ont donné la suite des princes de cette dynastie, mais avec très-peu de détails. Le prélat Et. Évode Assemani, dans son Catalogue des manuscrits Orientaux de la bibliothèque des Médicis à Florence, a pareillement fait connoître la suite de ces princes, d'après des tables chronologiques des dynasties Orientales, écrites en langue Turque: il ne l'a acccompagnée d'aucun fait. Dans la notice du *Nizam altéwarikh* dont j'ai déjà parlé, j'ai inséré ce que cet abrégé très-court m'offroit sur la même dynastie. Enfin M. l'abbé S. Assemani, de Padoue, a publié, dans le numéro de juin 1806 du journal qui s'imprime en cette ville, sous le titre de *Giornale dell'Italiana letteratura*, une dissertation où l'on trouve un peu plus de détails sur cette famille. Il les a puisés dans le Nighiaristan. Cela se réduit à quatre ou cinq pages, et il s'en faut beaucoup que l'on connoisse suffisamment par-là l'histoire de ces Ismaéliens.

Il est facile de suppléer à l'insuffisance de ces matériaux, en puisant dans le *Rouzat alsafa* de Mirkhond, où l'on trouve une histoire très-longue et très-détaillée de cette dynastie, et sur-tout de son fondateur Hasan ben-Sabbah. Enjoignant à cela ce que fournissent Elmacin, Abou'lféda, Abou'lfaradj et quelques autres écrivains, on suivra les progrès de cette puissance depuis son origine jusqu'à sa destruction.

M. Falconet, dans deux mémoires sur les Ismaéliens ou Assassins, insérés dans le recueil de l'Académie des belles-lettres, a très-bien développé plusieurs faits relatifs à ce sujet. Il a fait voir que les Assassins de Syrie étoient une dépendance des Ismaéliens du *Djébal* ou de la Perse, que le chef de la secte, *le*

Vieux de la montagne, résidoit à Alamout, et que c'étoit à lui que ressortissoient les Ismaéliens de Syrie. Il a aussi discuté l'origine du nom d'*Assassins*: mais, comme il ne connoissoit point les langues Orientales, il n'a pu fair usage, dans ces recherches, que des évrivains Orientaux dont il existoit des traductions imprimées, et de quelques extraits d'Abou'lféda que lui avoit communiqués M. de Guignes, fort jeune alors; aussi ce travail de M. Falconet est-il demeuré très-imparfait. Cependant, comme il a fort bien établi l'identité des Ismaéliens de Perse et des Assassins de Syrie, je ne m'arrêterai point à discuter ce point historique; je m'attacherai principalement à développer les rapports de cette branche d'Ismaéliens avec celle à laquelle appartenoient les khalifes d'Égypte; après quoi je rechercherai l'origine du nom des *Assassins*. Je joindrai à cela quelques observations sur les divers noms donnés aux Ismaéliens dans les historiens Orientaux.

L'histoire des Ismaéliens de Perse que donne Mirkhond, est assez intéressante pour mériter d'être traduite en entier; mais, comme ce travail est étranger aux travaux de la Classe, je le réserve pour le recueil des Notices, et je vais seulement tracer ici un tableau rapide de leurs commencemens.

Schahristani et Ebn-Khaldoun nous apprennent que les Ismaéliens se divisent en deux branches ou sectes, ou, pour me servir de leur propre expressions en deux *prédications* دعوة, l'une ancienne, l'autre nouvelle. L'ancienne remonte à l'époque même de l'imam Ismaël, fils de Djafar Sadek, ou plutôt de son fils Mohammed, vers le milieu du troisième siècle de l'hégire; la seconde commence à Hasan ben-Sabbah, vers l'an 483 de la même ère.

Les mêmes auteurs disent que chacune de ces deux branches d'Ismaéliens a ses dogmes et ses opinions particulières; mais elles se réunissent toutes deux sur plusieurs points capitaux qui forment l'essence de leur système. Ainsi tous les Ismaéliens reconnoissent les droits d'Ali et de ses enfans après lui à l'*imamat*, c'est-à-dire, à la souveraine puissance spirituelle et temporelle, et ne tiennent tous les princes qui ont exercé la souveraineté, au mépris des droits de la famille d'Ali, que pour des usurpateurs: ils n'admettent pas, comme beaucoup d'autres sectes des partisans d'Ali, une suite de douze imams. Les imams qu'ils reconnoissent sont au nombre de sept, et le septième est Ismaël, fils de Djafar Sadek: c'est de là qu'ils se donnent eux-mêmes le nom d'*Ismaéliens*. Ils croient qu'après Ismaël l'imamat est demeuré caché, et a reposé sur des personnages obscurs et ignorés des hommes: la vraie foi étoit alors confiée, comme un dépôt, aux daïs ou autres ministres, en attendant une nouvelle manifestation de l'imam. Elle a eu lieu en la personne d'Obaïd-allah, surnommé *le Mahdi*, qui, aidé du daï Abd-allah, fonda d'abord dans l'Afrique septentrionale la dynastie des khalifes Obaïdites ou Fatémites. Sous le quatrième prince de cette dynastie, l'Égypte fut ajoutée à leurs domaines; elle devint le centre de la puissance de ces pontifes, rivaux de ceux de Bagdad, et qui avoient un nombre infini de partisans dans les états de ces derniers, où ils entretenoient secrètement des *daïs* ou missionnaires, zélés pour la propagation de leur doctrine et prêts à profiter de toutes les occasions pour faire valoir leurs droits.

Hasan ben-Sabbah fut un de ces daïs. Son père se nommoit *Ali*; et si on l'appelle quelquefois *fils de Sabbah*, ou *fils de Mohammed ben-Sabbah*, c'est qu'il prétendoit descendre d'un personnage célèbre par ses vertus et par les miracles qu'on lui attribue, nommé *Mohammed ben-Sabbah Homaïri.*

Ali, père de Hasan, étoit un homme retiré due monde et livré à la vie mortifiée, mais qui passoit pour attaché à des opinions peu religieuses, et dont l'orthodoxie étoit fort suspecte. Pour détourner ces soupçons, il envoya son fils à Nichabour, étudier sous un scheïkh célèbre par la pureté de sa foi, ses lumières et ses vertus, l'imam Mowaffek Nischabouri. Hasan y fit une étroite connoissance avec un personnage qui devint très-illustre sous le nom de *Nizam-almulc*. Cette liaison lui procura dans la suite l'avantage d'être attachée au service du sultan Melicschah Seldjoukide, auprès duquel il fut introduit par son ancien compagnon d'études, devenu vizir sous le nom de *Nizam-almulc*. Il chercha ensuite à supplanter son bienfaiteur: mais, ayant échoué dans ce projet par les intrigues et l'adresse du vizir, il se vit obligé à quitter la cour, et se retira d'abord à Reï, et ensuite à Ispahan, où il se tint caché chez le reïs Abou'lfadhl. Hasan disoit lui-même: «J'ai été élevé dès ma jeunesse dans la doctrine des Schiites qui reconnoissent la succession des douze imams: j'avois formé une liaison avec un de ces sectaires qu'on nomme *réfik* رفيقان (j'expliquerai ce mot plus bas); il s'appeloit *Amirèh Zarrab*. J'étois persuadé que la doctrine de la secte des Ismaéliens étoit d'accord avec celle des philosophes: aussi avois-je toujours des disputes avec Amirèh, quand il vouloit prendre le parti de la secte des Ismaéliens, ou qu'il attaquoit ma croyance. Cependant ses discours firent impression sur mon esprit; et étant tombé dangereusement malade, il me vint en pensée que la doctrine des Ismaéliens étoit la vraie; que si je ne l'avois pas adoptée, ce n'étoit que par entêtement; et que si je venois à mourir dans cet état, je serois perdu sans ressource. Revenu de ma maladie, je fit connoissance avec un autre Ismaélien, puis avec un daï, que je priai de m'admettre dans la secte. Ensuite je fus moi-même promu au rang de daï, et envoyé en Égypte pour y jouir du bonheur de voir l'imam Mostanser.» Mostanser, flatté sans doute d'une circonstance qui pouvoit étendre sa puissance en Asie, prodigua les honneurs à Hasan, sans cependant l'admettre en sa présence; le khalife s'informoit de tout ce qu'il faisoit, et en parloit d'une manière si avantageuse, que personne ne doutoit que Hasan ne parvînt bientôt à la place la plus éminente. Sur ces entrefaites, il survint une vive altercation entre Hasan et l'*émir-aldjoyousch* ou généralissime de l'armée du khalife, qui avoit la direction de la secte des Ismaéliens, au sujet de la désignation faite par Mostanser, de Nézar, l'un de ses fils, pour son successeur. Le khalife avoit révoqué cette disposition, et l'*émir-aldjoyousch*, approuvoit cette mesure du prince. Hasan, au contraire, soutenoit l'irrevocabilité de la premiére disposition. Mostanser étroit pressé par l'*emir-aldjoyousch* qui peut-être étoit jaloux du crédit de Hasan, de le faire arrêter et enfermer dans la fortresse de Damiette; mais, comme le khalife ne voulut pas s'y prêter, les ennemis de Hasan l'embarquèrent sur un vaisseau avec des Francs, et l'envoyèrent dans le Magreb. Après quelques aventures qui sembloient tenir du prodige, Hasan aborda en Syrie, se rendit à Alep, puis à Bagdad, de là dans le Khouzistan, puis à Ispahan, et enfin à Yezd et dans le Kirman, faisant par-tout ses fonctions de daï, et ne négligeant rien pour la propagation de sa secte. Il revint ensuite à Ispahan, puis dans le Khouzistan, où il demeura trois ans. De là il vint à Damégan, où il séjourna aussi trois ans, et fit beaucoup de prosélytes. Il se rendit ensuite à Djordjan, d'où il passa par Damawend et Kazwin dans le Dilem. Enfin il se retira à Alamout, où il vécut occupé de la méditation et de la vie religieuse.

Il est inutile de raconter ici par quels moyens Hasan ben-Sabbah parvint à s'emparer de la forteresse d'Alamout, place située dans les environs de Kazwin, et qui appartenoit au sultan Melicschah: elle étoit gouvernée par un cotoual ou commandant, nommé *Mahdi*. Les prédications des daïs, sur-tout celles de Hosaïn Kaïni, avoient tellement multiplié dans ces canton les partisans de la doctrine des Ismaéliens qui reconnoissoient pour souverain l'imam établi en Égypte, qu'il ne fut pas difficile à Hasan de forcer le coutoual à lui céder, pour 3000 dinars, une étendue de terre égale à la peau d'un bœuf; mais Hasan, aussi fin que Didon, se trouva, par ce marché, maître d'un vaste emplacement qui comprenoit toute la citadelle. Il donna à Mahdi une assignation de 3000 dinars sur le gouverneur de Kirdcouh, qui avoit secrètement embrassé son parti, et il l'obligea à se retirer. Maître d'Alamout, il envoya le daï Hosaïn Kaïni avec d'autres *réfiks*, pour convertir et amener à la soumission les peuples du Kouhestan, contrée qui fait partie du Khorasan, et qui est située vers l'extrémité sud-ouest de cette grande province.

Il y a ici une circonstance importante à remarquer. Je vais traduire littéralement le texte de Mirkhond.

«Quand Hasan fils de Sabbah fut maître d'Alamout, il donna ordre de creuser un canal, et fit amener de fort loin des eaux au pied de la forteresse. Il fit planter au-dehors de la place des arbres fruitiers, et encouragea les habitans à ensemencer les terres et à les mettre en valeur. Par-là, l'air d'Alamout, qui étoit auparavant très-malsain, devint pur et salubre.»

Ceci n'auroit-il pas servi à accréditer l'idée des jardins délicieux des Assassins, dont je parlerai plus loin? Mais revenons à la suite des faits historiques.

Melicschah envoya des troupes contre Hasan, et elles firent inutilement le siége d'Alamout. Hasan, qui n'avoit alors avec lui que soixante-dix *réfiks*, tint tête aux assaillans, et, ayant reçu du dehors un renfort de trois cents hommes, il tomba de nuit sur les troupes du sultan, en fit un grand carnage, et prit un immense butin. La mort de Melicschah, arrivée en l'année 485 de l'hégire [1092 de J.C.], contribua ensuite à étendre et à consolider la puissance de Hasan.

Hasan avoit deux fils, qu'il fit mourir, l'un pour avoir bu du vin, l'autre parce qu'il étoit soupçonné d'avoir fait assassiner Hosaïn Kaïni. Le but de Hasan en cela étoit de faire connoître à toute le monde que son intention n'étoit point d'établir une souveraineté pour la faire passer à ses enfans. Il se livroit avec tant de zèle à l'administration de ses états, et donnoit tant de temps à répondre aux consultations qu'on lui adressoit touchant les dogmes de la secte, que, pendant trente-cinq ans qu'il passa à Alamout, il ne sortit que deux fois de son appartement pour monter sur la terrasse de son palais, et ne mit jamais le pied hors de la forteresse.

Je ne pousserai pas plus loin cet extrait historique. Il me suffira de dire que Hasan, lors de sa mort, arrivée en 519 de l'hégire, désigna pour son successeur Kia Buzurc-umid, dont les descendans conservèrent, sous le titre de *mokaddam* مقدم, la souveraineté d'Alamout et des autres lieux conquis par les Ismaéliens, et que, sous le règne due même Kia Buzurc-umid, on voit les

Ismaéliens prendre les armes à l'effet de réduire un descendant d'Ali, nommé *Abou-Haschem*, qui vouloit se faire reconnoître dans le Ghilan pour imam. Les Ismaéliens sont encore nommés, à cette occasion, par Mirkhond, *réfikan*.

Finissons par quelques traits de l'histoire des Ismaéliens.

En 498, ils pillèrent et massacrèrent, près de Reï, une caravane formée de la réunion de pélerins de l'Inde et du Mawara'lnahr, ou de la Transoxane, qui se rendoit à la Meque.

En 500, ils éprouvèrent un échec de la part du sultan Mélicschah.

Peu s'en fallut, en 502, qu'ils ne se rendissent maîtres de Schaïzer en Syrie.

En 591, mourut Hasan, fils de Sabbah, qui, dit Abou'lféda, interdisoit au commun des hommes la culture des sciences, et aux gens plus éclairés la lecture des livres des anciens philsophes.

La première conquête des Ismaéliens en Syrie est Panéas; ils s'en rendirent maîtres en 523.

En 525, ils prirent Mesyat en Syrie: cette place y devint leur chef-lieu.

En 559, Hasan, fils de Mohammed, et petit-fils de Kia Buzurcumid, abolit toutes les pratiques de l'islamisme, et au nom d'un imam caché, dont il prétendoit avoir reçu, un ordre exprès pour cela, il donna à ses sujets toute liberté de boire du vin, et de se permettre tout ce que défend la loi Musulmane. Il publia que la connoissance du sens allégorique des préceptes rendoit inutile l'observation de la lettre, et mérita à la secte le nom de *Molheds* ou impies.

Hasan, suivant Mirkhond et l'auteur du *Nighiaristan*, régna peu d'années: il mourut en 561 [1165], et son fils Mohammed, qui imita son impiété, régna quarante-six ans, et mourut en 606 [1209]. Au contraire, suivant l'auteur du *Nizam altéwarikh*, Hasan régna cinquante ans, et mourut en 607 [1210]: son fils n'eut qu'un règne très-court. Selon que l'on admet l'un ou l'autre de ces récits, l'ambassade du Vieux de la montagne au roi de Jérusalem Amaury I.er tombe sous le règne de Hasam ou sous celui de son fils. Il est donc vrai, comme le dit Guillaume de Tyr, que le prince qui l'envoya avoit banni toutes les pratiques de la religion Musulmane, renversé les mosquées, permis l'usage du vin et de la chair de porc, et les unions incestueuses. Quand on connoît les livres des Druzes, on croit aisément que ce même prince pouvoit avoir lu les livres saints des Chrétiens, et avoir conçu le desir, non pas d'embrasser la religion Chrétienne, mais d'en connoître plus à fond la doctrine et les pratiques.

En 588, meurt Sinan, chef des Ismaéliens de Syrie, et fondateur de la puissance de cette secte dans cette contrée.

En l'année 608, tous les Ismaéliens, tant de Syrie que de Perse, reprennent, par ordre de Djélal-eddin Hasan, émir d'Alamout, et sixième prince de cette dynastie, les signes extérieurs de la religion Musulmane, qu'ils avoient quittés par ordre de l'aïeul de ce prince, Hasan, fils de Mohammed et petit-fils de Kia Buzurc-umid.

En 644, des ambassadeurs d'Ala-eddin, émir des Ismaéliens de Perse, se trouvent à un *couriltaï* ou assemblée générale des chefs des tribus Mogoles pour l'election d'un khan des Tartares.

En 668, le sultan Bibars entre sur les terres des Ismaéliens de Syrie, et leur prend Mesyat.

Enfin la même prince, en 670, met fin à leur puissance en Syrie.

Elle avoit fini dans le Kouhestan dès 653, par la soumission du prince des Ismaéliens, Rocn-eddin Khourschah, à Holagou, la destruction d'Alamout, et le massacre de la famille de Rocn-eddin et d'un grand nombre de Molheds.

Lorsque je dis que les Ismaéliens ont été détruits, tant en Perse qu'en Syrie, avant la fin due VIIe siècle de l'hégire, il faut entendre cela, non pas de leur secte, mais de la souveraineté qu'ils avoient fondée. On les voit encore plus d'une fois, postérieurement à cette époque, paroître dans l'histoire, et continuer à exercer le métier d'assassins, qui les avoit rendus si redoubtables. Un des faits de ce genre sur lesquels les historiens Orientaux nous ont transmis le plus de détails, est leur conspiration plusieurs fois réitérée contre Karasankor. Cet émir, qui avoit été gouverneur ou viceroi d'Alep, pour le sultan d'Égypte Mélic-alnaser Mohammed, fils de Kélaoun, avoit été obligé de quitter les états de ce sultan, et de se retirer auprès des Mogols de Perse, descendans de Holagou, et auxquels commandoit alors Oldjaïtou-khan, nommé aussi *Khoda-bendèh*. Le sultan, qui le voyoit avec peine à l'abri de sa vengeance, essaya plusieurs fois de le faire assassiner par des Ismaéliens qu'il envoya exprès pour cela. Il en dépêcha à cet effet, en une seule fois, trente-quatre, qui étoient des gens domiciliés à Mesyat, ancien chef-lieu des Ismaéliens de Syrie. Karasankor échappa à leurs coups, et eut recours au même moyen, avec aussi peu de succès, pour faire périr le sultan. Cent vingt-quatre assassins Ismaéliens envoyés ensuite par Mélic-alnaser pour tuer Karasankor périrent victimes de sa vengeance, sans avoir pu exécuter leur projet. Les Ismaéliens avoient même encore, à cette époque, un chef à Mesyat; car Makrizi nous apprend que le sultan s'adressa à lui, et lui donna beaucoup d'argent pour qu'il lui envoyât quelques-uns de ses gens. Dans le récit de ces aventures, c'est toujours Mesyat qui paroît la résidence et l'asile de ces Assassins. Le sultan traita ensuite avec Karasankor et le vizir du prince Mogol, et s'engagea à ne plus envoyer d'Ismaéliens pour les assassiner; mais il observa mal ces conditions. Il chargea de nouveau de l'exécution de son projet un Ismaélien qu'on lui avoit envoyé de Mesyat, et qu'il nourrit trente-quatre jours avant de lui donner ses ordres et de l'expédier, lui fornissant chaque jour à boire et à manger, autant qu'il en auroit fallu pour plusieurs personnes. Cet homme, par une méprise, tua un autre émir pour Karasankor. En vain plusieurs de ces meurtriers furent mis à la torture, on n'en tira jamais aucun aveu.

La secte des Ismaéliens subsiste encore aujourd'hui, comme je le dirai plus loin.

Je passe à l'origine du nom des *Assassins.*

J'ai dit, au commencement de ce Mémoire, que les Ismaéliens ou Baténiens étoient connus, dans les historiens des croisades, sous le nom d'*Assassins.* Ce nom a été prononcé et écrit de diverses manières, soit, comme le dit M. Falconet, par la faute des copistes, soit par l'ignorance des auteurs mêmes. Parmi ces variations, celles qui ont le plus d'autorité sont les suivantes: *Assassini, Assessini* et *Heissessini.* Cette dernière, tirée d'Arnold de Lübeck, a l'avantage de conserver l'aspiration qui doit se trouver dans le mot original, puisque Benjamin de Tudèle écrit en hébreu *Haschischin* par un *heth*, et que les auteurs Grecs l'écrivent par un *χ*, nommant ces sectaires *χασισίοι.* Renaudot écrit aussi *Hassissini*, et quelquefois *Hassassini*; mais il ne donne pas l'étymoligie de ce mot.

On a proprosé diverses étymologies du mot *assassins.* Je ne ferois pas mention de l'opinion de M. De Caseneuve, qui veut dériver le nom des *Assassins* de l'ancien mot Teuton *sahs, sachs, sæhs,* coutelas, parce qu'elle semble se réfuter d'elle-même, rien n'étant moins naturel que de chercher dans le langage des Teutons l'origine d'une dénomination Orientale, si ce savant n'avoit cru pouvoir prouver que ce nom ne venoit point des langues de l'Asie et étoit inconnu aux Sarrasins, par l'autorité de Guillaume, archevêque de Tyr, qui dit: *Hos tam nostri quàm Saraceni, nescimus unde deducto vocabulo,* Assissinos *vocant.* M. De Caseneuve pousse évidemment beaucoup trop loin la conséquence qu'il tire de ce passage, dans lequel Guillaume convient qu'il ignore l'origine de ce nom, mais ne dit nullement qu'elle étoit ignorée des Sarrasins.

M. Court de Gébelin dérive aussi le mot *assassin,* du teuton *sachs;* mais le même mot, comme signifiant la *dynastie des Assassins,* lui paroît venir de شا. شا. *roi des rois.*

Th. Hyde, qui n'avoit sans doute jamais rencontré la dénomination dont il s'agit dans aucun écrivain Arabe, a cru que ce devoit être le mot *hassas* حساس , dérivé de la racine *hassa* حس , qui signifie, entre autres choses, *tuer, exterminer.* Cette opinion a été suivie par Ménage et par M. Falconet. M. De Volney a aussi adopté cette étymologie, sans en citer aucun garant.

Benjamin de Tudèle parle en deux endroits des Assassins: il écrit leur nom, la première fois en parlant des Assassins de Syrie, par un *heth,* אלחשישין; dans le second passage, parlant des Ismaéliens de Perse, qu'il nomme *Molahat* מולחאת, par corruption, pour *Mélahedèh* ملاحدة, il dit qu'ils reconnoissent l'autorité du vieillard qui réside dans le pays des *Caschischin* אלכשישין, comme l'a bien rendu Baratier, et non, comme l'avoit ridiculement traduit Constantin Lempereur, *seniorem suæ regionis Alcaschischin, quasi senes dicas, appellantes.* Je remarque ceci pour qu'on ne s'imagine pas, sur une fausse autorité, que le nom des *Assassins* signifiât *vieillard,* suivant l'opinion de Benjamin de Tudèle. Je ne sais si quelque manuscrit de cet écrivain Juif ne porteroit pas aussi, dans le second passage, *Haschischin* par un *heth,* au lieu d'un *eaf;* au reste, la substitution du *caf* au *heth* ne surprendra point les personnes instruites dans les langues de l'Orient. J'ajoute qu'en citant Benjamin de Tudèle, je ne prétends pas garantir la réalité de son voyage: mais, quoique vraisemblablement il n'ait jamais vu une grande partie des pays qu'il décrit, on ne peut nier qu'il n'ait eu d'assez bons matériaux.

Le savant auteur de la *Bibl. Or. Clem. Vaticana,* Joseph-Simon Assemani, ayant trouvé, dans le territoire de *Tacrit* en Mésopotamie, une ville nommée par les Arabes, *Hasasa* حصاصة , et par les Syriens, *Beth-hasosonoyè* ܒܝܬ ܚܣܘܣܢܝܐ, ou *Hasosonitho* ܚܣܘܣܢܝܬܐ, s'est imaginé que c'étoit de là que les *Assassins* dont les historiens des croisades ont parlé, avoient pris leur nom. Une telle conjecture ne repose sur aucun fondement historique, et ne méritoit pas d'être adoptée par l'auteur de l'*Oriens Christianus.* L'orthographe de ce nom n'a aucun rapport avec celle du véritable nom Arabe des *Assassins.* M. Falconet a rejeté cette conjecture d'Assemani; mais, par une autre méprise, il a confondu حصيصة *Hassasa* avec اعزاز *Azaz,* ou عزاز *Ezaz,* ville de

Mésopotamie, quoique ces deux noms n'aient aucune consonne commune entre eux.

M. Falconet a indiqué une autre origine du nom des *Assassins*, origine qu'il rejette lui-même, mais que je ne dois pas omettre, parce qu'elle pourroit trouver des approbateurs, et qu'effectivement elle a eu l'approbation de D. Carpentier, auteur du *Glossarium ad script. medii œvi.* D'ailleurs cela me donnera lieu de faire quelques observations utiles. Abou'lféda, dans sa Description de la Syrie, observe que *Mesyat*, ville qui étoit le chef-lieu de la secte des Ismaéliens en Syrie, est située sur la montagne nommée *Djabal-assikkin* جبل السكين. Comme *sikkin* veut dire *couteau, poignard*, le nom de cette montagne peut signifier *montagne du Couteau*, et il semble qu'il y ait quelque analogie entre cette dénomination, les atrocités reprochées aux *Assassins*, et leur nom même d'*Assassins*.

«Nous avons vu, dit M. Falconet, le mont *Assikkin*, la montagne du Poignard, être le domicile du commandant des *Assassins* en Syrie; les couteaux dont les *Assassins* se servoient, nommés *sikkin;* leur souverain qualifié, par Jacques de Vitry, du titre de *magister cultellorum;* ses sujets appelés *cultelliferi* dans Mathieu Paris, *sicarii* même, dans Guillaume de Neubridge. ... Mais, ajoute M. Falconet, toutes ces rencontres, quelqu'heureuses qu'elles soient, ne forment qu'une de ces allusions qui ne sont que trop souvent séduisantes dans la recherche de l'origine des mots, et ne sauroient prévaloir sur l'étymologie que nous avons d'abord proposée.»

Cette étymologie préférée par M. Falconet est, comme je l'ai déjà dit, celle que Hyde avoit proposée.

Les réflexions de M. Falconet sont très-justes: mais on peut ajouter, pour leur donner encore plus de poids (1) qu'il n'y a réellement pas une ressemblance bien grande entre le mot *alsikkin* ou *assikkin* et le nom des *Assassins;* (2) qu'il n'est pas certain que *Djabal-assikkin* signifie *la montagne du Poignard*. Abou'lféda ne le dit point. On lit, il est vrai, dans la traduction de Kœhler: *De hac denominatione montis, quâ* Assekkin *vocatur, quod cultrum significat, mirificè commentus est Ibn Saïd*. Mais ces mots, *quod cultrum significat,* sont ajoutés par le traducteur, et nous ignorons l'origine singulière que donnoit à cette dénomination Ebn-Saïd, dont l'ouvrage ne nous est point parvenu. Peut-être *Sekkin* est-il ici un nom d'homme, et faut-il traduire *la montagne de Sekkin*. Ce qu'il y a de certain du moins, c'est qu'un personnage nommé *Sekkin* a joué un grand rôle dans ce pays, vers le temps de Hakem et de l'établissement de la religion des Druzes, et que nous avons, dans le recueil des livres sacrés de cette secte, un diplôme daté de la dixième année de l'ère de Hamza, 418 de l'hégire, par lequel Sekkin fut nommé surintendant ou inspecteur général d'un diocèse, ou province ecclésiastique, désigné sous le nom de la *presqu'île de la Syrie supérieure,* et qui paroît avoir eu pour limites, au midi l'Arabie, au nord Hamat et son territoire, l'Irak à l'orient, et à l'occident la Méditerranée. Il étoit autorisé à avoir sous lui douze daïs ou missionnaires, et quelques autres ministres d'un rang inférieur. Les écrits des Druzes nous apprennent aussi que Sekkin ne se contenta pas de ce grade, et voulut s'arroger à lui-même un rang plus élevé dans la hiérarchie; qu'il commit beaucoup de brigandages qui rendirent odieux le nom des Druzes; enfin qu'il introduisit dans la religion, des nouveautés, un culte idolâtre et d'autres abominations. Ce Sekkin est vraisemblablement le même dont Abou'lféda raconte les intrigues et la mort sous l'an 434, en ces termes:

«En cette même année, au mois de redjeb, se souleva à Misr un homme appelé *Sekkin,* qui ressembloit à Hakem. Il prétendit être Haken; il fut suivi d'une troupe de gens qui comptoient sur le retour de Hakem. Ces gens marchèrent donc vers le palais, dans le moment où le khalife étoit seul et retiré dans ses appartemens, en criant: *Voici Hakem.* Ceux qui gardoient la porte en ce moment furent d'abord saisis d'effroi; mais ensuite, soupçonnant quelque erreur, ils arrêtèrent Sekkin, et il fut mis en croix avec ses partisans.»

Au reste, je ne donne ceci que comme une conjecture, à laquelle on pourroit même opposer que *Sekkin,* comme nom propre d'homme, n'a pas ordinairement d'article. Il est bon cependant d'observer que, dans un des écrits dirigés contre Sekkin, il est dit qu'*il met sa confiance dans les montagnes où il fait sa résidence*; ce qui fortifie beaucoup ma conjecture.

Passons à une autre étymologie, ou plutôt à deux étymologies différentes, proposées par un savant dont l'autorité est d'un grand poids quand il s'agit de littérature Arabe. C'est de Reiske que je veux parler. Cet habile orientaliste suppose que le mot *assassins* n'est qu'une corruption, et que les Ismaéliens ou Baténiens étoient nommés حسانيين *Hassanini* ou *Hassanici,* du chef de leur secte, Hasan ben-Sabbah. «Peut-être aussi, dit-il, comme ce nom est souvent écrit *chassassin,* ce que les Allemands rendent par *schassasin*, leur nom étoit-il en arabe *djassas* جساس: ce mot se prononce à-peu-près en arabe, comme en françois, *chassas,* ou en allemand, *schassas*, et veut dire *espion*.» Je n'ai pas besoin de m'arrêter à discuter ces deux étymologies, dont la première est fondée sur une supposition très-hardie, la seconde est dépourvue de toute vraisemblance. Il suffit de dire que si Reiske eût, comme moi, rencontré le nom des *Assassins* écrit en lettres Arabes, il n'auroit hasardé ni l'une ni l'autre de ces conjectures.

Une étymologie bien différente et beaucoup mieux fondée en apparence, est celle que M. l'abbé Simon Assemani, professeur de langues Orientales au séminaire de Padoue, a proposée nouvellement dans la dissertation dont j'ai déjà parlé, et qui se trouve insérée dans le numero de juin 1808 du Journal littéraire de Padoue. Elle a pour titre *Ragguaglio storico-critico sopra la setta Assissana, detta volgarmente degli Assassini*.

«Pendant, dit M. Simon Assemani, que je me trouvois à Tripoli de Syrie, ville voisine de certaines montagnes qui renferment un reste de cette secte, j'ai souvent entendu lâcher ce brocard rimé contre ceux qui venoient à la ville pour leurs affaires, *Assissani la moslem we la nasrani*, الصيصاني لا مسلم ولا نصراني, *l'Assissani n'est ni Musulman, ni Chrétien;* ce qui veut dire que ces gens n'ont aucune religion, précisément parce que, suivant la doctrine de Hasan, ils n'ont aucun culte extérieur. Observons que les historiens des croisades ont transposé ici les deux voyelles *i* et *a*, et qu'au lieu d'*Assissani* ils ont dit *Assassini;* et c'est ainsi que ce nom a passé dans notre langage, pour désigner les scélérats qui commettent un homicide de guet-apens. C'étoit par-là, en effet, que se distinguoient les souverains de cette secte, qui enjoyoient par-tout leurs sicaires pour massacrer quiconque leur déplaisoit.

«*Assissani*, ajoute le même écrivain, vient d'*assissa* الصيصة, *roche, forteresse, lieu fort et qui offre une retraite sûre;* et de là *Assissani* الصيصاني, en arabe, signifie un homme qui habite des rochers et des lieux forts, comme nous dirions *un montagnard, un habitant des montagnes*.»

Quelque estime que j'aie pour les talens de M. L'abbé Assemani, je ne puis point admettre son opinion sur l'origine due nom des *Assassins*. Voici mes raisons: (1) *sisa* صيصة, ou plutôt *sisiya* صيصية, ne signifie pas proprement un *rocher*, mais, en général, tout ce qui sert à la défense, *la corne d'un bœuf, l'ergot d'un coq, le bois d'un antilope,* et par la même raison une *citadelle*, une *place forte*. (2) صيصاني ne seroit point formé régulièrement de صيصية, ce devroit être صيصى; au contraire, صيصاني est formé régulièrement de صيصان, pluriel de صوص, *poulet,* d'où se forme aussi le verbe صوّص, *piauler comme un petit poulet;*

du pluriel صيصان doit se former صيصانى, *marchand de petits poulets,* comme de دجاجات, pluriel de دجاجة, *poule,* se forme دجاجاتى, *marchand de volailles;* de كتب, pluriel de كتاب, *livre,* كتبى, *libraire;* de لبود, pluriel de لبد, *feutre,* لبودى, *marchand de feutres;* de صناديق, pluriel de صناديق, *coffre,* صندوق, *marchand de coffres;* de حوايص, pluriel de حياصة, *ceinturon,* حوايصى, *marchand de ceinturons.* Le proverbe rapporté par M. Assemani peut donc s'appliquer aux montagnards ou aux villageois qui viennent vendre des volailles dans les villes, et il voudra dire que ces gens-là sont des hommes sans bonne foi et grossiers, n'appartenant, à cause de leur profonde ignorance, à aucune religion.

Je dois observer d'ailleurs que ce proverbe a cours aussi d'une autre manière, qui pourroit bien être plus conforme à son origine. Au lieu de الصيصانى, on dit souvent الساسانى, comme je le tiens de M. Michel Sabbagh d'Acca; ce qui signifie *de la famille de Sasan.* Or ce dernier terme est employé par les Arabes pour désigner un *vagabond,* un *aventurier,* un ***homme qui court le monde afin de gagner de l'argent sans rien faire.*** C'est en ce sens que Hariri fait dire, dans sa quarante-neuvième séance, à Abou-Zeïd Saroudji, personnage de ce genre:

ولم ار ما هو بارد المغنم لذيذ المطعم وافى المكسب صافى المشرب
الا الحرفة التى وضع ساسان اساسها ونوّع اجناسها.........اذ
كانت المتجر الذى لا يبور والمنهل الذى لا يغور والمصباح
الذى يعشو اليه الجمهور ويستصبح به العُمى والعُور وكان اهلها
اعزّ قبيل واسعد جيل............لا يتخذون اوطانًا ولا يتّقون
سلطانًا ولا يمتازون عمّا تغدوا خماصًا وتروح بطانًا.....................
إنّ الارتكاض بابها والنشاط جلبابها والفطنة مصباحها
والقِحة سلاحها..........ولا تسئم الطلب ولا تملّ الدأب فقد كان
مكتوبًا على عصا شيخنا ساسان من طلب جلب ومن جال نال

Je n'ai pas trouvé de gain plus facile, de subsistance plus agréable, de profession plus lucrative, de ruisseau dont l'eau soit plus pure, que le métier institué par Sasan, et dont il a imaginé diverses modifications. ... C'est un commerce qui ne languit jamais, un réservoir dont l'eau ne s'épuise point, un flambeau à la lueur duquel se rassemblent un grand nombre d'hommes, et qui éclaire les aveugles et les borgnes. Ceux qui exercent cette profession, sont le peuple le plus heureux, la race la plus fortunée. . . . Ils n'ont point de demeure fixe, ils ne cragnent aucune autorité: il n'ya nulle différence entre eux et les oiseaux qui se lèvent le ventre creux et se trouvent au soir la panse pleine. . . . Mais la première condition pour exercer cette profession, c'est de se donner beaucoup de mouvement; la première qualité requise, c'est une grande activité. Un esprit fécond en ressources doit être le flambeau de celui qui l'embrasse; l'impudence, l'armure dont il faut qu'il soit muni. . . . Ne vous lassez donc point de chercher, ne vous rebutez pas de faire toute sorte de diligence; car il étoit écrit sur le bâton de notre chef *Sasan:* Quiconque cherchera, trouvera; quiconque ira et viendra, obtiendra.

C'est aussi dans le même sens que, dans la seconde séance, Hariri dit, en parlant du méme Abou-Zeïd:

فيدّعى تارة انه من آل ساسان ويعتزى مرّة الى اقيال غسان

Il forgeoit toute sorte de généalogies pour se faire valoir, et il n'y avoit aucun moyen de tirer de l'argent qu'il ne mît en pratique: tantôt il disoit être de la famille de *Sasan,* et tantôt il se donnoit pour un descendant des rois de Gassan.

Motarrézi, commentateur de Hariri, explique ainsi le mot *Sasan:*

راس الشحّاذين وكبيرهم وهو ساسان الاكبر ابن بهمن بن
اسفنديار بن كشتاسف الملك وكان من حديثه على ما ذكر ابن
المقفّع انه لما حضر بهمن الموت دعا بابنته هماى وهى حامل
وكانت من اكمل الناس جمالا واعقل اهل ذلك العصر من
العجم فامر بالتاج فوضع على راسها وملّكها من بعده وامرها ان
ولدت غلاما ان يقوم بامر الملك فحين ادرك ابنها وبلغ ثلثين

سنة سلّمت اليه الملك فكان ابنه ساسان بن بهمن
حينيذ رجلا ذا رواء وادب وعقل وكمال فلم يشكّ الناس ان
الملك يفضى اليه فلما فوّض ابوه الملك الى اخته هماى انف
ساسان من ذلك انفا شديدا فانطلق فاشترى غنما وساقها الى
الجبل بنفسه فجعل يرعاها مع الاكراد غيظا مما صنع به ابوه
فى تقصيره به وصرفه الملك الى اخته فمن ثم يعتبر ساسان الى
اليوم براعى الغنم فيقال ساسان الكردى وساسان الراعى ثم نسب
اليه كل من يكدى او يباشر امرا حقيرا من الغُى والغُور
والمشعوذين والكلّابين والقرّادين وامثالهم وان لم يكونوا من
اولاده وهم جمع كثير وجمّ غفير واجناس لا موتلفة وانواع مختلفة
ذكرهم ابو دلف الخزرجى فى قصيدته التى قالها على لسانهم
وبيّن فيها حِرَفهم العجيبة وصنائعهم الغريبة وما لهم من نوادر
الخرافات وفنون الاصطلاحات وهى تعرف بالساسانية وقد
شرحها الصاحب بن عبّاد فمن طالعها وجد مجمل ما ذكرت
مفصّلا فيها

Sasan, dit-il, est le chef des mendiants et leur patron. Le Sasan dont il s'agit est Sasan l'ancien, fils de Bahman, fils d'Estendiar, fils du roi Ghischtasf. Voici comment son histoire est racontée par Ebn-Almokanna. Quand Bahman fut près de mourir, il fit venir sa fille Homaï, qui étoit enceinte. Elle surpassoit tous les mortels en beauté, et personne, parmi les Perses de ce temps-là, ne l'égaloit en sagesse. Ensuite le roi se fit apporter la couronne, la mit sur la tête de sa fille, et la déclara reine après lui, ordonnant que, si elle mettoit au monde un enfant mâle, elle conserveroit l'administration du royaume, jusqu'a ce que son fils eût atteint l'âge de trente ans, époque à laquelle elle lui remettroit le gouvernement. Sasan, fils de Bahman, étoit un homme d'une belle figure, bien élevé, et plein de sagesse et de toute sorte de perfections; personne ne doutoit qu'il ne dût hériter du trône. Bahman

> ayant donc disposé de son royaume en faveur de Homaï, sœur de Sasan, celui-ci en ressentit un dépit violent, s'en alla, acheta des brebis, les conduisit lui-même vers les montagnes, et s'occupa à les faire paître, habitant au milieu des Curdes, le tout par un effet de la collère qu'il avoit conçue, à cause du mépris que son père avoit témoigné pour lui en lui ôtant la couronne pour la donner à sa sœur. Depuis ce temps jusqu'à ce jour, le nom de *Sasan* a été pris métaphoriquement pour indiquer un homme qui conduit un troupeau de brebis, et l'on dit *Sasan le Curde*, ou *Sasan le berger*. On dénomme de là *Sasani* tout homme qui mendie, ou qui fait un métier vil, comme les aveugles, les borgnes, les joueurs de gobelets, ceux qui dressent et montrent des chiens ou des singes, et les autres gens de cette espèce, quoiqu'ils ne descendent pas de ce Sasan. Le nombre de ces hommes est très-grand, et il y en a beaucoup de classes et d'espèces différentes. Abou-Dolaf Khazradji en parle dans le poème où il décrit, en les faisant parler eux-mêmes, tous leurs métiers, leurs jongleries, leurs contes, et l'argot dont ils se servent entre eux. Ce poème, connu sous le nom de *Sasaniyyèh,* a été commenté par Saheb ben-Abbad; en le lisant, on y trouvera dans le plus grand détail ce que j'ai dit en raccourci.

On conçoit, par ce qu'on vient de lire, combien le proverbe, *c'est un Sasani, il n'est ni Musulman ni Chrétien,* présente un sens convenable, mais qui n'offre aucun rapport avec les *Assassins.*

Depuis M. Asseimani, un autre orientaliste, dans le premier numéro du journal intitulé *les Mines de l'Orient,* en rejetant l'étymologie de Hyde, qu'il attribue à M. De Volney, a proposé de dériver le mot *Assassins* de عَسَس, *guet nocturne.*

J'apprends aussi de M. Dominique Sestini, qu'un savant Arménien, consulté sur l'étymologie de ce même mot, le dérivoit de حبس حبس, *ramassis de gens de toute espèce.*

La première de ces deux étymologies auroit pu être admise, si l'on en étoit réduit, à cet égard, à des conjectures; la seconde n'est pas même proposable.

Puisque j'ai fait mention plus haut des Mémoires historiques sur les Assassins et le Vieux de la montagne par Mariti, je dois dire ici que cet écrivain se déclare pour l'une des étymologies les moins vraisemblables qui avoient été proposées du nom des

Assassins. Il croit que leur véritable nom étoit *Arsasides* ou *Arsacides*, et qu'ils étoient ainsi appelés parce que les premiers fondateurs de cette peuplade, qui, transportée en Syrie, y fut connue sous le nom d'*Assassins*, étoient des Curdes qui habitoient originairement dans les environs et sous la juridiction de la ville d'*Arsacia.* Ce seroit perdre le temps que de s'arrêter à réfuter un tel système.

On sera peut-être surpris que je n'aie pas parlé jusqu'ici d'une autre étymologie rapportée par Ménage, et dont l'auteur est M. Étienne Lemoine, ministre de la religion réformée, à Rouen. Elle se trouve dans une lettre de Lemoine à Ménage, que celui-ci a publiée dans son *Dictionaire étymologique de la langue Française*, au mot *Assassins.* Je n'en rapporterai que ce qui a trait à mon sujet.

«Le mot *Assassin*, dit M. Lemoine, a été dit du Vieux de la montagne, roi des *Assassin*, qui est ainsi nommé, comme qui diroit *roi des herbages*, *des prés*, *des jardins.* En effet, ce roi occupoit, au pied du Liban, une terre fort bonne, et qui pourroit bien tirer son nom de sa fertilité. *Assessa,* ou *Assissa*, signifie des herbes, des pâturages, des jardins, toutes choses qui se trouvent en abondance dans le pays de la domination de ce prince. Vous savez comme, à la faveur de ses jardins délicieux, il trompoit plusieurs de ses sujets, et comme il les engageoit à tout entreprendre, dans l'espérance qu'il leur donnoit qu'ils jouiroient après leur mort de tous ces lieux agréables. . . . Benjamin le nomme *scheïk el-chasisin*, et c'est aussi de la sorte qu'on le nomme dans tout l'Orient. De là vient que nous l'avons appelé *le roi des Assassins.* Mais ces paroles, comme je l'ai déjà dit, signifient le roi des prairies, des terres cultivées, des jardins où l'art et la nature fournissent à l'envi une infinité de choses délicieuses.»

Cette étymologie a été désapprouvée, au rapport de Ménage, par M. Ferrari, savant professeur de Padoue, qui aimoit mieux dériver le mot *assassin, ab assidendo;* et Ménage lui-même n'hésite pas à se ranger de l'opinion de M. De Caseneuve, qui tire ce mot du vieux teuton *sahs,* couteau. M. Falconet dit aussi sans aucun ménagement, que l'étymologie est aussi fausse que les conséquences qu'en tire M. Lemoine. Cependant c'est cette étymologie qui est la seule véritable, comme j'espère le démontrer; mais M. Lemoine a ignoré pourquoi les Ismaéliens portoient le nom de *Haschischin*, et il en a donné une très-mauvaise raison qui a fait rejeter son étymologie. J'espère offrir une autre raison beaucoup plus satisfaisante de cette dénomination. J'ai donc deux choses à faire voir ici: (1) que les Ismaéliens ou Baténiens portoient aussi le nom de *Haschischin*. (2) quel étoit le motif de cette dénomination.

La première proposition sera facile à établir. Observons seulement que dans le mot *Haschischin*, la terminaison *in* est le signe du pluriel. Dans l'arabe littéral, la terminaison du pluriel masculin est pour le nominatif *ouna* ونَ, et pour les deux autres cas, *ina* ينَ; dans le langage usuel, on supprime la voyelle finale *a*, et l'on dit, sans distinction de cas, *in*. Exemple: *Moslimin* مسلمين, les Musulmans; *Mouminin* مومنين, les croyants; *Kafirin* كافرين, les infidèles. *Haschischin*, ou plus grammaticalement *Haschischiyyin* حشيشيين, est donc le puriel de *Haschischi* حشيشى : ce même mot peut aussi faire au pluriel *Haschischiyyèh* حشيشية, ce qui est même plus élégant. Il ne faut pas perdre de vue cette observation triviale, mais que j'ai dû faire pour les personnes qui n'ont aucune notion de la langue Arabe.

Abou'lféda, dans ses *Annales*, et Boha-eddin, dans la *Vie de Saladin*, racontent qu'en l'année 571, tandis que ce prince faisoit le siége de la citadelle d'Ezaz, des Ismaéliens tentèrent de l'assassiner: c'étoit la seconde fois que sa vie étoit menacée par des gens de cette secte; il avoit déjà été attaqué en vain en 570. Le récit d'Abou'lféda étant plus détaillé, c'est à ce récit que je m'arrête.

«En l'année 570, Saad-eddin Camouschtékin enoya une grande somme d'argent à Sinan, chef des Ismaéliens, pour que ces gens-là tuassent Saladin. Sinan envoya donc plusieurs gens qui attaquèrent subitement Saladin; mais ils furent tués sans pouvoir lui ôter la vie.

«En l'année 571 . . . le sultan Saladin s'avança vers Ézaz; il mit le siége devant la place, le 3 de dhou'lkadèh, et la prit le 11 de dhou'lhiddjèh. Tandis qu'il assiégeoit cette place, un Ismaélien fondit sur lui, lui porta un coup de poignard à la tête, et le blessa. Saladin arrêta l'Ismaélien, qui continua à frapper, mais sans qu'aucun coup portât: il fut tué dans cette situation. Un second attaqua le sultan, et fut tué de même; puis un troisième eut le même sort. Le sultan, effrayé, rentra dans sa tente, fit faire la revue de ses troupes, et renvoya les gens qu'il ne connoissoit pas.»

Voyons maintenant en quels termes ces deux faits sont racontés par Abou'lschama, auteur du *Kitab alraudhataïn* كتاب الروضتين, histoire très-détaillée de Nour-eddin et de Saladin:

ورحل الى حماة فاخذها مستهلّ جمادى الاخرة ثم مضى ونزل
على حلب فحصرها ثالث الشهر فلما اشتدّ على الحلبيين الحصار
واعوزهم الانتصار استغاثوا بالاسماعيلية وعيّنوا لهم ضياعا
وبذلوا لهم من البذول انواعا فجاء منهم فى يوم بارد شاتٍ من
فتّاكهم كل عاتٍ فعرفهم الامير ناصح الدين خمارتكين صاحب
بوقتيش وكان مثاغر الاسماعيلية فقال لهم لاى شىء جئتم وكيف
تجاسرتم على الوصول وما خشيتم فقتلوه فجاء من يدفع عنه
واثخنوه وعدا احدهم ليهجم على السلطان فى مقامه وقد شهر
سكين انتقامه وطغريل امير خازندار واقف ثابت مساكن
ساكت حتّى وصل اليه فشمل بالسيف راسه وما قتل
الباقون حتى قتلوا عدّة ولاقى من لاقاهم شدّة وعصم الله
حشاشته فى تلك النوبة من سكاكين الحشيشيّة فاقام الى
مستهلّ رجب

En l'an 570, Saladin s'avança vers Hamat, et la prit le premier jour de djoumada second. De là il marcha vers Alep, et mit le siége devant cette ville, le 3 du même mois. Comme les habitans se voyoient serrés de très-près, et qu'ils avoient grand besoin de secours, ils s'adressèrent aux Ismaéliens, leur promirent certaines terres et leur firent différentes sortes de largesses. Un jour donc que le temps étoit très-froid, et que l'hiver se faisoit rudement sentir, il vint quelques-uns des plus déterminés de leurs scélérats. Ils furent reconnus par l'emir Nasih-eddin Khomartékin, maître de Boktisch, et dont les possessions étoient limitrophes de celles des Ismaéliens. Que voulez-vous faire, leur dit l'émir, et comment avez-vous eu l'audace de venir ici sans que la crainte vous ait retenus? Alors ils le tuèrent; un homme étant accouru pour le défendre, ils le blessèrent aussi. L'un d'eux s'avança soudain pour se précipiter sur le sultan: mais l'émir Togril Khazendar l'attendit de pied ferme, sans faire aucun mouvement et sans dire aucune parole; et au moment où il arrivoit, il lui abattit la tête avec son sabre. Les autres ne furent tués qu'après avoir tué eux-mêmes beaucoup de monde, et ceux qui se trouvèrent à leur rencontre coururent de grands dangers. Ainsi, pour cette fois, Dieu sauva la vie (à la lettre, *le dernier soupir*) du sultan, des poignards des *Haschischis*.

L'auteur fait ici un jeu de mots entre حشاشة *hoschaschèh*, le dernier soupir, et حشيشيّة *haschischiyyèh*, pluriel de *haschischi*; et c'est peut-être ce jeu de mots qui est cause que nous trouvons ici cette dénomination, au lieu de celle d'*Ismaéliens*.

Passons au second fait. Voici comment il est raconté:

فصل فى وثوب الحشيشيّة على السلطان مرّة ثانية على عزاز
وكان الاولى على حلب فـال العماد وفى حادى عشـر ذى القعـدة
قفز الحشيشيّة على السلطان ليـلة الواحد وهو نازل على عـزاز
وكان للامير جاولى الاسدى خيمة قـريبة من المنجنيقات وكـان
السلطان يحضر فيها كل يـوم لمشاهدة الالات وترتيب المقاتلات
وحضّ الرجال والحثّ على القـتال وهـو بارّ ببثّ اياديـه قارّ على
الدهر بكف عواديه والحشيشيّة فى زى الاجناد وقوف والرجال
عنده صفوف اذ قفز واحد منهم فضرب راسه بسكينه فعاقته
صفائح الحديد المدفونة فى كمّته عن تمكينه ولفحت المدية خده
فخدشته فقوّى السلطان قلبه وحاش راس الحشيشى اليـه
وجذبه ووقع عليـه وركبه وادركـه سيف الدين يازكـوج فاخذ
حشاشة الحشيشى وبضّعه وقطعه وجاء اخـر فاعترضه الامـير
داود بن منكـلان فمنعه وجـرحه الحشيشى فى جنبه فمات
بعد ايام وجاء اخر فعانقه الامير على بن ابى الفوارس وضمه من
تحت ابطيـه وبقـيت يد الحشيشى من ورائـه لا يتمكن من
الضرب ولا يتاتى له كشف ما عراه من الكرب فنادى اقتلونى
معه فقد قتلنى واذهب قوّتى واذهلنى فطعنـه ناصر الدين بن

شيركوه بسيفه وخرج اخر من الخيمة منهزما وعلى الفتك بمن
يعارضه مقدما فثار عليه اهل السوق فقطعوه

Chapitre contenant le récit de la seconde enterprise des *Haschischis* contre la vie du sultan: celle-ci eut lieu pendant qu'il assiégeoit Ézaz; la première s'étoit passée devant Alep.

Le 11 de dhou'lkadèh, dit Omad-eddin, dans la nuit du premier jour de la semaine, les *Haschischis* assaillirent le sultan, tandis qu'il étoit campé devant Ézaz. L'émir Djavali Asadi avoit sa tente auprès des machines, et le sultan se rendoit dans cette tente pour inspecter les machines, donner ordre aux affaires les plus importantes, et exciter l'ardeur des combattants. Tandis qu'il étoit occupé à distribuer des largesses, et à remédier aux maux que cause la malice de la fortune, des *Haschischis* se tenoient là déguisés sous le'extérieur de soldats, et les troupes rangées sur diverses lignes étoient près du sultan. Subitement l'un de ces Haschischis sauta sur le sultan et lui porta un coup de son poignard à la tête. Les plaques de fer dont son bonnet étoit garni intérieurement, empêchèrent le poignard de l'atteindre, et l'arme ne fit que le blesser légèrement à la joue. Le sultan, sans perdre courage, saisit la tête du *Haschischi* et la tira à lui, puis se jeta sur cet homme et se mit à cheval sur lui; alors Séif-eddin Yazkoudj survint, ôta la vie au *Haschischi*, et le tailla en pièces. Un autre s'avança; mais l'émir Daoud, fils de Menkélan, se jeta au-devant de lui et l'arrêta. Le *Haschischi* lui fit au flanc une blessure dont il mourut au bout de quelques jours. Un troisième survint: l'émir Ali, fils d'Abou'lféwaris, le saisit entre ses bras, et le tint fortement embrassé par-dessous les aisselles. La main du *Haschischi* resta derrière son dos, en sorte qu'il ne pouvoit ni frapper ni se débarrasser de la gêne où il se trouvoit. L'émir se mit donc à crier: «Tuez-moi avec lui; car il m'a porté un coup mortel, il m'a ôté mes forces, et m'a mis hors de combat.» Alors Nasir-eddin, fils de Schirkouh, perça cet homme de son épée. Un autre sortit de la tente et s'enfuit, prêt à frapper quiconque voudroit lui couper le chemin; cependant les valets de l'armée tombèrent sur lui et le tuèrent.

Je supprime le reste de ce récit.

L'auteur ajoute ensuite l'extrait d'une lettre du kadhi Fadhil, qui contient la relation du même événement, et où on lit que le *Haschischi* n'avoit fait au sultan qu'un égratignure, d'où il n'étoit coulé que quelques gouttes de sang.

Enfin, suivant l'usage des Orientaux, l'auteur rapporte encore une autre relation du même fait, tirée d'un écrivain nommé *Ebu-Abi'ltaï.* Je la traduirai aussi, malgré les répétitions que cela nécessite, parce que les expressions de ce récit méritent d'être pesées.

وقال ابن ابي الطي لما فتح السلطان حصن بزاغا ومنبج ايقن من
بحلب بخروج ما في ايديهم من المعاقل والقلاع فعادوا الى عادتهم
في نصب الحبائل للسلطان فكاتبوا سنانا صاحب الحشيشة
مرة ثانية ورغبوه بالاموال والمواعيد وحملوه على انفاذ من يفتك
بالسلطان فارسل لعنه الله جماعة من اصحابه فجاؤا بزيّ الاجناد
ودخلوا بين المقاتلة وباشروا بالحرب وابلوا فيها احسن البلاء
وامتزجوا باصحاب السلطان لعلّهم يجدون فرصة ينتهزونها
فبينما السلطان يوما جالس في خيمة جاولي والحرب قائمة
والسلطان مشغول بالنظر الى القتال اذ وثب عليه احد الحشيشيّة
وضربه بسكينه على راسه وكان رحمه الله محترزا خائفا من
الحشيشيّة لا ينزع الزردنة عن بدنه ولا صفائح الحديد عن راسه
فلم يصنع ضربة الحشيشي لمكان صفائح الحديد واحسّ
الحشيشي بصفائح الحديد على راس السلطان فسبح يده بالسكينة
الى خدّ السلطان فجرحه وجرى الدم على وجهه فتتعتع
السلطان لذلك ولما راى الحشيشي ذلك هجم على السلطان
وجذب راسه حتى وضعه على الارض وركبه لينحره وكان من
حول السلطان قد ادركتهم دهشة اخذت بعقولهم وحضر في
ذلك الوقت سيف الدين يازكوج وقيل انه كان حاضرا
فاخترط سيفه وضرب الحشيشي فقتله وجاء اخر من الحشيشيّة

ايضا يقصد السلطان فاعترضه الامير منكلان الكردى وضربه
بالسيف وسبق الحشيشى الى منكلان فجرحه فى جبهته
وقتله منكلان ومات منكلان من ضربة الحشيشى بعد ايام وجاء
اخر من الباطنيّة فحصل فى سهم الامير على بن ابى الفوارس
فهجم على الباطنى ودخل الباطنى فيه ليضربه فاخذه على تحت
ابطه وبقيت يد الباطنى من ورائه لا يتمكن من ضربه فصاح
على اقتلوه واقتلونى معه فجاء ناصر الدين محمد بن شيركوه
فطعن بطن الباطنى بسيفه وما زال يخضخضه فيه حتى سقط
ميّتا ونجا ابن ابى الفوارس وخرج اخر من الحشيشيّة منهزما
فلقيه الامير شهاب الدين محمود خال السلطان فتنكب
الباطنى عن طريق شهاب الدين فقصدوه اصحابه وقطعوه
بالسيوف واما السلطان فانه ركب من وقته الى سرادقه ودمه
على خده سائل

Voici, dit toujours l'auteur du *Raudhataïn,* de quelle manière s'exprime Ebn-Abi'ltaï: Quand le sultan se fut emparé de Bazaga et de Manbedj, ceux qui étoient maîtres d'Alep reconnurent bien qu'ils ne pouvoient manquer de se voir enlever successivement les places fortes et les citadelles qu'il possédoient. Ils revinrent donc à leurs menées accoutumées, et recommencèrent à tendre des piéges au sultan. Ils écrivirent en conséquence une seconde fois à Sinan, *maître du haschischa* (j'expliquerai plus loin cette expression), le gagnèrent à force d'argent, et le déterminèrent à envoyer des gens pour tuer le sultan. Sinan (que Dieu le maudisse!) envoya effectivement quelques-uns de ses gens, qui se rendirent à l'armée de Saladin, déguisés sous le costume de soldats. Ils se mêlèrent aux combattants, prirent part aux opérations militaires, et s'en acquittèrent avec beaucoup de bravoure. Ils eurent soin de se mêler aux gens du sultan, dans l'espérance de trouver une occasion d'exécuter leur projet et de la saisir. Un jour donc que le sultan étoit assis dans la tente de l'émir Djawali, pendant qu'on se battoit, et que le sultan considéroit le combat, un des *Haschischis* fondit sur lui, et lui porta sur la tête un coup de son poignard. Comme le sultan appréhendoit toujours quelque surprise de la part des *Haschischis*, il ne quittoit jamais sa cuirasse, et avoit toujours la tête garnie de plaques de fer: le coup porté par le *Haschischi* ne put pas entamer les plaques de fer qui couvroient la tête du sultan; et le *Haschischi,* ayant senti ces plaques de fer, laissa glisser sa main avec le poignard vers la joue du sultan, et lui fit une blessure dont le sang coula sur son visage. Cela fit chanceler le sultan: le *Haschischi* saisit cet instant, sauta sur le sultan, tira sa tête à lui, en sorte qu'il l'entraîna jusqu'à erre; et se mettant à cheval sur lui, il cherchoit à l'égorger. Ceux qui entouroient le sultan étoient dans un état de stupeur qui sembloit leur ôter la raison. En ce moment survint Séif-eddin Yazcoudj: d'autres disent qu'il étoit présent dès auparavant; il tira son sabre, en frappa le *Haschischi* et le tua. Un autre des *Haschischis* accourut pour se jeter sur le sultan; mais l'émir Menkélan le Curde lui barra le chemin, et lui porta un coup de son épée: le *Haschischi* cependant prévint Menkélan, et le blessa au front. Menkélan le tua; mais il mourut lui-même, quelques jours après, du coup que lui avoit donné le *Haschischi.* Un autre des Baténiens survint encore, et se trouva près de l'émir Ali fils d'Abou'lféwaris. L'émir fondit sur le Baténien; mais le Baténien s'avança sous le coup pour le frapper. Ali le saisit sous les aisselles; et la main du Baténien resta derrière lui, sans qu'il pût le frapper. L'émir Ali cria alors, *Tuez-le et moi avec lui;* et Nasir-eddin, fils de Schirkouh, s'avançant, enfonça son épée dans le ventre du Baténien, et ne cessa de l'y remuer en tout sens jusqu'à ce que cet homme tombât mort: ainsi échappa Ali fils d'Abou'lféwaris. Alors un autre des *Haschischis* sortit en fuyant; il fut rencontré par l'émir Schéhab-eddin Mahmoud, oncle maternel du sultan: le Baténien se détourna pour éviter l'émir; mais les gens de l'émir coururent à sa rencontre, et le taillèrent en pièces avec leurs sabres. Pour le sultan, il monta sur-le-champ à cheval, et retourna à sa tente: le sang couloit sur sa joue.

Un peu plus loin l'auteur du *Raudhataïn* ajoute:

«En l'année 572, la paix étant faite, le sultan se souvint de la vengeance qu'il avoit à prendre des Ismaéliens, et de la manière dont ils étoient venus l'attaquer pendant cette guerre. Il partit donc le vendredi 19 de ramadhan, vint assiéger leur place forte de Mesyat, et dressa contre elle de grandes machines de guerre. Il leur tua beaucoup de monde, fit un grand nombre de prisonniers, emmena les hommes, ravagea les habitations, détruisit les édifices, mit leurs maisons au pillage, jusqu'à ce que son oncle maternel Schéhab-eddin Mahmoud ben-Tacasch, prince de Hamat, intercéda en leur faveur, car ils avoient envoyé vers lui pour le prier de le faire, attendu qu'ils étoient ses voisins. Le sultan se retira donc de leur pays, ayant tiré vengeance d'eux.»

Après ce qu'on vient de lire, ce seroit perdre le temps que de s'arrêter à prouver que les *Haschischis*, les *Bateniens* et les *Ismaéliens* sont le même peuple, ou, si l'on veut, la même secte. On a vu qu'Ebn-Abi'ltaï emploie indifféremment les deux premiers noms, et que l'auteur du *Raudhataïn* nomme *Ismaéliens* ceux qu'il avoit appelés précédemment *Haschischis*.

Il seroit inutile de rechercher d'autres autorités pour prouver cette identité. Je remarquerai seulement qu'Ebn-alkhatib, historien Araba d'Espagne, en racontant la mort violente du khalife Amer-biahcam-allah, dit qu'il fut tué par des *Haschischis*, tandis que d'autres historiens, Abou'lféda, Mirkhond, Makrizi, disent que ce prince fut assassiné par des *Ismaéliens,* des *Bateniens,* ou des *Nazaris*. J'expliquerai ce dernier mot plus loin.

On ne doutera pas non plus, je crois, que le mot *haschischi,* au pluriel *haschischin,* ne soit l'origine des mots corrompus *heissessini, assassini, assissini.* On ne doit pas s'étonner que le *schin* Arabe ait été rendu dans tous nos écrivains qui se servoient de la langue Latine, par une *s*, et dans les historiens Grecs par un *σ*: ils ne pouvoient faire autrement. Il faut d'ailleurs observer que le *schin* se prononce moins fortement que le *ch* en françois. Ce que l'on demandera, et avec raison, c'est le motif qui avoit fait donner aux Ismaéliens ou Bateniens le nom de *Haschischis*. C'est la second chose que j'ai à examiner, et à laquelle je ne répondrai que par une conjecture, mais conjecture qui me paroît porter un grand caractère de vraisemblance.

M. Lemoine avoit peut-être connoissance de quelques passages d'auteurs Arabes où les Ismaéliens étoient désignés sous le nom de *Haschischis,* et il avoit vu que ce mot dérivoit nécessairement de *haschisch. Haschisch* حشيش signifie de l'*herbe,* du *fourrage:* mais cette signification ne présentant aucun rapport avec ce que l'histoire nous apprend des Assassins, il supposa que *haschisch,* qui signifie *herbe, fourrage,* pouvoit aussi se prendre pour des *prés*, des *prairies,* des *jardins délicieux.* Cette fausse conséquence a pu contribuer à discréditer dans l'esprit des savants l'étymologie qu'il proposoit, d'autant plus qu'il ne cite aucune autorité d'écrivain Arabe pour prouver que les Ismaéliens portoient effectivement en arabe le nom de *Haschischis*. Peut-être aussi n'en avoit-il point réellement d'autre que le passage de Benjamin de Tudèle, quoiqu'après avoir invoqué le témoignage de ce rabbin qui nomme le Vieux de la montagne *Scheikh alchassisin,* il ajoute que c'est ainsi qu'on le nomme dans tout l'Orient.

M. Lemoine ignoroit que parmi les substances simples ou composées dont les Orientaux se servent pour se procurer une ivresse plus ou moins violente, il en est une que l'on connoît sous le nom de *haschisch* et *haschischa*. J'ai publié, dans ma *Chrestomathie Arabe,* un chapitre fort curieux de la *Description historique de l'Égypte et du Caire*, de Makrizi; chapitre qui a pour objet cette espèce d'électuaire nommé communément *haschischia* حشيشة, *herbe,* mais dont le nom entier est *haschischat alfokara* حشيشة الفقراء, *l'herbe des fakirs*. Suivant Makrizi, c'est la feuille du chanvre qui porte ce nom; et c'est effectivement ce que dit aussi Prosper Alpin, dont je crois devoir citer ici les propres paroles:

«Je n'ignore pas que les Égyptiens usent, pour se procurer ces sortes de visions, de plusieurs médicaments composés, tels que l'électuaire nommé *bernavi,* que l'on apporte des contrées de l'Inde les plus voisines, le *bers* et le *bosa;* mais celui dont l'usage est le plus commun parmi eux, c'est tout simplement la plante du chanvre, qu'ils appellent *assis*. Ce mot ne signifie autre chose que *l'herbe,* en sorte qu'il semble qu'ils appellent le chanvre *herbe par excellence*. Cette manière proverbiale de s'exprimer, *prendre de l'herbe,* pour dire *prendre une drogue envirante,* vient de ce que le chanvre est, comme je l'ai ouï dire, la première substance dans laquelle on a reconnu la propriété d'exciter ces visions fantastiques, ou parce qu'elle possède cette vertu dans un degré supérieur à toutes les autres drogues.

«L'*assis* n'est autre chose qu'une poudre préparée avec les feuilles du chanvre, que l'on mêle avec de l'eau tiède, et dont on forme une pâte. On en avale cinq bols ou même plus, de la grosseur d'une châtaigne. Au bout d'une heure, ils font leur effet; et ceux qui les ont pris, tombant dans une sorte d'ivresse, font toute sorte de folies: ils restent long- temps dans un état d'extase, et jouissent de ces visions qu'ils recherchent tant. Le peuple surtout fait plus volontiers usage de cette drogue, parce qu'elle coûte moins que les autres. Vous ne servez point surpris que le chanvre produise cet effet; car Galien, comme vous le savez, dans son I.er livre *de alim. facult.* dit qu'il fait monter des vapeurs au cerveau, et frappe violemment cet organe. C'est par cette vertu singulière que cette plante a, comme je l'ai dit, mérité dans ce pays le nom d'*assis,* comme qui diroit *l'herbe par excellence.*»

Kœmpfer a décrit trois des substances que les Persans emploient de préférence pour se procurer cette espèce d'ivresse qu'ils appellent *kéif* كيف. Ces substances, prises du règne végétal, sont le tabac, l'opium et le chanvre. Il parle ainsi de la dernière:

«Je passe maintenant au chanvre. Ceux qui aiment à varier les drogues enivrantes, ou qui ont de la répugnance pour le goût de l'opium, se servent du chanvre pour se procurer cette sorte d'ivresse extatique. Je n'examinerai pas ici si cette plante est véritablement notre chanvre, ou bien une variété particulière appelée *bangue,* et décrite par les auteurs de l'*Hortus Malabaricus.* Quant à moi, elle m'a paru semblable, comme deux gouttes d'eau, à notre chanvre commun, tant le mâle que la femelle; je suis donc porté à croire que celui-ci doit sa vertu particulière au sol et au climat. Les parties de la plante qui produisent cette gaieté artificielle, sont la graine, appelée *schadanech;* la poussière des fleurs, qu'on nomme *djers,* et les feuilles, qui sont connues sous le nom de *beng.* . . . On emploie les feuilles en les faisant infuser dans l'eau froide. La boisson de cette eau procure une gaieté accompagnée d'une forte ivresse. Je vais indiquer les procédés employés pour sa préparation, comme je l'ai vu faire à quatre dervischs que je rencontrai dans une hôtellerie, sur les frontières de l'Inde. . . . Quelques personnes pétrissent la poudre des feuilles avec du sirop, et en font des pastilles et des bols qu'elles avalent dans la même intention. C'est des feuilles du chanvre, comme de la plus estimée de toutes les drogues enivrantes, qu'on appelle *benghi* dans la Perse et dans l'Inde, les hommes qui ont contracté l'usage des préparations enivrantes.»

Chardin nous apprend qu'en Perse les gens qui aiment à s'enivrer de tabac, y mêlent de la graine de chanvre, qui fait monter la vapeur au cerveau et étourdit en peu de temps.

Le chanvre et aussi en usage dans la Barbarie et à Maroc, comme substance enivrante, ainsi que l'attestent Hoest et Lamprière, et il y porte aussi le nom de *haschisch.* Léon Africain en a fait mention sous celui de *l'hasis,* qui n'est que le même mot avec l'article. A Alep, il sert au même usage et porte le même nom, selon que l'assure le docteur Russel. On le fume dans la même vue en plusieurs pays, et même en Afrique.

«Comme dans les villes, dit M. Niebuhr, les Arabes du commun veulent aussi avoir *keif*, c'est-à-dire, de la joie, mais qu'ils ne peuvent pas payer les liqueurs fortes, que souvent même il ne leur est pas possible d'en trouver, ils fument du *haschisch:* c'est une sorte d'herbe que M. Forskal et quelques autres qui nous ont précédés en Orient, ont prise pour des feuilles de chanvre. Ceux qui en sont amateurs assurent qu'elle donne du courage. Nous en vîmes un exemple dans le personne d'un de nos domestiques Arabes. Après avoir fumé du *haschisch*, il rencontra dans la rue quatre soldats qu'il lui prit fantaisie de chasser. Un d'eux le rossa d'importance, et le conduisit à la maison. Malgré ce petit revers, on ne put le tranquilliser, étant toujours très-persuadé que quatre soldats ne sauroient lui résister.»

Forskal, parlant du chanvre cultivé en Égypte, dit: *Cannabis. Arab.* sjadenek. *Colitur passim; floret fine april.; folia ad usus medicos; semina inebriantia. Usus textorum ignoratur.*

M. Olivier dit aussi, en parlant de l'Égypte: «Le peuple a substitué à l'usage de l'opium celui des feuilles de chanvre, comme beaucoup moins cher. Mises en poudre et mélangées avec le miel, et quelquefois avec des substances aromatiques, on en fait des bols que l'on prend dans la vue de se procurer des sensations agréables, mais dont l'effet le plus certain est le délire, l'hébétement, la consomption, et la mort, pour peu qu'on en continue l'usage. Cette plante, au reste, réussit assez mal en Égypte.»

Le même voyageur, après avoir parlé de l'usage qu'on fait de l'opium dans les cafés, en Perse, ajoute: «On a souvent distribué, dans ces mêmes cafés, un breuvage beaucoup plus fort, beaucoup plus enivrant: il étoit fait avec les feuilles et les sommités du chanvre ordinaire, auxquelles on ajoutoit un peu de noix vomique. La loi, qui permet ou tolère les autres breuvages, a toujours défendu celui-ci. Méhémet Khan, lorsque nous étions en Perse, punissoit du dernier supplice ceux qui le distribuoient et ceux qui le prenoient.»

M. Sonnini semble mettre quelque distinction entre le chanvre d'Europe et le végétal cultivé en Égypte, dont on fait le *haschischa*. Quoique le passage où il en parle soit un peu long, je le copierai en entier.

«Le chanvre se cultive dans les plaines des mêmes contrées (de la haute Égypte); mais l'on n'en tire pas due fil, comme en Europe, quoiqu'il pût vraisemblablement en fournir. Ce n'en est pas moins une plante d'un grand usage. Au défaut de liqueurs enivrantes, les Arabes et les Egyptiens en composent diverses préparations, avec lesquelles ils se procurent une sort d'ivresse douce, un état de rêverie qui procure de la gaieté et des songes agréables. Cette espèce d'anéantissement de la faculté de penser, cette espèce de sommeil de l'âme, n'a aucun rapport avec l'ivresse occasionnée par le vin et les liqueurs fortes, et notre langue n'a point de terme pour l'exprimer. Les Arabes nomment *keif* cet abandon voluptueux, cette sorte de stupeur délicieuse.

«La préparation de ce chanvre la plus usitée se fait en pilant les fruits avec leurs capsules (ou plutôt *enveloppes*) membraneuses; l'on met cuire la pâte qui en résulte avec du miel, du poivre et de la muscade, et l'on avale de cette confiture, gros comme une noix. Les pauvres, qui charment leur misère par l'étourdissement que le chanvre leur procure, se contentent de broyer avec de l'eau les capsules des graines, et d'en manger la pâte. Les Égyptiens mangent aussi ces capsules sans aucune préparation, et ils les mêlent encore avec le tabac à fumer. D'autres fois ils réduisent en poudre fine les capsules et les pistils seulement, en rejetant les graines. Ils mêlent cette poudre avec partie égale de tabac, et ils fument ce mélange dans une espèce de pipe, imitation très-simple, mais grossière, des pipes à la persane: ce n'est qu'un noix de coco creusée et remplie d'eau, au travers de laquelle on aspire une fumée âcre et enivrante. Cette manière de fumer est un des passetemps les plus ordinaires des femmes de la partie méridionale de l'Égypte.

«Toutes ces prépartions, ainsi que les parties de la plante qui servent à les faire, sont connues sous le nom Arabe de *haschisch,* qui, proprement, signifie *herbe,* comme si cette plante étoit l'herbe par excellence. On trouve du *haschisch,* dont la consommation est considérable, sur tous les marchés. Lorsqu'on veut désigner la plante elle-même, abstraction faite de ses vertus et de son usage, on l'appelle *basté.*

«Quoique le chanvre d'Égypte ressemble beaucoup au nôtre, il en diffère néanmoins par quelques caractères qui paroissent constituer une espèce particulière. En comparant attentivement ce chanvre avec celui d'Europe, on remarque que sa tige est beaucoup moins élevée, qu'elle acquiert en grosseur ce qui lui manque en hauteur; que le port de la plante est plutôt celui d'un arbuste dont le tronc a souvent plus de deux pouces de cironférence, et des branches nombreuses et alternes qui le garnissent depuis le pied:

ses feuilles sont aussi moins étroites et moins dentelées. La plante entière exhale une odeur plus forte, et les fruits sont plus petits et en même temps plus nombreux que dans l'espèce d'Europe.»

Après tout ce qui vient d'être dit, on sera sans doute disposé à penser que les Ismaéliens étoient nommés *Haschischis,* à cause de l'usage qu'ils faisoient du *haschisch,* comme ceux qui font usage du *beng* (soit que le *beng* soit aussi un électuaire formé des feuilles du chanvre, comme le dit Kœmpfer, ou plutôt un extrait de la plante narcotique nommée *datura,* ainsi que d'autres écrivains l'assurent), de l'opium, allelé *afyoun*, et d'autres drogues connues sous la dénomination générale de *teriak*, sont appelés *benghi, afyouni, teriaki.*

Et ce qui confirme bien ce que je dis de l'usage du *haschisch* chez les Ismaéliens, c'est ce passage de Makrizi:

«Vers ce temps-là [l'an 795], il vint au Caire un homme de la secte des *Molheds* ou Ismaéliens de Perse, qui composoit le *haschischa* en le mêlant avec du miel, et y joignoit diverses substances sèches, comme de la racine de mandragore et autres drogues du même genre: il nommoit cette composition *okda* [c'est-à-dire, gelée, confection], et la vendoit secrètement.»

Une observation qu'il n'est pas inutile de faire, c'est que du mot *haschisch,* ou *haschischa,* se forment également les deux adjectifs ou noms d'agent حشيشى *haschischi,* et حشاش *hasschasch*. On a vu le premier employé dans divers passages que j'ai cités, et c'est sûrement celui qe Makrizi avoit en vue en disant:

«J'ai vu un temps où les hommes de la classe la plus vile osoient seuls en manger; encore répugnoient-ils à s'entendre appeler d'un nom dérivé de cette drogue.» Le second, *hasschasch,* se trouve dans ce passage de Schems-eddin Mohammed, fils d'Abou'l-sourour: «Le pont neuf situé sur le grand canal est connu aujourd'hui sous le nom de *pont des hasschasch* [*kantarat alhasschaschin* قنطرة الحشاشين], à cause que c'est le lieu où les *mastouls* [comme qui diroit les ivrognes] d'entre les habitans du Caire prenoient le *haschisch.*»

Les mots *haschischin* et *hasschaschin* ont produit les deux dénominations *assissini* et *assassini* chez Joinville.

Je ne dois point dissimuler cependant que l'on peut faire contre ce que je dis ici deux objections: la première est que l'ivresse causée par le *haschisch* ne paroît consister que dans une sorte d'extase tranquille, et non dans une fureur propre à exalter le courage et l'imagination, et à faire entreprendre et exécuter des actions hardies et périlleuses; la seconde, c'est que, selon Makrizi, l'introduction du *haschisch* en Syrie et en Égypte, et même la découverte de la propriété enivrante du chanvre, sont postérieures au temps des Assassins.

Ma réponse à la première objection ne sera pas difficile. Ce qui est raconté de l'obéissance des Assassins à leur chef, et de la détermination avec laquelle ils exposoient leur vie pour faire périr les victimes qui leur avoient été désignées; les voyages qu'ils entreprenoient pour se rendre à leur destination; le sang-froid avec lequel ils épioient l'instant favorable à leur dessein, et savoient le saisir à propos; tout cela n'annonce pas des fruieux semblables aux Amoques des Indiens, et capables de tout entreprendre par une sorte de délire factice, mais des fanatiques persuadés qu'en se sacrifiant pour obéir aux ordres du ciel manifestés par ceux de leurs chefs, ils s'assuroient un bonheur éternel et toutes les jouissances des sens. Et c'est effectivement ainsi que les historiens nous les représentent. Quel étoit donc sur ces hommes l'effet du *haschischa!* C'étoit de leur procurer, quand il plaisoit à leur maître de leur faire prendre une dose de cet électuaire, dont lui seul possédoit le secret, un état extatique et une douce et profonde rêverie, pendant laquelle ils jouissoient ou s'imaginoient jouir de toutes les voluptés qui embellissent le paradis de Mahomet. Écoutons ce que nous raconte Marc-Pol, ou plutôt le rédacteur du texte Italien de sa relation; ce récit est le meilleur commentaire de ce que je viens de dire:

«Parlons maintenant du Vieux de la montagne. *Mulehet* est une contrée où demeuroit anciennement celui que l'on appeloit *le Vieux de la montagne:* car ce nom de *Mulehet* veut dire, en langue Sarasine, le lieu où résident les hérétiques; et du nom de ce lieu, on appelle ceux qui y demeurent, *Muléhétiques,* c'est-à-dire, hérétiques de leur religion, comme sont les Patarins parmi les Chrétiens. Voici ce que Marc-Pol racontoit de ce Vieux de la montagne, comme l'ayant ouï dire à plusieurs personnes. Ce prince se nommoit *Alaodin*, et étoit mahométan. Il avoit fait faire, dans une belle vallée renfermée entre deux montagnes très-hautes, un très-beau jardin, rempli de toutes les sortes de fruits et d'arbres qu'il avoit pu se procurer, et, alentour de ces plantations, différents palais et pavillons décorés de travaux en or, de peintures et d'ameublemens tout en soie. Là, dans de petits canaux qui répondoient à diverses parties de ces palais, on voyoit courir des ruisseaux de vin, de lait, de miel et d'une eau très-limpide. Il y avoit logé de jeunes filles parfaitement belles et pleines de charmes, instruites à chanter, à jouer de toute sorte d'instruments, à danser, et sur-tout à faire aux hommes toutes les avances les plus séduisantes que l'on puisse imaginer. On voyoit sans cesse ces jeunes filles, vêtues d'or et de soie, se promener dans ces jardins et ces palais: pour les femmes qui servoient le prince, elles étoient toujours renfermées, et ne paroissoient jamais au dehors. Voici le motif pour lequel ce Vieux avoit fait construire ce palais: Mahomet ayant dit que ceux qui obéiroient à ses volontés iroient dans le paradis, où ils trouveroient tous les plaisirs et toutes les délices du monde, de belles femmes et des fleuves de lait et di miel, celui-ci vouloit faire croire qu'il étoit prophète et compagnon de Mahomet, et qu'il pouvoit faire entrer qui'il vouloit dans ce même paradis. Personne ne pouvoit pénétrer dans le jardin dont nous avons parlé, parce qu'on avoit construit, à l'entrée del la vallée, un château très-fort et inexpugnable; on ne pouvoit y entrer que par un chemin secret. Ce Vieux avoit à sa cour des jeunes gens de douze à vingt ans, pris parmi ceux des habitants des montagnes qui lui paroissoient propres au maniement des armes, hardis et courageux. Il ne cessoit de les entretenir tous les jours de ce paradis de Mahomet, et du pouvoir qu'il avoit de les y faire entrer. Il faisoit, quand il lui plaisoit, donner à dix ou douze de ces jeunes gens une *certaine boisson qui les endormoit;* et quand its étoient comme à demi morts, il les faisoit transporter dans diverses chambres de ces palais. Lorsqu'ils venoient à se réveiller dans ces lieux, ils voyoient toutes les choses que nous avons décrites; chacun d'eux étoit entouré de ces jeunes filles qui chantoient, jouoient des instruments, faisoient toutes les caresses et les jeux qu'elles pouvoient s'imaginer, et leur présentoient les mets et les vins les plus exquis. De la sorte, ces jeunes gens, enivrés de tant de plaisirs et des ruisseaux de lait et de vin qu'ils voyoient, ne doutoient nullement qu'ils ne fussent dans le paradis, et auroient voulu n'en jamais sortir.

Au bout de quatre ou cinq jours, le Vieux les faisoit endormit de nouveau et retirer de ce jardin; puis, les faisant paroître devant lui, il leur demandoit où ils avoient été. Par votre grâce, Seigneur, disoient-ils, nous avons été dans le paradis: puis ils racontoient en présence de toute le monde ce qu'ils avoient vu. Ce récit excitoit dans tous ceux qui les entendoient, l'admiration et le desir d'une semblable félicité. Tel est, leur répondoit le Vieux, le commandement de notre prophète; il fait entrer dans le paradis quiconque combat pour défendre son seigneur: si donc tu m'obéis, tu jouiras de ce bonheur. Par de semblables discours, il avoit tellement disposé leurs esprits, que celui à qui il ordonnoit de mourir pour son service, s'estimoit heureux. Tous les seigneurs ou autres personnes qui étoient ennemis du Vieux de la montagne, étoient mis à mort par ces assassins qui étoient à son service; car aucun d'eux ne craignoit de mourir, pourvu qu'ils s'acquittassent des ordres et de la vontonté de leur seigneur, et ils e'exposoient volontiers à tous les dangers les plus évidents, ne comptant pour rien la perte de la vie présente. Aussi ce Vieux étoit-il redouté dans tous ces pays comme un tyran. Il avoit établi deux lieutenants, l'un dans les environs de Damas, l'autre dans le Curdistan; et ceux-ci se conduisoient de la même manière envers les jeunes gens qu'il leur envoyoit. Quelque puissant donc que fût un homme, s'il étoit ennemi du Vieux, il ne pouvoit manquer d'être tué.»

Tous les écrivains qui ont parlé des Assassins, Amauri, Hayton, Guillaume de Tyr, Jacques de Vitry, le sire de Joinville, Arnold de Lübeck, ne reconnoissent d'autre principe de leur conduite qu'une obéissance aveugle à leur chef, fondée sur l'espérance d'un bonheur futur sans bornes. Marc-Pol, ce qui est bien remarquable, fait mention d'*un breuvage enivrant* que le chef leur faisoit donner, quand il vouloit les faire transporter dans ses jardins enchantés. Or on a vu que-toutes les préparations enivrantes que l'on fait avec le chanvre, bols, confections, liqueurs, fumigations, s'appellent également du nom de *haschischa.* Au reste, je ne sais si l'on doit croire littéralement à l'existence de ces jardins enchantés, ou s'ils n'étoient pas uniquement un fantôme produit par l'imagination exaltée des jeunes gens enivrés par le *haschischia,* et que l'on avoit longtemps bercés de l'image de ce bonheur. Ce qu'il y a de certain, c'est qu'aujourd'hui même le preneurs d'opium ou de *haschisch* savent se procurer, sous les haillons de la pauvreté, et sans sortir d'une misérable taverne, un bonheur et des jouissances auxquels il ne manque de la réalité.

J'ai déjà observé que les travaux, les plantations, les eaux courantes, dont Hasan avoit embelli la forteresse et les environs d'Alamout, sa résidence, peuvent avoir contribué à répandre la fable de ces jardins enchantés. Arnold de Lübeck fait aussi mention de beaux palais situés dans les montagnes, où l'on élevoit les jeunes gens destinés à faire le métier d'assassins.

Écoutons comment Prosper Alpin rend les effets que les Égyptiens attribuent à l'usage de l'opium, du *haschisch* et des autres substances qu'ils prennent pour se procurer cet état, si recherché, de délire et de rêverie:

«Quelques-uns d'entre eux assurent que quand ils ont avalé une dose d'*opium,* d'*assis,* de *bousa,* ou de *bernavi,* ou enfin une prise de *bers,* ils voient, comme en songe, un grand nombre de magnifiques vergers et de belles filles, pleines d'attraits et de charmes; d'autres disent que, dans cet état, ils ne voient que les objets qui les flattent le plus: ceux que l'aspect des vergers réjouit, voient des vergers; les amants voient leurs maîtresses; les guerriers, des batailles.»

Russell, dans son Histoire naturelle d'Alep, dit avoir été témoin de la folie d'un de ces mangeurs d'opium, qui, se croyant pacha, avoit pris sans façon la place d'honneur sur le sofa, causoit familièrement avec le maître de la maison, entroit dans le détail des affaires de son prétendu gouvernement, condamnoit l'un à la bastonnade, l'autre à la prison, disgracioit quelques-uns de ses officiers, en créoit d'autres, et jouissoit ainsi de sa nouvelle fortune dont l'acquisition ne lui avoit coûté qu'une forte dose d'opium, jusqu'à ce qu'un bruit soudain fait à dessein derrière lui le tira de cette rêverie, et fit évanouir toute sa félicité.

L'usage immodéré et habituel du *haschisch* détruit, il est vrai, toutes les facultés, et paroîtroit peu propre à atteindre le but que se proposoient les Ismaéliens. Écoutons ce qu'en dit le médecin Ebn-Beïtar: «Il ya, c'est ainsi qu'il s'exprime, une troisième espèce de chanvre que l'on nomme *chanvre Indien.* Je n'en ai vu nulle autre part qu'en Égypte; on l'y cultive dans les jardins, et on le nomme *haschischa:* il enivre fortement, pour peu que l'on en prenne une ou deux drachmes. Quand on en fait un usage immodéré, il produit une sorte de démence: des gens qui en faisoient habituellement usage, en ont éprouvé ce pernicieux effet; il a affoibli leurs esprits, et a fini par les conduire à des affections maniaques; quelqufois même il mène à la mort. J'ai vu les fakirs l'employer de diverses manières: les uns font bien cuire les feuille de cette plante; ils les pétrissent avec leurs mains, jusqu'à en former une espèce de pâte dont ils font des pastilles; il y en a qui les laissent un peu sécher, qui ensuite les torréfient, les broient avec la main, y mêlent un peu de sésame dépouillé de sa pellicule, et du sucre, puis mangent cette drogue sèche en la mâchant longtemps. En même temps ils gesticulent et se réjouissent beaucoup; et comme elle les enivre, elle les fait tomber dans la folie, ou dans un état bien voisin de celui-là.»

Ala-eddin ben-Néfis, autre médecin cité par Makrizi, dit aussi qu l'usage de cette drogue produit des inclinations basses et avilit l'âme, et que, dans ceux qui en ont contracté l'habitude, toutes les facultés naturelles se dégradent, en sorte qu'à la fin il ne leur reste plus aucun des attributs de l'humanité.

Makrizi lui-même, confirme tout cela par ses propres observations, et il attribue à l'usage immodére du *haschischa* la dépravation des mœurs et l'abrutissement de ses contemporains.

Nous avons vu que, suivant M. Olivier, son effet le plus certain est le délire, l'hébétement, la consomption et la mort, pour peu qu'on en continue l'usage.

Enfin, dans un arrêté pris par le général François en Égypte, le 17 vendémiaire an IX, on lit: «L'usage de la liqueur forte faite par quelques Musulmans avec une certaine herbe forte nommée *haschisch,* ainsi que celui de fumer la graine de chanvre, sont prohibés par toute l'Égypte. Ceux qui sont accoutumés à boire cette liqueur et à fumer cette graine, perdent la raison, et tombent dans un violent délire qui souvent les porte à commettre des excès de tout genre.»

Cet inconvénient attaché à l'usage excessif et journalier du *haschisch,* et qu'on ne sauroit révoquer en doute, n'avoit certainement point lieu chez les Ismaéliens; it eût été directement contraire au but qu'ils proposoient, et l'on doit croire qu'un électuaire, ou, comme le dit Marc-Pol, une boisson qui n'étoit administrée que par l'ordre du chef, et dont peut-être lui seul avoit le secret, n'étoit point prodiguée, et que l'usage en étoit renfermé dans certaines bornes.

J'ai dit *dont le chef avoit seul le secret;* car c'est ainsi que j'entends ces mots d'un historien que j'ai cité ci-devant, et qui dit que ceux qui avoient le gouvernement d'Alep, voulant se défaire de Saladin, écrivirent à Sinan, *maître* ou *possesseur du* haschischah صاحب الحشيشة.

Ce que je viens de dire fournit aussi la réponse à la seconde objection que je me suis faite à moi-même, et qui résulte du récit de Makrizi, suivant lequel l'usage du *haschisch* ne se seroit introduit parmi les Musulmans que vers le commencement du VIIe siècle de l'hégire, et par conséquent longtemps après l'époque de la plus grande puissance des Ismaéliens, et peu avant leur destruction par Holagou.

Makrizi, en effet, d'après un grand nombre d'autorités, attribue la découverte des propriétés enivrantes de la feuille du chanvre au scheïkh Haïdar, mort en 618 de l'hégire. It ajoute que ce secret resta quelque temps concentré parmi les fakirs, disciples du scheïkh Haïdar; que cet usage du chanvre fut introduit dans l'Irak pour la première fois en 628, par deux princes souverains, l'un d'Ormuz, l'autre de Bahréïn, et qu'il ne parvint que plus tard en Syrie, en Égypte et dans l'Asie mineure.

On ne peut guère douter que l'usage du *haschisch,* du moins en Égypte, ne soit postérieur au VIe siècle de l'hégire, puisqu'Abdallatif, qui écrivoit en 605, n'en fait aucune mention; et, d'un autre côté, il doit s'y être introduit peu de temps après cette époque, attendu qu'Ebn-Beïtar, mort en 646, l'a déjà trouvé commun dans ce même pays parmi les fakirs.

Je ne serois point éloigné de croire cependant que le scheïkh Haïdar n'avoit point eu l'honneur de la découverte qu'on lui attribue. La dénomination de *konnab hindi,* قُنّب هندى [chanvre indien], donnée, suivant Ebn-Beïtar, à l'espèce de chanvre dont on se servoit sous le nom de *haschisch* en Égypte, me porte à croire que cet électuaire est venu originairement de l'Inde, que Haïdar pouvoit en avoir reçu la connoissance de quelque *djougui* indien, et que peut-être c'étoit de la même source que les Ismaéliens l'avoient reçue avant lui. Cela est d'autant moins invraisemblable, que l'on reconnoît dans la doctrine des Ismaéliens plusieurs traits de conformité avec les doctrines idiennes, telles que la transmigration des âmes, les incarnations de la divinité ou *avatars,* les émanations, &c. La conjecture que je propose ici, est appuyée par Makrizi lui-même qui dit:

«Cependant je tiens du scheïkh Mohammed Schirazi Kalendéri, que jamais le scheïkh Haïdar n'a usé du *haschischa,* et que les peuples du Khorasan ne lui attribuent l'origine de cette drogue que parce que ses disciples sont connus pour en faire un usage assidu. Le *haschischa* remonte, suivant ce qu'il m'a dit, à une époque bien antérieure au scheïkh Haïdar. Ce fut un scheïkh nommé *Biraztan,* qui vivoit dans l'Inde, qui apprit aux peuples du pays à manger le *haschischa;* ils ne l'avoient point connu avant lui. Cette drogue devint d'un usage si commun dans l'Inde, qu'elle s'introduisit jusque dans le Yémen; de là elle passa dans la province de Fars: enfin les habitants de l'Irak, de l'Asie mineure, de l'Égypte et de la Syrie, en entendirent parler pour la première fois, en l'année que j'ai marquée plus haut. Biraztan vivoit du temps des Chosroès; il vécut jusqu'à l'islamisme, et se fit Musulman.»

Au reste, quelque parti qu'on prenne sur cette question, on voit que le *haschischa* a pu être employé par les Ismaéliens long-temps avant le VIe siècle de l'hégire, sans que cela soit en contradiction avec les faits historiques qui en attribuent l'introduction, parmi les fakirs, au scheïkh Haïdar, et la propagation aux disciples de ce scheïkh.

Je dois maintenant faire connoître divers autres noms sous lesquels les Assassins sont quelquefois désignés dans les écrivains Orientaux.

Ebn-Khaldoun, dans ses *Prolégomènes historiques*, et Schahristani, ne font aucune mention des *Haschischis*. Le premier dit que les Ismaéliens sont aussi nommés *Baténis*, *Mazdakis* et *Karmates* dans l'Irak, et que dans le Khorasan on les nomme *Talimis* et *Molheds*, mais que pour eux ils s'appellent *Ismaéliens*. Nous allons rendre raison de chacun de ces noms.

Le nom de *Baténis* باطنى, c'est-à-dire, partisans du sens intérieur, est donné aux Ismaéliens, comme je l'ai dit ailleurs, parce qu'ils enseignent que tout ce qui est extérieur, comme les pratiques du culte, les préceptes de la loi, la profession de foi, &c., a un sens intérieur, *batin* باطن ; que tout révélation, *tenzil* تنزيل, a une signification allégorique: *tawil* تاويل. C'est là ce que dit aussi Schahristani; et Ebn-Khaldoun se trompe en disant qu'on les nomme *Baténis*, parce qu'ils reconnoissent un imam intérieur, *batin* باطن, c'est-à-dire, ajoute-t-il, caché, *mestour* مستور. Dans les textes que j'ai vus, l'imam caché n'est jamais nommé *batin*, mais bien *mestour* ou *maktoum* مكتوم. Les livres des Druzes déposent à chaque page en faveur de la première explication.

Mazdaki مزدكى signifie sectateur de *Mazdak* مزدك. C'est une dénomination injurieuse donnée aux Ismaéliens, à cause de la conformité vraie ou supposée de leur doctrine et de leur conduite licencieuse avec la morale et les pratiques de Mazdak, novateur qui avoit causé de grands troubles en Perse sous le règne de Kobad, et qui fut mis à mort sous celui de Khosrou Nouschirwan. On peut consulter, sur ce sujet, l'histoire de la dynastie des Sassanides de Mirkhond, que j'ai publiée dans mes *Mémoires sur diverses antiquités de la Perse* (1793).

Que les Ismaéliens aient été nommés *Karmates*, c'est une chose sur laquelle je n'ai pas besoin de m'arrêter, puisque j'ai déjà dit plus d'un fois que les Karmates étoient les mêmes que les Ismaéliens. Le nom de *Karmates* leur fut donné, parce que l'un de leurs chefs étoit ainsi surnommé, à cause, dit-on, qu'il avoit les jambes courtes, et ne faisoit que de petits pas.

Malahidèh ملاحدة ou *molhidoun* ملحدون, est le pluriel de *molhid* ملحد, qui veut dire *impie*. Ce nom ne fut donné aux Ismaéliens de Perse, suivant Mirkhond, que lorsque le quatrième prince de leur dynastie, Hasan fils de Mohammed, eut abjuré publiquement les dogmes et les pratiques de la religion Musulmane; mais il leur resta toujours depuis ce temps, et on l'étendit même aux princes qui avoient précédé cette apostasie, quoiqu'ils eussent été religieux Musulmans.

Enfin, toujours d'après Schahristani, les Ismaéliens étoient encore appelés, dans le Khorasan, *Talimi* تعليمى. Pour entendre cette dénomination, il faut savoir que parmi les sectes Musulmanes qui, étant d'accord sur les *dogmes* اصول, ne diffèrent que sur les *lois morales et pratiques* فروع, on distingue trois écoles. La première, nommée *ahl altalim* اهل التعليم, *les partisans de l'étude,* se décide par ces quatre autorités, l'*Alcoran*, la *Sunna*, le *consentement des imams* sur un point de doctrine اجماع, et les *raisonnements* fondés sur des inductions قياس. La seconde ne reconnoît que des *autorités positives écrites;* on l'appelle, à cause de cela, *ahl alnosous* اهل النصوص. La troisième suit principalement la *raison,* ou les probabilités: elle est, en conséquence, nommée *ahl alraï* اهل الراى. Hasan ben-Sabbah faisoit profession de suivre la première école. Comme ce système s'appelle *talim* تعليم, on donna à Hasan, ainsi qu'à ses sectateurs, le nom de *Talimi* تعليمى Schahristani, en exposant les quatre fondements de la doctine de Hasan, dit très-positivement que le premier établissoit la *nécessité de l'enseignement* تعليم, et étoit destiné à réfuter ceux qui n'admettoient d'autre autorité pour se décider dans les questions théologiques, que la *raison* et le *jugement* الراى والعقل. Le second fondment avoit pour objet de réfuter ceux qui n'admettoient d'autre autorité que les *traditions* الحديث.

On a quelquefois confondu les Assassins avec les Druzes et les Nosaïris. M. Venture, dans un mémoire sur les Druzes, dit que, suivant toutes les apparences, le Vieux de la montagne n'étoit autre que le chef de la nation des Druzes. D'un autre côté, M. de Volney ne doute point que les Assassins, dont parle Guillaume de Tyr, ne fussent les *Ansarièhs*. M. de Volney eût mieux fait de nommer ces sectaires, avec tous les auteurs Arabes et avec M. Venture, *Nosaïri* ou *Nosaïrèh* au pluriel. M. Falconet a aussi confondu les *Nosaïris* avec les Assassins, et a reproché à M. Assemani d'avoir substitué le mot *Nazaréens* aux *Nosaïris* ou *Nosroye* ܢܨܪܝܐ des historiens Syriens.

Il n'y a aucun doute que les *Nosaïris* ne soient une branche des Ismaéliens, qui tient de bien près aux Karmates, si même elle diffère de cette dernière secte dans son origine. Quant aux Druzes, quoiqu'ils aient pris leur naissance dans le sein de la secte des Ismaéliens, ils diffèrent cependant et des Nosaïris et des autres sectes des Ismaéliens par plusieurs dogmes importants, surtout par la croyance en la divinité du khalife Fatémite Hakem, par l'attente de son retour, et la soumission aux ordres de Hamza, son premier ministre. Ils anathématisent les autres sectes des Ismaéliens, et il se trouve dans leurs livres sacrés une réfutation expresse du système des Nosaïris. Au surplus, les Nosaïris, et même les Druzes, sont antérieurs aux *Haschischis;* car ce nom n'a, je crois, jamais été donné qu'aux Ismaéliens de la seconde époque, ou, pour me servir des termes de Schahristani, de la *seconde mission,* الدعوة الثانية. Hasan ben-Sabbah, instituteur de cette *seconde mission,* ne commença à paroître que vers l'an 483. C'est par lui que fut établie dans le Djébal la puissance de ces Ismaéliens, qui s'étendit plus tard en Syrie, vers l'an 520; et ce ne fut que depuis l'établissement de cette puissance à Alamout, que les Baténiens commencèrent à menacer la vie des rois et des grands. C'est donc un anachronisme que de confondre les Ismaéliens ou Baténiens, nommés *Assassins*, avec les Druzes et les Nosaïris. Mais je reviens à quelques autres noms donnés aux Assassins.

Une des raisons qui ont porté M. Venture à croire que les Druzes étoient les Assassins des historiens des croisades, et le chef ou l'émir des Druzes, le *Vieux de la montagne,* c'est, dit'il, que l'émir des Druzes a toujours eu à son service une troupe choisie qu'on appelle les *Fédawièhs,* c'est-a-dire, gens disposés à se sacrifier pour lui. Ils étoient autrefois tous Druzes de religion; ils sont maintenant preque tous Chrétiens. Il n'y a point de dangers et de périls auxquels cette troupe ne s'expose, lorsqu'il est question d'exécuter les ordres du prince, et l'on peut citer un exemple récent de cet aveugle dévouement dont ils font profession.

«Il ya environ dix-sept à dix-huit ans que l'émir Melhem . . . eut un vif démêlé avec un douanier de Seyde, envoyé auprès de lui par le pacha de la province, pour accélérer le paiement du tribut. L'émir Melhem lui jura dans sa colère qu'il le feroit périr, lorsqu'il le pourroit faire sans violer le droit des gens et l'hospitalité. Un jour que ce douanier étoit assis dans un kiosque découvert, qui sert d'entrepôt à la douane de Seyde, un de ces Fédawièhs se présente armé de son fusil et d'une paire de pistolets. Il examine tout de sang-froid, distingue le douanier au milieu de ses gens, le couche en joue et le tue. Lorsqu'il fut bien assuré qu'il n'avoit pas manqué son coup, il voulut regagner la porte de la ville, où il y avoit un cheval qui l'attendoit; mais, avant de pouvoir y arriver, il fut assommé par la populace.»

Il faut avouer que ces *Fédawièhs* فداوية ou *Fédawis* ont un grand rapport avec les ministres de la vengeance du chef des Ismaéliens ou Vieux de la montagne. Il y a cependant cette différence, qu'on ne les supposera point mus par un fanatisme religieux, puisque, suivant M. Venture, ce sont pour la plupart des Chrétiens qui font ce service pour l'émir des Druzes.

On peut ajouter, ce qui sembleroit d'abord fortifier l'opinion que je combats, que les sicaires ou assassins du chef des Ismaéliens sont aussi nommés assez souvent dans les auteurs Arabes et Persans, *Fédawi* فداوى , ou, ce qui es la même chose, فدائي *Fédaï*. Je ne citerai, pour le moment, qu'un seul passage où ce mot est appliqué aux Assassins; mais il suffira pour prouver ce que j'avance: c'est Abou'lfaradj qui me le fournira. Lorsque le mogol Holagou résolut de détruire la puissance des Ismaéliens dans la Perse, cette secte avoit pour chef Rocn-eddin Khourschah, fils d'Ala-eddin: «Ce prince, dit Abou'lfaradj, tenta d'abord plusieurs moyens d'en imposer à Holagou par une feinte soumission; mais le Tartare lui signifia qu'il n'avoit d'autre parti à prendre que de sortir de la place forte d'Alamout où il faisoit sa résidence, et de se rendre en personne au camp des Mogols, ou, s'il ne vouloit point le faire, de se préparer à soutenir un siége. Roch-eddin envoya un homme affidé pour dire à Holagou qu'il n'osoit point sortir de la place, de crainte que ceux de ses gens qui y étoient enfermés avec lui, n'attentassent à sa vie; mais que, dès qu'il en trouveroit l'occasion, il sortiroit. Holagou, convaincu que Rocn-eddin ne cherchoit qu'à gagner du temps, vint mettre le siége devant la forteresse; ce que Rocn-eddin voyant, il envoya dire à Holagou: Je n'ai différé jusqu'ici que parce que je n'étois pas assuré de votre arrivée; aujourd'hui ou demain, je me rendrai auprès de vous. Lorsqu'il voulut sortir, les plus fanatiques d'entre les Molheds se soulevèrent, et les *Fédaïs* se jetèrent sur lui, et s'opposèrent à sa sortie. Il envoya instruire Holagou de leur rebellion, et ce prince lui fit dire d'user de ménagement envers eux, et de les amadouer pour le moment, afin de mettre sa vie en sûreté contre leurs entreprises, mais d'aviser d'une manière ou d'une autre aux moyens de sortir, fût-ce même sous un déguisement. En même temps Holagou ordonna à ses émirs d'entourer la place de toutes parts, de dresser contre elle les machines, et de combattre, chacun de leur côté, ceux des Ismaéliens qui les attaqueroient. Pendant que les Molheds étoient occupés à cet engagement, Rocn-eddin sortit avec son fils et les personnes de sa cour, et vint se soumettre à Holagou.»

Dans la *Chronique Syriaque* du même Abou'lfaradj, on lit: «Quand Rocn-eddin voulut sortir, ses gens tirèrent leurs poignards contre lui, en disant: Si tu sors, nous te tuerons.»

Il est certain que, dans ce passage d'Abou'lfaradj, les *Fédaïs* ne sont pas les Ismaéliens ou Molheds en général, mais sont une classe particulière d'hommes, les plus fanatiques, les *dévoués,* en un mot vraisemblablement ceux que les Ismaéliens employoient pour donner la mort à leurs ennemis; il ne s'ensuit pas de là néanmoins que par-tout où l'on trouve des *Fédaïs*, ce soient des Ismaéliens. Chaque secte, chaque prince, peut avoir ses *Fédaïs*.

C'est ainsi que dans l'Inde, suivant le F. Vincent-Marie de Sainte-Catherine de Sienne, chaque prince, et même chaque église Chrétienne, a ses *Amoques*, qui jurent de défendre, aux dépens de leur vie, les droits, les privilèges, la propriété de leurs patrons envers et contre tous, même envers tout autre souverain.

M. Muradjea d'Ohsson ne s'est donc pas exprimé exactement, en disant que les sectateurs de Hasan ben-Sabbah, appelés de son nom *Huméiri* حميري, portèrent encore celui de *Fédaïs*, à cause de l'enthousiasme avec lequel ils exposoient leurs vies en marchant sous ses drapeaux.

Tenons donc pour certain que tous les Ismaéliens n'étoient point *Fédaïs*, quoique les assassins de profession, dévoués à la secte, soient désignés sous ce nom. On en verra plus loin de nouvelles preuves, lorsque je parlerai de ce nom comme appliqué aux Ismaéliens.

La confusion que l'on a faite des Assassins avec les *Nosaïris*, qu'Assemani nomme *Nazarei*, auroit sans doute été généralement admise, quoique très-mal fondée, si l'on eût su que les Ismaéliens de Perse et de Syrie ont aussi été nommés *Nazaris* نزاري. Je vais prouver ce fait, et donner en même temps l'origine et l'explication de cette dénomination.

En l'année 524 de l'hégire, le khalife Faémite Amerbiahcamallah fut tué par des Baténiens, comme le disent Abou'lfaradj, Abou'lféda, Renaudot, &c.; cependant Makrizi attribue ce meurtre à des *Nazaris*, et Mirkhond à des Baténiens et à des *Nazaris:* mais cette contradiction apparente s'explique facilement; car les Nazaris ne sont autre chose qu'une faction de Baténiens, qui a pris naissance à la mort du khalife Fatémite Mostanser-billah. Ce khalife eut pour successeur son fils Abou'kasem Ahmed Mostalibillah; mais, ainsi que je l'ai déjà insinué au commencement de ce Mémoire, Mostali ne succéda pas à son père d'un commun accord, son frère Nazar lui ayant disputé le trône. «Or, dit Makrizi, à cette occasion les Ismaéliens se divisèrent en deux partis, celui des *Nazaris*, qui regardoient Mostali comme illégitime khalife, et un autre, qui le reconnoissoit pour khalife légitime.» Renaudot a parlé de la révolte de Nazar contre Mostali; mais il n'a pas fait mention de la scission que cela occasionna parmi les Ismaéliens, et qui continua sous plusierus règnes. Je ne puis me dispenser de donner ici un extrait de Mirkhond, qui mettra ces faits dans le plus grand jour. Voici ce qu'il raconte, en traçant brièvement l'histoire des khalifes Fatémites d'Égypte:

«Mostanser avoit d'abord déclaré son fils aîné *Mostafalidin-allah Nazar* pour son successeur; mais ensuite, mécontent de lui, il ordonna par son testament que Nazar eût à renoncer à toute prétention à la souveraineté, et que la couronne fût déférée à son autre fils Mostali-billah. Quand Mostanser fut mort, les Ismaéliens se divisèrent en deux partis: les un prêtèrent le serment à Mostali, et le firent asseoir sur le trône; les autres, croyant, conformément aux dogmes de leur secte, que la première disposition devoit être maintenue, embrassèrent le parti de Nazar. Hasan ben-Sabbah Homeïri adopta ce second parti. En effet, le *Nazari* du Kouhestan est au nombre des partisans de Mostafalidin-allah Nazar, et le nom même de *Nazari,* qu'il porte, prouve cette assertion. Ces gens allèguent en faveur de leur opinion, que l'imam Djafar Sadek avoit d'abord déclaré pour héritier de l'imamat après lui son fils Ismaël; qu'ensuite, ayant reconnu qu'Ismaël se laissoit aller à boire du vin, il le destitua, et ordonna que, quand il auroit terminé ses jours, l'imamat passeroit à Mousa Cadhem. Mais comme les Ismaéliens pensent que la première disposition doit avoir toute sa force, ils considèrent Ismaël, et non pas Mousa, comme le successeur de Djafar Sadek dans la dignité d'imam. Mostali, se voyant en possession du khalifat, voulut se défaire de son frère Nazar; mais Nazar, pour mettre sa vie en sûreté, se retira à Alexandrie, auprès d'un serviteur de son père, qui en étoit gouverneur. Celui-ci déclara Mostali destitué du khalifat, et proclama Nazar khalife. Cependant Mostali fit marcher contre Alexandrie un grande armée. Le gouverneur de la ville, qui avoit embrassé le parti de Nazar, fut pris et mis à mort. Nazar fut fait prisonnier avec ses deux fils, et envoyé à Mostali, qui le fit renfermer au Caire; il y resta prisonnier jusqu'à sa mort. Il y avoit sept ans que Mostali régnoit, lorsqu'il fut tué, dit-on, d'un coup de poignard, à l'âge de vingt-huit ans, par quelques-uns des partisans de Nazar.

»Son fils Amer-biahcam-allah lui succéda. . . . Sous son règne, quelques *Nazaris,* ennemis de *l'émir-al-djoyousch* (ou généralissime des armées), qui étoit beaupère d'Amer, le tuèrent . . . Aksankar, l'un des principaux seigneurs de la cour du khalife, fut aussi tué dans la djami de Mosul, par quelques-uns des *Fédaïs* d'entre les *Nazaris,* d'un coup de poignard. Sous le règne d'Amer, la faction des *Nazaris* commença à paroître en Syrie, et quelques places fortes de cette province tombèrent entre leurs mains. Le 4 de dhou'lkadèh 524, une troupe de Baténiens et de fanatiques de la faction des *Nazaris* assassinèrent Amer, par représailles de la mort de Nazar. Hafedh-lidin-allah, qui lui succéda, ayant donné la charge de vizir à Abou-Ali Ahmed, fils de Fadhl *émir-aldjoyousch,* et l'ayant élevé en dignité, quelques *Fédaïs* des *Nazaris* le tuèrent dans les premiers jours de son administration; peu de jours après, ils tuèrent aussi celui qui avoit été nommé pour le remplacer, toujours pour venger le même sang.»

Ceci nous explique comment et pourquoi Hasan ben-Sabbah, qui ne s'étoit établi dans le Kouhestan que comme daï des khalifes Fatémites, et qui reconnoissoit leur souveraineté, et avoit reçu, dit-on, les patentes d'investiture de Mostanser, en vint non seulement à se rendre indépendant dans cette province, mais même à s'emparer de quelques places de la Syrie qui appartenoient aux Fatémites: c'est que, depuis le schisme survenu parmi les Ismaéliens à la mort de Mostanser, Hasan avoit embrassé le parti de Nazar, et ne regardoit plus Mostali et ses successeurs que comme des khalifes intrus.

Aussi, à sa mort, ordonna-t-il que Kia Buzurc-umid بزرك اميد et le *Dehdar* دهدار Abou-Ali administreroient, l'un les affaires de la secte, l'autre celles du divan, d'accord avec le généralissime Hasan Kasrani, jusqu'à ce que *l'imam vînt se mettre lui-même à la tête du gouvernement.* Mirkhond nous aprend qu'un des princes de la dynastie des Ismaéliens de Perse, Hasan fils de Mohammed, fils de Buzurc-umid, ayant dispensé ses sujets de toutes les observances légales, fut cause, par cette conduite, qu'on leur donna le nom de *Molheds,* qui s'étendit même à ses prédécesseurs, quoique ceux-ci eussent observé les lois de l'islamisme. Bien que ce prince se reconnût publiquement pour fils de Mohammed ben-Buzurc-umid, cependant, dans un grand nombre d'écrits qu'il envoyoit de divers côtés, il disoit, tantôt d'une manière ambiguë, tantôt ouvertement, qu'il étoit descendant de Nazar, fils du khalife Mostanser, et que c'étoit lui qui étoit le véritable khalife et l'imam.» Les *Nazaris,* ajoute Mirkhond, ont inventé toute sorte de fables et de contes ridicules pour jusifier cette prétention de Hasan. Du vivant même de son père, il avoit voulu se faire passer pour l'imam, promis par Hasan ben-Sabbah; mais Mohammed avoit coupé court à cette folie, en déclarant publiquement que hasan étroit son fils, et que pour lui n'étroit pas iman, mais seulement un des daïs de l'iman, et en faisant mourir un grand nombre de ceux qui avoient accueilli les extravagances de Hasan.»

C'est ici le lieu de remarquer, comme nous l'avons annoncé plus haut, que Mirkhond se sert toujours du mot *Fédaï* pour désigner les hommes que les Ismaéliens employoient pour assassiner leurs ennemis. Ainsi il dit que l'illustre Nizam-almulc, vizir de Mélicschah, fut assassiné par un *Eédaï,* par l'ordre de Hasan ben-Sabbah; que, sous le règne de Hasan ben-Sabbah, beaucoup de princes Musulmans qui avoient des querelles avec les Ismaéliens, furent assassinés par des *Fédaïs;* que, sous celui de son successeur Kia Buzurc-umid, les *Fédaïs* tuèrent un grand nombre de princes ou grands seigneurs Musulmans, tels que le grand kadhi Abou-Saïd de Hérat; un fils de Mostali, khalife d'Égypte, qui fut assassiné par sept personnes d'entre les *Réfiks;* Dauletschah, reïs d'Isaphan; Aksankar, gouverneur de Marage; Mostanser, khalife de Bagdad; le reïs de Tabriz, Hasan, fils d'Abou'lkasem, mufti de Kazwin, &c.; qu'il répète la même chose à la fin du règne de Mohammed, fils de Kia Buzurc-umid, &c. Le mot *Fédawi* est également employé dans le récit des entreprises du sultan Mélic-alnaser Mohammed, fils de Kélaoun, contre Karasankar, dont j'ai donné un extrait plus haut. Cette observation confirme ce que j'ai dit de la signification du most *fédaï,* et me fournit en même temps l'occasion d'expliquer une autre expression que j'ai souvent rencontrée dans Mirkhond; je veux parler du mot *réfik* رفيق , au pluriel *réfikan.*

Réfik signifie proprement en arabe, *compagnon, aide, camarade de voyage;* mais plusieurs passages de Mirkhond que j'ai rapportés dans ce *Mémoire*, et un grand nombre d'autres que je pourrois citer, prouvent que ce mot avoit, parmi les Ismaéliens, une signification propre, et, pour ainsi dire, technique.

Hasan ben-Ali ben-Sabbah, parlant de lui-même, disoit: «J'avois toujours, ainsi que mes pères, fait profession de la doctrine des Schiites, qui admettent la succession des douze imams. Il arriva par hasard que je rencontrai un homme d'entre les *Réfiks,* qui se nommoit *Amirèh Dharrab,* et il se forma une étroite liaison entre lui et moi. . . . Toutes les fois donc qu'Amirèh parloit pour soutenir la doctrine des Ismaéliens, je disputois avec lui à ce sujet. . . . Après cela, je contractai des liaisons avec un autre d'entre les Ismaéliens, nommé *Abou-Nadjm Sarradj,* et je le priai de m'instruire à fond de la doctrine des Ismaéliens. . . . Enfin je rencontrai un daï de cette religion, nommé *Moumin,* qui avoit reçu du scheïkh Abd-almélic ben-Atrousch, daï de la province d'Irak, la permission d'exercer le ministère de daï.»

Ce passage prouve que *Réfik* et *Ismaéli* sont deux mots synonymes, ou du moins que ceux qu'on désignoit sous le nom de *Réfik,* étoient des Ismaéliens. Il prouve aussi que cette dénomination étoit antérieure à Hasan ben-Sabbah; mais il donne lieu de soupçonner qu'il y avoit une différence entre les *daïs* et les *Réfiks.* Le passage suivant confirme cette opinion: «Hasan [c'est encore Mirkhond qui parle] s'étant affermi dans la possession d'Alamout et des lieux qui en étoient voisins, ne négligea rien pour se rendre maître par la force ou par la douceur de tout le gouvernement de Roudbar; après quoi il envoya le daï Hosaïn Kaïni avec une troupe de *Réfiks,* pour prêcher sa doctrine aux peuples due Kouhestan. Mélicschah fit marcher dans le Kouhestan un de ses généraux, Kézil Sarek, pour s'opposer aux progrès de Hosaïn Kaïni. En conséquence, Kézil Sarek fit les plus grands efforts pour repousser les Molheds du Kouhestan. Hosaïn Kaïni, avec les *Réfiks*, se renferma dans une forteresse du territoire de Moumen-abad. Tandis que Kézil Sarek l'assiégeoit, on reçut la nouvelle de la mort de Mélicschah; ce qui l'obligea à lever le siége.»

En racontant le siége d'Alamout par les troupes de Mélicschah, le même historien dit que Hasan n'avoit pas avec lui plus de soixante-dix *Réfiks*.

Lorsqu'il parle des princes et des personnes illustres qui furent assassinés sous le règne de Kia Buzurc-umid et par son ordre, il dit: «Pendant la durée du gouvernement de Buzurc-umid, les *Fédaïs* tuèrent plusieurs princes et personnes illustres. Au nombre de ceux qui furent tués, furent le kadhi de l'Orient et de l'Occident, Abou-Saïd de Hérat; un fils de Mostali, qui fut assassiné en Égypte par sept personnes d'entre les *Réfiks,* &c.»

Enfin, en racontant les événemens du règne de Buzurc-umid, Mirkhond emploie une multitude de fois le mot *Réfik.* Je vais donner un extrait de ce récit, et je conserverai ce mot toutes les fois qu'il se rencontrera.

Le sultan Mahmoud Seldjoukide, desirant faire la paix avec Kia Buzurc-umid, un de ses officiers fut chargé d'en faire les premières ouvertures au prince Ismaélien, qui envoya un député à Ispahan pour traiter cette affaire. Ce député, nommé *Khodja Mohammed Nasihi Schahristani,* en sortant de l'audience de sultan Mahmoud, fut tué par la populace avec un *Réfik,* dans un bazar. Le sultan envoya sur-le-champ faire des excuses à Buzurc-umid, et protester qu'il n'avoit eu aucune part à cet assassinat. Buzurc-umid fit dire au sultan qu'il devoit punir les meurtriers, ou s'attendre à la vengeance qu'il ne manqueroit pas de tirer d'une telle perfidie. Mahmoud n'ayant eu aucun égard aux demandes de Buzurc-umid, au commencement de l'année 523, les *Réfiks* vinrent à la porte de Kazwin, tuèrent quatre personnes, et enlevèrent beaucoup de bestiaux. Les habitants de Kazwin se mirent à leur poursuite; mais un des principaux de la ville fut tué, et ils se virent obligés à prendre la fuite. En l'année 525, mille hommes de troupes de l'Irak sétant approchés de la forteresse de Lanker, les *Réfiks,* instruits de leur marche, les mirent en fuite, sans qu'il y eût de sang répandu. Le sultan Mahmoud étant mort vers ce temps-là, les *Réfiks* firent une nouvelle incursion sur le territoire de Kazwin, enlevèrent des bestiaux, et tuèrent cent Turcomans et vingt habitants de Kazwin.

En l'année 526, l'armée d'Alamout s'avança dans le Ghilan pour faire la guerre à Abou-Haschem Aléwi, parce que celui-ci s'arrogeoit le titre d'imam, et envoyoit des lettres de tous côtés pour se faire reconnoître pour tel. Kia Buzurc-umid lui avoit d'abord écrit une lettre remplie d'avis et de représentations, pour le ramener, où avoir une preuve de son crime. Abou-Haschem donna pour toute réponse, que la secte des Ismaéliens professoit une doctrine qui renfermoit l'incrédulité, l'hérésie et le *zindaka* (ou magisme). Les *Réfiks* entrèrent donc dans le Dilem, et combattirent contre Abou-Haschem, qui fut mis en fuite, et se cacha dans une forêt: mais les *Réfiks* l'ayant poursuivi, se rendirent maîtres de sa personne; et après l'avoir vivement réprimand", ils le brûlèrent.

On voit, par ces extraits, que Mirkhond distingue les *Réfiks* ou *Réfikis* des *Daïs* et des *Fédaïs*. Je pense que les *Réfiks* sont tous les membres de la secte, à l'exclusion des *Daïs,* qui formoient le clergé, et des *Fédaïs,* qui étoient consacrés d'une manière particulière au ministère d'assassin.

Je ne sais si cette distinction ne doit pas aussi s'appliquer au nom de *Haschischis*. Je n'ai pas rencontré assez de passages où ce mot soit employé, pour avoir à cet égard une opinion assurée; mais je suis porté à croire que, chez les Ismaéliens, on ne nommoit *Haschischi* ou *Hasschasch*, que les gens que l'on élevoit spécialement pour la fonction d'assassin, et que l'on disposoit, par l'usage du *haschisch*, à cette résignation absolue aux volontés de leur chef. Cela n'aura point empêché que chez les autres peuples, et surtout chez les Occidentaux, cette dénomination n'ait été étendue à tous les Ismaéliens.

Il est vraisemblalbe que la secte des Ismaéliens a pu encore être connue sous quelques autres noms; car Schahristani dit que chez chaque nation elle a une dénomination différente. Abraham

Ecchellensis dit qu'on les appelle *Tatili* تعطيلي ; ce qui n'est pas sans vaisemblance, ce nom signifiant un partisan du dogme du *tatil* تعطيل , qui consiste à dépouiller Dieu de tout attribut, et qui se réduit au plus pur déisme, et va preque justqu'à l'athéisme. Suivant M. Muradjea, on les nomme aussi *Huméiri* حميرى , du nom de leur chef Hasan ben-Sabbah, surnommé *Homéiri.* Je n'ai, au surplus, trouvé aucune trace de cette dénomination.

Je finirai ce *Mémoire* par l'indication d'un passage du *Voyage* de M. Niebuhr, qui nous apprend qu'il existe encore des Ismaéliens en Syrie, et par l'extrait d'une lettre que M. Rousseau fils m'a écrite de Téhéran, en date du 1.er juin 1808.

«J'ai recueilli des notions assez exactes sur les Baténiens ou Ismaéliens nommés vulgairement *Mélahédèhs,* secte qui subsiste encore, et qui est répandue et tolérée, comme tant d'autres, dans les provinces de la Perse et dans le Sind. Comme j'ai très-peu de loisir, je vous prie d'agréer que je remette à un autre temps le soin de vous en entretenir d'une manière détaillée. Il est bon que je vous dise, en attendant, que ces *Mélahédèhs* ont, jusqu'aujourd'hui, leur imam ou pontife, qui descend, selon eux, de Djafar Sadek, chef de leur secte, et qui réside à Kéhek, village du district de Khom. Il s'appelle Scheïkh Khalil-allah, et a succédé dans l'imamat à Mirza Abou'lhasan son oncle, qui joua un grand rôle sous le règne des Zends. Le gouvernement persan ne l'inquiète point, parce qu'il en retire des revenus annuels. Aussi ce personnage, décoré par les siens du titre pompeux de khalife, jouit-il d'une grande reputation, et passe-t-il pour avoir le don des miracles. On m'a assuré que des Indiens musulmans viennent habituellement des bords de l'Indus pour recevoir ses bénédictions, en échange des riches et pieuses offrandes qu'ils lui apportent. Les Persans le connoissent plus particulièrement sous le nom de *Séid Kéheki.*»

4

THE HERO AS PROPHET. MAHOMET: ISLAM

Thomas Carlyle

From the first rude times of Paganism among the Scandinavians in the North, we advance to a very different epoch of religion, among a very different people: Mahometanism among the Arabs. A great change; what a change and progress is indicated here, in the universal condition and thoughts of men.

The Hero is not now regarded as a God among his fellow men; but as one god-inspired, as a Prophet. It is the second phasis of Hero-worship: the first or oldest, we may say, has passed away without return; in the history of the world there will not again be any man, never so great, whom his fellow men will take for a god. Nay we might rationally ask, Did any set of human beings ever really think the man they *saw* there standing beside them a god, the maker of this world? Perhaps not: it was usually some man they remembered, or *had* seen. But neither can this any more be. The Great Man is not recognised henceforth as a god any more.

It was a rude gross error, that of counting the Great Man a god. Yet let us say that it is at all times difficult to know *what* he is, or how to account of him and receive him! The most significant feature in the history of an epoch is the manner it has of welcoming a Great Man. Ever, to the true instincts of men, there is something godlike in him. Whether they shall take him to be a god, to be a prophet, or what they shall take him to be? that is ever a grand question; by their way of answering that, we shall see, as through a little window, into the very heart of these men's spiritual condition. For at bottom the Great Man, as he comes

Source: Carlyle, T., *On Heroes, Hero-Worship and the Heroic in History*, 1840, London, Chapman and Hall, pp. 39–71 (Lecture II).

from the hand of Nature, is ever the same kind of thing: Odin, Luther, Johnson, Burns; I hope to make it appear that these are all originally of one stuff; that only by the world's reception of them, and the shapes they assume, are they so immeasurably diverse. The worship of Odin astonishes us—to fall prostrate before the Great Man, into *deliquium* of love and wonder over him, and feel in their hearts that he was a denizen of the skies, a god! This was imperfect enough: but to welcome, for example, a Burns as we did, was that what we can call perfect? The most precious gift that Heaven can give to the Earth; a man of 'genius' as we call it; the Soul of a Man actually sent down from the skies with a God's-message to us—this we waste away as an idle artificial firework, sent to amuse us a little, and sink it into ashes, wreck and ineffectuality: *such* reception of a Great Man I do not call very perfect either! Looking into the heart of the thing, one may perhaps call that of Burns a still uglier phenomenon, betokening still sadder imperfections in mankind's ways, than the Scandinavian method itself! To fall into mere unreasoning *deliquium* of love and admiration, was not good; but such unreasoning, nay irrational supercilious no-love at all is perhaps still worse!—It is a thing forever changing, this of Hero-worship: different in each age, difficult to do well in any age. Indeed, the heart of the whole business of the age, one may say, is to do it well.

We have chosen Mahomet not as the most eminent Prophet, but as the one we are freest to speak of. He is by no means the truest of Prophets; but I do esteem him a true one. Farther, as there is no danger of our becoming, any of us, Mahometans, I mean to say all the good of him I justly can. It is the way to get at his secret: let us try to understand what *he* meant with the world; what the world meant and means with him, will then be a more answerable question. Our current hypothesis about Mahomet, that he was a scheming Impostor, a Falsehood incarnate, that his religion is a mere mass of quackery and fatuity, begins really to be now untenable to any one. The lies, which well-meaning zeal has heaped round this man, are disgraceful to ourselves only. When Pococke inquired of Grotius, Where the proof was of that story of the pigeon, trained to pick peas from Mahomet's ear, and pass for an angel dictating to him? Grotius answered that there was no proof! It is really time to dismiss all that. The word this man spoke has been the life-guidance now of a hundred-and-eighty millions of men these twelve-hundred years.

These hundred-and-eighty millions were made by God as well as we. A greater number of God's creatures believe in Mahomet's word at this hour than in any other word whatever. Are we to suppose that it was a miserable piece of spiritual legerdemain, this which so many creatures of the Almighty have lived by and died by? I, for my part, cannot form any such supposition. I will believe most things sooner than that. One would be entirely at a loss what to think of this world at all, if quackery so grew and were sanctioned here.

Alas, such theories are very lamentable. If we would attain to knowledge of anything in God's true Creation, let us disbelieve them wholly! They are the product of an Age of Scepticism; they indicate the saddest spiritual paralysis, and mere death-life of the souls of men: more godless theory, I think, was never promulgated in this earth. A false man found a religion? Why, a false man cannot build a brick house! If he do not know and follow *truly* the properties of mortar, burnt clay and what else he works in, it is no house that he makes, but a rubbish-heap. It will not stand for twelve centuries, to lodge a hundred-and-eighty millions; it will fall straightway. A man must conform himself to Nature's laws, *be* verily in communion with Nature and the truth of things, or Nature will answer him, No, not at all! Speciosities are specious—ah me!—a Cagliostro, many Cagliostros, prominent world-leaders, do prosper by their quackery, for a day. It is like a forged bank-note; they get it passed out of *their* worthless hands: others, not they, have to smart for it. Nature bursts-up in fire-flames, French Revolutions and such-like, proclaiming with terrible veracity that forged notes are forged.

But of a Great Man especially, of him I will venture to assert that it is incredible he should have been other than true. It seems to me the primary foundation of him, and of all that can lie in him, this. No Mirabeau, Napoleon, Burns, Cromwell, no man adequate to do anything, but is first of all in right earnest about; what I call a sincere man. I should say *sincerity*, a deep, great, genuine sincerity, is the first characteristic of all men in any way heroic. Not the sincerity that calls itself sincere; ah no, that is a very poor matter indeed—a shallow braggart conscious sincerity; oftenest self-conceit mainly. The Great Man's sincerity is of the kind he cannot speak of, is not conscious of: nay, I suppose, he is conscious rather of *in*sincerity; for what man can walk accurately by the law of truth for one day? No, the Great Man does not boast himself sincere, far from that; perhaps does not ask himself if he is so: I would say rather, his sincerity does not depend on himself; he cannot help being sincere! The great Fact of Existence is great to him. Fly as he will, he cannot get out of the awful presence of this Reality. His mind is so made; he is great by that, first of all. Fearful and wonderful, real as Life, real as Death, is this Universe to him. Though all men should forget its truth, and walk in a vain show, he cannot. At all moments the Flame-image glares-in upon him; undeniable, there, there!—I wish you to take this as my primary definition of a Great Man. A little man may have this, it is competent to all men that God has made: but a Great Man cannot be without it.

Such a man is what we call an *original* man; he comes to us at first-hand. A messenger he, sent from the Infinite Unknown with tidings to us. We may call him Poet, Prophet, God—in one way or other, we all feel that the words he utters are as no other man's words. Direct from the Inner Fact of things;—he lives, and has to live, in daily communion with that. Hearsays cannot hide it from him; he is blind, homeless, miserable, following hearsays; *it* glares-in upon him. Really his utterances, are they not a kind of 'revelation'—what we must call such for want of some other name? It is from the heart of the world that he comes; he is portion of the primal reality of things. God has made many revelations: but this man too, has not God made him, the latest and newest of all? The 'inspiration of the Almighty giveth *him* understanding': we must listen before all to him.

This Mahomet, then, we will in no wise consider as an Inanity and Theatricality, a poor conscious ambitious schemer; we cannot conceive him so. The rude message he delivered was a real one withal; an earnest confused voice from the unknown Deep. The man's words were not false, nor his workings here below; no Inanity and Simulacrum; a fiery mass of Life cast-up from the great bosom of Nature herself. To *kindle* the world; the world's Maker had ordered it so. Neither can the faults, imperfections, insincerities even, of Mahomet, if such were never so well proved against him, shake this primary fact about him.

On the whole, we make too much of faults; the details of the business hide the real centre of it. Faults? The greatest of faults, I should say, is to be conscious of none. Readers of the Bible above all, one would think, might know better. Who is called there 'the man according to God's own heart'? David, the Hebrew King, had fallen into sins enough; blackest crimes; there was no want of sins. And thereupon the unbelievers sneer and ask, Is this your man according to God's heart? The sneer, I must say, seems to me but a shallow one. What are faults, what are the outward details of a life; if the inner secret of it, the remorse, temptations, true, often-baffled, never-ended struggle of it, be forgotten? 'It is not in man that walketh to direct his steps.' Of all acts, is not, for a man, *repentance* the most divine? The deadliest sin, I say, were that same supercilious consciousness of no sin—that is death; the heart so conscious is divorced from sincerity, humility and fact; is dead: it is 'pure' as dead dry sand is pure. David's life and history, as written for us in those Psalms of his, I consider to be the truest emblem ever given of a man's moral progress and warfare here below. All earnest souls will ever discern in it the faithful struggle of an earnest human soul towards what is good and best. Struggle often baffled, sore baffled, down as into entire wreck; yet a struggle never ended; ever, with tears, repentance, true unconquerable purpose, begun anew. Poor human nature! Is not a man's walking, in truth, always that: 'a succession of falls'? Man can do no other. In this wild element of a Life, he has to struggle onwards; now fallen, deep-abased; and ever, with tears, repentance, with bleeding heart, he has to rise again, struggle again still onwards. That his struggle *be* a faithful unconquerable one: that is the question of questions. We will put-up with many sad details, if the soul of it were true. Details by themselves will never teach us what it is. I believe we misestimate Mahomet's faults even as faults: but the secret of him will never be got by dwelling there. We will leave all this behind us; and assuring ourselves that he did mean some true thing, ask candidly what it was or might be.

These Arabs Mahomet was born among are certainly a notable people. Their country itself is notable; the fit habitation for such a race. Savage inaccessible rock-mountains, great grim deserts, alternating with beautiful strips of verdure: wherever water is, there is greenness, beauty; odoriferous balm-shrubs, date-trees, frankincense-trees. Consider that wide waste horizon of sand, empty, silent, like a sand-sea, dividing habitable place from habitable. You are all alone there, left alone with the Universe; by day a fierce sun blazing down on it with intolerable radiance; by night the great deep Heaven with its stars. Such a country is fit for a swift-handed, deep-hearted race of men. There is something most agile, active, and yet most meditative, enthusiastic in the Arab character. The Persians are called the French of the East; we will call the Arabs Oriental Italians. A gifted noble people; a people of wild strong feelings, and of iron restraint over these: the characteristic of noblemindedness, or genius. The wild Bedouin welcomes the stranger to his tent, as one having right to all that is there; were it his worst enemy, he will slay his foal to treat him, will serve him with sacred hospitality for three days, will set him fairly on his way—and then, by another law as sacred, kill him if he can. In words too, as in action. They are not a loquacious people, taciturn rather; but eloquent, gifted when they do speak. An earnest, truthful kind of men. They are, as we know, of Jewish kindred: but with that deadly terrible earnestness of the Jews they seem to combine something graceful, brilliant, which is not Jewish. They had 'Poetic contests' among them before the time of Mahomet. Sale says, at Ocadh, in the South of Arabia, there were yearly fairs, and there, when the merchandising was done, Poets sang for prizes—the wild people gathered to hear that.

One Jewish quality these Arabs manifest; the outcome of many or of all high qualities: what we may call religiosity. From of old they had been zealous worshippers, according to their light. They worshipped the stars, as Sabeans; worshipped many natural objects—recognised them as symbols, immediate manifestations, of the Maker of Nature. It was wrong; and yet not wholly wrong. All God's works are still in a sense symbols of God. Do we not, as I urged, still account it a merit to recognise a certain inexhaustible significance, 'poetic beauty' as we name it, in all natural objects whatsoever? A man is a poet, and honoured, for doing that, and speaking or singing it—a king of diluted worship. They had many Prophets, these Arabs; Teachers each to his tribe, each according to the light he had. But indeed, have we not from of old the noblest of proofs, still palpable to every one of us, of what devoutness and noblemindedness had dwelt in these rustic thoughtful peoples? Biblical critics seem agreed that our own *Book of Job* was written in that region of the world. I call that, apart from all theories about it, one of the grandest things ever written with pen. One feels, indeed, as if it were not Hebrew; such a noble university, different from noble patriotism or sectarianism, reigns in it. A noble Book; all men's book! It is our first, oldest statement of the never-ending Problem—man's destiny, and god's ways with him here in this earth. And all in such free flowing outlines; grand in its sincerity, in its simplicity; in its epic melody, and repose of reconcilement. There is the seeing eye, the mildly understanding heart. So *true* everyway; true eyesight and vision for all things; material things no less than spiritual: the Horse—

'hast thou clothed his neck with *thunder*?'—he '*laughs* at the shaking of the spear!' Such living likenesses were never since drawn. Sublime sorrow, sublime reconciliation; oldest choral melody as of the heart of mankind—so soft, and great; as the summer midnight, as the world with its seas and stars! There is nothing written, I think, in the Bible or out of it, of equal literary merit.

To the idolatrous Arabs one of the most ancient universal objects of worship was that Black Stone, still kept in the building called Caabah at Mecca. Diodorus Siculus mentions this Caabah in a way not to be mistaken, as the oldest, most honoured temple in his time; that is, some half-century before our Era. Silvestre de Sacy says there is some likelihood that the Black Stone is an aerolite. In that case, some man might *see* it fall out of Heaven! It stands now beside the Well Zemzem; the Caabah is built over both. A Well is in all places a beautiful affecting object, gushing out like life from the hard earth—still more so in those hot dry countries, where it is the first condition of being. The Well Zemzem has its name from the bubbling sound of the waters, *zem-zem*; they think it is the Well which Hagar found with her little Ishmael in the wilderness: the aerolite and it have been sacred now, and had a Caabah over them, for thousands of years. A curious object, that Caabah! There it stands at this hour, in the black cloth covering the Sultan sends it yearly; 'twenty-seven cubits high;' with circuit, with double circuit of pillars, with festoon-rows of lamps and quaint ornaments: the lamps will be lighted again *this* night—to glitter again under the stars. An authentic fragment of the oldest Past. It is the *Keblah* of all Moslem: from Delhi all onwards to Morocco, the eyes of innumerable praying men are turned towards *it*, five times, this day and all days: one of the notablest centres in the Habitation of Men.

It had been from the sacredness attached to this Caabah Stone and Hagar's Well, from the pilgrimings of all tribes of Arabs thither, that Mecca took its rise as a Town. A great town once, though much decayed now. It has no natural advantage for a town; stands in a sandy hollow amid bare barren hills, at a distance from the sea; its provisions, its very bread, have to be imported. But so many pilgrims needed lodgings: and then all places of pilgrimage do, from the first, become places of trade. The first day pilgrims meet, merchants have also met: where men see themselves assembled for one object, they find that they can accomplish other objects which depend on meeting together. Mecca became the Fair of all Arabia. And thereby indeed the chief staple and warehouse of whatever Commerce there was between the Indian and the Western countries, Syria, Egypt, even Italy. It had at one time a population of 100,000; buyers, forwarders of those Eastern and Western products; importers for their own behoof of provisions and corn. The government was a kind of irregular aristocratic republic, not without a touch of theocracy. Ten Men of a chief tribe, chosen in some rough way, were Governors of Mecca, and Keepers of the Caabah. The Koreish were the chief tribe in Mahomet's time; his own family was of that tribe. The rest of the Nation, fractioned and cut-asunder by deserts, lived under similar rude patriarchal governments by one or several: herdsmen, carriers, traders, generally robbers too; being oftenest at war one with another, or with all: held together by no open bond, if it were not this meeting at the Caabah, where all forms of Arab Idolatry assembled in common adoration—held mainly by the *inward* indissoluble bond of a common blood and language. In this way had the Arabs lived for long ages, unnoticed by the world; a people of great qualities, unconsciously waiting for the day when they should become notable to all the world. Their Idolatries appear to have been in a tottering state; much was getting into confusion and fermentation among them. Obscure tidings of the most important Event ever transacted in this world, the Life and Death of the Divine Man in Judea, at once the symptom and cause of immeasurable change to all people in the world had in the course of centuries reached into Arabia too; and could not but, of itself, have produced fermentation there.

It was among this Arab people, so circumstanced, in the year 570 of our Era, that the man Mahomet was born. He was of the family of Hashem, of the Koreish tribe as we said; though poor, connected with the chief persons of his country. Almost at his birth he lost his Father; at the age of six years his Mother too, a woman noted for her beauty, her worth and sense: he fell to the charge of his Grandfather, an old man, a hundred years old. A good old man: Mahomet's Father, Abdallah, had been his youngest favourite son. He saw in Mahomet, with his old life-worn eyes, a century old, the lost Abdallah come back again, all that was left of Abdallah. He loved the little orphan Boy greatly; used to say, They must take care of that beautiful little Boy, nothing in their kindred was more precious than he. At his death, while the Boy was still but two years old, he left him in charge to Abu Thaleb the eldest of the Uncles, as to him that now was head of the house. By this Uncle, a just and rational man as everything betokens, Mahomet was brought-up in the best Arab way.

Mahomet, as he grew up, accompanied his Uncle on trading journeys and suchlike; in his eighteenth year one finds him a fighter following his Uncle in war. But perhaps the most significant of all his journeys is one we find noted as of some years' earlier date: a journey to the Fairs of Syria. The young man here first came in contact with a quite foreign world—with one foreign element of endless moment to him: the Christian Religion. I know not what to make of that 'Sergius, the Nestorian Monk,' whom Abu Thaleb and he are said to have lodged with; or how much any monk could have taught one still so young. Probably enough it is greatly exaggerated, this of the Nestorian Monk. Mahomet was only fourteen; had no language but his own: much in Syria must have been a strange unintelligible whirlpool to him. But the eyes of the lad were open; glimpses of many things would doubtless be taken-in, and lie very enigmatic as yet, which were to ripen in a strange way into views, into beliefs and insights one day. These journeys to Syria were probably the beginning of much to Mahomet.

One other circumstance we must not forget: that he had no school-learning; of the thing we call school-learning none at all. The art of writing was but just introduced into Arabia; it seems to be the true opinion that Mahomet never could write! Life in the Desert, with its experiences, was all his education. What of this infinite Universe he, from his dim place, with his own eyes and thoughts, could take in, so much and no more of it was he to know. Curious, if we will reflect on it, this of having no books. Except by what he could see for himself, or hear of by uncertain rumour of speech in the obscure Arabian Desert, he could know nothing. The wisdom that had been before him or at a distance from him in the world, was in a manner as good as not there for him. Of the great brother souls, flame-beacons through so many lands and times, no one directly communicates with this great soul. He is alone there, deep down in the bosom of the Wilderness; has to grow up so—alone with Nature and his own Thoughts.

But, from an early age, he had been remarked as a thoughtful man. His companions named him '*Al Amin*, The Faithful.' A man of truth and fidelity; true in what he did, in what he spake and thought. They noted that *he* always meant something. A man rather taciturn in speech; silent when there was nothing to be said; but pertinent, wise, sincere, when he did speak; always throwing light on the matter. This is the only sort of speech *worth* speaking! Through life we find him to have been regarded as an altogether solid, brotherly, genuine man. A serious, sincere character; yet amiable, cordial, companionable, jocose even—a good laugh in him withal: there are men whose laugh is as untrue as anything about them; who cannot laugh. One hears of Mahomet's beauty: his fine sagacious honest face, brown florid complexion, beaming black eyes—I somehow like too that vein on the brow, which swelled-up black when he was in anger: like the '*horse-show* vein' in Scott's *Redgauntlet*. It was a kind of feature in the Hashem family, this black swelling vein in the brow; Mahomet had it prominent, as would appear. A spontaneous, passionate, yet just, true-meaning man! Full of wild faculty, fire and light; of wild worth, all uncultured; working out his life-task in the depths of the Desert there.

How he was placed with Kadijah, a rich Widow, as her Steward, and travelled in her business, again to the Fairs of Syria; how he managed all, as one can well understand, with fidelity, adroitness; how her gratitude, her regard for him grew: the story of their marriage is altogether a graceful intelligible one, as told us by the Arab authors. He was twenty-five; she forty, though still beautiful. He seems to have lived in a most affectionate, peaceable, wholesome way with this wedded benefactress; loving her truly, and her alone. It goes greatly against the impostor theory, the fact that he lived in this entirely unexceptionable, entirely quiet and commonplace way, till the heat of his years was done. He was forty before he talked of any mission from Heaven. All his irregularities, real and supposed, date from after his fiftieth year, when the good Kadijah died. All his 'ambition,' seemingly, had been, hitherto, to live an honest life; his 'fame,' the mere good opinion of neighbours that knew him, had been sufficient hitherto. Not till he was already getting old, the prurient heat of his life all burnt out, and *peace* growing to be the chief thing this world could give him, did he start on the 'career of ambition;' and, belying all his past character and existence, set-up as a wretched empty charlatan to acquire what he could now no longer enjoy! For my share, I have no faith whatever in that.

Ah no; this deep-hearted Son of the Wilderness, with his beaming black eyes and open social deep soul, had other thoughts in him than ambition. A silent great soul; he was one of those who cannot *but* be in earnest; whom Nature herself has appointed to be sincere. While others walk in formulas and hearsays, contented enough to dwell there, this man could not screen himself in formulas; he was alone with his own soul and the reality of things. The great Mystery of Existence, as I said, glared-in upon him, with its terrors, with its splendours: no hearsays could hide that unspeakable fact, 'Here am I!' Such *sincerity*, as we named it, has in very truth something of divine. The word of such a man is a Voice direct from Nature's own Heart. Men do and must listen to that as to nothing else—all else is wind in comparison. From of old, a thousand thoughts, in his pilgrimings and wanderings, had been in this man: What am I? What *is* this unfathomable Thing I live in, which men name Universe? What is Life; what is Death? What am I to believe? What am I to do? The grim rocks of Mount Hara, of Mount Sinai, the stern sandy solitudes answered not. The great Heaven rolling silent overhead, with its blue-glancing stars, answered not. There was no answer. The man's own soul, and what of God's inspiration dwelt there, had to answer!

It is the thing which all men have to ask themselves; which we too have to ask, and answer. This wild man felt it to be of *infinite* moment; all other things of no moment whatever in comparison. The jargon of argumentative Greek Sects, vague traditions of Jews, the stupid routine of Arab Idolatry: there was no answer in these. A Hero, as I repeat, has this first distinction, which indeed we may call first and last, the Alpha and Omega of his whole Heroism, That he looks through the shows of things into *things*. Use and wont, respectable hearsay, respectable formula: all these are good, or are not good. There is something behind and beyond all these, which all these must correspond with, be the image of, or they are—*Idolatries*; 'bits of black wood pretending to be God;' to the earnest soul a mockery and abomination. Idolatries never so gilded, waited on by heads of the Koreish, will do nothing for this man. Though all men walk by them, what good is it? The great Reality stands glaring there upon *him*. He there has to answer it, or perish miserably. Now, even now, or else through all Eternity never! Answer it; *thou* must find an answer. Ambition? What could all Arabia do for this man; with the crown of Greek Heraclius, of Persian Chosroes, and all crowns in the Earth—what could they all do for him? It was not of the Earth he wanted to hear tell; it was of the Heaven above and of the Hell beneath. All crowns and sovereignties whatsoever, where could *they* in a few brief years be? To be Sheik of Mecca or Arabia, and have a bit of gilt wood put into your hand—will that be one's salvation? I decidedly think, not. We will leave it altogether, this impostor hypothesis, as not credible; not very tolerable even, worthy chiefly of dismissal by us.

Mahomet had been wont to retire yearly, during the month Ramadhan, into solitude and silence; as indeed was the Arab custom; a praiseworthy custom, which such a man, above all, would find natural and useful. Communing with his own heart, in the silence of the mountains; himself silent; open to the 'small still voices:' it was a right natural custom! Mahomet was in his fortieth year, when having withdrawn to a cavern in Mount Hara, near Mecca, during this Ramadhan, to pass the month in prayer, and meditation on those great questions, he one day told his wife Kadijah, who with his household was with him or near him this year, That by the unspeakable special favour of Heaven he had now found it all out; was in doubt and darkness no longer, but saw it all. That all these Idols and Formulas were nothing, miserable bits of wood; that there was One God in and over all; and we must leave all Idols, and look to Him. That God is great; and that there is nothing else great! He is the Reality. Wooden Idols are not real; He is real. He made us at first, sustains us yet; we and all things are but the shadow of Him; a transitory garment veiling the Eternal Splendour. '*Allah akbar*, God is great'—and then also '*Islam*,' that we must *submit* to God. That our whole strength lies in resigned submission to Him, whatsoever he do to us. For this world, and for the other! The thing He sends to us, were it death and worse than death, shall be good, shall be best; we resign ourselves to God. 'If this be *Islam*,' says Goethe, 'do we not all live in *Islam*? Yes, all of us that have any moral life; we all live so. It has ever been held the highest wisdom for a man not merely to submit to Necessity—Necessity will make him submit—but to know and believe well that the stern thing which Necessity had ordered was the wisest, the best, the thing wanted there. To cease his frantic pretension of scanning this great God's-World in his small fraction of a brain; to know that it *had* verily, though deep beyond his soundings, a Just Law, that the soul of it was Good—that his part in it was to conform to the Law of the Whole, and in devout silence follow that; not questioning it, obeying it as unquestionable.

I say, this is yet the only true morality known. A man is right and invincible, virtuous and on the road towards sure conquest, precisely while he joins himself to the great deep Law of the

World, in spite of all superficial laws, temporary appearances, profit-and-loss calculations; he is victorious while he coöperates with that great central Law, not victorious otherwise and surely his first chance of coöperating with it, or getting into the course of it, is to know with his whole soul that it *is*; that it is good, and alone good! This is the soul of Islam; it is properly the soul of Christianity—for Islam is definable as a confused form of Christianity; had Christianity not been, neither had it been. Christianity also commands us, before all, to be resigned to God. We are to take no counsel with flesh-and-blood; give ear to no vain cavils, vain sorrows and wishes: to know that we know nothing; that the worst and cruelest to our eyes is not what it seems; that we have to receive whatsoever befalls us as sent from God above, and say, It is good and wise, God is great! 'Though He slay me, yet will I trust in Him.' Islam means in its way Denial of Self, Annihilation of Self. This is yet the highest Wisdom that Heaven has revealed to our Earth.

Such light had come, as it could, to illuminate the darkness of this wild Arab soul. A confused dazzling splendour as of life and Heaven, in the great darkness which threatened to be death: he called it revelation and the angel Gabriel—who of us yet can know what to call it? It is the 'inspiration of the Almighty that giveth us understanding. To *know*; to get into the truth of anything, is ever a mystic act—of which the best Logics can but babble on the surface. 'Is not Belief the true god-announcing Miracle?' says Novalis. That Mahomet's whole soul, set in flame with this grand Truth vouchsafed him, should feel as if it were important and the only important thing, was very natural. That Providence had unspeakably honoured *him* by revealing it, saving him from death and darkness; that he therefore was bound to make known the same to all creatures: this is what was meant by 'Mahomet is the Prophet of God;' this too is not without its true meaning.

The good Kadijah, we can fancy, listened to him with wonder, with doubt: at length she answered: Yes, it was *true* this that he said. One can fancy too the boundless gratitude of Mahomet; and how of all the kindnesses she had done him, this of believing the earnest struggling word he now spoke was the greatest. 'It is certain,' says Novalis, 'my Conviction gains infinitely, the moment another soul will believe in it.' It is a boundless favour. He never forgot this good Kadijah. Long afterwards, Ayesha his young favourite wife, a woman who indeed distinguished herself among the Moslem, by all manner of qualities, through her whole long life; this young brilliant Ayesha was, one day, questioning him: 'Now am not I better than Kadijah? She was a widow; old, and had lost her looks: you love me better than you did her?' 'No, by Allah!' answered Mahomet: 'No, by Allah! She believed in me when none else would believe. In the whole world I had but one friend, and she was that!' Seid, his Slave, also believed in him; these with his young Cousin Ali, Abu Thaleb's son, were his first converts.

He spoke of his Doctrine to this man and that; but the most treated it with ridicule, with indifference; in three years, I think, he had gained but thirteen followers. His progress was slow enough. His encouragement to go on, was altogether the usual encouragement that such a man in such a case meets. After some three years of small success, he invited forty of his chief kindred to an entertainment; and there stood-up and told them what his pretension was: that he had this thing to promulgate abroad to all men; that it was the highest thing, the one thing: which of them would second him in that? Amid the doubt and silence of all, young Ali, as yet a lad of sixteen, impatient of the silence, started-up, and exclaimed in passionate fierce language, That he would! The assembly, among whom was Abu Thaleb, Ali's Father, could not be unfriendly to Mahomet; yet the sight there, of one unlettered elderly man, with a lad of sixteen, deciding on such an enterprise against all mankind, appeared ridiculous to them; the assembly broke-up in laughter. Nevertheless it proved not a laughable thing; it was a very serious thing! As for this young Ali, one cannot but like him. A noble-minded creature, as he shows himself, now and always afterwards; full of affection, of fiery daring. Something chivalrous in him; brave as a lion; yet with a grace, a truth and affection worthy of Christian knighthood. He died by assassination in the Mosque at Bagdad; a death occasioned by his own generous fairness, confidence in the fairness of others: he said, If the wound proved not unto death, they must pardon the Assassin; but if it did, then they must slay him straightway, that so they two in the same hour might appear before God, and see which side of that quarrel was the just one!

Mahomet naturally gave offence to the Koreish, Keepers of the Caabah, superintendents of the Idols. One or two men of influence had joined him: the thing spread slowly, but it was spreading. Naturally he gave offence to everybody. Who is this that pretends to be wiser than we all; that rebukes us all, as mere fools and worshippers of wood! Abu Thaleb the good Uncle spoke with him:

Could he not be silent about all that; believe it all for himself, and not trouble others, anger the chief men, endanger himself and them all, talking of it? Mahomet answered: If the Sun stood on his right hand and the Moon on his left, ordering him to hold his peace, he could not obey! No: there was something in this Truth he had got which was of Nature herself; equal in rank to Sun, or Moon, or whatsoever thing Nature had made. It was speak itself there, so long as the Almighty allowed it, in spite of Sun and Moon, and all Koreish and all men and things. It must do that, and could do no other. Mahomet answered so; and, they say, 'burst into tears.' Burst into tears: he felt that Abu Thaleb was good to him; that the task he had got was no soft, but a stern and great one.

He went on speaking to who would listen to him; publishing his Doctrine among the pilgrims as they came to Mecca; gaining adherents in this place and that. Continual contradiction, hatred, open or secret danger attended him. His powerful relations protected Mahomet himself; but by and by, on his own advice, all his adherents had to quit Mecca, and seek refuge in Abyssinia over the sea. The Koreish grew ever angrier; laid plots, and swore oaths among them, to put Mahomet to death with their own hands. Abu Thaleb was dead, the good Kadijah was dead. Mahomet is not solicitous of sympathy from us; but his outlook at this time was one of the dismalest. He had to hide in caverns, escape in disguise; fly hither and thither; homeless, in continual peril of his life. More than once it seemed all-over with him; more than once it turned on a straw, some rider's horse taking fright or the like, whether Mahomet and his Doctrine had not ended there, and not been heard of at all. But it was not to end so.

In the thirteenth year of his mission, finding his enemies all banded against him, forty sworn men, one out of every tribe, waiting to take his life, and no continuance possible at Mecca for him any longer, Mahomet fled to the place then called Yathreb, where he had gained some adherents; the place they now call Medina, or '*Medinal al Nabi*, the City of the Prophet,' from that circumstance. It lay some 200 miles off, through rocks and deserts; not without great difficulty, in such mood as we may fancy, he escaped thither, and found welcome. The whole East dates its era from this Flight, *Hegira* as they name it: the Year I of this Hegira is 622 of our Era, the fifty-third of Mahomet's life. He was now becoming an old man; his friends sinking round him one by one; his path desolate, encompassed with danger: unless he could find hope in his own heart, the outward face of things was but hopeless for him. It is so with all men in the like case. Hitherto Mahomet had professed to publish his Religion by the way of preaching and persuasion alone. But now, driven foully out of his native country, since unjust men had not only given no ear to his earnest Heaven's-message, the deep cry of his heart, but would not even let him live if he kept speaking it—the wild Son of the Desert resolved to defend himself, like a man and Arab. If the Koreish will have it so, they shall have it. Tidings, felt to be of infinite moment to them and all men, they would not listen to these; would trample them down by sheer violence, steel and murder: well, let steel try it then! Ten years more this Mahomet had; all of fighting, of breathless impetuous toil and struggle; with what result we know.

Much has been said of Mahomet's propagating his Religion by the sword. It is no doubt far nobler what we have to boast of the Christian Religion, that it propagated itself peaceably in the way of preaching and conviction. Yet withal, if we take this for an argument of the truth or falsehood of a religion, there is a radical mistake in it. The sword indeed: but where will you get your sword! Every new opinion, at its starting, is precisely in a *minority of one.* In one man's head alone, there it dwells as yet. One man alone of the whole world believes it; there is one man against all men. That *he* take a sword, and try to propagate with that, will do little for him. You must first get your sword! On the whole, a thing will propagate itself as it can. We do not find, of the Christian Religion either, that it always disdained the sword, when once it had got one. Charlemagne's conversion of the Saxons was not by preaching. I care little about the sword: I will allow a thing to struggle for itself in this world, with any sword or tongue or implement it has, or can lay hold of. We will let it preach, and pamphleteer, and fight, and to the uttermost bestir itself, and do, beak and claws, whatsoever is in it; very sure that it will, in the long-run, conquer nothing which does not deserve to be conquered. What is better than itself, it cannot put away, but only what is worse. In this great Duel, Nature herself is umpire, and can do no wrong: the thing which is deepest-rooted in Nature, what we call *truest*, that thing and not the other will be found growing at last.

Here however, in reference to much that there is in Mahomet and his success, we are to remember what an umpire Nature is; what a greatness, composure of depth and tolerance there is in her. You take wheat to cast into the Earth's bosom: your wheat may be mixed with chaff, chopped straw, barn-sweepings, dust and all imaginable rubbish; no matter: you cast it into the kind just Earth; she grows the wheat—the whole rubbish she silently absorbs, shrouds *it* in, says nothing of the rubbish. The yellow wheat is growing there; the good Earth is silent about all the rest—has silently turned all the rest to some benefit too, and makes no complaint about it! So everywhere in Nature! She is true and not a lie; and yet so great, and just, and motherly in her truth. she requires of a thing only that it *be* genuine of heart; she will protect it if so; will not, if not so. There is a soul of truth in all the things she ever gave harbour to. Alas, is not this the history of all highest Truth that comes or ever came into the world? The *body* of them all is imperfection, an element of light *in* darkness: to us they have to come embodied in mere Logic, in some merely *scientific* Theorem of the Universe; which *cannot* be complete; which cannot but be found, one day, *in*complete, erroneous, and so die and disappear. The body of all Truth dies; and yet in all, I say, there is a soul which never dies; which in new and ever-nobler embodiment lives immortal as man himself! It is the way with Nature. The genuine essence of Truth never dies. That it be genuine, a voice from the great Deep of Nature, there is the point at Nature's judgment-seat. What *we* call pure or impure, is not with her the final question. Not how much chaff is in you; but whether you have any wheat. Pure? I might say to many a man: Yes, you are pure; pure enough; but you are chaff—insincere hypothesis, hearsay, formality; you never were in contact with the great heart of the Universe at all; you are properly neither pure nor impure; you *are* nothing, Nature has no business with you.

Mahomet's Creed we called a kind of Christianity; and really, if we look at the wild rapt earnestness with which it was believed and laid to heart, I should say a better kind than that of those miserable Syrian Sects, with their vain janglings about *Homoiousion* and *Homoousion*, the head full of worthless noise, the heart empty and dead! The truth of it is embedded in portentous error and falsehood; but the truth of it makes it be believed, not the falsehood: it succeeded by its truth. A bastard kind of Christianity, but a living kind; with a heart-life in it; not dead, chopping barren logic merely! Out of all that rubbish of Arab idolatries, argumentative theologies, traditions, subtleties, rumours and hypotheses of Greeks and Jews, with their idle wire-drawings, this wild man of the Desert, with his wild sincere heart, earnest as death and life, with his great flashing natural eyesight, had seen into the kernel of the matter. Idolatry is nothing: these Wooden Idols of yours, 'ye rub them with oil and wax, and the flies stick on them'—these are wood, I tell you! They can do nothing for you; they are an impotent blasphemous pretence; a horror and abomination, if ye knew them. God alone is; God alone has power; He made us, He can kill us and keep us alive: '*Allah akbar*, God is great.' Understand that His will is the best for you; that howsoever sore to flesh-and-blood, you will find it the wisest, best: you are bound to take it so; in this world and in the next, you have no other thing that you can do!

And now if the wild idolatrous men did believe this, and with their fiery hearts lay hold of it to do it, in what form soever it came to them, I say it was well worthy of being believed. In one form or the other, I say it is still the one thing worthy of being believed by all men. Man does hereby become the high-priest of this Temple of a World. He is in harmony with the Decrees of the Author of this World; coöperating with them, not vainly withstanding them: I know, to this day, no better definition of Duty than that same. All that is *right* includes itself in this of coöperating with the real Tendency of the World: you succeed by this (the World's Tendency will succeed), you are good, and in the right course there. *Homoiousion*, *Homoousion*, vain logical jangle, then or before or at any time, may jangle itself out, and go whither and how it likes: this is the *thing* it all struggles to mean, if it would mean anything. If it do not succeed in meaning this, it means nothing. Not that Abstractions, logical Propositions, be correctly worded or incorrectly; but that living concrete Sons of Adam do lay this to heart: that is the important point. Islam devoured all these vain jangling Sects; and I think had right to do so. It was a Reality, direct from the great Heart of Nature once more. Arab idolatries, Syrian formulas, whatsoever was not equally real, had to go up in flame—mere dead *fuel*, in various senses, for this which was *fire*.

It was during these wild warfarings and strugglings, especially after the flight to Mecca, that Mahomet dictated at intervals his Sacred Book, which they name *Koran*, or *Reading*, 'Thing to be read.' This is the Work he and his disciples made so much of, asking all the world, Is not that a miracle? The Mahometans regard their Koran with a reverence which few Christians pay even to their Bible. It is admitted everywhere as the standard of all law and all practice; the thing to be gone-upon in speculation and life: the message sent direct out of Heaven, which this Earth has to conform to, and walk by; the thing to be read. Their Judges decide by it; all Moslem are bound to study it, seek in it for the light of their life. They have mosques where it is all read daily; thirty relays of priests take it up in succession, get through the whole each day. There, for twelve-hundred years, has the voice of this Book, at all moments, kept sounding through the ears and the hearts of so many men. We hear of Mahometan Doctors that had read it seventy-thousand times!

Very curious: if one sought for 'discrepancies of national taste,' here surely were the most eminent instance of that! We also can read the Koran; our Translation of it, by Sale, is known to be a very fair one. I must say, it is as toilsome reading as I ever undertook. A wearisome confused jumble, crude, incondite; endless iterations, long-windedness, entanglement; most crude, incondite—insupportable stupidity, in short! Nothing but a sense of duty could carry any European through the Koran. We read in it, as we might in the State-Paper Office, unreadable masses of lumber, that perhaps we may get some glimpses of a remarkable man. It is true we have it under disadvantages: the Arabs see more method in it than we. Mahomet's followers found the Koran lying all in fractions, as it had been written-down at first promulgation; much of it, they say, on shoulder-blades of mutton, flung pell-mell into a chest: and they published it, without any discoverable order as to time or otherwise—merely trying, as would seem, and this not very strictly, to put the longest chapters first. The real beginning of it, in that way, lies almost at the end: for the earliest portions were the shortest. Read in its historical sequence it perhaps would not be so bad. Much of it, too, they say, is rhythmic; a kind of wild chanting song, in the original. This may be a great point; much perhaps has been lost in the Translation here. Yet with every allowance, one feels it difficult to see how any mortal ever could consider this Koran as a Book written in Heaven, too good for the Earth; as a well-written book, or indeed as a *book* at all; and not a bewildered rhapsody; *written*, so far as writing goes, as badly as almost any book ever was! So much for national discrepancies, and the standard of taste.

Yet I should say, it was not unintelligible how the Arabs might so love it. When once you get this confused coil of a Koran fairly off your hands, and have it behind you at a distance, the essential type of it begins to disclose itself; and in this there is a merit quite other than the literary one. If a book come from the heart, it will contrive to reach other hearts; all art and authorcraft are of small amount to that. One would say the primary character of the Koran is this of its *genuineness*, of its being a *bona-fide* book. Prideaux, I know, and others have represented it as a mere bundle of juggleries; chapter after chapter got-up to excuse and varnish the author's successive sins, forward his ambitions and quackeries: but really it is time to dismiss all that. I do not assert Mahomet's continual sincerity: who is continually sincere? But I confess I can make nothing of the critic, in these times, who would accuse him of deceit *prepense*; of conscious deceit generally, or perhaps at all—still more, of living in a mere element of conscious deceit, and writing this Koran as a forger and juggler would have done! Every candid eye, I think, will read the Koran far otherwise than so. It is the confused ferment of a great rude human soul; rude, untutored, that cannot even read; but fervent, earnest, struggling vehemently to utter itself in words. With a kind of breathless intensity he strives to utter himself; the thoughts crowd on him pellmell: for very multitude of things to say, he can get nothing said. The meaning that is in him shapes itself into no form of composition, is stated in no sequence, method, or coherence—they are not *shaped* at all, these thoughts of his; flung-out unshaped, as they struggle and tumble there, in their chaotic inarticulate state. We said 'stupid:' yet natural stupidity is by no means the character of Mahomet's Book; it is natural uncultivation rather. The man has not studied speaking; in the haste and pressure of continual fighting, has not time to mature himself into fit speech. The panting breathless haste and vehemence of a man struggling in the thick of battle for life and salvation; this is the mood he is in! A headlong haste; for very magnitude of meaning, he cannot get himself articulated into words. The successive utterances of a soul in that mood, coloured by the various vicissitudes of three-and-twenty years; now well uttered, now worse: this is the Koran.

For we are to consider Mahomet, through these three-and-twenty years, as the centre of a world wholly in conflict. Battles with the Koreish and Heathen, quarrels among his own people, backslidings of his own wild heart; all this kept him a perpetual whirl, his soul knowing rest no more. In wakeful nights, as one may fancy, the wild soul of the man, tossing amid these vortices, would hail any light of a decision for them as a veritable light from Heaven; *any* making-up of his mind, so blessed, indispensable for him there, would seem the inspiration of a Gabriel. Forger and juggler? No, no! This great fiery heart, seething, simmering like a great furnace of thoughts, was not a juggler's. His life was a Fact to him; this God's Universe an awful Fact and Reality. He has faults enough. The man was an uncultured semi-barbarous Son of Nature, much of the Bedouin still clinging to him: we must take him for that. But for a wretched Simulacrum, a hungry Impostor without eyes or heart, practising for a mess of pottage such blasphemous swindlery, forgery of celestial documents, continual high-treason against his Maker and Self, we will not and cannot take him.

Sincerity, in all senses, seems to me the merit of the Koran; what had rendered it precious to the wild Arab men. It is, after all, the first and last merit in a book; gives rise to merits of all kinds—nay, at bottom, it alone can give rise to merit of any kind. Curiously, through these incondite masses of tradition, vituperation, complaint, ejaculation in the Koran, a vein of true direct insight, of what we might almost call poetry, is found straggling. The body of the Book is made-up of mere tradition, and as it were vehement enthusiastic extempore preaching. He returns forever to the old stories of the Prophets as they went current in the Arab memory: how Prophet after Prophet, the Prophet Abraham, the Prophet Hud, the Prophet Moses, Christian and other real and fabulous Prophets, had come to this Tribe and to that, warning men of their sin; and been received by them even as he Mahomet was—which is a great solace to him. These things he repeats ten, perhaps twenty times; again and ever again, with wearisome iteration; has never done repeating them. A brave Samuel Johnson, in his forlorn garret, might con-over the Biographies of Authors in that way! This is the great staple of the Koran. But curiously, through all this, comes ever and anon some glance as of the real thinker and seer. He has actually an eye for the world, this Mahomet: with a certain directness and rugged vigour, he brings home still, to our heart, the thing his own heart has been opened to. I make but little of his praises of Allah, which many praise; they are borrowed I suppose mainly from the Hebrew, at least they are far surpassed there. But the eye that flashes direct into the heart of things, and *sees* the truth of them; this is to me a highly interesting object. Great Nature's own gift; which she bestows on all; but which only one in the thousand does not cast sorrowfully away: it is what I call sincerity of vision; the test of a sincere heart.

Mahomet can work no miracles; he often answers impatiently: I can work no miracles. I? 'I am a Public Preacher;' appointed to preach this doctrine to all creatures. Yet the world, as we can see, had really from of old been all one great miracle to him. Look over the world, says he; is it not wonderful, the work of Allah; wholly 'a sign to you,' if your eyes were open! This Earth, God made it for you; 'appointed paths in it;' you can live in it, go to and fro on it. The clouds in the dry country of Arabia, to Mahomet they are very wonderful: Great clouds, he says, born in the deep bosom of the Upper Immensity, where do they come from? They hang there, the great black monsters; pour-down their rain-deluges 'to revive a dead earth,' and grass springs, and 'tall leafy palm-trees' with their date-clusters hanging round. Is not that a 'sign?' Your cattle too—Allah made them; serviceable dumb creatures; they change the grass into milk; you have your clothing from them, very strange creatures; they come ranking home at evening-time, 'and,' adds he, 'and are a credit to you!' Ships also—he talks often about ships: huge moving mountains, they spread-out their cloth wings, go bounding through the water there, Heaven's wind driving them; anon they lie motionless, God has withdrawn the wind, they lie dead, and cannot stir! Miracles? cries he: What miracle would you have? Are not you yourselves there? God made *you*, 'shaped you out of a little clay.' Ye were small once; a few years ago ye were not at all. Ye have beauty, strength, thoughts, 'ye have compassion on one another.' Old age comes-on you, and gray hairs; your strength fades into feebleness; ye sink down, and again are not. 'Ye have compassion on one another:' this struck me much: Allah might have made you having no compassion on one another—how had it been then! This is a great direct thought, a glance at first-hand into the very fact of things. Rude vestiges of poetic genius, of whatsoever is best and truest, are visible in this man. A strong untutored intellect; eyesight, heart: a strong wild man—might have shaped himself into Poet, King, Priest, any kind of Hero.

To his eyes it is forever clear that this world wholly is miraculous. He sees what, as we said once before, all great thinkers, the rude Scandinavians themselves, in one way or other, have contrived to see: that this so solid-looking material world is, at bottom, in very deed, Nothing; is a visual and tactual Manifestation of God's power and presence—a shadow hung-out by Him on the bosom of the void Infinite; nothing more. The mountains, he says, these great rock-mountains, they shall dissipate themselves 'like clouds'; melt into the Blue as clouds do, and not be! He figures the Earth, in the Arab fashion, Sale tells us, as an immense Plain or flat Plate of ground, the mountains are set on that to *steady* it. At the Last Day they shall disappear 'like clouds;' the whole Earth shall go spinning, whirl itself off into wreck, and as dust and vapour vanish in the Inane. Allah withdraws his hand from it, and it ceases to be. The universal empire of Allah, presence everywhere of an unspeakable Power, a Splendour, and a Terror not to be named, as the true force, essence and reality, in all things whatsoever, was continually clear to this man. What a modern talks-of by the name, Forces of Nature, Laws of Nature; and does not figure as a divine thing; not even as one thing at all, but as a set of things, undivine enough—saleable, curious, good for propelling steam-ships! With our Sciences and Cyclopædias, we are apt to forget the *divineness*, in those laboratories of ours. We ought not to forget it! That once well forgotten, I know not what else were worth remembering. Most sciences, I think, were then a very dead thing; withered, contentious, empty—a thistle in late autumn. The best science, without this, is but as the dead *timber*; it is not the growing tree and forest—which gives ever-new timber, among other things! Man cannot *know* either, unless he can *worship* in some way. His acknowledge is a pedantry, and dead thistle, otherwise.

Much has been said and written about the sensuality of Mahomet's Religion; more than was just. The indulgences, criminal to us, which he permitted, were not of his appointment; he found them practised, unquestioned from immemorial time in Arabia; what he did was to curtail them, restrict them, not on one but on many sides. His religion is not an easy one: with rigorous fasts, lavations, strict complex formulas, prayers five times a day, and abstinence from wine it did not 'succeed by being an easy religion.' As if indeed any religion, or cause holding of religion, could succeed by that! It is a calumny on men to say that they are roused to heroic action by ease, hope of pleasure, recompense—sugar-plums of any kind, in this world or the next! In the meanest mortal there lies something nobler. The poor swearing soldier, hired to be shot, has his 'honour of a solider,' different from drill-regulations and the shilling a day. It is not to taste sweet things, but to do noble and true things, and vindicate himself under God's Heaven as a god-made Man, that the poorest son of Adam dimly longs. Show him the way of doing that, the dullest daydrudge kindles into a hero. They wrong man greatly who say he is to be seduced by ease. Difficulty, abnegation, martyrdom, death are the *allurements* that act on the heart of man. Kindle the inner genial life of him, you have a flame that burns-up all lower considerations. Not happiness, but something higher: one sees this even in the frivolous classes, with their 'point of honour' and the like. Not by flattering our appetites; no, by awakening the Heroic that slumbers in every heart, can any Religion gain followers.

Mahomet himself, after all that can be said about him, was not a sensual man. We shall err widely if we consider this man as a common voluptuary, intent mainly on base enjoyments—nay on enjoyments of any kind. His household was of the frugalest; his common diet barley-bread and water: sometimes for months there was not a fire once lighted on his hearth. They record with just pride that he would mend his own shoes, patch his own cloak. A poor, hard-toiling, ill-provided man; careless of what vulgar men toil for. Not a bad man, I should say; something better in him than *hunger* of any sort—or these wild Arab men, fighting and jostling three-and-twenty years at his hand, in close contact with him always, would not have reverenced him so! They were wild men, bursting ever and anon into quarrel, into all kinds of fierce sincerity; without right worth and manhood, no man could have commanded them. They called him Prophet, you say? Why, he stood there face to face with them; bare, not enshrined in any mystery; visibly clouting his own cloak, cobbling his own shoes; fighting, counselling, ordering in the midst of them: they must have seen what kind of a man he *was*, let him be *called* what you like! No emperor with his tiaras was obeyed as this man in a cloak of his own clouting, during three-and-twenty years of rough actual trial. I find something of a veritable Hero necessary for that, of itself.

His last words are a prayer; broken ejaculations of a heart struggling-up, in trembling hope, towards its Maker. We cannot say that his religion made him *worse*; it made him better; good, not bad. Generous things are recorded of him: when he lost his Daughter, the thing he answers is, in his own dialect, everyway sincere, and yet equivalent to that of Christians, 'The Lord giveth, and the Lord taketh away; blessed be the name of the Lord.' He answered in like manner of Seid, his emancipated well-beloved Slave, the second of the believers. Seid had fallen in the War of Tabûc, the first of Mahomet's fightings with the Greeks. Mahomet said, It was well; Seid had done his Master's work, Seid had now gone to his Master: it was all well with Seid. Yet Seid's daughter found him weeping over the body—the old gray-haired man melting in tears! 'What do I see?' said she 'You see a friend weeping over his friend.' He went out for the last time into the mosque, two days before his death; asked, If he had injured any man? Let his own back bear the stripes. If he owed any man? A voice answered, 'Yes, me three drachms,' borrowed on such an occasion. Mahomet ordered them to be paid: 'Better be in shame now,' said he, 'than at the Day of Judgment.' You remember Kadijah, and the 'No, by Allah!' Traits of that kind show us the genuine man, the brother of us all, brought visible through twelve centuries—the veritable Son of our common Mother.

Withal I like Mahomet for his total freedom from cant. He is a rough self-helping son of the wilderness; does not pretend to be what he is not. There is no ostentatious pride in him; but neither does he go much upon humility: he is there as he can be, in cloak and shoes of his own clouting; speaks plainly to all manner of Persian Kings, Greek Emperors, what it is they are bound to do; knows well enough, about himself, 'the respect due unto thee.' In a life-and-death war with Bedouins, cruel things could not fail; but neither are acts of mercy, of noble natural pity and generosity wanting. Mahomet makes no apology for the one, no boast of the other. They were each the free dictate of his heart; each called-for, there and then. Not a mealy-mouthed man! A candid ferocity, if the case call for it, is in him; he does not mince matters! The War of Tabûc is a thing he often speaks of: his men refused, many of them, to march on that occasion; pleaded the heat of the weather, the harvest, and so forth; he can never forget that. Your harvest? It lasts for a day. What will become of your harvest through all Eternity? Hot weather? Yes, it was hot; 'but Hell will be hotter!' Sometimes a rough sarcasm turns-up: He says to the unbelievers, Ye shall have the just measure of your deeds at the Great Day. They will be weighed-out to you; ye shall not have short weight! Everywhere he fixes the matter in his eye; he *sees* it: his heart, now and then, is as if struck dumb by the greatness of it. 'Assuredly,' he says: that word, in the Koran, is written down sometimes as a sentence by itself: 'Assuredly.'

No *Dilettantism* in this Mahomet; it is a business of Reprobation and Salvation with him, of Time and Eternity: he is in deadly earnest about it! Dilettantism, hypothesis, speculation, a kind of amateur-search for Truth, toying and coquetting with Truth: this is the sorest sin. The root of all other imaginable sins. it consists in the heart and soul of the man never having been *open* to Truth—'living in a vain show.' Such a man not only utters and produces falsehoods, but *is* himself a falsehood. The rational moral principle, spark of the Divinity, is sunk deep in him, in quiet paralysis of life-death. The very falsehoods of Mahomet are truer than the truths of such a man. He is the insincere man: smooth-polished, respectable in some times and places; inoffensive, says nothing harsh to anybody; most *cleanly*—just as carbonic acid is, which is death and poison.

We will not praise Mahomet's moral precepts as always of the superfinest sort; yet it can be said that there is always a tendency to good in them; that they are the true dictates of a heart aiming towards what is just and true. The sublime forgiveness of Christianity, turning of the other cheek when the one has been smitten, is not here: you *are* to revenge yourself, but it is to be in measure, not overmuch, or beyond justice. On the other hand, Islam, like any great Faith, and insight into the essence of man, is a perfect equaliser of men: the soul of one believer outweighs all earthly kingships all men, according to Islam too, are equal. Mahomet insists not on the propriety of giving alms, but on the necessity of it: he marks-down by law how much you are to give, and it is at your peril if you neglect. The tenth part of a man's annual income, whatever that may be, is the *property* of the poor, of those that are afflicted and need help. Good all this: the natural voice of humanity, of pity and equity dwelling in the heart of this wild Son of Nature speaks *so*.

Mahomet's Paradise is sensual, his Hell sensual: true; in the one and the other there is enough that shocks all spiritual feeling in us. But we are to recollect that the Arabs already had it so; that Mahomet, in whatever he changed of it, softened and diminished all this. The worst sensualities, too, are the work of doctors, followers of his, not his work. In the Koran there is really very little said about the joys of Paradise; they are intimated rather than insisted on. Nor is it forgotten that the highest joys even there shall be spiritual: the pure Presence of the Highest, this shall infinitely transcend all other joys. He says, 'Your salutation shall be, Peace.' *Salam*, Have Peace!—the thing that all rational souls long for, and seek, vainly here below, as the one blessing. 'Ye shall sit on seats, facing one another: all grudges shall be taken away out of your hearts.' All grudges! Ye shall love one another freely; for each of you, in the eyes of his brothers, there will be Heaven enough!

In reference to this of the sensual Paradise and Mahomet's sensuality, the sorest chapter of all for us, there were many things to be said, which it is not convenient to enter upon here. Two remarks only I shall make, and therewith leave it to your candour. The first is furnished me by Goethe; it is a casual hint of his which seems well worth taking note of. In one of his Delineations, in *Meister's Travels* it is, the hero comes-upon a Society of men with very strange ways, one of which was this: 'We require,' says the Master, 'that each of our people shall restrict himself in one direction,' shall go right against his desire in one matter, and *make* himself do the thing he does not wish, 'should we allow him the greater latitude on all other sides.' There seems to me a great justness in this. Enjoying things which are pleasant; that is not the evil: it is the reducing of our moral self to slavery by them that is. Let a man assert withal that he is king over his habitudes; that he could and would shake them off, on cause shown: this is an excellent law. The Month Ramadhan for the Moslem, much in Mahomet's Religion, much in his own Life, bears in that direction; if not by forethought, or clear purpose of moral improvement on his part, then by a certain healthy manful instinct, which is as good.

But there is another thing to be said about the Mahometan Heaven and Hell. This namely, that, however gross and material they may be, they are an emblem of an everlasting truth, not always so well remembered elsewhere. That gross sensual Paradise of his; that horrible flaming Hell; the great enormous Day of Judgment he perpetually insists on: what is all this but a rude shadow, in the rude Bedouin imagination, of that grand spiritual Fact, and Beginning of Facts, which it is ill for us too if we do not all know and feel: the Infinite Nature of Duty? That man's actions here are of *infinite* moment to him, and never die or end at all; that man, with his little life, reaches upwards high as Heaven, downwards low as Hell, and in his threescore years of Time holds an Eternity fearfully and wonderfully hidden: all this had burnt itself, as in flame-characters, into the wild Arab soul. As in flame and lightning, it stands written there; awful, unspeakable, ever present to him. With bursting earnestness, with a fierce savage sincerity, half articulating, not able to articulate, he strives to speak it, bodied it forth in that Heaven and that Hell. Bodied forth in what way you will, it is the first of all truths. It is venerable under all embodiments. What is the chief end of man here below? Mahomet has answered this question, in a way that might put some of *us* to shame! He does not, like a Bentham, a Paley, take Right and Wrong, and calculate the profit and loss, ultimate pleasure of the one and of the other; and summing all up by addition and subtraction into a net result, ask you, Whether on the whole the Right does not preponderate considerably? No; it is not *better* to do the one than the other; the one is to the other as life is to death, as Heaven is to Hell. The one must in nowise be done, the other in nowise left undone. You shall not measure them; they are incommensurable: the one is death eternal to a man, the other is life eternal. Benthamite Utility, virtue by Profit and Loss; reducing this God's-world to a dead brute Steam-engine, the infinite celestial Soul of Man to a kind of Hay-balance for weighing hay and thistles on, pleasures and pains on. If you ask me which gives, Mahomet or they, the beggarlier and falser view of Man and his Destinies in this Universe, I will answer, It is not Mahomet!

On the whole, we will repeat that this Religion of Mahomet's is a kind of Christianity; has a genuine element of what is spiritually highest looking through it, not to be hidden by all its imperfections. The Scandinavian God *Wish*, the god of all rude men—this has been enlarged into a Heaven by Mahomet; but a Heaven symbolical of sacred Duty, and to be earned by faith and welldoing, by valiant action, and a divine patience which is still more valiant. It is Scandinavian Paganism, and a truly celestial element superadded to that. Call it not false; look not at the falsehood of it, look at the truth of it. For these twelve centuries, it has been the religion and life-guidance of the fifth part of the whole kindred of Mankind. Above all things, it has been a religion heartily *believed*. These Arabs believe their religion, and try to live by it! No Christians, since the early ages, or only perhaps the English Puritans in modern times, have ever stood by their Faith as the Moslem do by theirs—believing it wholly, fronting Time with it, and Eternity with it. This night the watchman on the streets of Cairo when he cries, 'Who goes?' will hear from the passenger, along with his answer, 'There is no God but God.' *Allah akbar, Islam*, sounds through the souls, and whole daily existence, of these dusky millions. Zealous missionaries preach it abroad among Malays, black Papuans, brutal Idolaters displacing what is worse, nothing that is better or good.

To the Arab Nation it was as a birth from darkness into light; Arabia first became alive by means of it. A poor shepherd people, roaming unnoticed in its deserts since the creation of the world: a Hero-Prophet was sent down to them with a word they could believe: see, the unnoticed becomes world-notable, the small has grown world-great; within one century afterwards, Arabia is at

Granada on this hand, at Delhi on that—glancing in valour and splendour and the light of genius, Arabia shines through long ages over a great section of the world. Belief is great, life-giving. The history of a Nation becomes fruitful, soul-elevating, great, so soon as it believes. These Arabs, the man Mahomet, and that one century—is it not as if a spark had fallen, one spark, on a world of what seemed black unnoticeable sand; but lo, the sand proves explosive powder, blazes heaven-high from Delhi to Granada! I said, the Great Man was always as lightning out of Heaven; the rest of men waited for him like fuel, and then they too would flame.

5

ISLAMISM AND SCIENCE

Ernest Renan

I have already so frequently proved the indulgent attention of this audience, that I ventured to choose for my subject to-day a question of the most subtle nature, full of these delicate distinctions into which it is necessary to enter resolutely, when we wish to make history leave the domain of inexactitude. The causes of historical error are nearly always to be found in a failure of precision in the use of words denoting nations and races. We speak of the Greeks, of the Romans, of the Arabs, as though these words designated human groups ever identical with themselves, without taking into account the changes due to military, religious, and linguistic conquests, to fashion, and to the great currents of every description which traverse the history of humanity. Reality does not govern itself in accordance with such simple categories. We French, for instance, are Roman by language, Greek by civilisation, and Jewish by religion. The matter of race, of capital importance in the beginning, has a constant tendency to lose that importance, when the great universal facts, known as Greek civilisation, Roman conquest, Teutonic conquest, Christianity, Islamism, the Renaissance, philosophy, and revolution pass, like grinding millstones, over the primitive varieties of the human family, and force them to mingle themselves in more or less homogeneous masses. It is my desire to unravel with you one of the greatest confusions of ideas made in this respect—that is to say, the equivocation contained in these expressions: Arabic science, Arabic philosophy, Arabic art, Mohammedan science, Mohammedan civilisation.

Source: Renan, E., *The Poetry of the Celtic Races and Other Studies*, 1896, London, Water Scott, pp. 84–108. Lecture delivered at the Sorbonne, 29 March 1883.

From the vague ideas current on this matter result many false judgments, and even practical errors that are, at times, of some gravity.

Every person, however slightly he may be acquainted with the affairs of our time, sees clearly the actual inferiority of Mohammedan countries, the decadence of states governed by Islam, and the intellectual nullity of the races that hold, from that religion alone, their culture and their education. All those who have been in the East, or in Africa, are struck by the way in which the mind of a true believer is fatally limited, by the species of iron circle that surrounds his head, rendering it absolutely closed to knowledge, incapable of either learning anything, or of being open to any new idea. From his religious initiation at the age of ten or twelve years, the Mohammedan child, who occasionally may be, up to that time, of some intelligence, at a blow becomes a fanatic, full of a stupid pride in the possession of what he believes to be the absolute truth, happy as with a privilege, with what makes his inferiority. This foolish pride is the radical vice of the Mussulman. The apparent simplicity of his creed inspires him with an unjustifiable contempt for other religions. Persuaded that God gives fortune and power at his good pleasure, without taking account either of education or personal merit, the Mussulman has the most profound disdain for instruction, for science, for everything that constitutes the European spirit. This bent of mind inculcated by the Mohammedan faith is so strong, that all differences of race and nationality disappear by the fact of conversion to Islam. The Berber, the Sudanese, the Circassian, the Malay, the Egyptian, and the Nubian, once they have become Mussulmans, are no longer Berbers, Sudanese, Egyptians, etc.; they are simply Mussulmans. To this Persia is the only exception; she has been able to keep her own genius, for Persia has known how to take a place by herself in Islam. At bottom she is more Shîite than Moslem.

To diminish the inferences hostile to Islam, which one is compelled to draw from this generally observed state of things, many persons point out that this decadence, after all, can only be a transitory phase. To reassure themselves for the future, they make appeal to the past. This Mohammedan civilisation, now so debased, was once very brilliant. It had men of science and philosophers. It was for centuries the mistress of the Christian West. Why should that which has been, not be once more? That is the precise point which I wish to discuss. Was there really a

Mohammedan science, or at least a science recognised by Islam, tolerated by Islam?

There is undoubtedly in the facts alleged a partial truth. Yes; from about the year 775 to nearly the middle of the thirteenth century, that is to say, for about five hundred years, there were in Mohammedan countries learned men, thinkers of very high distinction. It might almost be said that, during this period, the Mohammedan world was superior in intellectual culture to the Christian world. But this fact must be carefully analysed, if we are to avoid drawing from it erroneous conclusions. We must follow, century by century, the history of Eastern civilisation, in order to appreciate, at their true value, the diverse elements which brought about this momentary superiority, so soon transformed into a distinct inferiority. There is nothing more alien to all that can be called philosophy or science, than the first century of Islam. The result of a religious warfare which lasted for several centuries, and held the conscience of Arabia in suspense between the different forms of Semitic monotheism, Islam is a thousand leagues from all that can be called rationalism or science. The Arab cavaliers who espoused its cause, as a pretext for conquest and pillage, were, in their time, the finest warriors in the world; but they were assuredly the least philosophical of men. An Oriental writer of the thirteenth century, Aboul-Faradj, tracing the character of the Arabian people, thus expresses himself: "The science of this people, that which gave it glory, was the science of language, the knowledge of its idioms, the texture of verse, the skilful composition of prose. As for philosophy, God had taught them none, and had not fitted them for it." Nothing can be truer. The nomad Arab, the most literary of men, is of all men the least mystical, the least inclined to meditation. The religious Arab contents himself, for the explanation of things, with a creative God, governing the world directly, and revealing himself to man by successive prophets. Thus, so long as Islam was in the hands of the Arab race, that is to say, under the first four Caliphs and under the Omeyyades, there was born within it no intellectual movement of a profane character. Omar did not burn—as we are often told—the library of Alexandria; that library had, by his time, nearly disappeared. But the principle which he caused to triumph in the world was, in a very real sense, destructive of learned research and of the varied work of the mind.

All underwent a change when, towards the year 750, Persia took the upper hand, and made the dynasty of the children of Abbas victorious over that of the Beni-Omeya. The centre of Islam found itself transported into the region of the Tigris and Euphrates. But this country was still full of the traces of one of the most brilliant civilisations that the East has ever known, that of the Persian Sassanidæ, which had reached its highest point under the rule of Chosroes Nuschirvan. For centuries past art and industry had flourished in these lands. Chosroes added intellectual activity. Philosophy, banished from Constantinople, came to Persia for refuge. Chosroes had translations made of the books of India. The Nestorian Christians, who formed the most considerable element of the population, were versed in Greek science and philosophy; medicine was entirely in their hands. Their bishops were logicians and geometricians. In the Persian epics, of which the local colour is borrowed from Sassanian times, when Rustem desires to construct a bridge, he summons to his aid a *djathalik* (*Catholicos*, the name of the Nestorian patriarchs or bishops), in the capacity of engineer.

The terrible blast of Islam completely checked, for the space of a century, all this fine Iranian development. But the advent of the Abbasides seemed like a revival of the brilliancy of Chosroes. The revolution that gave the throne to this dynasty was brought about by Persian troops under Persian leaders. Its founders, Aboul Abbas, and, above all, Mansour, were always surrounded by Persians. These were in some measure the Sassanians resuscitated. The privy councillors, the preceptors of the princes, and the prime ministers were the Barmecides, a highly enlightened family of ancient Persia, which had remained faithful to the old Persian religion, to Parsiism, and had been tardily, and without conviction, converted to Islam. The Nestorians soon surrounded those somewhat sceptical caliphs, and became, by a kind of exclusive privilege, their chief physicians. Harran, a town which, in the history of the human mind, has taken a place by itself, had remained Pagan; and had retained the whole scientific tradition of Greek antiquity. To the new school it furnished a large contingent of learned men, indifferent to revealed religion; and including, above all, skilful astronomers.

Bagdad arose as the capital of this renascent Persia. Arabic, the language of the conquest, could not be supplanted, nor its religion be disowned; but the spirit of the new civilisation was essentially a mingled one. Parsis and Christians took the leading part; the administration, the police in particular, was in the hands of the latter. All those brilliant caliphs, the contemporaries of our

Carlovingian monarchs, Mansour, Haroun al-Raschid, Mamoun, can scarcely be called Mussulmans. Externally they practise the religion of which they are the chiefs, or popes, if one can thus express one's self; but in spirit they are elsewhere. They are curious to know all things, and chiefly things exotic and Pagan; they question India, ancient Persia, above all, Greece. At times, it is true, the Moslem pietists cause strange reactions at court; at certain moments the Caliph becomes devout, and proceeds to sacrifice his infidel or free-thinking friends. Then the independent influence takes the upper hand once more; the caliph recalls his men of science, and his boon companions; and a free life begins anew, to the great scandal of the puritanical Mussulmans.

Such is the explanation of that strange and fascinating civilisation of Bagdad, the features of which the fables of the *Thousand and One Nights* have fixed in every imagination, a curious medley of official rigour and private relaxation, an age of youth and inconsequence, in which the serious arts and the arts of the life of pleasure flourished; thanks to the protection of the hostile chiefs of a fanatical religion; in which the libertine, though always under the menace of the most cruel punishments, was flattered and a favourite at court. Under the rule of those Caliphs, now tolerant, now reluctant persecutors, free thought developed; the *Motecallemîn* or "disputants" held debates, where all religions were examined in the light of reason. in some measure we have an account of one of those debates given by a highly devout person. Allow me to read it to you, as M. Dozy has translated it.

A doctor in Kairawan asks a pious Spanish theologian, who has journeyed to Bagdad, whether, during his stay in that town, he has ever been present at the meetings of the *Motecallemîn*. "I was twice present," replies the Spaniard; "but I shall take good care not to go again." "And why?" asks his interlocutor.

"You will judge," responds the traveller. "At the first meeting to which I went there were not only Mussulmans of every kind, orthodox and heterodox, but also unbelievers, fire-worshippers, atheists, materialists, Jews, and Christians—in fact, sceptics of every species. Each sect had its leader, whose duty it was to defend the opinions that it held; and every time one of these leaders entered the room, all rose in token of respect, and no one resumed his place until the leader was seated. The room was soon full, and, when the meeting was seen to be complete, one of the sceptics took up the discourse. 'We are gathered together for the purpose of reasoning,' he said; 'you know all the conditions. You

Mussulmans will not allege reasons drawn from your Book, or based on the authority of your Prophet; for we believe in neither one nor the other. Every one must confine himself to arguments adduced from reason.' All applauded these words. You can understand," added the Spaniard, "that after hearing such things, I returned no more to that assembly. I was induced to visit another; but it was the same scandal over again."

A genuine philosophical and scientific movement was the consequence of this momentary relaxation of orthodox rigour. The Syrian Christian physicians, successors to the later Greek schools, were well versed in the Peripatetic philosophy, in mathematics, in medicine, and in astronomy. The Caliphs employed them to translate into Arabic the Encyclopædia of Aristotle, Euclid, Galen, Ptolemy—in a word, the whole of Greek science, as it was then known. Active minds, like that of Alkindi, began to speculate on the eternal problems that man puts to himself, and is powerless to solve. They were called *Filsouf (Philosophos)*, and from that time this exotic word was taken in bad part, as designating something foreign to Islam. With the Mussulmans *Filsouf* became a name to be feared, often bringing death or persecution like *Zendik* (unbeliever) and later still *Farmaçoun* (Free-Mason). It must be admitted that the rationalism produced in the bosom of Islam was of the most thorough character. A sort of philosophical society, which called itself the *Ikhwan es-safa*, "the brethren of sincerity," set itself to publish a philosophical encyclopædia, remarkable for its wisdom, and for the elevation of its ideas. Two very great men, Alfarabi[1] and Avicenna,[1] soon ranked with the deepest thinkers who have ever lived. Astronomy and algebra had, especially in Persia, remarkable developments. Chemistry pursued its long subterranean labours, revealing itself to the outer world by astonishing results, such as distillation and perhaps gunpowder. Moslem Spain followed the East in the pursuit of these studies; the Jews lent an active collaboration. Ibn Badja, Ibn Tofail, and Averroes raised philosophical thought, in the twelfth century, to heights it had never reached since antiquity.

Such is that great philosophical system which we are accustomed to call Arabic, because it is written in Arabic, but which is in reality Græco-Sassanian. It would be more precise to say Greek, for the really fruitful element of all this came from Greece. One's value, in those days of abasement, was proportionate to what one knew of ancient Greece. Greece was the one source of knowledge and of exact thought. The supremacy of Greece and Bagdad over the Latin West was due to this fact alone—that, in the former, men were much closer to the Greek tradition. It was an easier matter to have a copy of Euclid, or Ptolemy, or Aristotle, at Bagdad, or at Harran, than at Paris. If the Byzantines had only been less jealous guardians of the treasures, which at that moment they scarcely read, if in the eighth or the ninth century had lived a Bessarion[2] or a Lascaris,[2] there would have been no need for that strange detour, by which Greek science reached us in the twelfth century, after passing through Syria, Bagdad, Cordova, and Toledo. But that species of mysterious providence which causes the torch of humanity, when it begins to expire in the hands of one people, to pass into the hands of another which uplifts and lights it anew, gave a value of the highest order to the work, otherwise apt to be obscure, of those poor Syrians, of those persecuted *Filsouf*, of those Harranians, whose scepticism put them under the ban of their contemporaries. It was by those Arabic translations of Greek works of philosophy and science that Europe was plunged into the ferment of ancient tradition, needful for the birth of her genius.

In fact, while Averroes, the last of the Arabic philosophers, was dying in Morocco, in sadness and abandonment, this West of ours was fully awakening out of its slumber. Abelard had already given the cry of renascent rationalism. Europe had found her genius, and was commencing upon that extraordinary evolution, the last term of which will be the complete emancipation of the human mind. Here on the mount of St Geneviève, a new *sensorium* was created for the work of the mind. One thing was wanting—books, the pure sources of antiquity. At a first glance, it would seem as though the more natural thing to have done would have been to go and ask for them in the libraries of Constantinople, where the originals were to be found, than to have depended upon translations, often mediocre, and in a language but ill fitted to render Greek thought. But religious controversy had created between the Latin world and the Greek world a deplorable antipathy which the fatal crusade of 1204 only served to intensify. And then we had no Greek scholars; it was necessary to wait for three hundred years before we had a Budè,[3] a Lefèvre d'Étaples.[3]

In default of the true and authentic Greek philosophy which was in the Byzantine libraries, it was incumbent to go to Spain, and seek there a Greek science translated badly and sophisticated. I shall not speak of Gerbert,[4] about whose travels among the Mussulmans there hangs much doubt. But even in the eleventh century, Constantine the African[4] was superior in learning to his age and country, because he had received a Moslem education. From 1130 to 1150 an active college of translators, established at Toledo under the patronage of Archbishop Raymond, put into Latin the most important works of Arabic science. In the early years of the thirteenth century, the Arabic Aristotle made its triumphant entrance into the University of Paris. The West threw off its inferiority, which had lasted for four or five hundred years. Till then Europe had been, as regarded science, tributary to the Mussulmans. Towards the middle of the thirteenth century the balance was still uncertain. Starting from about the year 1275, two easily discernible movements are apparent. On the one hand, the Mohammedan countries plunge into the most pitiable intellectual decadence; on the other, Western Europe resolutely enters on its own account into that great highway of the scientific search for truth, that immense curve, the amplitude of which cannot yet be gauged.

Woe to him that becomes useless to human progress. He is almost instantly cast aside. When the so-called Arabic science had inoculated the Latin West with its germ of life, it disappeared. While Averroes was arriving in the Latin schools of thought as a celebrity almost equal to that of Aristotle himself, he was forgotten by his co-religionists. After about the year 1200 there was no longer a single Arabic philosopher of any renown. Philosophy had ever been persecuted in the bosom of Islam, but by means that had not succeeded in suppressing it. From the year 1200, the theological reaction carried it away altogether. Philosophy was abolished in Mohammedan countries. The historians and other writers only speak of it as a memory, and that an evil memory. The philosophical manuscripts were destroyed, and have become rare. Astronomy is only tolerated for the sake of that part of it which serves to determine the direction of prayer. Soon the Turkish race assumed the hegemony of Islam, and caused the universal prevalence of its total lack of the philosophic and scientific spirit. From that moment, with some rare exceptions, like Ibn Khaldoun,[5] Islam no longer counted among its members any man of great mind. It has slain the science and philosophy within itself.

I have not sought to diminish the rôle of that great science, known as Arabic, which marks such an important stage in the history of the human mind. On some points its originality has been exaggerated, notably with regard to astronomy; but we need not go to the other extreme, and depreciate it beyond measure. Between the disappearance of ancient civilisation in the sixth century, and the birth of the European genius in the twelfth and thirteenth, there was what can be called the Arabic period, during which the traditions of the human spirit were continued by the regions conquered by Islam. In reality what was Arabic in this so-called Arabic science? The language, and nothing but the language. The Moslem conquest had borne the language of the Hedjaz to the very ends of the earth. It was with Arabic as with Latin, which in the West became the vehicle of feelings and thoughts that had nothing to do with ancient Latium. Averroes, Avicenna, Albateni,[6] were Arabs, as Albertus Magnus,[7] Roger Bacon, Francis Bacon, and Spinoza were Latins. It is as great a mistake to give the credit of Arabic science and philosophy to Arabia, as to put all the Latin Christian literature, all the Scholastic Philosophy, all the Renaissance, and the whole of the science of the fifteenth, and in part of the sixteenth centuries, to the credit of the city of Rome; because all this was written in Latin. What is in fact a very remarkable thing is, that among the philosophers and learned men called Arabic, there was but one alone, Alkindi, who was of Arabic origin; all the others were Persians, Transoxians, Spaniards, natives of Bokhara, of Samarcand, of Cordova, of Seville. Not only were those men not Arabs by blood, but they were in nowise Arabs in mind. They made use of Arabic; but they were fettered by it, as the mediæval thinkers were fettered by Latin, and modified it for their own use. Arabic, which lends itself so well to poetry, and to a certain eloquence, is a very unsuitable instrument for metaphysics. The Arabic philosophers and men of science were in general somewhat bad writers.

This science, then, is not Arabic. Is it at least Mohammedan? Has Islamism lent any tutelary aid to rational research? In no way. This splendid advance in learning was entirely the work of Parsees, of Christians, of Jews, of Harranians, of Ismaelians, of Mussulmans in internal revolt against their own religion. From orthodox Mussulmans it only reaped curses. Mamoun, the Caliph who showed most zeal for the introduction of Greek philosophy, was pitilessly damned by the theologians; the misfortunes that afflicted his reign were represented as penalties for his tolerance of doctrines alien to Islam. It was no rare circumstance for the books of philosophy and astronomy to be burnt in public places, or cast into wells and cisterns, to please the populace, aroused by the Imams. Those who cultivated these studies were called *Zendiks*; they were stoned in the streets, their houses were set on fire, and very frequently the authorities, when they desired to secure popularity, would put them to death.

Islamism has then, in reality, constantly persecuted science and philosophy. It ended by stifling it. It is, however, necessary to distinguish in this respect two periods in the history of Islam—one from its commencement to the twelfth century, the other from the thirteenth century to our own days. In the former period Islam, undermined by sects, and tempered by a species of protestantism (known as *Motazelism*), was much less organised and less fanatical than it has been in the latter, when it has fallen into the hands of the Tartar and Berber races—races which are heavy, brutal, and without intelligence. Islamism offers this peculiarity: that it has obtained from its disciples a faith ever tending to grow stronger. The first Arabs engaged in the movement scarcely believed in the mission of the Prophet. During two or three centuries incredulity was scarcely dissimulated. Then came the absolute reign of dogma, without any possible separation of the spiritual from the temporal, the reign of coercion and corporeal punishments for him who did not practise religion; a system, finally, which has only been exceeded, in regard to persecutions, by the Spanish Inquisition. Liberty is never more grievously wounded than by a social organisation, in which religion absolutely dominates civil life. In modern times we have seen only two examples of such a rule—on the one hand the Moslem States, on the other the former Papal State, in the days of its temporal power. And it ought to be remarked that the temporal papacy only weighed upon a country of very limited extent; while Islamism oppresses vast portions of our globe, and in them maintains the idea most opposed to progress—the state founded on a pseudo-Revelation, theology governing society.

The liberals who defend Islam do not know its real nature. Islam is the close union of the spiritual and the temporal; it is the reign of a dogma, it is the heaviest chain that humanity has ever borne. In the first half of the Middle Ages, I repeat, Islam supported philosophy because it could not prevent it; it could not prevent it, because it was itself lacking in cohesion, and only poorly equipped against terrorism. The police was, as I have said, in the hands of the Christians; and was chiefly occupied in checking the attempts of the followers of Ali.[8] A multitude of things passed through the meshes of that loosely held net. But when Islam had at its disposal masses of ardent believers, it destroyed all. Religious terror and hypocrisy were the order of the day. Islam has been liberal in its day of weakness, and violent in its day of strength. Do not let us honour it then for what it has been unable to suppress. To do honour to Islam for the philosophy and science that it did not annihilate from the very first, is as though we were to do honour to the theologians for the discoveries of modern science. These discoveries are made in spite of the theologians. Western theology has not persecuted less than that of Islamism; only it has not been successful, it has not crushed out the modern spirit, as Islamism has trodden out the spirit of the lands it has conquered.

In our Western Europe theological persecution has only succeeded in a single country—Spain. There a terrible system of oppression has stifled the scientific spirit. Let us hasten to say that that noble land will have her revenge. In Moslem countries has come to pass what would have happened in Europe, if the Inquisition, Philip II, and Pius V had succeeded in their design of arresting the human mind. Frankly, I have much difficulty in being grateful to people for desisting from the evil that they have been unable to achieve. No; religions have their great and beautiful hours, when they console and raise the feeble parts of our poor humanity; but we need not compliment them for what has been born in spite of them, for what they have sought to smother in the cradle. We do not inherit the possessions of the people whom we assassinate; we ought not to allow persecutors to profit from the things that they have persecuted.

That is, however, the error that we commit, by an excess of generosity, when we attribute to the influence of Islam a movement which produced itself in spite of Islam, against Islam, and which Islam has happily been unable to prevent. Doing honour to the Islam of Avicenna, of Avenzoar,[9] of Averroes, is like doing honour to the Catholicism of Galileo. Theology impeded Galileo; it was not sufficiently strong to fetter him altogether. That is no reason for his owing it any great gratitude. Far from me be it to speak, with words of bitterness, against any of the symbols in which the human conscience has sought for rest, amongst the insoluble problems presented to it by the universe and its destiny. Islamism has its beauties as a religion; I have never entered a mosque without a vivid emotion—shall I even say without a certain regret in not being a Mussulman? But to the human reason Islamism has only been injurious. The minds that it has shut from the light were, no doubt, already closed in by their own internal limits; but it has persecuted free thought, I shall not say more violently than other religions, but more effectually. It has made of the countries that it has conquered a closed field to the rational culture of the mind.

What is, in fact, essentially distinctive of the Mussulman is his hatred of science, his persuasion that research is useless, frivolous, almost impious—the natural sciences, because they are attempts at rivalry with God; the historical sciences, because, since they apply to times anterior to Islam, they may revive ancient heresies. One of the most curious evidences of this is that of the Sheik Rifaa, who resided in Paris for several years, as chaplain of the Egyptian school; and after his return to Egypt wrote a work full of the quaintest observations on French society. His fixed idea is that European science, above all by its principle of the permanence of natural laws, is from one end to the other a heresy; and it must be admitted that, from the point of view of Islam, he is not altogether wrong. A revealed dogma is always opposed to the free research that may contradict it. The result of science is not to banish the divine altogether, but ever to place it at a greater distance from the world of particular facts in which men once believed they saw it. Experience caused the supernatural to draw back, and restrains its domain. But the supernatural is the basis of all theology. Islam, in treating science as an enemy, is only consistent; but it is a dangerous thing to be too consistent. To its own misfortune Islam has been successful. By slaying science it has slain itself; and is condemned in the world to a complete inferiority.

When one starts from the idea that scientific research is a thing that infringes on the rights of God, one inevitably comes to sloth of mind, to lack of precision, to incapacity for exactitude. *Allah aalam*: "God knoweth best what it is," is the last word of all Moslem discussion. It is a good thing to believe in God, but not to such an extent as that. In the early days of this sojourn at Mossoul, Sir Henry Layard desired, clear-minded as he was, to acquire some information on the population of the town, on its commerce, and on its historical traditions. He addressed himself to the Cadi, who gave the following response, the translation of which has been kindly furnished to me.

"O my illustrious friend, O joy of living men! What thou askest of me is both useless and harmful. Albeit all my days have been spent in this land, I have never sought to count the houses, or to inform myself of the number of their inhabitants. And as to what merchandise this man putteth upon his mules, and that man in the hold of his ship, in very truth these are things that concern me not at all. As for the former history of this city, God alone knoweth it; and He alone could say with how many errors its dwellers were filled before it was overcome by Islam. The knowledge of it would be dangerous for us.

"O my friend, O my lamb, seek not to know the things that concern thee not. Thou hast come amongst us, and we have made thee welcome; go in peace! Verily, all the words that thou hast said unto me have done me no ill; for he that speaketh is one, and he that giveth ear is another. After the manner of the men of thy nation, thou hast journeyed through many lands, but not the more hast thou found happiness anywhere. We (blessed be God!) were born here, and have no desire to go hence.

"Hearken unto me, my son; there is no wisdom like unto that of faith in God. He hath created the world; who are we that we should strive to equal Him by seeking to fathom the mysteries of His creation? Behold that star that goeth round another star; behold yet another star that draweth a tail behind it, and is so many years in coming, and so many years in departing. Leave it, my son; He whose hands have fashioned it, knoweth well how to lead and direct it.

"But it may be that thou shalt say: 'O man, get thee gone; for I am wiser than thou, and have looked upon things whereof thou knowest not.' If thou thinkest that these things have made thee better than I, be doubly welcome; but as for me, I bless God that I have not sought after that of which I have no need. Thou art learned in things that have no interest for me; and what thou hast seen, I disdain. Shall greater knowledge give thee a second belly, and shall thine eyes, that go prying everywhere, make thee find a Paradise?

"O my friend, if it be that thou hast a desire to be happy, let this be thy cry, 'God alone is God!' Do no evil, and then thou shalt fear neither men nor death itself, for thine hour shall come."

This Cadi is very philosophical after his own fashion; but note the difference. We consider the Cadi's letter charming; but he, on the contrary, would deem what we are saying here to be abominable. Besides, it is for society that the consequences of such a way of thinking are fatal. Of the two evils that follow in the train of lack of the scientific spirit, superstition and dogmatism, the latter is perhaps worse than the former. The East is not superstitious; its great evil is the narrow dogmatism imposed by the whole force of society. The goal of humanity is not repose in a resigned ignorance; it is an implacable war with falsehood, a struggle with the powers of darkness.

Science is the very soul of a society; for science is reason. It creates military superiority and industrial superiority. Some day it will create social superiority—that is to say, a state of society in which the amount of justice compatible with the essence of the universe will be attained. Science gives force for the service of reason. In Asia there are elements of barbarism analogous to those that formed the early Moslem armies, and the great cyclones of Attila and Genghis Khan. But science bars their way. If Omar or Genghis Khan had found good artillery confronting them, they would never have passed the borders of their desert. We need not stop at momentary aberrations. What was not said at the beginning against fire-arms, which nevertheless have contributed much to the victory of civilisation? For my own part, I am convinced that science is good, that it alone can furnish weapons against the evil that can be wrought by it; and that in the end it will only serve progress—I mean true progress—that which is inseparable from respect for humanity and freedom.

APPENDIX TO THE PRECEDING LECTURE[10]

The very judicious reflections which my last lecture at the Sorbonne suggested to Sheik Gemmal Eddin were read yesterday with the interest which they deserved. There is nothing more instructive than thus to study, in its original and sincere manifestations, the conscience of the enlightened Asiatic. It is by listening to the most diverse voices, coming from the four quarters of the horizon in favour of rationalism, that one comes to the conclusion that if religion divides men, reason tends to unite them; and that, at bottom, there is but one reason. The unity of the human mind is the great and consoling consequence which results from the peaceful encounter of ideas, when the antagonistic pretensions of so-called supernatural revelations are put on one side. The league of the whole world's honest thinkers against fanaticism and superstition is apparently composed of an imperceptible minority; essentially it is the only league destined to endure, for it rests upon truth, and will end by winning the day, after the fables that rival it have been exhausted in lengthened series of powerless convulsions.

Nearly two months ago I made the acquaintance of the Sheik Gemmal Eddin, thanks to my dear colleague, M. Ganem. Few persons have produced a more vivid impression upon me. It was in great measure my conversation with him that decided me in choosing for the subject of my lecture at the Sorbonne the relation between the scientific spirit and Islamism. The Sheik Gemmal Eddin is an Afghan, entirely emancipated from the prejudices of Islam; he belongs to those energetic races of the Upper Iran bordering upon India, in which the Aryan spirit still flourishes so strongly, under the superficial garb of official Islamism. He is the best proof of that great axiom, which we have often proclaimed, that the worth of religions is to be determined by the worth of the races that profess them. The freedom of his thought, his noble and loyal character, made me believe, when in his presence, that I had before me, in a resuscitated state, one of my old acquaintances, Avicenna, Averroes, or some other of those great sceptics who for five centuries represented the tradition of the human spirit. The contrast was especially apparent to me when I compared this striking similarity with the spectacle presented by Moslem countries other than Persia, countries where scientific and philosophical curiosity is so rare a thing. The Sheik Gemmal Eddin is the finest case of racial protest against religious conquest that could be cited. He confirms what the intelligent orientalists of Europe have frequently said, namely, that Afghanistan is in all Asia, Japan alone excepted, the country which presents most of the constituent elements of that which we call a nation.

In the Sheik's learned article I can only see a single point on which we really differ. The Sheik does not admit the distinctions, which historical criticism leads us to make, in these great and complex facts called empires and conquests. The Roman Empire, with which the Arabic conquest has so much in common, made the Latin language the organ of the human spirit through the whole of the Western world up to the sixteenth century. Albertus Magnus, Roger Bacon, and Spinoza wrote in Latin. They are not however, for us, Latins. In a history of English literature we assign a place to Bede and Alcuin, in a history of French literature we place Gregory of Tours and Abelard. It is not that we think lightly of the action of Rome in the history of civilisation, any more than we fail to recognise Arabic action. But these great currents of humanity demand analysis. All that is written in Latin is not to the glory of Rome; all that is written in Greek is not Hellenic work; all that is written in Arabic is not of Arabic production; all that is done in a Christian country is not the result of Christianity; all that is done in a Mohammedan country is not the fruit of Islam. This is the principle which the profound historian of Moslem Spain, M. Reinhart Dozy, whose loss learned Europe is at this moment deploring, applied with so rare a sagacity. These sorts of distinctions are necessary, if we do not wish history to be a tissue of inexactitude and misunderstanding.

One aspect in which I have appeared unjust to the Sheik, is that I have not sufficiently developed the idea that all revealed religion is forced to show hostility to positive science; and that, in this respect, Christianity has no reason to boast over Islam. About that there can be no doubt. Galileo was not treated more kindly by Catholicism than was Averroes by Islam. Galileo found truth in a Catholic country despite Catholicism, as Averroes nobly philosophised in a Moslem country despite Islam. If I did not insist more strongly upon this point, it was, to tell the truth, because my opinions on this matter are so well known that there was no need for me to recur to them again before a public conversant with my writings. I have said, sufficiently often to preclude any necessity for repeating it, that the human mind must be detached from all supernatural belief if it desires to labour at its own essential task, which is the construction of positive science. This does not imply any violent destruction or hasty rupture. It does not mean that the Christian should forsake Christianity, or that the Mussulman should abandon Islam. It means that the enlightened parts of Christendom and Islam should arrive at that state of benevolent indifference in which religious beliefs become inoffensive. This is half accomplished in nearly all Christian countries. Let us hope that the like will be the case for Islam. Naturally on that day the Sheik and I will be at one, and ready to applaud heartily.

I did not assert that all Mussulmans, without distinction of race, are, and always will be, sunk in ignorance: I said that Islamism puts great difficulties in the way of science, and unfortunately has succeeded for five or six hundred years in almost suppressing it in the countries under its sway; and that this is for these countries a cause of extreme weakness. I believe, in point of fact, that the regeneration of the Mohammedan countries will not be the work of Islam; it will come to pass through the enfeeblement of Islam, as indeed the great advance of the countries called Christian commenced with the destruction of the tyrannical church of the Middle Ages. Some persons have seen in my lecture a thought hostile to the individuals who profess the Mohammedan religion. That is by no means true; Mussulmans are themselves the first victims of Islam. More than once in my Eastern travels I have been in a position to notice how fanaticism proceeds from a small number of dangerous men who keep the others in the practice of religion by terror. To emancipate the Mussulman from his religion would be the greatest service that one could render him. In wishing these populations, in which so many good elements exist, a deliverance from the yoke that weighs them down, I do not believe that I have any unkindly thought for them. And, let me say also, since the Sheik Gemmal Eddin desires me to hold the balance equally between different faiths, I should not any the more believe that I was wishing evil of certain European countries if I expressed a hope that Christianity should have a less dominant influence upon them.

The lack of agreement between liberal thinkers on these different points is not very serious, since, favourable or not to Islam, all come to the same practical conclusion, the necessity for spreading education among Mohammedans. This is perfectly right, if by education is meant serious education of a character to cultivate the reason. If the religious leaders of Islamism contribute to this excellent work I shall be delighted. To be frank, I am a little doubtful of their doing so. Distinguished individualities—there will be few so distinguished as the Sheik Gemmal Eddin—will be formed who will sever their connection with Islam as we ourselves have separated from Catholicism. Certain countries in time will almost break with the religion of the Koran; but I suspect that the movement of Renaissance will be made without the support of official Islam. The scientific Renaissance of Europe was to no greater extent carried on with the assistance of Catholicism; at the present hour—and we have no reason to be surprised at it—Catholicism still struggles to prevent the full realisation of that which sums up the rational cloud of humanity, the neutral state outside so-called revealed dogmas.

Above all else, as a supreme law, let us put freedom and respect for men. Not to destroy religions, even to treat them with kindliness as free manifestations of human nature, but not to guarantee them, most of all not to defend them against such of their own members as desire to leave them—this is the duty of civil society. Thus reduced to the condition of free and independent studies, like literature or taste, religions will be entirely transformed. Deprived of the official or temporal bond, they will disintegrate and lose the greater part of their drawbacks. All this is Utopian at the present hour; all this will be reality in the future. How will each religion comport itself under the reign of liberty, which, after many actions and reactions, is destined to impose itself upon human societies? It is not in a few lines that such a problem can be examined. In my lecture I merely wished to treat an historical question. The Sheik Gemmal Eddin seems to me to have brought considerable arguments in support of my two fundamental theses: During the first half of its existence Islam did not prevent the scientific movement from growing in Mohammedan soil; during the second half of its existence it stifled the scientific movement within it, and that to its own misfortune.

NOTES

1 Alkindi (known to the Latin schoolmen as Alkindius) lived in the reigns of Al-Mamûm and Al-Motassem, and is said to have written two hundred treatises on scientific and philosophical subjects, only a few of which, however, have survived. Alfarabi (Alfarabius) died at Damascus in 950. According to legendary accounts he was a man of great learning, and knew seventy languages. "He gave the tone and direction to nearly all subsequent speculations among the Arabians." Avicenna (980–1037), by his medical and philosophical works, was the most illustrious of the oriental Arabic writers. Ibn Badja (Avempace) died at Fez in 1138. His principal work was an essay on the *Republic of the Solitary*. The same theme was developed by Ibn Tofail (Abubacer), who died in Morocco in 1185.

2 Bessarion (1395–1472) was one of the earliest of the scholars of the Renaissance. As Bishop of Nicæa in the Greek Church, he accompanied the Greek Emperor to Italy in 1439, in order to effect a union between the Eastern and Western Churches. On joining, soon after, the latter church, he was created a cardinal. Constantine Lascaris, a famous Greek scholar of the fifteenth century, was born at Constantinople; but on the capture of that city by the Turks in 1453, he sought asylum in Italy, where he lived till his death in 1493. He did much, both by teaching and writing, to revive the study of Greek.

3 Budé (Budaeus) was born in 1467, and died in 1540. He wrote many Greek and Latin commentaries, was the most learned Frenchman of his time, and enjoyed the friendship of Erasmus. Lefèvre d'Étaples (1450–1537) was a scholar of great eminence, and a writer on theological and literary subjects.

4 Gerbert, who afterwards became Pope Sylvester II, was born in Auvergne about 930. He pursued scientific studies among the Arabs in Spain, and is said to have introduced Arabic numerals and clocks

into France. Constantine the African was a Carthaginian scholar of the eleventh century. He was said to have studied in Egypt and India, and wrote principally on medical subjects.

5 Ibn Khaldoun (1322–1406) was an Arabian historian, his chief work being a universal history which treats especially of the Arabs and Berbers.

6 Albateni (Albategnius), who was born in Mesopotamia about 850 and died in 929, was mainly noted for his astronomical and mathematical writings, including commentaries on Ptolemy.

7 Albertus Magnus (1193–1280) was one of the most distinguished of the scholastic philosophers and a member of the Dominican order. He studied at Padua and Bologna, taught theology and philosophy at Paris and Cologne, and was for a short time Bishop of Ratisbon (Regensburg). His fame chiefly rests on the fact that he was the first of the scholastics to reproduce Aristotle's philosophy, and transform it in accordance with Catholic dogma.

8 Ali, born at Mecca about 600, killed at Kufa 661, was the adopted son of Mohammed and the fourth Caliph. The Shîite sect among the Mohammedans regard Ali with veneration as the first rightful Caliph.

9 Avenzoar, an Arabian physician, was born in Spain about 1072 and died in 1162. He was the teacher of Averroes, who spoke highly of his wisdom.

10 A remarkably intelligent Afghan sheik, visiting Paris, having published in the *Journal des Débats* of May 18th, 1883, some remarks upon the preceding lecture, I replied next day in the same journal, as follows. *Author's Note.*

6

MOHAMMED AND THE KORAN

D.S. Margoliouth

From the definition of the name *Moslem* given above, it follows that the place filled by the founder in the system is exceedingly prominent; if it is man's business to obey God, it is from Mohammed only that his business can be learned. As compared with some other systems, Islam possesses great advantages for the application of this principle. The text of the Koran, or divine revelation, verbally communicated by the Prophet, was finally settled within thirty years of the latter's death; and though the earliest biography of him which we possess is one hundred and thirty years later, the bulk of it is connected with later history by continuous chains: many of the personages who figure therein played a historic part after their master's death; and in many cases the sources of the narrative can be traced with certainty. The amount, then, which negative criticism would reject could never be a considerable fraction of the whole; both eulogists and detractors are agreed as to the main facts of the career, however much their judgment of it may differ.

Owing to the absence of written chronicles, the history of Arabia before Islam is exceedingly obscure; the difficulty of communication, and the poverty of the central portions of the peninsula, kept it away from the main currents of history. Its condition at the time when Islam arose is therefore imperfectly known. It is, however, clear that the bulk of the peninsula was still pagan, and indeed primitively pagan, the objects of worship being fetishes, which had names, but about which there was little

Source: Margoliouth, D.S., *Mohammedanism*, 1911, London, Williams and Norgate, pp. 42–74.

theological speculation. One particular sanctuary, that of Bakkah (in the ordinary language Meccah), and its god Allah, had acquired fame by supernatural resistance to an Abyssinian expedition, of which the purpose had been destruction of the cult; and it seems that there was an arrangement between the tribes whereby warfare should cease for four months in each year in order to permit of safe pilgrimage to the sanctuary, whose keepers enjoyed various privileges. The process of pilgrimage came to involve a number of ceremonies, of which the meaning was naturally forgotten. Among the pagans there was in the main only tribal government, though at Meccah itself, the town that had grown up round the sanctuary, there were the beginnings of municipal government, as perhaps elsewhere. The two great empires of the time, the Byzantine and the Persian, had their spheres of influence—the former in the north, the latter in the south of the peninsula, where indeed it appears to have maintained a governor; it seems doubtful, however, whether tribute was paid to either power.

Both Christianity and Judaism were represented in Arabia, and indeed in many provinces; a third monotheistic community, the Sabians, or Mandæans, also had representation. The Jewish tribes lay outside the ken of their Palestinian and Persian brethren; but for Islamic history posterity would not have known of their existence. Christianity, as the court religion of the Byzantine Empire, had been adopted in two states which disappeared shortly before the rise of Islam, and there were quite a number of Christian tribes; even in Meccah something seems to have been known of Christianity. Since the prosperity of the place was due to the carrying trade, the participators in which regularly visited Syria and Yemen, and at times perhaps Egypt and Abyssinia, the Meccan merchants on their travels had the opportunity of learning about it in Christian cities. Moreover, the modern Arabic script appears to have become known in Meccah about the time of Mohammed's birth, and this fact facilitated the introduction of the Christian or Jewish scriptures.

Mohammed, when he first meets us, is in middle life. He belonged to a numerous and apparently powerful clan in his native city; several of his near relations, his uncles, aunts, and cousins, play an important part in his career. We know the name of his first wife, Khadijah, said to have been fifteen years his senior, yet the mother of a considerable family—four daughters and one or more sons. The son or sons died in infancy, but the daughters lived to maturity, and were all married to men of note. He seems, like most of the Meccans, to have carried on a trade; at first, we are told, that of conducting or accompanying caravans, afterwards that of selling dry goods retail. We even know the name of his partner in the latter business.

In studying the work of a prophet it is necessary to distinguish the historical from the theological attitude. What the Prophet claims is to be absolute dictator to his community; and if there have been communities in which the prophets were content with a humbler rôle, it is because in them the initiative came from the questioner, who was at liberty to reject the divine mandate when it was intelligible, though of course at his own risk. Thus the Greek oracles communicated the wishes of the gods, but only when they were questioned, and demanded a fee for their services. The Hebrew prophets appear to have aimed somewhat higher; the initiative ordinarily came from them, but they did not aim at displacing existing authority, though they demanded that it should be guided by their advice. The part to be played by a prophet was suggested to Mohammed by a few cases wherein the divine messenger was also the founder, leader, and legislator of a community. Where those to whom such a claim is addressed dispute it, the theological attitude is that of sympathy with one of the parties; it either brands the disputers as stiffnecked and bigoted or the prophet himself as an impostor. And where the prophet claims supernatural powers, it is difficult to avoid holding one or other of these opinions. An Isaiah who could make the shadow on a sundial go back might well claim the obedience of his community; an Isaiah who made it appear to go back by some artful contrivance would be a disreputable charlatan. But in Mohammed's case no miracle of this convincing kind was claimed during his lifetime; for in whatever sense the miracle of the Koran be interpreted, command of either language or archæology is a different thing from command over the forces of nature. It is quite possible for one critic to find ideal eloquence where another is not even moved to admiration. Hence the historical attitude, which sympathizes with both sides, admits of easy application in dealing with the origins of Islam.

It is quite clear that reforms have ordinarily been effected by men who believed absolutely in the efficacy of their expedients; it is also clear that none of these expedients have ever been as wholly beneficent in their results as the reformers had hoped. It must also be remembered that the scientific settling of moral values is a matter of slow growth, and that many a prophet has in consequence assigned what seem to us wholly disproportionate values in his assessment of acts. Thus probably the most violent language with which crime was ever denounced has been launched against idolatry, which does not obviously harm society, or sabbath-breaking, which few communities have regarded as even immoral.

If we attempt to sum up the evils current in Meccah which roused the Prophet's deepest indignation, they seem to have been of three classes.

One set were theological, i.e. false notions about the Divine Being, and a system of superstitious ceremonies. The latter were some harmless, some silly, and some disgusting. The Prophet swept them all away, just as the Founder of Christianity swept away the Mosaic law of purity; His disciples would eat meat without washing their hands. Such of these taboos as are recorded are usually connected with the camel, which was the basis of Meccan civilization. In general, however, Mohammed seems to have abhorred the Meccan beliefs more than the Meccan practices. The former, being known to us only from the statements in the Koran, are in the highest degree obscure; it is certain that there were minor deities, mostly goddesses, who were privileged in some way above the chief Deity, Allah, to whom the sanctuary and in the main the people of Meccah belonged. The true religion was, in Mohammed's opinion, that of the founder of the community, Abraham and his son Ishmæl, and it was his function to restore the ancient purity of the cult. It is a psychological puzzle that this destroyer of idols maintained the ceremony of kissing the Black Stone, which at any rate bears a close resemblance to idolatry. But however that may be explained, the Prophet seems from the first to have waged implacable war against idols, and never rested till he had banished their cult from Arabia.

A second set of evils might be described as social. The society of Arabia was founded on the theory of the joint responsibility of the tribe, especially for bloodshed; and it would seem that the death of a tribesman at the hands of a member of another tribe led to a long and complicated series of battles and assassinations, the purpose of which was not to gain any decisive results, such as the acquisition of territory or the subjugation of a community, but retaliation with interest. When the warring communities got tired or exhausted, the numbers of slain on either side were counted up, and any surplus paid for. The distinction between voluntary and involuntary slaughter seems to have been wholly ignored. Either, then, a tribe lived in a perpetual state of warfare, or the fear of this internecine strife caused impunity in crime. That there was no need for reform in this matter, and that such reform could only be effected by the complete destruction of the tribal system and the substitution for it of orderly government, is obvious.

We gather too from the Koran that much injustice was prevalent in Meccah, and that there were various disabilities from which chiefly strangers suffered.

Thirdly, there were offences against morality which very rightly shocked the Prophet. Most notable amongst these was infanticide, the horrible practice of burying girls alive. Doubtless the Arabs in the main were endeavouring by this practice to deal with the problem of a surplus female population, which in modern times also occupies the attention of thinkers; but that in reprobating the custom Mohammed was helping on the cause of good is clearly true. That there was also much irregularity of morals in Meccah is historically attested, yet the nature of the innovations cannot be precisely made out. Perhaps the formula "regulation of sexual relations" would be sufficiently precise and sufficiently vague to describe what was done.

The task, then, which the Prophet set himself—or, if the phrase be preferred, received—was the execution of a scheme of theological, social, and moral reform. To a certain extent a reformer is less an innovator than an interpreter of the ideas of his age; to a certain extent his work has to be experimental, and even opportunist: he has not an answer ready for every question which arises.

The stages of the Prophet's career become clearer after the Flight to Medinah; before that epoch, which afterwards became the era of Islam, they are faint. He commenced by an appeal to his own household, and won converts in his wife Khadijah, his adopted son, his young cousin Ali, and his uncle Hamzah. For a period of three years the mission was conducted privately: meetings were held in secret, and, unless the religious observances of the Meccans differed very much from those of other communities, some external participation in the national worship must have been maintained by both the Prophet and his followers. Conversion of persons who were not of the privileged caste was comparatively easy, and several adherents were won from among these: but some persons of importance also joined. One of the earliest adherents was Abu Bakr, son of Abu Kuhafah, afterwards the Prophet's father-in-law and his first successor, said to be an authority on Arabian pedigrees: a man of unswerving loyalty, ready to fulfil all the obligations which the most uncompromising theorists ever demanded of a friend, yet not honoured with that name by his Master; but also a man of astuteness, of forethought, of resolution. Unlike his three successors, also early adherents of the Prophet, he died in his bed. Othman Ibn Affan, the third successor, married successively two of the Prophet's daughters; he seems to have been a respected personage, who, till he became sovereign, made few enemies. Omar, the second successor, converted after the mission had been made public, and when its fortunes were at a low ebb, is represented as the strenuous partisan, who persecuted the sect before he joined it. His accession to the cause in its early days turned the scale in its favour just as the battle of Badr did after the Flight; titles, indicating this service, were conferred both on him and it.

At the end of these three years some open breach occurred, and the pagan Meccans were astonished that one of their number claimed to be the messenger of their God, bringing them a strange message, wholly subversive of their former beliefs and practices: claiming, in short, to be their dictator, though dictating not his own words, but God's. There is no example in history of such a claim being at the first favourably received, unless by any chance it is made by one already sovereign. In most communities it has meant death, or at least condign punishment, for the person who makes it. The better the order of the community, the less chance has a prophet. The execution of Socrates took place after a legal trial, in the most highly civilized and most tolerant state of antiquity. The charge was that Socrates did not worship the city's gods and shook other people's belief in them. The Book of Deuteronomy urges that the man who introduces a new cult should be stoned without mercy and without a hearing. Some citizens of Baghdad a few months ago clamoured for the execution of a man who preached the equalization of the sexes in defiance of the Koran. People suppose that the favour of the gods is necessary for the well-being of their communities: if the gods are offended, their vengeance falls not upon the individual offender, but upon the community, taking the form of plague, famine, or defeat in war. Hence it is with the view of self-preservation that the community defends the honour of its gods.

The problem, then, is not why did Mohammed for eighteen years fail to convince the bulk of his citizens? but, How was it that he escaped death when once his mission had been proclaimed? And the reply is, Because there was no orderly government. In the first place it seems clear that all Meccah was *sanctuary*, no blood might be shed there under any pretext: when first the Prophet became dangerous, the Meccan plan was to *starve* him to death. Justice, it would seem, could only be executed within the tribe, and the tribe seems to have recognized the authority of some sort of patriarch: the patriarch of Mohammed's tribe was his uncle, Abu Talib, who accorded protection to his nephew, without acknowledging his mission. For some time, then, it was possible to attack the adherents of the Prophet, while impossible to assail the Prophet himself. For such an assault would have led to civil war between the Meccan tribes, a consequence which it was their common interest to avert.

For his persecuted followers the Prophet presently succeeded in finding a refuge in Axum, the capital of Christian Abyssinia, where a few fell away to Christianity, but most remained Moslems, in the wretchedness of exile, till recalled in triumph some fourteen years later, when Arabia was fast becoming Mohammed's. It is creditable to the obscure potentate of Abyssinia that he should so long have tolerated a community whose opinions evidently differed on some important matters from his, and that he should have refused the demand for their extradition made by wealthy Meccans and enforced with presents. Naturally the latter were enraged by this diplomatic success of the Prophet, and proceeded to the measure which has been mentioned—the blockade of the whole clan of Abu Talib, who were to be starved into submission. The blockade seems to have terminated with the death of the patriarch, whose successor, apparently Abbas, eponymus of the Abbasid Dynasty, was less quixotic than his brother. Mohammed fled in consequence from Meccah to Taif, where he attempted an abortive mission; nor did he venture to quit the hospitality of the place until he had, after many failures, secured the protection of another Meccan patriarch.

But the notion of reconquering Meccah from the outside having once suggested itself to him, his chance lay in finding a refuge with some of the tribes who presented themselves at the sanctuary in the pilgrim month, and many further negotiations were started before chance or providence brought him what he required. That a city should actually require a *prophet of the Rahman* was not to be expected, but it occurred. In Yathrib, where there were Jews who called God by this name, and civil war waged between the two Arab tribes Aus and Khazraj, the accession of a Jewish force—ordinarily, of course, the Jews would not fight—had turned the battle of Bu'ath in favour of the former; in other words, the Rahman had given victory to the Aus; the Khazraj had sent envoys to Meccah to implore aid, and found there "a prophet of the Rahman" who was in a position to make a permanent peace. There is reason for believing that the Jews readily accepted this solution of the difficulty, since what they wanted was peace and quiet, and these were all the more welcome with honour. The Prophet, whose selection of agents was extraordinarily felicitous, sent a trusty follower to represent him at Yathrib, where conversions began to take place with extraordinary rapidity. Refuge and hospitality were offered by the new converts, henceforth called the *Helpers*, to their persecuted brethren of Meccah, to be called the *Refugees*. Gradually, as the news came of the progress of affairs at Yathrib, they slunk away thither, till only the Prophet and a few of his immediate adherents or relatives remained. And then only did the Meccans learn what was taking place, viz. that the Prophet whom they had persecuted had been offered and had accepted the tyranny of a city which could intercept their Syrian caravans.

There are dangers in the presence of which all scruples are abandoned, and at this crisis the Meccans resolved to shed blood, first making an arrangement whereby the guilt should be spread over as large a number of tribes as possible, and indeed taking so many precautions that the time passed in which the act could have been perpetrated. The Flight from Meccah to Medinah taxed to the uttermost the resourcefulness, the astuteness, and the daring of both the Prophet and Abu Bakr, and to some extent of Ali, but they were equal to the demand. The first two were secure for three days in a cave south of Medinah while the Meccans were searching every path that led to the north. The Meccans confiscated the property of the Refugees; but their war was in future to be not with a sect, but with a state.

The coincidence of Mohammed's arrival at Kuba, a few hours from Yathrib (afterwards known as "the City," i.e. Mohammed's City), with the Jewish Day of Atonement, gives us the date 20 September, 622, for this event, and is one of the few definite synchronisms which the history of this period offers.

The seizure of the Moslems' goods and the attempt on the Prophet's life undoubtedly justified him in regarding his relations with the Meccans as a state of war, giving him the right to waylay their caravans.

At Medinah it was his object to conciliate the different parties, and so far as possible unite them, in some cases by establishing artificial brotherhoods, in others by extinguishing the memory of past disputes. The principle which he adopted and even formulated was that man's conscience was God's concern: he was a Moslem who professed Islam. Although, then, during the whole of his despotism there was a disaffected party among the Arabs, called in the Koran "the hypocrites," or "the sick-hearted," their ostensible acceptance of Islam secured them the mildest possible treatment. With the Jews, on the other hand, various compromises were attempted; they failed because the Jews obstinately refused to acknowledge his prophetic title, and regularly taunted him with ignorance of the Scriptures which he claimed to confirm. Moreover, he regarded them as useless for military purposes, and (except as bankers) utterly untrustworthy. His judgment was shown by their conduct to be sound; hostilities between him and them broke out ere he had been despot of Medinah for a year; the various Jewish tribes refused each other assistance, whence he was able to deal with them one by one, his measures becoming severer after each victory. The tribe which he left till the end was massacred to a man in the year 5. The reader of these narratives fancies himself with Josephus at the siege of Jerusalem. The same qualities which ruined the revolters against the Roman power ruined the Jewish tribes which opposed Mohammed.

Those Moslem historians seem right who assert that Meccah was the key to Arabia, and that if the Prophet was already planning the conquest of the latter, it was necessary for him to take Meccah first.

For the first five years of the Medinah period, then, the Prophet was occupied mainly with his enemies of Meccah, who nerved themselves to great efforts, which, however, were frustrated by the Prophet's superior ability and the discipline and earnestness of the Moslems. The Meccan leader, Abu Sufyan, father to the founder of the Umayyad Dynasty, had no influence over his followers compared with that of Mohammed; and his timid and incompetent generalship appears to have paralysed the Meccan fight for independence. The series of events consisted in a pitched battle in the year 2, at Badr, caused by a raid on a Meccan caravan. The caravan escaped, but the army sent to succour it came to an engagement with Mohammed's host, and, though somewhat superior in numbers, was defeated with considerable loss. The following year the Meccans invaded Medinese territory with the view of avenging their defeat; they were satisfied with killing a number of Mohammed's followers equal to the victims of Badr, and returned when this exploit had been accomplished. The constant and successful raiding of their caravans by Mohammed led to a vigorous assault on Medinah in the year 5, the Meccans being aided by a powerful confederation of Arab tribes. Mohammed, however, succeeded in sowing dissension among them, and bad weather did the rest. The confederates broke up, having accomplished nothing. The next three years were marked by a series of peaceful negotiations ending with the capitulation of Meccah. During the course of them the leading men, weary of Abu Sufyan's incompetence, had one by one joined the victorious side, till at last Abu Sufyan himself joined it. In dealing with his countrymen, the Prophet, in accordance with Koranic doctrine, began with severity, and then became gentler and gentler; his proscription list when Meccah capitulated was reduced to two.

In Medinah itself the Prophet had to deal with three parties, which gradually were extinguished. These three were pagans, Jews, and disaffected converts. The first disappeared shortly after his arrival; paganism was not to be tolerated in Medinah or elsewhere. With the second he did his best to make terms; it was impossible, and the Jews was therefore exterminated. The disaffected converts gave occasional trouble, but their leader seems to have been cowardly and incompetent, and these to had ceased to count as a party by the end of the Prophet's life.

The conception of converting Arabia probably arose, as has been seen, before the end of the Meccan period, when the Prophet was temporarily exiled to Taif, and after his return to Meccah was compelled to devote his proselytizing efforts to foreign visitors at the feasts. It was not, however, before the eve of the taking of Meccah that he was conscious that his mission extended not only to Arabia, but to the world; and he despatched a number of missives to all known potentates bidding them embrace Islam. The missives appear to have been effective in South Arabia, and not without results in Abyssinia and Egypt; in Persia and the Byzantine Empire their effect was less noticeable. It would appear, however, that in the latter case the message led to the first struggle between Moslems and Byzantines, culminating after the Prophet's death in the seizure by the former of some of the fairest provinces of the empire.

It does not lie within the province of this work to treat in further detail the events of this extraordinary career, which terminated on 6 June 632. These have been narrated over and over again by friends, by foes, and by neutrals. Those who can express no approval of his moral qualities cannot refrain from admiring his intellectual ability; and it might seem uncertain whether the quality of persistence admirably displayed by him in the maintenance of an opinion against fierce opposition, for a number of years, should be reckoned to the head or to the heart.

Although, as has been seen, there were various reasons which led to the accurate preservation of much of the Prophet's biography, it is not surprising that a legendary biography should also grow up and gradually become imbedded in the genuine material. The thirst after the wondrous was not sufficiently gratified by a record which for the most part deals with commonplace causes and effects. There were, indeed, in the original biography a few places in which supernatural beings, angels and demons, had played a part; but it was a modest one, scarcely, if at all, affecting the course of events. The Prophet, besides the miracle of the Koran, to be presently considered, had scarcely done anything publicly that could be called miraculous; he rarely even foretold the immediate future. His contact with the supernatural had in the main been confined to private experiences, of which the most remarkable was his ascent into heaven, or at least his miraculous transference from the Temple in Meccah to the "Furthest place of prostration," i.e. the Temple of Jerusalem, long before destroyed; on which perhaps a new light is thrown by that ADVENTURE published this year, by two ladies who were transferred at Trianon to the days of Marie Antoinette. Similarly subjective was the miracle whereby he had preached to and converted certain of the *Jinn*. Since the founders of other systems were known to have shown more striking signs and wonders, many felt that here was a gap in the prophetic biography which ought to be supplied. Of the stories which owe their origin to this feeling some have obtained wide circulation, e.g. that he fed multitudes miraculously, and that he split the moon.

But there are many which have acquired less celebrity, but are to be found recorded in the works of the pious. One, called *The Removal of Grief*, composed some three hundred years ago, is a mine of them. One Tha'labah, we are told, asked the Prophet to pray that his wealth might increase; the Prophet declined twice, but the third time yielded to the request. Immediately Tha'labah's flocks and herds grew so numerous that there was no room for them in Medinah, and he had to find a valley for them, etc. At a comparatively early period the Ascent to Heaven lent itself to amplification in a variety of ways. M. le Châtelier records a tradition that on this night the Prophet was led by his conductor, the Angel Gabriel, into a palace sparkling with jewels, where was a box containing garments of various colours. the Prophet brought these garments down with him, and after having worn them himself transmitted them to his favoured disciples, who handed them on. This is the origin of the coloured stuffs worn by the ascetics.

Besides the Prophet's works, his qualities and privileges became a popular subject of study and exercise for the imagination. The character of saint and ascetic was substituted for that of the commander, statesman, and man of affairs.

We proceed to describe the miracle which he certainly claimed, the Koran.

ISLAMIC NOTION OF REVELATION

The Word of God is regarded by Islamic theology as literally God's composition, whence the Divine Being is cited as an authority for grammatical forms and rhetorical figures. The theory of "colouring by the medium," adopted by Christian theologians in order to explain discrepancies in their Scriptures, is wholly unknown to Islamic orthodoxy. The language of the Koran is God's language, and its eloquence is miraculous; any one who tries to rival it can prove that for himself. And being the communication of the All-wise, it is an infallible guide to conduct; the authority for both statements and precepts is paramount. It is therefore absolutely and uniquely consistent; inconsistency, which would have been the sign of human effort, cannot be found in it.

Although it is unlikely that we possess the whole Koran, i.e. revelations produced from the beginning to the end of the Prophet's mission, this theory of its nature seems to have prevailed from beginning to end. In what is supposed to be the earliest revelation God declares that he has "taught man with the pen, taught him what he did not know." To teach with the pen is evidently to write a book for general guidance, and the Koranic view is that the earlier revelations were of the same sort. The fact that the Jewish and Christian Scriptures are written in a style which conflicts with this theory is to the Moslem an argument against their genuineness.

The main difference between the ancient book and the modern is that the seat of the former was the mind, the seat of the latter is the paper. In works emanating from Jewish circles we can trace the effects of this "How readest thou?" in the New Testament means "What is the written text?" implying that in this case there was an authentic copy somewhere; whereas had the question been "How recitest thou?" it would have implied that there was none. The "Word of God" is therefore thought of as the two Tables of Stone were thought of—as an authentic but concealed record; and J. Smith's idea of the original of the "Book of Mormon," i.e. Tables of gold containing characters which he could only read by the grace of God, was the same. To this eternal record, "the well-guarded Table," the Koran was referable; the process by which it became communicated to Mohammed might be different at different times or be thought of differently. In the main the prevailing opinion is that the Angel Gabriel communicated its contents to Mohammed in a trance, but Gabriel is sometimes represented as taking human form, and indeed the form of a well-known man. Usually, however, the Prophet was in trance when revelations were communicated, and they were taken down by trustworthy scribes.

GENERAL CHARACTER OF REVELATION

The prophetic style is ordinarily ejaculatory, and a case of a continuous paragraph is noticed as exceptional in the Koran itself. This feature it shares with the two styles of Arabic literary art, which are thought to be earlier than the Koran, rhymed prose and verse. In the former the unit is a couplet—which may be extended—of sentences ending with the same consonant: "I would not *care* In such an enterprise to *share*" would illustrate this style. In the latter the unit is a couplet of sentences *rhythmically* alike. If, however, several verses are joined to make a poem, they must all rhyme in the same letter. Some passages of the Koran, but not many, show signs of the union of both systems. The following is a noteworthy example:

alam nashraḫ laka ṣadrak
wawaḏa'nā 'anka wiẓrak
warafa'nā laka dhikrak

Ordinarily, however, the former system only is in use, and in the later revelations the rhyme is limited to *ūna* or *īna*, which is furnished by many grammatical inflexions. The rhyme, however, is in all cases far looser than that which the literary style called rhymed prose permits.

Hence it is denied that the Koran is either in rhymed prose, or in verse; it is in a style *sui generis*, which is inimitable. If we had merely the evidence of language before us, we should undoubtedly argue that both rhymed prose and verse were later than the Koran, and represent a later stage of evolution. The present writer is not convinced that this is not the case, but it cannot be discussed here.

CONTENTS OF THE KORAN

A branch of the later Koranic literature consists in treatises on the *Occasions of Revelation*, i.e. accounts of the historic occasions in the Prophet's life when texts were revealed. The later we get in the Prophet's career the more certain such tracing becomes. At times the persons to whom they refer are mentioned in the text—e.g. the Prophet's wives and his adopted son Zaid; or the allusions to events are unmistakable—e.g. the battles of Badr and Hunain, the taking of Khaibar, the taking of Meccah, the exclusion of pagans from the pilgrimage, the building of the rival mosque at Kuba. Hence Sprenger compared these portions of the Koran with the modern leading articles on current events in the official chronicle of a government. But the earlier we go back in the Prophet's career the less certain do such allusions become. In one case indeed a personal name—Abu Lahab, said to belong to an uncle of the Prophet—figures in an imprecation, and the Persian conquest of the nearer East is mentioned in a prophecy. Even in these days only a high degree of education or unusual critical ability enables a man to distinguish between historic truth and historic conjecture; in the greater number of cases these identifications of occasions are conjectural, and even among orthodox Moslem writers they have no good name. The earlier revelations appear to be *oracular*, ejaculations, brief admonitions or warnings, whether directed to the Prophet himself or intended for others. There are also some brief historical pictures, naturally pointing morals. The main doctrines of Islam, the Unity of God, the Future Life, with certain moral precepts, are also found. Some few are personal, and may be said to refer to the psychology of the Prophet. The intermediate revelations, i.e. those from the public promulgation of Islam to the Flight, are homiletic, very largely the "Stories of the Prophets," i.e. accounts of the mission of various prophets, both Hebrew and Arabian, and the vengeance which fell on those who disobeyed them. One Surah, which deals with Gospel history, is supposed to belong to the time of the Abyssinian Exile, and to have been an account of the Islamic theory of the nature and work of Christ for communication to the Abyssinian King. Some portions must have been intended for liturgical use, but about this little certain is known; some legislation, though little, also belongs to this period. The revelations after the Flight are either legislation, in some cases minute, or in the style of political manifestors; the bulk of the second Surah, which is regarded as the most eloquent of all, is of this type. The nature of the arrangement of the Koran is such that the historical order of the Surahs is much more nearly from end to beginning than conversely.

PRESERVATION OF THE KORAN, AND PROBABILITY OF ITS AUTHENTICITY

One fact that emerges from a study of our authorities is that the Prophet kept no official copy of his revelations. The teachers of the Koran had, like other teachers of the time, to satisfy themselves that their pupils had committed certain portions to memory; and when we hear of as many as seventy missionaries being sent to a single tribe—doubtless the ordinary round number—the multitude is explained by this consideration. But when once the matter was committed to memory, the material on which it was written was of no further use. The real Koran was on the "Well-guarded Table": those who took down the matter communicated to them by the Prophet did so only as a temporary expedient. The project of collecting it is said to have originated with Omar, the second Caliph, after the Prophet's death. It met at first with serious opposition on the ground that it was *ultra vires* to endeavour to do what the Prophet might have done, but had not; and when Abu Bekr agreed, the task of collecting it was found to be of great difficulty: for where was it? *In people's breasts*, unless there happened to be an ostrakon, or bit of parchment or of papyrus here and there containing a memorandum of it. Zaid Ibn Thabit was entrusted with this work, and he compiled an official copy, only intended for the sovereign's use. We have no memoir of his procedure, but he is supposed to have settled the text by the principle which underlies the later treatment of Tradition—credibility of witnesses. The Korashite dialect was declared to be the true language of the Koran: doubtless there were differences between that and the dialect of Medinah.

The main difficulty of the Koran in its existing form is the import of the word *Surah*, or Chapter. The origin of the word, which is employed in the Koran itself, is unknown; most probably it means a *layer*, or *course* of bricks in a wall, the bricks of which must in certain ways—i.e. at least two dimensions—be symmetrical. Rhythmical agreement between the texts, *āyāt*, literally signs or miracles, of each separate chapter only exists to a rudimentary extent; and it is generally admitted that the Surahs contain materials belonging to different dates. It seems difficult to think of any theory of their construction which is not unnatural. The task of arranging the sacred texts in fixed groups might very well have appalled a Moslem; we could scarcely credit a contemporary of the Prophet with having the courage to attempt it. On the other hand, the notion that the Surahs existed as frames, which gradually became filled as revelations descended, has little to commend it, and involves the existence of an official copy, which we have seen to be excluded by the evidence.

The work of the third Caliph was to provide a public edition. The reason appears to have been that unofficial copies were being circulated in the vast regions which were being, or had been, won over to Islam, and for which copies of the Sacred Book had become indispensable. All these were destroyed, and official copies despatched to the chief capitals. The same editor was employed, perhaps because, in the extreme ambiguity and imperfection of the Arabic script, he alone could interpret the first edition with certainty. Whether there was any fresh revision at this time is unknown. There is at best reason for thinking that some of the controversies which cropped up within the score of years following the Prophet's death left traces in the volume. The traditions preserve fragments of the edition of the Koran by learned followers of the Prophet, but the variations which they offer are slight, and it is likely that the Caliphs chose the best man who could be found for the purpose.

The official copies were, after all, only *memoriæ technicæ*. One who had read the text with a teacher would afterwards be able to check his memory thereby; one who saw the text for the first time would be confronted with an enigma. Towards the end of the century such improvements were introduced into Arabic writing as would enable a man acquainted with the language to make it out for himself. Yet certain systems of intonation were introduced, which were considered necessary for liturgical purposes; the Koran, if otherwise intoned in prayers, would have no value. Whether the Jewish system of accentuation comes from the Islamic doctrine or conversely is not certain. The systems permissible were afterwards stereotyped as seven or ten. These of course can only be acquired orally.

INTERPRETATION OF THE KORAN

Of the Sacred Book the least intelligible portion consists in certain letters of the alphabet prefixed to a certain number of Surahs; they are pronounced like our letter-names (*aitch*, *zed*, etc.). Much ingenuity has been spent on solving this enigma; most probably they are no more than what they profess to be, trials of the pen or voice before starting the writing or recitation: probably of the latter, since very early traditions treat them as part of the revelation. The meaning of the text is otherwise ordinarily simple and clear; there are few archaisms in the sense of obsolete and obscure words: nevertheless the Koran offered many opportunities for commentary. Since it divides itself into two parts, the distinct and the equivocal, or the genuine and the doubtful, it was a matter of necessity to know to which portion any text belonged. There is reason for thinking this division identical with the division into valid and abrogated; for that texts could be revealed and afterwards abrogated is distinctly stated in the volume, and the theory of abrogation is defended by the procedure of the Christian revelation. If Christ could abrogate the Mosaic law, Mohammed could abrogate the Christian and since God's ordinances could have merely temporary value, there was nothing to extend their duration necessarily to an age: it might be limited to some days. It is also hinted in the Koran that Prophets were liable to have their revelations interpolated by the devil and the word used in this place, where God is said to *revise* this text, is used in the above division, where its participle has been rendered "distinct."

In any case this text is a justification for comment; for where, as is frequently the case, the obvious sense of the passages involve difficulties, the student ought to know which of the two or more is to be the permanent authority. The differences between Islam sects to some extent arise from different views on this matter; if, e.g., the Koran is determinist texts which seem to favour free will have to be explained in the light of the others; if it be in favour of the freedom of the will, the others must be explained away. The same holds good the principle of religious toleration and of others.

SOURCES OF THE KORAN

The source of the Koran in the orthodox opinion is, as we have seen, Divine revelation; the only way in which the question could be put from this point of view is, To what extent do the contents of the book correspond with other known pre-existing literature? In the first place it claims to confirm the Law and the Gospel, or in general "what was before it." In the main this is the fact. The story of Joseph, that of the Fall, that of the Deliverance from Egypt, are told much as the Old Testament tells them; in several cases the matter of the Koran is nearer that of apocryphal books and collections of traditions than the Bible. The persons who figure most in the Koran are Old Testament characters. Among New Testament persons only Zacharias, John (Yahya), Mary, and Jesus ('Isā) figure. The apostles are just mentioned by their Abyssinian name, but none of them is specified. Some prophets have been identified with Old Testament characters though their names differ considerably; others belong clearly to Arabian narratives, and their sphere of work is located in Arabia. One of these, Lukman, was said to be the author of a Book of Wisdom, in the hands of some of the Arabian tribes before the Prophet's time.

The verses ascribed to a contemporary poet, Umayyah, son of Abu' l-Salt, show a considerable likeness to certain parts of the Koran, and those who believe them to be genuine regard them as one of the sources of the Koran, especially as the Prophet, who by no means favoured poetry, is said to have admired this bard. It seems far more likely that the Koran is the source of the verses than that the converse could be the case.

The Koran is therefore cast in a different mould from those sacred books which treat directly of historical matters, whether as a record of God's dealings with a chosen people or as an authentic chronicle of the Founder's life. So far as the Koran introduces history, it is with the view of enforcing morals; this is the case even with its allusions to current events. "Ye have had a warning in two parties that met"—this introduces a brief notice of the Battle of Badr; the text does not set itself to tell the story, but reminds the hearer of the events in order to enforce the warning.

7

ESSENTIAL ELEMENTS OF RELIGION WITNESSED IN THE HISTORY OF THREE UNIVERSAL RELIGIONS

W. Boyd Carpenter

'Hereafter ye shall see heaven open and the angels of God ascending and descending.'

St John i. 51.

The position which we have reached is as follows. We have seen that there are reasons for believing that religion will survive; the grounds for this are to be found in the fact that man everywhere shows invincible religious tendencies, coupled with the fact that man's nature seems to be permanent. There are certain laws or principles of man's spiritual and moral nature which appear to be constant. These point to the permanence of man's nature, and also to the elements which the future religion must possess if it is to survive. Some idea of the form which the religion of the future is likely to take may be derived from the elements which appear to be essential. These elements are Dependence, Fellowship, Progress.

In proof of the need of these three elements we must turn to the witness of religious history. We found their need attested in the history of the Mexican religion. We saw hints of the same in the language of Hellenism, and in the religious conceptions of the Hebrews.

Source: Carpenter, W.B., *The Permanent Elements of Religion*, 1894, London and New York, Macmillan, pp. 78–90, 131–45, 297–8.

These, however, only touch the hem of the subject. The religious history of the world centres in those religions which are called universal. We can only make approximate guesses at the population of the world; but recent authorities seem agreed that three-fourths, if not four-fifths, of the population of the world will be found distributed among the three universal religions—Islamism, Buddhism, Christianity.[1]

We are about to interrogate the history of these three great religions, and ascertain whether we find in them evidence that the elements of Dependence, Fellowship, and Progress are essential to the completeness of the religious idea. One point needs, perhaps, to be made clear before we go further. We must understand what we mean when we speak of a religion as universal. We may recall the distinction pointed out by Kuenen. A religion may be regarded as universal, because as a fact it has shown itself capable of transcending the limits of the land of its birth. But this by no means implies that it has within it the essential elements or qualities calculated to ensure its complete universalism. It is universal in fact—as Kuenen would say—because it has shown itself more than national; whether it is universal in quality demands further investigation. This distinction is important, and it enters deeply into the drift of these Lectures, the aim of which is to ascertain what are the elements without which a religion cannot be said to be possessed of the quality of universalism, and then to ask how far the great religions truly possess it.

In the present Lecture our inquiry is whether the history of the three universal religions bears witness to the need of the three elements of Dependence, Fellowship, and Progress. In the next lecture we shall ask how far these three elements are native to the religions in whose history we have found them; for the three elements may appear in the history of a religion, and yet not be of its essence; they may be accretions, rather than developments; additions, and not evaluations; adoptions, not children born in its home; proselytes of the gate rather than children of the covenant. In this Lecture we are merely regarding the history of these religions as attesting what are the elements which man demands in the faith which aspires to permanence. And our inquiry will show us that Dependence, Fellowship, and Progress are asked for by the spirit of man, whether we interrogate the story of Islamism, Buddhism, or Christianity.

ISLAMISM

The figure of Mohammed loomed large and terrible upon those who saw him only through the fog which dread and ignorance spread around him. To them he was an object of horror against which anything evil might be said. He was the first-born of Satan, the dealer in black arts; his very name became an epithet of reproach. But, now the mists of prejudice have cleared away, we can afford to see the founder of Islamism in a fairer light. We can understand him better as we recall his traditional portraiture. A lithe and slender figure, broad-shouldered, and upbearing proudly his majestic head, crowned with dark, flowing and curling hair; an oval face bronzed by the sun; the nose, 'the rudder of the face, the index of the will,' strong and masterful; teeth brilliant as hailstones, and eyes bright as stars; soft, small, nervous hands: all made up a figure goodly to look upon. His peculiarities also are known to us: the deep blood-vessel on the forehead that darkened with passion; the strange egg mark between the shoulders, the so-called seal of prophecy; and the gracious gait, light and springing, as of one stepping downwards. Joyous he was and loving as a child, patient as a woman; ready now to romp with the children, to tell them stories, now to sit patiently in a foul dense atmosphere, nursing the sick child till it died with its head on his bosom; full of a sweet, soft courtesy which would not willingly offend by gesture or by manner; never the first to withdraw his hand from another's grasp, or to turn aside from another's converse. Altogether you would say a delicate organisation, sensitive, passionate, responsive; drawn to a strange, sad love of solitude, yet longing for the solace and soothing of a woman's hand, and flying to her sheltering arms as to a safe place from the wild terrors which at times fell upon him. Briefly, he is a man with that mixture of qualities which Coleridge declared needful for the highest genius, that blending of masculine and feminine qualities which is called androgynous; full of contradictions with his timidity and his courage, his passionate indulgence and his wondrous modesty, his outbursts of cruelty and his patient tenderness; terrified at the weight of the task laid upon him, yet finding it impossible to shrink from it; hating conflict, yet preferring it to the inward torment of the spirit that, Jonah-like, refuses its errand; gaining in his self-surrender the power which was needful to weld others together, and to inspire them with that loyalty to God which was the essence of his teaching.[2] From this picture of the Prophet, we may, after allowing for natural exaggerations, understand him and his system better. Dependence is at the root of Islamism. This may be called its initial idea. It is seen in the very word by which the religion is described. The religion is not Mohammedanism. The religion is Islâm: submission. It teaches that man is of small account. In the view of the Prophet, God was all; the varied and grotesque divinities and saints which were brought into the worship of men, Christian or Pagan, were impertinences. Man could only be religious in a complete self-surrender; he depended wholly upon God; he was but a slave of the Most High, who owned him and demanded from him the most absolute service. All other divinities were usurpers, standing between the sovereign and his subjects; man was God's slave, no other could share that proprietorship, and to the sense of this relationship with the Creator the Prophet would restore man. 'Obedience to God and His messenger is the strength of the Moslem system.'[3] 'Man lives on content with himself, but he must one day return to his Creator and Lord and give account to Him. This is in a sense the material principle of the oldest faith of Islâm.'[4] We can see that the principle of Dependence shows itself here. The exalted idea of the sovereign and sole God, and the necessity of the most complete obedience to Him, are the emphatic statements of this Dependence. Islamism starts with this as its essential idea.

We must note next its relation to the idea of Fellowship or communion, which is the second element we are seeking. The alien gods and intermediate divinities, the worship of saints and the devotion to shrines were offensive in the eyes of the Prophet; they savoured of the usurpation which he denounced; they robbed God of His glory. But Mohammed thought more of the glory of God than of the needs of man. He seems to promise, indeed, the restoration of union with the Divine, but he practically makes no provision for it. His mind is full of God and God's greatness; God is the Ruler, man is the subject; God is the Creator, man is the creature; God is the owner and arbiter of all, man is His possession, and must surrender to God's will and submit to His decree. The profoundness of his conviction of the one truth overshadowed the other needful element; and he forgot that the subject, the creature, the slave, had been made in God's image, and had a heart which asked for real fellowship with the Divine. Mohammed hardly saw this; the emphasis with which he affirmed the one truth made the realization of the fellowship of man with his Maker difficult, indeed impossible. The idea of God's greatness, and of the absolute authority exercised by the fiat of His will, dazzled the popular mind for a while, but it had the effect of seeming to push man very far away from God. True Fellowship was impossible; the link between the Creator and the creature was that of power on the one side and Dependence on the other; the idea of holiness which satisfies the ethical feeling, and the idea of love which captivates the heart, were wanting. No wonder that Fellowship seemed impossible.

But the after history exhibits a reaction, and shows eloquently man's desire for some nearness or fellowship with the Divine. The followers of Mohammed could not rest in the pure Theism which the Prophet sought to preach and on his death they commenced the worship of Mohammed, viewing him as a mediator still living and pleading with Allah; and Medina became, in sanctity, second only to Mecca. Nor was this all; the worship of Walis, or saints, quickly followed. The sense of the need of some points of contact between man and the object of his worship led to saint-worship. If a power high and great cannot minister to this strong yearning of man's breast, humanity will invent some other mode of bringing the Divine near itself. And this is what happened in the history of Islamism. It was expressed in the saint-worship of which we have spoken, but it found its most important expression in the movement called Súfism. Súfism is a motley phrase; it covers a wide area; but from whatever source it sprang, its significance is clear. The Súfite is the Mohammedan mystic. He realizes the double yearning of the human soul: the longing for reconciliation which springs from the conscience; the longing for Fellowship which springs from the heart. The splendid absolutism with which Mohammed invested his idea of God made direct Fellowship between the Creator and the creature difficult, for the creature was the slave of the Divine will; and there can be no Fellowship where the will is enslaved. According to the saint-worshipper, if man must have Fellowship with the Divine, let him have it with those who are nearest to the great God, seeing that God Himself dwells beyond the reach of human fellowship. But where shall this be found, if not with the Prophet and with those great heroes of Islâm who have been the highest servants of God? The Súfite, moved by the same yearning, took a bolder line and claimed man's right to go straight to God. These movements in various ways sought to supply the element of Fellowship. 'If the mystic element,' says Kuenen, 'was almost entirely wanting at first, and if the pressure of the sense of sin was unrelieved, Súfism and the belief in the mediation of Mohammed himself and of the saints so assiduously honoured, filled up the gap.'[5] This movement, or rather, element, is of importance; for in the eyes of many its presence in the heart of Islamism is the omen of its future advance. The only path in Islamism towards reformation lies in this doctrine of mysticism, is the language of one writer.[6]

The third element to be sought in the history of Islamism is that of Progress. Dogmatism is prone to be jealous of this element. True theology understands that it has a place within her fold. The laws of God are in Himself: they can work outside the range of all human institutions, and they do not therefore end with the dogmas of any prophet, however great. Dogmas may express truth or they may not, but at their best they are no more than expressions of it: they do not originate it; they may reveal, but they do not create truth. The vice of dogmatism appears in its virtual denial of God, or, what is the same thing, the limiting of the range of His rule. A doctrine is true and living when it declares anything which is; but it must declare what *is*, not what merely may or might be. The glory of doctrinism lies in the capacity which it has for declaring what exists as an unalterable fact or truth; the sin of dogmatism lies in its attempt to pose as a final authority for the truth, and to limit the operation of the truth to the system which is conscious of and which formulates it. It is like the attempt of an astronomer to prove that the planets move by the laws of motion, only when his glass is upon them. Truths can never be invented: they can only be discovered. The dogmatist is, in this, different from the prophet. The prophet perceives and declares truth, which is true whether people hear or forbear, whether the prophet speaks or is silent; the dogmatist is one who speaks of truth as though it were his monopoly, and insists that nothing is genuine without the trade-mark of his firm upon it. But truth is of God, and God's truth remains whether we formulate it wisely or unwisely, or do not formulate it at all. The righteous Ruler of the world rules the world in righteousness, and works with the growing thoughts and endeavours of mankind. Religion must recognise this, if it is to live. Man asks for the presence of God working in all history according to right. Righteousness is of God wherever it is found. Submission to the will of God may be an element of religious life; the recognition of the righteousness of God's universal rule is needful for the religious life of mankind. The submission of my will to God's will may be a religious submission or not; but the submission of my will to a system which says it is God's will, and enforces rules without grounding them on principles of righteousness, is neither religious nor wise. This is proved even in the history of Mohammedanism; for in the morning of its history we find those who resented the hard doctrines of predestination, who asked for the recognition of ethical principles, who reverenced will in man and righteousness in God, and who could not acquiesce in blind and unconscientious surrender to God's will merely because He was mighty. It is needless to tell the story of this movement. It is enough to say that those who called themselves the upholders of God's unity and righteousness, and who, together with those who, resembled them in teaching, are called the Mo'tazilites, or Dissidents, flourished for a time; but, notwithstanding the patronage of some of the Caliphs, the day came when the so-called orthodox, unable to see the worthlessness of a religion divorced from righteousness, rose against the Freethinkers, as they were styled. 'It was not in the God of the Mo'tazilites whose essence was righteousness, but in the God of orthodoxy, the Almighty, subject to no other rule than his own caprice, that they recognized their own and Mohammed's Allah.'[7] The Mo'tazilites fell; but their influence is sufficient to show that, within the history of Islamism, the plea for the third element of Progress was put forward. The movement would have freed Islamism from difficulties of its own creation; it would have enabled men to recognise the width of God's work in the world; it would have opened their eyes to the revelation of God in nature; and in giving this knowledge, it would have saved Islâm from the stagnation which has befallen it. 'This is *true*,' must ever be the voice of the prophet; 'this *only* is true,' is the voice of the fanatic and the dogmatist. The difference is slight: but the voice of the prophet is heard to the end of time, and the truth, which he declared, mingles with the flowing life of the world and keeps it pure; the voice of the fanatic is heard, and it calls up the spirit of frenzy; it wins a victory, it binds and imprisons its foe, but its mad temper is its destruction, for the bound victim pulls down its sanctuary and slays the faith of the fanatic in its ruins. Islâm crushed the life within its bosom, and so doomed itself to prolonged barrenness. But notwithstanding this, the history of Islamism has yielded evidence of the three elements of which we have spoken. Dependence was its point of departure; something to satisfy the instinct for Fellowship was demanded and conceded in its growth; and the element of freedom and Progress was demanded and refused in its history.

I ISLAMISM

1. We have already seen that the element of Dependence is supplied by Islamism. It is admitted that this element belongs to its very essence. Islamism would not be Islamism without this quality, for it is the religion of dependence. Submission is the whole of Mohammedanism.[8] To lose this idea would be to drop the keystone out of the arch of its structure; it would be the breaking down of the bridge which it sought to build between earth and heaven. The ladder by which man climbs towards Paradise is the ladder of dependence and submission. Islamism is surrender. The element of Dependence is essentially in Islamism.

2. Is the element of Fellowship there also? Historically it is present. We have seen that a mystical element began to show itself among the followers of Mohammed. This mystical tendency covers and embraces the element of Fellowship. Man yearns for more than the sense of his dependence upon one greater than himself; he asks for the sense of the nearness of one who is kin with himself. The worship of the Walis or Saints is the expression of this yearning. Greatness does not satisfy; omnipotence appals; fitness and kinship are more attractive than arbitrary and irresistible might. If man cannot creep into the heart of God, he will crouch close under the shadow of those who seem to him god-like. He will worship the heroes, and rain tears upon the shrines of saints, and invoke their aid, feeling sure of their sympathy. The Súfite movement exhibits in bolder form the same tendency. It supplied a sense of nearness by saying that men might go straight to God and that God was One who felt with them and fought for them. So the missing element of Fellowship was supplied in two ways. On the one hand men had looked up to God with wonder and awe; but they could not feel the beating of the divine heart in sympathy with their own: that was too much to expect; Allah was too great a monarch for that; therefore the sympathy, which the conception of God failed to convey, was sought in the Prophet or the Saint. On the other hand the Súfite movement, teaching gentler thoughts of God, grew and became popular because it also met a want in human nature.

But it was not an indigenous plant. It arose because man wanted it; it did not spring spontaneously out of the heart of the religion itself. It is using far too mild an expression when we say it was not indigenous. It is far more exact to say that it was alien from the original spirit of Islamism. Those features, which give evidence of the craving of man for fellowship with the divine, are features which had no place in the religion as it came from its founder's hands.

Take Saint-worship. In the reverence paid to Walis or Saints, in the worship given to the Prophet, the mystical feeling found expression. But such a movement was out of harmony with the original faith. The adoration of the Walis 'might lead us to regard it as a product of Islam itself. But, as a fact, it is far from being so. It is rather a protest against the very religion in which it occupies so prominent a place. The Moslem seeks what his faith withholds from him, and seeks it where the authority which he himself recognises forbids him to look.' Again: 'If it is only in this form that Islam can satisfy the demands of the pious soul, then it has become a religion of the world in the teeth of its own proper nature.'[9]

Take the reverence paid to sacred places. The disposition from which this proceeds is akin to the impulse to Saint-worship. But this reverence for holy shrines is as alien from the original faith as is the worship of the Walis. The Ka'ba was reverenced, but its veneration 'is in such glaring contradiction with the Moslem's otherwise pure conceptions of God, that a reconciliation can only be effected by the most far-fetched theories, and even then imperfectly.'[10]

Take Súfism. Súfism exists in the bosom of Islamism; but she is like Israel, a stranger in the land of Ham; she is tolerated, but the son of the bondwoman cannot be co-heir with the son of the free woman. 'The Moslem who makes terms with Súfism thereby gives his own religion a certificate of poverty, and the true Súfite is a Moslem no more.'[11]

We need scarcely be surprised at this. The conception of God presented by Islamism will account for it. Islamism is a Deism. God is infinitely great, dwelling afar off, removed by His majesty to an immeasurable distance from His creatures. 'Mohammed pointed the world to the solitary majesty of God, but he left it a solitary majesty; he did not bring the object of his reverence into union with the human soul.' Parallel is the conception of man: man is a slave, the mechanical executor of God's will, finding 'his highest goal only in absolute submission to a will he cannot resist, and may not try to comprehend.'[12] This conception excluded mysticism, for 'Deism and mysticism'[13] it has been truly said, 'cannot really go together.' We cannot find the element of Fellowship naturally in Islamism. It is there, but not as a daughter born in the house. It is there as a historical fact, but it is of alien, not of native growth. We must admit, therefore, that Fellowship is not an indigenous element in Islamism.

3. Can we find there the element of Progress? Our first impulse would certainly be to answer 'Yes.' Memory and imagination are at hand ready to paint the glories of the culture and civilization which have flourished under the shadow of the Prophet's name. We cannot forget all that has been said of Arabian Science. Side by side with the conquerors came the teachers. Victorious in Africa and Europe, they brought gifts of surpassing value in their hands. We cannot ignore the venerable walls of Cordova and the great stream of knowledge which flowered throughout Spain, carrying with it fertilizing power, and regenerating the intellectual life of Europe.[14] We might acknowledge that from the middle of the eighth century to the middle of the thirteenth there were not merely great thinkers and scholars in the Moslem world, but that its average culture and intelligence were in advance of those of Christendom.[15] We do not undervalue the services rendered to civilization under the rule of certain princes who held the faith of Islâm.

Thus then, as a historical fact, Progress was fostered at periods of Mohammedan ascendency; but this does not show that Islamism allied itself naturally and sympathetically with the progress of the race. This question is one of great and present interest. No apology is needed for giving it as full consideration as our time will allow. One thing is clear. The relation of Islamism to Progress was not always one of sympathy. How is it, we may ask, that the earlier years of Moslem rule do not show any intellectual movement? Under the auspices of the first four Caliphs and under the guidance of the Omayyads, there was no zeal for culture, no thirst for knowledge, no desire of progress. Intellectual life drooped. Whatever growth and knowledge existed, withered at the touch of Islamism, like vegetation beneath the fiery breath of the desert.

But, when the sovereign power passed from Arab to Persian hands,[16] a change took place. The throne of the Moslem world was moved eastward, and its sceptre was wielded by the Abbasids. When new conditions are followed by new results, we can hardly refuse to admit the probability that the new conditions have contributed to the new results. The land to which the Moslem power came was a land of culture. Unlike the Arab, who was destitute of all the instincts of higher civilization, and changeless as his changeless deserts, the Persian welcomed knowledge, loved science, and kept alive his intellect. It was on the soil of Persia, and under the rule of intelligent princes like the Abbasids, that the forward movement took place. That is, under Persian, rather than Moslem influence, civilization and knowledge began to flourish. Euclid, Galen, and Ptolemy were translated, and became the heritage of the eastern lands. There arose great thinkers, among whom Alfarabi, Avicenna, and Averroes reached the front rank.[17] Astronomy and algebra were studied, a fresh development of chemistry took place, the theory of distillation was reached, and, as some think, the invention of gunpowder belongs to this epoch.

We cannot argue *Post hoc, ergo propter hoc*. We cannot say that because culture and civilization advanced after the rise of Islamism, therefore the advance was due to Islamism. But we may, perhaps, argue—*ante hoc, ergo non propter hoc*—we may plead that if before the rise of Moslem influence there was a cultivated soil in Persia, therefore the advance was probably due not to Mohammedan but to Persian influence.[18] Are we then to consider the state of the case to be this: to the Arabs culture was nothing; to the Persians it was much? The transference of the Faith from the one soil to the other was the transference of religion from a soil which was unlikely to develop culture to a soil which was pre-eminently likely to do so. It dwelt then in a country open to a twofold stream of thought and culture from the West and from the East. Influences reached it alike from India and from Greece. Are we to assign, therefore, the whole of that culture to the soil? Are we to conclude that Islamism as such is actually hostile to culture? The answer of Renan is that what we are accustomed to call Arabian science, 'because it is written in Arabic, is, in reality, Greco-Sassanidean; or, more strictly, Greek, for the fertile element of it springs from Greece.' The answer may be challenged on the ground that it does not sufficiently recognise the influences which came from India; but few will challenge its accuracy as regards the Arab. But if not Arabian, might it be called Moslem science? Did the religion of Mohammed reach forth a fostering hand for its progress? If the race of Mohammed was heedless of culture, was the faith of Mohammed equally so? The answer is a sad one. The growing culture only 'won from the orthodox Moslem his malediction.' 'Islâm persecuted philosophy and science.'[19]

Progress has always had to fight against timid conservatism and hot-house religionism, against ignorance and self-opinionatedness.

Hence it is a fair question to ask: Was the persecution and opposition to culture the work of an individual or of a party, or was it of the very tendency of the faith? The answer of Renan is that in treating science as an enemy, Islamism had only been consistent.[20] Notwithstanding this opinion, some may be tempted to ask: 'What is there in Islamism hostile to science?' Are there dogmas, held to be of the essence of Mohammedanism, which make the maintenance of the faith inconsistent with the spirit of Progress? The doctrine of the uncreated Koran, which is accepted by orthodox Islamism, affirms the changeless infallibility and, in most uncompromising form, the verbal inspiration of the sacred book.[21] This foolish dogma necessarily creates a collision between the creed of Islâm and the growing life of the world of thought. But it may be suggested that the faith of Islâm could freely surrender this ossified idea of inspiration without damaging the essential elements of her creed, and so become free to welcome those discoveries which reveal the unity of the world, the unity of the race, and the unity of nature. But even were this possible, which it is not, for the doctrine of the uncreated Koran forbids it, there still would be wanting a real link between the faith of Islâm and the spirit of culture and progress. It is not enough that a religion which aspires to universality should be passive towards culture—it must at least be sympathetic. But in Islamism there is no encouragement to culture. It offers no benediction to the student of nature; it speaks no cheering words to the pioneers of progress. God is far away from human life; His sovereignty too august to heed the arts and thoughts of men. He is great, we are little; it is as vain to study His world as to try and understand His ways. The answer of the Caliph, when Sir H. Layard asked information respecting the population, commerce, and history of Mossoul, may illustrate this: 'What you ask,' he said, 'is both useless and harmful. You know much which does not interest me, and what you have seen I despise. Will greater knowledge improve your digestion, and can your wandering eyes discover Paradise?'[22] Whatever springs from such a faith is cut and dried, barren and limited. It has no sap, no seed of future life in itself; and its impotence is the more apparent, when we find behind it the conception of a God, who does not care to touch dead things to make them live. The inspirations of God cannot be claimed for man's art and science, man's songs and implements. He has bestowed inspiration once, and it lies within the covers of a book, and there is no inspiration for the working or for the thinking sons of men, to consecrate thought and dignify art. Man may paint,[23] and sing, and study, and discover; he may explore and explain the wonders of God's works; he may alleviate by his discoveries the burden of life; but it is not by a divinely-given wisdom he has done these things. God takes no delight in such things. It is little wonder that a hopeless fatalism has become a part of the creed of the Moslems.

The movement commenced by the Wahhábites,[24] who have been called the Puritans of Islamism, has, in the opinion of many, reasserted the purest and most essential features of the faith of the Prophet. Under their auspices the dogma of the uncreated Koran reigns supreme. Commenting on the phrase, 'Puritans of Islam,' Kuenen says: 'The comparison is not unjust. But whereas no serious historian would ever dream of simply identifying Puritanism and Christianity, Wahhábism really is Islâm itself—Islâm, the whole of Islâm, and nothing but Islâm.'[25]

The conclusion, then, seems to be this: Islamism has been, and still is, a great power in the world. There is much in it that is calculated to purify and elevate mankind, at a certain stage of history. It has the power of reclaiming the slaves of a degraded polytheism from their low grovelling conception of God to conceptions which are higher:[26] it has set an example of sobriety to the world, and has shielded its followers from the drink-plague which destroys the strength of nations. And, in so far as it has achieved this, it has performed a work which entitles it to the attention of man, and no doubt has been a factor in God's education of the world. But when we come to the wider question, and ask whether Islamism possesses those elements which will qualify her to stand the crisis of the future, and to emerge from its trials as a religion fitted to guide the future of humanity, to satisfy the demands of man's heart, and to be considered universal in gift and quality, we are bound to answer 'No. It can teach man reverence and service. It can meet his instinct of dependence; but to minister to the higher needs of man, it is powerless.' For the spirit of man, when it cries aloud in its agony, 'Oh, that I knew where I might find Him! that I might come even to His seat!' (Job xiii.3) Islâm has no answer. For the cry of him who asks that our fair world with all its beauty shall be regarded as a thing growing up under the inspiring hand of God, Islâm has no sympathy. It is like one of those countries in which the verdure is luxuriant, the flowers are of glorious colours, and the birds soar over our heads resplendent in plumage and majestic in flight; but where the flowers lack fragrance, where the birds lack song, and where the homes of men are not. The mirage-fever of the desert is upon us; we dream of water, we wake to thirst; we think of shelter, and we wake to yearn for the shadow of a rock in the weary land. Such faith can never be universal; it provides for Dependence, but not for Progress, and it supplies no link of Fellowship between the spirit of man and the Spirit of God who made him.

We have now to ask, whether these religions meet the requirements which the religion of the future must fulfil, by possessing unifying force and that characteristic which raises them above any special time, and is the pledge of perpetuity.

We commence with Islamism. Has it unifying force? Has it power to meet the hopes and desires of men for a religion which shall embrace every race, complexion and character? The answer must be that Islamism is essentially rigid and frigid. Islamism is great, but great as an iceberg is great; its tendency is to stiffen and harden. Whenever, under more genial influences, it melts to meet the needs of humanity, it ceases to be Islamism. It was destined—such is the view of those who have studied it—to stereotype itself once for all and assume unalterable shape. 'Almost as old as Islam itself, and destined to last as long, there stood and there stand immoveable the Koran and the tradition.'[27]

So while the world rolls on from change to change,
And realms of thought expand,
The letter stands without expanse or range,
Stiff as a dead man's hand.

It can hardly supply the unifying force requisite in a great religion of humanity.

It cannot claim perpetuity. There are indeed elements in it which never die, but these are common to other creeds. In its special characteristics it is limited; it is of an epoch; 'it is a side branch of Christianity, or, better still, as we should now say, of Judaism: a selection, as it were, from Law and Gospel, made by an Arab and for Arabs.'

NOTES

1 There is considerable difficulty in ascertaining the exact number of the adherents of various religions throughout the world. The estimated population of the world varies from twelve to fourteen hundred millions. M. Hubner sets it at 1,392½ millions. Of these, from

150,000,000 to 200,000,000 may at the utmost be claimed for Mohammedanism. M. Hubner's estimate is 80 millions. The number ranged under the complex term of Buddhism have been placed at from 400,000,000 to 500,000,000, while Christianity claims from 300,000,000 to 400,000,000. *Cf.* Rhys Davids, *Buddhism*, p. 6 (SPCK); W. Scawen Blunt's article in *Fortnightly Review*, 1881, vol. ii. p. 208; also an article on 'Missions' in *Quarterly Review*, July, 1886. De Quatrefages, *Human Species*, p. 485.

2 'Mohammed was a man of middle height, but of commanding presence; rather thin, but with broad shoulders and a wide chest; a massive head, a frank, oval face with a clear complexion, restless black eyes, long heavy eyelashes, a prominent aquiline nose, white teeth, and a full thick beard are the principal features of the verbal portraits historians have drawn of him.

'He was a man of highly nervous organisation, thoughtful, restless, inclined to melancholy, and possessing an extreme sensibility, being unable to endure the slightest unpleasant odour or the least physical pain. . . . From youth upwards he had suffered from a nervous disorder which tradition calls epilepsy, but the symptoms of which more closely resemble certain hysterical phenomena well known and diagnosed in the present time, and which are almost always accompanied with hallucinations, abnormal exercise of the mental functions, and not unfrequently with a certain amount of deception, both voluntary and otherwise.' Palmer, Introduction to vol. vi. of *Sacred Books of the East* (Qur'ân), p. xix.

The following may illustrate some of the positions adopted in the Lectures:

'For three days they lay concealed, their enemies once coming so near that Abu Bekr, trembling, said, 'We are but two.' 'Nay,' said Mohammed, 'we are three; for God is with us.' *Ibid.*, p. xxxiii.

'Mohammed, in one point at least, used his supreme authority as prophet to make provision for the flesh' (J. Wellhausen, article on '*Mohammedanism,' Encyc. Brit.*, 9th ed.). This refers to the affairs of his harem. One of these marriages, it is well known, 'gave great scandal to the faithful, namely, that with the wife of his adopted son, Zâid, whom her husband divorced and offered to surrender to Mohammed on finding that the latter admired her. This also required a revelation to sanction it.' Palmer, Introduction to vol. vi. of *Sacred Books of the East*, p. xxix.

'It is a fact that the politician in him outgrew the prophet more and more, and that in many cases where he assigned spiritual motives he merely did so to give a fair appearance to acts that emanated from secular regards.'—Wellhausen, '*Mohammedanism,' Encyc. Brit.*, 9th ed.

'It is less easy to free him from the reproach of perfidy and cruel vindictiveness. The surprise of Nakhla in the month Rajab (ordered by him, though he afterwards repudiated it), the numerous assassinations which he instigated, the execution of the 600 Jews at the close of the war of the Fosse, burden the Prophet heavily, and sufficiently explain the widespread antipathy in which he is held.' *Ibid.*

'Mohammed, though deeply grieved at losing, as he feared, his uncle's protection and goodwill, exclaimed in reply, 'By Allâh! if they placed the sun on my right hand and the moon on my left, to persuade me, yet while God bids me, I will not renounce my purpose!' and bursting into tears turned to leave the place.' Palmer, Introduction to vol. vi. of *Sacred Books of the East*, p. xv.

'I demand no reward of you for my preaching unto you; I expect my reward from no other than the Lord of all creatures.' Sale's *Koran*, ch. 26 (The Poets), vol. ii. p. 207.

Compare also Sir William Muir's *Life of Mohammed, passim* and article on "*Islam*" by E. Deutsch in *Quarterly Review*, vol. cxxvii, reprinted in *Essays and Remains.*

3 Art. in *Encyclopaedia Britannica* on 'Mohammed' by J.Wellhausen, p. 534.

4 Ibid., p. 548.

5 'Hibbert Lectures,' p. 37. Mirza Kasem Beg, quoted by Kuenen, 'Hib. Lectures,' p. 45.

6 Súfism—'the mysticism of Islâm'—among Moslems was believed to have been founded by a woman, *Rabi'a* by name, who lived in the first century of the Hijra.

'Her doctrine was simply the theory of Divine Love. She taught that God must be loved above all things, because He alone is worthy of love; and that every thing here below must be sacrificed in the hope of one day attaining to union with God.' (S. Guyard, *Encyc. Brit.*) One feels a sense of high fitness on reading that this woman was buried at Jerusalem.

It has been thought that this movement, which carries the hope of reformation for Islâm, may supply the bridge by which the Moslem may yet pass to a higher faith.

'It is to the progress of Súfism, which is constantly spreading amongst the people of Persia, that we must look for that preparation of the Mohammedan mind, which in due time may lead to the overthrow of Islâm for a purer creed.' *Persian Literature,*' by E. B. Cowell, *Oxford Essays*, 1859.

In some cases Súfism led to Pantheism. 'In the reign of Moktadir, a Persian Súfi, named Halláj, who taught publicly that every man is God, was tortured and put to death.' Guyard, *Encyc. Brit.*, '*Mohammedanism*,' 9th ed.

'The Khárijites are the most interesting feature of the then phase of Islam (time of Alí, Caliph). In the name of religion they raised their protest against allowing the whole great spiritual movement to issue in a secular and political result, in the establishment within the conquered territories of an Arabian kingdom, a kingdom which diametrically contradicted the theocratic ideal. ... The Khárijites protested, not merely against the dynastic principle and the rule of the Omayyads, but also against orthodoxy; they disputed the doctrine of predestination and the proposition that a great sinner could yet be a good Moslem because they did not understand how to divorce religion from practice. To some degree they call to mind the Montanists, but their opposition was much more energetic in its expression.' J. Wellhausen, article on '*Mohammedanism*,' *Encyc. Brit.* 9th ed.

7 Kuenen, 'Hibbert Lectures,' p. 49.

8 The absolutism in Islâm Theology can hardly be more strongly expressed than in the following:

'Dieu a implanté le bien et le mal dans la nature humaine, ainsi qu'il l'a dit lui-même dans le Coran: "la perversité et la vertu arrivent a l'âme humaine par l'inspiration de Dieu."' Ibn Khaldoun, i., 268.

'The central idea of this religion,' writes Archbishop Trench, 'in its noblest aspect is just the surrendering of oneself to God as the absolute Power.' In the same strain Wellhausen puts God and His mastery as the strength of the Moslem system; and thus the view which Bishop Butler expressed is seen to be true, when he said, 'Submission is the whole religion of Mohammed.' Cf. *Mohammed and Mohammedanism*, by R. Bosworth Smith, p. 161, 2nd ed.

'Who will be averse to the religion of Abraham but he whose mind is infatuated? . . . When his (Abraham's) Lord said unto him, Resign thyself unto Me; he answered, I have resigned myself unto the Lord of all creatures. And Abraham bequeathed this religion to his children,' &c. *Al Koran*, ch. ii., Sale's ed., 1812, vol. i, pp. 24–25. Cf. *Mohammed and Mohammedanism*, by R. Bosworth Smith, p. 161, 2nd ed.

9 Kuenen, 'Hib. Lect.,' pp. 43, 45.

10 Sprenger, l.c. ii. 346, quoted by Kuenen, 'Hib. Lect.,' p. 32.

11 Kuenen, 'Hib. Lect.,' p. 46.

12 Matheson, *The Growth of the Spirit of Christianity*, vol. i., p. 336.

13 Kuenen, 'Hib. Lect.,' p. 46. Sale calls attention to one verse in the Koran, which he thinks, perhaps, indicates that the Mohammedans were no strangers to Quietism. He speaks, however, doubtfully. The words on which he lays stress are these: "O thou soul that art at rest!" He thinks that these may indicate the deep soul-quiet so dear to the mystic; but he admits that they may have a more superficial meaning, and may be understood of the soul secure of salvation and free from fear. The words afford a very slender foundation on which to build any superstructure of Quietism. It is ill hanging doctrines on the frayed threads of a doubtful text. The Quietism which appeared in the history if Islâm sprang from other sources than the Koran. It had a much securer foundation in the heart of mankind than in the language of the Prophet, from whom, according to Wellhausen, "contemplative piety received only the praise of words." See *Encyc. Brit.*, "Mohammed," 9th ed.

14 See Bosworth Smith, *Mohammed and Mohammedanism*, p. 287, 2nd ed. *Cf.* Matheson, *Growth of the Spirit of Christianity*, pp. 342–345.

15 M. Renan, *L'Islamisme et la Science*, p. 4. 'De l'an 775 a peu près, jusque vers le milieu du treizième siècle, c'est-à-dire pendant 500 ans environ, il y a eu dans les pays musulmans des savants, des penseurs très distingués. On peut même dire que, pendant ce temps, le monde musulman a été supérieur, pour la culture intellectuelle, au monde chrétien.'

16 It will be understood that this paragraph only refers to the questions of culture and progress. The question of corruptions of the faith of

Islam in Persia is distinct. According to Mr Bosworth Smith, 'in no nation in the Mohammedan world has the religion less hold on the people as a restraining power' than in Persia? *Mohammed and Mohammedanism*, pp. 290, 2nd ed.

17 Renan, *L'Islamisme et la Science*, p. 10.

18 The influences it met with on this (Persian) soil, and out of which peculiar religious tendencies were developed, were foreign, Indo-Germanic; and these tendencies besides have always been regarded by Moslem orthodoxy as aberrations and heresies, and were therefore soon, with a greater or less degree of decision, expelled from Islam.' Pfleiderer, *Phil. of Rel.*, vol. iii, p. 180. Cf. also vol. iv, 98–100.

19 *L'Islamisme et la Science*, pp. 11.

20 *Ibid.*, p. 20.

21 'The tendency to deify Scripture only reached satisfaction in the dogma that the Koran, just as it is written, its very letters and breathings, was "uncreated," and had an eternal and independent existence as God's own word, having no part in the conditions and the imperfection of all created things.' Pfleiderer, *Phil. of Rel.*, vol. iv, p. 63.

With this we may compare:

'Dans le Coran, un grand nombre de versets témoignent que ce livre fut communiqué au Prophète sous la forme d'une lecture (*Coran*) faite à haute voix et dont chaque sourate était un miracle (de style) qui surpassait le pouvoir des hommes.' Ibn Khaldoun, *Proleg.*, vol. i, p. 195.

An orthodox and authoritative Moslem treatise (used as a textbook in all Turkish schools and colleges), entitled *Risála-i-Berkevi*, says: 'The Koran is the word of God, and is eternal and uncreated.' See Sell's *Faith of Islam*, p. 118.

22 Renan, *L'Islamisme et la Science*, pp. 21, 22.

23 As a fact Islamism discourages painting. Mohammed cursed the painter or drawer of men and animals (*Mishkāt*, bk. xii, ch. I, pt 1) and consequently they are held to be unlawful.' Hughes *Dictionary of Islam*, Pictures, p. 458.

'The making of carved, graven, or sculptured figures is understood to be forbidden in the Qur'ān. . . . Consequently sculpture is not allowed according to Muslim law.' *Ibid.*, *Sculpture*, p. 566.

Ibn Khaldoun (see Canon MacColl's account of him in the *Contemp. Review*, April 1888) gives a dissertation on the arts generally (*Proleg.*, French ed., vol. ii, pp. 357–406), but says nothing about painting and sculpture, because they are forbidden by the sacred law. And even of the arts which are allowed, he observes, 'La pratique des arts est en général très-limitée dans le pays dont les Arabes sont originaires et dans les contrées dont ils se sont emparés depuis la promulgation de l'islamisme.' *Proleg.*, vol. ii, p. 365.

Mohammed had no love for the poets: 'They rove as bereft of their senses in every valley,' he said. But he had a shrewd appreciation of the advantage which he and his cause might derive from the employment of satire: 'Ply them with satires,' he once said to Caba Ebn Malec; 'for, by him in whose hand my soul is, they wound more deeply than arrows.' Sale's *Koran*, vol. ii, p. 211, and note.

24 *Cf.* Bosworth Smith, *Mohammed and Mohammedanism*, p. 315, 2nd ed., and Kuenen's 'Hibbert Lectures,' p. 52.

25 'Hibbet Lectures,' p. 52.

26 Bosworth Smith, *Mohammed and Mohammedanism*, pp. 161, 308, 2nd ed. 'Mohammedism is the only form in which the knowledge of the true God has ever made way with the native races of Africa; and the form of Christianity which it supplanted in the North—that of the Donatists and of the Nitrian monks; of Cyril, strangely called a saint; and of the infamous George of Cappadocia, still more stangely transformed into St. George of England—was infinitely inferior to Mohammedism.' Bosworth Smith, *Mohammed and Mohammedanism*, p. 285, 2nd ed.

27 Kuenen, 'Hibbert Lectures,' p. 54.

With this we must compare what is said by Pfleiderer:
'We must, however, observe that Islam cannot be called a universal religion in quite the same sense as Christianity and Buddhism. Its founder certainly contemplated the universal spread of his religion; but he certainly lacked the true universal human spirit. Though the founder of a religion he never ceased to be an Arab, and he impressed on his religious community forms of thought and life, which however well they answered the genius of the Arabs, were to the members of all other peoples nothing but a heavy yoke, and a fetter which prevented all sound and living development. Even the customary spread of Islam by force of arms shows that the religion now before us is not a religion of humanity, which overcomes the limits of race by the inner influence of spiritual universality.' *The Philosophy of Religion*, vol. iii, p. 180.

8

DIE HANDWERKE BEI DEN ARABERN

Ignaz Goldziher

Die Beduinen der arabischen Wüste liegen wenig Achtung vor dem Handwerke und den Handwerkern. Unter diesen ist es besonders der Schmied, den ihre Verachtung trifft.[1] Burkhardt berichtet von den „Aneze-Beduinen, dass sie das Schmiedehandwerk für herabwürdigend betrachten und ihre Schmiedebedürfnisse von Arabern besorgen lassen, die aus dem Dschôf in ihr Gebiet eingewandert sind. Niemand würde seine Tochter mit einem sonna" (d. h. Handwerker, Schmied) oder dem Abkömmling eines solchen verheiraten; diese heiraten nur untereinander, oder nehmen die Töchter von Sklaven der 'Aneze zu Frauen.[2] Auch viele arabische Stümme in Afrika teilen diese Verachtung vor dem Schmiedehandwerk.[3]

Die altarabische Litteratur ist überreich an Spuren dieses Gefühles.

„Fürwahr, abscheulich ist der Speiseort des Hundes—
Und fürwahr, der Schmied arbeitet au tiefern Orte"[4]

In der Satire der altarabischen Dichter ist es gleichsam ein Gemeinplatz, jemandem, den man arg verhöhnen will, vorzuwerfen, dass sein Ahn mit dem Blasbalg (kir) zu thun hatte. Umejja b. Chalaf glaubt, den medinenser Dichter Hassân b. Thâbit, der sich in der mohammedanischen Litteratur als Ruhmesposaune des Propheten und als poetische Geissel seiner Feindo einen Ehrenplatz erworben, nicht sicherer treffen zu können, als wenn er ihn mit folgenden Epigramm verhöhnt:

Source: *Goldziher Globus: Illustratierte Zeitschrift für Länder und Volker Kunde*, 1894, vol. 66, pp. 203–5.

„Wer trügt mir zu Hassan eins Botschaft, die is nach ‘Okaz hin sohleicht“?
„War dein Vater nicht ein Schmied unter uns, neben den Ständen der Weinverkäufer, von niedriger Gesinnung in der Treue;
Ein Jemenite, der immer den Blasbalg festigte und fortwährend die Flammen des Feuers blies.“[5]

Hassân war ein Städter; in seiner Heimat waren Ackerbau und Handwerke nicht verachtete Beschäftigungen. Seine Landsleute, die auch für die Aufnahme der neuen Religion günstig gestimmt waren, hatten immerfort den Spott der Stockaraber zu erdulden),[6] die sie nicht als ebenbürtig betrachteten und mit dem verachteten Nabat gleichstellten).[7] Desto merkwürdiger und bewisender für den bloss formelhaften. Wert dieser Art von Spott ist es, wenn wir beobachten, dass derselbe Hassân auch seinerseits wieder den Gegenständen seiner Feindschaft, den „Schmied“ und den „Blasbalg“, vorwirft. Auch er glaubt, die Familie des Kurejshiten Al-‘Âsî b. al-Mughîra, den man den „Blödesten des Kurejshstammes“ zu nennen pflegte; aufs tiefsto zu erniedrigen, wenn er gegen ihn folgende Satire verbreitet:

„Schmiedesöhne! wenn ihr euch eures Stammsitzes rühmt, so prahlt ihr nur mit dem dem Blasbalg vor dem Thore des Ibn Gunda,
Den euer Vater errichtet hatte, noch bevor er sein Haus erbaut in Hars; so machet denn ein Geheïmnis aus dem verstossenen Schmied;
Und werfet fort die Asche des Blasbalges“ n. a. w.[8]

Und auch sonst nennt er die Familie der Mughîra „Schmiedeknechte“ (abîdu kujûn), deren Vater „vor dem Blasbalg die Asche sammelt.“[9]

„Dies ist euer Handwerk, das seit ewigen Zeiten bekannt ist, Pfeile verfertigen und sein Kessel flicken.“[10]

Auch den Dichter Nâbigha lässt man in einem, sicherlich nicht echten Gedichte, den ihm unholden König No‘mân von Hira damit verhöhnen dass er „der Erbe eines sâ’igh“, eines Goldschmiedes sei, womit er das Epitheton des „Feiglings“ verbindet.[11] Die Philologen haben in der That herausgefunden, dass der mütterliche Grossvater des Königs in Fadak Goldschmied war.[12] Und auch der

Mu'allaka-Dichter 'Amr b. Kulthûm benutzt diesen Flecken, der die Abstammung desselben Königs verunziert haben soll, zur Verspottung seiner Mutter (der Tochter eben jenes Goldschmiedes aus Fadak):

„Sulejma erwartet doch nicht, dass in dem Königsschloss Chawarnak Sohmiedse- und Panzerverfertiger[13] sein werden!"

und zu ihrem Sohne, dem König No'man, gewendet, ruft er:

„Möge Gott verpönen den, der unter uns ain nächsten ist zur Schmach, der schimpflichste ist vermöge seines (mütterlichen) Oheims und der schwächste, hinsichtlich seines Vaters;
Und der würdigste, dass sein Oheim am Balge blase, in Jathreb (Medina), Ohrgehänge und Weiberschmuck schmiede."[14]

Der Dichter war wohl, als er dem König seine Schmähworte zurief, in gehöriger Entfernung von dessen Machtkreise.

In der ersten Zeit des Islam waren bei den arabischen Dichtern für Ehre und Schmach noch immer die Ideen und Gesichtspunkte des Heidentums in Geltung. Darum schwindet auch der „Schmied" und der „Blasbalg" nicht von der Liste ihrer Schmähworte, in welchen man leicht gewisse ständige Typen nachweisen könnte. Der Dichter Gerîr, dessen Wettstreit mit seinem Rivalen Al-Farazdak zu den fruchtbarsten poetischen Anlässen der alteren Umejjadenzeit gehörte, wirst seinem Gegner die Beschuldigung entgegen:

„Der Zügel war deinem Vater versagt, aber nicht war ihr der Blasbalg versagt."[15]

d. h. er war weit entfernt ein Ritter zu sein hingegen war er ein gemeiner Handwerker. Und solche Anschauungen beherrschten zu jener Zeit auch noch die allgemeine Gesellschaft. In Kufa war eine zum Stamm Asad gehörige Familie, nach dessen einem Mitglied sogar eine Moschee (Sinnâk) ihren Namen erhielt, Gegenstand des Spottes darüber, weil sie unter ihren Urahnen einen gewissen Hâlîk b. 'Amrzählte, der ein Schwefeger gewesen sein soll.[16] Er ist der Heros eponyme für dies Handwerk; man nennt die, welche es ausüben mit dem schwer erklärbaren Namen Hâlîkî.[17]

Kremer hat in grossen Zügen die Einflüsse auf kennzeichnet, unter welchen auf dem weiteren Entwickelungsgange des Islam die Handwerke aufhörten eine blosse Sklavenbeschäftigung zu sein, sondern stetem Fortschritt sich ihre Stellung in der freien Gesellschaft errangen.[18] Zu diesen Faktoren ist jede noch der Einfluss der religiösen Weltanschauuing hinaus zunehmen, welche der Verachtung vor den Handwerken wie sie das heidnische Arabertum hegte, ein Gegengewicht bot. Hat ja die mohammedanische Tradition einigen Propheten Handwerke zugewiesen; die biblische Könige David und Salomo waren berühmte Panzerverfertiger.[19]

Aber innerhalb dieser Weltanschauung bildeten sich wieder anderseits herabsetzende Vorurteile gegen bestimmte Erwerbsgattungen heraus. Man klassifiziert zunächst die verschiedenen Beschäftigungsarten nach Massgabe der ihnen zugemuteten Würdigkeit. Charakteristisch ist unter anderm die dem Khalifen Wazugeschriebene Meinung, welche er in einem Serschreiben an einem seiner Statthalter kundgethan haben soll: „Stelle den Weber und den Schuhmacher auf einen Rangstufe, auf eine andere den Schröpfmeister und dem Tierarzt, auf eine andere den Trödler und Wechsler, auf eine andere den Schullehrer und den Eunuchen; die Sklavenhändler und der Satan sind auf der gleichen Stufe".[20]

An mehrere Einzelheiten dieser Rangordung liess sich mannigfache kulturhistorische Bemerkungen knüpfen die bei dieser Gelegenheit zu weit führen würden, wohl es sehr verlockend wäre, z. B. die niedrige Stellung welche dem Pädagogen zugeeignet wird, näher zu leuchten. Dies ist jedoch nicht der Ort dafür, da es hier lediglich mit den Handwerken zu thun haben. Unter diesen hat man besonders einige als sehr ber; würdigend hingestellt. „Drei Beschäftigungen—heisst es weiter—wurden immer nur von den niedrigsten Menschen geübt: die Weberei, dass Schröpfen und die Gerberei".[21] Der Erwerb des Schröpfers wird in eine Tradition in einem Atemzuge mit dem „Lohn fei Dirnen und dem Vorkaufspreis für Hunde" (vergl. diese beiden zusammen, Deuteron. 23, 19) genannt.[22] „Die Araber desselben Stammes)—so heisst es a. a. O.—sind einander gleichwertig, nur der Weber und der Schröpfer sind ihren Stammesgenossen nicht ebenbürtig zu achten".[23]

An Stelle des veralteten Schimpfwortes „Schmied" und „Schmiedesohn" treten nun neue Schmähungsarten aus dem Kreise der Gewerb ein. „Weber, Sohn eines Webers" (ha'ik ibn hâ'ik).[24] Der tamimitische Wohlredner Châlid b. Safawân, Zeitgenosso des ersten.

Abbâsidenkhalifen schmäht den Stamm der Banû Hârith b. Ka'b in folgender Weise: „Ein Volk, in welchem man keine andere Leute findet als Mantelweber, Häutegerber und Affenführer".[25] Dies letztere im II, III. Jhd. d. H. Sehr häufig vorkommende Gewerbe[26] scheint schon zur Zeit der Entstchung das Islam geübt worden zu sein. Hassân nennt in einem Epigramm seinen Gegner Chālid b. Usejd einen „dressierten Affen" (kird mu'addab).[27] Man muss danach voraussetzen, dass man zu jener Zeit in Medina abgerichtete Affen sehen konnte; sonst hätte der Dichter diese Vergleichung nicht anwenden können.

Ein Odium ganz besonderer Art lastete auf dem Beruf des Webers. Auch bei den Römern galt der textor bis Repräsentant des ungeschlachten Handwerkes.[28] Bei den Arabern ist noch im II. Ihd. das Weben besonderes Attribut der Sklaven,[29] und Sklavinnen werden zuweilen als Weberinnen (hajjâka) bezeichnet.[30] Während aber Gerber und Schröpfer wegen der Natur ihres Gewerbes missachtet wurden, scheint man beim Weber auch intellektuelle Mängel als Folgen seiner Beschäftigung vorausgesetzt zu haben. „Von den zehn Zelmteln Dummheit, welche in der Welt vorhanden sind, findet man nenn Zehntel bei den Webern". Die Legende bemächtigte sich der Vergangenheit der Weberzunft, und man fand es natürlich, ihnen alle denkbaren Missethaten anzudichten, um sie auch aus religiösen Gesichtspunkten missliebig zu machen. Von 'Ali citiert man folgende Sprüche: „Wer mit einem Weber auf der Strasse einhergeht, geht seines täglichen Broles verlustig; wer sich mit ihm in ein Gespräch einlässt, dem haftet das Ominöse an, welches dem Weber innewohnt; wer seinen Laden besucht, dessen Körperfarbe wird gelb". Ein Zuhörer befragte den 'Ali um den Grund dieser Warnung, „da doch die Weber unsere Brüder sind". Da sprach Ali: „Sie haben die Sandalen des Propheten gestohlen, haben im Vorhof der Ka'ba uriniert; sie sind die Sippe des Satan und das Gefolge des Daggâl (Antichrist). Sie haben den Kopfbund des Jahjâ b. Zakarijja, den Mantelsack des Chidr, das Webestück der Sara gestohlen; der 'A'isha haben sie einen Fisch aus dem Ofen herausgestohlen. Maria fragte sie einmal um den richtigen Weg, da führten sie sie irre und sie verfluchte sie damit, dass sie Gott zum Gegenstand des Gespöttes mache und in ihrer Hände Arbeit keinen Segen Schicke".[31]

Es gab aber auch Leute, welche sich von solchen Anschauungen befreit hatten und die ehrliche Handarbeit in jeder Form würdigten. Dazu waren zumeist jene Moralisten geeignet, welche eine von allen konfessionellen und gesellschaftlichen Vorurteilen befreite

Sittlichkeit und Weisheit lehrten. Ihre Ansicht verdolmetscht der buddhistisch[32] angehauchte asketische Dichter Abû-l-'Atahija (Zeitgenosse des Khalifen Hârun al-Rashid) mit seinen Worten:

„Fürwahr Gottesfurcht ist Glanz und Adel—die Liebe zur Welt ist Not und Armut;
Wein ein frommer Mann in richtiger Weise gottesfürchtig ist, so thut es nichts zur Sache, mag er auch weben und schröpfen".[33]

NOTES

1 Ich habe über diese Dinge ausführlich gehandelt in meinem: *Mythos bei den Hebräern* (1876), S. 97 bis 06 (englische Ausgabe, S. 81 bis 89); obige Daten wollen als Nachlese zu den dortigen Ausführungen gelten.
2 *Reise in Arabien* (französische Ausgabe), III, S. 47.
3 Nachtigal, *Sahara und Sudan*, I, S. 443 bis 444.
4 Al-Ia'in al-Minkari, *Lisan al-'arab* (s. v. bkj), XVIII, S. 86.
5. Al-'Ajnî, IV, p. 568.
6 Vergl. meine *Muhammedanischen Studien*, I, S. 93.
7 z. B. *Aghani*, XIII, 120, 5, nabat bi-Jathriba.
8 *Dîwân* des Hassân ed. Tunis, 1281, p. 63 ult.
9 Ebend, S. 96, 1.
10 Ebend. S. 95, 2.
11 *Six poëts* ed. Ahlwardt, Nab. App. 41, 2.
12 *A'ghânî*, I, p. 169, 2.
13 Nassâg, *Weber*; im Arabischen wird das Wort nag auch von der Verfertigung des Ringelpanzers gebraucht und an dieser Stelle ist wohl dies Geschäft gemeint.
14 *Aghani*, ebend, S. 124.
15 *Chizânat al-adab*, II, p. 468, 3.
16 Al-Baladhori ed. De Goeje, p. 264.
17 Der *Dîwân des Garwal b. Aus*, zu 29, S (Separat ausgabe S. 154).
18 *Kulturgeschichte des Islam unter den Khalifen*, II, S. 189 bis 186.
19 Vergl. *Dîwân des Garwal b. Aus* zu 11, 11 (S. der Separatausgabe). Es ist immer verdächtig, wenn dar in vorislamischen Gedichten, wie das ja so häufig zu finde ist, Bezug genommen wird; siehe *Wiener Zeitschr. für die Kunde des Morgenlandes*, III, 1889, 363.
20 Al-Râghî al-Isfahânî, *Muhâdarât al-udabâ*, p. 284.
21 Im babylonischen Talmud, Kiddûschîn fol. 82a, weine Reihe von bedenklichen Handwerken aufgezäblt; die erwähnten drei sind unter denselben genannt.
22 Muslim, *Traditionssammlung*, IV, S, 41.
23 Al-Dahabi, *Mîzân al-i'tidâl*, II, 210, 250.
24 So lässt Al-Gâhîz den Ash'ath b. Keja Schwagen des Khalifen Abû Bekr charakterisieren, *Aghâni*, XIV, p. 143, 2, Vergl. Al-Tabarî II, p. 1121, 1.

25 *Muhadârât al-udabâ*, 1, p. 215.
26 Siehe *Muhammedanische Studien*, II, S. 164. Vergl. die *Makamen* des Hamadânî (Beirut 1889), S. 93, so ein Karrad, Affenführer, austritt der deas Publikum belustigt.
27 *Diwän*, p. 25, 5.
28 Vergl. Friedländers *Cena Trimalchionis*, p. 211.
29 Ghulâm ha'ik, *Aghânî*, IV, p. 174, 4. Vergl. al-abd al-ha'lk, al-Tabari II, p. 245, 14.
30 Zum Belspiel *Lisân al-'arab* (a.v. r'an), XVII, p. 42, 3 unten.
31 *Muhâdarât al-udabâ'*, I, p. 284.
32 Transactions of the Ninth Internat. Congress of Orientalists (London, 1893), II, p. 114.
33 *Diwân* ad Beirut 1886, p. 243, 5; *Aghânâ*, III, p. 127, penult: wa'in hâka au hagama.

9

LA FIN DE L'EMPIRE DES CARMARTHES DU BAHRAÏN

M.J. De Goeje

Lorsque je publiai, en 1888, mon *Mémoire sur les Carmathes du Bahraïn et les Fatimides*, je me suis vu dans l'obligation d'avouer que je n'avais pu trouver une seule notice sur l'histoire de ces sectaires depuis la visite de Nâcir ibn Khosrau à Lahsa, en 442. Je viens d'en découvrir une dans le commentaire sur la grande qaçida en *mīm* d'Ibn Moqarrab. Ce poète distingué du commencement du VIIe siècle de l'hégire, étant originaire de Lahsa et descendant du prince qui avait mis fin à leur dynastie, devait être bien informé. Le commentateur ne se nomme pas, mais à en juger d'après sa connaissance du Bahraïn et de l'histoire de ce pays, on est en droit de conclure qu'il en était originaire lui aussi. Il me semble avoir écrit peu de temps après la mort du poète.

Les troubles sérieux qui amenèrent la chute de l'empire des Carmathes commencèrent dans l'île d'Owal peu de temps après la visite de Nâcir. Un certain Abou'l-Bahloul (al-ʿAuwam ibn Mohammed ibn Yousouf ibn az-Zaddjādj), de la tribu autrefois dominante au Bahrain des Abdalqais, et son frère Abou'l-Walīd Moslim, orateur (*khatīb*) de l'île, tous les deux pieux sonnites, s'adressèrent au gouverneur (ناظر) carmathe, nommé Ibn ʿArham, sollicitant son intervention auprès du gouvernement de Lahsa pour leur concéder le droit de bâtir une mosquée, parce que les marchands étrangers évitaient de venir à Owal, où ils trouvaient pas de place convenable pour célébrer les prières du vendredi. En fréquentant les marchés de l'île, ils y apporteraient le bien-être et

Source: Journal Asiatique, 1895, January–February, pp. 5–30.

beaucoup d'autres avantages indirects. En outre, Abou'l-Bahloul et son frère offrirent pour la concession une somme de 3,000 dinars. Sur le rapport d'Ibn ʿArham, la permission fut donnée. Lorsque la mosquée fut construite, Abou'l-Walid monta en chaire et récita la *khotba* au nom du khalife abbāside al-Qāim bi-amrillah. Les partisans des Carmathes se récrièrent: «C'est, dirent-ils, une innovation damnable qu'Abou'l-Bahloul a introduite par ruse et fraude; il faut la leur interdire.» Abou'l-Bahloul répondit: «Il est vrai que notre but véritable n'était pas d'attirer les marchands, mais bien de remplir nos devoirs religieux. Nous avons fait pour cela des sacrifices considérables. Si l'on ne veut pas le permettre, on n'a qu'à rendre la somme versée et nous obéirons.» Le gouverneur écrivit à Lahsa et obtint pour Abou'l-Bahloul et les siens la permission du libre exercice du culte sonnite et même celle de dire la *khotba* au nom du khalife de Bagdad. La restauration du culte musulman attira les marchands des ports du golfe persique, et le marché d'Owal prit un grand essor. Mais bientôt les partisans des Carmathes manifestèrent une opposition nouvelle. «La personne, dirent-ils, à laquelle vous portez hommage dans la *khotba* n'a plus d'autorité. On fait la *khotba*, même en ʿIraq, au nom d'al-Mostancir, le prince d'Egypte; c'est son nom que vous devez citer dans la priere et non pas celui d'un homme dont la dignité n'est plus reconnue.» Ces paroles fournissent la preuve que cette opposition se produicit en 450, puisque l'inauguration de la souveraineté du prince fatimide et la restauration du khalifat abbāside ont eu lieu dans cette même année. Abou'l-Bahloul écrivit à Lahsa pour prier le gouvernement de lui permettre de continuer à faire la *khotba* au nom du khalife abbāside, ayant soin de joindre à sa lettre un riche cadeau et de belles promesses. Les chefs de Lahsa lui accordèrent ce qu'il demandait, et Abou'l-Bahloul vit s'accroître, de jour en jour, ses ressources et son influence. Peu de temps après, le gouvernement de Lahsa, ayant besoin d'une forte somme d'argent,[1] ordonna à Ibn ʿArham d'en répartir une partie sur les habitants d'Owāl, mais de la manière la moins onéreuse. In ʿArham, étant peu disposé à obéir, eut une entrevue secrète avec Abou'l-Bahloul et les siens, leur communiqua les ordres qu'il avait reçus et se concerta avec eux sur les mesures à prendre. Ensuite il écrivit au gouvernement de Lahsa que les habitants d'Owāl refusaient de payer l'impôt; qu'il n'avait pas les moyens de les y contraindre et qu'il s'était vu obligé de laisser l'ordre sans exécution. En même temps, il conseillait au gouvernement de revenir sur sa résolution. Cette lettre irrita les chefs de Lahsa. Ils envoyèrent un gouverneur pour remplacer Ibn ʿArham, avec ordre de 's'emparer de ceux qui s'opposaient aux mesures du gouvernement et de leur faire payer la somme fixée. Cependant Abou'l Bahloul n'avait pas seulement convoqué les siens, mais il s'était assuré de l'alliance d'Ibn abi'l-ʿOryān, un des seigneurs les plus puissants de l'île, et ensuite de l'aide des principaux fermiers, en leur disant: «Le *kharādj* doit être payé par les seigneurs (*domini soli*, ارباب الضياع), non par les cultivateurs (اصحاب الضياع).» On s'accorda à déclarer aux chefs carmathes qu'on refuserait de leur obéir, à moins qu'Ibn ʿArham ne fût rétali, et qu'on s'opposerait à l'installation du nouveau gouverneur. Celui-ci, après avoir vainement essayé de s'emparer d'Aou'l-Bahloul et d'Ibn abi'l-ʿOryān, se vit obligé de reculer devant les troupes des insurgés qui comptaient 30,000 hommes, et de se réembarquer au plus vite après avoir perdu plusieurs des siens. Les insurgés écrivirent de nouveau aux chefs carmathes pour demander le retour d'Ibn ʿArham. Mais cette fois la réponse fut menaçante. Ibn ʿArham ne reviendrait pas, mais on enverrait une armée pour mettre ordre aux affaires d'Owāl. Le vizir des Carmathes, Abou Abdallah ibn Sanbar,[2] expédia un de ses fils à Omān pour aller quérir des armes et de l'argent. A son retour, les chefs des insurgés le surprirent, le tuèrent lui et quarante de ses hommes et s'emparèrent de 5,000 dinars et de 3,000 lances qu'il avait apportés, et qu'ils distribuèrent parmi leurs gens. Ibn Sanbar comprit, mais un peu tard, qu'il fallait employer d'autres moyens. Il s'engagea secrètement envers Ibn abi'l-ʿOryān à lui conférer le gouvernement de l'île, à condition qu'il tâcherait de ruiner l'influence d'Aou'l-Bahloul. Ibn abi'l-ʿOryān se laissa gagner. «Nous avons entrepris une chose très dangereuse; commença-t-il à dire à ses amis; les Carmathes ont le pouvoir de nous écraser et ils ne manqueront pas de le faire. Tâchons de réparer les fautes que nous avons commises.» Son avis fut écouté, ce qui inquiéta Abou'l-Bahloul, parce qu'Ibn abi'l-ʿOryān avait une influence prépondérante. Peut-être avait-il eu connaissance aussi du plan suivant arrêté entre son adversaire et Ibn Sanbar: le vizir viendrait avec sa flotte et quand elle serait en vue, Ibn abi'l-ʿOryān s'emparerait d'Aou'l-Bahloul et le tuerait. Dans un conseil de famille convoqué par Abou'l-Bahloul, on résolut de faire assassiner Ibn abi'l-ʿOryān. Celui-ci avait coutume de se baigner dans un ruisseau situé sur ses terres, accompagné d'un seul serviteur. C'est là qu'un soir sa famille le trouva mort. Abou'l-Bahloul, accusé de ce meurtre, fit les *quarante serments*[3] et réussit à apaiser les parents du défunt. Sur ces entrefaites, Ibn Sanbar partit de la côte avec une flotte de cent quatre-vingts galères (شذاة) dont l'équipage se composait pour la plupart d'Arabes des ʿAmir Rabīʿa (branche des ʿAmir in Çaʿçaʿa), avec leurs chevaux au nombre de cinq cents qu'Ibn Sanbar avait emmenés, ne s'attendant pas à la résistance. Abou'l-Bahloul n'avait à lui opposer que cent galères équipées en toute hâte. Au moment de s'embarquer, il eut le malheur de tomber de cheval et de se casser la jambe. Cet accident fut cause de la défaite des Carmathes. Cédant aux instances de son frère, Abou'l-Bahloul donna l'ordre de battre en retraite. Or les chevaux des Bédouins, déjà excités par l'embarquement et le mouvement des galères, s'effarouchèrent tout à fait à la vue des drapeaux flottants, au son des tambours et des trompettes, et causèrent le naufrage d'un certain nombre de vaisseaux. Les Bédouins, perdant la tête; se jetèrent dans la mer et Ibn Sanbar prit la fuite. Abou'l-Bahloul s'empara du reste des galères et de deux cents chevaux, de grandes quantités d'armes et de bon nombre de prisonniers. Les gens de l'équipage jurèrent qu'ils avaient été forcés par les Carmathes de prendre part à l'expédition et furent graciés, mais quarante chefs carmathes furent tués. Cette victoire consolida la puissance d'Abou'l-Bahloul. Il nomma vizir son frère Abou'l-Walīd et lui ordonna d'entrer en correspondance avec Ibn abī Mançour[4] ibn Yousouf, le chef du diwan de Bagdad, pour obtenir la sanction et l'appui du gouvernement afin de combattre les Carmathes sur le continent et d'y rétalir la souveraineté des Abbāsides.

Nous lisons dans le commentaire sur un autre vers du même poème que la ruine des ʿAmir Rabīʿa datait d'une expédition malheureuse contre l'île d'Owāl, enterprise pour soumettre Abou'l-Bahloul qui avait chassé les fonctionnaires des Carmathes et s'était proclamé émir. L'armée expéditionnaire, commandée par Bishr ibn Moflih al-ʿOyounī, fut jetée à la mer près de l'île, dans une localité appelée *Keshloush Owāl.* On ne peut affirmer, mais il est probable que cette expédition est la même que celle qu'avait organisée Ibn Sanbar. Or l'affaiblissement des Amir Rabīʿa qui étaient les protecteurs (خفراء) du Bahraïn c'est-à-dire qui fournissaient des troupes aux Carmathes, en échange d'une partie des récoltes, obligea ces derniers à appeler à leur aide des Arabes de la tribu d'Azd de l'Oman. Ceci se passait trois ans avant qu'Abdallah in ʿAli eût commencé la guerre contre les Carmathes. Or cetto guerre ayant duré sept ans et s'étant terminée en 469, l'arrivée des Azdites eut donc lieu en 459.

Abou'l-Bahloul ne jouit pas longtemps du résultat de sa victoire. Car nous lisons que déjà, en 469, l'île d'Owāl était soumise au seigneur d'al-Katīf, Yahya in 'Abbās. On peut donc criore sans témérité que ce Yahya profita du désastre des Carmathes près d'Owāl pour s'emparer d'al-Katīf. Le commentateur nous raconte que ce chef entama des négociations avec un Alide nommé *Ibn az-Zarrād* qui était au service de Kadjkina (كجكينا), chambellan du sultan Malikshāh. Il demandait au gouvernement de Bagdad deux cents cavaliers pour conquérir Lahsa et y rétablir la souveraineté des Abbāsides, s'engageant de son côté à verser, chaque année, une somme considérable au trésor. Kadjkīna parvint à trouver des alliés pour la conquête de Lahsa à la condition que le khalife et le sultan auraient chacun 1/11e du butin, les ministres Nizām al-Molk et Sa'd-ad-daula Kouhrāy ensemle 1/11e, Kadjkīna et Ibn Moharish, le chef des 'Oqail, chacun 4/11e. Kadjkīna partit de Basra avec quatre cents cavaliers arabes et turcs et leur suite; après avoir été harcelé en route par des Bédouins; il arriva à 4 parasanges d'al-Katīf et annoñça son arrivée à Ibn 'Abbās. Celui-ci répondit froidement qu'il avait demandé deux cents cavaliers pour être sous ses ordres, que si Kadjkina était disposé à les lui donner, il aurait soin de le faire reconduire sain et sauf à Basra. «Sinon, ajoutait-il, le désert est devant vous; allez à votre guise.» Kadjkīna, furieux, tenta de soumettre Ibn 'Abbās à sa volonté par la force et eut un commencement de succès. Mais le rusé Ibn 'Abbās sut si bien faire avec ses Bédouins que Kadjkina et les siens furent dépouillés de tout ce qu'ils possédaient et leur camp fut mis au pillage; obligés de rebrousser chemin, ils rentrèrent à Basra en l'année 468, épuisés de fatigue et dans la condition la plus misérable.

Cependant un ennemi beaucoup plus terrible s'était levé contre les Carmathes dans la personne de Abdallah in 'Ali. Le district le plus septentrional de la province de Lahsa porte le nom d'*al-'Oyoun*, «les Sources», parce qu'il y a quatre cents sources d'eau courante qui arrosent les plantations de dattiers et les champs.[5] C'est là que résidait la famille d'Irahim ibn Mohammed, appartenant aux Banou Morra ibn 'Amir ibn al-Hārith, frères des Banou Mālik (Wüstenfeld, *Geneal. Tabulæ*, A, 17), de la tribu des Abdalqaïs. En 462, le chef de cette famille, Abdallah ibn Ali ibn Mohammed ibn Ibrahim, commença la guerre contre Lahsa. A la tête de quatre cents hommes il battit les Carmathes qui comptaient alors quatre-vingts chefs bien armés et de nombreuses troupes recrutées parmi les Azdites et les 'Amir Rabi'a. Par cette victoire Abdallah prit place parmi les guerriers les plus renommés, comme autrefois le Carmathe Abou Tāhir. Nous ne savons pas au juste quand cette bataille eut lieu, mais il est assez probable qu'à la suite de cette première défaite les Carmathes durent se retirer dans leur capitale et y soutenir un siège de sept ans. Abdallah, voyant que ses forces ne suffisaient pas à prendre Lahsa, ouvrit des négociations avec la cour de Bagdad où elles furent bien accueillies. En 467, Oksok-Salār, surnommé *Ibn Toubek* (توبك), feudataire (مقطع) de Holwān et dépendances, fut expédié avec sept mille cavaliers seldjoucides, que le poète nomme *Shorsikiya*.[6] Arrivés à Basra, ces soldats se livrèrent, pendant trois jours, à toutes sortes d'exactions envers les habitants, et refusèrent de continuer leur route si l'on ne leur donnait mille chameaux de monture et cinq cents chameaux pour porter les outres d'eau, cinq cent mille *mann* de farine et autant d'orge et de dattes; enfin 19,000 dinars. Après avoir reçu une grande partie de cette contribution de guerre, Oksok-Salār se mit en route pour al-Katīf, afin de punir tout d'abord Yahya ibn ʿAbbās de ses mauvais procédés à l'égard de Kadjkīna, comme on l'a vu plus haut. Il s'ensuit que l'expédition ne partit de Basra au plus tôt qu'au commencement de l'année 468. A l'approche de l'armée, Ibn ʿAbbās alla se réfugier à Owāl; et Oksok-Salār continua sa route sur Lahsa. Grâce à ses troupes auxiliaires, Abdallah ibn ʿAli pouvait enfin bloquer sérieusement la capitale. Bientôt la disette obligea les Carmathes à entrer en composition. Ils consentirent à se soumettre et à payer au khalife une grosse somme d'argent, à la condition d'otenir l'amān pour leur vie et leurs biens et un mois de délai pour le payement. Comme garantie de ces propositions, ils s'engagèrent à fournir treize otages. Le délai ayant été accordé, les Carmathes en profitèrent pour se ravitailler dans des magasins secrets et se mettre de nouveau en état de défense. Ils savaient que les Turcs étaient dans l'impossibilité de prolonger leur séjour au Bahraïn à cause de la chaleur (l'an 468 finit un des premiers jours d'août) et de la dévastation de la campagne. Oksok-Salār, dans sa fureur, tua une partie des otages, mais se voyant obligé de quitter le pays immédiatement, il laissa à Abdallah ibn ʿAli deux cents cavaliers sous le commandement de son frère al-Baghoush, promettant de revenir bientôt pour achever la conquête du Bahraïn.

Lorsque Oksok-Salār arriva à Bagdad, il se présenta au diwan et y rendit compte de la guerre contre les Carmathes et de la victoire que Dieu lui avait accordée, annonçant en même temps son intention de retourner immédiatement pour réduire Lahsa. On communiqua ces nouvelles au khalife, sur l'ordre duquel on rédigea le diplôme suivant pour être lu devant Oksok-Salār:

مَضْمونُ نُسْخَةَ التَّوْقيع

بسم الله الرحمن الرحيم الحمدُ لله المتوحّد بالجمال والبَهاء المتفرّد بالقدرة والكبرياء المنجى من غياهب الشرك بانوار الحقّ المختار لرسالته ودينه اكرمْ خلقه محتداً واصلاً واشرفهم درجةً ومحلّاً النبىّ العربىّ سيّد الانبياء وخاتم الاصفياء صلى الله عليه وسلّم ارسله بالهدى ودين الحقّ ليظهره على الدين كلّه ولو كره المشركون والحمدُ لله الذى عضد الاسلام بالخلفاء الراشدين من بنى العبّاس المهديّين الذين ازال الله بهم البدع والمنكر وجعل ولاءهم سبيل النَّجاة يوم الفزع الاكبر وقَرَنَ طاعتهم بطاعته وطاعة رسوله فقال عزّ من قائل (Qor., IV, vers. 62) واطيعوا الله واطيعوا الرسول واولى الامر منكم حتّى صار الى امير المؤمنين وشرَّف الامامة ارثه بالوجوب واضحت قلوب اهل الزَّيغ بعزّ ايامه [لى] الهلع والوجوب وغدت رايات اوليائه حيث امَّتَ منصورةً ظاهرةً وامداد الفتوح اليهم متقاطرةً متناظرةً والله يمتّع امير المؤمنين بالنعمة فيه ولا يخلى دولته من حميد مساعيه ففى الاثر ان رسول الله صلى الله عليه وسلّم قال اتانى جبرئيل عليه السلام وعليه قباء اسود وفى وسطه كالخنجر فقلت يا جبرئيل ريلستهم ى من تكون فقال لى ولد العبّاس ابن عبد المطلب فقلت يا جبرئيل اتباعهم ممّن يكون (l. تكون) فقال من اهل خراسان اصحاب المناطق ومن وراء دهاقنة الصعيد وترك اليغرغر (l. التغزغز) او اهل الخناجر من اهل

الجبال قلت يا جبرئيل اى شىء تملك ولد العبّاس فقال يا محمد تملك ولد العباس المدر والوبر والاحمر والاصفر والمروة والمشعر والصّفا والحجر والقبّة والمخبر والسرير والدنيا الى الحشر ذلك فضل الله يؤتيه من يشاء وليعلم ان توبك بن اكسب (?ابن توبك اكسك .l) الوقوف على خدمته والامتثال على طاعته (correction du copiste pour الطاعة) والاجهاد لساعيه فى جهاد المبطلين والقرامطة الملحدين وليستفزّ معه متاجرة الله تعالى فى استيصال ذكرهم وتطهير تيك البقعة من دنس كفرتهم قال تعالى (Qor., IX, vers. 14.) قاتلوهم يعذّبهم الله بايديكم ويخزهم وينصركم عليهم ويشفِ صدور قوم مؤمنين وليعتمد احاد السريرة والسيرة فيما يفتتحه من الاعمال وليقدم امدًا بعيدًا ويحذّركم الله نفسه والله رؤف بالعباد (Qor., III, vers. 28.)

Au nom de Dieu, le clément, le miséricordieux. Louanges à Dieu qui est unique dans la possession de la beauté et de la splendeur, qui est seul dans le maintien de la puissance et de la grandeur; qui, par les lumières de la vérité, a sauvé des ténèbres du polythéisme celui qu'il a élu pour sa mission et son culte, la plus noble de ses créatures d'origine et de souche, le plus élevé des hommes en degré et en rang, le prophète arabe, le seigneur des prophètes, le sceau des élus. Que Dieu lui accorde sa bénédiction et sa paix! Il l'a envoyé avec la direction et la vraie religion pour la faire triompher de toute autre religion, nonobstant la résistance des polythéistes. Et louanges à Dieu qui a soutenu l'Islam par les khalifes orthodoxes des Banou 'l-ʿAbbās qui, conduits eux-mêmes sur la voie droite, sont l'instrument par lequel Dieu fait disparaître les hérésies et tout ce qui est blamable! Leur patronage a été établi par Dieu comme le chemin du salut au jour de la terreur suprême; l'obéissance qui leur est due a été jointe par lui à celle qu'on doit à Dieu et à son envoyé.

Car il a dit (son nom soit exalté!): «Obéissez à Dieu, à l'Apôtre et à vos chefs.» Jusqu'au jour où l'Empire échut au Prince des Croyants et qu'il honora la dignité héréditaire de l'imamat en en rendant la reconnaissance indispensable pour tout le monde, la gloire de ses combats faisant palpiter de crainte les cœurs des dissidents, les drapeaux de ses armées étant couronnés partout de victoires, ses conquêtes se suivant dans une série continuelle. Que Dieu accorde au Prince des Croyants la jouissance de ses bienfaits et qu'il ne permette pas que les efforts louables du Prince fassent jamais défaut à la dynastie! La sainte tradition nous apprend que le prophete (à qui Dieu accorde sa bénédiction et sa paix!) a dit: «Gabriel, (la paix soit sur lui!) vint à moi, vêtu d'une robe noire, ayant à la ceinture une arme semblable à un poignard. Je lui dis: «O Gabriel qui aura la principauté sur eux (sur les Mussulmans)?» Il répondit: «Les fils d'al-ʿAbbās ibn Abd-al-Mottalib.» Je continuais: «O Gabriel, et quels seront leurs soutiens?»—«D'abord, dit-il, les Khorāsaniens, les porteurs de ceintures, ensuite les chefs cantonaux de la Haute-Egypte et les Turcs Toghozhoz,[7] ou bien les gens au poignuard de la Médie.» Je demandai encore: «O Gabriel, quelle sera l'étendue du domaine des fils d'al-ʿAbbās?»—«O Mohammed, répondit-il, les fils d'al-ʿAbbās régneront sur les gens à demeure fixe et les habitants des tentes; sur les hommes à peau rouge et à peau jaune; sur les lieux saints et les marchés; sur la coupole (d'Ozaïn) et sur le trône (le Caucase); enfin sur le monde entier jusqu'au jour de la résurrection. C'est la faveur de Dieu et il l'accorde à qui il veut.»

Or il faut qu'Ibn Toubek Oksok sache qu'on a pris connaissance de ses hommages, qu'on désire récompenser son dévouement, et qu'on applaudit à ses éxploits dans la guerre sainte contre les mécréants et les Carmathes hérétiques. Puissent ceux qui espèrent mériter les récompenses de Dieu dans la vie future, se sentir animés de zèle pour l'aider dans l'effacement de leur souvenir, dans la purification des souillures et de l'impiété de ces contrées! Le Très-Haut a dit: «Faites-leur la guerre, Dieu les punira par vos mains et les confondra. Il vous concédera la victoire sur eux et donnera satisfaction aux cœurs des fidèles.» Qu'il fasse son possible pour que ses intentions et ses

> actions dans les contrées qu'il ya conquérir soient dignes de louanges, et qu'il se procure «un long ajournement! Et Dieu nous exhorté à le Craindre car Dieu est miséricordieux envers ses serviteurs.»

Après la lecture de ce document, Oksok-Salār se leva, baisa la terre, exprima ses remerciements et ses vœux, puis s'en alla. On lui offrit de la part du khalife, outre les cadeaux ordinaires faits aux hôtes, des vêtements, un cheval avec une selle dorée et ornementée (بمركوب مغموس ومنموق) et trois galères (شذاة). Il avait sollicité cette marque de distinction qu'il ambitionnait et pour laquelle il s'était rendu à la cour. Ensuite il descendit le Tigre jusqu'à Wāsit, dans l'intention de continuer son voyage jusqu'à Basra. Mais un courrier vint lui remettre des lettres de la part de son frère qui était resté à Lahsa avec Abdallah ibn ʿAli. Il lui communiqua qu'après son départ les Carmathes et les Azd s'étaient réunis aux ʿAmir Rabīʿa et menaçaient de l'écraser lui et Abdallah qui n'avaient pas le cinquantième de troupes à opposer aux leurs. «Bien que nous désespérions presque de pouvoir leur tenir tête (disait ce message), nous résolûmes de les attaquer, et nous commençâmes par les ʿAmir Rabiʿa que nous mîmes en fuite. Puis nous marchâmes contre les Carmathes et les Azdites que nous attaquâmes au lieu nommé «Entre les deux places» (ما بين الرحبتين). Nous leur tuâmes un très grand nombre d'hommes et les contraignîmes à réfugier au château. La plus grande partie des guerriers ayant péri, ils demandèrent à se soumettre à condition d'avoir la vie et la liberté sauves. Abdallah ibn ʿAli les leur accorda et prit possession du château où il entra au son des trompettes. Mais il ne permit pas aux Turcs d'y monter avec lui.»

Cette lettre finit au milieu de la phrase et elle est suivie de la continuation d'un autre récit dont le commencement nous manque. Mais nous avons une seconde relation de ces événements. On lit ce qui suit dans le commentaire sur un autre vers du même poème: «Lorsque Abdallah in ʿAli eut fait la conquête de Lahsa et que les Turcs furent partis, à l'exception d'un petit nombre, il laissa les Carmathes et les Azd tranquilles, sans tuer ni bannir personne. Ceux-ci en profitèrent pour entrer en négociations avec les ʿAmir Rabiʿa, qui bientôt arrivèrent en grand nombre camper dans Lahsa; requérant d'Abdallah ibn ʿAli les contributions en céréales, etc., qu'ils avaient reçues du temps des Carmathes comme protecteurs du pays. Sur le refus d'Abdallah, ils s'armèrent, eux et leurs chevaux, et s'avancèrent en poussant les chameaux devant eux pour écraser les soldats d'Abdallah ibn ʿAli. La rencontre eut lieu entre les ruisseaux Nahr Mohallim et Solaïsil. Abdallah, entrevoyant le stratagème de l'ennemi, fit battre les tambours et les timbales et sonner les trompettes, tandis que les Turcs décochaient leurs flèches contre les chameaux. Épouvantés par le bruit et frappés par les flèches, ces animaux s'effarouchèrent, firent volte-face et foulèrent aux pieds les cavaliers des ʿAmir Rabīʿa, aussitôt poursuivis par la cavalerie d'Abdallah. Les ʿAmir Rabīʿa éprouvèrent une défaite complète. Il ne se sauva qu'un seul chef avec un émir allié, lesquels arrivèrent dans la condition la plus misérable au camp des Montafik, dans les environs de Basra. Abdallah épargna les femmes et les enfants et déféndit aux Turcs d'y toucher. Plus tard il les fit déporter en Omān. Il s'empara de quatre mille chamelles avec leurs étalons et leurs bergers et de beaucoup de chevaux et d'autre butin, mais il ne prit pour lui que quelques coursiers, cédant tout le reste à ses hommes et aux Turcs. Après la défaite des ʿAmir Rabīʿa, Abdallah attaqua les Carmathes. La rencontre eut lieu entre la rivière dite *al-Khandak* (le fossé) et la porte *Bāb al-Açfar*, au nord de la ville. La bataille fut sanglante; quatre-vingts chefs de Carmathes armés de pied en cap y périrent. Elle eut lieu en l'année 470.»

Nous avons vu qu'al-Baghoush avait écrit à son frère qu'Abdallah n'avait pas admis les Turcs au château. Ce refus paraît les avoir exaspérés. Abdallah, ayant appris qu'al-Baghoush nourrissait le projet de lui arracher la souverainété, le fit arrêter et tuer dans la prison. Lorsqu'on apprit cela en Irāk, Rokn-ad-daula partit avec deux mille cavaliers pour Lahsa afin de punir Abdallah. Bon gré mal gré les habitants de Lahsa se soumirent à lui, de sorte qu'Abdallah resta seul au château avec ses parents et ses fidèles partisans, et fut assiégé pendant une année. Enfin Rokn-ad-daula, lassé des lenteurs du siège, fit sàvoir à Abdallah qu'il consentirait à lever le blocus et à retourner en Irāk s'il lui livrait son fils aîné pour expier le sang d'al-Baghoush. Adallah refusa et offrit, mais en vain, le double de l'argent d'expiation. Ali, le fils d'Abdallah, l'ayant appris, sortit du château à l'insu de son père et alla se livrer à Rokn-ad-daula qui l'emmena avec lui et l'enferma dans un château au Kirmān, d'ou Abdallah parvint à le sauver plus tard. Au départ de Rokn-ad-daula plusieurs seigneurs du pays, craignant la vengeance d'Abdallah, s'apprêtèrent à le suivre. Mais Abdallah s'empressa de proclamer l'amnistie générale. Seulement il annexa au domaine plusieurs terres qu'il avait données en fief aux seigneurs au commencement de sa carrière, et depuis ce temps il mit une certaine distance entre sa maison et les familles seigneuriales du pays.

A peine ce danger était-il surmonté qu'il en survint un autre. Deux émirs, le kādhī de Qārout, district aux environs de Wāsit, et un des officiers de Khomārtekīn qui, après le départ d'Oksok-Salār pour la Syrie, ayait la plus grande autorité dans le pays de Basra, entreprirent une expédition à Lahsa pour s'en rendre maîtres. Abdallah, faisant contre mauvaise fortune bon visage, les reçut avec une grande bienveillance, sans toutefois les inviter au château, et leur donna le conseil de poursuivre leur chemin vers Omān où ils trouveraient des trésors immenses. Prié de leur fournir des guides, il fit venir quelques khāridjites du désert entre l'Omān et le Bahraïn, et leur donna secrètement l'instruction de les faire marcher jusqu'au jour où la provision d'eau serait épuisée, puis de les abandonner en un lieu dépourvu de puits. De tous ces hommes il n'en revint qu'un seul qui s'était enfui sans savoir où son cheval le menait. Cet événement se passait en 474.

Abdallah n'était pas encore entièrement maître du Bahraïn; la province d'al-Katīf et l'île d'Owāl obéissaient à la famille de Yahya in ʿAbbās. Il est probable que ce prince mourut peu de temps après la défaite finale des Carmathes, car nous trouvons dans la troisième qacīda en *mīm* la preuve que son fils al'Hasan avait été en guerre avec Abdallah et obligé d'acheter la paix par des présents considérables en or, en perles et en dattiers. Cet al'Hasan sut attirer à lui un petit-fils d'Abdallah[8] qui avait pris part à ses expéditions contre Lahsa, et il se donna beaucoup de peine pour engager d'autres membres de la famille d'Abdallah à faire cause commune avec lui; c'est ce que nous lisons dans le commentaire. Dans la glose de la grande qaçīda, le commentateur raconte qu'al-Hasan fut tué par son frère Zakarīya et que celui-ci conduisit son armée vers Lahsa. Mais Abdallah fondit sur lui à Nāzira (ناظرة), mit son armée en fuite, prit al-Katīf et donna à son fils al-Fadhl l'ordre de poursuivre Zakarīya qui s'était réfugié dans l'île d'Owāl. Fadhl s'illustra en tuant de sa propre main l'homme le plus fort de l'île, un certain al-ʿOkrout (العكروت), et en dispersant les troupes de Zakarīya. Celui-ci s'enfuit à al-ʿOqaïr, d'où il fit une dernière tentative pour reconquérir al-Katīf avec l'aide de tribus bédouines. Mais il perdit la bataille et la vie, et Abdallah devint enfin maître de tout le Bahrain.

«Alors les cœurs des Abdalqaïs furent rafraîchis; on voyait rire joyeusement ceux qui avaient enfin pu assouvir leur vengeance», dit le poète. Ces paroles nous ramènent à l'époque du fondateur de la dynastie des Carmathes, Abou Sa'īd. Sur ce personnage aussi le commentaire donne les détails suivants qui ne sont pas sans intérêt. Lorsque les Abdalquaïs étaient divisés entre eux et se faisaient la guerre les uns contre les autres, leur puissance au Bahrain s'était affailie. Le Carmathī, c'est-à-dire Abou Sa'īd al-Hasan ibn Bahram,[9] en profita pour se rendre maître d'al-Katīf. Il était fermier des droits de port pour les seigneurs de cette province (فرضتها ضامن ملوكها وضامن, *sic)*, les fils d'Abou'l Hasan 'Ali ibn *Mismār*, famille apparentée aux Djadhīma in 'Auf.[10] Avec les richesses qu'il sut amasser grâce à ses fonctions, il s'était fait à al-Katīf beaucoup d'amis. Alors ayant formé une armée composée d'habitants de cette province, de Bédouins du voisinage et d'Omaniens, il attaqua les Banou Mismār et se rendit maître du pays, après avoir saccagé et brûlé la résidence d'al-Zāra. Puis il se dirigea sur Lahsa. Les deux familles les plus puissantes, les Banou'l-'Ayāsh et les Banou'l-'Oryān; ayant repoussé l'ordre qu'il leur donna de se retirer avec les leurs, se virent obligés après une bataille sanglante de se soumettre au vainqueur avec tous les autres seigneurs du Lahsa. Abou Sa'īd les réunit tous dans un quartier de la ville nommé *ar-Rammāda*, qu'il fit incendier après en avoir fait occuper toutes les issues par ses soldats. Il n'en échappa pas un seul; ceux qui tâchaient de se sauver du feu furent tués par les gardes. Ils périrent en grand nombre et parmi eux plusiers «porteurs du Koran» (حملة القران). Un peu plus haut, le commentateur dit qu'al-'Ayāsh ibn Sa'īd, le chef des Mohārib (de Abdalqaïs), avait sa résidence dans la montagne d'al-Sha'bān, près de Hadjar, au milieu de ruisseaux et de jardins, et qu'al-'Oryān ibn Ibrāhim était le chef des Banou Mālik ibn 'Amir ibn al-Hārith (les frères des Banou Morra auxquels appartenait la famille d'Abdallah ibn 'Ali al-'Oyounī).

Ces détails qu'on trouve dans le commentaire sur la septième qaçīda en *noun* forment avec ceux que donnent Masoudi dans son *Tanbīh*, pages 392 et suivantés, et Hamdānī dans sa description de l'Arabie, page 36, un supplément important à l'histoire du commencement de l'empire des Carmathes au Bahraïn. Hamdānī avait reçu ses renseignements d'un certain Ibn Çabbāh al-Yashkori qui doit les avoir reçueillis antérieurement aux premières expéditions d'Abou Sa'īd. Cet auteur et Masoudi nomment également 'Ayāsh le Mohāribī, seigneur de Hadjar, et 'Ali ibn Mismār, des Banou Djadhīma, seigneur d'al-Katīf. Masoudi décrit en détail la marche victorieuse d'Abou Sa'īd, Ibn Çabbāh ne fait pas mention de Djowātha, la résidence d'al-ʿOryān, ni de ce chef lui-même, quoique celui-ci soit bien connu par sa résistance contre l'Alide qui, en 255, organisa l'insurrection terrible des esclaves nègres (les Zendj) dans le pays de Basra. A cause de ce silence, je crois devoir donner à son rapport la date de l'année 250 environ. Les deux auteurs disent que Lahsa, avec son fameux marché d'al-Djarʿa (Gerra), situé sur une colline, appartenait aux Banou Saʿīd, branche des Tamīm. Puisque les Tamīm avaient secondé l'Alide Çāhib az-Zendj et qu'ils nourrissaient un ancien ressentiment contre les Abdalquaïs (voir *Tanbîh*, p. 393, dans les poèms du Chef des nègres), il est très probable qu'ils embrassèrent le parti d'Abou Saʿīd et que Lahsa doit à ce fait l'honneur d'être devenu la résidence des Carmathes, au lieu de la capitale Hadjar.

Si j'avais connu, en 1888, les renseignements fournis par Masoudi, je me serais épargné la conjecture que j'ai avancée, pages 35 et 135 de mon *Mémoire*, à savoir qu'Abou Zakarīya, qu'on disait avoir prêché au Bahraïn la doctrine des Carmathes avant Abou Saʿīd, en 281, serait identique au Zakrī qui, en 319, parut au milieu des Carmathes comme rejeton de la maison royale des Persans. En avançant ce fait, je m'appuyais sur Birouni qui a confondu les deux personnages. Mais ma conjecture était fausse. Abou Zakarīya se nommait Yahya ibn al-Mahdī aç-Çammamī et il fut emprisonné et tué par Abou Saʿīd. Quant à Zakarī, le jeune homme de vingt ans qui a été vénéré et obéi comme une incarnation de la divinité, Dhahabī, qui le nomme *Abou'l-Fadhl le Mage* (al-Madjousī), donne sur lui des détails qu'il doit à un médecin nommé *Hamdān* qui l'avait vu lorsqu'il pratiquait son art à al-Katif (autographe de Leide, ms. 1721, fol. 2011°).

Pour tout le reste, le commentaire ne nous donne sur les Carmathes que des faits déjà çonnus. Le seul fait que j'ignorais c'est qu'Abou Tāhair avait le surnom de «court d'étrier». (الركاب قصير). Le nom d'al-Carmathī est toujours écrit sans voyelles, à l'exception d'un seul passage où l'on trouve *Qacr al-Qirmithī*. (comp. *Mémoire*, p. 203).

Pour la géographie du pays, les poèmes et les commentaires fournissent quelques données. Ainsi la capitale de la province d'al-Katīf y est nommée très souvent *al-Khott* (الخطّ). C'est probablement la même place qu'on appelait aussi *al-Khatt*, l'un et l'autre nom signifiant proprement «chemin»; c'est de là que les lances fameuses de bambou avaient reçu le nom de *khattīya*. Hadjar porte encore le nom de «capitale de la province de Lahsa». Dans les poèmes ce dernier nom, proprement al-Ahsā, est plusieurs fois écrit al-Hasā. On célebrait encore au temps du commentateur les grandes fêtes de l'islam à al-Djarʿa.

Le *Diwan* d'al-Moqarrab fait partie d'une belle collection de manuscrits dont M. Houtsma a fait le catalogue et qui appartient à la maison Brill. Les chefs de cette maison ont eu la générosité de me confier ce manuscrit, faisant pour moi une exception à leur règle de ne rien communiquer de leur collection. Il est assez correctement écrit et donne les poèmes selon l'ordre alphabétique des rimes. La plupart de ces poèmes ont été l'objet de commentaires et on y trouve beaucoup d'*excursus* importants, spécialement pour l'histoire de la dynastie des 'Oyounides et celle de la tribu des Abdalquaīs. Outre cet exemplaire du *Diwan*, il y en a un au Musée britannique (catal., p. 288, n. DCVII, add. 7598 Rich.) qui est incomplet et donne les poèmes sans aucun ordre et sans commentaire. Le premier poème de ce manuscrit est le huitième rimé en *bā* du manuscrit de MM. Brill, qui commence par le vers:

بِينِى هما انت من جِدّى ولا لَعِبِ
ما لى بشَىْء سِوَى العَلْياء من أرَبِ

Le texte de ce vers, comparé avec le même vers dans le catalogue du Musée britannique, est une preuve évidente de la supériorité du manuscrit de Brill sur celui de Londres. Ce dernier manuscrit se termine par un poème panégyrique adressé au vizir Sharaf-ad-dīn ʿAmīd ad-daula, à Bagdad, mais qui ne se trouve pas dans le manuscrit Brill, le prototype de cette copie ayant eu une lacune. On pàsse d'une phrase incomplète du commentaire sur un vers d'une qaçīda en *āilo* au beau milicu de l'introduction sur une qaçīda en *āmoha*. Par la même raison, la qaçīda adressée à l'émir de Moçoul Badr-ad-dīn Loulou que cite Yaqout (III, 766) manque dans le manuscrit. Yaqout avoue qu'il ne trouve pas beaucoup de mérite dans ce poème; et, en effet, les panégyriques composés par Ibn Moqarrab en l'honneur de cet émir et d'autres, pour lesquels le poète n'était inspiré que par la reconnaissance du bon accueil qu'il avait trouvé auprès d'eux, témoignent bien de son habileté, mais non pas de ses dons poétiques. Son talent se montre dans les poémes ou, célébrant les faits et gestes de sa famille et de sa tribu, il tâche de réveiller parmi ses contemporains et spécialement chez le prince régnant la noblesse d'âme et l'énergie des ancêtres. Il faut louer aussi les poésies où il se plaint de l'injustice dont il a été l'objet et dénonce ceux qui l'ont obligé de quitter sa patrie comme ennemi de la dynastie. On peut opposer, du reste, au témoignage de Yaqout le jugement très favorable de Mohibb ad-dīn Abou'l-baqā al-ʿOkbarāwī, qui a été inséré dans le catalogue du Musée britannique.

NOTES

1 Le texte présente ici une lacune que je crois devoir combler comme je l'ai fait.
2 Le manuscrit porte *Shanbar.*
3 C'est-à-dire le grand serment. Dans les livres de droit musulman, tant orthodoxes que shîites, le nombre des serments est de cinquante. (Comp. le *Minhadj* de Nawawi, par M. van den Berg, III, 191; Querry, *Recueil de lois concernant les Musulmans shyites,* II, 583 et suiv.)
4 Ibn al-Athir l'appelle «Abou Mancour».
5 Le commentateur dit qu'une partie de ce district a été envahie plus tard par les sables.
6 Dans un autre poème, le nom est vocalisé *Sharsakiya*, avec l'explication suivante: يعنى بالشرسكية السلجوقية ملوك الاعاجم. Je n'ose pas décider laquelle des deux prononciations est préférable. La forme du mot semble exclure une dérivation du turc جريشه—شوره (comp. Houtsma, *Ein Türkisch-Arabisches Glossar*, p. 79, هارى) qui donnerait *Sharishkiya.* Une dérivation du persan شورش s'accorderait avec la prononciation *Shorskikiya*, mais je ne said pas si ce mot s'employait communément dans le sens de «guerre».
7 Nous savons maintenant qu'on doit prononcer ainsi et non pas *Toghozghour*, par les *Alttürkische Inschriften der Mongolei* publiées par M. Radloff, p. 10, 61 (Togus-Ogus). Voir aussi la note de M. Nöldeke que j'ai donnée dans la préface du septième volume de ma *Bibliotheca geogr. arab.*
8 Nommé *Abou Saʿīd al-Hasan*, fils de Ali le fils aîné d'Abdallah.
9 Le manuscrit a souvent *Bokrām*; le grand-père d'Abou Saʿīd est nommé ibn Behrest بهرست, une fois بهرشت.
10 Le commentateur donne la généalogie qui peut servir à compléter la table A de Wüstenfeld.

10

ÉPIGRAPHIE DES ASSASSINS DE SYRIE[1]

Max van Berchem

I UNE INSCRIPTION DES ASSASSINS À L'ÉPOQUE DE SAINT LOUIS

Au XIIe siècle, pendant les premières croisades, l'ordre des Assassins, cette secte d'Ismaïliens qui se rendit célèbre par ses redoutables attentats,[2] avait élu domicile en Syrie, dans la région comprise entre Tripoli et Lattakeih, entre la mer et la vallée de l'Oronte. Au cœur de ces montagnes sauvages, ils avaient pris et réparé quelques forteresses, repaires inaccessibles où le Vieux de la Montagne, c'est-à-dire le chef de la secte, se dérobait impunément à la vengeance de ses victimes.

Ces forteresses sont en grande partie détruites, mais leur emplacement est connu et leur nom s'est conservé dans celui du village le plus voisin. Elles ont été visitées par plusiers explorateurs, mais les renseignements qu'ils nous donnent sont incomplets, surtout en ce qui concerne l'epigraphie.[3]

Quand je partis pour le nord de la Syrie en 1895, j'étais préparé à une excursion dans le district des Assassins. On peut l'aborder de deux côtés opposés, par la côte, ou par la vallée de l'Oronte. En passant à Hamah, je songeai à Masyâd, la résidence principale du Vieux de la Montagne, où quelques voyageurs ont signalé des textes arabes. L'occasion était bonne, la route facile; plusiers raisons me décidèrent à renoncer à ce détour. D'ailleurs je craignais, une fois de plus, d'être déçu dans mon attente et de ne trouver dans ces châteaux que des documents de basse époque.

Source: *Journal Asiatique*, 1897, May–June, pp. 453–501.

Le mystère qui entoure l'histoire des Assassins me faisait présumer qu'ils n'avaient, peur-être à dessein, laissé aucune trace épigraphique. Toutefois, à mon retour, pris de scrupules tardifs, je signalai à quelques explorateurs l'intérêt d'une nouvelle étude archéologique de ces châteaux.

Un jeune archéolgue, qui recueille avec ardeur les insrciptions grecques de Syrie, M. Fossey, élève de l'Ecole français d'Athènes, voulut bien répondre à ce désir. En passant à Masyâd en automne 1896, il y prit quelques photographies d'inscriptions arabes et les mit à ma disposition avec une obligeance dont je suis heureux de le remercier ici.[4]

Deux de ces photographies reproduisent un texte gravé sur deux blocs séparés, encastrés à droite et à gauche de la porte sud de l'enciente de la ville.

Ces blocs, de grandeur inégale, semblent mesurer environ 60 et 80 centimètres de longueur, sur 50 de hauteur. Ils renferment chacun quatre lignes en naskhi cursif, à caractères moyens. Sur chaque bloc, la quatrième ligne est gravée dans le cardre, en plus petits caractères. Le style rappelle celui de plusiers inscriptions ayoubites de Syrie; il est assez grossier, d'un aspect provincial, et offre des negligences qui trahissent une main peu exercée. Sur le bloc A, celui de droite, les lettres sont bien conservées; elles sont plus frustes sur le bloc B, qui fait suite au premier, à gauche de la porte. Sur le cliché de M. Fossey, la lecutre de quelques mots reste douteuse. Voir planche, fig. 1 et 2.

A

(1) أُمر بعمارة صور مدينة مصياف وعمل (2) هذا الباب المبارك
المولا الصاحب (3) تاج الدنيا والدين أبو الفتوح بن محمد
(4) أعزّ الله أنصاره ۞

B

(1) بولاية أحد (?) عبيد الدعوة الهادية (2) عبد الله بن
أبى الفضل بن عبد الله (3) رحمه الله فى شهر ذى القعدة
(4) [un mot] ستّة وأربعين وستّمائة ۞

A

A ordonné la construction du mur d'enciente de la ville de Masyâf et l'edification de cette porte bénie, le seigneur, le maître Tâdj ad-dunyâ wad-din Abu l-futûh, fils de Muhammad, qu'Allah glorifie ses victoires!

B

Sous le gouvernement de l'un (?) des serviteurs de la secle qui conduit dans le droit chemin, 'Abdallâh, fils d'Abu l-faḍl, fils de ʿAbdallâh, qu'Allah aie pitié de lui! Au mois de dhu l-qaʿdah de l'année (?) 646 (février–mars 1249).

Ce texte a été découvert par Burckhardt en 1812. Le célèbre voyageur a copié les trois premières lignes du bloc A, mais il ne parle pas du bloc B. Sa copie est reproduite dans sa relation de voyage; quoique médiocre, ell est d'un bon observateur, si l'on songe qu'elle date des premières années de ce siècle; on peut y lire une partie du texte.[5] En l'étudiant il y a quelques années, je n'y avais découvert aucune allusion à l'histoire des Assassins. Burckhardt, il est vrai, prétend qu'au d'un habitant de Tripoli, la troisième ligne, renfermerait le nom de quelques divinités adorées par les Ismaïliens. Mais il est facile de voir sur son dessin que cette assertion est erronée; la photographie de M. Fossey ne laisse aucun doute à cet égard. La marque incontestable de la secte n'apparaît que sur le bloc B, dont Burckhardt ne fait pas mention.

Voici l'analyse du texte:

BLOC A. Un certain Tâdj ad-dîn Abu l'futûh, dont le nom et les titres seront discutés plus loin, a décrété la construction de la muraille de Masyâd et de sa porte méridionale.

Ligne 1. L'orthographe du mot صور pour سور n'est pas rare en épigraphie. Peur-être le rédacteur était-il d'origine persane, comme tant de partisans de la secte. Mais cette erreur ne le prouve pas absolument, car on trouve chez les Arabes eux-mêmes, et dès l'epoque classique, de nombreux exemples de la confusion du *sîn* et du *ṣâd*.[6]

L'orthographe du nom de Masyâd est celle qui figure le plus souvent chez les auteurs.[7]

Je lis *ʿamalin*, comme nom de verbe, parallèle à *ʿimâratin* et dépendant du verbe *amara*. On pourrait lire *ʿamala*, comme verbe parallèle à *amara*, mais il est évident que le verbe *amara* régit les deux membres de la phrase et que le personnage qui a ordonné la construction de la muraille n'a pas bâti la porte lui-même.

Bloc B. Le travail a été exécuté sous le gouvernement d'un certain ʿAbdallâh, en 646 de l'hégire.

Ligne 1. Le terme *bi-wilâyah* n'est pas absolument certain, le mot est un peu fruste. On voit assez bien les trois premières lettres; les deux dernières, plus effacées, se distinguent encore. L'*alif* d'allongement, qui a disparu, peut trouver place à gauche du *lâm*; il semble qu'on en voit encore la tête vers le haut de la ligne.

Ce mot n'est pas indifférent; voici pourquoi. On sait que les textes de construction débutent en général par le nom de l'instigateur des travaux, introduit par les mots: «A ordonné la construction . . .», *amara bi-ʿamal*, *bi-ʿimârah bi-inchâ*, etc. Ce premier nom est suivi souvent du nom du fonctionnaire chargé d'exécuter le travail, lequel est introduit par diverses formules; or, autant que j'en puis juger jusqu'ici, ces formules correspondent au titre porté par le fonctionnaire. Ainsi les formules les plus fréquentes, *bi-ichârah*, *fî mubâcharah*, *bi-naẓr*, *bi-wilâyah*, *bi-tawalli*, indiquent que le fonctionnaire était *muchîr* «conseiller», *mubâchir* «intendant», *nâẓir* «inspecteur», *wâlî* ou *mutawallî* «gouverneur, commandant». Quelques-uns de ces titres, tels que *mubâchir*, *nâẓir*, désignent des fonctions spécifiques créées pour la construction ou l'entretien des monuments. En revanche, le titre *wâlî*, et par conséquent la formule correspondante *bi-wilâyah*, désigne une charge d'administration politique. En d'autres termes, la personne dont le nom suit était gouverneur du district ou commandant de la place de Maṣyâd. Notons ce détail dont l'importance ressortira plus loin.[8]

Le mot suivant est beaucoup plus douteux. On distingue un *alif*, puis une lettre effacée, surmontée du signe en queue d'aronde v, qui sert dans la règle à distinguer le *sîn* du *chîn*, mais qu'on trouve aussi sur d'autres lettres; enfin une finale à queue qui peut être un *kâf* ou un *lâm*, à la rigueur un *dâl*. Le mot suivant est écrit paléographiquement عىد ou عىىد .

Je lis أحد عبيد, (l'un des serviteurs). Le premier mot n'est pas très satisfaisant, mais rien ne s'oppose absolument à cette lecture. Quant au mot *ʿabîd* au pluriel, il suppose deux jambages entre le *ʿain* et le *dâl*. Ils sont indistincts, mais on voit clairement trois points diacritiques, un à droite et deux à gauche de la queue de la dernière lettre du mot précédent; ainsi le mot est bien ponctué عبيد.

Les deux mots suivants forment la pierre de touche de l'inscription. Le premier, *ad-da'wah*, saute aux yeux. C'est le terme don't tous les auteurs se servent pour désigner la mission, c'est-à-dire la secte des Ismaïliens.[9] Je cherchais le sens du second mot, quand le passage suivant me tomba sous les yeux: Au rapport de l'auteur du *Masâlik*, les Ismaïliens se désignaient eux-mêmes sous le nom de «partisans de la secte qui conduit dans le droit chemin» *àṣḥâb ad-da'wah al hâdiyah.*[10] Le mot *al-hâdiyah*, est certain. Seules les deux dernières lettres, gravées en surcharge au-dessus du *dâl*, ont un peu l'aspect d'un ornement; cette apparence s'explique soit par le peu de place qui restait au graveur, soit par le petit format de la photographie.

Ligne 3. La formule *raḥimahu allâhu* suit d'ordinaire le nom de personnes décédées. Il ne faudrait pas en conclure que le gouverneur était mort durant les travaux. D'ailleurs la terminologie religieuse des chiïtes s'écarte beaucoup de celle des sunnites; elle est pleine de sous-entendus. La secte des Ismaïliens, notamment, possédait toute une langue allégorique, curieux mélange d'éléments disparates, empruntés à diverses croyances et dont le sens échappait à ceux qui n'étaient pas initiés. Justement le terme *raḥmah* («miséricorde») avait pour eux le sens allégorique d'*unspiration.*[11] Peut-être *raḥimahu allâhu* signifie-t-il ici «au-Allâh luí donne l'inspiration?»

Reste la date, dont l'examen va nous ramener au premier personnage.

Le nom du mois *al-qa'dah* est gauchement écrit. Il semble que le graveur ait commencé un *dâl* à la fin de la ligne; puis, s'avisant que la place allait lui manquer, il l'a répété au-dessus, avec le *hâ* final. En tout cas, le mois est certain; il n'en est pas de même de l'année, écrite dans la quatrième ligne en petits caractères un peu frustes.

Ligne 4. Le premier mot paraît indéchiffrable sur le cliché. Il est suivi du mot سنه, avec le signe en queue d'aronde sur le *sîn*. A première vue, on lit ici *sanah* «année». Mais après vient le groupe, *wa-arba'ín* «et quarante», le préfixe *wa* est très distinct; il suppose nécessairement un chiffre d'unités. Il faut alors lire le mot précédent *sittah* «six», et reporter le mot «année» (*'âm* ou *sanah?*) dans le groupe in distinct au début de la ligne.

Le chiffre des centaines peut se lire خمسمائة «500» ou ستمائة «600», en liant ou en séparant les deux éléments du mot. Les lettres sont si petites qu'il est difficile de se décider. Cependant, en dehors de toute considération, la deuxième leçon semble mieux répondre à l'original. La première lettre, qui peut être un *khâ* un peu fruste, a plutôt l'air d'un *sîn* à queue d'aronde; elle est suivie d'une petite queue précédent immédiatement l'élément ىـا du mot *mi'ah*; il est bien difficile de trouver là les trois lettres du mot *khams*. Ainsi nous aurions le choix entre 546 et 646, avec une forte présomption en faveur de la seconde date.

C'est isi qu'il faut interroger rapidement l'histoire des Assassins. Cette histoire est entourée de beaucoup d'obscurités; on n'en trouve nulle part le récit complet et suivi, le fil chronologique. On ne l'entrevoit que dans quelques échappées, aux points précis où elle est mêlée aux événements contemporains; avant et après, elle s'efface dans les coulisses de la politique, où ses principaux acteurs la ramenaient à dessein. C'est par ces percées rapides que Maṣyâd apparaît, surtout à trois reprises, dans les chroniques générales.

En 535 (1140–41), les Ismaïliens de Syrie s'emparent de Maṣyâd. Elle appartenait alors au prince de Chaizar, qui l'avait achetée des émirs de la famille de Mirdâs.[12]

Vers 557 (1162), un émissaire du grand maître d'Alamût, le siège de la secte mère persane, arrive en Syrie dans les montagnes occupées par la secte. Il se présente au maître[13] Abû Muḥammad, muni d'un diplôme officiel. Bientôt il le remplace et commande à la secte. On connaît l'histoire du célèbre Sinân, ses allures mystérieuses et terrifiantes, ses multiples assassinats, ses tentatives contre Saladin et son alliance avec le sultan, enfin sa mort, survenue en septembre 1192.[14]

Enfin en 658 (1260), sous le maître Riḍâ' ad-dîn Abu l-ma'âlî, les Tartares s'emparent momentanément de Maṣyâd. Mais après la victoire du sultan d'Egypte Qutuz, à 'Ain Djâlût, les forteresses ismaïliennes sont rendues aux Assassins. Ils ne devaient pas les garder longtemps. Vers 660 (1262), sous le maître Nadjm ad-dîn Ismâ'îl, le sultan Baibars s'ingère dans les affaires de la secte, réclame un tribut, puis dépose le maître et le remplace par son gendre Sârim ad-dîn Mubârak, auquel il retire Maṣyâd. Celui-ci étant rentré dans la place, Baibars l'en déloge et l'emprisonne au Caire. L'ancien maître Nadjm ad-dîn et son fils Chams ad-dîn, dépouilles de toute autorité, ne sont plus que les otages du sultan, qui achève bientôt la conquête des places ismaïliennes (671).[15] Dès lors, les Assassins deviennent les serviteurs du sultan d'Égypte; ils n'ont plus d'organisation politique.

Ainsi, quelle que soit la solution qu'on adopte pour la date, elle conduit à une période obscure de l'histoire de Maṣyâd, et les auteurs les plus connus nous laissent en défaut. Cherchons dans le texte même les éléments d'une opinion.

La paléographie offre un premier point d'appui. On sait que le caractère carré (coufique) s'est maintenu dans les inscriptions syro-égyptiennes jusque-vers le milieu du VIe siècle de l'hégire, et que l'introduction du caractère arrondi en épigraphie se rattache en Syrie au règne de Nûr ad-dîn. Une étude comparée des inscriptions de ce sultan m'a permis de fixer approximativement, pour l'introduction du nouveau caractère à Alep l'année 543, à Damas l'année 549, à Hamah l'année 552.[16] En revanche, les inscriptions des Atâbeks de Damas jusqu'en 544 sont en coufique, et ce caractère paraît pour la dernière fois dans un texte damasquin de Nûr ad-dîn, daté de 561. Si notre inscriptions datait de 546, on s'attendrait à trouver du coufique encore à Damas ou à Hamah, à plus forte raison dans une ville comme Maṣyâd, perdue dans la montagne en dehors des grandes routes politiques et commerciales.

D'autres présomptions tout aussi fortes découlent des termes de l'inscription et des titres donnés au premier personnage, Abu l-futûḥ. En comparant ces indices à divers passages des auteurs, j'arrivais à la conviction qu'Abu l-futûḥ était maître de la secte en Syrie en 646 de l'hégire. A ce moment, M. Casanova, que j'avais consulté à ce sujet, voulut bien m'indiquer un curieux passage inédit qui confirme directement cette hypothèse.[17]

Voici ce texte:

> En l'an 637, le qâḍi de Sindjâr, Badr ad-dîn, voyageant en Syrie, passa chez les Ismaïliens pour implorer leur protection contre le sultan de Damas, Malik Ṣaliḥ. *Le chef (muqaddam) des Imaïliens était alors un Persan venu d'Alamût, qui s'appelait Tâdj ad-dîn.*[18]

Une fois de plus, l'histoire et l'épigraphie se complètent l'une par l'autre. L'histoire affirme ce que l'inscription lasse deviner c'est qu'Abu l-futûḥ Tâdj ad-dîn était le maître de la secte syrienne. Mais celle-ci donne quelques détails omis par l'historien. Ils confirment l'identification du maître et la date de son règne, et jettent une nouvelle lumière sur la politique et l'organisation de la secte. Voici, je crois, les plus importants.

La fonction de ʿAbdallâh. On a vu que la formule *bi-wilâyah* désigne une fonction de *wâlî*; en d'autres termes, que le second personnage, ʿAbdallâh, devait être le gouverneur de Maṣyâd au nom du premier, Abu l-futûḥ. Qui donc pouvait avoir un commandant à Maṣyâd, si ce n'est le chef de la secte lui-même? Preuve de plus qu'Abu l-futûḥ était maître.

D'autre part, le peu que nous savons de l'histoire de la secte avant Sinân nous la montre répandue un peu partout en Syrie, sans organisation centralisée, sans hiérarchie fixe, surtout sans noyau stratégique. Abû Muḥammad, le prédécesseur de Sinân, concentre le premier, dans les monts de la Qadmûsiyyah, la secte dispersée. Sinân l'organise pour une forte résistance; il bâtit ou répare la plupart de ses forteresses et les confie à des commandants placés sous ses ordres, qui portaient justement le titre de *wâlî* ou *mutawallî*. Mais rien ne trahit l'existence de ces commandants avant le règne de Sinân.[19] Preuve de plus que l'inscription est bien datée de 646, non de 546.

Les titres du maître. Abu l-futûḥ est appelé *maulâ* et *ṣâḥib*: or ces deux titres sont donnés par les auteurs au chef de la secte;[20] preuve de plus qu'Abu l-futûḥ était maître. D'autre part, je ne trouve aucun exemple de ces deux titres avant Sinân;[21] preuve de plus pour la date de l'inscription.

Le surnom du maître. Il est appelé Tâdj ad-dunyâ wad-dîn; or on sait, par de multiples exemples, que les surnoms de cette forme désignaient alors des souverains, ou du moins de très grands personnages. La formule *aʿazza allâh anṣârahu*, qui suit son nom propre, s'adressait aussi à des souverains.[22] Preuve de plus qu'Abu l-futûḥ était maître.

Enfin ce surnom fournit une dernière preuve pour la date 646. Mais ici la question se complique et demande à être examinée de plus haut, car elle touche aux rapports de la secte de Syrie avec la secte mère persane, dont les grands maître résidaient à Alamût.

Si l'on parcourt la liste des grands maîtres d'Alamût, on verra qu'à partir de Hasan III, qui monta sur le trône en 607, leurs noms sont précédés d'un surnom en *ad-dîn*.[23] Ce détail n'a frappé personne, car l'étude des titres comme élément critique en histoire n'a pas été tentée jusqu'ici. Elle ne pouvait l'être sérieusement sur les manuscrits, où les titres officiels, souvent raccourcis ou défigurés, perdent leur caractère de précision. De fait, des le Ve siècle de l'hégire, les titres en *ad-dîn* sont portés couramment en Orient par des fonctionnaires de tout order, civils, religieux et militaires, par de hauts dignitaires, par des souverains. Dans les manuscrits, rien ne les distingue le plus souvent les uns des autres. Or l'étude des monnaies et des inscriptions prouve que dès le VIe

siècle et encore plus au VIIe, les titres en *ad-dîn* portés par des souverains ont officiellement la forme en *ad-dunyâ wad-dîn*.[24]

Mais les titres officiels des souverains n'étaient pas pris arbitrairement par les titulaires. Ils leur étaient conférés par le calife de Bagdad, alors dépouillé de sa puissance temporelle, mais reconnu comme le pontife ou imâm, c'est-à-dire comme le chef spirituel, seul capable de déléguer la souveraineté qu'il tenait d'Allâh.[25] Il y avait une Église orthodoxe, ou si l'on veut, catholique, dont la chancellerie pouvait seule déliverer des diplômes orthodoxes. Ces titres sont donc, pour ceux qui les portent, la marque extérieure et visible de leur *légitimité*.

Ceci posé, les maîtres d'Alamût prétendaient-ils à la souveraineté? Alors, de qui la tenaient-ils? On sait que les doctrines des chiïtes, «nées en Perse et alimentées par les antiques croyances de l'Iran, se résument surtout dans la théorie d'une perpétuelle incarcation de la divinité en un imâm».[26] Mais cet imâm n'est pas l'imâm orthodoxe abbasside; il est issu de la famille d'Ali. De là le perpétuel antagonisme entre sunnites et chiïtes, de là leurs luttes politiques toutes les fois que ces derniers ont visé au pouvoir termporel. Ainsi, tous les ambitieux repoussés par les partis orthodoxes étaient fatalement conduits à s'appuyer sur les idées chiïtes.

La vie du fondateur de l'ordre des assassins, Hassan Sabbâḥ, son séjour en Égypte, ses relations avec les Fatimites, issus eux-mêmes d'une secte chiïte, tout montre qu'il se rattachait d'abord au califat du Caire.[27] Mais une fois établi dans son repaire d'Alamût, il abandonne la dynastie régnante pour voler de ses propres ailes. Sans oser se proclamer imâm lui-même, il reprend à son profit les vieilles idées messianiques, et se donne pour le lieutenant du fatimite Nizâr, l'imâm disparu qui doit revenir un jour régner sur la tere.[28] Ainsi Ḥasan, qui n'obéissait dès lors à aucun pouvoir établi, ne pouvait recevoir aucun titre officiel. De fait, il n'en portait pas d'autre que celui de *sayyidnâ* «notre seigneur», qu'il se donnait sans doute à lui-même.[29] Les curieuses monnaies de son second successeur, Muḥammad ibn Buzurg-ûmîd, publiées récemment par M. Casanova, ne donnent aucun titre au grand maître. On y lit son nom tout seul, après ceux d'Ali et de Nizâr, alors décédé, mais reconnu fictivement comme imâm, et substitué comme tel au calife fatimite.[30]

En 559, le quatrème grand maître, Hasan II, dit *'alâ dhikrihi as-salâm*, monté depuis peu sur le trône d'Alamût, jette le masque et se proclame lui-même imâm, en se donnant pour un descendant d'Ali par les Fatimites.[31] Des lors, la fiction de Nizâr est abandonnée; moins que jamais le grand maître dépend d'une dynastie régnante. M. Casanova a prédit que si l'on retrouve la monnaie de ce grand maître, le nom de Nizâr ne s'y lira plus à la place d'honneur; ajoutons qu'on n'y trouvera aucun des titres souverains que délivrait alors la chancellerie de Bagdad. On peut le prédire d'autant plus hardiment que Ḥasan, non content d'attaquer les traditions orthodoxes, rejetait jusqu'aux pratiques extérieures du culte et se mettait ainsi au ban de la société musulmane.[32]

Il semble que Ḥasan, ait fait un pas de clerc; il eût été plus politique de continuer à s'abriter derrière un imâm invisible et responsable dont on pouvait jouer à sa guise et sans crainte, puisqu'il était mort. D'ailleurs la réaction sunnite, portée par les souverains mongols, par Nûr ad-dîn et Saladin, frappait de rudes coups sur les doctrines chiïtes. Bientôt la chute du califat d'Égypte, miné par les attaques des Croisés et de Saladin, rendait au califat de Bagdad tout son prestige spirituel. Décidément, on ne pouvait plus se passer de sa sanction suprême. En 608 (1211–12), le grand maître Ḥasan III, à peine monté sur le trône d'Alamût, rentre publiquement au giron de l'Église. Il fait amende honorable, brûle en public les livres secrets de la secte, renie ses prédécesseurs, rétablit dans ses châteaux et dans ceux de Syrie les pratiques musulmanes abolies par Ḥasan II, bâtit des mosquées et impose à sa famille le pèlerinage de la Mecque. Il échange de ambassadeurs avec le souverain pontife et les rois ses vassaux, et comme marque extérieure de sa soumission, il reçoit de la chancellerie de Bagdad *les titres réservés aux souverains, titres que jusque-là aucun grand maître n'avait pu obtanir*.[33] Comme Henri IV à Canossa, le grand maître avait courbé la tète; la secte n'était plus qu'une des nombreuses dynasties gravitant autour du trône pontifical.

Or Ḥasan III est surnommé Djalâl ad-dîn, et ses successeurs s'appellent ʻAlâ' ad-dîn Muḥammad et Rukn ad-dîn Khûrchâh. N'est-il pas permis de supposer que ces surnoms étaient officiellement en *ad-dunyâ wad-dîn* et qu'on les retrouverait sous cette forme dans des documents authentiques?[34]

On voit comment l'évolution des grands maîtres d'Alamût, repprochée du surnom que porte Abu l-futûḥ, confirme encore la date de l'inscription. En 546, ce surnom tomberait pour ainsi dire dans le vide. A cette époque, les maîtres de Syrie ne sont que des émissaires du grand maître d'Alamût, et ce dernier ne reconnaît d'autre autorité que celle de l'imâm fictif Nizâr. Bien plus, les surnoms en *addanyâ wad-dîn* n'étaient pas encore en usage en Syrie.[35] En 646 au contraire, la secte persane et la syrienne sont rentrées dans le giron de l'Église orthodoxe et les grands maîtres reçoivent leurs titres de Bagdad. Son surnom de forme souveraine, le maître Abu l-futûḥ le tanait sans doute aussi de Bagdad, par l'entremise du grand maître d'Alamût.

Résumons nos conclusions:

1. Abu l-futûḥ ibn Muḥammad était maître des Assassins de Syrie dès l'année 637, d'après Ibn Wâṣil; il l'était encore en 646, date de l'inscription;

2. ʿAbdallâh ibn Abi l-faḍl était, à cette dernière date, son lieutenant dans la place de Maṣyâd;

3. L'inscription est datée de 646, époque où le maître de Syrie était reconnu comme souverain légitime. Cette assertion repose sur deux faits corrélatifs: dès l'année 608, la secte s'était rapprochée du califat de Bagdad, et notre maître porte un surnom dont la forme, à cette époque, est une marque de légitimité.

Pour terminer, rappelons un curieux épisode de l'histoire de croisades, qui donne à l'inscriptions de Maṣyâd une saveur particulière.

En mai 1250, saint Louis, échappé au désastre de Manṣûrah, vint débarquer à Saint-Jean-d'Acre. Il y reçut des messagers du Vieux de la Montagne, qui venaient réclamer un tribut au roi de France, ou la suspension du tribut que le Vieux payait alors au Temple et à l'Hôpital. Sur la réponse indignée des deux grands maîtres de ces ordres, les envoyés s'en retournèrent les mains vides et rapportèrent au roi des présents de laur maître, des jeux d'échecs, un éléphant et une girafe en cristal, mêlés d'ambre et d'or fin. Cette fois, le roi renvoya les messagers avec de riches présents. Il leur adjoignit Yves le Breton, de l'ordre des Frères prêcheurs, qui savait l'arabe (le sarrasinois). Frère Yves s'enquit avec ardeur des croyances de la secte. «Il trouva un livre au chevet du lit du Vieux, où étaient écrites plusieurs paroles que Notre-Seigneur dit à saint Pierre quand il était sur terre. Et frère Yves lui dit: «Ah! pour Dieu, Sire, lisez souvent ce livre, car ce sont de très bonnes paroles». Et il dit qu'ainsi faisait-il: «Car j'aime beaucoup monseigneur saint Pierre . . .» Alors le Vieux lui raconte que l'âme d'Abel passa dans le corps de Noé, puis dans le corps d'Abraham, puis dans le corps de saint Pierre.[36] «Quand frère Yves eut ouï cela, il lui montra que sa croyance n'était pas bonne, et lui enseigna beaucoup de bonnes paroles; mais il ne le voulut pas croire.»

Au retour de sa mission infructueuse, frère Yves rapporte au roi de curieux détails sur les idées religieuses des Assassins, que Joinville a conservés dans son récit naïf et plein de traits charmants.[37] Cet essai d'histoire religieuse au XIIIe siècle ferait sourire aujourd'hui les savants dominicains de Jérusalem, les successeurs du vaillant frère Yves.

Joinville n'a pas conservé le nom du Vieux qui reçut l'envoyé de saint Louis. L'inscription de Maṣyâd est datée de février–mars 1249, c'est-à-dire de quinze mois avant l'épisode raconté par Joinville. Ainsi le Vieux qui lisait dans son lit les paroles de Jésus à saint Pierre était probablement ce même Abu l-futûḥ Tâdj ad-dunyâ wad-dîn qui fit relever les murailles et la porte de Maṣyâd.

II NOUVELLES INSCRIPTIONS DES ASSASSINS

A l'époque où M. Fossey visitait Maṣyâd, un autre archéologue français, M. Dussaud, déjà connu par l'exploration d'une partie du nord de la Syrie, faisait un second voyage dans la même région. Il voulut bien se charger de recueillir les inscriptions arabes qu'il trouverait en chemin, dans les localités que je lui désignai d'avance, notamment dans les châteaux des Assassins. Au moment où je terminai le mémoire précédent, M. Dussaud, de retour en France, me remit, avec une obligeance dont je ne saurais trop le remercier, ses copies, ses estampages et ses photographies.

Ces documents proviennent pour la plupart de quatre châteaux des Assassins: Maṣyâd, le Kahf, Qadmûs et 'Ullaiqah. Ils complètent fort à propos les relevés de MM. Hartmann et Fossey, et jettent un jour nouveau sur les questions soulevées dans le précédent mémoire, en révélant toute une épigraphie de la secte. Voici les plus importants.[38]

Inscription du château de Maṣyâd

Ce text est gravé au-dessus d'une porte intérieure du château, sur une sorte de large linteau composé de plusieurs blocs et formant coussinet entre un linteau monolithe à moulures et un arc de décharge grossièrement appareillé. M. Fossey m'en avait envoyé une photographie un peu pâle, sur laquelle je n'avais pu déchiffrer que quelques mots. Je renonçais à ce travail au moment où la photographie de M. Dussaud me permit de le reprendre avec succès, mais non sans peine.

L'inscription comprend deux lignes en beau naskhi, à caractères moyens, sans points ni voyelles, mais gravés avec soin et entremêlés de rinceaux qui compliquent un peu la lecture. Elle est encadrée d'une bordure à denticules et offre un aspect plus monumental que les autres inscriptions de la région. Voir planche, fig. 3.

(۱) عُمِّر هذا المكان المبارك بدوام أيّام المولا الأعظم شاه
شاه (sic) المعظّم علاى الدنيا (۲) والدين محمّد بن الحسن بن
محمّد بن الحسن خلّد الله أيّامه في أيّام المولى الصاحب كمال
الدنيا والدين الحسن بن مسعود أدام (؟) الله ظلّه ۝

Cette demeure bénie a été entretenue pendnt le règne du très grand seigneur, le roi des rois vénéré, 'Alâ' ad-dunyâ wad-dîn Muḥammad, fils d'al-Ḥasan, fils de Muḥammad, fils d'al-Ḥasan, qu'Allâh éternise son règne! Sous le règne du seigneur et maitre Kamâl ad-dunyâ wad-din al-Ḥasan, fils de Mas'ùd, qu'Allah prolonge sa puissance!

Ce texte confirme les conclusions tirées de la première inscription de Maṣyâd et soulève quelques nouveaux problèmes intéressants.

Ligne 1. On sait que le verbe neutre *'amara* (ou *'amira*) a le sens général d'«être prospère, habité, florissant, cultivé», et le verbe actif *'amara* (ou *'ammara* à la deuxième forme) celui de «rendre prospère, habité, etc.». De là sens spéciaux de ce verbe, suivant les cas. Ainsi *'amara al-arḍ* «cultiver la terre»; *'amara al-binâ'* «bâtir ou réparer l'édifice».[39] De la encore la formule: *'amara allâhu bika baitaka* «qu'Allâh rende ta maison prospère par toi», c'est-à-dire: «qu'il fasse reposer sur toi la prospérité de ta demeure!» C'est donc par erreur qu'on accuse de plagiat les souverains qui se servent de ce terme pour indiquer de simples restaurations dans un monument plus ancien, sous prétexte qu'ils voudraient s'en attribuer la paternité. Ils n'entendent pas dire qu'ils ont *fondé* l'édifice, mais qu'ils lui ont conservé ou rendu sa *prospérité*, soit par des constructions, soit par des fondations pieuses.[40]

Ainsi la première phrase de l'inscription ne signifie pas simplement que le château a été bâti (*'umira*) pendant (*bi-dawâm*) le règne du personnage nommé ci-après, mais que la *prospérité* de l'édifice est fondée sur la *durée* de ce règne. Il y a là une nuance à souligner, puisque le premier personnage, on va le voir, était le grand maître d'Alamût.

Le mot *makân* «demeure» confirme ce que nous savions déjà, c'est que le château de Maṣyâd servait de résidence au maître de Syrie.

Le personnage dont les titres et le nom suivent, c'est le grand maître d'Alamût, 'Alâ' ad-dîn Muḥammad III, qui règne de 618 à 653. On se souvient que son père, Ḥasan III, avait renié l'hérésie des fondateurs de la secte et que, rentré au giron de l'Église, il avait obtenu du calife les titres souverains, aven la reconnaissance officielle de sa légitimité.[41] Dès lors, chaque mot a sa valeur.

C'est d'abord le titre *maulâ* («seigneur») porté également par les maîtres de Syrie.[42] Il paraît ici sous une forme qui trahit de hautes prétentions: *al-maulâ al-a'ẓam* «le très grand seigneur», rimant avec *châhinchâh al-mu'aẓẓam* «le roi des rois vénéré».[43]

Le vieux titre persan *châhânchâh* a passé dès longtemps dans la titulature musulmane, notamment chez les dynasties orientales.[44] En vertu d'une loi générale, les titres dégénèrent avec le temps; leur usage abusif les fait tomber de plus en plus bas dans la hiérarchie officielle. Il s'agit donc de savoir quelle était la valeur du titre *châhinchâh* à l'époque de l'inscription, c'est-à-dire dans la première moitié du XIIIe siècle. Un passage de Nasawi nous le dit très clairement. Le sultan du Khârizm, Djalâl ad-dîn Mankubirti, à l'époque où son règne débutait dans l'Inde, c'est-à-dire vers 620, réclamait en vain du calife le titre de sultan. A la suite de nombreuses démarches, il obtint les insignés de sultan avec le titre *al-djanâb al-'âlî ach-châhinchâhi.*[45] Ainsi vers 620, à la date de notre insciption, le titre *châhinchâh* était de rang souverain, et 'Alâ' ad-dîn, qui ne pouvait le tenir que du calife, était réconnu comme souverain légitime.

Enfin le surnom 'Alâ' ad-dunyâ wad-dîn confirme ce que j'ai avancé plus haut, à savoir que les grands maîtres d'Alamût, à partir de Ḥasan III, devaient porter un surnom officiel en *ad-dunyâ wad-dîn*, indice de leur souveraineté.

Ligne 2. Le nom de grand maître est suivi de celui de son père, Ḥasan III, puis de ceux de son aïeul, Muḥammad II, et de son arrière-grand-père, Ḥasan II, ce même Ḥasan *'alâ dhikrihi as-salâm* qui avait rejeté en 559 la tutelle de l'imâm fictif Nizâr pour se proclamer lui-même imâm et descentant des Fatimites.[46] On voit tout l'intérêt de cette généalogie, parfaitement confirme aux récits des auteurs.

Enfin la formule *khallada allâh ayyâmahu*, qui d'ordinaire est souveraine, du moins à cette époque, vient clore cette série de preuves à l'appui de la souveraineté reconnue des grands maîtres d'Alamût.

L'inscription nomme ensuite un certain Ḥasan, fils de Masʿûd, qui ne peut être que le maître de Syrie gouvernant alors sous la tutelle d'Alamût. La formule *fî ayyâm* «sous le règne de» trahit déjà ses prétentions souveraines; dans l'épigraphie syro-égyptienne elle ne figure que devant le nom des sultans. Les titres *maulâ* et *ṣâḥib* sont ceux que l'autre inscription de Maṣyâd donne au maître Abu l-futûḥ. Le surnom Kamâl ad-dunyâ wad-dîn est la réplique du surnom Tâdj ad-dunyâ wad-dîn, porté par ce même Abu l-futuḥ. Enfin la formule finale *adâma*[47] *allâh ẓillahu* est bien caractéristique. Le mot *ẓill* «ombre, protection», signifie aussi «autorité, puissance, pouvoir souverain», en vertu d'une tradition attribuée à Mahomet: *as-sulṭânu ẓill allâh fi l-arḍ* «la souveraineté est l'ombre protectrice d'Allâh sur la terre».[48]

Ce Ḥasan était-il bien le maître de Syrie et à quelle époque? Voici un texte qui semble répondre à ces deux questions. Au cours des démêlés du sultan Mankubirti avec les Ismaïliens de Perse, un personnage surnommé Al-Kamâl, qui avait été quelque temps le lieutenant en Syrie du chef des Ismaïliens, c'est-à-dire du grand maître d'Alamût, vint trouver le sultan pour lui faire entendre des réclamations.[49]

Nasawi dit que cet ambassadeur était *surnommé* Al-Kamâl, ce qui revient à dire qu'il portait le surnom Kamâl ad-dîn, puisque les surnoms en *ad-dîn* sont désignés couramment, dès cette époque, sous cette forme abrégée.[50] Enfin l'on sait maintenant que ce surnom doit se traduire officiellement par Kamâl ad-dunyâ wad-dîn. On peut donc identifier cet Al-Kamâl avec le maître Ḥasan, fils de Masʿûd, Kamâl ad-dunyâ wad-dîn.

Quant à la date, on peut la fixer approximativement. Nasawi écrit le passage cité dans le récit des événements de l'année 624. D'après lui, Al-Kamâl n'était alors plus maître de Syrie. D'autre part, ʿAlâ' ad-dîn était monté sur le trône d'Alamût en 618. L'inscription aurait donc été rédigée entre ces deux dates, vers l'année 620.

Les autres inscriptions relevées à Maṣyâd n'ayant qu'un intérêt secondaire, passons au Kahf. On sait que ce château s'élève dans la montagne, à l'ouest de Maṣyâd, dans un district encore mal exploré.

Inscription du château du Kahf

Une copie de ce texte m'a été énvoyée il y a deux ans, par M. Hartmann, avec d'autres de la même forteresse. Elles avaient été faites à la hâte et par un temps pluvieux. Le savant professeur de Berlin me priait très modestement de les accepter avec réserve. M. Dussaud ayant rapporté deux photographies et un estampage de ce texte, j'ai pu le déchiffrer à l'aide de tous ces documents.

L'inscription est gravée sur un linteau monolithe d'environ 190 × 50, sur la porte d'un petit édifice en ruine, à côté du sentier qui monte à la forteresse. Elle comprend quatre lignes en naskh: cursif, à petits caractères allongés, d'un travail négligé, mais avec de nombreux points et signes. Une profonde cassure, qui traverse le milieu du linteau, a endommagé quelques mots; voir planche, fig. 4.[51]

(1) بسمله ... ادخلوها بسلام آمنين وعلى الله فليتوكل
المؤمنون ۱ أمر بعمارة (2) هذه الحمّام المباركة المولى الصاحب
العالم العادل سراج الدنيا والدين مظفّر بن الحسين أعزّ الله
(3) أنصاره فى ولاية العبد الفقير إلى رحمة الله تعالى وشفاعة
مواليه الأئمّة الأطهار صلوات الله عليهم (4) أجمعين حسن
بن إسماعيل العجمى الألموتى فى رمض[ان] سنة خمس وثلثين و
ستّمائة هجريّة طاعة حقّ ه

A ordonné la construction de ce bain béni, le seigneur, le maître, le savant, le juste, Sirâdj ad-dunyâ wad-dîn Muẓaffar, fils d'al-Ḥusain, qu'Allâh glorifie ses victoires! Sous le gouvernement du serviteur que a besoin de la miséricorde d'Allâh et de l'intercession de ses seigneurs les imâms purs—que les bénédictions d'Allâh soient sur eux tous!—Ḥasan, fils d'Ismâîl, le Persan d'Alamût. En ramaḍân de l'an 635 de l'hégire. Fait par ordre supérieur (?).

Ce text important confirme les précédents et fixe un nouveau jalon dans l'histoire des Assassins de Syrie.

Ligne 1. C'est la première fois que des versets du Coran figurent dans une inscription des Assassins.

Ligne 2. Le mot *al-ḥammâm* paraît certain. Le premier *mim* est très indistinct sur l'estampage et sur les deux photographies de M. Dussaud, mais on en voit un fragment au-dessus de la ligne. D'ailleurs la copie de M. Hartmann porte bien الحمّام هذه الحمّام ; on sait que ce mot peut etre féminin.[52]

Ce bain a été bâti par un personnage du nom de Muẓaffar, fils d'al-Ḥusain, que les titres de *maulâ* et *ṣâḥib*, le surnom Sirâdj al-dunyâ wad-dîn et la formule *a'azza allâh anṣârahu* trahissent à première vue pour le maître de Syrie. Il porte en outre les titres honorifiques *al-'âlim* et *al-'âdil*; ils étaient alors si communs qu'on n'en peut guère tirer d'induction nouvelle.

C'est encore Nasawi qui nous permet d'identifier ce personnage, et cette fois d'une manière certaine. En 625 ou 626, le sultan de Rûm (c'est-à-dire le sultan seldjoukide d'Asie Mineure Kaiqubâdh) envoya au sultan Mankubirti une lettre qu'il avait reçue de Sirâdj ad-dîn al-Maẓaffar ibn al-Ḥusain, *lieutenant en Syrie du grand maître d'Alamût* 'Alâ' ad-dîn (c'est-à-dire Muḥammad III, celui dont le nom figure sur l'inscription du château de Maṣyâd).[53] Ne retenons que les noms de ce personnage, identiques à ceux de l'inscription, et sa fonction de maître de Syrie, toujours sous la tutelle d'Alamût.

Ligne 3. Le nom suivant est introduit par la formule *fî wilâyah*, étudiée à propos de la première inscription de Maṣyâd. J'ai tâché de montrer qu'elle désigne la fonction de gouverneur, c'est-à-dire ici du gouverneur du Kahf.

La formule banale *al-'abd al-faqîr ilâ raḥmat allâh* est suivie des mots caractéristiques: *wa-chafâ'al mawâlihi al-a'immah al-aṭhâr*; *ṣalawât allâh 'alaihim* «et l'intercession de ses maîtres les imâms purs, que les bénédictions d'Állâh soient sur eux!»

On sait que la formule *ṣalawât allâh 'alaihi*, réservée d'abord à Mahomet, est donnée souvent aux califes, comme successeurs du Prophète, notamment aux Abassides, qui s'entourèrent d'une pompe orientale inconnue aux Omayades.[54] Pour toutes les sectes chiïtes, qui se fondent sur l'imamat d'Ali, cette formule est naturellement réservée à Ali et aux imâms ses successeurs, quels que soient d'ailleurs l'ordre et la série de ces imâms. Quant au terme *aṭ-ṭâhirûn*, *les purs*, il désigne pour les sunnites la famille du Prophète en général, pour les chiïtes, plus spécialement celle d'Ali.[55] Or tous les imâms chiïtes, se considérant comme les descendants direct d'Ali, donnent cette épithète *à leurs ancêtres*. De là la formule des imâms chiïtes, notamment des califes fatimites: *ṣalawât allâh 'alaihi wa-'alâ abâ'ihi (al-a' immah) aṭ-ṭâhirîn* (ou *al-aṭhâr*) «que les bénédictions d'Allâh reposent sur lui (l'imâm) et sur ses ancêtres (les imâms) les purs!»[56]

Cette formule, les imâms ismaïliens se l'attribuent à leur tour, ainsi qu'il résulte d'un document authentique.[57] Naturellement, le gouverneur du Kahf n'appelle pas la bénédiction divine sur ses ancêtres, mais sur ses *seigneurs* les imâms purs. Ces imâms, qui sont'ils? Les maîtres de Syrie? Évidemment non, puisqu'ils n'étaient alors que les lieutenants d'Alamût et qu'aucun d'eux ne semble avoir renouvelé la tentative d'indépendance de Sinân. Les maîtres d'Alamût? C'est peu probable, puisqu'ils avaient abandonné, par leur soumission au calife, toute prétention officielle à l'imâmat. Je pense qu'ici la formule n'a plus de valeur politique et désigne simplement la série des imâms adoptée par les dogmes ismaïliens. Elle montre du moins que les idées religieuses de la secte s'affichaient encore, malgré l'apparente soumission des grands maîtres.[58] C'est ainsi que le terme de *maulâ* «seigneur» qui désignerait ici les imâms de la secte, est resté l'un des titres spécifiques des grands maîtres persans et des maîtres syriens, même après leur conversion. Il le restera jusqu'à la fin, comme on le verra dans l'inscription suivante.

Ligne 4. Le premier mot est illisible sur l'estampage et les photographies de M. Dussaud. La copie de M. Hartmann porte جه من ou quelque chose d'approchant; celle de M. Dussaud donne اجوبين . Il faut lire sans doute اجمعين «tous»; ce mot figure souvent dans les formules de bénédiction.

Le nom du personnage que je considère comme le gouverneur du Kahf, Ḥasan, fils d'Ismâ'îl, n'a probablement pas été conservé par les auteurs. Retenons du moins son patronymique: le Persan d'Alamût. Comme Abu l-futûḥ et tant d'autres chefs de la secte syrienne, ce Ḥasan venait de la célèbre forteresse, dont le nom paraît ici pour la première fois dans un document authentique.

Le nom du mois est fruste à la fin, sur tous les documents que je possède, mais on peut le restituer facilement. En revanche, les chiffres de l'année sont parfaitement clairs. Le mot *thalâthîn* «trente», est écrit d'une manière bizarre, avec une queue dans le *lâm* tournée en bas et à droite. Il semble que le graveur, s'étant aperçu qu'il avait sauté l'alif d'allongement, ait voulu l'indiquer sous cette forme assez gauche; en tout cas, la ponctuation des deux *thâ* rend le mot certain. Ainsi Muẓaffar Sirâdj ad-dîn, qui gouvernait la secte en 626, était encore maître en l'année 635.

L'inscription se termine, sur les copies de MM. Hartmann et Dussaud, par le groupe طا هو حو . Ces lettres énigmatiques ne donnant aucun sens, j'ai cru qu'elles cachaient la date en chiffres, ou quelque formule propre à la secte, mais j'en cherchai vainement l'explication. En examinant l'estampage de M. Dussaud, je vis que la quatrième lettre a la forme d'un petit ـهـ final et que la dernière porte deux points distincts. Dès lors, ces lettres prennent un sens: il faut lire, je pense, طاعةً حقّ «en obéissant à un ordre, à un devoir impératif», c'est-à-dire que le gouverneur a exécuté un ordre du maître, ou que ce dernier a suivi un ordre du grand maître.[59]

Les autres insciptions du château du Kahf sont toutes postérieures à la prise de la forteresse par le sultan Baibars, autant que j'en puis juger par les documents que j'ai sous les yeux; par conséquent, elles n'ont plus trait à la secte en tant qu'organisme politique. L'une est au nom de Baibars et de son fils Malik Sa'îd; une autre est datée de 691, une troisième est du début du VIIIe siècle de l'hégire.

Tel est aussi le cas d'un curieux texte de la forteresse de 'Ullaiqah, daté de 670, et que la photographie de M. Dussaud permet de lire intégralement. Passons à Qadmûs, la troisième des principales forteresses de la secte syrienne, située dans la montagne au nord du Kahf.

Inscription de la mosquée de Qadmûs

Les inscriptions de Qadmûs sont fort nombreusses. Ce renseignement, fourni par M. Hartmann, est confirmé par M. Dussaud, qui en a estampé plusieurs. Malheureusement, elles paraissent dans un état pitoyable, en partie effacées, brisées ou dispersées. Voici la seule qui donne un lecture satisfaisante. Ce texte, gravé sur le mur à l'entrée de la mosquée de Qadmûs, a été copié par un indigène, et M. Dussaud n'en possède pas d'estampage. Je le donne donc sous toute réserve, quoique la copie paraisse exacte.

بسم الله الرحمن (الرحيم) أمر بعمارة هذا الجامع المبارك
الموالى الأصحاب نجم الدين وشمس الدين أعزّ الله نصرهما

Ont ordonné la construction de cette mosquée bénie les seigneurs, les maîtres Nadjm ad-dîn et Chams ad-dîn, qu'Allâh glorifie leur victoire!

Ainsi la mosquée a été bâtie ou plutôt restaurée par Nadjm ad-dîn, le dernier grand maître indépendant, ce vieillard que Baibars dépouilla peu à peu de son autorité, et par son fils Chams ad-dîn, dont le nom figure souvent avec celui de son père, dans les démelés de la secte avec le sultan d'Égypte. Ce texte suggère deux observations.

D'abord on y trouve les deux titres habituels des maîtres de Syrie, *maulâ* et *ṣâḥib*. Ces titres sont au pluriel: par conséquent, Chams ad-dîn était associé à son père dans la maîtrise. L'emploi du pluriel au lieu du duel, fréquent dans l'arabe médiéval, trahit un acheminement de la langue vers les dialectes modernes, où le duel est d'un emploi beaucoup plus rare et tend à disparaître.

Ensuite on observera que, pour la première fois, les surnoms des grands maîtres en *ad-dîn* paraissent sous la forme courante, non sous la forme officielle en *ad-dunyâ wad-dîn*. S'il n'y a là ni faute de copie, ni négligence du rédacteur, c'est peut-être un indice de la situation politique des maîtres de Syrie à l'epoque où fut gravée l'inscription. L'absence d'une date nous laisse le champ libre à cet égard.

En effet, ce n'est point en un jour que Baibars mit fin à l'autonomie politique des Assassins. Dès son avènement en 658, le sultan s'ingère dans les affaires de la secte, prétend nommer son chef, lui réclame un tribut et lui reprend une partie de ses forteresses. Jusqu'ici, malgré l'affaiblissement de la secte, malgré la chute du grand maître d'Alamût, qu'Houlagou venait de renverser, le maître de Syrie semble avoir gardé sa souveraineté. Mais en 668, à la suite de nouveaux démêlés, Nadjm ad-dîn, alors âgé de 90 ans, et son fils Chams ad-dîn font acte de soumission; ils se présentent humblement au camp du sultan. Celui-ci se laisse fléchir, confère à Nadjm ad-dîn le titre de son lieutenant, conjointement avec son gendre Sârim ad-dîn, et leur impose un nouveau tribut. Puis il garde auprès de lui Chams ad-dîn, sous prétexte de l'avoir à sa cour, en réalité pour conserver un otage.

La lutte renaissant encore, Baibars contraint le père et le fils à demeurer auprès de lui, en promettant un fief au premier, au second le grade d'emir avec un commandement dans son armée; puis il dépose et emprisonne Ṣârim ad-dîn. Après de nouveaux incidents, Chams ad-dîn est arrêté et conduit en Égypte, et le sultan s'empare en 671 des derniers châteaux ismaïliens.[60]

Durant cette agonie de douze années, Najdm ad-dîn et Chams ad-dîn passent par degrés successifs du rang de maîtres à l'état de prisonniers du sultan. Mais dès l'année 668, Nadjm, simple lieutenant de Baibars, et Chams, simple officier de son armée, ne pouvaient plus prétendre aux titres souverains. Dès lors, ils ne portaient plus officiellement qu'un surnom en *ad-dîn*, comme tous les fonctionnaires du royaume égyptien. C'est probablement à cette époque que remonte l'inscription de Qadmûs.

En comparant ces quatre inscriptions aux auteurs cités dans ce mémoire, on peut ébaucher le tableau suivant, encore bien incomplet, des maîtres de Syrie au XIIIe siècle:

Kamâl ad-dîn Ḥasan était maître vers l'année 620, date approximative de l'inscription du château de Maṣyâd, fixée sur un passage de Nasawi.

Sirâdj ad-dîn Muẓaffar était maître vers 626, comme l'indique un autre passage de Nasawi. L'inscription du château du Kahf nous le montre encore en place en l'an 635.

Tâdj ad-dîn Abu l-futûh était maître en 637, suivant Ibn Wâṣil. Il l'était encore en 646, date de l'inscription de l'enceinte de Maṣyâd.

Riḍâ' ad-dîn Abu l-ma'âlî était maître en 656 et en 658, lors de l'invasion des Tartares.

Nadjm ad-dîn Ismâ'îl régnait depuis 659 ou 660, d'abord seul ou avec Riḍâ', plus tard avec son gendre Ṣârim ad-dîn Mubârak, fils de Riḍâ', et avec son fils Chams ad-dîn. Il fut définitivement déchu en 668 (mars 1270).

Ainsi tous les maîtres syriens connus à partir du début du VIIe siècle de l'hégire portent un surnom en *ad-dîn*, comme les grands maîtres d'Alamût contemporains. Or ces surnoms sont officiellement en *ad-dunyâ wad-dîn* et trahissent le rapprochement qui se fit en 608 entre la secte et Bagdad. On peut en conclure qu'avant cette date, aucun des grands maîtres d'Alamût ni des maîtres de Syrie n'a porté un surnom officiel en *ad-dunyâ wad-dîn*.

Cette conclusion est certaine pour les grands maîtres d'Alamût, parce qu'aucun d'entre eux, avant 608, ne figure dans les auteurs avec un surnom en *ad-dîn*. Mais parmi les maîtres de Syrie antérieurs à cette date, le plus célèbre, Sinân, s'appelait Râchid ad-dîn. Serait-ce l'indice d'un surnom officiel Râchid ad-dunyâ wad-dîn et d'un rapprochement entre Sinân et la cour de Bagdad?

La question, on l'avouera, était bien tentante. Il eût été curieux de montrer, par un simple détail emprunté à l'épigraphie, que le célèbre maître qui s'était émancipé de la tutelle d'Alamût et pouvait alors suivre sa propre politique,[61] avait compris, avant le chef de la secte persane, l'opportunité d'un rapprochement avec le calife. En cherchant attentivement, j'ai réuni quelques vagues indices qui semblaient autoriser cette hypothèse: le sens su surnom de Sinân (*râchid* signifie «qui suit la bonne voie, orthodoxe»); sa brusque alliance avec Saladin, zélé sunnite et défenseur des intérêts du calife, alliance dont les motifs, après la lutte acharnée entre Sinân et Saladin, ne semblent pas encore suffisamment éclaircis;[62] enfin l'anecdote XIII de l'attachant récit de Guyard, où l'ambassade du calife auprès du maître de Syrie semble trahir une tentative de négociations politiques.[63]

En relisant les pages que j'avais rédigées d'un premier jet, je m'aperçus qu'elles ne satisfaisaient pas aux exigences d'une saine méthode historique. En l'absence d'un document positif, il vaut mieux admettre que Sinân portait, comme tant d'autres, un surnom en *ad-dîn* sans valeur politique, et que ces surnoms chez les maîtres de Syrie ne cachent un titre souverain qu'à partir de l'évolution de la secte en l'année 608.[64]

NOTES

1 Ce mémoire a été lu en partie à l'Académie des inscriptions et belles-lettres, les 2 et 9 avril 1897; il en a paru un résumé dans les *Comptes rendus* de l'Académie. Sauf indication spéciale, les pages des mémoires cités ici sont celles des tirages à part.

2 Sur l'origine du mot *assassin*, voir de Sacy, *Mémoire su la dynastie des Assassins*, 21 et suiv.

3 Voir *Journal asiatique*, IXe série, VI, 511. Les seuls relevés que je possédais jusqu'ici sont ceux de M. Hartmann.

4 Outre ces documents, M. Fossey m'a communiqué la copie d'inscriptions confiques qu'il a relevées au cours d'un voyage antérieur dans le Hauran. Tous ces matériaux seront classés et prendront place dans le *Corpus*.

5 Burckhardt, *Travels in Syria*, éd. de 1822, 150; *Ileisen*, éd. Gesenius, 255 et planche I, n° 7.

6 Voir les cas cités dans Harîri, *Durrat al-gauwâṣ*, éd. Thorbecke, 15. J'avoue que j'ai beaucoup de peine à les distinguer dans la langue vulgaire.

7 On trouve dans les auteurs مصيات , مصياث , مصياف et مصياب . D'aprés de Sacy, *op. cit.*, 17, note 1, et Guyard, *Fragments relatifs à la doctrine des Ismaêlis*, 3, note 2, la première forme serait la bonne. Je croirais plutôt, avec M. Derenbourg, *Autobiographie d'Ousâma*, 43, note 1, que la forme originale est la deuxième, parce qu'elle est intermédiaire entre la première et la troisième, qui en dérivent toutes deux par un procédé fréquent en arabe; voir Spitta, *Grammatik*, 4 et 1.2. La quatrième, donnée par Yâqût, est peut-être une erreur de copie. La forme *maṣyâf* (ainsi vocalisée) est la plus fréquente *chez les auteurs*;

elle figure sur la carte arabe publiée à Beyrouth en 1889. Au temps de Burckhardt, c'était la forme *officielle*, mais on *prononçait maṣyâd*, comme au moyen âge (cf. le *Messiat* des auteurs médiévaux). Aujourd'hui l'on prononce toujours ainsi, si mes souvenirs sont exacts, mais M. Fossey m'apprend que les lettrés de l'endroit épellent encore مصيان.Citons enfin, comme formes excentriques, le *miṣyâf* du texte de Dimachqi, éd. Mehren, 208, et le مصياثا de Khalîl Ẓàhiri, éd. Rayaisse, 49. Sur l'orthographe du nom, voir encore Quatremère, *Notice historique sur les Ismaïliens*, dans *Mines de l'Orient*, IV, 340; Defrémery, *Nouvelles recherches sur les Ismaïliens*, 45; Guyard, *Un grand maître des Assassins*, 71, note 1.

Je crois en somme qu'il s'agit d'un vieux nom indigène que les Arabes ont cherché à ramener à une forme de leur grammaire (*maf'àl, mif'âl*) et à une racine de leur dictionnaire (*ṣaif, ṣaid, ṣaub, ṣaut*). De là ces hésitations, qu'on observe souvent en pareil cas.

8 Ainsi *wilâyah* correspond à *wâli*, comme *niyâbah, kifâlah* à *nâ'ib, kâfil*, etc.

Sous les Ayoubites, les places fortes étaient commandées par des *wâlis* et des *mutawallis*. Voir, par exemple, Abû Châmah, *Kitâb arrauḍatain*, I. p. 50; Guyard, *Un grand maître*, 31, 74 et 135, où il s'agit justement des forteresses des Assassins. Plus tard, sous les Mamlouks, les gouverneurs de forteresse prennent le titre de *nâ'ib*, et celui de *wôli* désigne les gouverneurs de district.

Ces détails ressortent d'un grand nombre d'inscriptions et de passages dans les receuils administratifs. Je l'ai montré, en ce qui concerne le titre de *nâ'ib*, dans *C. I. A.*, I, 210 et *passim*; il me reste à donner un exemple de la valeur du titre *wâli* sous les Mamlouks.

On sait, par les recueils, qu'à cette époque les provinces (*mamlakah*) étaient subdivisées en districts (*wilâyah*). Ainsi la mamlakah de Gazzah comptait, parmi ses districts, la wilâyah de Ramleh; *Ta'rif*, éd. Caire, 177. Or, dans une inscription du sultan Baibars à Yabneh (673 H.), l'instigateur de l'assassinat d'Édouard d'Angleterre, Khalîl ibn Châwir, est appelé *wâli* de Ramleh, et, dans un texte du sultan Muḥammad à Ramleh (714 H.), on lit: ... *bi-niyâbat Djâwli ... bi-wilâyat Ḥasan*, etc., c'est-à-dire: «Djâwlî étant *nâ'ib* de la province de Gazzah, et Ḥasan étant *wâli* du district de Ramleh». A cette époque, l'emir Djâwlî était en effet gouverneur de la province de Gazzah; voir *C. I. A.*, I. 160.

On sait qu'aujourd'hui, en Turquie, les wâlîs sont les gouverneurs civils des provinces.

J'ajoute qu'il ne faut pas fair grand fonds des termes techniques qu'on trouve *chez les auteurs*, à part les ouvrages spéciaux sur l'administration. Ainsi le gouverneur de Bosra appelé *wâli* dans le passage cité d'Abû Châmah, est nommé *nâ'ib* par Nu'aimi et 'Il-mawi (Sauvaire, *Description de Damas*, 79), parce qu'à l'époque de ces auteurs, les gouverneurs de place portaient ce dernier titre. Ainsi encore, le même gouverneur de Maṣyâd, sous Sinân, est appelé successivement *mutawalli, wâli* et *na'ib* (Guyard, *Un grand maître*, 135 et 141). Il n'y a là que des indices à ajouter aux documents plus certains fournis par les recueils et les inscriptions.

La loi de correspondance entre la formule et le titre demande d'ailleurs à être vérifiée. Il faudra pour cela dépouiller les inscriptions et chercher dans les auteurs quelles fonctions remplissaient les personnages visés par les formules.

Je n'ai rien dit de la formule *'alâ yad* («par la main de»), qui semble désigner un rôle plus immédiat, quelque chose comme l'entreprise des travaux. On trouve parfois, en dernier lieu, les mots *'amal* ou *rasm* suivis d'un nom propre: c'est la signature du tailleur de pierre.

9 De Sacy, *Chrestomathie*, II, 240; Guyard, *Un grand maître*, 31, note 2; *Fragments*, 104.

10 Quatremère, *Notice historique*, *op. cit.*, 368; *Mémoires sur l'Égypte*, II, 505; Defrémery, *Nouvelles recherches sur les Ismaéliens*, 116. Voici le passage du *Masâlik*, que j'ai contrôlé sur le manuscrit que M. Schefer a bien voulu mettre à ma disposition: أنفسهم بأصحاب الدعوة الهادية ويسمّون Voir aussi Guyard, *Un grand maître*, 145, où ce terme est employé par un auteur de la secte.

11 Guyard, *Fragments*, 104 et 135–136.

12 Quatremère, *Notice*, *op. cit.*, 340; Defrémery, *Recherches*, 45; Guyard, *Un grand maître*, 30; Derenbourg, *op. cit.*, 281, et les chroniques arabes, par exemple Nuwairi, cod. Leide 2er, f° 222 r[e]. De Sacy, 17, dit par erreur: en 525.

13 Pour éviter toute confusion, j'appelle *grand maître* le chef de la secte mère persane, résidant à Alamût, et *maître* le chef de la secte syrienne, résidant d'ordinaire à Maṣyâd.

14 Voir les sources citées, notamment Guyard.

15 De Sacy, *op. cit.*, 19; Quatremère, *op. cit.*, 364; De Hammer, *Histoire de l'ordre des Assassins*, 313 et suiv.; Defrémery, *Recherches*, 91 et suiv.; Guyard, *Un grand maître*, 52; *Sultans Mamlouks*, I, *passim*, et la fin de ce mémoire.

16 Voir mes *Inscriptions de Syrie*, dans *Mémoires de l'Institut égyptien*, III, 450.

17 Ibn Wâṣil, *Histoire des Ayoubites*. Paris 1702, fol. 333 V[e]. L'auteur a été mêlé lui-même à une partie des événements qu'il raconte et son livre a une grande valeur documentaire. Dans le passagé cité ici, il ajoute qu'il connaissait personnellement le chef de la secte.

Le manuscrit de Paris est malheureusement fragmentaire, et ses cahiers incomplets sont interpolés dans le plus grand désordre. M. Casanova, qui s'occupe à démêler cet écheveau et à analyser le contenu du volume, rend un grand service à nos études. C'est à lui que je dois tous les passages d'Ibn Wâṣil cités dans ce mémoire; je suis heureux de le remercier, une fois de plus, du concours empressé qu'il apporte à mes recherches. Sur l'auteur, voir *Historiens orientaux des croisades*, I, LV; Reinaud, *Chroniques arabes des croisades*, XXV; Wüstenfeld, *Geschichtschreiber*, 149.

18 مضى إلى الإسمعيلية مستجيرًا بهم خائفًا من الملك الصالح عماد
الدين وكان مقدّم الإسمعيلية يومئذ رجل من العجم وَرَدَ من الالموت
يقال له تاج الدين ... فأجاره تاج الدين ۝

Le terme *muqaddam* désigne souvent, dans les auteurs, le chef de la secte syrienne; voir, par exemple, Ibn al-Athir, *passim*: de Sacy, *op. cit.*, 17. Sur le sens technique de ce terme, voir Guyard, *Fragments*, 119.

19 D'après Guyard, *Un grand maître*, 31, Abû Muḥammad aurait déjà gouverné les forteresses au moyen de mutawallîs placés sous ses ordres. Mais l'auteur emprunte visiblement ce terme au récit IV de son historien arabe (p. 74 et 135), qui parle du mutawallî ou wâlî de Maṣyâd *sous Sinân.*

20 Pour le premier, voir Guyard, *Fragments*, 17 et 70; *Un grand maître*, 131 et suiv. Pour le deuxième, Defrémery, *Recherches*, 93, note 3; 95, note 1; Nuwairi, *cod. cit.* f° 221 v° et *passim*. On y lit, entre autres, que Baibars conféra à Sârim ad-dîn les titres inhérents à la dignité de ṣâḥib, ou simplement qu'il le nomma ṣâḥib, *suivant l'usage des gouverneurs de la secte*:

نعت صارم الدين بالصوبية على عادة نواب الدعوة ۵

Le mot *nâ'ib*, qui désigne ici le chef de la secte, ne prouve pas qu'il ait porté officiellement ce titre. Il était très répandu sous les Mamlouks, et les auteurs de l'époque l'emploient dans un sens général, comme on l'a vu plus haut, 460.

21 Abû Muḥammad, le prédécesseur de Sinân, est appelé d'ordinaire le *chaikh*, titre que portait aussi Sinân avant sa maîtrise; Defrémery, *Recherches*, 55; Guyard, *Un grand maître*, 33, 71 et suiv. C'est évidemment ce titre que les historiens des croisades ont traduit par *Vieil* ou «Vieux de la Montagne» (*chaikj al-djabal*): «Il n'ont mic seigneur par heritage, ainçois eslisent à escient le meilleur home de la terre por cus governer et deffendre; *ne le vuclent apeler empereur ne roi ne conte; sanz plus, le noment le Vieil*»; Guillaume de Tyr, éd. Paris, II, 357; Bongars, *Gesta Dei*, I, 994: magistrum solent sibi praeficere ... quem spretis aliis dignitatum nominibus *senem* vocant; cf. Jacques de Vitry, *ibid.*, 1062. On remarquera que le récit de Guillaume se raporte à l'année 1173, c'est-à-dire avant l'époque où les maîtres de Syrie, comme on verra plus loin, reçurent des titres officiels du calife de Bagdad.

Le rapprochement de *chaikh* et *vieil* a déjà été fait par de Sacy, *op. cit.* (extrait du *Moniteur*, 6; ce passage ne figure pas dans l'édition plus complète du *Mémoire* que j'ai citée jusqu'ici). Le célèbre orientalist voit dans le *Vieil* des Croisés le grand maître d'Alamût. Mais il est probable, comme l'observe de Hammer, *op. cit.*, 205, que les Croisés ne connaissaient pas directement le grand maître d'Alamût et que, pour eux, le Vieil était le maître de Syrie, Sinân et ses successeurs.

22 Voir *C.I.A.*, *passim.*

23 De Hammer, *op. cit.*, *passim*; Defrémery, *op. cit.*, 83, et *Journal asiatique,* 4ᵉ série, XIII, 43 et suiv.

24 Voir *C. I. A.*, 82 et *passim*, et les catalogues des monnaies du British Museum et du Cabinet des médailles. Ces titres figurent dès le début

du VIe siècle, parmi ceux des Seldjoukides, puis de leurs atâbeks. Il y aurait une curieuse étude à faire sur leur origine. Sur les monnaies et les inscriptions de Nûr ad-dîn, cette forme du surnom ne figure pas encore; je crois donc que pour la Syrie, l'origine en remonte à Saladin.

25 Voir *C.I.A.*, 82, note 2; 83, note 3; 144, note 3. Pour les surnoms en *ad-dunyâ wad-dîn*, cf. *Historiens orientaux des croisades*, IIb, 193. – Sur les théories du souverain, voir surtout de Kremer, *Geschichte der herrschenden Ideen*, livre III.

26 Casanova, *Monnaie des Assassins de Perse*, dans *Revue numismatique*, III (série XI), 345.

27 De Sacy, *op. cit.*, 77.

28 De Sacy, *loc. cit.*; Defrémery, *Journal asiatique, tom. cit.*, 27; Casanova, *op. cit.*, 347, rectifiant Guyard.

29 Dozy, *Histoire de l'islamisme*, 302; de Hammer, *op. cit.*, 89; Defrémery, *Essai sur l'histoire des Ismaéliens*, 66 et suiv.

30 Casanova, *op. cit.*, 344. On remarquera que les formules qui suivent le nom de Nizâr sont celles qui figurent sur les monnaies et les inscriptions fatimites.

31 De Sacy, *op. cit.*, 18; Defrémery, *Essai*, 101 et suiv. (d'après Djuwaini); *Journal asiatique, tom. cit.*, 41 (d'après Hamdallâh); Guyard, *Un grand maître*, 25; de Hammer, *op. cit.*, 168 et suiv.; Dozy, *op. cit.*, 310.

32 Nous n'avons encore aucun document officiel de Ḥasan II. D'après Djuwaini, les inscriptions gravées sur les murs et les portes de ses château et les protocoles de ses lettres portaient simplement: Ḥasan fils de Muḥammad fils de Buzurg-ûmîd; Defrémery, *Essai*, 104. Suivant Mirkhond, on lisait sur la porte de la bibliothèque d'Alamût: «Avec l'aide de l'Éternel, le maître du monde (le salut soit sur son nom) a secoué le joug de la loi»; Jourdain, *Notice de l'histoire de Mirkhond*, etc., 54; de Hammer, *op. cit.*, 171. Enfin, d'après Ḥamdallah, Ḥasan, qui se faisait appeler *khudâwand* (le *sayyidnâ* de Ḥasan Ier), prit un titre de calife: *al-qâhir bi-quwwat allâh*, et créa son ère propre, qu'il mit dans les inscriptions des monuments ismaïliens; Defrémery, *Journal asiatique, tom. cit.*, 40–43. Il est impossible de proclamer plus hardiment son indépendance. Quelque explorateur ne rapportera-t-il pas une inscription oubliée dans les ruines de ces châteaux?

33 Tous les auteurs persans et arabes racontent cet évenement, qui fit sensation dans le monde musulman. De Sacy, *op. cit.*, 29; Jourdain (Mirkhond), *op. cit.*, 59; Defrémery (Ḥamdallâh), *Journal asiatique, tom. cit.*, 44, et *Recherches*, 83; de Hammer, *op. cit.*, 220 (donnant par erreur l'année 607); Dozy, *op. cit.*, 312; Ibn al-Athîr, XII, 195; Abu l-fidâ', III, 120; *Historiens orientaux des croisades*, I, 86. Parmi les sources citées par Defrémery, figure le *Djihân Kuchây* de Djuwaini, dont le regretté savant a commencé la traduction dans son *Essai*; ce travail s'arrête avant l'époque où nous sommes arrivés. M. Schefer a bien voulu mettre à ma disposition ses trois manuscrits de cet ouvrage, où l'on trouve le chapitre sur les Ismaïliens; il était trop tard pour en tirer parti dans ce mémoire. Je suppose que Djuwaini ne parle qu'incidemment des châteaux de Syrie. Rachîd ad-dîn (éd. Quatremère), qui raconte en détail la conquête des châteaux persans par

Houlagou, parle à peine des premiers. En revanche, voici un passage inédit d'Ibn Wâṣil, ms. cité, fol. 169 r° (année 608):

وفي هذه السنة أظهر الكيا جلال الدين حسن صاحب الالموت إمام
الباطنية شعائر الإسلام وأمر رعيّته بالصلوات.والحجّ إلى بيت الله الحرام
وصيام شهر رمضان وإقامة وضائف (sic) الشريعة وكتب إلى الخليفة الإمام
الناصر لدين الله والملوك يعلّمهم بذلك وبعث والدته إلى مكة لتحجّ فحجّت
كما ذكرنا وأكرمت ببغداد لمّا دخلتها إكرامًا عظيمًا وبعث جلال الدين
حسن إلى الحصون التى لهم بالشأم يلزمهم أن يفعلوا نظير ما فعله ببلاد
العجم فأعلنوا بالأذان وإقامة الجمع وأظهروا أنّهم قد التزموا بمذهب
الشافعي ۞

En résumé: Le Kiyâ Djalâl ad-dîn Ḥasan, le grand maître d'Alamût, embrasse publiquement l'islamisme et impose à ses sujects les devoirs religieux. Il annonce sa conversion au calife Nâṣir et aux rois. Il envoie sa mère en pèlerinage à la Mecque; elle est accueillie à Bagdad avec les plus grands honneurs. Enfin il impose les mêmes obligations aux sectaires des châteaux de Syrie, qui adoptent le rite chafiïte.

Voici un passage d'Abû Châmah, tiré d'un ouvrage inédit: *adh-dhail fi r-rauḍatain*, l'«Appendice au livre des deux jardins». M. Schefer a bien voulu mettre son manuscrit à ma disposition, avec une inépuisable obligeance; le style, comme on verra est peu soigné.

وفيها (٦٠٨) قدم رسول جلال الدين حسن صاحب الالموت يخبر بأنّهم قد
تبرا (sic) من الباطنية وبنوا الجوامع والمشاهد وأقمت (sic) الجمعة والجماعات
عندهم وصلّوا (sic) رمضان فسرّ الناس والخليفة بذلك وقدمت خاتون
بنت جلال الدين حاجّة فاحتفل لها الخليفة ۞

En cette année 608 vint un ambassadeur de Djalâl ad-dîn Ḥasan, le grand maître d'Alamût, pour annoncer qu'ils s'étaient affranchis du batinisme, qu'ils avient bâti des mosquées et des chapelles et rétabli le culte et les réunions de prière, et le jêune du ramaḍân. Le public et le calife en conçurent une grande joie. La princesse fille de Djalâl ad-dîn entreprit le pèlerinage et reçut un bon accueil du calife.

Un peu plus loin, l'auteur ajoute:

وفيها تظاهرت الإسماعيلية بالالموت وكروكور (sic) وما والاها من بلاد
العجم بالاسلام وإقامة شعائره والرجوع عمّا كانوا عليه من الفساد وأرسل
زعيمهم جلال الدين حسن إلى الخليفة الناصر يبذل الطاعة ويستدعي
قضاة وفقهاء يفقّهوهم ويقضون بينهم فأجيب وبعث إلى الحصون الشأمية
مصياف والخوابي والقُلَيْعة وما ينضاف إليها ممّا ينسب إلى الإسماعيلية مَن
أظهر فيها شعائر الإسلام وتجديد المساجد وإقامة الحدّ على من ارتكب
محرّمًا ۞

> En cette année 608, les Ismaïliens d'Alamût, de Kirdkûh et des districts voisins en Perse affichèrent l'islâm et ses pratiques, abjurant leur hérésie. Leur chef, Djalâl ad-dîn Ḥasan, envoya un ambassadeur au calife Nàṣir pour lui offrir sa soumission et pour lui demander des juges et des légistes . . . Aux châteaux de Syrie, Maṣyâf, Khawâbî, Qulai'ah, et à tous ceux qui appartenaient à la secte, il envoya des messagers pour y proclamer le retour à l'islàm et édicter des peines rontre ceux qui commettraient des actes illicites.

Dans ces récits, relevons deux points intéressants: la secte syrienne, un moment émancipée sous Sinân, était rentrée sous la tutelle d'Alamût; cf. Defrémery, *Recherches*, 82; Guyard, *Un grand maître*, 52. En second lieu, les nouveaux convertis, en Syrie du moins, se rattachent officiellement au rite chafiïte. Ibn Wâṣil est le seul auteur, à ma connaissance, qui signale ce fait. On verra plus loin que cette conversion politique ne détruisit pas les doctrines de la secte.

34 Voir plus loin, 482 [291], une inscription qui confirme directement cette hypothèse.

35 Voir plus haut, note 23.

36 Cette phrase est un reflet de la théorie des *nâṭiq* et des *asâs*; voir Guyard, *Fragments*, 13 et *passim*. Abel semble prendre ici la place d'Adam, le premier nâṭiq.

37 Joinville, éd. Wailly, 246 et suiv.; cf. Quatremère, *Notice*, *op. cit.*, 362; Defrémery, *Recherches*, 90. L'*Eracles* (*Historiens occidentaux des croisades*, II, 624) dit quelques mots de cette ambassade.

38 M. Dussaud a visité deux autres forteresses des Assassins, al-Khawâbî et al-Manîqah (*sic*). Il n'y a trouvé aucune inscription, non plus que dans les ruines de Sâfîthâ, al-'Arîmah, Burdj Mïâr, Qal'at Yaḥmûr et Tortose, mais il en signale une sur une autre porte de l'encient de Maṣyâd. Les autres textes qu'il m'a remis proviennent de 'Akkâr et de Mariamîn.

39 Lane, *Dictionary*, *s. v.* ظلّ.

40 Voir *C.I.A.*, I, 99.

41 Voir plus haut, 475 [288].

42 Voir plus haut, 469 [286]. Le titre *sâḥib* est aussi donné au grand maître d'Alamût; Nasawi, *Histoire du sultan Mankubirti*, éd. Houdas, 12.

43 Sur la valeur politique des épithètes *a'ẓam* et *mu'aẓẓam* dans les titres souverains, on culsultera un mémoire sur les Ayoubites, que M. Casanova prépare en ce moment.

44 Sur l'évolution de ce titre chez les anciens rois de Perse, voir Humann et Puchstein, *Reise in Klein-Asien*, 281, note 1. Pour les dynasties musulmanes, notamment les Samanides et les Bouïdes, voir *Siyâset Nâmch*, trad. Schefer, 200, etc.

45 Nasawi, trad. Houdas, 413. Cet ouvrage offre un intérêt particulier, car l'auteur raconte des événements auxquels il a été mêlé lui-même, par ses fonctions politiques. Le récit de son ambassade à Alamût est des plus captivants et nous autorise à accepter avec confiance les renseignements de l'auteur sur les Assassins, dont il sera tiré parti plus loin.

Voici encore une preuve de la valeur du titre *châhinchâh*: en 604, c'est-à-dire quelques années auparavant, le sultan Malik ʿÂdil, le frère de Saladin, reçut du calife Nâṣir un diplôme qui lui concédait la souveraineté des pays qu'il avait conquis. Or ce document officiel lui donnait le titre *châhinchâh*; Abul-fidâ', *Historiens orientaux des croisades*, I, 84 (cf. IIb, 193); *C.I.A.*, I, 83, note 3.

46 Voir plus haut, 388.

47 Le mot أعلام n'est pas parfaitement sur; il semble que le texte porte امان ou ظِل اعلام.. Ce détail a peu d'importance; l'intérêt de la formule réside dans le mot *ẓill*.

48 Lane, *Dictionary*, *s. v.* ظِل

49 Nasawii, trad. 220; texte, 132:

شخص يلقّب بالكمال وقد ناب
عن صاحبهم زمانًا ببلاده الشآمية ۞

50 Quatremère, *Notice*, *op. cit.*, 359, raconte cet épisode d'après Nasawi et le prétendu Ḥasan ibn Ibrâhîm (c'est-à-dire ʿAini, Paris 1543, f°s 30 v° et 16 r°). Il nomme le personnage Kamâl ad-dîn, ce qui confirme mon hypothèse. C'est peut-être ainsi que l'appelle ʿAini, que je n'ai pas eu l'occasion de consulter.

51 *Coran*, XV, 46; et III, 118 (ou III; 154; ou V, 14; ou IX, 51; ou XIV, 14; ou LVIII, 11; ou LXIV, 13).

52 Voir Lane, *Dictionary*.

53 Nasawi, trad. 280; texte, 1681: بالناحية الشآمية سراج الدين المظفر بن الحسين نائب علاء الدين صاحب الموت. J'ai dégà dit que le titre *nâ'ib*, alors très fréquent, n'a pas nécessairement ici un caractère officiel. Il est pris souvent dans le sens général de *représentant*.

54 Goldziher, *Muhammedanische Studien*, II, 55, note 5, citant Bundâri, 240 *ult.*

55 *Âluhn* (ou *ahl baitihi*) *aṭ-ṭâhirûn*, formule très fréquente sur les tombeaux musulmans. L'attribution de cette formule à la famille d'Ali pour les chiïtes semble remonter à Ali lui-même, en tout cas à son fils Ḥasan; Masʿûdi, *Prairies d'or*, V, 13.

56 Voir toutes les inscriptions fatimites, dan *C.I.A.*, I, *passim*, notamment dans le texte de Mustanṣir à Rabwah (*Notes d'archéologie arabe*, I, 84), où cette prétention est clairement exprimée. J'ai réuni plusiers documents à l'appui dans *C.I.A.*, I, 25, note 1.

57 Casanova, *op. cit.*, 344.

58 Alors comme toujours en Orient, les doctrines chiïtes couvaient et se transmettaient en secret, en plein sunnisme officiel, quend les circonstances politiques n'étaient pas favorables à leur application. En voici deux examples caractéristiques, empruntés à Ibn Wâṣil, ms. cité f°s 273 r° et 233 r°:

1. Après la mort du sultan Mankubirti (628 H.), sunnite declaré et vassal du calife de Bagdad, plusiers habitants du Khârizm attendaient son retour messianique.

2. Le calife Nâṣir, celui-là même qui reçut la soumission du grand maître d'Alamût en 608, penchait vers le chiïsme et la doctrine imamienne (يتشيّع ويميل إلى مذهب الإماميّة). Faut-il voir dans ce fait le secret du rapprochement entre le calife et le grand maître?

59 Peut-être faut-il traduire: «Pour obéir à Allâh?» On sait que le mot *ḥaqq* est des épithètes divines. Ce mot désignant aussi le Coran et l'islâm, il y a peut-être ici quelque allusion au retour de la secte à l'orthodoxie? Sur un sens analogue, voir Dozy, *Supplément*. J'avoue que ces explications ne me satisfont guère.

60 Quatremère, *Notice*, 364; Defrémery, *Recherches*, 92–109; Guyard, *Un grand maître*, 53 et suiv.; cf. plus haut, 465 [284].

J'ai suivi dans cet exposé le récit détaillé de Defrémery, qui cite un grand nombre d'auteurs arabes. Ils offrent entre eux bien des divergences de détail. Ainsi, suivant Ibn Muyassar, Riḍâ' ad-dîn Abu l-ma'âlî mourut en 660 et eut pour successeur Nadjm ad-dîn Ismâ'îl, tandis que pour le continuateur d'Al-Makin, ces deux chefs furent quelque temps associés au pouvoir. D'autre part, Maqrîzi donne à Nadjm ad-dîn le nom de Ḥasan. Mais tous les auteurs cités s'accordent à fair de Chams le fils de Nadjm, et de ce dernier un vieillard.

Quand je montrai à M. Casanova l'inscription de Qadmûs, il me signala un passage d'Ibn Wâṣil relatif à l'ambassade que les Ismaïliens envoyèrent à Baibars en 661, près du mont Thabor (voir Defrémery, 94). L'auteur, f° 416 v°, dit que les messagers apportaient des présents et ajoute: ووصل ولدين الصاحبين مقدّمي الدعوة. Ce passage, d'un style fort négligé, semble dire qu'avec les messagers arrivèrent deux enfants qui etaient alors les deux ṣâḥibs ou chefs de la secte. En le rapprochant de l'inscription de Qadmûs, où Nadjm et Chams sont associés sans aucune distinction hiérarchique, M. Casanova se demandait avec raison si ce n'étaient pas là ces deux enfants dont parle Ibn Wâṣil et si les auteurs ne s'étaient pas trompés en faisant du premier le père du second.

Mais Nuwairi, cité par Defrémery en note, reproduit le passage d'Ibn Wâṣil, et cette fois sous une forme plus claire: ووصلا ولدا الصاحبين مقدّمي الدعوة «et arrivèrent les deux fils des deux ṣâḥibs, chefs de la secte». Dès lors, je crois que tout s'explique. On vient de voir que suivant un auteur arabe, Nadjm fut quelque temps associé à Riḍâ'. Or ce dernier avait un fils, Ṣârim ad-dîn Mubârak, qui était gendre de Nadjm. Les deux enfants envoyés à Baibars étaient sans doute Chams, fils de Nadjm, et Ṣârim, fils de Riḍâ' et beau-frère de Chams, que les deux maîtres envoyaient à Baibars pour gagner sa confiance. Il est vrai que, d'après les auteurs, Riḍâ' était déjà mort en 661, mais ce détail ne suffit pas à infirmer ma supposition. Dès lors, il n'y a plus de raison de douter du témoignage unanime des auteurs arabes qui font de Chams le fils de Nadjm.

L'inscription ne parle ni de Riḍâ' ni de son fils Ṣârim, d'où l'on peut induire qu'ils n'étaient plus chef de la secte. Or Riḍâ' mourut vers 660 et Ṣârim fut définitivement dépossédé et emprisonné par Baibars en 668, l'anné même où le sultan ôtait à Nadjm et à Chams tout reste de souveraineté, c'est-à-dire tout droit à porter un surnom en *ad-danyâ wad-dîn*. Tous ces indices s'accordent pour fixer à l'inscription la date approximative de 668–670.

61 Guyard, *op. cit.*, 42 et suiv.

62 Sur la lutte de Sinân avec Nûr ad-dîn et Saladin: Defrémery, *Recherches*, 58 et suiv.; Guyard, *op. cit.*, 45 et suiv., et anecdote VII; Ibn Khallikân, trad. de Slane, III, 340, etc. Sur son alliance avec Saladin, Defrémery, *op. cit.*, 73; Guyard, *op. cit.*, 48, et le très curieux mémoire de M. Casanova, *Journal asiatique*, 8e série, XVII, 329.

63 Guyard, *op. cit.*, 104 et suiv. D'après ce récit, l'enboyé du calife, un célèbre docteur, n'avait d'autre mission que de réfuter les dogmes de la secte; mais on sait qu'à cette époque, les envoyés politiques étaient presque toujours des docteurs en renom. En tout cas, si cette mission avait un but politique, il est naturel que Sinân en ait caché le vrai sens à ses partisans.

64 A la liste des maîtres dy Syrie au XIIIe siècle, il convient peut-être d'ajouter un certain Madjd ad-dîn, qui reçut en 624 les envoyés de l'empereur Frédéric II. L'auteur arabe auquel j'emprunte ce passage (Ḥamawi, texte dans Amari, *Bibliotheca arabico-sicula, seconda appendice*, 30; traduction dans Amari, *Estratti del Tarih Mansuri*, 20) dit qu'il était alors mutawallî des châteaux ismaïliens de Syrie. On a vu que ce titre désigne non le maître de Syrie lui-même, appelé *maulâ*, *ṣâḥib* ou *muqaddam*, mais les commandants des châteaux sous les ordres du maître. Toutefois je pense que l'auteur arabe s'est servi de ce terme par inexactitude et que Madjd ad-dîn était bien le maître, puisque c'est lui qui reçoit les ambassadeurs et qui les adresse au grand maître d'Alamût, que l'auteur appelle Djalâl ad-dîn: autre inexactitude, puisque Djalâl ad-din Ḥasan III était mort en 618 et qu'en 624 régait son fils 'Alâ' ad-din Muḥammad III. C'est en raison de ces incertitudes que je n'ai pas classé Madjd ad-dîn dans la liste précédente.

On trouve un bon résumé des sources sur les Assassins dans *Historiens grecs des croisades*, II; 423–426, et un curieux aperçu dans l'ouvrage cité d'Amari, *Estratti*, 8–10.

11

LIFE OF MAHOMET

Washington Irving

I PRELIMINARY NOTICE OF ARABIA AND THE ARABS

During a long succession of ages, extending from the earliest period of recorded history down to the seventh century of the Christian era, that great chersonese or peninsula formed by the Red Sea, the Euphrates, the Gulf of Persia, and the Indian Ocean, and known by the name of Arabia, remained unchanged and almost unaffected by the events which convulsed the rest of Asia, and shook Europe and Africa to their centre. While kingdoms and empires rose and fell; while ancient dynasties passed away; while the boundaries and names of countries were changed, and their inhabitants were exterminated or carried into captivity, Arabia, though its frontier provinces experienced some vicissitudes, preserved in the depths of its deserts its primitive character and independence, nor had its nomadic tribes ever bent their haughty necks to servitude.

The Arabs carry back the traditions of their country to the highest antiquity. It was peopled, they say, soon after the deluge, by the progeny of Shem the son of Noah, who gradually formed themselves into several tribes, the most noted of which are the Adites and Thamudites. All these primitive tribes are said to have been either swept from the earth in punishment of their iniquities, or obliterated in subsequent modifications of the races, so that little remains concerning them but shadowy traditions and a few passages in the Koran. They are occasionally mentioned in Oriental history as the "old primitive Arabians" – the "lost tribes."

The permanent population of the peninsula is ascribed, by the same authorities, to Kahtan or Joctan, a descendant in the fourth

Source: Irving, W., *Life of Mahomet*, 1911, London, J.M. Dent & Sons, pp. 3–52.

generation from Shem. His posterity spread over the southern part of the peninsula and along the Red Sea. Yarab, one of his sons, founded the kingdom of Yemen, where the territory of Araba was called after him; whence the Arabs derive the names of themselves and their country. Jurham, another son, founded the kingdom of Hedjaz, over which his descendants bore sway for many generations. Among these people Hagar and her son Ishmael were kindly received, when exiled from their home by the patriarch Abraham. In the process of time Ishmael married the daughter of Modâd, a reigning prince of the line of Jurham; and thus a stranger and a Hebrew became grafted on the original Arabian stock. It proved a vigorous graft. Ishmael's wife bore him twelve sons, who acquired dominion over the country, and whose prolific race, divided into twelve tribes, expelled or overran and obliterated the primitive stock of Joctan.

Such is the account given by the pensinsular Arabs of their origin;[1] and Christian writers cite it as containing the fulfilment of the covenant of God with Abraham, as recorded in Holy Writ. "And Abraham said unto God, O that Ishmael might live before thee! And God said, As for Ishmael, I have heard thee. Behold, I have blessed him, and will make him fruitful, and will multiply him exceedingly: *twelve princes* shall he beget, and I will make him a great nation." (Genesis xvii. 18, 20.)

These twelve princes with their tribes are further spoken of in the Scriptures (Genesis xxv. 18) as occupying the country "from Havilah unto Shur, that is before Egypt, as thou goest towards Assyria;" a region identified by sacred geographers with part of Arabia. The description of them agrees with that of the Arabs of the present day. Some are mentioned as holding towns and castles, others as dwelling in tents, or having villages in the wilderness. Nebaioth and Kedar, the two first-born of Ishmael, are most noted among the princes for their wealth in flocks and herds, and for the fine wool of their sheep. From Nebaioth came the Nabathai who inhabited Stony Arabia; while the name of Kedar is occasionally given in Holy Writ to designate the whole Arabian nation. "Woe is me," says the Psalmist, "that I sojourn in Mesech, that I dwell in the tents of Kedar." Both appear to have been the progenitors of the wandering or pastoral Arabs; the free rovers of the desert. "The wealthy nation," says the prophet Jeremiah, "that dwelleth without care; which have neither gates nor bars, which dwell alone."

A strong distinction grew up in the earliest times between the Arabs who "held towns and castles," and those who "dwelt in tents." Some of the former occupied the fertile wadies, or valleys, scattered here and there among the mountains, where these towns and castles were surrounded by vineyards and orchards, groves of palm-trees, fields of grain, and well-stocked pastures. They were settled in their habits, devoting themselves to the cultivation of the soil and the breeding of cattle.

Others of this class gave themselves up to commerce, having ports and cities along the Red Sea; the southern shores of the peninsula and the Gulf of Persia, and carrying on foreign trade by means of ships and caravans. Such especially were the people of Yemen, or Arabia the Happy, that land of spices, perfumes, and frankincense; the Sabæa of the poets; the Sheba of the sacred Scriptures. They were among the most active mercantile navigators of the eastern seas. Their ships brought to their shores the myrrh and balsams of the opposite coast of Berbera, with the gold, the spices, and other rich commodities of India and tropical Africa. These, with the products of their own country, were transported by caravans across the deserts to the semi-Arabian states of Ammon, Moab, and Edom or Idumea, to the Phœnician ports of the Mediterranean, and thence distributed to the western world.

The camel has been termed the ship of the desert, the caravan may be termed its fleet. The caravans of Yemen were generally fitted out, manned, conducted, and guarded by the nomadic Arabs, the dwellers in tents, who, in this respect, might be called the navigators of the desert. They furnished the innumerable camels required, and also contributed to the freight by the fine fleeces of their countless flocks. The writings of the prophets show the importance, in scriptural times, of this inland chain of commerce by which the rich countries of the south, India, Ethiopia, and Arabia the Happy, were linked with ancient Syria.

Ezekiel, in his lamentations for Tyre, exclaims, "Arabia, and all the princes of Kedar, they occupied with thee in lambs, and rams, and goats; in these were they thy merchants. The merchants of Sheba and Raamah occupied in thy fairs with chief of all spices, and with all precious stones and gold. Haran, and Canneh, and Eden,[2] the merchants of Sheba, Asshur, and Chelmad, were thy merchants." And Isaiah, speaking to Jerusalem, says: "The multitude of camels shall cover thee; the dromedaries of Midian and Ephah; all they from Sheba shall come; they shall bring gold and incense. . . . All the flocks of Kedar shall be gathered together unto thee; the rams of Nebaioth shall minister unto thee." (Isaiah lx. 6, 7.)

The agricultural and trading Arabs, however, the dwellers in towns and cities, have never been considered the true type of the race. They became softened by settled and peaceful occupations, and lost much of their original stamp by an intercourse with strangers. Yemen, too, being more accessible than the other parts of Arabia, and offering greater temptation to the spoiler, had been repeatedly invaded and subdued.

It was among the other class of Arabs, the rovers of the desert, the "dwellers in tents," by far the most numerous of the two, that the national character was preserved in all its primitive force and freshness. Nomadic in their habits, pastoral in their occupations, and acquainted by experience and tradition with all the hidden resources of the desert, they led a wandering life, roaming from place to place in quest of those wells and springs which had been the resort of their forefathers since the days of the patriarchs; encamping wherever they could find date-trees for shade, and sustenance and pasturage for their flocks, and herds, and camels; and shifting their abode whenever the temporary supply was exhausted.

These nomadic Arabs were divided and subdivided into innumerable petty tribes or families, each with its Sheikh or Emir, the representative of the patriarch of yore, whose spear, planted beside his tent, was the ensign of command. His office, however, though continued for many generations in the same family, was not strictly hereditary; but depended upon the good-will of the tribe. He might be deposed, and another of a different line elected in his place. His power, too, was limited, and depended upon his personal merit and the confidence reposed in him. His prerogative consisted in conducting negotiations of peace and war; in leading his tribe against the enemy; in choosing the place of encampment, and in receiving and entertaining strangers of note. Yet, even in these and similar privileges, he was controlled by the opinions and inclinations of his people.[3]

However numerous and minute might be the divisions of a tribe, the links of affinity were carefully kept in mind by the several sections. All the Sheikhs of the same tribe acknowledge a common chief called the Sheikh of Sheikhs, who, whether ensconced in a rock-built castle, or encamped amid his flocks and herds in the desert, might assemble under his standard all the scattered branches on any emergency affecting the common weal.

The multiplicity of these wandering tribes, each with its petty prince and petty territory, but without a national head, produced frequent collisions. Revenge, too, was almost a religious principle among them. To avenge a relative slain was the duty of his family, and often involved the honour of his tribe; and these debts of blood sometimes remained unsettled for generations, producing deadly feuds.

The necessity of being always on the alert to defend his flocks and herds made the Arab of the desert familiar from his infancy with the exercise of arms. None could excel him in the use of the bow, the lance, and the scimitar, and the adroit and graceful management of the horse. He was a predatory warrior also; for though at times he was engaged in the service of the merchant, furnishing him with camels and guides and drivers for the transportation of his merchandise, he was more apt to lay contributions on the caravan or plunder it outright in its toilful progress through the desert. All this he regarded as a legitimate exercise of arms; looking down upon the gainful sons of traffic as an inferior race, debased by sordid habits and pursuits.

Such was the Arab of the desert, the dweller in tents, in whom was fulfilled the prophetic destiny of his ancestor Ishmael. "He will be a wild man; his hand will be against every man, and every man's hand against him."[4] Nature had fitted him for his destiny. His form was light and meagre, but sinewy and active, and capable of sustaining great fatigue and hardship. He was temperate and even abstemious, requiring but little food, and that of the simplest kind. His mind like his body was light and agile. He eminently possessed the intellectual attributes of the Shemitic race: penetrating sagacity, subtle wit, a ready conception, and a brilliant imagination. His sensibilities were quick and acute, though not lasting; a proud and daring spirit was stamped on his sallow visage and flashed from his dark and kindling eye. He was easily aroused by the appeals of eloquence, and charmed by the graces of poetry. Speaking a language copious in the extreme, the words of which have been compared to gems and flowers he was naturally an orator; but he delighted in proverbs and apophthegms, rather than in sustained flights of declamation, and was prone to convey his ideas in the Oriental style by apologue and parable.

Though a restless and predatory warrior, he was generous and hospitable. He delighted in giving gifts; his door was always open to the wayfarer, with whom he was ready to share his last morsel; and his deadliest foe, having once broken bread with him, might repose securely beneath the inviolable sanctity of his tent.

In religion the Arabs, in what they term the Days of Ignorance partook largely of the two faiths, the Sabæan and the Magian, which at that time prevailed over the Eastern world. The Sabæan, however, was the one to which they most adhered. They pretended to derive it from Sabi the son of Seth, who, with his father and his brother Enoch, they supposed to be buried in the pyramids. Others derive the name from the Hebrew word, Saba, or the Stars, and trace the origin of the faith to the Assyrian shepherds who, as they watched their flocks by night on their level plains, and beneath their cloudless skies, noted the aspects and movements of the heavenly bodies, and formed theories of their good and evil influences on human affairs; vague notions which the Chaldæan philosophers and priests reduced to a system, supposed to be more ancient even than that of the Egyptians.

By others it is derived from still higher authority, and claimed to be the religion of the antediluvian world. It survived, say they, the deluge, and was continued among the patriarchs. It was taught by Abraham, adopted by his descendants, the children of Israel, and sanctified and confirmed in the tablets of the law delivered unto Moses, amid the thunder and lightning of Mount Sinai.

In its original state the Sabæan faith was pure and spiritual; inculcating a belief in the unity of God, the doctrine of a future state of rewards and punishments, and the necessity of a virtuous and holy life to obtain a happy immortality. So profound was the reverence of the Sabæans for the Supreme Being that they never mentioned his name, nor did they venture to approach him but through intermediate intelligences or angels. These were supposed to inhabit and animate the heavenly bodies, in the same way as the human body is inhabited and animated by a soul. They were placed in their respective spheres to supervise and govern the universe in subserviency to the Most High. In addressing themselves to the stars and other celestial luminaries, therefore, the Sabæans did not worship them as deities, but sought only to propitiate their angelic occupants as intercessors with the Supreme Being; looking up through these created things to God the great creator.

By degrees this religion lost its original simplicity and purity, and became obscured by mysteries, and degraded by idolatries. The Sabæans, instead of regarding the heavenly bodies as the habitations of intermediate agents, worshipped them as deities; set up graven images in honour of them, in sacred groves and in the gloom of forests; and at length enshrined these idols in temples, and worshipped them as if instinct with divinity. The Sabæan faith too underwent changes and modifications in the various countries through which it was diffused. Egypt has long been accused of reducing it to the most abject state of degradation; the statues, hieroglyphics, and painted sepulchres of that mysterious country being considered records of the worship, not merely of celestial intelligences, but of the lowest order of created beings, and even of inanimate objects. Modern investigation and research, however, are gradually rescuing the most intellectual nation of antiquity from this aspersion; and as they slowly lift the veil of mystery which hangs over the tombs of Egypt, are discovering that all these apparent objects of adoration were but symbols of the varied attributes of the one Supreme Being, whose name was too sacred to be pronounced by mortals. Among the Arabs the Sabæan faith became mingled with wild superstitions, and degraded by gross idolatry. Each tribe worshipped its particular star or planet, or set up its particular idol. Infanticide mingled its horrors with their religious rites. Among the nomadic tribes the birth of a daughter was considered a misfortune, her sex rendering her of little service in a wandering and predatory life, while she might bring disgrace upon her family by misconduct or captivity. Motives of unnatural policy, therefore, may have mingled with their religious feelings, in offering up female infants as sacrifices to their idols, or in burying them alive.

The rival sect of Magians or Guebres (fire worshippers), which, as we have said, divided the religious empire of the East, took its rise in Persia, where, after a while, its oral doctrines were reduced to writing by its great prophet and teacher Zoroaster, in his volume of the *Zendavesta*. The creed like that of the Sabæans, was originally simple and spiritual, inculcating a belief in one supreme and eternal God, in whom and by whom the universe exists: that he produced, through his creating word, two active principles; Ormusd, the principle or angel of light or good, and Ahriman, the principle or angel of darkness or evil: that these formed the world out of a mixture of their opposite elements, and were engaged in a perpetual contest in the regulation of its affairs. Hence the vicissitudes of good and evil accordingly as the angel of light or darkness has the upper hand: this contest would continue until the end of the world, when there would be a general resurrection and a day of judgment; the angel of darkness and his disciples would then be banished to an abode of woeful gloom, and their opponents would enter the blissful realms of ever-during light.

The primitive rites of this religion were extremely simple. The Magians had neither temples, altars, nor religious symbols of any kind, but addressed their prayers and hymns directly to the Deity, in what they conceived to be his residence, the sun. They reverenced this luminary as being his abode, and as the source of the light and heat of which all the other heavenly bodies were composed; and they kindled fires upon the mountain tops to supply light during its absence. Zoroaster first introduced the use of temples, wherein sacred fire, pretended to be derived from heaven, was kept perpetually alive through the guardianship of priests, who maintained a watch over it night and day.

In process of time this sect, like that of the Sabbaeans, lost sight of the divine principle in the symbol, and came to worship light or fire as the real Deity, and to abhor darkness as Satan or the devil. In their fanatic zeal the Magians would seize upon unbelievers, and offer them up in the flames to propitiate their fiery deity.

To the tenets of these two sects reference is made in that beautiful text of the wisdom of Solomon: "Surely vain are all men by nature who are ignorant of God, and could not, by considering the work, acknowledge the work master; but deemed either fire, or wind, or the swift air, or the circle of the stars, or the violent water, or the lights of heaven, to be gods which govern the world."

Of these two faiths the Sabæan, as we have before observed, was much the more prevalent among the Arabs, but in an extremely degraded form, mingled with all kinds of abuses, and varying among the various tribes. The Magian faith prevailed among those tribes which, from their frontier position, had frequent intercourse with Persia; while other tribes partook of the superstitions and idolatries of the nations on which they bordered.

Judaism had made its way into Arabia at an early period, but very vaguely and imperfectly. Still many of its rites and ceremonies, and fanciful traditions, became implanted in the country. At a later day, however, when Palestine was ravaged by the Romans, and the city of Jerusalem taken and sacked, many of the Jews took refuge among the Arabs; became incorporated with the native tribes; formed themselves into communities; acquired possession of fertile tracts; built castles and strongholds and rose to considerable power and influence.

The Christian religion had likewise its adherents among the Arabs. St. Paul himself declares in his epistle to the Galatians that, soon after he had been called to preach Christianity among the heathens, he "went into Arabia." The dissensions, also, which rose in the Eastern church, in the early part of the third century, breaking it up into sects, each persecuting the others as it gained the ascendancy, drove many into exile into remote parts of the East, filled the deserts of Arabia with anchorites, and planted the Christian faith among some of the principal tribes.

The foregoing circumstances, physical and moral, may give an idea of the causes which maintained the Arabs for ages in an unchanged condition. While their isolated position and their vast deserts protected them from conquest, their internal feuds, and their want of a common tie, political or religious, kept them from being formidable as conquerors. They were a vast aggregation of distinct parts; full of individual vigour, but wanting coherent strength. Although their nomadic life rendered them hardy and active; although the greater part of them were warriors from infancy, yet their arms were only wielded against each other, excepting some of the frontier tribes, which occasionally engaged as mercenaries in external wars. While, therefore, the other nomadic races of Central Asia, possessing no greater aptness for warfare, had, during a course of ages, successively overrun and conquered the civilised world, this warrior race, unconscious of its power, remained disjointed and harmless in the depths of its native deserts.

The time at length arrived when its discordant tribes were to be united in one creed, and animated by one common cause; when a mighty genius was to arise, who should bring together these scattered limbs, animate them with his own enthusiastic and daring spirit, and lead them forth, a giant of the desert, to shake and overturn the empires of the earth.

II BIRTH AND PARENTAGE OF MAHOMET – HIS INFANCY AND CHILDHOOD

Mahomet, the great founder of the faith of Islam, was born in Mecca, in April, in the year 569 of the Christian era. He was of the valiant and illustrious tribe of Koreish, of which there were two branches, descended from two brothers, Haschem and Abd Schems. Haschem, the progenitor of Mahomet, was a great benefactor of Mecca. This city is situated in the midst of a barren and stony country, and in former times was often subject to scarcity of provisions. At the beginning of the sixth century Haschem established two yearly caravans: one in the winter to South Arabia or Yemen; the other in the summer to Syria. By these means abundant supplies were brought to Mecca, as well as a great variety of merchandise. The city became a commercial mart, and the tribe of Koreish, which engaged largely in these expeditions, became wealthy and powerful. Haschem, at this time, was the guardian of the Caaba, the great shrine of Arabian pilgrimage and worship, the custody of which was confided to none but the most honourable tribes and families in the same manner as, in old times, the temple of Jerusalem was intrusted only to the care of the Levites. In fact, the guardianship of the Caaba was connected with civil dignities and privileges, and gave the holder of it the control of the sacred city.

On the death of Haschem, his son, Abd al Motâlleb, succeeded to his honours, and inherited his patriotism. He delivered the holy city from an invading army of troops and elephants, sent by the Christian princes of Abyssinia who at that time held Yemen in subjection. These signal services rendered by father and son confirmed the guardianship of the Caaba in the line of Haschem, to the great discontent and envy of the line of Abd Schems.

Abd al Motâlleb had several sons and daughters. Those of his sons who figure in history were, Abu Taleb, Abu Lahab, Abbas, Hamza, and Abdallah. The last named was the youngest and best beloved. He married Amina, a maiden of a distant branch of the same illustrious stock of Koreish. So remarkable was Abdallah for personal beauty and those qualities which win the affections of women, that, if Moslem traditions are to be credited, on the night of his marriage with Amina, two hundred virgins of the tribe of Koreish died of broken hearts.

Mahomet was the first and only fruit of the marriage thus sadly celebrated. His birth, according to similar traditions with the one just cited, was accompanied by signs and portents announcing a child of wonder. His mother suffered none of the pangs of travail. At the moment of his coming into the world a celestial light illumined the surrounding country, and the new-born child, raising his eyes to heaven, exclaimed: "God is great! There is no God but God, and I am his prophet."

Heaven and earth, we are assured, were agitated at his advent. The Lake Sawa shrank back to its secret springs, leaving its borders dry; while the Tigris, bursting its bounds, overflowed the neighbouring lands. The palace of Khosru the king of Persia shook to its foundations, and several of its towers were toppled to the earth. In that troubled night the Kadhi, or Judge of Persia, beheld, in a dream, a ferocious camel conquered by an Arabian courser. He related his dream in the morning to the Persian monarch, and interpreted it to portend danger from the quarter of Arabia.

In the same eventful night the sacred fire of Zoroaster, which, guarded by the Magi, had burned without interruption for upwards of a thousand years, was suddenly extinguished, and all the idols in the world fell down. The demons, or evil genii, which lurk in the stars and the signs of the zodiac, and exert a malignant influence over the children of men, were cast forth by the pure angels, and hurled, with their arch leader, Eblis, or Lucifer, into the depths of the sea.

The relatives of the new-born child, say the like authorities, were filled with awe and wonder. His mother's brother, an astrologer, cast his nativity, and predicted that he would rise to vast power, found an empire, and establish a new faith among men. His grandfather, Abd al Motâlleb, gave a feast to the principal Koreishites, the seventh day after his birth, at which he presented this child, as the dawning glory of their race, and gave him the name of Mahomet (or Muhamed), indicative of his future renown.

Such are the marvellous accounts given by Moslem writers of the infancy of Mahomet, and we have little else than similar fables about his early years. He was scarce two months old when his father died, leaving him no other inheritance than five camels, a few sheep, and a female slave of Ethiopia, named Barakat. His mother, Amina, had hitherto nurtured him, but care and sorrow dried the fountains of her breast, and the air of Mecca being unhealthy for children, she sought a nurse for him among the females of the neighbouring Bedouin tribes. These were accustomed to come to Mecca twice a year, in spring and autumn, to foster the children of its inhabitants; but they looked for the offspring of the rich, where they were sure of ample recompense, and turned with contempt from this heir of poverty. At length Halêma, the wife of a Saadite shepherd, was moved to compassion, and took the helpless infant to her home. It was in one of the pastoral valleys of the mountains.[5]

Many were the wonders related by Halêma of her infant charge. On the journey from Mecca, the mule which bore him became miraculously endowed with speech, and proclaimed aloud that he bore on his back the greatest of prophets, the chief of ambassadors, the favourite of the Almighty. The sheep bowed to him as he passed; as he lay in his cradle and gazed at the moon, it stooped to him in reverence.

The blessing of heaven, say the Arabian writers, rewarded the charity of Halêma. While the child remained under her roof everything around her prospered. The wells and springs were never dried up; the pastures were always green; her flocks and herds increased tenfold; a marvellous abundance reigned over her fields, and peace prevailed in her dwelling.

The Arabian legends go on to extol the almost supernatural powers, bodily and mental, manifested by this wonderful child at a very early age. He could stand alone when three months old; run abroad when he was seven, and at ten could join other children in their sports with bows and arrows. At eight months he could speak so as to be understood; and in the course of another month could converse with fluency, displaying a wisdom astonishing to all who heard him.

At the age of three years, while playing in the fields with his foster-brother Masroud, two angels in shining apparel appeared before them. They laid Mahomet gently upon the ground, and Gabriel, one of the angels, opened his breast, but without inflicting any pain. Then taking forth his heart, he cleansed it from all impurity, wringing from it those black and bitter drops of original sin, inherited from our forefather Adam, and which lurk in the hearts of the best of his descendants, inciting them to crime. When he had thoroughly purified it, he filled it with faith and knowledge and prophetic light, and replaced it in the bosom of the child. Now, we are assured by the same authorities, began to emanate from his countenance that mysterious light which had continued down from Adam, through the sacred line of prophets, until the time of Isaac and Ishmael; but which had lain dormant in the descendants of the latter, until it thus shone forth with renewed radiance from the features of Mahomet.

At this supernatural visitation, it is added, was impressed between the shoulders of the child the seal of prophecy, which continued throughout life the symbol and credential of his divine mission; though unbelievers saw nothing in it but a large mole, the size of a pigeon's egg.

When the marvellous visitation of the angel was related to Halêma and her husband, they were alarmed lest some misfortune should be impending over the child, or that his supernatural visitors might be of the race of evil spirits of genii, which haunt the solitudes of the desert, wreaking mischief on the children of men. His Saadite nurse, therefore, carried him back to Mecca, and delivered him to his mother Amina.

He remained with his parent until his sixth year, when she took him with her to Medina, on a visit to her relatives of the tribe of Adij, but on her journey homeward she died, and was buried at Abwa, a village between Medina and Mecca. Her grave, it will be found, was a place of pious resort and tender recollection to her son at the latest period of his life.

The faithful Abyssinian slave Barakat now acted as a mother to the orphan child, and conducted him to his grandfather Abd al Motêlleb, in whose household he remained for two years, treated with care and tenderness. Abd al Motâlleb was now well stricken in years, having outlived the ordinary term of human existence. Finding his end approaching, he called to him his eldest son Abu Taleb, and bequeathed Mahomet to his especial protection. The good Abu Taleb took his nephew to his bosom, and ever afterwards was to him as a parent. As the former succeeded to the guardianship of the Caaba at the death of his father, Mahomet continued for several years in a kind of sacerdotal household, where the rites and ceremonies of the sacred house were rigidly observed. And here we deem it necessary to give a more especial notice of the alleged origin of the Caaba, and of the rites and traditions and superstitions connected with it, closely interwoven as they are with the faith of Islam and the story of its founder.

III TRADITIONS CONCERNING MECCA AND THE CAABA

When Adam and Eve were cast forth from Paradise, say Arabian traditions, they fell in different parts of the earth; Adam on a mountain of the Island of Serendib, or Ceylon; Eve in Arabia, on the borders of the Red Sea, where the port of Joddah is now situated. For two hundred years they wandered separate and lonely about the earth, until in consideration of their penitence and wretchedness, they were permitted to come together again on Mount Arafat, not far from the present city of Mecca. In the depth of his sorrow and repentance, Adam, it is said, raised his hands and eyes to heaven, and implored the clemency of God, entreating that a shrine might be vouchsafed to him similar to that at which he had worshipped when in Paradise, and round which the angels used to move in adoring processions.

The supplication of Adam was effectual. A tabernacle or temple formed of radiant clouds was lowered down by the hands of angels, and placed immediately below its prototype in the celestial paradise. Towards this heaven-descended shrine, Adam thenceforth turned when in prayer, and round it he daily made seven circuits in imitation of the rites of the adoring angels.

At the death of Adam, say the same traditions, the tabernacle of clouds passed away, or was again drawn up to heaven; but another of the same form, and in the same place, was built of stone and clay by Seth, the son of Adam. This was swept away by the deluge. Many generations afterwards, in the time of the patriarchs, when Hagar and her child Ishmael were near perishing with thirst in the desert, an angel revealed to them a spring or well of water, near to the ancient site of the tabernacle. This was the well of Zem Zem, held sacred by the progeny of Ishmael to the present day. Shortly afterwards two individuals of the gigantic race of the Amalekites, in quest of a camel which had strayed from their camp, discovered this well, and, having slaked their thirst brought their companions to the place. Here they founded the city of Mecca, taking Ishmael and his mother under their protection. They were soon expelled by the proper inhabitants of the country, among whom Ishmael remained. When grown to man's estate, he married the daughter of the ruling prince, by whom he had a numerous progeny, the ancestors of the Arabian people. In process of time, by God's command, he undertook to rebuild the Caaba, on the precise site of the original tabernacle of clouds. In this pious work he was assisted by his father Abraham. A miraculous stone served Abraham as a scaffold, rising and sinking with him as he built the walls of the sacred edifice. It still remains there an inestimable relic, and the print of the patriarch's foot is clearly to be perceived on it by all true believers.

While Abraham and Ishmael were thus occupied, the angel Gabriel brought them a stone, about which traditional accounts are a little at variance; by some it is said to have been one of the precious stones of Paradise, which fell to the earth with Adam, and was afterwards lost in the slime of the deluge, until retrieved by the angel Gabriel. The more received tradition is, that it was originally the guardian angel appointed to watch over Adam in Paradise but changed into a stone and ejected thence with him at his fall, as a punishment for not having been more vigilant. This stone Abraham and Ishmael received with proper reverence, and inserted it in a corner of the exterior wall of the Caaba, where it remains to the present day, devoutly kissed by worshippers each time they make a circuit of the temple. When first inserted in the wall it was, we are told, a single jacinth of dazzling whiteness, but became gradually blackened by the kisses of sinful mortals. At the resurrection it will recover its angelic form, and stand forth a testimony before God in favour of those who have faithfully performed the rites of pilgrimage.

Such are the Arabian traditions, which rendered the Caaba and the well of Zem Zem objects of extraordinary veneration from the remotest antiquity among the people of the East, and especially the descendants of Ishmael. Mecca, which incloses these sacred objects within its walls, was a holy city many ages before the rise of Mahometanism, and was the resort of pilgrims from all parts of Arabia. So universal and profound was the religious feeling respecting this observance, that four months in every year were devoted to the rites of pilgrimage, and held sacred from all violence and warfare. Hostile tribes then laid aside their arms; took the heads from their spears; traversed the late dangerous deserts in security; thronged the gates of Mecca clad in the pilgrim's garb; made their seven circuits round the Caaba in imitation of the angelic host; touched and kissed the mysterious black stone; drank and made ablutions at the well Zem Zem in memory of their ancestor Ishmael; and having performed all the other primitive rites of pilgrimage, returned home in safety, again to resume their weapons and their wars.

Among the religious observances of the Arabs in these their "days of ignorance", that is to say, before the promulgation of the Moslem doctrines, fasting and prayer had a foremost place. They had three principal fasts within the year; one of seven, one of nine, and one of thirty days. They prayed three times each day: about sunrise, at noon, and about sunset; turning their faces in the direction of the Caaba, which was their kebla, or point of adoration. They had many religious traditions, some of them acquired in early times from the Jews, and they are said to have nurtured their devotional feelings with the book of Psalms, and with a book said to be by Seth, and filled with moral discourses.

Brought up, as Mahomet was in the house of the guardian of the Caaba, the ceremonies and devotions connected with the sacred edifice may have given an early bias to his mind, and inclined it to those speculations in matters of religion by which it eventually became engrossed. Though his Moslem biographers would fain persuade us his high destiny was clearly foretold in his childhood by signs and prodigies, yet his education appears to have been as much neglected as that of ordinary Arab children; for we find that he was not taught either to read or write. He was a thoughtful child, however, quick to observe, prone to meditate on all that he observed, and possessed of an imagination fertile, daring, and expansive. The yearly influx of pilgrims from distant parts made Mecca a receptacle for all kinds of floating knowledge, which he appears to have imbibed with eagerness and retained in a tenacious memory; and as he increased in years, a more extended sphere of observation was gradually opened to him.

IV FIRST JOURNEY OF MAHOMET WITH THE CARAVAN TO SYRIA

Mahomet was now twelve years of age, but, as we have shown, he had an intelligence far beyond his years. The spirit of inquiry was awake within him, quickened by intercourse with pilgrims from all parts of Arabia. His uncle Abu Taleb, too, beside his sacerdotal character as guardian of the Caaba, was one of the most enterprising merchants of the tribe of Koreish, and had much to do with those caravans set on foot by his ancestor Haschem, which traded to Syria and Yemen. The arrival and departure of those caravans, which thronged the gates of Mecca and filled its streets with pleasing tumult, were exciting events to a youth like Mahomet, and carried his imagination to foreign parts. He could no longer repress the ardent curiosity thus aroused; but once, when his uncle was about to mount his camel to depart with the caravan for Syria, clung to him, and entreated to be permitted to accompany him: "For who, oh my uncle," said he, "will take care of me when thou art away?"

The appeal was not lost upon the kind-hearted Abu Taleb. He bethought him, too, that the youth was of an age to enter upon the active scenes of Arab life, and of a capacity to render essential service in the duties of the caravan; he readily, therefore, granted his prayer, and took him with him on the journey to Syria.

The route lay through regions fertile in fables and traditions, which it is the delight of the Arabs to recount in the evening halts of the caravan. The vast solitudes of the desert, in which that wandering people pass so much of their lives, are prone to engender superstitious fancies; they have accordingly peopled them with good and evil genii, and clothed them with tales of enchantment, mingled up with wonderful events which happened in days of old. In these evening halts of the caravan, the youthful mind of Mahomet doubtless imbibed many of those superstitions of the desert which ever afterwards dwelt in his memory, and had a powerful influence over his imagination. We may especially note two traditions which he must have heard at this time, and which we find recorded by him in after years in the Koran. One related to the mountainous district of Hedjaz. Here, as the caravan wound its way through silent and deserted valleys, caves were pointed out in the sides of the mountains once inhabited by the Beni Thamud, or children of Thamud, one of the "lost tribes" of Arabia; and this was the tradition concerning them:

They were a proud and gigantic race, existing before the time of the patriarch Abraham. Having fallen into blind idolatry, God sent a prophet of the name of Saleh to restore them to the right way. They refused however, to listen to him, unless he should prove the divinity of his mission by causing a camel, big with young, to issue from the entrails of a mountain. Saleh accordingly prayed, and lo! a rock opened, and a female camel came forth, which soon produced a foal. Some of the Thamudites were convinced by the miracle, and were converted by the prophet from their idolatry: the greater part, however remained in unbelief. Saleh left the camel among them as a sign, warning them that a judgment from heaven would fall on them should they do her any harm. For a time the camel was suffered to feed quietly in their pastures, going forth in the morning, and returning in the evening. It is true, that when she bowed her head to drink from a brook or well, she never raised it until she had drained the last drop of water; but then in return she yielded milk enough to supply the whole tribe. As, however, she frightened the other camels from the pasture, she became an object of offence to the Thamudites, who ham-strung and slew her. Upon this there was a fearful cry from heaven, and great claps of thunder, and in the morning all the offenders were found lying on their faces, dead. Thus the whole race was swept from the earth, and their country was laid for ever afterward under the ban of heaven.

This story made a powerful impression on the mind of Mahomet, insomuch that, in after years, he refused to let his people encamp in the neighbourhood, but hurried them away from it as an accursed region.

Another tradition, gathered on this journey, related to the city of Eyla, situated near the Red Sea. This place, he was told, had been inhabited in old times by a tribe of Jews, who lapsed into idolatry and profaned the Sabbath by fishing on that sacred day; whereupon the old men were transformed into swine, and the young men into monkeys.

We have noted these two traditions especially because they are both cited by Mahomet as instances of divine judgment on the crime of idolatry, and evince the bias his youthful mind was already taking on that important subject.

Moslem writers tell us, as usual, of wonderful circumstances which attended the youth throughout this journey, giving evidence of the continual guardianship of heaven. At one time, as he traversed the burning sands of the desert, an angel hovered over him unseen, sheltering him with his wings; a miracle, however, which evidently does not rest on the evidence of an eye-witness; at another time he was protected by a cloud which hung over his head during the noontide heat; and on another occasion, as he sought the scanty shade of a withered tree, it suddenly put forth leaves and blossoms.

After skirting the ancient domains of the Moabites and the Ammonites, often mentioned in the sacred Scriptures, the caravan arrived at Bosra, or Bostra, on the confines of Syria, in the country of the tribe of Manasseh, beyond the Jordan. In Scripture days it had been a city of the Levites, but now was inhabited by Nestorian Christians. It was a great mart, annually visited by the caravans; and here our wayfarers came to a halt and encamped near a convent of Nestorian monks.

By this fraternity Abu Taleb and his nephew were entertained with great hospitality. One of the monks, by some called Sergius, by others Bahira,[6] on conversing with Mahomet was surprised at the precocity of his intellect and interested by his eager desire for information, which appears to have had reference, principally, to matters of religion. They had frequent conversations together on such subjects, in the course of which the efforts of the monk must have been mainly directed against that idolatry in which the youthful Mahomet had hitherto been educated; for the Nestorian Christians were strenuous in condemning not merely the worship of images, but even the casual exhibition of them; indeed so far did they carry their scruples on this point, that even the cross, that general emblem of Christianity, was in a great degree included in this prohibition.

Many have ascribed that knowledge of the principles and traditions of the Christian faith displayed by Mahomet in after life to those early conversations with this monk; it is probable, however, that he had further intercourse with the latter in the course of subsequent visits which he made to Syria.

Moslem writers pretend that the interest taken by the monk in the youthful stranger arose from his having accidentally perceived between his shoulders the seal of prophecy. He warned Abu Taleb, say they, when about to set out on his return to Mecca, to take care that his nephew did not fall into the hands of the Jews, foreseeing with the eye of prophecy the trouble and opposition he was to encounter from that people.

It required no miraculous sign, however, to interest a sectarian monk, anxious to make proselytes, in an intelligent and inquiring youth, nephew of the guardian of the Caaba, who might carry back with him to Mecca the seeds of Christianity sown in his tender mind; and it was natural that the monk should be eager to prevent his hoped-for convert, in the present unsettled state of his religious opinions, from being beguiled into the Jewish faith.

Mahomet returned to Mecca, his imagination teeming with the wild tales and traditions picked up in the desert, and his mind deeply impressed with the doctrines imparted to him in the Nestorian convent. He seems ever afterwards to have entertained a mysterious reverence for Syria, probably from the religious impressions received there. It was the land whither Abraham the patriarch had repaired from Chaldæa taking with him the primitive worship of the one true God. "Verily," he used to say in after years, "God has ever maintained guardians of his word in Syria; forty in number; when one dies another is sent in his room; and through them the land is blessed." And again – "Joy be to the people of Syria, for the angels of the kind God spread their wings over them."[7]

NOTE. The conversion of Abraham from the idolatry into which the world had fallen after the deluge is related in the sixth chapter of the Koran. Abraham's father, Azer, or Zerah, as his name is given in the Scriptures, was a statuary and an idolater.

"And Abraham said unto his father, Azer, 'Why dost thou take graven images for gods? Verily, thou and thy people are in error.'

"Then was the firmament of heaven displayed unto Abraham, that he might see how the world was governed.

"When night came, and darkness overshadowed the earth, he beheld a bright star shining in the firmament, and cried out to his people who were astrologers: 'This, according to your assertions, is the Lord.'

"But the star set, and Abraham said, 'I have no faith in gods that set.'

"He beheld the moon rising, and exclaimed, 'Assuredly, this is the Lord.' But the moon likewise set, and he was confounded, and prayed unto God, saying, 'Direct me, lest I become as one of these people, who go astray.'

"When he saw the sun rising, he cried out, 'This is the most glorious of all; this of a certainty is the Lord.' But the sun also set. Then said Abraham, 'I believe not, oh my people, in those things which ye call gods. Verily, I turn my face unto Him, the Creator, who hath formed both the heavens and the earth.'"

V COMMERCIAL OCCUPATIONS OF MAHOMET – HIS MARRIAGE WITH CADIJAH

Mahomet was now completely launched in active life, accompanying his uncles in various expeditions. At one time, when sixteen years of age, we find him with his uncle Zobier journeying with the caravan to Yemen; at another time acting as armour-bearer to the same uncle, who led a warlike expedition of Koreishites in aid of the Kenanites against the tribe of Hawazan. This is cited as Mahomet's first essay in arms, though he did little else than supply his uncle with arrows in the heat of the action, and shield him from the darts of the enemy. It is stigmatised among Arabian writers as al Fadjar, or the impious war, having been carried on during the sacred months of pilgrimage.

As Mahomet advanced in years he was employed by different persons as commercial agent or factor in caravan journeys to Syria, Yemen, and elsewhere; all which tended to enlarge the sphere of his observation, and to give him a quick insight into character and a knowledge of human affairs.

He was a frequent attender of fairs also, which in Arabia were not always mere resorts of traffic, but occasionally scenes of poetical contests between different tribes, where prizes were adjudged to the victors, and their prize poems treasured up in the archives of princes. Such, especially, was the case with the fair of Ocadh; and seven of the prize poems adjudged there were hung up as trophies in the Caaba. At these fairs, also, were recited the popular traditions of the Arabs, and inculcated the various religious faiths which were afloat in Arabia. From oral sources of this kind, Mahomet gradually accumulated much of that varied information as to creeds and doctrines which he afterwards displayed.

There was at this time residing in Mecca a widow named Cadijah (or Khadijah), of the tribe of Koreish. She had been twice married. Her last husband, a wealthy merchant, had recently died, and the extensive concerns of the house were in need of a conductor. A nephew of the widow, named Chuzima, had become acquainted with Mahomet in the course of his commercial expeditions, and had noticed the ability and integrity with which he acquitted himself on all occasions. He pointed him out to his aunt as a person well qualified to be her factor. The personal appearance of Mahomet may have strongly seconded this recommendation; for he was now about twenty-five years of age, and extolled by Arabian writers for his manly beauty and engaging manners. So desirous was Cadijah of securing his services that she offered him double wages to conduct a caravan which she was on the point of sending off to Syria. Mahomet consulted his uncle Abu Taleb, and, by his advice, accepted the offer. He was accompanied and aided in the expedition by the nephew of the widow, and by her slave Maïsara, and so highly satisfied was Cadijah with the way in which he discharged his duties, that, on his return she paid him double the amount of his stipulated wages. She afterwards sent him to the southern parts of Arabia on similar expeditions in all which he gave like satisfaction.

Cadijah was now in her fortieth year, a woman of judgment and experience. The mental qualities of Mahomet rose more and more in her estimation and her heart began to yearn toward the fresh and comely youth. According to Arabian legends, a miracle occurred most opportunely to confirm and sanctify the bias of her inclinations. She was one day with her handmaids, at the hour of noon, on the terraced roof of her dwelling, watching the arrival of a caravan conducted by Mahomet. As it approached, she beheld, with astonishment, two angels overshadowing him with their wings to protect him from the sun. Turning, with emotion, to her handmaids, "Behold!" said she, "the beloved of Allah, who sends two angels to watch over him!"

Whether or not the handmaidens looked forth with the same eyes of devotion as their mistress and likewise discerned the angels, the legend does not mention. Suffice it to say, the widow was filled with a lively faith in the superhuman merits of her youthful steward, and forthwith commissioned her trusty slave, Maïsara, to offer him her hand. The negotiation is recorded with simple brevity. "Mahomet," demanded Maïsara, "why dost thou not marry?" "I have not the means," replied Mahomet. "Well, but if a wealthy dame should offer thee her hand – one also who is handsome and of high birth?" "And who is she?" "Cadijah!" "How is that possible?" "Let me manage it." Maïsara returned to his mistress, and reported what had passed. An hour was appointed for an interview, and the affair was brought to a satisfactory arrangement with that promptness and sagacity which had distinguished Mahomet in all his dealings with the widow. The father of Cadijah made some opposition to the match, on account of the poverty of Mahomet, following the common notion that wealth should be added to wealth: but the widow wisely considered her riches only as the means of enabling her to follow the dictates of her heart. She gave a great feast, to which were invited her father and the rest of her relatives and Mahomet's uncles Abu Taleb and Hamza, together with several other of the Koreishites. At this banquet wine was served in abundance and soon diffused good-humour round the board. The objections to Mahomet's poverty were forgotten; speeches were made by Abu Taleb on the one side, and by Waraka, a kinsman of Cadijah, on the other, in praise of the proposed nuptials; the dowry was arranged, and the marriage formally concluded.

Mahomet then caused a camel to be killed before his door, and the flesh distributed among the poor. The house was thrown open to all comers; the female slaves of Cadijah danced to the sound of timbrels, and all was revelry and rejoicing. Abu Taleb, forgetting his age and his habitual melancholy, made merry on the occasion He had paid down from his purse a dower of twelve-and-a-half okks of gold, equivalent to twenty young camels. Halêma, who had nursed Mahomet in his infancy, was summoned to rejoice at his nuptials, and was presented with a flock of forty sheep, with which she returned, enriched and contented, to her native valley, in desert of the Saadites.

VI CONDUCT OF MAHOMET AFTER HIS MARRIAGE – BECOMES ANXIOUS FOR RELIGIOUS REFORM – HIS HABITS OF SOLITARY ABSTRACTION – THE VISION OF THE CAVE – HIS ANNUNCIATION AS A PROPHET

The marriage with Cadijah placed Mahomet among the most wealthy of his native city. His moral worth also gave him great influence in the community. Allah, says the historian Abulfeda, had endowed him with every gift necessary to accomplish and adorn an honest man; he was so pure and sincere, so free from every evil thought, that he was commonly known by the name of Al Amin, or The Faithful.

The great confidence reposed in his judgment and probity caused him to be frequently referred to as arbiter in disputes between his townsmen. An anecdote is given as illustrative of his sagacity on such occasions. The Caaba having been injured by fire, was undergoing repairs, in the course of which the sacred black stone was to be replaced. A dispute arose among the chiefs of the various tribes as to which was entitled to perform so august an office, and they agreed to abide by the decision of the first person who should enter by the gate al Hâram. That person happened to be Mahomet. Upon hearing their different claims, he directed that a great cloth should be spread upon the ground, and the stone laid thereon; and that a man from each tribe should take hold of the border of the cloth. In this way the sacred stone was raised equally and at the same time by them all to a level with its allotted place, in which Mahomet fixed it with his own hands.

Four daughters and one son were the fruit of the marriage with Cadijah. The son was named Kasim, whence Mahomet was occasionally called Abu Kasim, or the father of Kasim, according to Arabian nomenclature. This son, however, died in his infancy.

For several years after his marriage he continued in commerce visiting the great Arabian fairs and making distant journeys with the caravans. His expeditions were not as profitable as in the days of his stewardship, and the wealth acquired with his wife diminished, rather than increased, in the course of his operations. That wealth, in fact, had raised him above the necessity of toiling for subsistence and given him leisure to indulge the original bias of his mind, a turn for reverie and religious speculation, which he had evinced from his earliest years. This had been fostered in the course of his journeying by his intercourse with Jews and Christians, originally fugitives from persecution, but now gathered into tribes, or forming part of the population of cities. The Arabian deserts, too, rife as we have shown them, with fanciful superstitions, had furnished aliment for his enthusiastic reveries. Since his marriage with Cadijah, also, he had a household oracle to influence him in his religious opinions. This was his wife's cousin Waraka, a man of speculative mind and flexible faith; originally a Jew, subsequently a Christian; and withal a pretender to astrology. He is worthy of note as being the first on record to translate parts of the Old and New Testaments into Arabic. From him Mahomet is supposed to have derived much of his information respecting those writings, and many of the traditions of the Mishnu and the Talmud, on which he draws so copiously in his Koran.

The knowledge thus variously acquired and treasured up in an uncommonly retentive memory, was in direct hostility to the gross idolatry prevalent in Arabia, and practised at the Caaba. That sacred edifice had gradually become filled and surrounded by idols, to the number of three hundred and sixty, being one for every day of the Arab year. Hither had been brought idols from various parts, the deities of other nations, the chief of which, Hobal was from Syria, and supposed to have the power of giving rain. Among these idols too, were Abraham and Ishmael, once revered as prophets and progenitors, now represented with divining arrows in their hands, symbols of magic.

Mahomet became more and more sensible of the grossness and absurdity of this idolatry, in proportion as his intelligent mind contrasted it with the spiritual religions which had been the subjects of his inquiries. Various passages in the Koran show the ruling idea which gradually sprang up in his mind until it engrossed his thoughts and influenced all his actions. That idea was a religious reform. It had become his fixed belief, deduced from all that he had learnt and meditated, that the only true religion had been revealed to Adam at his creation and been promulgated and practised in the days of innocence. That religion inculcated the direct and spiritual worship of one true and only God, the creator of the universe.

It was his belief furthermore, that this religion, so elevated and simple, had repeatedly been corrupted an debased by man, and especially outraged by idolatry; wherefore a succession of prophets, each inspired by a revelation from the Most High, had been sent from time to time, and at distant periods, to restore it to its original purity. Such was Noah, such was Abraham, such was Moses, and such was Jesus Christ. By each of these, the true religion had been reinstated upon earth, but had again been vitiated by their followers. The faith, as taught and practised by Abraham when he came out of the land of Chaldæa, seems especially to have formed a religious standard in his mind, from his veneration for the patriarch as the father of Ishmael, the progenitor of his race.

It appeared to Mahomet that the time for another reform was again arrived. The world had once more lapsed into blind idolatry. It needed the advent of another prophet, authorised by a mandate from on high, to restore the erring children of men to the right path, and to bring back the worship of the Caaba to what it had been in the days of Abraham and the patriarchs. The probability of such an advent, with its attendant reforms, seems to have taken possession of his mind, and produced habits of reverie and meditation, incompatible with the ordinary concerns of life and the bustle of the world. We are told that he gradually absented himself from society, and sought the solitude of a cavern on Mount Hara, about three leagues north of Mecca, where, in emulation of the Christian anchorites of the desert, he would remain days and nights together, engaged in prayer and meditation. In this way he always passed the month of Ramadhan, the holy month of the Arabs. Such intense occupation of the mind on one subject, accompanied by fervent enthusiasm of spirit, could not but have a powerful effect upon his frame. He became subject to dreams, to ecstasies and trances. For six months successively, according to one of his historians, he had constant dreams bearing on the subject of his waking thoughts. Often he would lose all consciousness of surrounding objects, and lie upon the ground as if insensible. Cadijah, who was sometimes the faithful companion of his solitude, beheld these paroxysms with anxious solicitude, and entreated to know the cause; but he evaded her inquiries, or answered them mysteriously. Some of his adversaries have attributed them to epilepsy, but devout Moslems declare them to have been the workings of prophecy; for already, say they, the intimations of the Most High began to dawn, though vaguely, on his spirit; and his mind laboured with conceptions too great for mortal thought. At length, say they, what had hitherto been shadowed out in dreams was made apparent and distinct by an angelic apparition and a divine annunciation.

It was in the fortieth year of his age when this famous revelation took place. Accounts are given of it by Moslem writers as if received from his own lips, and it is alluded to in certain passages of the Koran. He was passing, as was his wont, the month of Ramadhan in the cavern of Mount Hara, endeavouring by fasting, prayer and solitary meditation, to elevate his thoughts to the contemplation of divine truth. It was on the night called by Arabs Al Kader, or the Divine Decree; a night in which, according to the Koran, angels descend to earth, and Gabriel brings down the decrees of God. During that night there is peace on earth, and a holy quiet reigns over all nature until the rising of the morn.

As Mahomet, in the silent watches of the night, lay wrapped in his mantle, he heard a voice calling upon him; uncovering his head, a flood of light broke upon him of such intolerable splendour that he swooned away. On regaining his senses, he beheld an angel in a human form, which, approaching from a distance, displayed a silken cloth, covered with written characters. "Read!" said the angel.

"I know not how to read!" replied Mahomet.

"Read!" repeated the angel, "in the name of the Lord, who has created all things, who created man from a clot of blood. Read in the name of the Most High, who taught man the use of the pen, who sheds on his soul the ray of knowledge and teaches him what before he knew not."

Upon this Mahomet instantly felt his understanding illumined with celestial light, and read what was written on the cloth, which contained the decrees of God, as afterwards promulgated in the Koran. When he had finished the perusal, the heavenly messenger announced, "O Mahomet, of a verity, thou art the prophet of God! and I am his angel Gabriel."

Mahomet, we are told, came trembling and agitated to Cadijah in the morning, not knowing whether what he had heard and seen was indeed true, and that he was a prophet decreed to effect that reform so long the object of his meditations; or whether it might not be a mere vision, a delusion of the senses, or worse than all the apparition of an evil spirit.

Cadijah, however, saw everything with the eye of faith, and the credulity of an affectionate woman. She saw in it the fruition of her husband's wishes and the end of his paroxysms and privations. "Joyful tidings dost thou bring!" exclaimed she. "By him, in whose hand is the soul of Cadijah, I will henceforth regard thee as the prophet of our nation. Rejoice," added she, seeing him still cast down; "Allah will not suffer thee to fall to shame. Hast thou not been loving to thy kinsfolk, kind to thy neighbours, charitable to the poor, hospitable to the stranger, faithful to thy word, and ever a defender of the truth?"

Cadijah hastened to communicate what she had heard to her cousin Waraka, the translator of the Scriptures; who, as we have shown, had been a household oracle of Mahomet in matters of religion. He caught at once, and with eagerness, at this miraculous annunciation. "By him in whose hand is the soul of Waraka," exclaimed he; "thou speakest true, oh Cadijah! The angel who has appeared to thy husband is the same who, in days of old, was sent to Moses the son of Amram. His annunciation is true. Thy husband is indeed a prophet!"

The zealous concurrence of the learned Waraka is said to have had a powerful effect in fortifying the dubious mind of Mahomet.

NOTE. Dr. Gustav Weil, in a note to *Mohammed der Prophet*, discusses the question of Mahomet's being subject to attacks of epilepsy; which has generally been represented as a slander of his enemies and of Christian writers. It appears, however, to have been asserted by some of the oldest Moslem biographers, and given on the authority of persons about him. He would be seized, they said, with violent trembling, followed by a kind of swoon, or rather convulsion, during which perspiration would stream from his forehead in the coldest weather; he would lie with his eyes closed, foaming at the mouth and bellowing like a young camel. Ayesha, one of his wives, and Zeid, one of his disciples, are among the persons cited as testifying to that effect. They considered him at such times as under the influence of a revelation. He had such attacks, however, in Mecca, before the Koran was revealed to him. Cadijah feared that he was possessed by evil spirits, and would have called in the aid of a conjuror to exorcise them, but he forbade her. He did not like that any one should see him during these paroxysms. His visions, however, were not always preceded by such attacks. Hareth Ibn Haschem, it is said, once asked him in what manner the revelations are made. "Often," replied he, "the angel appears to me in a human form, and speaks to me. Sometimes I hear sounds like the tinkling of a bell, but see nothing. [A ringing in the ears is a symptom of epilepsy.] When the invisible angel has departed, I am possessed of what he has revealed." Some of his revelations he professed to receive direct from God, others in dreams; for the dreams of prophets, he used to say, are revelations.

The reader will find this note of service in throwing some degree of light upon the enigmatical career of this extraordinary man.

VII MAHOMET INCULCATES HIS DOCTRINES SECRETLY AND SLOWLY – RECEIVES FURTHER REVELATIONS AND COMMANDS – ANNOUNCES IT TO HIS KINDRED – MANNER IN WHICH IT WAS RECEIVED – ENTHUSIASTIC DEVOTION OF ALI – CHRISTIAN PORTENTS

For a time Mahomet confided his revelations merely to his own household. One of the first to avow himself a believer was his servant Zeid, an Arab of the tribe of Kalb. This youth had been captured in childhood by a freebooting party of Koreishites, and had come by purchase or lot into the possession of Mahomet. Several years afterwards his father, hearing of his being in Mecca, repaired thither and offered a considerable sum for his ransom. "If he chooses to go with thee," said Mahomet "he shall go without ransom: but if he chooses to remain with me, why should I not keep him?" Zeid preferred to remain, having ever, he said, been treated more as a son than as a slave. Upon this, Mahomet publicly adopted him, and he had ever since remained with him in affectionate servitude. Now, on embracing the new faith, he was set entirely free, but it will be found that he continued through life that devoted attachment which Mahomet seems to have had the gift of inspiring in his followers and dependants.

The early steps of Mahomet in his prophetic career were perilous and doubtful, and taken in secrecy. He had hostility to apprehend on every side; from his immediate kindred, the Koreishites of the line of Haschem, whose power and prosperity were identified with idolatry; and still more from the rival line of Abd Schems, who had long looked with envy and jealousy on the Haschemites, and would eagerly raise the cry of heresy and impiety to dispossess them of the guardianship of the Caaba. At the head of this rival branch of Koreish was Abu Sofian, the son of Harb, grandson of Omeya, and great-grandson of Abd Schems. He was an able and ambitious man, of great wealth and influence, and will be found one of the most persevering and powerful opponents of Mahomet.[8]

Under these adverse circumstances the new faith was propagated secretly and slowly, insomuch that for the first three years the number of converts did not exceed forty; these, too, for the most part, were young persons, strangers and slaves. Their meetings for prayer were held in private, either at the house of one of the initiated, or in a cave near Mecca. Their secrecy, however, did not protect them from outrage. Their meetings were discovered; a rabble broke into their cavern and a scuffle ensued. One of the assailants was wounded in the head by Saad, an armourer, thenceforth renowned among the faithful as the first of their number who shed blood in the cause of Islam.

One of the bitterest opponents of Mahomet was his uncle, Abu Lahab, a wealthy man, of proud spirit and irritable temper. His son Otha had married Mahomet's third daughter, Rokaia, so that they were doubly allied. Abu Lahab, however, was also allied to the rival line of Koreish, having married Omm Jemil, sister of Abu Sofian, and he was greatly under the control of his wife and his brother-in-law. He reprobated what he termed the heresies of his nephew, as calculated to bring disgrace upon their immediate line, and to draw upon it the hostilities of the rest of the tribe of Koreish. Mahomet was keenly sensible of the rancorous opposition of this uncle, which he attributed to the instigations of his wife, Omm Jemil. He especially deplored it, as he saw that it affected the happiness of his daughter Rokaia, whose inclination to his doctrines brought on her the reproaches of her husband and his family.

These, and other causes of solicitude, preyed upon his spirits, and increased the perturbation of his mind. He became worn and haggard, and subject more and more to fits of abstraction. Those of his relatives who were attached to him noticed his altered mien, and dreaded an attack of illness; others scoffingly accused him of mental hallucination; and the foremost among these scoffers was his uncle's wife, Omm Jemil, the sister of Abu Sofian.

The result of this disordered state of mind and body was another vision, or revelation, commanding him to "arise, preach, and magnify the Lord." He was now to announce, publicly and boldly, his doctrines, beginning with his kindred and tribe. Accordingly, in the fourth year of what is called his mission, he summoned all the Koreishites of the line of Haschem to meet him on the hill of Safa, in the vicinity of Mecca, when he would unfold matters important to their welfare. They assembled there accordingly, and among them came Mahomet's hostile uncle Abu Lahab, and with him his scoffing wife, Omm Jemil. Scarce had the prophet begun to discourse of his mission, and to impart his revelations, when Abu Lahab started up in a rage, reviled him for calling them together on so idle an errand and catching up a stone, would have hurled it at him. Mahomet turned upon him a withering look, cursed the hand thus raised in menace, and predicted his doom to the fire of Jehennam, with the assurance that his wife, Omm Jemil, would bear the bundle of thorns with which the fire would be kindled.

The assembly broke up in confusion. Abu Lahab and his wife, exasperated at the curse dealt out to them, compelled their son, Otha, to repudiate his wife, Rokaia, and sent her back weeping to Mahomet. She was soon indemnified, however, by having a husband of the true faith, being eagerly taken to wife by Mahomet's zealous disciple, Othman Ibn Affan.

Nothing discouraged by the failure of his first attempt, Mahomet called a second meeting of the Haschemites at his own house, where, having regaled them with the flesh of a lamb, and given them milk to drink, he stood forth and announced, at full length, his revelations received from heaven and the divine command to impart them to those of his immediate line.

"Oh children of Abd al Motâlleb," cried he with enthusiasm, "to you, of all men, has Allah vouchsafed these most precious gifts. In his name I offer you the blessings of this world and endless joys hereafter. Who among you will share the burden of my offer? Who will be my brother: my lieutenant, my vizier?"

All remained silent; some wondering, others smiling with incredulity and derision. At length Ali, starting up with youthful zeal, offered himself to the services of the prophet, though modestly acknowledging his youth and physical weakness.[9] Mahomet threw his arms round the generous youth, and pressed him to his bosom. "Behold my brother, my vizier, my vicegerent," exclaimed he; "let all listen to his words, and obey him."

The outbreak of such a stripling as Ali, however, was answered by a scornful burst of laughter of the Koreishites, who taunted Abu Taleb, the father of the youthful proselyte, with having to bow down before his son, and yield him obedience.

But though the doctrines of Mahomet were thus ungraciously received by his kindred and friends, they found favour among the people at large, especially among the women, who are ever prone to befriend a persecuted cause. Many of the Jews, also, followed him for a time, but when they found that he permitted his disciples to eat the flesh of the camel, and of other animals forbidden by their law, they drew back and rejected his religion as unclean.

Mahomet now threw off all reserve, or rather was inspired with increasing enthusiasm, and went about openly and earnestly proclaiming his doctrines, and giving himself out as a prophet sent by God to put an end to idolatry, and to mitigate the rigour of the Jewish and the Christian law. The hills of Safa and Kubeis, sanctified by traditions concerning Hagar and Ishmael, were his favourite places of preaching, and Mount Hara was his Sinai, whither he retired occasionally, in fits of excitement and enthusiasm, to return from its solitary cave with fresh revelations of the Koran.

The good old Christian writers, on treating of the advent of one whom they denounce as the Arab enemy of the church, make superstitious record of divers prodigies which occurred, about this time, awful forerunners of the troubles about to agitate the world. In Constantinople, at that time the seat of Christian empire, were several monstrous births and prodigious apparitions, which struck dismay into the hearts of all beholders. In certain religious processions in that neighbourhood, the crosses on a sudden moved of themselves, and were violently agitated, causing astonishment and terror. The Nile, too, that ancient mother of wonders, gave birth to two hideous forms, seemingly man and woman, which rose out of its waters, gazed about them for a time with terrific aspect, and sank again beneath the waves. For a whole day the sun appeared to be diminished to one-third of its usual size, shedding pale and baleful rays. During a moonless night a furnace light glowed throughout the heavens, and bloody lances glittered in the sky.

All these, and sundry other like marvels, were interpreted into signs of coming troubles. The ancient servants of God shook their heads mournfully, predicting the reign of anti-Christ at hand, with vehement persecution of the Christian faith, and great desolation of the churches; and to such holy men who have passed through the trials and troubles of the faith, adds the venerable Padre Jayme Bleda, it is given to understand and explain these mysterious portents, which forerun disasters of the church, even as it is given to ancient mariners to read in the signs of the air, the heavens, and the deep, the coming tempest which is to overwhelm their bark.

Many of these sainted men were gathered to glory before the completion of their prophecies. There, seated securely in the empyreal heavens, they may have looked down with compassion upon the troubles of the Christian world; as men on the serene heights of mountains look down upon the tempests which sweep the earth and sea, wrecking tall ships, and rending lofty towers.

VIII OUTLINES OF THE MAHOMETAN FAITH

Though it is not intended in this place to go fully into the doctrines promulgated by Mahomet, yet it is important to the right appreciation of his character and conduct, and of the events and circumstance set forth in the following narrative, to give their main features.

It must be particularly borne in mind, that Mahomet did not profess to set up a new religion, but to restore that derived in the earliest times from God himself. "We follow," says the Koran, "the religion of Abraham the orthodox, who was no idolater. We believe in God and that which hath been sent down to us, and that which hath been sent down unto Abraham and Ishmael, and Isaac and Jacob and the tribes, and that which was delivered unto Moses and Jesus, and that which was delivered unto the prophets from the Lord: we make no distinction between any of them, and to God we are resigned."[10]

The Koran[11] which was the great book of his faith, was delivered in portions from time to time, according to the excitement of his feelings, or the exigency of circumstances. It was not given as his own work, but as divine revelation; as the very words of God. The Deity is supposed to speak in every instance. "We have sent thee down the book of truth, confirming the scripture which was revealed before it, and preserving the same in its purity."[12]

The law of Moses, it was said, had for a time been the guide and rule of human conduct. At the coming of Jesus Christ it was superseded by the Gospel; both were now to give place to the Koran, which was more full and explicit than the preceding codes, and intended to reform the abuses which had crept into them through the negligence or the corruptions of their professors. It was the completion of the law; after it there would be no more divine revelations. Mahomet was the last, as he was the greatest, of the line of prophets sent to make known the will of God.

The unity of God was the corner-stone of this reformed religion. "There is no God but God," was its leading dogma. Hence, it received the name of the religion of Islam,[13] an Arabian word, implying submission to God. To this leading dogma was added, "Mahomet is the prophet of God;" an addition authorised, as it was maintained, by the divine annunciation, and important to procure a ready acceptation of his revelations.

Beside the unity of God, a belief was inculcated in his angels or ministering spirits; in his prophets; in the resurrection of the body; in the last judgment and a future state of rewards and punishments, and in predestination. Much of the Koran may be traced to the Bible, the Mishnu and the Talmud of the Jews,[14] especially its wild though often beautiful traditions concerning the angels, the prophets, the patriarchs, and the good and evil genii. He had at an early age imbibed a reverence for the Jewish faith, his mother, it is suggested, having been of that religion.

The system laid down in the Koran, however, was essentially founded on the Christian doctrines inculcated in the New Testament as they had been expounded to him by the Christian sectarians of Arabia. Our Saviour was to be held in the highest reverence as an inspired prophet, the greatest that had been sent before the time of Mahomet to reform the law; but all idea of his divinity was rejected as impious, and the doctrine of the Trinity was denounced as an outrage on the unity of God. Both were pronounced errors and interpolations of the expounders; and this, it will be observed, was the opinion of some of the Arabian sects of Christians.

The worship of saints, and the introduction of images and paintings representing them, were condemned as idolatrous lapses from the pure faith of Christ, and such, we have already observed, were the tenets of the Nestorians with whom Mahomet is known to have had much communication.

All pictures representing living things were prohibited. Mahomet used to say, that the angels would not enter a house in which there were such pictures, and that those who made them would be sentenced in the next world to find souls for them, or be punished.

Most of the benignant precepts of our Saviour were incorporated in the Koran. Frequent almsgiving was enjoined as an imperative duty; and the immutable law of right and wrong, "Do unto another as thou wouldst he should do unto thee," was given for the moral conduct of the faithful.

"Deal not unjustly with others," says the Koran, "and ye shall not be dealt with unjustly. If there be any debtor under a difficulty of paying his debt, let his creditor wait until it be easy for him to do it; but if he remit it in alms, it will be better for him."

Mahomet inculcated a noble fairness and sincerity in dealing. "Oh, merchants!" he would say, "falsehood and deception are apt to prevail in traffic, purify it therefore with alms; give something in charity as an atonement; for God is incensed by deceit in dealing, but charity appeases his anger. He who sells a defective thing, concealing its defect, will provoke the anger of God and the curses of the angels.

"Take not advantage of the necessities of another to buy things at a sacrifice; rather relieve his indigence.

"Feed the hungry, visit the sick, and free the captive if confined unjustly.

"Look not scornfully upon thy fellow man; neither walk the earth with insolence; for God loveth not the arrogant and vain-glorious. Be moderate in thy pace, and speak with a moderate tone; for the most ungrateful of all voices is the voice of asses."[15]

Idolatry of all kinds was strictly forbidden; indeed it was what Mahomet held in most abhorrence. Many of the religious usages, however, prevalent since time immemorial among the Arabs, to which he had been accustomed from infancy, and which were not incompatible with the doctrine of the unity of God, were still retained. Such was the pilgrimage to Mecca, including all the rites connected with the Caaba, the well of Zem Zem, and other sacred places in the vicinity, apart from any worship of the idols by which they had been profaned.

The old Arabian rite of prayer, accompanied or rather preceded by ablution, was still continued. Prayers, indeed, were enjoined at certain hours of the day and night; they were simple in form and phrase, addressed directly to the Deity with certain inflexions, or at times a total prostration of the body, and with the face turned towards the Kebla, or point of adoration.

At the end of each prayer, the following verse from the second chapter of the Koran was recited. It is said to have great beauty in the original Arabic and is engraved on gold and silver ornaments, and on precious stones worn as amulets. "God! There is no God but He, the living, the ever living; he sleepeth not, neither doth he slumber. To him belongeth the heavens, and the earth, and all that they contain. Who shall intercede with him unless by his permission? He knoweth the past and the future but no one can comprehend anything of his knowledge but that which he revealeth. His sway extendeth over the heavens and the earth, and to sustain them both is no burden to him. He is the High, the Mighty!"

Mahomet was strenuous in enforcing the importance and efficacy of prayer. "Angels," said he, "come among you both by night and day; after which those of the night ascend to heaven, and God asks them how they left his creatures. We found them, say they, at their prayers, and we left them at their prayers."

The doctrines in the Koran respecting the resurrection and final judgment were in some respects similar to those of the Christian religion, but were mixed up with wild notions derived from other sources; while the joys of the Moslem heaven, though partly spiritual, were clogged and debased by the sensualities of earth, and infinitely below the ineffable purity and spiritual blessedness of the heaven promised by our Saviour.

Nevertheless, the description of the last day, as contained in the eighty-first chapter of the Koran, and which must have been given by Mahomet at the outset of his mission at Mecca, as one of the first of his revelations, partakes of sublimity:

"In the name of the all merciful God! a day shall come when the sun will be shrouded and the stars will fall from the heavens.

"When the camels about to foal will be neglected, and wild beast will herd together through fear.

"When the waves of the ocean will boil, and the souls of the dead again be united to the bodies.

"When the female infant that has been buried alive will demand, for what crime was I sacrificed? and the eternal books will be laid open.

"When the heavens will pass away like a scroll, and hell will burn fiercely; and the joys of paradise will be made manifest.

"On that day shall every soul make known that which it hath performed.

"Verily, I swear to you by the stars which move swiftly and are lost in the brightness of the sun, and by the darkness of the night, and by the dawning of the day, these are not the words of an evil spirit, but of an angel of dignity and power, who possesses the confidence of Allah, and is revered by the angels under his command. Neither is your companion Mahomet, distracted. He beheld the celestial messenger in the light of the clear horizon, and the words revealed to him are intended as an admonition unto all creatures."

NOTE. To exhibit the perplexed maze of controversial doctrines from which Mahomet had to acquire his notions of the Christian faith, we subjoin the leading points of the jarring sects of Oriental Christians alluded to in the foregoing article; all of which have been pronounced heretical or schismatic.

The Sabellians, so called from Sabellius, a Libyan priest of the third century, believed in the unity of God, and that the Trinity expressed but three different states or relations, Father, Son, and Holy Ghost, all forming but one substance, as a man consists of body and soul.

The Arians, from Arius, an ecclesiastic of Alexandria in the fourth century, affirmed Christ to be the Son of God, but distinct from him and inferior to him, and denied the Holy Ghost to be God.

The Nestorians, from Nestorius, Bishop of Constantinople in the fifth century, maintained that Christ had two distinct natures, divine and human; that Mary was only his mother, and Jesus a man, and that it was an abomination to style her, as was the custom of the church, the Mother of God.

The Monophysites maintained the single nature of Christ, as their name betokens. They affirmed that he was combined of God and man, so mingled and united as to form but one nature.

The Eutychians, from Eutyches, abbot of a convent in Constantinople in the fifth century, were a branch of the Monophysites, expressly opposed to the Nestorians. They denied the double nature of Christ, declaring that he was entirely God previous to the incarnation, and entirely man during the incarnation.

The Jacobites, from Jacobus, bishop of Edessa, in Syria, in the sixth century, were a very numerous branch of the Monophysites, varying but little from the Eutychians. Most of the Christian tribes of Arabs were Jacobites.

The Mariamites, or worshippers of Mary, regarded the Trinity as consisting of God the Father, God the Son, and God the Virgin Mary.

The Collyridians were a sect of Arabian Christians, composed chiefly of females. They worshipped the Virgin Mary as possessed of divinity, and made offerings to her of a twisted cake, called collyris, whence they derived their name.

The Nazaræans, or Nazarenes, were a sect of Jewish Christians, who considered Christ as the Messiah, as born of a Virgin by the Holy Ghost, and as possessing something of a divine nature; but they conformed in all other respects to the rites and ceremonies of the Mosaic law.

The Ebionites, from Ebion, a converted Jew, who lived in the first century, were also a sect of judaizing Christians, little differing from the Nazaræans. They believed Christ to be a pure man, the greatest of the prophets, but denied that he had any existence previous to being born of the Virgin Mary. This sect, as well as that of the Nasaræans, had many adherents in Arabia.

Many other sects might be enumerated, such as the Corinthians, Maronites, and Marcionites, who took their names from learned and zealous leaders; and the Docetes and Gnostics, who were subdivided into various sects of subtle enthusiasts. Some of these assert the immaculate purity of the Virgin Mary, affirming that her conception and delivery, were effected like the transmission of the rays of light through a pane of glass, without impairing her virginity; an opinion still maintained strenuously in substance by Spanish Catholics.

Most of the Docetes asserted that Jesus Christ was of a nature entirely divine; that a phantom, a mere form without substance, was crucified by the deluded Jews, and that the crucifixion and resurrection were deceptive mystical exhibitions at Jerusalem for the benefit of the human race.

The Carpocratians, Basilidians, and Valentinians, named after three Egyptian controversialists, contended that Jesus Christ was merely a wise and virtuous mortal, the son of Joseph and Mary, selected by God to reform and instruct mankind; but that a divine nature was imparted to him at the maturity of his age, and period of his baptism, by St. John. The former part of this creed, which is that of the Ebionites, has been revived, and is professed by some of the Unitarian Christians, a numerous and increasing sect of Protestants of the present day.

It is sufficient to glance at these dissensions, which we have not arranged in chronological order, but which convulsed the early Christian church, and continued to prevail at the era of Mahomet, to acquit him of any charge of conscious blasphemy in the opinions he inculcated concerning the nature and mission of our Saviour.

NOTES

1 Beside the Arabs of the peninsula, who were all of the Shemitic race, there were others called Cushites, being descended from Cush the son of Ham. They inhabited the banks of the Euphrates and the Persian Gulf. The name of Cush is often given in Scripture to the Arabs generally as well as to their country. It must be the Arabs of this race who at present roam the deserted regions of ancient Assyria, and have been employed recently in disinterring the long-buried ruins of Nineveh. They are sometimes distinguished as the Syro-Arabians. The present work relates only to the Arabs of the peninsula, or Arabia proper.

2 Haran, Canna, and Aden, ports on the Indian Sea.

3 In summer the wandering Arabs, says Burckhardt, seldom remain above three or four days on the same spot; as soon as their cattle have consumed the herbage near a watering-place, the tribe removes in search of pasture, and the grass again springing up, serves for a succeeding camp. The encampments vary in the number of tents, from six to eight hundred; when the tents are but few, they are pitched in a circle; but more considerable numbers in a straight line, or a row of single tents, especially along a rivulet, sometimes three or four behind as many others. In winter, when water and pasture never fail, the whole tribe spreads itself over the plain in parties of three or four tents each, with an interval of half-an-hour's distance between each party. The Sheikh's tent is always on the side on which enemies or guests may be expected. To oppose the former, and to honour the latter, is the Sheikh's principal business. Every father of a family sticks his lance into the ground by the side of his tent, and ties his horse in front. There also his camels repose at night. Burckhardt, *Notes on Bedouins*, vol. i. p. 33.

The following is descriptive of the Arabs of Assyria, though it is applicable, in a great degree, to the whole race.

"It would be difficult to describe the appearance of a large tribe when migrating to new pastures. We soon found ourselves in the midst of wide-spreading flocks of sheep and camels. As far as the eye could reach, to the right, to the left, and in front, still the same moving crowd. Long lines of asses and bullocks, laden with black tents, huge cauldrons, and variegated carpets; aged women and men, no longer able to walk, tied on the heap of domestic furniture; infants crammed into saddle-bags, their tiny heads thrust through the narrow opening, balanced on the animal's back by kids or lambs tied on the opposite side; young girls clothed only in the close-fitting Arab shirt, which displayed rather than concealed their graceful forms; mothers with their children on their shoulders; boys driving flocks of lambs; horsemen armed with their long tufted spears, scouring the plain on their fleet mares; riders urging their dromedaries with their short-hooked sticks, and leading their high-bred steeds by the halter; colts galloping among the throng; such was the motley crowd through which we had to wend our way." Layard's *Nineveh*, i. 4.

4 Genesis xvi. 12.

5 The Beni Sad (or children of Sad) date from the most remote antiquity, and, with the Katan Arabs, are the only remnants of the primitive tribes of Arabia. Their valley is among the mountains which range southwardly from the Tayef. Burckhardt, *On the Bedouins*, vol. ii. p. 47.

6 Some assert that these two names indicate two monks, who held conversations with Mahomet.

7 *Miscât-ul-Masâbih*, vol. ii. p. 812.

8 Niebuhr (*Travels*, vol. ii.) speaks of the tribe of Harb, which possessed several cities and a number of villages in the highlands of Hedjaz, a mountainous range between Mecca and Medina. They have castles on precipitous rocks, and harass and lay under contribution the caravans. It is presumed that this tribe takes its name from the father of Abu Sofian, as did the great line of the Omeyades from his grandfather.

9 By an error of translators, Ali is made to accompany his offer of adhesion by an extravagant threat against all who should oppose Mahomet.

10 Koran, ch. ii.

11 Derived from the Arabic word Kora, to read or teach.

12 Koran, ch. v.

13 Some etymologists derive Islam from Salem or Aslama, which signifies salvation. The Christians form from it the term Islamism, and the Jews have varied it into Ismailism, which they intend as a reproach, and an allusion to the origin of the Arabs as descendants of Ishmael.

From Islam the Arabians drew the terms Moslem or Muslem, and Musulman, a professor of the faith of Islam. These terms are in the singular number and make Musliman in the dual, and Muslimen in the plural. The French and some other nations follow the idioms of their own languages in adopting or translating the Arabic terms, and form the plural by the addition of the letter s; writing Musulman and Musulmans. A few English writers, of whom Gibbon is the chief, have imitated them, imagining that they were following the Arabian usage. Most English authors, however, follow the idiom of their own language, writing Moslem and Moslems, Musulman and Musulmen; this usage is also the more harmonious.

14 The Mishnu of the Jews, like the Sonna of the Mahometans, is a collection of traditions forming the Oral law. It was compiled in the second century by Judah Hakkodish, a learned Jewish Rabbi, during the reign of Antoninus Pius, the Roman Emperor.

The Jerusalem Talmud and the Babylonish Talmud are both commentaries on the Mishnu. The former was compiled at Jerusalem, about three hundred years after Christ, and the latter in Babylonia, about two centuries later. The Mishnu is the most ancient record possessed by the Jews, except the Bible.

15 The following words of Mahomet, treasured up by one of his disciples, appears to have been suggested by a passage in Matthew xxv. 35–45:

"Verily, God will say at the day of resurrection, 'Oh, sons of Adam! I was sick, and ye did not visit me.' Then they will say, 'How could we visit thee? For thou are the Lord of the universe, and art free from sickness.' And God will reply, 'Knew ye not that such a one of my servants was sick, and ye did not visit him? Had you visited that servant, it would have been counted to you as righteousness.' And God will say, 'Oh, sons of Adam! I asked you for food, and ye gave it me not.' And the sons of Adam will say, 'How could we give thee food, seeing thou are the sustainer of the universe, and art free from hunger?' And God will say, 'Such a one of my servants asked you for bread, and ye refused it. Had you given him to eat, ye would have received your reward from me.' And God will say, 'Oh, sons of Adam, I asked you for water, and you gave it me not.' They will reply, 'Oh, our supporter! How could we give thee water, seeing thou are the sustainer of the universe, and not subject to thirst?' And God will say, 'Such a one of my servants asked you for water, and ye did not give it to him. Had ye done so, ye would have received your reward from me.'"

12

ISLAM UND KALIFAT

Paul Wittek

Der Glaube an den einen, überweltlichen, persönlichen, ethischen Gott ist eine spezifisch morgenländische Konzeption. Sowohl in Aegypten wie im Zweistromlande darf von einem «latenten Monotheismus» gesprochen werden,[1] hat er sich hier auch gegen bereits systemisierte, von Priesterschaften erfolgreich verteidigte polytheistische Religionen nicht durchzusetzen vermocht. Erst mit der Jahwe-Religion der Juden kommt in dem Durchzugsland zwischen den beiden Zentralländern der alten morgenländischen Kultur ein ausgeprägter Monotheismus zur Herrschaft und beansprucht alsbald trotz seiner Beschränkung auf eine relativ sehr kleine Gemeinde universale Geltung: Jahwe hat Macht über die ganze Welt; auch Israels Feinde sind nur sein Werkzeug, mit welchem er sein Volk prüfen oder strafen will. Diese geschichtlichen Tatsachen werden keineswegs erklärt, wohl aber in einen offenbar notwendigen Zusammenhang gebracht durch den Hinweis auf die Rolle, welche in den Fruchtländern des Niltals und des Zweistromlandes der als «Ebenbild des Götterherren» göttliche Verehrung geniessende Herrscher spielt. Dort wo nicht der Regen, sondern künstliche Bewässerung und Stromregulie-rung die Ernte sichert, ist die Möglichkeit einer absoluten Herrschaft am ehesten gegeben: der «König» verfügt über die zum Bau von Kanälen notwendigen Arbeitskräfte und sichert das Funktionieren des Systems durch seine Verwaltung. Damit ist auch eine Möglichkeit für das Emporkommen der Vorstellung von dem einen Gott gegeben, «der die Erde und den Menschen nicht, wie sonst meist, gezeugt, sondern aus dem Nichts ‚gemacht' hat auch die Wasserwirtschaft des Königs schafft ja die Ernte im Wüstensand aus dem Nichts. Der König schafft sogar das Recht durch Gesetze

Source: *Archiv für Sozialwissenschaft und Sozialpolitik*, 1925, vol. 53, pp. 370–426.

und rationale Kodifikationen – etwas, was die Welt hier in Mesopotamien zum erstenmal erlebte».[2] Der Jahwe der Juden trägt sichtlich die Züge dieser morgenländischen Könige. Aber entsprechend der politischen Ohnmacht seines Volkes ist er zu einer ausserweltlichen, ethischen Macht unerforschlichen Ratschlusses geworden. In diesen sich fügen heisst Anwartschaft auf die Verheissungen erlangen, die er seinem Volke, d. h. für die Folgezeit: den seinem Gesetze Getreuen, gegeben hat. Als Pariareligion war der Monotheismus schliesslich Wilklichkeit geworden.

Neue Nahrung bot die römische Weltreichbildung. Als der Monotheismus mit dem Christentum den entscheidenden Impuls und die über den Kaiserkult siegreiche Form empfangen hatte, war ihm ein weiter, vorbereiteter Raum geöffnet. Seit Alexander waren West und Ost, die sich mit Salamis einst deutlichst geschieden hatten (die auf Insel und Schiffe geflüchteten Athener schaffen, nach der Seeschlacht in ihre zerstörte Stadt heimkehrend, auf mutig eingeebneten Trümmern einer innerlich night wenig vom Osten her bestimmt gewesenen Vergangenheit in völliger innerer Freiheit aus dem nationalen Genius heraus ein neues Dasein), zur Einheit gefügt gewesen, schliesslich aufs festeste zusammengefasst und auf das meiste einander angeglichen im Imperium Romanum, das nur im äussersten Osten das Perserreich als Residuum nahezu unberührten morgenländischen Daseins und im Westen die noch ungestalte Germanenwelt, Hort unverbrauchter europäischer Volkskraft, ausserhalb seiner Grenzen liess. Die Gleichförmigkeit der materiellen Kultur dieses römischen Raumes war eine weitgehende. Im Geistigen half der weitherzige Synkretismus des Pantheon über die Gegensätze hinweg. Doch als die neue Lehre zur Einigung im Letzten und Tiefsten drängte, als die Entscheidung für den einen Gott nicht mehr aufschiebbar war, da wurde diese Welt ihrer Gegensätzlichkeit sich bewusst und brach auseinander.

Der universalistische Monotheismus des Christentums ist eine Fortsetzung des Judentums, wird aber durch die Idee der Erlösung durch den Menschengott stark relativiert. Gott, der die Welt aus dem Nichts erschaffen hat, tritt zu ihr in ein wesentlich anderes Verhältnis, wenn er in seiner Kreatur den ihm wesensgleichen Sohn zeugt – ein Widerspruch, der an der Bestimmung der Natur dieses Sohnes deutlich sichtbar werden muss. So ist denn auch die Kirche ein halbes Jahrtausend nach ihrem Stifter immer noch uneins über die Naur desselben. Der erregte Streit, der deshalb zwischen dem Osten und Westen tobt, ist keineswegs Ausdruck eines sich mit gleichgültigen, unverständlichen Formeln bewaffnenden ‚Nationalismus', ist vielmehr die natürliche Auswirkung viel tiefer liegender ‚nationaler' Gegensätze, die auch in nationalistischen Tendenzen zutage treten mögen, in den christologischen Diskussionen jedenfalls viel sinnfälligeren Ausdruck ihres Wesens gefunden haben als in jenen.[3] Wenn der Westen an der Wesensgleichheit von Vater und Sohn und an des letzteren göttlicher und menschlicher Natur in einer Person festhielt, so bewies er damit, dass ihm ein schlecht verhüllter Verstoss gegen den strengen Monotheismus erträglicher war als die Preisgabe des gottmenschlichen Heilands und der Eigenschaft Marias als ‚Gottesgebärerin'. Der Osten aber hing am Monotheismus, ob er nun mit den Nestorianern im Menschen Christus – Maria ist also *ἀνθρωποτόκος* – die göttliche Natur *κατὰ χάριν*, d. i. ‚aus Gnade', ‚wie in einem Tempel' wohnen lässt und damit die Einheit der Person so gut wie preisgibt, oder ob er als Monophysitismus Christus nur eine, ‚gottmenschliche' Natur zuschreibt, frei von sünde, Leiden und Tod – dann sind die letzteren lediglich *κατὰ χάριν* übernommene Zustände, die mit der besonderen (im Grunde genommen doch einfach göttlichen) Natur Christi in keinem notwendigen Zusammenhang stehen und ist das Menschtum des Heilands so gut wie geleugnet.[4]

Schon hatte sich der ganze Osten: Aegypten, Syrien, Armenien und was es östlich davon an Christen gab, durch Schaffung eigener Kirchen aus der ursprünglichen Gemeinschaft gelöst, und hätte nicht Justinian aus politischer Rücksichtnahme auf den Westen die eigene Neigung zum Monophysitismus zurückgestellt, so hätte sich schon damals die griechisch redende Welt von der lateinischen religiös geschieden. Diese Stellungnahme der staatlichen Gewalt gegen eine notwendige, weil aus innerstem Antrieb eingeleitete Entwicklung hielt den Osten des Reiches dauernd in erregtester Spannung. Aus dieser Spannung heraus erwuchs im äussersten Winkel der antiken Oikumene, schon ausserhalb ihres politischen Machtbereichs und daher an der gegebenen Zufluchtstätte alles Sektierertums, die Tat, die alles ‚Morgenland' aus der Bindung an den Westen herausnahm und in einem, entschiedenen Monotheismus einigte – die Gründung des Islams.[5]

Geschichtlich an das ihm übrigens nur in getrübter und apokrypher Form und nur durch mündliche Mitteilungen bekannte Christentum anknüpfend, bog Mohammed – in der ihm als aus Vater, Sohn und Maria zusammengesezt bekannten Trinität den schlecht verhüllten Polytheismus richtig erkennend –

entschieden zur Gottesvorstellung des Judentums zurück, aber keineswegs zu dessen reifster, ‚rationalisiertester', vielmehr zu einer ihre Verwandtschaft mit dem morgenländischen Herrschertum noch durchaus erkennen lassenden ursprünglicheren, sinnlicheren Form (vgl. den im Islam viel rezitierten ‚Thronvers', Koran II 256: «Allah, ausser ihm ist kein Gott! Er ist der Lebendige, der Beständige; ihn fasst nicht Schlummer noch Schlaf; sein ist alles in den Himmeln und auf Erden; wer legt Fürsprache bei ihm ein als wem er es erlaubt? Er weiss, was vor und hinter euch liegt, die Menschen aber erfassen nichts von seinem Wissen als was er will. Sein Thron umfasst Himmel und Erde, und die Hütung beider ermüdet ihn nicht. Er ist der Hohe, der Grosse.») Der in ganz Vorderasien siegreiche Monotheismus hatte schon ver Mohammed auch in Arabien Allah, «den Gott», den generellen Befriff der Gottheit, zum Eigennamen eines allen Stämmen gemeinschaftlichen grossen Gottes erhoben.[6] Aber die Ausschliesslichkeit der Geltung von Mohammeds Allah und das alles dominierende, dem Christentum entlehnte eschatologische Moment, vor allem aber der politische Zug, den die Lehre sehr rasch gewann[7] und der ihr die weltgeschichtliche Bedeutung verliehen hat, sind Mohammeds persönlichste Leistung.

Diese Wendung ins Politische, auf deren Psychologie hier nicht einzugehen ist, hat die Tatsache der koranischen Gesetzgebung und des Medinensischen Staates geschaffen, von dessen mit der ‚Flucht' unmittelbar zusammenhängender Begründung die islamische Welt mit Recht ihre Jahre zählt. Erst als ‚Staat' ist der islam Realität geworden. Mohammed, erst nur Prophet – doch der eigenliche Inhalt seiner Prophetie ist rasch erschöpft –, wird dank des Charismas der ekstatischen Rede, die ihn als ‚Gesandten Gottes' kennzeichnet und ihm selber Kraft und Mittel zu politischem Wirken gibt, alsbald zum Herrscher. Neben dem, die kultischen Vorschriften hinzugerechnet, unendlich dürftigen Inhalt von Mohammeds religiöser Verkündigung stehen die zahlreichen 'politischen' Gesetze des Korans – nur ein Bruchteil der Willensakte des Herrschers, die nach der ständig wiederholten Mahnung: «Glaubet an Gott und gehorchet seinem, Propheten» sämtlich religiös verbindlich sind.

Der Prophet ist ja der Vermittler des sonst unbekannten Willens Gottes, der die Welt aus dem Nichts erschaffen hat und in uneingeschränkter Willkür regiert, kraft seiner Allwissenheit ihren Lauf von Ewigkeit her wissend. Dem Menschen ziemt es, in dieser Schicksalsfügung mit frommer ‚Ergebung' (*islām*) zu stehen, dem ihm durch den Propheten bekanntgewordenen Willen Gottes gehorsam, im übrigen auf Allah vertrauend.

Von Anfang an ist mit der Offenbarung, dem Koran, eine ausserpersönliche Instanz von Gesetzescharakter vorhanden, die zugleich Grundlage eines Staates ist, der ihr hinwiederum Geltung und Ausbreitung verbürgt: also eine von ethischer Prophetie ausgehende Theokratie.[8] Der grundsätzliche Gegensatz zum Christentum (und die nähere innere Verwandtschaft mit dem Judentum) ist auch hier wieder klar: das Christentum ist im wesentlichen durchaus exemplarische Prophetie, die zu einer über dem Staate stehenden Gemeinschaft, zur Kirche führt. Es stehen einander gegenüber: die ‚Muslims', d. s. die dem Gesetze ‚Ergebenen', und die ‚Christen', d. s. die, welche an sich in Nachfolge den Christus sichtbar machen wollen.[9] Das worauf der Akzent liegt, ist hier: ‚lieb', dort: ‚Gesetz'.

Das von Mohammed verkündete Gesetz ist aber keineswegs systematisch ethischen Charakters, spiegelt vielmehr – bei Aufnahme von sehr viel religiös an sich indifferentem Gewohnheitsrecht und mitunter grossen Zugeständnissen an lokale oder politische Bedürfnisse und sogar eigene Wünsche – sehr naiv und vielfach widerspruchsvoll die ethischen Ideale zwar nicht gerade der arabischen Welt, wohl aber des östlichen Raumes, soweit er von der allgemeinen monotheistischen Bewegung ergriffen war – ist also schon dadurch ein rechtes Kind der morgenländischen Welt. Die Versuche der Folgezeit, Dogma und Ethik des Islams im Sinne einer einheitlichen Grundintention zu rationalisieren, sind gegenüber der zu immer grösserer ‚Weltangepasstheit' führenden, rein formalistischen, religiös und ethisch indifferenten Kasuistik nahezu ganz wirkungslos geblieben: das religiöse Gesetz entwickelt sich zum immer genaueren Ausdruck, zu einer Art Kodifizierung morgenländischer Daseinsform mit ständiger Anpassungsfähigkeit an den einzelnen Bedarfsfall. Ergebung in diese Daseinsform, nicht Erhöhung des Menschen über eine ihm zur Gestaltung aufgegebene Welt ist der eigentliche Sinn des Islams.[10]

Hat so der Islam schon mit seiner Grundurkunde, dem Koran, ein hohes Ausmass von Weltangepasstheit erreicht, so war zu deren Ausgestaltung mehr als eine Möglichkeit geboten. Schon die Notwendigkeiten des politischen Lebens müssen in der Theokratie die Religion modifizieren und bereits der Koran selbst weist mit der zunehmenden Politisierung eine Herabsetzung der religiösen Forderungen auf. «Allah wünscht es Euch leicht und nicht schwer zu machen.» «Allah hat Euch in der Religion keine Beengung auferlegt».[11] Mit solchem Trumpf gegen die erheblich schwierigeren Forderungen vor allem des Christentums wirbt der Politiker Mohammed für seinen Gottesstaat. Dort, wo die Anordnungen des Korans in der Folgezeit als den Anforderungen eines von der ursprünglichen Primitivität sehr weit entfernten Kulturlebens im Wege stehend empfunden werden, deutet und dehnt man sie auf das kunstvollste und unbedenklichste, bis zwischen Lehre und Leben der innere Einklang hergestellt ist, der beiden eine so aussergewöhnliche Lebenskraft verbürgt. Als Anhaltspunkt der Deutung und als Quelle neuer gesetzlicher Vorschriften dienen das Leben des Propheten und seines Kreises und seine Aussprüche (*sunna* und *hadīs*), letztere wo es nottut mit dem ruhigsten Gewissen auch frei erfunden und mit erdichteter Reihenfolge von Gewährsmännern (*isnād*) legitimiert, aus dem in dieser streng formalistischen Welt geltenden Grundsatze heraus: was immer an guter Rede gesagt wird, ist so als ob es der Prophet selbst gesagt hätte.[12] Die aus dieser unversieglichen Quelle beliebig vermehrbaren Gesetze erstreckt nun die Rechtsgelehrsamkeit nach den Methoden des Schlusses und der Analogie, ja selbst auf Grund freier Spekulation grundsätzlich auf die gesamte Lebenspraxis, immer neue Gesetze findend, welche sämtlich dem dogmatischen Bestande einverleibt werden, sobald sie nur die Anerkennung der Gemeinde gefunden haben, eine Anerkennung, die nicht auf Konzilien oder von organisatorisch bestimmten Stellen ausgesprochen wird, sondern als ein stillschweigender Consensus (*idjmā*) spontan sich auswirkt. Manche zunächst auf schroffen Widerstand stossende Neuerung hat sich so, vom Leben immer weider der Lehre aufgedrängt, erst bis zur Duldung, dann bis zur Einverleibung in den Dogmenbestand durchsetzen können.

Abschluss und Festigkeit gewennt das Lehr- und Gesetzesgebäude des Islams zunehmend seit dem 9. Jahrh. (also gegen Ende des 2. Jahrh.s seines Bestendes),[13] seit den grossen Sammelwerken der Prophetenaussprüche und der systematischen Entwicklung eines kanonischen Rechtes sowie bestimmter Methoden zu dessen kasuistischer Weiterbildung, also seit der Begründung der grossen Rechtsschulen, vor allem auch seit dem Werke des Asch'arī (st. 935), der die auf einen reineren Gottesbegriff und eine ethisch-rationale Regelung der Lebenspraxis hinzielenden Bestrebungen des Rationalismus besiegte, indem er dessen Methoden der Orthodoxie dienstbar machte, in deren

Stoffmassen System brigend und sie festigend. Von da an gibt es erst eine greifbare «Orthodoxie» mit in bestimmtem Studiengang herangezogenen Trägern. Bis dahin war Irrlehre durch politische Loslösung von der Gesamtgemeinde, also Proklamierung eines eigenen politischen Oberhauptes und Bekämpfung des von der Gesamtgemeinde anerkannten (und zwar ist letzteres erst das Ausschlaggebende) charakterisiert gewesen – die Vielheit der übrigen Lehrmeinungen hatte in reger Wechselwirkung nebeneinander gestande. Jetzt aber wird jede freiere Spekulation und Auslegung zur Irrlehre. Unverständlichem oder Widerspruchsvollem in der Lehre ist nicht nachzugehen, um es aufzulösen, sondern es ist einfach gläubig hinzunehmen. Die Aufrollung grosser Probleme ist schon dadurch unmöglich gemacht, dass ein Zurückgreifen auf die primären Glaubensquellen zu eigener Auslegung (*idjtihād*), über die durch den Consensus bereits geheiligte hinaus, streng untersaft ist. Das «Tor des *Idjtihād*» wird geschlossen.

Nun ist der Islam eine verhältnismässig kleine Summe von Glaubenssätzen neben einem (eigentlich sind es mehrere, dem Gläubigen zur Wahl überlassene) prinzipiell die ganze Lebenspraxis regelnden unendlich einlässlichen Komplex (auch hier wird die Bezeichnung ‚System' besser vermieden) von Pflichten. Diesen auch nur in seinen Hauptzügen zu kennen ist dem gewöhnlichen Gläubigen unmöglich. Er weiss, dass er sich notwendig beinahe mit jedem Atemzug gegen das heilige Gesetz (*Scherīʿa*) versündigt, und zwar «durch Wissen, Willen und Vorherbestimmung Gottes»[14] versündigt. Der sündige Mensch kann in solch heilloser Verstrickung nur demütig auf Gottes Nachsicht hoffen. Und Gott ist gnädig. Er verzeiht dem Sünder, woferne dieser nur glabut. Ja er verzeiht sogar eine wissentliche schwere Sünde, wenn sie als Sünde empfunden und bereut wird.[15] Den Ungläubigen aber trifft sichere Verdammnis. Eine starre und doch nicht ganz ernst genommene Gesetzeswelt. Das religiöse Leben neight, sich in leerem, blutlosem, zur Formel entwertetem Bekenntnis zu erschöpfen. Das menschliche Ideal verkörpern in dieser Welt die *ʿUlemā*, ‚die Wissenden', die sich erst nach und nach, zusammen mit der Herausbildung der Orthodoxie, zu einem, Stand zusammenschliessenden Theologen-Juristen – nicht Träger oder Vermittler charismatischer Gnaden, auch nicht exemplarische Führer oder tröstende Seelsorger der Gemeinde; auch nicht Instrument einer einheitlichen geistlichen Leitung; nicht einmal notwendig die Leiter der rituellen Uebungen; aber als Bewahrer und souveräne Ausleger des in verwirrender Fülle ausgebreiteten heiligen Gesetzes sind sie in gewissem Sinne die Nachfolger des Propheten und die Herrscher in der islamischen Gemeinde, jedenfalls eine privilegierte Schichte, mit der jede weltliche Macht zu rechnen hat. Indem die 'Ulemā, freizügig über alle Grenzen der islamischen Staatenwelt hinweg und untereinander in steter Verbindung, durch die für den gesamten Islam verbindliche gemeinsame Weiterbildung des Gesetzes die Fiktion einer einheitlichen muslimischen Gemeinde aufrechterhalten, werden sie die Repräsentanten des Islams, der – von der Wallfahrt nach Mekka abgesehen – vorzugsweise an ihnen sich seiner ideellen Einheit und seiner Ausdehnung bewusst wird.

In viel weniger einheitlicher Weise, dafür mit grösserer Glut und Vehemenz fungieren in gleichem Sinne die Derwische, die Träger der der Gesetzeskasuistik polar entgegengesetzten anderen Entwicklungsmöglichkeit, der aus dem Grundgefühl der Ergebung gespeisten Mystik, welche seit dem 8. Jahrh. – von verwandten fremden Einflüssen gefördert – von klösterlichen Gemeinschaften gepflegt und verbreitet wird. Hatte jene Gesetzeskasuistik eine Art ‚religiöser Depression' eintreten lassen, in die nun von allen Seiten Anregungen und fremde Religiosität einströmen, so ist die Mystik geeignet, die Religion als festes Lehr- und Gesetzesgebäude durch die Ueberfülle des subjektiven Erlebens zu zersprengen. Gazālī (st. IIII) hat die noch in orthodoxen Bahnen verbliebene Mystik für die schon erkaltete offizielle Lehre gerettet und diese vor dem leersten Formalismus bewahrt. Dennoch verbleibt dieser das primäre. So empfiehlt Gazālī mit einem *Hadīs* denen, die sich bei der Koranrezitation nicht zu Tränen gerührt fühlen, sich doch so zu stellen, als ob sie es wären und weiten. «Denn» – fügt er hinzu – «in diesen Dingen legt man sich anfangs einen Zwang auf, aber schliesslich kommt alles von selbst».[16] Das ist aber doch auch ein Wegstreben vom Formalismus, wenn es auch weit entfernt ist von der Forderung nach natürlicher, naiver Einheit von Geste und Gesinnung, Ueberzeugung und Tat.

In der Mystik an sich war eine Richtung auf diese Forderung hin durchaus nicht enthalten. Zumal in ihren heterodoxen Formen neigt sie dazu, den Zuständen der Versenkung in Gott gegenüber alles Irdische, auch die Gesetze (denen immerhin zumeist ein relativer Wert zuerkannt wird), als nichtig anzusehen. Skrupelloseste Gleichgültigkeit gegenüber den religiösen Vorschriften, gegenüber Sittlichkeit und Sitte ist mit Heiligkeit im Sinne des islamischen Mystikers durchaus vereinbar, ja sie ist sogar ein Mittel zur

Heiligkeit, weil sie Verachtung der Mitwelt einbringt und ertragen lehrt, ganz abgesehen von der ekstasefördernden Wirkung der Rauschmittel und geschlechtlichen Ausschweifung. Hier also versinkt die Tat in einem Gefühlsrausch, wie sie ort im Formalismus erstickt.

Erst die durch Gazālī systemisierte Vermählung der beiden Sphären, die sich vorher heftig befehdt hatten – waren sie auch oft genug in einer Person vereinigt gewesen –, bedeutet eine jetzt entschieden und allgemein einsetzende Wendung zu realistischer Lebensauffassung, über Formelwesen und Mystik hinaus. Die Erfüllung der gesetzlichen Vorschriften wird nun auch als Mittel zur Erweckung aller jener Gefühle gewertet, welche Gott nahe bringen und die mystische Vereinigung mit ihm vorbereiten. Man denke in diesem Zusammenhange an die Wirkung des täglich fünfmal, womöglich gemeinschaftlich zu verrichtenden und in allen Einzelheiten des Wortlautes und der Körperhaltung genau vorgeschriebenen rituellen Gebetes mit seinen Neigungen, Beugungen, Prosternationen und den ihm vorangehenden Reinigungszeremonien! Schon dies allein sichert eine dauernde Erfüllung des Daseins mit religiöser Stimmung und hat sicherlich seinen Anteil an dem würdevollen Ernste, der den Muslim schmückt und den immer wieder zu sich selbst zurückkehrenden, hier seinen festen Halt findenden Menschen auszeichnet. Dieses ‚Training' auf die Erweckung religiöser Gefühle durch Befolgung der Vorschriften, worauf wieder in frommer Wallung eine erhöhte, werktätige Befolgung der Vorschriften folgt, hält den Bekenner des Islams ungemein empfänglich für die Gefühle plötzlicher Rührung und Zerknirschung und lässt ihn sich aus diesen Gefühlen (sie dürfen ruhig als Sentimentalität gewertet werden) immer wieder – wobei Gelübde naturgemäss eine grosse Rolle spielen – zu Gott wohlgefälligen Taten erheben. Eine wüchsige Durchdringung des Lebens mit Heiligkeit ist das keineswegs – sie ist auch unmöglich in einer Welt, in der der Mensch als Einzelner sich zerknirscht als armselig willenlose, notwendig sündhafte Kreature vor Allah empfindet, in der er, mit Allah durch mystische Vereinigung verbunden, all sein wildes, dunkles Tun als gleichgültig und als Schein ansieht, der seiner Erwähltheit, sich mit Gott vereinigen zu dürfen, nichts anhaben kann.

Das heilige Gesetz, diese ‚Kodifikation morgenländischen Daseins', ist immerhin vor gänzlicher Idealität seiner Forderungen bewahrt und zeichnet sich aus der Gefühlsregung jedes einzelnen Bekenners im Stoffe ab.[17] In dieser Verknüpfung überdauern morgenländische Kultur und Islam ohne einheitliches weltliches Oberhaupt und ohne kirchliche Organisation die Ueberflutung durch noch heidnische Völkerschaften als Einheit, über alle sich ständig verschiebenden Staaten- und Völkergrenzen hinweg – als eine Lebensform, die im wesentlichen in allen Stürmen, die über sie hinweggegangen sind, dieselbe geblieben ist, wie sie uns auf den Denkmälern altorientalischer Geschichte entgegentritt.

Es soll hier nicht behauptet werden, dass diese Lebensform eine Sache des Bodens sei, auf dem sie so paradigmatische Ausprägung erlangt hat. Immerhin gibt es zu denken, dass der Islam – von seinem Vordringen in Gebiete kultureller und religiöser Depression abgesehen – in dauernden Besitz doch nur schon von der altorientalischen Kultur ergriffene Gebiete genommen hat. Trotzdem die Spätantike dem morgenländischen Wesen eine breite Gasse nach dem Westen gebahnt hatte, war dieser in seiner Art genügend befestigt, damit der Versuch einer Einigung im Letzten zum Bruche führen musste. Das Christentum des Westens ist trotz fernster Herkunft seines Gedanken- und Formengutes der gemässe Abschluss antiken Lebens, unter diesem sinngemäss die von Hellas ihren Ursprung nehmende geschichtliche Einheit verstanden, die auch in fremdestem Gewand noch ihrer Herkunft gewiss ist. Und trotz noch so vieler aufzeigbarer genetischer Zusammenhänge ist der Islam nach zu Recht bestehendem Mommsen-Wort der ‚Henker der Antike'. Mit ihm ist ein neues Kristallisationszentrum morgenländischen Daseins erstanden, welches alles ihm Zugehörige an Ländern und Kulturgütern, geistigen und materiellen, aus der Verbindung mit dem Westen herauslöst, an sich zieht und sich eingliedert.[18] Der Sonderungsprozess dauert, so wie er nicht unvorbereitet einsetzt, geraume Zeit. Um das jahr 1000 tritt er in das Stadium seines Ausreifens.[19] Der Weg, den der Islam hier zurückzulegen hatte, wird auf das deutlichste gekennzeichnet durch die Wandlung, welche in seinem Bereich das oberste Herrscheramt in Theorie und Praxis durchzumachen hatte. Die Hauptphasen dieser Wandlung und deren vielfältige Verknüpfung mit geistigen, politischen, sozialen, ökonomischen, schliesslich ethnischen Momenten sichtbar zu machen ist Aufgabe des folgenden.

Mohammeds Herrschaft in Medina ruhte auf dem Charisma der Prophetie, dessen Bewährung in den Kämpfen gegen Mekka die Gefolgschaft der Beduinenstämme Arabiens sicherte. Wenn diesen zugerufen wird: «Der Glaube ist zwar och nicht in eure

Herzen eingegangen; doch wenn ihr Gott und seinem Gesandten gehorcht, so wird er euch von euren Werken nichts entziehen» (Kor. IL 14), so zeight das, wie die religiösen Forderungen den politischen Notwendigkeiten zuliebe zurückgestellt werden, zugleich aber auch, dass doch Gott, die Prophetie und das Jenseits deutlich auch das Politische beherrschen. Und dieses gilt auch für die nächsten Nachfolger des Propheten, unter denen sich das Reich in raschem Siegeslauf weit über Arabien hinaus bis an den Oxus und bis Westafrika ausdehnt. Abu Bekr und Omar herrschen kraft ihres Charismas als durch Verdienst und Ansehen ausgezeichnete engste Gefährten des Propheten, den sie in der Leitung des Staates wie beim Gottesdienst ersetzen, ohne dass diesbezüglich für den Fall seines Ablebens von Mohammed eine Verfügung getroffen worden war. Sie nannten sich ‚Stellvertreter des Gesandten Gottes' (*chalīfat rasūl Allah*), ‚Beherrscher der Gläubigen' (*Emīr al mu'minīn*),[20] als ‚Vorbeter' der Gesamtgemeinde auch schlechtweg ‚*Imām*'. Vor ihnen hielt 'Alī, der Vetter und Eidam des Propheten, mit seinem auf die Verwandtschaft sich stützenden Herrschaftsanspruch noch zurück.

Nach 'Omar war ein ähnlich charismatisch ausgezeichneter Kandidat nicht mehr vorhanden. Das Charisma, auf welches 'Alī sich berief, fand nur geteilten Anklang, auch als er dann die Herrschaft erlangte.[21] Zunächst wurde noch durch ein vom sterbenden 'Omar eingesetztes Sechsmännerkollegium (schūra) nach mühevoller Beratung ihm 'Osmān vorgezogen: mit diesem zeight sich die Leitung der Gemeinde durch einen ‚Stellvertreter des Gesandten Gottes', bisher spontan durch einen unbezweifelbar hiezu berufenen Prophetengenossen ausgeübt, zu einer legalen Institution, zum ‚Kalifat' entwickelt, freilich auch als noch sehr auf die persönlichen, in diesem Falle fehlenden, Qualitäten ihres Trägers angewiesen und noch durchaus bar der Stützung durch die für diesen Herrschaftstypus unentbehrliche Beamtenhierarchie.[22] 'Osmān fiel in einer den Staat als solchen schlechtweg aufhebenden Revolution. Die Wiederaufrichtung der Staatsautorität geschah nicht durch 'Alī und nicht auf charismatischer, sondern auf ganz anderer Grundlage durch seine Gegner und Nachfolger, die 'Umajjaden.

Wie unter Mohammed selbst, so hat auch unter den von einer späteren Legende mit politischer Absicht zu idealen, ‚rechtgeleiteten' Kalifen (den *Rāschidūn*) verklärten vier ersten Herrschern der politische Gesichtspunkt stark den religiösen alteriert.[23] Es war kaum ein religiöses Motiv – etwa die notwendige Auswirkung eines universellen, die Theokratie notwendig zur ‚Kosmokratie', zur Universalmonarche treibenden Monotheismus –, welches nach der Einigung Arabiens zur Eroberung Syriens, Persiens, Aegyptens drängte. Vielmehr waren deren Bewohner vom Islam aus gesehen als ‚Buchbesitzer', d. h. Angehörige geoffenbarter und schriftlich fixierter Religionen - wenn auch in einer mehr oder weniger verdunkelten, der ursprünglichen Reinheit verlustigen Lehre befangen - ohnedies Diener des einen Gottes. Als solche wurden die neuen Untertanen gar nicht zum Islam geladen, ja, man erschwerte ihnen, als sie diesem später aus innerer Neigung oder wohl noch mehr um des Vorteils willen in Scharen zuströmten, den Uebertritt, sobald dem Fiskus und der privilegierten islamischen Kriegerschicht daraus eine Schmälerung der Einkünfte aus der Untertanensteur zu erwachsen drohte. Der wahre Antrieb zur Eroberung des hundert Jahre nach der medinensischen Staatsgründung bereits Transoxanien und Spanien einschliessenden islamischen Länderkomplexes wird heute mit Recht nicht in irgendeiner einheitlichen Absicht als vielmehr in der Zwangsläufigkeit gesehen, mit welcher die nun einmal vom Erfolg erhitzten und nach neuer Beute gierigen Beduinenstämme zu immer neuen Aktionen verwendet werden mussten, schon damit man sie los wurde. Den Anstoss aber, dass die Beduinen, statt sich gegenseitig in endlosen Stammesfehden zu zerfleischen, überhaupt zu einheitlicher Aktion zusammengefasst wurden, hatte eben der theokratische Staat von Medina gegeben, wie er es auch war, der hinter allen den nun folgenden, vielfach von ihm missbilligten, zumindest aber gewiss nicht von ihm initiierten Aktionen doch überall mit seinen Ansprüchen nachrückte und damit das so blindings Eroberte zur, wenn auch nur lockeren, Einheit zusammenfügte und zasammenhielt. Jedenfalls war in den anderthalb Jahrtausenden arabischer Völkerwanderung trotz mehrfacher Ansätze zur Staatenbildung keine Gründung von einiger Dauer geglückt. Wenn jetzt die Gründung eines Weltreiches möglich war, so ist dies eben einzig der ‚morgenländischen' Bewegung zuzuschreiben, die im Islam ihr Stichwort und ihren Organisator, in den arabischen Beduinen das Werkzeug ihrer Verwirklichung gefunden hat.[24] Die nächste Phase der islamischen Geschichte ist so stark vom Arabertum beherrscht, dass J. Wellhausen seiner Darstellung derselben den Titel «Das arabische Reich» geben durfte. Doch es ist das nur ein Intermezzo von nicht hundert Jahren. Durch Ausdehnung und äusseren wie inneren Krieg verbraucht, seiner Machtstellung nicht gewachsen, vielmehr in ihr verlotternd, unterhöhlt vom ihm durchaus entgegengesetzten Islam, hat das Arabertum sehr rasch dem sich aus anfangs verhältnismässig schwacher Position zur Herrschaft emporringenden Geist des Morgenlandes und dessen immer adäquater werdendem religiösen Ausdruck Platz machen müssen.[25]

Zunächst verlor Arabien bereits mit der Ermordung des Kalifen 'Osmān das Privileg, Sitz der Regierung zu sein, an das alte Kulturland. Medina hat dieser, von irakensischen und ägyptischen Kriegern verübten Tat passiv zugesehen und damit war ihre Rolle als Hauptstadt des Weltreichs – die sie auch sonst schon ihrer Lage wegen kaum auf die Dauer hätte behaupten können – ausgespielt. 'Alī residierte zu Kufa im Irak, dessen Truppen ihn zum Kalifen proklamiert hatten. Mu'āwia, der syrische Statthalter, der als Vetter und berufener Rächer des ermordeten 'Osmān 'Alī das Herrscheramt streitig machte, wählte – über die von Parteien zersetzten, launenhaften Krieger der irakensischen Lagerstädte mit seinen disziplinierteren; an das Zusammenarbeiten mit der Syrien beherrschenden politischen Macht seit Jahrhunderten gewöhnten Beduinentruppen siegreich – Damaskus zur Residenz, wo seine Familie, die Banū 'Umajja, 90 Jahre lang im Besitz des Kalifates regieren sollte (660–750).[26]

Trotz dieser frühen Abwanderung des politischen Schwerpunktes nach dem Kulturland trägt die 'Umajjadenherrschaft doch ausgesprochenen, allerdings nicht immer gleich stark betonten, sondern deutlich auf Zersetzung hinsteuernden national-arabischen Charakter. Auf arabische Anschauung stützt sich die Legitimität des Hauses: gegen den nach ihrer Behauptung an der Ermordung 'Osmāns mitschuldigen 'Alī den Kampf aufzunehmen war nach arabischer Anschauung ihre Verwandtschafts-Pflicht – er führte notwendig zur beanspruchung des Kalifates, denn anders war er kaum zu führen. Mu'āwia beanspruchte – auch hierin arabischer Anschauung folgend – die Herrschaft für sein Haus als ein diesem gebührendes Erbe nach dem 'Umajjaden 'Osmān, und da das Haus 'Umajja zu demselben Stamm, den Kuraisch, gehörte wie die Banū Hāschim, das Haus des Propheten, so war wieder arabischer Anschauung entsprochen, welche die Herrschaft vor allem als Eigentum des Stammes ansieht. Die 'Umajjaden vereben die Herrschaft – auch dies ist arabisch – in ihrem Hause durch Verfügung über die nächste, auch übernächste Nachfolge, wobei die zunächst hervortretende Tendenz zur Vererbung vom Vater auf den Sohn der altarabischen Senioratserbfolge wieder weichen muss.[27] Trotz der politischen Degradierung Arabiens empfängt der

Kalifenhof von Damaskus sein entscheidendes Gepräge doch von der nationalen Lebensform, wie sie in Mekka und Medina gerade jetzt emporgedeiht. Die 'Umajjaden haben den Zusammenhang mit ihrer Heimat nie verloren. So sicher fühlen sie sich in der Wüste, dass sie ihre prächtigen, bildergeschmückten Schlösser hier errichten, Stätten echt arabischen Jäger-, Reiter- und Sängerlebens, inmitten von Gärten, die sie mit den reichen Mitteln, die ihnen zu Gebote stehen, vor allem mit den aus der Kriegsbeute stammenden Sklavenherden durch künstliche Bewässerung dem Wüstenboden abringen. Gleich ihnen machen es die Grossen des Reichs. Schon Mohammed hatte die Gefährten seiner Auswanderung nach Medina, die dort seine Leibgarde bildeten, mit den den Juden, den bis dahin einzigen Bestellern des Bodens, abgenommenen Oasen ausgestattet. Nun ziehen sich die Ex-Statthalter nach der Aussangung der Provinzen prinzipiell nach Mekka und Medina zurück und treiben mit ihren Schätzen und Sklaven ringsum Plantagenwirtschaft, während die Städte des Propheten selbst Mittelpunkte des Vergnügens, des Luxus und verwegenen Gesanges werden.[28] Arabisch ist die sehr freie Art, mit der sich zunächst die grosse Menge dem Kalifen gegenüber verhält, der zumindest am Freitag als Vorbeter der hauptstädtischen Gemeinde fungiert: die Moschee ist Fortsetzerin der alten Stammesversammlungen, als solche auch Ort rein weltlicher Zusammenkünfte – hier diskutiert der Kalife in oft stürmischer Versammlung die öffentlichen Angelegengeiten mit dem Volke. Nicht anders steht es in den einzelnen Heerstädten zwischen den dort angesiedelten arabischen Kriegern und den ihnen «für Krieg und Gebet» vorgesetzten Statthaltern (Emīren). Ein solcher Statthalter von Kufa lässt wohlweislich den Kiesboden der Moschee durch Steinpflaster ersetzen, weil die Kufenser sogar beim Gottesdienst den unliebsamen Vorgesetzten mit Steinen zu bewerfen pflegten. Die natürliche Beredsamkeit des Arabers kam in den Moscheenversammlungen zu voller Wirkung. Vor allem aber beruht die Herrschaft der 'Umajjaden auf der klugen Verwendung der Beduinenstämme, die sie durch Verschwägerung, Geld oder Gunstbezeugungen an sich fesseln und denen sie in regelmässigen Sommerfeldzügen gegen Ostrom immer wiederkehrende Gelegenheit zu neuer Beute bieten. Freilich hat ebendieses Stammeswesen, das auch die Heerstädte durchsetzte und «durch eine Art Integrierung» zur Bildung eines unüberbrückbaren, alle politischen und sonstigen Streitfragen mitvertretenden Gegensatzes zwischen zwei grossen Sammelgruppen führte, zum Untergang des ʿUmajjadenreiches entscheidend beigetragen.

Die hier beigebrachten züge charakterisierten das Kalifat von Damaskus als eine traditionale Herrschaft, die sich als Königtum (*mulk*) fühlt und gibt. Die Emire der Provinzen sind zur Zeit Muʿāwias eher dessen ‚Bundesgenoseen' als Beamte. Den Beistand ʿAmrs, des Eroberers von Aegypten erwarb sich Muʿāwia, indem er ihm diese Landschaft mitsamt deren Steuerertrag überliess.[29] In der Chronik des Theophanes (Weltjahr 6169. 6171 = 661. 663 D) erscheint dieser Kalife als *πρωτοσύμβουλος* unter den *σύμβουλοι*, den Grossen seines Hofes, die eine Art von bisweilen tumultuösem Parlament bilden. Diese Mischform von ‚primärem Patriarchalismus' und ‚Gerontokratie' – neben dem durch sein Erbrecht legitimierten Herrscher stehen die ‚Aeltesten', ihnen gegenüber die übrigen Muslims als ‚Genossen' mit traditionaler Bindung; ein persönlicher Verwaltungsstab fehlt noch fast gänzlich – muss sich modifizieren: die ‚Genossen' werden zu allerdings den Ungläubigen gegenüber privilegierten ‚Untertanen', die Emire werden geflissentlich nicht mehr aus der alten, sich dem Herrscherhaus gleichberechtigt fühlenden Aristokratie, sondern aus zuverlässigen Klienten des Hauses und aus Emporkömmlingen gewählt. Mit der Autorität seiner Person hatte der Kalife ʿOmar I. die grossen Eroberungen seiner Regierungszeit für den Staat gerettet, indem durch ihn «das arabische Beuterecht zur Seite geschoben wurde und der Staat zwischen Heer und Unterworfene trat», das eroberte Land als sein Eigentum (d. h. das der Gesamtgemeinde) ansprechend, aus welchem den Kriegern lediglich eine jährliche Ertragsrente auszuzahlen war. Jetzt beginnt sich, anknüpfend an die vorgefundenen, erst in der zweiten Generation – und auch da nur der Sprache nach und nicht hinsichtlich der Sache und des Personals – arabisierten Institutionen der Byzantiner und Perser eine Verwaltung auszubilden, die keineswegs nur auf die von den Provinzen einfliessenden Zahlungen angewiesen war, sondern durch den Ertrag der staatlichen Plantagenwirtschaft von sich aus der Regierung die Mittel bot, die in den Heerstädten immer mehr verlotternden Krieger durch ergebene Beduinenstämme und Söldnertruppen zu ersetzen. Freilich: erstere waren auch ein reichlich unsicheres, entscheidend von der Gesamtkonstellation der Stammesfehden bestimmtes Element, welches der Dynastie gegenüber selbstbewusst und selbständig sich hielt.[30] Um so grösser die Rolle der Söldnertruppen, mit denen die ganzen inneren Kämpfe der letzten ʿUmajjadenzeit ausgefochten werden.

Mit ihrer Hilfe, zuweilen auf eine fremdländische Sklavenleibwache gestützt, brachten rücksichtslos energische Statthalter die unruhigsten Heerstädte zum Schweigen. Wenn ein Mann wie Hadjdjādj die Kanzel bestieg, in stürmische Versammlung seine Drohungen zu donnern, da erstarb der spöttische Zwischenruf auf den Lippen und sank der Arm herab, der schon bereit gewesen war, den Kiesel auf den Redner herabregnen zu lassen. Die Tribüne, von der herab einst heissatmige politische Rede die Massen entzündet hatte, wird zur Kanzel: schweigend hat das Volk die im schweren, langgezogenen Ton der medinensischen Suren hergesagten Enunziationen der Regierung hinzunehman.[31]

Auch äusserlich tritt der Kalife jetzt anders auf: in seiner Titulatur wird er vom ‚Stellvertreter des Gesandten Gottes' zum ‚Stellvertreter Gottes'.[32] Den in stolzen Palästen Residierenden hebt die Pracht der Lebensführung hoch über die Menge der Untertanen, die ein reicher Hofstaat und eine zu hierarchischer Abstufung neigende Verwaltung von dem Herrscher sondert. Dieser liebt es mit seiner Majestät zu prunken. Er verbietet, in seiner Gegenwart viel zu reden oder ihm zu widersprechen.[33] Bei Audienzen thront er nach Chosroenart mit untergeschlagenen Beinen auf erhöhtem Polstersitz. Haremswesen und dessen unerlässliche Patrone die Verschnittenen – letztere von Byzanz herübergenommen[34] – stellen auch an diesem morgenländischen Hofe bald sich ein. Fröhlicher, des koranischen Verbotes offen spottender Weingenuss vereinigt mit dem Herrscher begünstigte ‚Zechgenossen' (nudamā).

Aber diese typisch traditionale Herrschaft enthält doch auch ein, zuweilen von den Herrschern missachtetes, aber nie preisgegebenes legales Moment, welches auf der Verbindung des Herrscheramtes mit der Religion beruht. Wie weltlich das Regime nach Ursprung und Gestion immer war, seine Träger heissen doch Stellvertreter des Propheten oder Allahs, Beherrscher der Gläubigen, daneben auch Imame, und regierten auf dieser Grundlage. Sie hatten religiöse Funktionen zu verrichten, setzten ihre Statthalter «für Krieg und Gebet» ein – äusserlich wie auch in ihrem und ihrer Untertanen Bewusstsein nahm die Religion die bestimmende Stelle ein: sie nennen sich auf Inschriften vorzugsweise «Knecht Gottes». Keiner dieser ‚Könige' hat an eine Erbteilbarkeit seines ‚Eigentumes' (*mulk*) gedacht und von einem ihrer Reihe, von ʿOmar II darf man sagen, dass er auf die legale Herrschaftsform als auf sein Ideal hingearbeitet hat – «es war nicht *Mulk*, was seine Herrschaft darstellen wollte».[35]

Dieser Kalife war – im Gegensatz zu den anderen Prinzen des Hauses – in dem Kreise der medinensischen Frommen aufgewachsen, die abseits von dem Damaszener Regime und in deutlicher Oppositionsstellung dazu die *Sunna* des Propheten[36] und vor allem das legendär erhöhte Ideal der Zeit der *Rāschidūn* hgeten und pflegten. Das ‚weltliche' Gebaren der 'Umajjaden – dieses dem Propheten am erbittersten widerstrebenden, erst durch Gewalt bekehrten Hauses – mit seinem Anknüpfen an die heidnischen Traditionen des Arabismus und seiner Anpassung and die Erfordernisse und Verlockungen des Kulturlandes gab den treuen Nachfolgern des Gesetzes und der Lebensweise des alten Islams sicherlich tiefes und ständiges Aergernis. Hinzu kam, dass die alte Aristokratie des Islams – die Prophetengenossen und deren Söhne – sich um ihren Anteil an der Herrschaft betrogen und in Mekka und Medina abseits und übergangen fühlten. Mochte man den Mu'āwia hingenommen haben, ein erbliches 'Umajjadenkalifat ertrug man nicht ohne bewaffneten Widerstand. Zwölf Jahre lang (680–692) behauptete sich Ibn Zubair gegen die Damaszener als Kalife in Mekka, das er, den geistlichen Charakter seiner Stellung betonend, trotz seiner Anerkennung im Irak nicht verleiss. Nach dem Zusammenbruch dieses Gegenkalifates haben sich die Frommen mit der Sachlage abgefunden, um jetzt durch vorwiegend geheime Wühlarbeit den Staat nur noch mehr zu unterhöhlen, aus ihrem sichern Schmollwinkel heraus die von überall zusammenströmenden Muslims, deren religiöse Erregung an den heiligen Stätten nutzend, wirksam zu bearbeiten. Empfänglich für diese Hetze war und blieb vor allem der Irak mit den von ihm aus eroberten und mit Militärkolonien besiedelten iranischen Provinzen: der Osten konnte es nicht verschmerzen, dass er mit 'Alīs Untergang die Teilnahme an der Herrschaft verloren hatte – schon, dass die Bezüge seiner Krieger hinter denen der syrischen zurückstanden, zeigte ihm deutlich, wie er zur Provinz herabgesunken war, weshalb hier auch immer wieder von der Schī'a (*schī'at 'Alī* ‚Partei des 'Alī') propagierte alidische Prätendenten Gefolgschaft fanden. Auch blühte unter dem Einfluss persischer Elemente hier – man denke an die Schulen von Basra und Kufa – ein reiches religiöses Leben empor, einig mit dem Hidjāz in der Opposition gegen die ‚weltliche' 'Umajjadenherrschaft. Hinzu kamen die Forderungen der Neubekehrten vor allem persischer Nationalität, sie mit den arabischen Eroberern gleichzustellen, sie also von den Lasten, die sie als Unterworfene zu leisten hatten, zu befreien und ihre Teilnahme am Kriegsdienst durch Einbeziehung in die Jahrespensionen zu entlohnen – Forderungen, die dem Staatshaushalt schwere Verlegenheiten zu bereiten drohten, von den nur nach religiösen Gesichtspunkten urteilenden Frommen jedoch gebilligt werden.

Die Sammlung all dieser oppositionellen Elemente in dem Lager der Rechtgläubigkeit war eine um so dringendere Gefahr, je mehr das Arabertum für die Dynastie an Bedeutung verlor. Die Halbinsel selbst hatte sich aus dem Zusammenhang mit dem Gesamtreich schon sehr früh gelöst – hier herrschten unter eigenen Anführern seit den Tagen ʿAlīs die von der übrigen Gemeinde deutlich geschiedenen Charidjiten, nicht selten nur in blutigen Kämpfen vom Kulturland ferngehalten.[37] Die Stämme des Kulturlandes, teils in Zusammenhang mit diesem ein halbnomadisches Dasein führend, teils angesiedelt in den Heerstädten, waren in ihrem politischen Verhalten keineswegs mehr ausschliesslich vom Kalifen bestimmt, nahmen vielmehr in den Auseinandersetzungen zwischen Damaskus und den einzelnen aufrührerischen Provinzen oder Statthaltern oder Parteien wechselnde, von autonomen Interessen, hauptsächlich aber von der Entscheidung ihres Stammverbandes diktierte Stellung.

Unter diesen Umständen musste eine ihres religiösen Fundamentes nie ganz vergessene Herrschaft es sich doppelt angelegen sein lassen, ihren Gegnern im Namen der Religion entgegenzutreten. Die Möglichkeit dazu bot die Gefolgschaft, die ein Teil der Frommen selbst leistete, hiefür vom Herrscher und dessen Statthaltern mit Richter- oder Vorbeterämtern oder durch Heranziehung an den Hof belohnt. Den in unbeugsamer Opposition Verharrenden war solch ein öffentliches Amt ein Greuel – wirklich war seine Annahme nur bei grosser Willfährigkeit gegenüber den Wünschen der Regierung möglich. So wird uns von einem dieser regierungstreuen Frommen berichtet, dass er ein Heft angeblicher Prophetenaussprüche ohne weiteres mit seinem Namen autorisierte, als es ihm von einem ʿUmajjadenprinzen zu diesem Zwecke überreicht wurde. Mit solchen Traditionen nämlich suchte die Regierung ihre Massnahmen und Einrichtungen gegenüber dem, was die Opposition als *Sunna* propagierte, zu rechtfertigen.[38] Der Kampf mit den Verfectern eines legalen Kalifates zwang sie, auch ihrerseits die legalen Grundlagen ihrer Herrschaft zu betonen und auf religiöse Motivierung ihres Tuns und Lassens Gewicht zu legen. «Der Islam machte Fortschritte in der herrschenden Familie.» «Muʿāwia, ʿAbdalmalik, Walid, Sulaiman stellen insofern eine aufsteigende Reihe dar – Omar II. steht an der Spitze».[39] Letzterer, dem Religion durchaus kein Mittel zur Herrschaft, sondern allen Ernstes die bestimmende Macht bedeutete, blieb nun freilich eine Ausnahme in seinem Hause. Aber, dass er in diesem Hause bis zur höchsten Würde aufsteigen konnte, zeigt doch immerhin, wohin die Entwicklung strebte und andererseits hat seine drei Jahre währende Regierung einen so starken Eindruck hinterlassen, dass durch sie das Kalifat oder doch wenigstens die Vorstellung davon bestimmende Züge erhielt. Die 'Umajjaden haben nicht nur auf die Gesetzesentwicklung, sondern auch auf Ritus und Dogma modifizierend eingewirkt. So haben sie gegen die Verfechter der menschlichen Willensfreiheit energisch Stellung genommen und als Rechtgläubigkeit propagiert, alle bestehenden Glaubenssätze auch mit ihren Widersprüchen hinzunehmen und an die Vorherbestimmung des Schicksals zu glauben – solche Gessinnung liess am ehesten erwarten, dass man sich auch mit der nun einmal die Macht besitzenden Dynastie abfinden, diese sogar als ‚gottgewollt' bejahen und unterstützen würde.

Erschien die 'Umajjadenherrschaft einmal als legales Kalifat, dann konnte ihr ein charismatisches Moment, das solche heilige Würde notwendig ihrem Träger verleihen muss, nicht lange vorenthalten bleiben.[40] Die Wandlung in Titulatur und Auftreten (s. o.) bringt es deutlich zum Ausdruck. Den Herrschern selbst war diese Verbrämung ihrer Machtstellung mit legalen und charismatischen Zügen – soweit sie ihnen überhaupt bewusst geworden sein mögen – kaum mehr als Mittel für ihre weltlichen Zwecke. So wie sie wenig davon innerlich ergriffen waren, taten sie auch alles, um durch offene Zucht- und Sittenlosigkeit den in Ausbildung begriffenen schützenden Nimbus zu zerstören. Als ihnen die Leitung der überdies durch gegenseitige Kämpfe aufgeriebenen, in den Städten rasch verlotterten arabischen Stämme entglitt und die ökonomische, soziale, nationale Unzufriedenheit der Neubekehrten in religiös-politischen Bewegungen ihre Organisationsform fand, besassen sie kein Machtmittel mehr, sich auf dem Thron zu halten. Ein blutiger Zwist im Herrscherhause selbst bahnte den so gesammelten feindlichen Kräften den Weg zum Sieg.

Als Mandatare der Frommen, mit der seit den Tagen 'Alīs im Irak und in Iran nicht mehr verstummten Losung ‚Das Kalifat dem Hause des Propheten', die Missgunst des Ostens gegen Syrien, den Hass der neubekehrten Perser gegen die national-arabische Herrschaft nutzend, hatten die Abbasiden die 'Umajjaden besiegt und sich an ihre Stelle gesetzt (750). Ein Zweig der vielgespaltenen *Schī'at 'Alī* – sie gehörten, wie die Aliden als Banū Hāschim dem Hause des Propheten an, diesem zwar entfernter verwandt als jene, dafür auf eine Erbrechtsübertragung seitens eines Aliden pochend – rissen sie durch ihre Emissäre mit der klugerweise weit genug gewählten Losung die Ostprovinzen mit sich und proklamierten, glücklicher als all die vielen erfolglos untergegangenen alidischen Prätendenten, ihren ‚Gottesstaat', von Anfang an den legalen, geistlichen Charakter ihres Amtes und das persönliche Charisma von dessen Träger betonend. Sie geben vor, «auf den Trümmern einer von den Frommen als gottlos verschrieenen Regierung ein der Sunna des Propheten, den Anforderungen der göttlichen Religion entsprechendes Regiment zu begründen».[41] Prinzipiell wird in ihrem Staate alles und jedes nach Koran und Sunna entschieden. Der dadurch benötigte Apparat von theologisch-juristisch gebildeten Beamten rekrutiert sich aus den 'Ulemā, die damit beginnen, sich auf die Verwendung im Staatsdienst einzurichten[42] und zu einem ausgesprochenen Stand zu werden – sehr in Gegensatz zu ihrer bisherigen gänzlich unabhängigen, ökonomisch von andersartiger Berufstätigkeit oder von Vermögensbesitz ermöglichten Stellung. Auch in dogmatischen Streitigkeiten zu entscheiden, dünkt diesen Kalifen ihre Sache zu sein. Während bisher die Lehrmeinungen – sofern sie nicht zu akuter politischer Abspaltung führten – nebeneinander gestanden hatten, kommt nun eine harte Unduldsamkeit auf, die den Gegner verketzert, überall aufspürt und mit Machtmitteln verfolgt. Das hatte die ethisch-rationale Richtung der *Mu'tazila* in den Islam gebracht, dem solche Intoleranz schon wegen seiner wenig gefestigten, die grössten Widersprüche beherbergenden Form an sich fremd sein musste. Im Gefolge einer auf ein streng rationales System hinzielenden Bewegung dagegen, die mit so viel Widersprüchen aufräumen musste, ist intolerante Härte durchaus verständlich. Doch so wie die alte Rechtgläubigkeit sich mit Asch'arī die Denkmethoden des mu'tazilitischen Gegners dienstbar gemacht hat, übernahm sie von diesem auch die Unduldsamkeit und als vornehmstes Kampfmittel die Ketzerverfolgungen. In dem vorübergehenden Bündnis – es war ein unnatürliches – von Mu'tazila und Kalifat war die ganze weltliche Macht im Dienste der mu'tazilitischen Intoleranz gestanden. Als das Kalifat zur orthodoxen Lehre den Rückweg gefunden hatte (847, 20 Jahre, nachdem das Dogma vom Erschaffensein des Korans als Staatsgesetz verkündet worden war) – die reinere Gottesvorstellung und

Ethik der Muʿtazila stand in tiefem, bald fühlbarem Gegensatz zur Despotie – lieh es seinen Arm in gleicher Weise dem früheren Gegner, der sich in diesem kampfe den Hang nach einem festen – wenn auch keineswegs rationalen – System und einen bis dahin unbekannten Fanatismus, mit dem er sich verteidigte und durchsetzte, angeeignet hat.

Den geistlichen Charakter ihrer Stellung betonend, nennen sich die abbasidischen Kalifen vorzugsweise ‚Imāme' ‚Vorbeter der Gemeinde'. Als ‚Herren der zwei Schwerter' haben sie «die Grenzen des Reichs zu schützen und zu verteidigen, anderseits den Glauben in seiner dogmatischen Form zu sichern und Unglauben und Häresie zu bestrafen».[43] Der Titel ‚Kalife' wird jetzt durchgängig als ‚Kalife Allahs' verwendet, daneben kommt die Bezeichnung ‚Schatten Gottes auf Erden' auf, eine Wiederbelebung der alten morgenländischen Vorstellung von dem Herrscher als dem lebenden ‚Bild Gottes' (Schatten = Schattenbild).[44] Als Inkarnation der Gottheit wurde von einer Gruppe seiner Anhänger schon der zweite Abbaside – gegen seinen Willen – verehrt; die späteren haben solche Verehrung als übermenschliche Wesen nicht nur hingenommen, sondern verlangt.

Es ist der altorientalische Herrschergott, der hier wiederersteht, als solcher das Ebenbild des morgenländischen, nach dem Bilde des weltlichen Herrschers konzipierten Weltengottes, wie er in der gegen alle Rationalisierungsversuche erfolgreich verteigdigten Orthodoxie weiterlebt. Wie Allah in schrankenloser Willkür über die Welt, so waltet der Kalife in seinem Reich. Was Koran III 25 von Gott gesagt ist: «Du erhebst wen Du willst und Du erniedrigst wen Du willst. In Deiner Hand ist das Gute. Siehe, Du hast Macht über jedes Ding», gilt auch von ihm. Wie der Gläubige als ‚Knecht Allahs' sich im Gebete vor dem ‚Herren der Welten' niederwirft und mit der Stirn den Boden berührt, so prosterniert er sich auch vor dessen ‚Stellvertreter'. Dieser liebt es, seine durch ihre Willkür der Allahs durchaus wesensgleiche Macht durch Unerwartetes manifest zu machen: märchenhafte Gunstbezeugungen lassen den davon ganz unvorbereitet Betroffenen vor Staunen erstarren; aber neben dem Thron steht auch der kenker und liegt ein Leder ausgebreitet, auf dem ein ebenso Ahnungsloser, der sich eben noch im Vollbesitz der Gnade gedünkt, im Angesicht des Herrschers enthaptet wird. Und der geheimnisvolle, von der Orthodoxie verteidigte Widerspruch, dass Allah trotz der Existenz des unerschaffenen Korans in absoluter Willkür herrscht, findet auf Erden eine einfache Lösung: zwar geschieht hier alles im Namen des heiligen Gesetzes, aber es sind die Theologen-Juristen zur Hand, die jedem Wunsch des Herrschers die formale Rechtfertigung erklügeln, so dass dieser faktisch in unbeschränkter Willkür herrscht. Z. B. werden, um den Luxus des Kalifenhofes zu rechtfertigen, jetzt Traditionen von dem Luxus, der angeblich im Kreise des Propheten geherrscht hat, in Umlauf gesetzt – nicht weniger frei erfunden wie die früher gegen die ʿUmajjaden geschmiedeten Hadīse der medinensischen Frommen, die nicht genug die Schlichtheit jenes goldenen Zeitalters hatten dartun können.

Den ihrer Herrschaft gemässen Formenschatz schöpfen die Abbasidenkalifen vornehmlich aus den Traditionen des mit ihnen hochgekommenen Persertums. Ein Jahrhundert nach der Vernichtung der Sassaniden (651), genährt von der nie erloschenen Gemeinschaft des Feuerkultes und von den zahlreichen, der Wiederherstellung der nationalen Freiheit geltenden oder doch in irgendeinem Gewande nationale Aspirationen mitvertretenden Aufsänden, hat dieses Persertum die dünne arabische Erobererschichte im ganzen östlichen Bereiche assimiliert (sinnbildlich dafür: die iranische Hose verdrängt den arabischen Burnus) und steigt nun in dem ihm näher gerückten neuen Zentrum des Islams zur höchsten Bedeutung empor. Der Sassanidenstaat war die Festung ungebrochenen morgenländischen Daseins gewesen, in der sich dieses gegen die hellenistisch-römische Vermählung von Ost und West erfolgreich gewehrt hatte; indem er nun einen seinem Sinne nach ‚morgenländischen' Staat aus seinen Traditionen speist, wird auch genetisch ein strukturell bereits bestehender Zusammenhang mit dem Alten Orient geschaffen und eine notwendige, bereits im Zuge begriffene Entwicklung rasch zur letzten Reife geführt. Die Anknüpfung geschah nicht unbewusst: ein Prinz des Hauses kann den regierenden Kalifen mit «dem Perser Ardeschir» vergleichen, «als dieser das erschütterte Reich erneuerte».[45] Das persische Regierungsideal der Verschwisterung von Religion und Staat, dieses «sichtbare Programm der sassanidischen Herrschaft», ist mit dem der Abbasidenkalifen identisch: Religion nicht bloss Staatsinterresse, sondern zentrale politische Angelegenheit. Auch die religiöse Unduldsamkeit hat ihre sassanidischen Vorbilder.[46]

Zwischen den in prunkvollstes Zeremoniell gehüllten Herrschergott und die Untertanen schiebt sich der mit grösster Vollmacht ausgestattete Wezir, welcher der ʿUmajjadenzeit gefehlt hatte,[47] aber durchaus zur Vorstellung von einem morgenländischen Staat gehört – so ist im Koran Aron der Wezir des Moses;

Salomon, der Prototyp morgenländischen Herrschertums für die islamische Welt, hat ebenfalls einen Wezir, den berühmten Asāf – und auch im Sassanidenstaat nicht gefehlt hat.[48] Der Wezir steht zu seinem Herrscher so wie der Prophet zu Gott – beide fordern Gehorsam nicht aus eigener Gewalt, sondern kraft ihrer Erwählung durch Gott, bzw. den Kalifen, der denen, welche zum Gehorsam gerufen werden, wesensfremd und unerreichbar ist.[49] Dem Wezir zur Seite steht eine streng abgestufte Hierarchie von Beamten und Offizieren (die beiden Laufbahnen ‚Schwert' und ‚Feder' sind genau geschieden). Dabei werden die Würdenträger vorzugsweise aus begabten, dann skrupellos nach oben drängenden Söhnen der unteren Schichten genommen (nicht selten aus christlichen oder zoroastrischen Kreisen). Vornehmheit der Abstammung und irgendein auf persönliche Beziehungen gegründeter Rückhalt machen nur suspekt. Die ʿUmajjaden waren schon im Kampf um das Kalifat ausgerottet worden – die um die Herrschaft betrogenen alidischen Vettern hatten in der Folge ungezählte Mordtaten zu erdulden. Auch auf Vornehmheit der Abstammung mütterlicherseits wird kein Wert mehr gelegt: die ehedem durch Verschwägerung zu gewinnenden Stämme hatten ausgespielt. In dem verfeinerten Dasein hatten raffiniert erzogene persische, türkische, griechische oder slawische Sklavinnen den stolzen Töchtern des arabischen Adeis den Rang abgelaufen, sich auch leichter in die Erniedrigung des Harems fügend. Bis auf drei hatten sämtliche Abbasidenkalifen Unfreie zu Müttern. Das Prinzip der Trennung des Herrschers von seinen Untertanen wurde so nirgends sichtbar durch verwandtschaftliche Beziehungen durchbrochen.

Die kriegerischen Machtmittel, die das Kalifat nach aussen und innen benötigte, waren nicht mehr aus dem Lande selbst zu gweinnen. Man trug nur der gänzlich veränderten Sachlage Rechnung, wenn man den jetzt nur mehr fälschlich so genannten ‚Kriegern' der ‚Heerstädte' die Jahrespensionen strich.[50] Die Völkerkammer Arabien selbst war wieder ganz in den alten Gegensatz zum von periodischen Beduineneinfällen heimgesuchten Kulturland zurückgesunken,[51] so dass zum notdürftigen Schutz der Pilgerfahrt eigene Wachposten und Festungen unterhalten werden mussten.[52] Das militärische Schwergewicht lag alsbald bei den vorzugsweise aus türkischen Sklaven gebildeten, von türkischen Führern befehligten Söldnern – eine schwere Plage für das Land, mit dem sie nichts verband, und – falls die Kunst, die einzelnen Regimenter gegenseitg in Schach zu halten, versagte oder das Geld für den Sold versiegte – eine ernste Gefahr für die Herrschaft.

Als deren Sitz wird nach kurzem Schwanken und Tasten an schicksalsvoller Stätte – unweit der einstigen Welthauptstadt Babylon und der Sassanidenresidenz Ktesiphon – Bagdad gegründet (762). Der Irak war den Abbasiden, die ja an alidische Traditionen anknüpften, als Sitz der Herrschaft vorherbestimmt. Aber nicht das zu Unruhen geneigte Kufa, wo die neue Dynastie die erste allgemeine Huldigung entgegengenommen hatte, entsprach ihren Bedürfnissen. Besser emphfahl sich eine Neugründung im Lande zwischen den Strömen, entrückter der fremd und feindlich gewordenen Wüste und näher dem persischen Osten, aus dem die Dynastie zur Macht gekommen war; hier brauchte man auch night mit eingewurzelten alten Bräuchen zu rechnen oder erst zu brechen. Schliesslich ward an dem gegebenen Mittelpunkt des dem Lande zu glänzendem Ernteertrag verhelfenden Kanalsystemes Bagdad gegründet.[53] Die Abbasiden lassen sich die wirtschaftliche Hebung des Landes, das bisher als Provinz zurückgestanden hatte, auf das grosszügigste angelegen sein. Bald ist es durch die wiederhergestellten alten und durch neue Bewässerungsanlagen, über welche eine ausgebreitete Verwaltung wacht, weider zu einer Blüte gediehen, die mit dem in früheren Glanzzeiten Erreichten gewiss sich messen kann und die ökonomische Grundlage der Abbasidenherrschaft bedeutet.[54] Der Kalife ist damit zum Herrschergott des Fruchtlandes geworden, der, indem er die Ernte schafft, unsichtbar waltend seinen Untertanen die Existenz verbürgt. Es ist auffällig, dass das alidische Gegenkalifat der Fatimiden, das noch im 9. Jahrh. in Afrika emporkam, schliesslich in dem anderen der beiden alten Fruchtländer, in Aegypten seinen Sitz nahm, in allem ein sehr getreues, das Vorbild vielfach noch überbietendes Gegenstück des Bagdader Rivalen. Damit steht wider dem ‚König von Babylon' der ‚Pharao des Niltals' gegenüber – es ist unzweifelhaft der Höhepunkt dieser letzten Phase morgenländischen Daseins was Verwaltung, Sicherheit, Handel, Wirtschaft und Wissenschaft betrifft – keineswegs freilich hinsichtlich der rasch herabgeminderten äusseren Macht.

So wie die Weltreiche des alten Orients war auch das der Kalifen bald (um 935 ist der prozess beendigt) in die uralten geographischen Einheiten wieder auseinandergebrochen. Die ‚Diadochenstaaten' – der Vergleich stammt von den arabischen Historikern – anerkannten nicht einmal alle die theoretische Oberhoheit des Kalifen: seit 909 nannten sich die hernach in Aegypten residierenden Fatimiden (angebliche Nachkommen

ʿAlīs aus der Prophetentochter Fātima) ‚Fürsten der Gläubigen', also ‚Kalifen', ein Beispiel, das die in Spanien noch regierenden ʿUmajjaden veranlasste, ihren bisherigen Titel ‚Kalifen söhne' mit dem des Kalifen zu vertauschen (961), den sich sogar ein magrebinischer Duodezfürst ein paar Jahre vorher zugelegt hatte.[55] Die Emire in Nordsyrien, Mesopotamien und in den persischen Ostprovinzen sind so gut wie unabhängig, wenn sie auch ihr Bestallungsdiplom und ihre klingenden Titel[56] vom Kalifen beziehen, den sie ihrerseits im Freitagsgebet (*chutba*) und auf der Münze nennen. Aber auch in seinem ureigensten Herrschaftsgebiet, im Fruchtland von Bagdad, wird der Kalife ohnmächtig. Etwa seit 833 waren die türkischen Leibgarden die Träger der militärischen Gewalt.[57] Ein Jahrhundert später endet der Kalife Al-Kāhir Billāh, «der Mächtige durch Gott», als geblendeter Bettler an der Pforte einer Moschee – nur eines der Opfer dieser Türken. Deren Generäle erhalten mit dem Amt des ‚*Emīr al-Umerā*' (des ‚Oberemirs') eine systemisierte Machtstellung, die schliesslich auch die Funktionen des Wezirs an sich zieht. Damit ist die ganze Verwaltung in die Hand des mächtigsten Gardekommandanten übergegangen und der Kalife zu einem Schattendasein verurteilt. Dieser Zustand ist mit Ar-Rādi (934–940) erreicht, welcher «der letzte Kalife ist, von dem Gedichte gesammelt sind, der letzte, der allein geherrscht hat, der das Freitagsgebet öffentlich auf der Kanzel gesprochen hat, der mit seinen Zechgenossen zusammensass, zu dem die Gelehrten Zutritt gehabt, unter dem Rangverleihungen, Gunstbeweise und Dienststellen nach den Regeln der früheren Kalifen geordnet waren».[58] Auch die ökonomische Grundlage des Kalifates war aufgehoben. Die Ländereien der Domäne, aber auch Privatbesitz, ebenso die Einkünfte aus dem Untertanenland mussten den Offizieren, Beamten und Söldnern zu Lehen gegeben werden. Das Fruchtland hörte auf, für den Staat zu steuern, und war der staatlichen Ueberwachung entzogen. Die Dämme und Kanäle, die dem Land erst seine Fruchtbarkeit gaben, gingen so zugrunde. Die Bauern fielen dem Elend anheim und verliessen teilweise das Land. Die systematische Bodenbestellung hörte überhaupt auf, die Organisation derselben war aufgelassen, das technische Personal verlief sich, die notwendigen Kenntnisse gerieten in Vergessenheit.[59] Das gilt gewiss auch schon für die Zeit vor 945, dem Jahre, mit dem ein arabisch. Autor dies alles in Verbindung bringt, in welchem nämlich – unter Ar-Rādis zweitem Nachfolger – Bagdad in die Hand des (seit etwa 935) in West- und

Mittelpersien mächtigen Geschlechtes Būje gelangt, das – entschieden der Schī'a geneigt – wenig prädestiniert war, des nunmehr ihm zufallenden Amtes eines *Emīr al-Umerā'* besonders rücksichtsvoll zu walten.

Die Schī'a war die hartnäckigste Opposition der 'Umajjaden gewesen, unermüdlich, ungeachtet aller Misserfolge, den Usurpatoren immer wieder neue alidische Kandidaten entgegenstellend, die sie – den Gegensatz zu jenen unterstreichend – ‚*Imām al-mahdī*' ‚rechtgeleiter Imām' nennt.[60] Die Schī'a ist es gewesen, welche die Abbasiden auf den Thron geführt hat, deren dritter Herrscher sich *al-Mahdī* als Thronnamen wählt. Man ersieht schon daraus, dass die Schī'a als solche noch keineswegs eine abgespaltene Sekte, sondern lediglich eine innerhalb des Islams besondere politische Ziele verfolgende Richtung war, die den Gesamtislam sehr nachhaltig beeinflussen konnte. Sowie die 'Alīden sich durch das Haus Abbas betrogen sehen, sowie ihre von der Furcht diktierte Verfolgung durch die glücklicheren Vettern beginnt, anderseits die Abbasiden-Kalifen zusehends verweltlichen, stellt diesen die Opposition der Schī'a ihre eigenen alidischen ‚Imāme' gegenüber als die wahren, rechtgeleiteten Herrscher, umbekümmert um äusseren Erfolg und um Anerkennung. Den durch ihre Heiligkeit und Lehrautorität zum Herrscheramt Berufenen wird dieses Charisma durch ihre Stellung im Hause 'Alī verbürgt. Dem 'Alī hatte der Prophet, so heisst es, geheime, allen anderen Genossen vorenthalten Offenbarungen anvertraut und diese gehen nun, als ein sorgsam weitergegebener Schatz, von einem Oberhaupt der Familie auf das andere über. Ja noch mehr: Die göttliche Lichtsubstanz, die einst in Adam gelegt worden war, geht in ununterbrochener Folge durch die Propheten in die Familie des 'Alī und wird inner halb dieser von Oberhaupt zu Oberhaupt, d. i. von Imām zu Imām weitergegeben. Daraus folgt für diese in den gemässigten Richtungen Sündlosigkeit und Unfehlbarkeit, in den extremsten werden sie zur Inkarnation der Gottheit – sehr in Gegensatz zu ihrer irdischen Machtlosigkeit. Es ist nur ein folgerichtiger Schritt, wenn die Imām-Reihe schliesslich zu einem Abschluss gelangt, indem man sich einen von ihnen als an einen unsichtbaren Ort entrückt vorstellt, wo er – ein anderer Kaiser Karl im Untersberg – seine Zeit abwartet, da er als Mahdī erscheinen und der trostlosen Ungerechtigkeit ein Ende bereiten wird, kanpp vor dem Jüngsten Tage noch ein Gottesreich begründend. Ein klarerer Verzicht auf irdische Wirksamkeit kann nicht mehr geleistet werden. Die Schī'a wird damit zu einer rein religiösen, politisch indifferenten Partei, die nunmehr freillich als (wenigstens mit ihren extremeren Richtungen) offenkundige Sekte, die alle heterodoxen Anschauungen in sich einsog, vollen Grund hatte, in den sich als Schutzmacht der Orthodoxie mit Ketzerverfolgungen eifrig betätigenden Abbasiden ihre sehr zu fürchtenden Gegner zu sehen. Muʿtazila und Mystik besassen in der Schīʿa eine Zufluchtsstätte wie sie ihnen die erstarrende, erkaltende Orthodoxie nicht bieten konnte. Die Weltabgewandtheit der Mystik findet in der Schīʿa ihren Ausdruck in der Lehre vom verborgenen Imām Mahdī.[61]

Im Zeichen der Schīʿa war das fatimidische Gegenkalifat errichtet worden, im Zeichen der Schīʿa wurde die ‚Entweltlichung' der Bagdader Kalifen zu Ende geführt. Die Bujiden, die 945 Bagdad in Besitz nehmen, kommen aus einer nur schwer für den Islam und nur für dessen oppositionelle schīʿitische Form gewonnenen persischen Landschaft, in der die Schīʿa hundert Jahre lang unter eigenen alidischen Herrschern offizielle Geltung besessen hatte. Nunmehr wird die Schīʿa sogar in der Residenz des Hauptes der Rechtgläubigkeit geschützt und gefördert: an den Türen der Bagdader Moscheen wird die Fluchformel gegen die drei ersten, den Orthodoxen hochheiligen, den Schīʿiten als usurpatoren fluchwürdigen Kalifen geschrieben. Der Kalife kann dem nicht wehren – er ist nicht weniger ohnmächtig als der verborgene Imām. Einige Wochen nach dem Einzug der Bujiden war der offenbar doch nicht ganz gefügige Kalife einfach vom Thron gezerrt und geblendet worden. Aber das Abbasiden-kalifat als solches blieb doch unangetastet bestehen. Die – im Islam gewiss nicht zu begründende – Ausstattung des Herrschers mit persönlichem, erblichem Charisma (eine Vorstellung, die ja gerade in schīʿitischen Kreisen gepflegt wurde) kam ihnen zugute: das Kalifat beginnt sich als rein ‚geistliche' Institution einzuleben und betont auch diesen seinen Charakter mehr als vorher. Die einzelnen Kalifen regieren jetzt ungewöhnlich lang, auch festigt sich der Uebergang der Herrschaft vom Vater auf den Sohn.[62] Bei öffentlichen Empfängen steht der bujidische Herr von Bagdad nicht an, dem Kalifen göttliche Ehren zu erweisen.[63] Und im Jahre 1017 darf der Kalife Kādir, der eine Bujidenprinzessin zur Frau hat, – unbehindert im Verkehr mit den auswärtigen Fürstenhöfen – eine allgemeine Ketzerverfolgung, die sich auch gegen die Schīʿiten richtet, veranstalten. In Bagdad werden nur erprobt sunnitische Moscheenprediger geduldet. Kādir wirkt nicht nur als Organisator dieser streitbaren Kirche, sondern er tritt auch als

Theologe mit dem Anspruch auf Lehrautorität für den rechten Glauben ein.[64]

Die Orthodoxie, in ihrer prinzipiellen Systemlosigkeit jederzeit zu Kompromissen fähig, hatte über die Schīʿa den Sieg davongetragen. Gegen die so überaus elastische Idjmāʿ-Kirche, welche einerseits das, was den Sekten ihren Zulauf bringt, leicht übernimmt, um die wesentliche Abweichung desto schärfer zu bekämpfen, anderseits doch ein einheitliches Ganzes ist, konnten die vielen, durch die verschiedenen Autoritäten auf verschiedene Einzelheiten festgelegten Spaltungen der Schīʿa nicht aufkommen. Doch musste bei diesem Stand der Dinge die Orthodoxie – zumal es schīʿitische Richtungen gab, die von ihr nur wenig abwichen und sich durchaus in ihr einbegriffen empfanden – sich manches vom schīʿitischen Glaubensbestand einverleiben. So wird die Mahdī-Idee, freilich losgelöst von der Imāmreihe, von der Orthodoxie übernommen, die angesichts der von den Schīʿiten an ihren Imām gestellten Forderung nach absoluter Tugendhaftigkeit gezwungen war, dem Kalifat der Wirklichkeit als einem nur ‚unvollkommenen' das vollkommene der Rāschidūn[65] und dessen Erneuerung vor dem Weltende durch den Mahdī gegenüberzustellen. Um den Preis solchen Zugeständnisses aber hat das Kalifat als Realität seine Existenz gerettet, ja indem es sich auf die Religion als seine eigentliche Basis gewiesen sah und sich ernsthaft dementsprechend einrichtete, erwuchsen ihm neue Kräfte.

So wie in der kasuistisch gerichteten Orthodoxie das heilige Gesetz eine zwar das gesamte Dasein zu regeln beanspruchende, in Wirklichkeit jedoch nur ‚geglaubte' aber nicht ‚befolgte' Instanz war, so war bis zur Bujidenzeit die macht des Kalifates eine theoretisch universale, faktisch aber null: man ‚glaubt' an das Kalifat, d. h. gibt ihm formale Ehrerbietung, ‚befolgt' aber keinen von dessen Befehlen und verfährt mit dem jeweiligen Träger wie man will. Und so wie sich die Mystik mit einer rein idealen Welt höchster Vollkommenheit abfand, der gegenüber die Welt als gleichgültiges Nichts versank, so war auch der Imām der Schīʿa aller Einwirkung auf das rettungslos verdorbene Irdische entrückt. In der Bujidenzeit werden die beiden Sphären, Orthodoxie und Schīʿa (Mystik) gewaltsam zusammengeführt zu einem Austauschprozess, dessen Abschluss das Werk Gazālīs bedeutet. Das Resultat ist eine Wendung zum Realismus. Das Kalifat taucht im Verfolg dieser Wendung neu gestärkt empor. Nicht mehr zu einer, die islamische Gemeinde umspannenden, politischen Herrschaft steigt es auf, dazu reichen hier die Kräfte ebensowenig, wie auf dem Gebiet der Sittlichkeit es nicht zu einer dauernden Einheit von Tat und Gesinnung kommt; aber es wird das Kalifat zu einem wichtigen Zentrum des nun immer ernsthafter das Leben beeinflussenden Glaubens.[66] Die grossen Traditionswerke und Rechtssystem, welche eine ‚Orthodoxie' als greifbare Realität überhaupt erst möglich gemacht hatten, waren nicht ohne weitgehende Beeinflussung, Anregung und Unterstützung seitens der theokratischen Herrschaft in Bagdad zustandegekommen. Nun gilt es, aus dem überreichlich vorhandenen Material auszuwählen und der Auswahl kanonische Geltung zu verschaffen, womit die Orthodoxie erst volle Festigkeit gewinnt. Auch an dieser zweiten, nicht minderwichtigen Periode in der Genesis der Orthodoxie haben die Kalifen noch ihren Anteil, wenn sie auch dabei schon von neuen Mächten in den Hintergrund gedrängt sind. Doch davon weiter unten.

Im Anschluss an die grosse Bestands-Aufnahme und -Sichtung wird auch das auf das Kalifat bezügliche Material, wie es die geschichtliche Wirklichkeit und daneben eine mehr oder weniger tendenziös entstellte oder erfundene Ueberlieferung bot, zusammengetragen und mit harmonistischen Künsten notdürftig zu einem System vereinigt, soweit dies eben ging. Aus der letzten Bujidenzeit ist uns das Staatsrecht der Māwerdī[67] (st. 1058) erhalten, eines Bagdader Oberkādī unter Kādir und Kāim. Die hier niedergelegte kalifatstheorie ist im wesentlichen bereits die, welche in die späteren Katechismen Eingang fand:[68] es wird ein in die goldene Zeit der Rāschidūn zurückprojizierter Idealtyp entworfen, welcher nur in den Legitimitätsbestimmungen auch für die ganze 'Umajjaden- und Abbasidenzeit stimmt, im übrigen aber nichts als eine schlechtweg unerfüllbare, erst vom Mahdī zu bewältigende Aufgabe darstellt.

«Das Kalifat als Stellvertretung des Prophetentums ist eingerichtet worden, damit die Religion und die weltlichen Angelgenheiten geschützt und geleitet werden.» Gleichwie die Heeresfolge im heiligen Krieg oder das Studium der Wissenschaften ist die Anerkennung des jeweils mit den Funktionen des Kalifates Betrauten eine von der muslimischen Gesamtheit als solcher zu erfüllende Verpflichtung. Ist das Kalifat vakant, dann hat ein recht unbestimmt durch die Eingenschaften der Gerechtigkeit, des Wissens um die Bedingungen des passiven Wahlrechts, und der Einsicht in die Eignung des zu Wählenden definierter Kreis von Wahlberechtigten[69] aus einem schärfer umgrenzten Kreis von Kandidaten den Kalifen zu wählen, falls nicht eine Verfügung des früheren Kalifen vorliegt, die – sobald es sich nicht um Uebertragung an Vater oder Sohn handelt – ohne weitere Zustimmung der Wähler gültig ist. Auch mehrere Nachfolger mit bestimmter Reihenfolge des Anspruches darf der Kalif designieren.[70] Zur passiven Wahlberechtigung ist neben Unbescholtenheit, Besitz der zur Rechtsfindung erforderlichen Kenntnisse,[71] Unversehrtheit der Sinne und Gesundheit der Körperglieder – Spätere fügen als weitere Bedingungen Grossjährigkeit und männliches Geschlecht hinzu – erforderlich: die nötige Einsicht zur Herrschaft über das Volk und zur Leitung der Staatsgeschäfte, Mut und Tapferkeit, damit er das islamische Gebiet verteidigen und die Ungläubigen bekriegen kann, endlich – und damit ist der sonst rein legale Charakter durch ein Moment traditioner Art durchbrochen – Zugehörigkeit zum Stamme Kuraisch. (Die Praxis der Abbasidenzeit hat, wieder aus traditionalen Gründen, sich auf die Mitglieder der Familie Abbās beschränkt – in die Theorie, welche auch die ʿUmajjaden und die Râschidrūn einbegreifen musste, war diese Einschränkung nicht einführbar.) An die Wahl schliesst sich die Huldigung durch Handschlag.

Deutlich wird der fiktive Charakter dieser Theorie in den zehn Pflichten, die der Kalif übernimmt: Schutz der orthodoxie gegen Ketzerei, Aufrechterhaltung der Gerechtigkeit, Schutz des islamischen Staatsgebietes, Schutz der von Gott gegebenen Gebote durch Verhängung der gesetzlichen Strafen, Vorsorge für eine ausreichende Streitmacht, Krieg gegen die Ungläubigen, Einhebung der Untertanen- und Armensteuer, Auszahlung der Jahresdotationen (im II. Jahrh.!), Sorge für eine gute Verwaltung, persönliches Interesse an den Staatsangelegenheiten. Erfüllt der Kalife diese Pflichten, dann kann er von seinen Untertanen Gehorsam und Unterstützung verlange. (Wann war also praktisch der Fall solcher Pflicht gegeben? Natürlich nie. Doch hört darum das Kalifat nicht auf, denn:) Der Kalife geht seiner Würde (erst) verlustig, wenn er durch verwerfliche Handlungen oder Unglauben seine Unbescholtenheit oder wenn er die körperlichen Vorbedingungen verliert oder wenn er seine Freiheit eingebüsst hat, also z. B. ohne Hoffnung auf Befreiung in Feindeshand gefallen ist. Doch wird ausdrücklich bemerkt, dass eine solche das Kalifat ungültig machende Freiheitsberaubung nicht vorliegt, «wenn einer seiner Gehilfen dazu gelangt, ihn völlig zu beherrschen und die Macht an sich zu reissen, ohne dass er sich dabei des Ungehorsams oder offenen Widerstandes schuldig erweist.» Eine deutliche Konzession an die Zeitverhältnisse. Immerhin wird das Interesse der Orthodoxie gewahrt: «Es müssen die Handlungen desjenigen, der sich diesen Einfluss auf die Macht des Kalifen verschafft, genau geprüft werden. Wenn sie nämlich den Grundsätzen der Religion und den Anforderungen der Gerechtigkeit entsprechen, so darf man den Betreffenden in seiner Stellung belassen und seine Anordnungen sollen ausgeführt werden, damit nicht die Staatsgeschäfte in Verzögerung geraten, die zu einer Unordnung im Volke führen könnte. Entsprechen aber seine Handlungen nicht den Vorschriften der Religion und den Erfordernissen der Gerechtigkeit, so darf er nicht in seiner Stellung belassen werden, damit diesem Usurpator die Gewalt entrissen und sein Einfluss auf den Kalifen zunichte gemacht werde.»

Nicht um die Freiheit des Kalifen geht es hier – kein Wort ist von der Wiederherstellung seiner Machtvollkommenheit gesagt – nur für die Wahrung der Orthodoxie wird Vorsorge getroffen; es ist ihren Forderungen Genüge geschehen, wenn ein neuer Machthaber die Herrschaft an sich reisst, woferne er eben nur der Orthodoxie entspricht. Noch zu Māwerdīs Lebzeiten ist solcher Machthaberwechsel Wirklichkeit geworden, ward die nicht zuverlässige Familie Būje von den streng sunnitischen Seldschuken abgelöst (1055). Noch bedarf der neue Machthaber der Bestätigung des Kalifen; aber es wird eine Theorie der ‚Statthalterschaft durch Usurpation' entwickelt, wonach der Kalife dem Usurpator die Bestätigung nicht vorenthalten darf, wenn dieser die Souveränität des Kalifen nur anerkennt, sich in religiöser Hinsicht der Autorität des Kalifen unterwirft, Freundschaft und Hilfe zum Wohl der Muslims gelobt, die Verleihung religiöser Würden dem Kalifen anheimstellt, in den Steuern und allem übrigen sich an das heilige Gesetz hält und dieses sowie den rechten Glauben gegen Verletzung schützt.[72]

Es nimmt hier die Orthodoxie dem Abbasiden-Kalifat gegenüber eine durchaus selbständige Stellung ein. Dessen Legitimität wird nicht bestritten, aber auch nicht begründet: dass gerade die Familie Abbās zum Kalifat erkoren sei, hat, wie wir sahen, in die Theorie nicht Eingang gefunden. Ist so die traditionale Grundlage der Stellung der Abbasiden ignoriert, so wird die charismatische entschieden abgelehnt. Von einer Vergöttlichung der Person des Kalifen, wie sie faktisch nahezu allgemein stattfand, ist keine Rede. Nicht einmal der Titel ‚Kalife Gottes' wird zugebilligt, trotzdem man ihm eine rechtfertigende Deutung findet.[73] Die Abbasiden hatten ihren Staat als ‚Gottesstaat' einrichten wollen, hatten im Namen der Orthodoxie und in engster Verbindung mit den zumal in der Rechtsprechung zahlreich beschäftigten ʿUlmā regieren wollen, freilich die Anpassungsfähigkeit des Islams für ihren politischen Willen nutzend und in keiner ihrer Absichten aus religiösen Gründen gebunden. Die wirklich Frommen haben darum bald auch ihnen den Rücken gekehrt und sich auf keine Weise in die korrumpierende Staatsmaschinerie einfügen lassen.[74] Immer wieder hat es Männer gegeben, die aus dem Koranwort (XXII 50) «Wer Opfer einer Ungerechtigkeit ist, den wird Allah triumphieren machen» die Ermutigung schöpften, dem in prunkvollstes Zeremoniell gehüllten Herrschergott Trotz zu bieten und ihn auf die Ebene stolzer Demut herabzuzwingen, auf der alle Muslims ohne Unterschied des Ranges und der Macht vor Allah stehen. Solcher Mut und das Martyrium, das diese Männer oft auf sich zu nehmen hatten, trug seine Früchte. Die von den Abbasiden grossgezogenen ʿUlemā, von Anfang an im Besitz der gesetzgeberischen Gewalt,[75] wuchsen den Kalifen über den Kopf. Bei Māwerdī ist das Kalifat nur mehr ein Symbol für etwas was einst war und einst weider sein wird. Die Obliegenheiten des Kalifates werden bereits von anderen erfüllt, mit denen zu paktieren es sich besser lohnt.

Immerhin lag auch unter diesen Verhältnissen noch ein solches Ansehen auf der Kalifenwürde, dass deren Träger die Gunst der Verhältnisse seit Ende des 12. Jahrhunderts zu neuem, letzten Aufstieg nutzen konnten. Schon machte kein Nebenkalifat mehr Bagdad ernstliche Konkurrenz – die ʿUmajjadenherrschaft in Spanien, längst in Emirate zersplittert, war mit der Konstituierung der Adelsrepublik von Kordova (1031) erloschen, ja die seit Mitte des 10. Jahrhunderts im Westen aufsteigenden Almorawiden sahen in ihrem Bekenntnis zu Bagdad ein «Symbol ihrer Zugenhörigkeit zum Islam».[76] 1171 hatten die von dem Kurden Saladin geführten Truppen des Türken Nur ed-dīn Zengi dem Fatimidenkalifat ein Ende gemacht und auch das junge – schon als solches nicht ebenbürtige – Almohadenkalifat des Westens geriet seit etwa 1200 in schwierige Lage. Mit dem Emporkommen der türkischen Sultane, der Gaznewiden und Seldjuken, die wie Saladin und dessen Nachfolger (die Ajubiden) fanatische Bekenner der Sunna waren, hatte der Islam wieder kriegerische Kraft erhalten: vom II. Jahrh. an gehören grosse Landstriche von Indien und Kleinasien zum ‚Haus des Islam' und wird damit der Name des Kalifen in bisher ungläubig gewesenen Gebieten im Freitagsgebet genannt. 1187 war mit der Wiedereroberung Jerusalems gegen die Kreuzfahrer ein entscheidender Erfolg errungen. Innerhalb der in der Folge rasch auseinanderbröckelnden Staatenwelt der Sultanate war der Kalif dank der seinem Amte anhaftenden Autorität der gegebene Mittelpunkt. Nach langer, schwerer Bedrängnis war er 1152 wieder unabhängiger Herr des Fruchtlandes geworden. Mit grosszügigster und skrupellosester Politik versuchte Nāsir (1180 bis 1225), das Kalifat noch einmal zu iniversaler weltlicher Machtstellung zu führen.[77] Der Versuch musste scheitern: diese atomisierte Welt war zu solchen Leistungen aus sich selbst heraus nicht mehr fähig – mit Intrigen war ihr nicht mehr aufzuhelfen. Uebermächtig drängten gegen sie die ungebrochenen Volkskräfte Zentralasiens. In Chwarezm hatten gewaltige türkische Herrscher ein bald den grössten Teil Vorderasiens umspannendes Reich begründet, in dem unvermittelt neben der islamischen Kultur als Träger der militärischen Macht zum Teil noch heidnische türkische Stämme standen. Nāsir empfand diesen Staat als unbequemen Erben der eben glücklich überstandenen Seldschukenherrschaft und als Hindernis für den Aufstieg des Kalifates. Unbedenklich rief er gegen den – allerdings infolge seiner Opposition zu Bagdad nicht sehr verlässlich orthodoxen – Sultan die Mongolen ins Land,[78] die Chwarezm auch überrannten und für den Augenblick halfen. Aber schon ein Menschenalter später machten die Welteroberer, ganz anders als die islamisierten Türken vorher, auch vor dem ‚Hause des Heiles' (Bagdad) und dessen Herrscher nicht Halt. 1258 ist das Kalifat als ungebrochen von den Anfängen des Islams her bestehende und daraus seine in allen Stürmen und Demütigungen und Wandlungen bewährte Autorität schöpfende Institution zu Ende. Die angeblichen Abbasiden, die dann in Kairo neben den dortigen weltlichen Herrschern ein mit wenigen Ausnahmen ohnmächtiges Dasein rein dekorativer Wirkung führen durften, um Aegypten einen Vorrang in der islamischen Welt zu sichern, waren keineswegs allgemein anerkannt.[79] Dort, wo von ihm Notiz genommen wird, verfestigt es die schon in der Bujiden- und Seldschukenzeit aufgekommene Ansicht von seinem rein ‚geistlichen' Charakter. Bereits zu Anfang des 13. Jahrh.s kursierte ein Prophetenausspruch, nach welchem Sache des Kalifen das Gebet ist; Einmischung des Kalifen in das irdische Regiment hat keinen Sinn, das ist den Sultanen zu überlassen.[80] Christen und Muslims pflegen unter dem Eindruck dieses Kalifates Papst und Kalif als Mächte gleicher Ordnung anzusehen,[81] sogar die

Gleichsetzung mit dem jedweder weltlichen Macht entratenden Patriarchen von Konstantinopel ist nachweisbar.[82]

Aber auch in dieser reduzierten Form hat das Kairiner Kalifat nicht einmal in Aegypten selbst besondere Beachtung gefunden.[83] Auf der Münze wurde des Kalifen Name nicht genannt. Der ägyptische Biograph eines Mamlukensultans äussert um 1440 die Ansicht: «So wie der Sultan der Kalife Gottes auf Erden und der Vikar seines Propheten ist in allem, was die Regierungsangelegenheiten betrifft, ebenso sind die ʿUlema die Erben der Propheten in der Anwendung und Durchführung der göttlichen Satzungen».[84] Für den Kalifen ist da kein Platz mehr vorhanden – die Welt ist zwischen Sultan und Schriftgelehrten aufgeteilt. Das war eigentlich schon von Māwerdī ausgesprochen gewesen.[85] Es war sinnfällig zutage getreten, als der Mongolechan Hulagu, ob erschreckender, das Weltende androhender Gerüchte zögernd, den Kalifen in den Tod zu schicken, bei einem muslimischen (allerdings vielleicht schīʿitisch gesinnten) Gelehrten sich Rat holt und die Auskunft erhält, schon so mancher bessere Vorgänger dieses Kalifen sei beseitigt worden, ohne dass dies eine Störung des Weltalls hervorgerufen hätte.[86] Und als derselbe Hulagu dann die ʿUlemā von Bagdad in ihrer Universität versammelt und ihnen die Frage vorlegt, ob der gerechte Heide oder der ungerechte Muslim als Herrscher den Vorzug verdiene, da entschieden diese nach einigem Zögern für den ersteren.[87] Der ‚Herrschergott' an der Spitze der islamischen Theokratie war eben ein Widerspruch, den man, solange man musste, hinnahm – so wie man in der Folgezeit sich mit den geistlichen Aspirationen rein weltlicher Herrscher abfand –, zu dessen Verteidigung jedoch die Orthodoxie keinen Anlass mehr hatte, zumal sich ihre Vertreter, die ʿUlemā, dem Kalifen wie jedem anderen Herrscher gegenüber ihrer autonomen Macht bewusst geworden waren. Der weltliche Herrscher, so unbequem er sein mochte, schien doch das kleinere, eher beeinflussbare Uebel zu sein; er stand ausserhalb der religiösen Sphäre, war also kein Konkurrent, hingegen dank seiner Machtmittel als ein notwendiges Werkzeug zu gebrauchen. Nach drei Jahrhunderten des Nebeneinander löst der Sultan den Kalifen endgültig ab.

Mit dem Worte «Sultan» taucht ein altes morgenländisches Wort, das schon auf assyrischen Inschriften den Herrscher bezeichnet, wieder auf.[88] Zunächst im Arabischen in der Bedeutung «die Herrschaft» verwendet, wird es Bezeichnung eines Trägers der staatlichen Macht[89] und schliesslich Titel der die weltliche Gewalt repräsentierenden Personen. Die Ausbildung der weltlichen als von der geistlichen gesonderten Gewalt wird einleuchtend mit der zunehmenden Bestallung nichtarabischer, zumal türkischer Krieger als Statthalter oder kleinere Kommandanten in Zusammenhang gebracht.[90] Die des Arabischen nur unzureichend mächtigen Funktionäre mussten die Obliegenheiten des Kultes und des Gerichtes den berufsmässig fungierenden ʿUlemā überlassen, deren Zahl und Ansehen dadurch gewaltig steigt und die sich zu einem Stand entwickeln. Dazu führte die Verselbständigung der Statthalter, die noch im 9. Jahrh. einsetzt, zu einem neuen, bisher dem Islam fremd gewesenen Herrschaftsbegriff, für welchen das Wort «Sultanat» die gegebene Bezeichnung war. Noch bedurfte es erst der bujidischen Drangsale und der notgedrungen bewussten Einstellung des Kalifen auf den geistlichen Charakter seines Amtes, ehe der Titel Sultan vom Kalifen selbst an Träger rein weltlicher Herrschaft verliehen wurde und damit die höchste Sanktionierung empfing.

Die Bujiden waren die ersten faktischen Sultane, wenn sie auch kaum noch diesen Titel geführt haben dürften. Man hat darauf aufmerksam gemacht, dass das Aufhören der verbreitetsten Imām-Reihe, der der sog. ‚Zwölfer', nämlich die Entrückung ihres letzten (zwölften) Gliedes als Mahdī, in dieselbe Zeit gesetzt wird (940), in der in Bagdad die schīʿitischen Bujiden zur Herrschaft kamen (945). Dieser der Schīʿa nahestehenden Dynastie nicht mit eigenen Prätendenten in den Rücken zu fallen und ihren Aspirationen freie Bahn zu geben, sei der zwölfte Imām als Mahdī zu verborgenem Warten entrückt worden.[91] Ein solcher Zusammenhang ist gewiss ausgeschlossen. Die Wendung von politischem Willen zu eschatologischer Erwartung ist viel zu sehr im Gesamtzug der Zeit begründet, als dass sie auf bewusster, politischer Ueberlegung entspringende Absicht zurückgeführt werden müsste.[92] Dennoch bleibt das Zusammentreffen der beiden Daten höchst bedeutungsvoll – es schafft von schīʿitischer Seite die Vorbedingung für ein sich als gottgewollt empfindendes, selbstbewusstes weltliches Herrschertum. Es ist klar, dass, während die vordem nach Selbständigkeit strebenden Machthaber sich, auch wenn sie schīʿitisch gesinnt waren, letzten Endes doch selbst als Rebellen empfinden mussten, nunmehr die Bujiden dem Mahdī und nicht weniger dem Kalifate gegenüber sich innerlich vollkommen frei fühlen konnten. Sie lehren die islamische Welt, weltliche Gewalt mit dem guten Gefühl der Gottgewolltheit üben und in keiner auf den Glauben gegründeten Instanz mehr ein Hindernis ihrer Aspirationen erblicken.

Dass die Kalifen mit den schī'itischen Machthabern schliesslich einen modus vivendi gefunden hatten, sich auf den geistlichen Charakter ihres Amtes beschränkend, haben wir gesehen. Die Orthodoxie aber hielt Ausblick, wie man «dem Usurpator, dessen Handlungen nicht den Vorschriften der Religion entsprechen, die Gewalt entreissen und seinen Einfluss auf den Kalifen zunichte machen» könne.[93] Dass damit nicht mehr an das Kalifat selbst, sondern nur an einen anderen, genehmeren Machthaber gedacht war, haben wir ebenfalls bereits vermerkt. Wo man ihn suchte, zeigt ein ‚Prophetenausspruch' aus dem Ende des 10. Jahrh.s, nach welchem ein Held aus Chorasan, von den Fremdvölkern stammend, den Bujiden ein Ende machen soll.[94] Der Held, mit diesem Spruche wohl kaum ad personam wohl aber allgemein dem Kreise seiner Herkunft nach apostrophiert, ein Türke aus dem transoxanisch-chorasanischen Samanidenreiche, der diesen Ruf hätte hören können – ihm Folge zu leisten war einem wenig Späteren bestimmt – war bald eine konkrete Hoffnung. Um 1000 eröffnet Mahmūd von Gaznas Reich die Reihe türkischer Staaten auf islamischem Boden.

Nicht handelt es sich hier um den schon früher zu verzeichnenden Fall, wo es einzelnen türkischen Statthalter-Generälen gelungen war, gestützt auf eine beschränkte Anzahl gekaufter Kriegersklaven, im Reiche des Kalifen sich unabhängig zu machen. Sondern hier kommt eine Türkendynastie zur Herrschaft in unmittelbarer Nachbarschaft, ja teilweise auf dem Boden ihrer Heimat und mit ständigem Kontakt mit ihr, getragen von dem breiten Zustrom türkischer Stämme, denen damit der Weg nach Vorderasien gebahnt ist, in ununterbrochener Reihenfolge (bis auf die Osmanen und die persischen Dynastien herunter) gefolgt von anderen Türkendynastien, die immer umfassenderen Besitz von der islamischen Welt ergreifen.

Mahmūd von Gazna ist zugleich der erste rechtgläubige weltliche Herrscher in dem neuen, unter den Bijiden möglich gewordenen Sinne: der Kalife selbst verleiht ihm als erstem den Titel Sultan,[95] von nun an die zustehende Bezeichnung für die Häupter unabhängiger Dynastien, denen der Kalife theoretisch seine Ansprüche auf weltliche Herrschaft in einem bestimmten Landstrich Übertragen hat und in diesem Sinne später den Titel ‚Mitregent des Beherrschers der Gläubigen' verleiht.[96] Zu diesen die weltlichen Funktionen bezeichnenden Titeln spendet der Kalife jetzt Ehrennamen, welche neben der weltlichen Macht sogar eine die Religion betreffende Funktion ihrer Träger zum

Ausdruck bringen. So heisst Mahmūd von Gazna ‚Jamīn eddaula Amīn el-mila' d. i. ‚Rechte Hand der (sc. Abbasiden-) Dynastie und Getreuer der Ecclesia'.[97]

Mit Ausnahme des durch die weltlichen Aspirationen des Kalifates in das alidische Lager gedrängten Chwarezmsultans (s. o. S. 411) waren alle diese türkischen Herrscher treue Söhne der Sunna, so leidenschaftlich in deren Dienst und so eifrige Verfolger von deren Feinden, dass mit einem Hinweis auf die natürliche Eignung dieser geraderen, primitiveren, trotz ihrer inneren Widersprüche doch abgeschlossenen und festen Form des Islams für ein einfaches Kriegervolk es nicht getan ist. Auch die Abneigung der Türken gegen die Perser und die von ihnen bevorzugten Sekten ist keine zureichende Erklärung. Dass die Türken überhaupt gerade Sunniten wurden, ergibt sich einfach aus dem Umstand, dass die entscheidende Missionierung in Transoxanien unter den bis rund 1000 dort mächtigen Samaniden stattgefunden hatte, einer Statthalterdynastie, die ihre freilich nur Formsache bleibende Ergebenheit gegenüber Bagdad nicht genug betonen konnte, darin eine wertvolle Legitimierung ihrer Herrschaft im fernen Osten mitten unter schīitischen Nachbarn findend. Aber dass die Türken so treue und leidenschaftliche Anhänger der Sunna blieben, das ist angesichts der religiösen Indifferenz, welche die vorislamischen Türken den Glauben ihrer Väter mit grösster Leichtigkeit nacheinander mit den verschiedenen, in Zentralisien aufeinander stossenden Weltreligionen hatte vertauschen lassen, nur aus einer besonderen Verwandtschaft des sunnitischen Islams mit der spezifisch türkischen Seelenlage zu erklären. Solches ist, mit einseitiger Betonung des quitistischen Momentes, für den Buddhismus behauptet worden.[98] Dieses kommt aber auch im Islam nicht zu kurz, besonders seitdem die Mystik ihren festen Platz in der Orthodoxie einnimmt – gerade die Mystik hat vom Türkentum eine gewaltige Belebung erfahren. Doch auch der andere Grundtrieb der türkischen Psyche erhält Nahrung aus dem sunnitschen Islam: ihr Fernenhang, ihr Wandertrieb, ihr Durst, das hindämmernde Ich – es ist eher ein ‚Es' – rauschhaft an kühnste Träume und masslose Taten zu verlieren – das, was die Nomaden Zentralasiens immer, wenn eine Hochkultur im Osten, Süden oder Westen des eurasischen Erdteils brüchtig und verteidigungsunfähig geworden war, als ‚Gottesgeissel' zu Zerstörungen welthistorischen Ausmasses auf den Plan führte, nun jedoch in den Dienst einer religiös unterbauten Kultur gestellt wird und dieser ungeheure Impulse, allerdings auch innere Erstarrung bringt. Der Islam, durch die Türken wieder wehrhaft, begegnet jetzt dem Ansturm der Kreuzzüge, trägt seine Grenzen im Glaubenskrieg nach Osten und Westen, in Indien und Kleinasien, vor. Was er an Elementen einer Kriegerreligion enthält, gewinnt nun Gewicht, vor allem eben der Glaubenskampf, als welchen die spätere muslimische Geschichtsschreibung die frühislamischen Eroberungskriege ansieht und der einen wichtigen Bestandteil der Sunna bildet, wird von den Türken neben den anderen Erinnerungen an die nomadische Heldenzeit des Frühislams begeistert aufgenommen und mit ihren kriegerischen Instinkten, ihrem Wandertrieb und Fernenhang durchdrungen.[99] Der durch bestimmte, die Lebenspraxis regelnde Vorschriften und durch zeremonielle Riten aufgewogene Mangel an ethischen Anforderunge, der durchaus männliche Charakter des religiösen Lebens, das Gebet um Sieg oder Aufnahme in einen Heldenhimmel, das alles sind Züge, die nun entsprechende Betonung finden und den islam zu einrer echten Kriegerreligion stempeln. Dazu dringt allenthalben in die ganz formalistisch gesinnte islamische Welt ein nüchterner, zuweilen hart anmutender Realismus ein.[100]

Mit alledem werden die weltlichen Herrscher, die Sultane, zu Schirmherren des Islams und die Kalifen neben ihnen mehr und mehr überflüssig. Einem so strenggläubigen Herrscher wie Mahmūd von Gazna, der es an Zeichen der Verehrung für den Bagdader Kalifen nicht fehlen liess und der dessen Aufforderung zur allgemeinen Ketzerverfolgung getreulich nachkam, wird ein Geschichtswerk gewidmet, das in seiner Einleitung eine wichtige Theorie vom Sultanat enthält:[101] «Es sind Religion und Herrschaft Zwillingsgeschwister: denn die Religion ist das Fundament und die Herrschaft (*mulk*) der Hüter; was aber ohne Hüter ist, geht verloren und was ohne Grund ist, wird zerstört. Der Sultan ist Gottes Schatten auf dessen Erde und sein Kalife in seiner Schöpfung, als sein Vertrauter mit der Beaufsichtigung seines Gesetzes beauftragt. Durch ihn steht fest die Verwaltung und auf ihn stützt sich Vornehm und Gering, durch seinen Schrecken verschwinden die Neuerungen und Empörungen ... ohne ihn würde die Ordnung sich auflösen ... und würden die Seelen zu ihrem natürlichen Trachten nach Hader und Betrug sich wenden, so dass sie davor gänzlich das versäumten, was ihrem jetzigen und künftigen Leben frommt. ... Es zügelt den Menschen mehr der Sultan als der Koran, denn die meisten scheuen mehr das Sichtbare der politischen Macht, und Furcht vor Strafe hält sie zurück, vom rechten Pfad abzulenken. ... Für den grossen Haufen ist das Schwert aufgestellt, der Koran aber für die Seltenen, wenn auch alle übereinstimmend an seine Gebote und Verbote sich binden. Jedoch der gemeine Mann sieht das Schwert und erschrickt, der Seltene aber sieht die Wahrheit und gehorcht. Und ein Unterschied ist zwischen dem, der sich durch etwas Anderes als die Wahrheit leiten und zwingen lässt und dem, den nur das Licht seines Herrn läutert und bildet... Das Schwert ist der Beweis Gottes wider den, der leugnet und widerspenstig ist. ... Es ist klar, dass der Sultan der Kalife Gottes in dessen Schöpfung ist, weil ihn Gott mit seinem Schwerte umgürtet und ihm auf der Erde Macht gab und bezüglich der Fürsten die Bestimmung machte, der solle glücklich, ruhmvoll und bei Gott geehrt sein, der sich so viel als möglich um den Sieg der Religion und die Beschützung des Islams und der Muslims bemüht und der die Feinde, die von Gottes Gesetz abweichen und seine Gebote und Satzungen übertreten, mit seiner eigenen Person und seinem Vermögen, mit seinen Verwandten und Mannen so bekämpft, dass er die Beklemmung der Brust möglichst aufhebt.»

Der Machthaber, der Herr des Schwertes, der Sultan, den die orthodoxe Staatslehre des Māwerdī legitimiert, wird hier – allerdings in einem versteckter schī'itischer Neigungen verdächtigen Werke[102] – als Kalife und Ebenbild Allahs angesprochen. Das ist mehr, als die Sultane selbst in der nächsten Zeit für sich in Anspruch nehmen. Noch anerkennen sie den Kalifen von Bagdad, dessen Bestallungsdiplom sie als Legitimierung ihrer Stellung den arabisch-persischen Untertanen gegenüber nicht missen wollen. Aber ihr Selbstgefühl wächst mit den Erfolgen, die sie in Kreuzzugs- und Tatarenstürmen im Dienst des Islams erringen, im selben Mass wie das Prestige des in ebendiesen Krisen versagenden Kalifen sinkt.

Dazu kam ihnen aus dem Bündnis mit den Theologen-Juristen ein gewaltiger Zuwachs an macht und Weihe. An der Schaffung eines zuverlässigen Theologenstandes, wie er den fremden Barbaren bei der Verwaltung der Kulturländer unentbehrlich war, äusserst interessiert, richten sie zum erstenmal im Islam von Staats wegen hohe Schulen (Medresen) ein, aus denen ein ihnen treu ergebener Stand von 'Ulemā hervorgeht. Wieder erscheint die Regierung des Mahmūd von Gazna als Epoche eröffnend: die erste staatliche Medrese wird von seinem Bruder Nasr zu Nischapur gegründet. Zu grösster Bedeutung steigt dann die von dem grossen Seldschukenwezir ins Leben gerufene und nach ihm benannte Nizāmījje zu Bagdad, die wohl als erste auch für den Lebensunterhalt der Studenten Sorge trug und damit erst so richtig die Schaffung von Nachwuchs garantierte.[103] Die alten Akademien (*dār al-ʿilm*, ‚Haus des Wissens') der Fatimiden- und Abbasidenzeit, in denen neben den religiösen Disziplinen auch die von Griechen und Persern ererbten: Astronomie, mathematik, Medizin, Philosophie gepflegt worden waren, hatten diesen Medresen und den gleichzeitig entstehenden Traditionsschulen weichen müssen. Die eklektisch-liberale Gesinnung machte starrer, einseitiger, fanatischer Orthodoxie Platz.[104] Erst jetzt kann man von einem Stande der ʿUlmā sprechen. Anfangs hatte der Lehrbetrieb[105] bei nahezu völliger Lehrfreiheit – jeder Muslim guten Rufes, der sich befähigt fühlte, war zum Lehren berechtigt – in den Moscheen stattgefunden, wo jedermann freien Zutritt hatte, und der Lehrer musste, falls er nicht Vermögen besass, sich sein Brot durch irgendeinen Beruf erwerben. Die zunehmende Verwendung der ʿUlemā als Beamte, wie sie schon in der ʿUmajjadenzeit beginnt, schafft dann die Vorstufe des mit den Medresen zur vollen Ausbildung gelangenden Gelehrtenstandes, wo nach einer bestimmten, in staatlichen Schulen von diplomierten Professoren geleiteten Studienlaufbahn die Diplomempfänger durchwegs Anwärter besoldeter Stellungen werden, innerhalb ihres Kreises – nicht selten in die Familie des Lehrers – heiraten und ihre Kinder in der ererbten Laufbahn erhalten und fördern (so dass die mühsam errungene Stelle des Vaters der nächsten Generation ein leicht erworbenes Erbe und der Ausgangspunkt zu weiterem Aufstieg wird). Diese ʿUlemā finden jetzt in allen erdenklichen öffentlichen und privaten Funktionen, als Richter, Anwälte, Verwaltungsbeamte, Polizeioffiziere, Minister, Gesandte, Sekretäre, als Professoren und Lehrer, Erzieher und Ratgeber Verwendung und gewinnen eine ungeheure Macht, auch über den Souverän, den sie ihrerseits mit ihrem moralischen Ansehen stützen.

Innerhalb diese Standes und seines geregelten Lehrbetriebs kommt nun die Orthodoxie zur abschliessenden Ausbildung: jetzt wird der Kanon der gültigen Traditionswerke, Kommentare, Gesetzbücher aufgestellt und ein Zurückgreifen über die kanonisierte Auslegung hinaus untersagt – nur ein Weiterarbeiten auf dem Boden des bisher Erreichten ist verstattet.

Alle die Pflanzstätten der Orthodoxie lebten von frommen Stiftungen. Je mehr Einfluss die ʿUlemā erwerben, zu desto reicherer Stiftungstätigkeit können sie die Gläubigen bewegen, was wieder zu ihrer geistigen Macht die ökonomische hinzufügt und neue Möglichkeiten ihrem numerischen Anwachsen bietet. Bei dem realistischen Zug der Zeit und vor allem des Türkentums, welches den leergewordenen islamischen Formalismus ehrlich mit Wirklichkeit zu füllen bestrebt war, traf diese Tendenz der 'Ulemā auf gutgewillte Laien. Nun setzt jene von Herrschern und Privaten geübte reiche Stiftungstätigkeit ein, der die islamische Welt ihren grossen Reichtum an Moscheen, Schulen, Bädern, Fremdenherbergen, Krankenhäusern und Brunnen verdankt – ein Moment, das durch Schaffung einer zahlreichen Pfründnerklasse und durch Stillegung von Gütern (mit Ruinierung derselben!) wieder seinerseits in dem grossen Erstarrungsprozess dieser Welt eine Rolle spielt.[106]

Mit Mahmūd von Gazna hebt die Reihe der grossen Herrschergestalten an, die von nun an die Geschicke des Orients bestimmen. Eine erst jetzt zur Ausbildung gelangende Biographik macht sie zum Gegenstand historischer Darstellung.[107] Wie fremd diese Sultane in der islamischen Welt stehen und wie viel verwandter sie sich etwa ihren christlichen Gegnern, den Kreuzfahrern, fühlten, erhellt aus einem Briefe Saladinis[108] an den Kalifen Nāsir vom Jahre 1191: «Der Islam hat es hier mit einem Volke zu tun, das den Tod liebt, das Land und Leute im Stiche lässt, seinem Priester gehorsam, seinem Marzuis ergeben. Sie eifern dem von ihnen Angebeteten (sc. Christus) nach und verteidigen die Glaubensgenossen. . . . Nicht einmal in der Not verlangen sie Geld, halten aber im übrigen in allen Mühsalen und Schicksalsproben mutig und heiter aus und beweisten mit den Waffen in der Hand grosse Tapferkeit. . . .» Und nach diesem Panegyrikus auf den fränkischen Gegner folgt bittere Klage über die eigenen Glaubensgenossen: «Nicht so die Muslims. Sie sind unwillig, ohne Ausdauer, zersplittert, unfähig zur Eintracht, sie entziehen sich ihren Pflichten und wollen höchstens einen Beitrag leisten. Kommen sie, so geschieht es mit Widerwillen, mit dem deutlichen Gefühl, dass der Islam durch Allahs Hilfe gerettet werden wird, auch ohne menschliches Zutun, und dass der Unglaube schon untergeht, weil Allah es will.»

Was den Kreuzfahrern entgegentritt und sich ihnen als gewachsen erweist, in seinem ‚Rittertum' dem europäischen Gegenspieler so ähnlich, gehört der neuen Kriegerschichte an, welche über der arabisch-persischen Bevölkerung als türkische Herrenklasse sitzt und den Islam wieder wehrfähig macht. Die Ideale dieser Klasse knüpfen an die nomadische Heldenzeit des

Frühislams an sowie an die eben jetzt unter Mahmūd von Gazna durch Firdusi zu neuem Leben erweckte Heldensage Irans. In dem gleichzeitig zur definitiven Ausbildung gelangenden Lehenswesen findet die neue soziale Struktur ihre gemässe wirtschaftliche Unterlage.[109]

Die Position dieser Sultane ihren Türken gegenüber beruht auf durchaus traditionalen Momenten. In dem Reiche Chwarezm z. B. sind die einzelnen Stämme an den Herrscher durch das Treuverhältnis geknüpft, in dem sie zu seiner ihnen entstammenden, resp. verwandten Mutter stehen – einer von mehreren Zügen des ursprünglich in Zentralasien herrschenden Matriarchates. Anders stehen diese Sultane natürlich gegenüber der arabisch-persischen Schicht. Ihr Bündnis mit den ʿUlemā macht ihre Stellung hinsichtlich dieser Untertanen zu einer legalen. «Der Sultan der Kalife Gottes in den weltlichen Angelegenheiten wie die ʿUlemā in den geistlichen» – auf diese Formel sahen wir unter dem Mamlukensultan Dschakmak die Vorstellung von der weltlichen Herrschaft gebracht.[110] Derselbe Sultan macht damit den Anfang, sich inschriftlich ‚den erhabensten Imām' zu nenne und sich so die Würde eines Vorbeters der Gesamtgemeinde, also gerade die am meisten geistliche Seite des Kalifates, zu arrogieren. Das in Aegypten, in unmittelbarer Gegenwart der Abbasidenkalifen! Mehr als ein Jahrhundert vorher hatte in der politischen Theorie des Aegypters Ibn Djamāʿa (st. 1333) die Gleichung ‚Gewaltherrscher = Kalife' Aufnahme gefunden: «Die letzte Alternative, die Herrschaft zu erlange, ist die Gewalt. Wenn nämlich kein legitimer Imām vorhanden ist und niemand von denen, die zur Führerschaft befähigt sind, sich um das Imāmat bewirbt, jemand aber mit Gewalt den Besitz der Herrschaft erringt, ohne gewählt worden zu sein oder die Souveränitätsrechte durch Uebertragung erlangt zu haben, so ist seine Herrschaft anzuerkennen und ist ihm Gehorsam zu leisten, um die Gemeinde der Muslime zusammenzuhalten und Parteibildungen zu vermeiden. Es ändert auch nichts hieran, wenn der Herrscher unwissend oder gottlos ist. Hat aber einer sich durch Gewalt zur Herrschaft emporgeschwungen, es erhebt sich dann aber ein anderer und besiegt wiederum den ersteren, so ist der zweite als gesetzlicher Imām anzuerkennen».[111] Auch die Vorschrift der Glaubenslehre, dass der Kalife aus dem Stamm Kuraisch sein müsse, wird weginterpretiert, indem man sie dahin deutet, dass das jeweilige Oberhaupt des Islams der mächtigsten und vornehmsten Familie seiner Zeit entstammen solle.[112] Eine unbedingte

Kapitulation vor der Gewalt, eine ‚Loyalitätserklärung für alle Fälle' seitens der 'Ulemā als der Repräsentanten der muslimischen Gemeinde an die Machthaber!

Die Gemeinde als solche nimmt an den Ereignissen, die innerhalb der kriegerischen Herrenschichte stattfinden, geflissentlich keinen Anteil – weder respektiert und unterstützt sie die traditionalen Bindungen, auf denen dort die Herrschaft beruht, noch negiert sie dieselben durch Parteinahme gegen den Herrscher. Was in jener Machtspäre an Kämpfen ausgetragen wird, ist ihr gleichgültig, nur das Resultat nimmt sie als Gottesurteil hin. «Schmahet nicht die Herrschenden – so wird die Gemeinde in einem Hadis ermahnt – wenn sie rechttun, wird ihnen Lohn zuteil und ihr habt dankbar zu sein; tun sie abe Böses, dann liegt auf ihnen die Last und ihr habt Geduld zu üben. Wahrlich, sie sind ein Werkzeug der Rache Gottes – er rächt sich mit ihm an wem er will; nehmet Gottes Rache nicht mit Erregung und Zorn hin, sondern empfanget sie mit Ruhe und Demut».[113]

Der Herrscher ist – gleichgültig ob gut oder böse – von Allah eingesetzt und ist Gottes Lohn oder seine Prüfung und Bestrafung für die Gemeinde. Keine andere Zuflucht gegen Tyrannei als die Stärkung des Herzens im Gebet und in der Versenkung, als die Gewissheit, dass Allah schliesslich seine Gläubigen triumphieren machen wird; keine andere Möglichkeit, eine schlechte Regierung zu beseitigen, als die ängstliche Gesetzesbefolgung seitens der Gläubigen, denn nur sie kann Gottes Zorn abwenden und nur Gott kann der Tyrannis ein Ende machen, indem er den Sinn des Machthabers ändert oder diesen durch einen frommen Herrscher beseitigen lässt. Nur wenn ein Mahdī ersteht und die Muslims ruft, erheben sich diese zu leidenschaftlichem Aufruhr.

Ein frommer Herrscher folgt in allem und jedem seinen geistlichen Ratgebern. Im Osmanenreiche haben diese dann eine feste Organisation und im Ober-Mufti (obersten Fetwa-Erteiler), dem ‚*Scheich ul-Islām*', eine beamtete Spritze mit genau umschriebener Kompetenz erhalten. Lockerung in den traditionalen Bindungen der Kriegerschicht wies die Herrscher immer mehr an die 'Ulemā, diese immer mächtiger werdenden Wortführer des muslimischen Volkes, das, vom politischen Leben ganz abgewendet, sich dem religiösen mit um so grösserer Hingabe weiht. Schliesslich fühlt sich der Herrscher selbst nicht anders denn als ein Werkzeug in der Hand Allahs, als sein ‚Stellvertreter' auf Erden, betraut mit der Wahrung des Gesetzes, legitimiert durch den Willen Gottes, der ihm die Macht verliehen hat, geheiligt durch das Charisma des Erfolgs. In diesem Sinn – wir sahen ihn schon in der Theorie aus der Zeit Mahmūds von Gazna ausgesprochen – haben unter anderen die späteren Mamluken-Sultane, die Timuriden, die Osmanen als Inhaber des Kalifates gegolten,[114] zumal die letzteren, die noch einmal den ganzen islamischen Bereich – mit Ausnahme der in einem schī'itischen Reich zusammengefassten und damit endgültig aus der Orthodoxie ausgeschiedenen, sowie der auf diese Weise räumlich getrennten Ostgebiete – zu einer Weltmacht zusammenfassten. Ihr Werk war von vornherein ein totgeweihtes. Die Welt, der sie ihre Kräfte weihten, war eine innerlich erstarrte und atomisierte: das Gesetz, das jeder einzelne für sich ängstlich befolgte, während die Gesamtheit nur noch durch stammesfremde Eroberer geführt werden konnte, war ja der Ausdruck einer uralten, längst erstarrten Kultur – der bewegte Entwicklungsprozess, der das Morgenland in den ersten Jahrhunderten des Islams ergiffen zu haben schien, war nichts als die Loslösung vom Fremden und die Heimkehr zu sich selbst gewesen. Die Türken konnten dieser Welt kaum Neubelebung, höchstens Konservierung bringen. Dass Europa sich seit etwa 1300 gleichsam auf sich selbst zu ungeheurer Kraftansammlung zurückzog und die vorgeschobenen Posten seines mittellater lichen Expansionsdranges geistig und politisch preisgab, hat es den Osmanen möglich gemacht, den Islam zeitweilig tief in die christlichen Länder vorzutragen und aus diesen Siegen die Mittel zu einer letzten Glanzzeit der islamischen Geschichte zu gewinnen. Dieses ‚Einkommen' hat für eine Zeit den Ausfall wettmachen können, den ökonomisch die Verlegung des politischen Zentrums aus dem eigentlichen Bereich des Morgenlandes heraus auf einen Boden mit ganz anderen Lebensbedingungen mit sich bringen musste. Der Islam war damit ‚sinnlos' geworden. Er hat die neu eroberten Gebiete eben darum auch nicht gewinnen können. Die nationalen Kräfte, die ihm die letzte Scheinblüte ermöglicht hatten, waren in der mächtigen Expansion rasch aufgezehrt. Je mehr Europa, überlegen in seiner Erneuerung seit den Tagen der Renaissance, den alten Machtbereich zurückgewinnt und mit den Waffen seiner Kultur, Zivilisation und Politik die islamischen Gebiete erobert, desto deutlicher tritt der ‚Pariacharakter' des Islams hervor. A. Salz hat in dieser Zeitschrift[115] dargelegt, wie Hand in Hand mit solcher ‚Dekadenz' der Islam eben wegen dieses Pariacharakters heute eine Steigerung seines Umfangs und seiner geistigen Macht erlebt.

NOTES

1 Vgl. die Zumsammenfassung und Hinweise bei V. Christian, ‚Untersuchungen zur Paläoethnol. des Orients.' *Mitt. d. Anthrop. Ges. Wien* LIX (1924) 2 ff.
2 M. Weber, *Wirtschaft und Gesellschaft* S. 256.
3 Vgl. O. Spengler, *Untergang des Abendlandes*, II 314 ff.
4 A. Harnack, *Dogmengesch.* II[4] 341 ff., 410 ff.
5 Die Geschichte dieses Aktes ist recht prekär geworden, seit die Kritik des französischen Jesuiten H. Lammens den Wert unserer Quellen darüber mit Recht in Frage gestellt hat (s. sein: Qoran et Tradition, comment fut composé la vie de Mahomet. *Rech. des Sciences rel., 1910*), vergleichbar der auf dem Gebiet frührömischer Geschichte von dem Italiener E. Pais betätigten. Beide haben damit der Geschichtsschreibung einer ganzen Epoche den Todesstoss versetzt; dass sie selbst in ebendemselben Rahmen noch grotesk zu nennende Versuche einer historischen Erkenntnis unternehmen, macht die Sachlage nur noch augenfälliger (vgl. C.H. Becker, Grundsätzliches zur Leben-Muhammed-Forschung. *Islamstudien* 520 ff.). Wie für jede Frühzeit (für die römische vgl. meine «Zenturienordnung», *Vierteljahrschr. f. Soz. u. Wirtschaftsgesch. XVI* [1922]) werden auch hier in einer Betrachtung des ‚Kairos', der geschichtlichen Situation der Geburtsstunde, und in der Deutung des in seiner Objektivierung fassbaren geschichtlichen Aktes, zuverlässigere Quellen als in der Ueberlieferung zu suchen sein.
6 H. Grimme, *Mohammed* II 36.
7 H. Ritter, *Muhammed* (in Meister der Politik III) 152.
8 Ueber die Begriffe: ‚ethische' – ‚exemplarische' Prophetie s. M. Weber, a. a. O. S. 255 ff.
9 Auch der islam kennt eine *imitatio* Mohammeds; aber gerade was jede der beiden Welten unter der *imitatio* versteht – mit Berücksichtigung des jeweils Wesentlichen und bewusster Abstraktion von da wie dort vorhandenen gegenläufigen Tendenzen – macht ihren Unterschied sinnfällig: im Islam ist die Imitatio nicht so sehr ethische als rituelle Uebung; so trachtet ein Frommer, sein Gebet dort zu verrichten, wo der Prophet es getan, das Kamel am gleichen Orte lagern zu lassen wie er (vgl. I. Goldziher, *Vorlesungen über den Islam*, S. 30 f.). Das Tun und Lassen des Propheten, selbst in den kleinsten Einzelheiten des täglichen Lebens, wird allgemein zur Quelle einer religionsgesetzlichen Regelung der gesamten lebenspraxis: auch die gestalt Mohammeds, wahrlich eine gewaltige, wenn auch nie sich exemplarisch empfindende, steht in dieser Welt als in eine Summe einzelner Bestimmungen zerfallende gesetzliche Instanz.

Gegenüber den im wesentlichen exemplarischen Heiligen der Kirche kennt der islam zunächst seinem Prinzipe nach überhaupt keine Heiligen. Mohammed selbst betont, dass er ein schwacher sterblicher Mensch sei, nicht imstande, ausser seiner (der willkürlichen Gnade Gottes verdankten) Prophetie irgendein Wunder zu wirken. Der spätere islam hat dann – den Forderungen der Volksreligiosität Rechnung tragend – die Heiligenverehrung aufgenommen; aber diese muslimischen Heiligen sind wenig exemplarische Gestalten, vielmehr – der Prophet an der Spitze – grosse Wundertäter und Zauberer, die konkurrierend mit ihren willkürlichen Werken neben den ebenso willkürlichen Allah treten. Vgl. I. Goldziher, Die Heiligenverehrung im Islam. *Muhammedanische Studien*, II 275 ff.

10 Auch hier wieder der Gegensatz zum Christentum: die Intention von dessen Gesetz ist durch die Gestalt Christi klar bestimmt und – wenigstens solange die Kirche heil ist – gegen kasuistische Auflösung oder Verkehrung gefeit.

11 Koran II 181. XXII 77. Vgl. I. Goldziher, *Vorlesungen*, S. 60.

12 I. Goldziher a. a. O.

13 Der älteste Katechismus (*ʿakāda*), das *fikh al-akbar*, wird 199 H = 814/15 D angesetzt. A. v. Kremer, *Gesch. d. herrschenden Ideen des islams*, S. 43.

14 Freilich nicht «durch Gottes Liebe, Wohlgefallen und Befehl», die bei den Gott wohlgefälligen Werken ausserdem noch mitwirken. *Fikh al-akbar* bei Kremera. a. O.

15 Katechismus des Nasafī (st. 537/1142 zu Bagdad), kommentiert von Taftazānī (st. 791/1389 zu Buchara), beides franz. bei Mouradgead'Ohsson, *Tableau gén. de l'empire Othoman* I 21 ss. Art. 16 verlangt zu glauben, ... que de tous les péchés énormes il n'est d'irrémissible auprès la justice de Dieu que celui du polythéisme (schirk) qui attaque son unité; qu'il ne dépend que de la volonté de Dieu de pardonner entièrement ou de punir les grands péchés commes les moindres, pourvu toutefois qu'il ne s'y mêle aucune impiété, laquelle consisteroit à regarder comme licite ce que la foi condamne, le défaut de croyance seul emportant par lui même le caractère d'infidélité. Kommentar: ... Il est enfin de foi que le repentir, l'acte de componction, efface ou plutôt diminue l'énormité du péché. Art. 18 verspricht den Gläubigen, dass sie nicht ewig im höllischen Feuer verweilen werden.

16 Kremer, *Herrschende Ideen* S. 130 (Ihjā II 344).

17 Die orientalischen Geschichtswerke noch des 13. Jahrh.s berichten fast auf jeder Seite die unerhörtesten Treulosigkeiten und Lügen, ohne ein Wort tadelnden Urteils hinzuzusetzen. Ja zuweilen erzählen Leute von sich selbst uns moralisch höchst verwerflich erscheinende Taten (z. B. Nesawī, *Hist. du Sultan Djelal ed-din Mankobirti*, trad. p. O. Houdas [*Publications de l'école des langues orient. vir.* 3e ser. IV] 337 ss.) – ein Beweis, wie wenig man an eine ernstliche Berücksichtigung der doch vorhandenen sittlichen Forderungen dachte. Aber schon ist eine Tendenz zu ethischer Beurteilung – wie sie in späteren Werken durchaus angetroffen wird – unverkennbar. Um 1300 berichtet der Autor des ‚Fürstenspiegels' *El-Fachrī* (trad. p. E. Amar [*Arch. Maroc.* XVI] 112 ff. eine Gemeinheit, die deren Verüber selbst erzählt hat, worauf der Autor: «Ich weiss wahrhaftig nicht, worüber ich mich mehr wundern soll: über die Täuschung seines Auftrraggebers ... oder über die Art, mit der er von sich selbst eine Aufführung wie diese berichtet.»

18 Also nicht nur nach der Herkunft der ‚Spolien', sondern vor allem

nach ihrer Bedeutung und nach dem Geist, in welchem sie verwendet werden, ist zu fragen. Wenn etwa der Kalifenhof von den Byzantinern das Eunuchenwesen übernimmt, so ist das doch wohl nur als Rückwanderung morgenländischen Gutes und nicht als Abhängigkeit von der Antike zu werten.

19 Einen Querschnitt durch diese so ungemein wichtige Epoche legt das nachgelassene Werk von A. Mez, *Die Renaissance des Islams*, eine stattliche Materialsammlung.

20 Angeblich hat ʿOmar diesen Titel gewählt, um der Schwerfälligkeit seiner ganz korrekt ‚Kalife des Kalifen des Gesandten Gottes' lautenden Titulatur auszuweichen (Tabarī I 2748. Vgl. L. Caetani, *Annali dell'Islam*, zu A. H. 13, § 140).

21 Schon unter dem Kalifen ʿOsmān soll ʿAlī von seinen Anhängern erst zum Wezir des Propheten bis zu dessen erwarteter Wiederkehr erklärt, als Kalife aber geradezu zur Gottheit erhoben worden sein; nach seinem Tode wartete man auf seine Wiederkunft als gerechter herrscher. Weil, *Gesch. d. Kalifen* II 36 ff.

22 M. Webera. a. O. 124 ff.

23 Doch ist auch noch durch das Medium der von der frommen Opposition als Waffe gegen die weltlichen ʿUmajjaden in Umlauf gesetzten ‚Geschichte' der Rāschidūn erkennbar, einer tendenziösen Utopie, die später in der Abbasidenzeit zum Dogma erhoben wurde und dann von den Theologen-Juristen mit Vorliebe benützt ward, um in ihr erst nachträglich entwickelte Zustände der Folgezeit unterzubringen, denen so, indem man sie in diese dem Propheten noch nahe Frühzeit projizierte, religiöse Weihe verliehen wurde. Vgl. z. B.J. Wellhausen, *Das arabische Reich und sein Sturz*, S. 177 f.

24 Die arab. Völkerwanderung, d. i. das Ausschwärmen arab. Stämme in den Wüsten-Raum zwischen dem syrischen und dem mesopotamischen Kulturland, belegt bereits eine Inschrift Salmanassars II. von 854 v. Chr., auf der in der um Damaskus gescharten Koalition gegen Assur neben Ahab von Israel auch ein Gindibu, der Aribi, erscheint (H. Winkler, Auszug aus der *Vorderasiat. Gesch.* S. 71). Der bedeutendste vorislamische Versuch, einen arabischen Staat zu gründen, war von Palmyra aus unternommen worden, das aus der Oase und dem Karawanenhandel ein selbständigen Bestand und politische Aspirationen ermöglichendes Einkommen bezog. In Roms Bedrängnis kann sein Regent sich «selbständiger Statthalter des Kaisers für den Osten» nennen und Zenobia, die Witwe nach ihm, für ihren unmündigen, zum römischen Kaiser ausgerufenen Sohn auch in Aegypten und Kleinasien gebieten, bis Aurelian 273 der Herrlichkeit von Staat und Stadt ein Ende macht (Mommsen, *Röm. Gesch.* V 428 ff.). Was hernach an arabischen Staaten selbständig besteht – wenn es überhaupt diesen Namen verdient – hat die Subsidien des persischen, bzw. römischen Nachbarn zur Voraussetzung, durch welche die Könige, ein ihnen die Herrschaft verbürgendes Kriegerkorps zu unterhalten, instand gesetzt sind. Ein Ausbleiben der oströmischen. Subsidien lässt den Gassaniden-‚Staat' augenblicklich in Stämme zerfallen, die zur Beute der Perser werden (613/4).

25 Unter ‚Arabertum' ist hier – im Gegensatz zu der sprachlich allerdings rasch arabisierten aramäischen Bevölkerung des Kulturlandes – das Städtertum der Halbinsel und der Standlager sowie die Beduinen der Wüste verstanden.
26 Für die 'Umajjadenzeit vgl., falls kein anderer Hinweis, J. Wellhausen, *Das arab. Reich und sein Sturz*.
27 A. v. Kremer, *Herrschende Ideen*, S. 392 ff. Unter den Herrschern der Dynastie sind der 2., 3., 5. und 6. als Nachfolger des Vaters auf den Thron gelangt.
28 H. Lammens, *Le berceau de l'Islam*. 94 ff., 154 ff.
29 A. v. Kremer, *Kulturgeschichte des Orients* I 160.
30 Stolz lässt der Dichter Farazdak die Beduinen seiner Zeit dem Herrscherhause (das nach Merwān I [683–685] hier apostrophiert wird) zurufen (Hamāsa, Uebers. von F. Rückert):

Haus Merwans gebt uns unser Recht und nah sind wir euch gerne.
Doch wenn ihr dieses uns versagt, so lasst uns in die Ferne.
Denn offen steht und frei uns noch von euch ein Weg, ihr Fürsten,
Mit unsern Falben, welche nach dem Hauch der Wüste dürsten ...

31 H. Lammens, l. c. 227 f.
32 I. Goldziher, Du sens propre des expressions Ombre de Dieu, Khalife de Dieu etc. in *Rev. de l'hist. des religions* XXXV (1897) 331 ff. will das ‚*Chalīfat Allah*' als ursprünglich ‚den von Gott gebilligten Kalifen' bedeutend verstanden wissen. Das mag für einzelne Theologen-Juristen zutreffen, in der Allgemeinheit konnte der Titel gewis nur so wörtlich verstanden werden, wie er gemeint war. Einen anderen theologischen Versuch, den Titel für den Rechtgläubigen zu retten s. u. Anm. 73.
33 So als erster 'Abd al Mālik (685–705). Al-Fachrī (trad. p. Amar), 95.
34 Kremer, *Kulturgesch.* I 148.
35 I. Goldziher, *Muh. Studien* II 34.
36 d. h. der (angeblich) «auf direkte Anordnung, stillschweigende Billigung oder unzweideutige Uebung des Propheten» sich stützende, «in der alten muhammedanischen Gemeinde lebende Usus mit Bezug auf ein religiöses oder gesetzliches Moment.» a. a. O. II 11, 16.
37 Sie sind durch ihre politische Loslösung die erste Sekte im Islam, eine ethisch es durchaus ernst meinende, auf keine Kompromisse sich einlassende ‚puritansiche' Bewegung, jeder Anpassung des Islamds an die Welt, sei diese nun das Kulturland oder das Wüstenarabertum, strenge feind.
38 I. Goldziher, *Muh. Stud.* II 34 ff.
39 J. Wellhausen, a. a. O. 167.
40 Vgl. I. Goldziher, *Vorlesungen* S. 85.
41 I. Goldziher, a. a. O. 49. Vgl. *Moh. Studien* II 52 ff.
42 Auch jetzt hat es nicht an Frommen gefehlt, die lieber Verfolgung litten, als sich im Staatsdienst ihrer Unabhängigkeit zu begeben. Vgl. A. Mez, *Renaissance des Islams* 209 f.
43 I. Goldziher, ‚Ueber Dualtitel.' *Wr. Ztschr. z. Kunde d. Morgenl.* XIII (1899) 325, Anm. 3.
44 Die Vorstellung lässt sich für den Hellenismus und im Neuen

Testament mehrfach belegen [vgl. die Bemerkungen und Hinweise bei F. Babinger, Zwei türk. Schutzbriefe usw. in *Monde orientale* [1920] 128 Anm. 2], sie findet sich bei einem Engländer des 12. Jahrh.s (s. K. Burdach, *Rienzo* S. 239 Anm. I): est ergo ... princeps in terra quaedam divinae majestatis imago. Die Erklärung I. Goldzihers (Du sens propre des expressions Ombre de Dieu usw. in *Rev. de l'hist. d. rel.* XXXV [1897] 331 ff.) als ‚Asyl der Bedrückten' ist zwar belegbar, stellt aber nur einen Ausweg dar, den sich die Theologen angesichts des seinem wirklichen Sinne nach mit dem Islam unvereinbaren Herrschertitels gefunden haben.

45 Gedicht des Ibn al-Mutazz auf Al-Mutadid (892–902). *Ztschr. d. deutsch. Morgenl. Ges.* XL (1886) 563 f.

46 Vgl. I. Goldziher, Islamisme et Parsisme in *Rev. de l'hist. d. rel.* XLIII (1901) 7 ff.

47 *El-Fachrī*, 243 ff. Ueber die Befugnisse des Wezirs vgl. M. Enger in *Ztschr. d. deutsch. Morgenl. Ges.* XIII (1859) 239 ff.

48 Ueber den Wazurg-Framadār der Sassaniden vgl. A. Christensen, *L'emp. Des Sassanides* 32 ff.

49 *El-Fachrī* a. a. O. wird ein vom Kalifen (es ist Nāsir, 1180–1225) eigenhändig ausgestelltes Wezirsdiplom angeführt: «N. N. ist unser Stellvertreter in dem was unser Land und unsere Untertanen betrifft. Wer ihm gehorcht, gehorcht uns, wer uns gehorcht, gehorcht Allah, und wer Allah gehorcht, der kommt ins Paradies. Und wer ihm nicht gehorcht, der gehorcht uns nicht usw. und wer Allah nicht gehorcht, der kommt ins Höllenfeuer.» Das ist nur eine erweiterte Form der Formel: «Glaubet an Gott und gehorchet seinem Propheten.»

50 C.H. Becker, Steuerpacht und Lehenswesen. *Islamstud.* 240 f. setzt die Massregel als eine allgemeine in d. J. 833, obwohl seine Quelle (s. Becker, *Beiträge zur Gesch. Aegyptens* 134) höchstens für Aegypten gilt. Doch darf man annehmen, dass wirklich die Massregel, die von den Verhältnissen längst gefordert war, bald überall durchgeführt worden ist.

51 Seit 844 machen für ein Jahrhundert die Karmaten den Irak zum Ziel ihrer Einfälle; um 1050 dringen Beduinen über den Nil nach Afrika. Seither gilt die Perspektive, aus der um 1400 Ibn Chaldūn schreibt (zitiert bei Kremer, *Herrsch. Ideen* 404 f.): «Betrachtet alle Länder, welche die arabischen Beduinen seit den ältesten Zeiten erobert haben: die Kultur ist ebenso dahingeschwunden wic die Bevölkerung und der Boden selbst scheint seine Natur geweschselt zu haben ...» Die letzte grosse Beduinenbewegung war die Mitte des 18. Jahrh.s einsetzende, noch heute nicht abgeschlossene der Wahhabiten. Als zu Ende des Weltkriegs die den Schutz des Kulturlandes ausübende türkische Armee Syrien räumen musste, waren die Städter – arabisch rendende Muslims und Christen – bis zum Eintreffen der Engländer in tötlicher Angst vor Beduinenüberfällen, ein beweis, dass der uralte Gegensatz auch heute noch latent fortwirkt und empfunden wird.

52 Das unter den ʿUmajjaden so blühende Hidjāz war verödet: mit dem Aufhören der Sicherheit war auch die Plantagenwirtschaft unmöglich geworden. Die Frommen waren zumeist nach dem Sitz der Theokratie,

nach Bagdad abgewandert. Die Pilgerzüge unterblieben zeitweilig wegen der Beduinen, die vorübergehend sogar den schwarzen Stein aus Mekka entführten. Um die Mitte des 10. Jahrh.s werden dann in den beiden hl. Städten die alidischen Scherīfe unabhängig.

53 Vgl. Kremer, *Kulturgesch.* I 274 f.

54 Kremer, a. a. O. 263–379. Hier im Fruchtland liegen vor allem die Krondomänen. Vgl. Kremer, Ueber das Einnahmebudget des Abbasiden-Reiches v. J. 306 H. (*Denkschr. d. Wr. Ak. d. W., phil.-hist. Kl.* XXXVI), S. 14.

55 A. Mez, *Renaissance des Islams* I f.

56 Dass diese Ehrentitel, wenn auch weniger eine Spezielle Bedeutung, so doch einen die religiösen und politischen Tendenzen jedes Zeitalters im grossen und ganzen widerspiegelnden Inhalt besitzen, zeigt M. von Berchem, Eine arab. Inschrift aus dem Ostjordanlande, in *Ztschr. d. deutsch. Palästina-Ver.* XVI (1893) 90 ff. Die in der Abbasidenzeit so überaus häufig werdenden Ehrentitel haben zunächst ausschliesslich religiösen Anstrich. In der Verfallszeit tragen die weltlichen Herrscher, selbst die Wezire, die weltliche Machtbefugnis anzeigende Ehrennamen (mit *daula* ‚Dynastie', *mulk* ‚Königtum', *mulūk* ‚Könige' zusammengesetzt), die sie dem Kalifen gegen Anerkennung seiner geistlichen Autorität zu entreissen wussten (seit etwa 900).

57 S. o. Anm. 50.

58 *El-Fachrī* a. a. O. 484 f. In tiefer Resignation klagt dieser letzte Erbe (vgl. Weil, *Gesch. d. Kalifen* II 677 Anm. 2. das Original bei Abu'l-Mahäsin, *Annales* ed. Juynboll II 294 und Abu'l-feda, ed. Reiske-Adler II 410):

Alles Klare bald wird trübe, Sicherheit verwandelt sich in Sorge nur.
Jugend führt zu Alter, führt zu Tod.
Tut der Menschheit neben Grauhaar noch ein Mahner not?
Hoffnung, die du in ein Meer der Täuschung dich verlierst –
Wo sind unsere Väter – losch von ihnen nicht jedwede Spur?

59 Vgl. Amedroz, Abbasid Administration in its decay, *Journ. Roy. Asiat. Soc.*, 1913, 823 ff.

60 Snouck Hurgronje, Der Mahdi. *Verspreide Geschriften* I 147 ff.

61 Ueber den Zusammenhang von Mystik und Schī'a vgl. I. Goldziher, *Vorlesungen* 159 f. R. Hartmann, Zur Frage nach der Herkunft und den Anfängen des Sufismus. *Islam* VI (1916) 40 f.

62 Mutī' 945–973, also 28 Jahre; dessen Sohn Tāī 973–991, 18 Jahre; Kādir 991–1031, 40 Jahre; dessen Sohn Kāīm 1031–1075, 44 Jahre!

63 Vgl. die Investitur eines bujidischen Emīr al-Umarā vom Jahre 979 bei A. Mez, *Die Renaissance des Islāms*, 136: «Der Kalife sass im Empfangshofe, vor ihm der Koran 'Osmāns, auf den Schultern der Mantel, in der Hand der Stab des Propheten, angetan mit dem Schwert des Kalifen. Adlige standen zu beiden Seiten. Die Türken und Deilemiten zogen auf ohne Waffen, dann ihr Fürst. Als diesem gesagt wird, jetzt sei der Blick des Kalifen auf ihn gefallen, küsst er die Erde, so dass sein General ihn erschreckt auf persisch fragt: ‚O König, ist das Gott? . . .'.»

64 Wie stolz klingen gegenüber dem oben Anm. 53 mitgeteilten Gedichte des Ar-Rāḍī die von Kādir überlieferten Verse (Kremer, *Gesch. d. herrsch. Ideen* 127 f.):

Pietät ist es nicht, wenn du auf die Welt verzichtest und nicht aufhörst zu fasten und zu beten.
Pietät ist es, die Lande und Menschen beherrschen, und dabei gerecht und gottsfürchtig sein.

65 Nasafī (s. o. Anm. 15) Art. 32: «Que le véritable Kaliphat ne dura que trente ans et qu'après ce période il n'y eut que dominations, puissances, souverainités, Emaréth. Kommentar: C'est point est appuyé sur cette parole du Prophète (natürlich!): «Le Kaliphat après moi sera de trente années; après ce terme il n'y a que des puissances établies par la force, l'usurpation, le tyrannie» L'évènement vérifia cette prédiction, puisqu' Aly eut la couronne du martyre à 40e année de l'Hégire et la 30e de la mort du Prophète; de sorte que le vicariat des quatre premiers Kaliphes est distingué sous le nom de Khilaféth-Kéamilé, Khaliphat parfait, par opposition à celui des Kaliphes postérieurs, caracterisé du nom de Khilaféth-ghayr'y-Kéamilé, Khaliphat imparfait ...»

66 Vgl. zu dem ganzen Absatz das oben S. 377–381 Gesagte.

67 *Constitutiones politicae.* ed. M. Enger, franz. von L. Comte Ostorog, *Traité de droit pub. mus.* und Fagnon, *Les Status gouverne-mentaux* etc. (Alger 1915). Die hier herangezogenen Partien nach Kasi, Das Kalifat nach islam. Staatsrecht, in *Welt d. Islams* V (1917) 228 ff.

68 Nasafī, a. a. O. Art. 31–38.

69 «Die Bewohner der Hauptstadt geniessen keinen Vorzug vor den übrigen Volksgenossen; nur die Gewohnheit und die Praxis, nicht aber das Gesetz bestimmt, dass sie, weil sie den Tod des Herrschers früher erfahren, auch früher zur Wahl des neuen Souveräns schreiten können. Es ist zu bemerken, dass die passiv Wahlberechtigten sich gewöhnlich in der Hauptstadt aufhalten.» So Māwerdī. Praktisch haben in der Abbasidenzeit die Wezire, Diwanvorstände, Nachkommen des Propheten, Kadis, Abbasiden und Notabeln der Hauptstadt die Wahl vorgenommen (s. M.J. Müller, Die oberste Herrschergewalt nach dem musl. Staatsr. *Abh. d. bayr. Ak. d. W., philos.-philol. Kl.* IV [1847] 3. Abt., S. 53 nach Abulfeda, *Ann.* II 412 und Freytag, Gesch. d. Hamdaniden, *Ztschr. d. deutsch. morgenl. Ges.* X 467).

70 Die Designierung ist für beide Teile verbindlich und keiner darf sie für sich allein rückgängig machen. Der Sinn der sehr ausführlichen diesbezüglichen Erörterungen liegt in der Fiktion, dass hier alles nach bestem Wissen und Gewissen erfolgt und es sich hier überhaupt um Wissbares handelt. Die Wirklichkeit bot ein sehr anderes Bild. Es war keine leichte Sache für den Autor, die Fülle von Willkür, welche die Kalifatsgeschichte gerade in bezug auf die Nachfolgerbestimmung enthält, mit der Theorie wenigstens halbwegs in Einklang zu bringen. Alles was mit Zustimmung oder auch nur stillschweigender Duldung der ʿUlemā, dieser Repräsentanten der Gemeinde, sich eingebürgert hatte, galt ja als durch Idjmāʿ sanktioniert und musste irgendwie

untergebracht werden. Wie z. B. kann von Wahl oder Designation beim Emporkommen des ersten ʿUmajjaden oder des ersten Abbasiden gesprochen werden, die beide ihre Herrschaft dem Schwert verdanken? Davon wird aber kein Wort gesagt. Hier ist eben auch die kunstvertigste Kasuistik am Ende.

71 D. h. er muss als Theologe-Jurist ein kanonisches Urteil abgeben können (*Mudjtehid* sein), doch halten nach Schahrastanī (st. 1153) die Sunniten es für genügend, wenn er einen Mudjtehid als Berater ständig in seiner Nähe hat und sich jederzeit bei diesem über das Erlaubte oder Verbotene ein Gutachten (Fetwa) einholen kann.

72 Kremer, *Herrschende Ideen.* 421 f.

73 «Ob man den Herrscher auch ‚Kalifen Gottes' nennen darf, darüber herrscht Streit. Die einen lassen es zu, dass er so genannt wird und begründen es damit, dass es die Rechte Gottes unter den Menschen wahrnimmt, und Gott spricht im Koran (VI 165): «Und er ist, der euch zu Kalifen auf der Erde machte und einen von euch über die andern um Stufen erhöhte.» Aber die Mehrzahl der Rechtsgelehrten lässt das nicht zu . . . Als der Kalife Abu Bekr mit dem Titel, ‚Kalife Gottes' angeredet wurde, erwiderte er: Ich bin nicht der ‚Stellvertreter Gottes', sondern der 'Stellvertreter des Propheten' (Māwerdī).

74 S. o. Anm. 42.

75 Sie bildeten ja – theoretisch in voller Unabhängigkeit vom Herrscher – das Gesetz selbständig weiter und sogar in administrativen Fragen musste sich die Regierung von Rechts wegen bei Neuerungen ein Fetwa holen.

76 Barthold-Becker, Studien über Kalif und Sultan, in *Islam* VI (1916) 359.

77 Ein schmeichlerischer Dichter hatte Nāsir das Epitheton eines ‚Mahdī' gegeben, neben dem die Erwartung eines messianischen Mahdī überflüssig geworden sei! Goldziher, *Vorl.* 230 Anm. I.

78 Die Schuld, die Mongolen gerufen zu haben, fällt unzweifelhaft Nāsir zur Last. Wenn die von dem sehr viel späteren Mīrchond (st. 1498) berichtete Gesandtschaft an Djingizchan auch bei den zeitgenössischen Autoren wie Nesawī und Ibn Asīr fehlt (von einem Briefwechsel d. J. 1217 weiss übrigens schon Raschīd ed-dīn [um 1300]), so findet sich doch bei dem letzteren eine Bemerkung (Weil, *Gesch. d. Kalifen* III 380), die zeigt, dass schon damals diesbezügliche Gerüchte umliefen, die freilich der ergebene Bagdader Beamte «nicht aufs Papier setzen wollte». Nesawī hat die Neigung, alles dem Ansehen des Kalifen Unzuträgliche zu unterdrücken. Immerhin entschlüpft ihm eine verräterische Mitteilung: Eine Karawane soll abgefasst werden, bei der sich Gesandte der Tataren mit für den Bagdader Diwan verfänglichen Schriftstücken befinden (*Hist. de Djelal-ed-din*, trad. p. Houdas, p. 262). Die Behandlung der Frage durch Barthold in dessen mir unzugänglichem: *Turkestan im Zeitalter der Mongolen* II 430 (zitiert *Islam* VI 365 Anm. 2) muss hier leider unberücksichtigt bleiben.

79 *El-Fachrī*, um 1300 in Mossul, also ausserhalb der Einflusssphäre Aegyptens, geschrieben, lässt das Kalifat ausdrücklich 1258 zu Ende

sein und weiss nichts von einem Fortbestand desselben anderswo (p. 571).

80 Barthold-Becker, a. a. O. 361.

81 A. a. O. 359 werden als Belege spanische Münzen des 12. Jahrh.s, der Geograph Jakut (13. Jahrh.) und Marco Polo (Ende des 13. Jahrh.s) angeführt.

82 So in der anonym. *Seldschukengeschichte* Blochet (Coll. Schéfer) Par. pers. nr 1553, referiert von M. Th. Houtsma in *Mededeel. d. Kon. Ak. v. Wetensch. Afd. Letterk.* III/9 (Amsterdam 1893) p. 141. Nach Mirchond, *Seldschukengesch.* (deutsch von Vullers) 62 will der byzantinische Kaiser (Romanus IV. Diogenes) in Bagdad an die Stelle des Kalifen einen ‚Katholikos' (so! nicht einen ‚Katholiken'! vgl. den pers. Text, ed. Vullers p. 69) setzen. Katholikos heisst der armenische Patriarch, also ebenfalls ein nur geistlicher Würdenträger. Der von Nallino *(Appunti sulla Natura del Callifato* etc. [Rom, Minist. delle Colonie, 1919, p. 10, n. i] beigebrachte Vergleich eines um 1681 schreibenden arab. Autors zwischen dem Kalifen und dem römisch-deutschen Kaiser (Karl V) dagegen hat – in sehr später Zeit gezogen – die Glanzzeit des Kalifates im Auge.

83 Barthold-Becker, a. a. O. 369, 379.

84 Ibn 'Arabschah, *Biographie des Sultans Djakmak* (vgl. Strong, *Journ. Asiat. Soc.* 1907, S. 395 ff.), hier nach Kremer, *Herrsch. Ideen* zitiert. – Der Parole: ‚Die 'Ulemā sind die Erben des Propheten' stellen die Derwische einen Prophetanausspruch entgegen, wonach vom jahr 200 (sc. d. Hidjra) an das Mönchstum im Islam die Stellung der Propheten einnehmen werde (Goldizher, *Ztschr. f. Assyr.* XXII 342 f.). – Ein mystisches Kalifat vertritt der 1191 auf Saladins Befehl als Ketzer hingerichtete Suhra-werdī, der den 'Ulemā und deren Gelehr samkeit seine charismatische Auf-fassung von der Wissenschaft gegenüberstellt: «Die Wissenschaft ist keine Pfründe, die ausschliesslich nur einer Klasse von heuten zukommt, hinter welschen die Pforte der Geisterwelt abgesperrt wird ... sondern jener, der uns die Wissenschaft in Gnade verlieh, geizt nicht mit den übersinnlichen Geheimnissen!» «Die Welt war nie ganz ohne Philosophie und ohne einen Mann, der sie pflegte und welchen Beweise und offenkundige Tatsachen als solchen kennzeichneten. Dieser ist der Stellvertreter Allahs (*chalīfat Allah*) auf Erden und so wird es bleiben solange Himmel und Erde dauern ... Unter dieser Herrschaft verstehe ich aber keine Gewaltherrschaft, sondern der Imam, der zugleich Theosoph ist, kann öffentlich die Herrschaft übernehmen und ausüben oder auch insgeheim. In letzterem Falle nennt ihn das Volk den « ‚[mystischen] Pol' (Kutb); ihm gebührt die Herrschaft und lebte er auch in der tiefsten Armut. Kommt nun wirklich die politsche Macht in seine Hand, so ist sein Zeitalter lichterfüllt; geniesst aber das Zeitalter keine solche göttliche Leitung, so wird es von der Finsternis überwältigt» (Kremer, *Herrsch. Ideen* S. 92 ff.). – Die von der Mystik ausgegangen politische Organisation, der Assasinen-Bund, ging darauf aus, auf terroristisch-anarchistischer Basis einem schmalen Kreis von Auserwählten die Möglichkeit zu schaffen, ein ihrer mystischen Geheimlehre gewidmetes Dasein zu leben.

85 S. o. S. 408–409.

86 *El-Fachri*, p. 225. Diese Antwort hat Hulagus Bedenken zerstreut. Der Gelehrte aber rechtfertigt seinen Bescheid später höchst bezeichnend mit dem Schrecken, den der Mongole einflösste, und dem Zorn desselben, der zu befürchten war: er hätte nicht gewagt etwas anderes als die Wahrheit zu sagen! D. h. dass das Charisma, das in den Augen der Menge den Kalifen vergottete, für den Theologen nicht existierte.

87 A. a. O. S. 25.

88 Ravaisse bei Seybold, *Ztschr. d. deutsch. Morgenl. Ges.* LXIII 329.

89 «Man spricht von ‚Sultan', wenn man den Vertreter eines Amtes, von ‚Emīr', wenn man die Person meint.» C.H. Becker bei Seybold a. a. O. und in *Islam* VI 355.

90 A. a. O.

91 A. Müller, *Der Islam im Morgen- und Abendland* II 10 f.

92 S. o. S. 404 die Einverleibung der Mahdī-Idee in die Orthodoxie. Eine andere Sekte der Schī'a, die ‚Siebener' (= ‚Isma'iliten'), lässt die Reihe mit dem 7. Imām, mit Mohammed, dem Sohn des 762 verstorbenen Ismā'il, schliessen. Die ihm nachfolgenden Imāme sind verborgen. Als dann um 900 ein angeblicher Imām dieser Reihe als ‚Mahdī' das Fatimidenreich gegründet hatte (das spätere ägyptische Gegenkalifat), da bedurfte es nur einer so merkwürdigen Erscheinung wie des Kalifen Hākim, um diesen zur Inkarnation Gottes und, nach seinem geheimnisvollen Verschwinden im Jahre 1021, zum verborgen fortlebenden Mahdī zu erklären.

93 S. o. S. 408 den Māwerdī.

94 Zitiert bei Barthold-Becker, *Islam* VI 357. Die Samaniden können nicht wegen des «von den Fremdvölkern stammend» gemeint sein, die Gaznewiden kommen zeitlich nicht in Betracht. Also war hier ganz allgemein an einen türkischen Heerführer des Ostens gedacht.

95 A. Mez, *Renaissance des Islams* 133, wonach C.H. Becker, *Islam* VI 355 wohl zu berichtigen sein wird.

96 Z. B. dem berühmten Seldjukensultan von Konia, 'Alā ed-dīn Kaikobad I (1210–1236). Vgl. die Inschrift Nr. 53 bei C l. Huart, Epigr. arabe d'Asie Mineure in *Rev. Sem.* III (1895) 354, sowie die von B. Moritz mitgeteilte vom Sultan Han: F. Sarre, *Reise in Kleinasien.* 85. Nach Ibn Bibi, ed. Houtsma (= Rec. II) 221 hatte der Kalife dem Kaikobad ein Diplom über «Sultanat und Stellvertreterschaft (nijābet) von Rum (= Kleinasien), Armenien und Diarbekir» übersendet.

97 Zu den weltlichen Ehrentiteln mit *daula*, *mulk* usw. treten nun seit etwa 1000 die mit *islām, milla* (geistige Seite des Islams, also etwa «Ecclesia») und besonders die mit *dīn* zusammengesetzten. M. van Berchem, a. a. O. (s. o., Anm. 56).

98 L. Cahun, *Introduction à l'hist. de l'Asie.*

99 M. van Berchem, *Mat. pour un Corp. Inscr. Arab.* I passim, bes. 106 ff. 260 ff.

100 So berichtet *El-Fachrī*, p. 28 s, dass unter den Mongolen sich der Geschmack der Fürsten von den formalistischen philogischen Wissenschaften (Syntax, Lexikographie, Poesie, Geschichte; «oft

verdankte man eine Rangerhöhung der Erzählung einer einzigen Anekdote, der Rezitation eines einzigen Verses, sogar lediglich dem glücklichen Gebrauch eines einzigen Ausdruckes») weg den Finanz- und Verwaltungswissenschaften, sowie der Medizin und Astrologie zuwandte.

101 ʿUtbī, *Kitāb Jemīnī,* verf. etwa 1015. Hier mit einigen Kürzungen die Uebersetzung von Th. Nöldeke, Ueber das Kit. Jem. *S.-B. d. Wr. Ak. d. W., ph.-h Kl.* XXIII (1857) 38 ff.

102 A. a. O. S. 88. Der schīʿitische Ursprung dieser – später allgemein gültigen – ‚Sultanatstheorie' stimmt sehr gut zu dem o. S. 414–415 über den Anteil der Schīʿa an dem Ursprung des Sultanates überhaupt Gesagten.

103 Ibn Khallikan, ed. Slane I p. XXVIII s. (Die erste Medrese ist die von Abu Ishāk al Isfarainī (st. 1027), einem Anhänger des Aschʿarī, in Nischapur gegründet – eine private Lehranstalt).

104 M. van Berchem *Matériaux u.s.w.* s. Index ‚Medrese'.

105 Vgl. D. Haneberg, Schul- und Lehrwesen der Muhammedaner im Mittelalter. München (*Ak. d. w.*) 1850.

106 Vgl. C.H. Becker, Islam und Wirtschaft. *Islamstudien* S. 62.

107 So den Mahmūd von Gazna, Saladin und den Chwarezmier Djelāl ed-dīn. s. C. Brockelmann, *Gesch. d. arab. Lit.* 157 f.

108 Dass er zufällig ein Kurde war, ist belanglos. Das Folgende nach Görgen-Röhricht, *Arab. Quellen z. Gesch. d. Kreuzz.* 145 f.

109 C.H. Becker, Steuerpacht und Lehenswesen. *Islamstud.* I 234 ff.

110 S. o. S. 412.

111 Kremer, *Herrsch. Ideen* 416.

112 Ibn Chaldūn (um 1400), *Prolégomènes* 350 ff.

113 *El-Fachrī* S. 55.

114 Vgl. Barthold-Becker a. a. O. 374 ff. Die Frage nach der (angeblichen) Uebertragung des Kalifates an Selim I durch den Kairiner Abbasiden (a. a. O. 386 ff.) ist gegenüber der neuen Auffassung vom Kalifat durchaus von sekundärer Bedeutung.

115 *Arch. f. Sozialwiss.* XLVII (1920) 376 ff.: ‚Ueber das Problem der Dekadenz im Islam.'

13

DIE ARABISCHE *ḤIJAL*-LITERATUR

Ein Beitrag zur Erforschung der islāmischen Rechtspraxis[1]

Joseph Schacht

1

Es ist in der Geschichte des islāmischen Gesetzes tief begründet, dass es sich mit dem Entstehen des Rechtsstudiums als solchen und des Standes der Fuqahā' in immer schärfer werdenden Gegensatz zur Praxis, zum täglichen Leben stellen musste und immer weniger Einfluss darauf ausüben konnte. Nichtsdestoweniger erhob es stets den Anspruch, das Leben seiner Bekenner in seinem vollen Umfang ohne Einschränkung zu beherrschen. Jedoch das Bild, das die Rechtsgelehrten von der muslimischen Idealgemeinde, die ganz nach den Vorschriften des göttlichen Gesetzes eingerichtet ist, entwerfen, kann nach ihrer eigenen auf Weissagungen des Propheten[2] gestützten Überzeugung nur für die den Augen der späteren Generationen paradiesisch erscheinenden ersten Jahrzehnte des Islām und für das am Ende der Tage kommende Reich des Mahdī gelten und in der verderbten und immer schlechter werdenden Gegenwart nicht in die Praxis umgesetzt werden. Gleichwohl bildet das Gesetz Allāhs den einzigen Gegenstand wahrer Wissenschaft, und wenngleich der Staat und die Gesellschaft, in der die Fuqahā' lebten, in mancher Beziehung unabhängig von ihrer Weisheit sich entwickelten, sie behielten die Herrschaft über die Geister. Das Gesetz, das im praktischen Leben dem Brauch und der Sitte der Völker und der Willkür der

Source: *Der Islam*, 1996, vol. 15, pp. 211–32.

Herrscher immer mehr Platz einräumen musste, gewann also auf der andern Seite als Ideal bedeutenden Einfluss auf das geistige Leben der Muhammedaner.

Der Islām besitzt aber Mittel, um ohne das geringste Nachgeben in den Grundsätzen diesen Widerstreit zwischen Theorie und Praxis zu überbrücken, einen annehmbaren modus vivendi mit den von ihm verurteilten Gewohnheiten zu finden. Zwei Sätze kommen hier vor allem in Betracht: die bereits erwähnte Überzeugung von dem bis zur Zeit des Mahdī stets fortschreitenden Verfall der islāmischen Gemeinde und die ausdrücklich anerkannte Lehre, dass die «Notwendigkeit die Gesetze bricht» und dass es infolgedessen unter Umständen erlaubt ist, die gesetzlichen Vorschriften nicht zu erfüllen, ja sogar ihnen geradezu zuwiderzuhandeln, wenn nämlich ein Zwang zu diesen Übertretungen vorliegt. Daher gibt es sogar Gelehrte, die da, wo der Konflikt zwischen den Bedürfnissen des Lebens und den Anforderungen des Gesetzes ihnen zu stark wird, sich praktisch ohne jegliche Ausrede über diese hinwegsetzen. Überhaupt gilt ja das Übertreten eines Verbotes für viel weniger sündhaft als seine Nichtigerklärung, die in den meisten Fällen als Unglaube anzusehen ist.

Die Muslims betrachten zwar das ganze Fiqh als göttlichen Ursprungs, machen aber gleichwohl einen bedeutenden Unterschied zwischen seinen verschiedenen Kapiteln in bezug auf ihren religiösen Charakter. Von den Zeremonialgesetzen versteht es sich von selbst: wer sich dárum nicht kümmert, ist ein Sünder. Aber auch die Familiengesetze haben ihre besondere Heiligkeit: Vergehen gegen sie werden ganz anders beurteilt als etwa Abweichungen vom Sachenund Obligationenrecht. Zwar gilt die Übertretung des Wucherverbots als eine schwere Sünde, aber sonst steht es dem Eigentümer frei, über das Seinige in anderer als der vom Gesetz angeordneten Weise zu verfügen. So hat die Bedeutung gerade des Sachen- und Obligationenrechtes sowie des Strafrechtes des Islām für das wirkliche Leben immer mehr abgenommen. Es gibt aber zu allen Zeiten und Orten Fromme, die, wenn es ohne allzugrosse Schwierigkeiten geht, in ihren Privatgeschäften dem kanonischen Rechte gern Rechnung tragen,[3] und überhaupt ist es hier im einzelnen oft ungemein schwer, die Stelle zu finden, wo die theoretische Forderung nicht mehr Ideal bleibt, sondern zum praktischen Lebenseinfluss wird; auch spielt ja zweifellos die Frage der persönlichen Gewissenhaftigkeit und der allgemeine Volkscharakter hinein, weshalb man sich sehr vor unberechtigten Verallgemeinerungen hüten muss.[4]

2

Hier liegt nun der Ausgangspunkt für die *hijal*- oder Rechtskniffliteratur: um dem Gläubigen die Befolgung der Vorschriften der *šarīʿa* möglichst zu erleichtern, um die Fälle offener Übertretung des Gesetzes auf Grund der Notwendigkeit möglichst einzuschränken, werden – abgesehen von freierer Interpretation der gesetzlichen Bestimmungen, wie sie in älterer Zeit namentlich die kūfische Theologenschule übte[5] – Geschäfte erdacht, die formal allen Anforderungen des Gesetzes entsprechen, in ihrem Resultat aber auf die Umgehung einer hinderlichen Vorschrift hinauslaufen, richtige Scheingeschäfte, bei denen es häufig die Billigkeit ist, die durch ein solches oft äusserst kompliziertes Verfahren in den Beziehungen zweier Kontrahenten zueinander hergestellt werden soll, während sie, wenn man lediglich die Bestimmungen der *šarīʿa* auf das faktisch zwischen ihnen bestehende Verhältnis anwendete, nicht gewahrt bliebe. Die Fiqh-Bücher selbst geben nicht selten solche *hijal* an[6] und von da ist nur ein Schritt bis zur Zusammenstellung derartiger Kniffe in eigens ihnen gewidmeten Werken. Hier ist eine Seite des Fiqh, die mit der Praxis eng verbunden ist, und hier handelt es sich nicht nur um die wenigen oben genannten Kapitel, die stets praktische Bedeutung hatten, sondern um das Gesetz in seinem wenn auch nicht ganzen, so doch grössten Umfange;[7] suchen doch die *hijal* Theorie und Praxis, Ideal und Wirklichkeit zu versöhnen, und je grösser die Unwirklichkeit und Weltfremdheit ist, desto mehr Kniffe sind nötig. So lassen die *hijal*-Bücher die am unangenehmsten und hinderlichsten empfundenen Gesetzesbestimmungen und die zu ihrer faktischen Umgehung und formalen Beobachtung üblichen Kniffe erschliessen. Hier ist jedoch Vorsicht am Platze. Denn neben Kniffen, denen man ihre Wichtigkeit für die Praxis auf den ersten Blick ansieht, finden sich auch solche, die ihrem ganzen Wesen nach nie praktisch durchgeführt worden sein können, in denen wir vielmehr nur Proben des Scharfsinns und doch auch der Spitzfindigkeit der Fuqahāʾ zu erblicken haben.[8] Unter diesem Vorbehalt aber können die *hijal*-Bücher als ein vorzügliches Hilfsmittel für die Kenntnis der Rechtspraxis gelten, die sich sonst ja zum grossen Teil der Erforschung entzieht.[9]

Noch aus einem andern Grund ist wenigstens das *kitāb al-hijal* des al-Ḫaṣṣāf für die Rechtspraxis besonders aufschlussreich: hier sind nämlich zahlreiche Nachrichten über *šurūṭ* erhalten, die ganz auf die Praxis zugeschnitten sind[10] und an Alter hinter den ältesten erhaltenen ḥanafitischen *šurūṭ*-Werken kaum zurückstehen;[11] und gerade auch in den *šurūṭ* war al-Ḫaṣṣāf Spezialist, da er zwei leider verlorene Schriften eigens diesem Gegenstand gewidmet hat.

3

Nun sind die *ḥijal* gegen eine zu einem gewissen Grade ähnliche Erscheinung, die *taqīja*, abzugrenzen: dies ist die Verleugnung des Glaubensbekenntnisses und die Übertretung von Allāhs Gesetz aus Furcht vor Lebensbedrohung durch eine ungläubige oder irrgläubige Regierung, die bei den Sunniten unter Ausschluss aller den Nächsten schädigenden Handlungen als Konzession theoretisch gestattet wurde, praktisch jedoch kaum zur Anwendung gelangen konnte, bei den Šī'iten aber im Interesse der Gesamtheit oft sogar als Pflicht verlangt und in mehr oder weniger weitem Umfange geübt wurde.[12] Wie die *taqīja*, bei der man sich zunächst doppeldeutiger Ausdrücke bedienen soll, die eine reservatio mentalis ermöglichen, der Begünstigung des zweideutigen Verhaltens in allen Beziehungen des Lebens förderlich ist, so ist sie es vornehmlich auf dem Gebiete des Eides. Überhaupt hat die muḥammedanische Ethic die Billigung der zweideutigen Schwüre und der Kniffe im Eideswesen aus dem vorislāmischen Arabertum ererbt),[13] und der Ansicht, dass man durch zweideutige Ausdrücke der Lüge entgehen könne, hat sie in aufrichtig gemeinten Sentenzen ganz unverhohlen Ausdruck gegeben, so in einem auf 'Umar zurückgefürten Ḥadit: *inna fi ma'āriḍ al-kalām lamandūḥa 'anil-kādb*).[14] In solchen Eidkniffen trifft die juristische *ḥijal*-Literatur mit den Äusserungen über die *taqīja* zusammen. Allerdings bleibt die grundsätzliche Einstellung und wesentliche Zielsetzung auf beiden Seiten stets weit verschieden: die *ḥijal* wendet man an, um selbst unter ungünstigen äusseren Verhältnissen das Gesetz nicht übertreten zu müssen, um hinderliche Vorschriften der *šarī'a* zu umgehen und unerwünschten Rechtsfolgen vorzubeugen, die *taqīja* dagegen übt man, um sich selbst und seine Glaubensgenossen durch offenes Hervortreten mit seinen Überzeugungen nicht in Gefahr zu bringen. Ein Moment der Ähnlichkeit liegt in der Zwangslage, durch die sowohl *ḥijal* wie auch *taqīja* hervorgerufen sind; sie verhalten sich dazu aber in ganz verschiedener Weise, und nur in der Anwendung doppeldeutiger Ausdrücke beim Eide gehen sie zusammen. Gleichwhol können die Rechtskniffe «der in politischer Freiheit lebenden herrschenden Schule der Ḥanafiten» eine gute Folie «zur gerechteren Würdigung des Versteckten und Zweideutigen bei den unter *taqīja* lebenden Sekten» bilden.[15]

4

Soviel mag über den Entstehungsgrund der *ḥijal*-Literatur und ihre Stellung im Fiqh gesagt sein; darüber, welcher Art die Verfahren sind, die zur Anwendung kommen, und welche Elemente sich etwa an den oben gekennzeichneten Grundstock angeschlossen haben, wird später (S. 229ff.) etwas bemerkt werden müssen. Bevor wir uns jetzt einem Überblick über die *ḥijal*-Werke, von denen wir überhaupt Kunde haben, zuwenden, sei noch eine Bemerkung gestattet. Ebenso wie die Fuqahāʾ sich nach *mādāhib* gliedern, führen natürlich auch die Literaturen der einzelnen Rechtsschulen ein Sonderleben: materielle Entlehnungen aus Schriften eines andern *maḏhab* sind teils wegen des *iḫtilāf*, besonders aber wegen des *taqlīd* innerhalb des *maḏhab* recht selten. Formelle Anregungen über die Grenzen des *maḏhab* hinaus sind zwar etwas häufiger; im allgemeinen aber schliesst sich, auch was den Interessenkreis und die Probleme anlangt, die sich in den einzelnen Rechtsschulen in bestimmten Zeiträumen nachweisen lassen, – abgesehen von Fällen von Polemik – jeder *maḏhab* gegen die andern Richtungen ab, was seinen Ausdruck darin findet, dass Schriften über gewisse Spezialfragen[16] innerhalb eines *maḏhab* immer wiederkehren, während sie in den andern Rechtsschulen nur ganz selten auftauchen. So kann und muss die Literatur jedes einzelnen *maḏhab* für sich betrachtet werden. Nun wurde die *ḥijal*-Literatur von Ḥanafiten begründet; deshalb finden wir auch unter ihren Vertretern meist Ḥanafiten und aus andern *maḏāhib* nur drei Šāfiʿiten, über deren Verhältnis zu jenen noch zu sprechen sein wird, während die nicht unbedeutende šīʿitische Literatur über die *taqīja*, die hier im übrigen ausser Betracht bleiben kann, unabhängig entstanden ist und sich entwickelt hat. Es ist ferner äusserst beachtenswert und unsere bereits gewonnene Überzeugung von dem ursprünglich wesentlich praktischen Charakter der *ḥijal* nur bestätigend, dass sie sich innerhalb der ḥanafitischen Fiqh-Literatur mit einer Reihe von andern durchaus praktischen Themen zu einer Gruppe zusammenschliessen, die sich durch eine Reihe von Jahrhunderten verfolgen lässt. Hier ist die Kontinuität und die Macht der literarischen Tradition mit Händen zu greifen: immer dieselben Themen treten in denselben Verbindungen bei den einzelnen Schriftstellern auf, zwar nicht so, dass jeder Autor sie alle bearbeitet hätte, aber doch so, dass diese Gruppe sich von den andern ḥanafitischen Rechtswerken deutlich abhebt.[17] Zu ihr gehören: *ḥijal*, *wuqūf*, *waṣājā*, *šurūṭ* und *mawāṭiq*, *maḥāḍir* und *siğillāt* sowie, in einem gewissen Abstande, *nafaqāt*. Alle diese Themen haben, wie schon bemerkt, auch heute noch praktische Bedeutung und sind, wenigstens zum grossen Teil, auch innerlich verwandt. Auf diesen Zusammenhang möchte ich nachdrücklich hingewisen haben.

5

Am Anfang der ḥanafitischen Rechtskniff-Literatur[18] ist allerdings nicht abū Ḥanīfa zu nennen, auf den wir noch zurückkommen werden, wohl aber abū Jūsuf (st. 182); sein *kitāb al-ḥijal*[19] ist leider verloren[20] und nur ein ausdrückliches Zitat daraus ist erhalten;[21] hauptsächlich auf Grund dieses Buches galt abū Jūsuf dem Witze des Volkes und der Literaten als Typus des spitzfindigen Faqīh, eine Eigenschaft, in der er uns noch begegnen wird. Ein weiteres Rechtskniffbuch rührt her von seinem Schüler Muḥammad ibn al-Ḥasan aš-Šaibānī (st. 189), das anonym in einer Kairiner Handschrift[22] vorliegt; dass dies Werk wirklich das des aš-Šaibānī ist, ergibt sich u. a. daraus, dass er sich selbst als Verfasser nennt; häufig zitiert er Ansichten des abū Jūsif, allerdings nie mit Nennung seines *kitāb al-ḥijal*, das aber doch auf grössere Strecken hin zugrundeliegt. Von aš-Šaibānis Schrift werden uns zwei *riwājas* genannt, die seines Zeitgenossen abū Ḥafṣ al-kabīr Aḥmad ibn Ḥafṣ al-Buḫārī und die des abū Sulaimān Mūsā ibn Sulaimān al-Ǧuzağānī (st. 244), es wird aber noch andere gegeben haben. Entweder die des abū Ḥafṣ selbst oder eine ihr nahestehende wurde von al-Ḥākim aš-Šahīd abul-Faḍl Muḥammad ibn Muḥammad al-Marwazī (st. 344) verkürzend bearbeitet, und dieser Auszug wurde von Šams al-a'imma abū Bakr Muḥammad ibn Aḥmad ibn abī Sahl as-Saraḫsī (st. 483) kommentiert: diese Bearbeitung as-Saraḫsīs ist uns erhalten.[23] Von anderen

Be-arbeitungen des Buches aš-Šaibānīs durch Šams al-a'imma 'Abdal'aziz ibn Aḥmad al-Ḥalwā'ī (st. 456)[24] und durch den Šaiḫ al-islām abul-Ḥasan 'Alī ibn Ḥusain as-Suġdī (st. 461) haben wir wenigstens einzelne Zitate.[25] Ein *kitāb al-ḥijal aš-šar'īja* wird ferner dem eben genannten al-Ǧūzaǧānī (st. 244), einem Schüler des aš-Šaibānī zugeschrieben;[26] da es aber ausdrücklich heisst, dass er keine eigenen Werke verfasst, sondern nur die Schriften des aš-Šaibānī tradiert habe,[27] wird es sich um seine oben behandelte *riwāja* der Schrift von aš-Šaibānī handeln.[28] Auf uns gekommen ist das *kitāb al-ḥijal wal-maḫāriǧ* des abū Bakr Aḥmad ibn 'Amr ibn Muhair aš-Šaibānī al-Ḥaṣṣāf (st. 261), des Hofjuristen des Kalifen al-Muhtadī, der bei Ḥāǧǧi Ḫalīfa (III 120) als bekanntester Vertreter der *ḥijal*-Literatur bezeichnet wird,[29] und zwar in zwei Rezensionen, einer kürzeren älteren, die einen treuen, nur wenig gekürzten Auszug aus dem in äusserst starkem Masse von aš-Šaibānī abhängigen[30] Werke des al-Ḫaṣṣāf bietet, und einer ausführlicheren jüngeren, die eine freie, durchaus selbstständige Bearbeitung darstellt.[31] In ihrem Verfasser, denn so muss man ihn nennen, gewinnen wir demnach einen weiteren, leider anonymen Autor eins *ḥijal*-Buches, der während des vierten Jahrhunderts geschrieben haben muss, wie sich aus inneren und äusseren Argumenten ergibt[32] Zu al-Ḫaṣṣāfs längerer Rezension sind mehrere Kommentare bekannt, einer – noch in Zitaten vorliegend – von dem oben genannten Šams al-a'imma al-Ḥalwā'ī (st. 456), ein weiterer von abū Bakr ibn Muḥammad, bekannt als Ḫwāherzāde (st. 483) und ein dritter von dem gleichfalls erwähnten Šams al-a'imma as-Saraḫsī (st. ebenfalls 483). Endlich sind noch *ḥijal*-Schriften von zwei Autoren zu nennen, die bei Hāǧǧi Ḫalīfa (III 120) erwähnt werden, sonst aber nicht nachzuweisen sind, von Muḥammad ibn 'Ali an-Naḫa'ī, der vielleicht der 324 gestorbene Ḥanafit 'Alī ibn Muḥammed an-Naḫa'ī sein soll, und von Sa'īd ibn 'Alī as-Samarqandī al-Ḥanafī, über dessen Schrift genaue Angaben gemacht werden.

Was die gegenseitigen Beziehungen dieser Werke, soweit sie nicht erhalten sind, anlangt, so können wir natürlich nichts Genaueres feststellen; gleichwohl werden wir kaum fehlgehen, eine engere Abhängigkeit zu vermuten. Über die Beziehungen der erhaltenen Schriften zueinander cf. aš-Šaibānī, Einleitung.

6

Bei der verhältnismässig geringen Menge des von der ḥanafitischen *ḥijal*-Literatur Erhaltenen ist es äussertst erfreulich, dass wir aus der Zeit des al-Ḫaṣṣāf eine zwar sehr wenig umfangreiche, in ihrer Bedeutung aber geradezu einzigartige Quelle für die Kenntnis der älteren ḥanafitischen *ḥijal* in dem *Ṣaḥīḥ* des al-Buḫārī (st. 256) besitzen. Das *kitāb al-ḥijal* dieser Traditionssammlung ist eine einzige Polemik gegen die Rechtskniffe.[34] Wie nicht selten[35] sind auch hier al-Buḫārīs Kapitelüberschriften durchaus tendenziös, da er in ihnen seine Abneigung gegen die *ḥijal* deutlich hervortreten lässt.[36] Aber auch der Text muss seinen Zwecken dienen: mit deutlicher Missbilligung stellt er in ausführlichen Darlegungen die Ansichten der Vertreter der *ḥijal* seinen Traditionen gegenüber, das Urteil über ihre Nichtvereinbarkeit und daher die Verwerflichkeit der Kniffe dem Leser überlassend. Auch die Kommentatoren alʿAinī und al-Qaṣtallānī heben die Tendenz al-Buḫārīs, die über den einfachen Wortlaut der Ḥadīte hinausgehe, hervor und nenne zum Überfluss abū Ḥanīfa und seine Schule als die bekämpften Gegner[37] Im ganzen sind es 14 Stellen, an denen al-Buḫārī die gegnerische Ansicht zu Worte kommen lässt, und aus ihrer genaueren Prüfung ergibt sich Folgendes: die Formulierungen der gegnerischen Ansicht rühren im wesentlichen nicht von al-Buḫārī selbst her, sondern sind Zitate aus den Schriften der von ihm bekämpften Schule, wenn auch hier und da wohl etwas retouchiert; es sind nicht Exzerpte aus einer einzigen Schrift, sondern aus mehreren, wie aus dem Vorkommen von Parallelformulierungen folgt. An mindestens einer Stelle – in Kapitel 15 – hat al-Buḫārī aller Wahrscheinlichkeit nach das *ḥijal*-Buch seines Zeitgenossen al-Ḫaṣṣāf (83, 18–20) oder dessen Quelle, die Schrift des aš-Šaibānī (24, 18–21) benutzt, und zwar, wenn es wirklich al-Ḫaṣṣāf ist, in der kürzeren Rezension, nicht in der längeren (23, 15 f.), was unsere auf anderm Wege gewonnene Ansicht von dem Verhältnis der beiden Rezensionen zueinander durchaus bestätigen würde. Deshalb brauchen aber alle Zitate bei al-Buḫārī nicht etwa auf eigene *ḥijal*-Schriften zurückgeführt zu werden, wenngleich die oben angeführten älteren ḥanafitischen Werke als Quellen natürlich ebenfalls in Betracht kommen;[38] wir wissen ja,[39] dass die *ḥijal* bisweilen auch ausserhalb der Rechtskniffbücher behandelt werden. Wir sehen, wie zu erwarten, eine sehr starke Ähnlichkeit zwischen den Parallelformulierungen, aber zu genaueren Feststellungen, geschweige denn zur Zuweisung einzelner Fragmente an bestimmte Persönlichkeiten, reicht das Material bei weitem nicht aus.

Ein weiteres Hilfsmittel ist das *kitāb al-ḥijal* in dem grossen ḥanafitischen Rechtswerk *al-fatāwā al-ʿālamgīrīja*, wo die in den bedeutenderen Fiqhbüchern der Schule zerstreuten Kniffe mit Angabe der Quelle gesammelt sind; auch die erhaltenen Rechtskniffbücher sind verwertet; einige *ḥijal*-Werke sind nur in diesen Zitaten erhalten. Übrigens sind manche Bestimmungen von den angeführten Autoren garnicht als Kniffe gemeint, sondern erst von den Sammlern, Šaiḫ Niẓām und seinen Helfern, unter den Gesichtspunkt der *ḥīla* gebracht.

Auch ibn Nuǧaim (st. 970; Brockelmann II 310) gibt in dem den *ḥijal* gewidmeten fünften *fann* seines *kitāb al-ašbāh wannaẓāʾir* eine Zusammenstellung zahlreicher Kniffe aus der Literatur des *maḏhab*, allerdings ohne Quellenangabe und lange nicht so ausführlich wie Saiḫ Niẓām.[40]

7

Wir haben oben angedeutet, dass von abū Ḥanīfa (st. 150 oder 151) ein Rechtskniffbuch nicht bekannt ist; nichtsdestoweniger ist auch er hier zu erwähnen: er und sein *maḏhab* nach ihm betonten – allerdings nicht als erste – das spekulative Element bei der Feststellung gesetzlicher Vorschriften, und das *raʾj* ist wirklich aufs engste mit den *ḥijal* verknüpft, sodass es kein Zufall ist, dass die Rechtskniffliteratur gerade von Ḥanafiten besonders gepflegt wurde. Das *raʾj* erschien abū Ḥanīfas Zeitgenossen oft als müssige Spitzfindigkeit, und eben Kniffe sind es, die als Beispiele dafür dienen müssen. So erzählt Ḥammād ibn Salama: es war ein Wegelagerer zur Zeit des Heidentums, der das geraubte Hab und Gut der Pilger mittels eines Krummstabes zu sich heranzuziehen pflegte. Des Raubes angeklagt, pflegte er die Entschuldigung zu gebrauchen: nicht ich, sondern dieser Krummstab hat sich fremdes Gut angeeignet. Ḥammād sagt: lebte dieser Mann noch heute, so gehörte er gewiss zu den Genossen abū Ḥanīfas.[41] Andererseits galten den Anhängern des *al-imām al-aʿẓam* jedenfalls in späterer Zeit seine scharfsinnigen Eidkniffe als besonderer Ruhmestitel ihres Meisters in den *manāqib*,[42] auf den, wie wir sehen werden (cf. unten die Šāfiʿiten nicht wenig neidisch waren, und abū Ḥanīfa erscheint schon bei aš-Šaibānī und al-Ḫaṣṣāf als Überlieferer des obersten Grundsatzes für alle Eidkniffe;[43] aber auch *ḥijal*, die nicht auf dem Gebiete des Eides liegen, werden bei aš-Šaibānī und al-Ḫaṣṣāf[44] auf ihn zurückgeführt. So ist abū Ḥanīfa, mag man über seine Stellung seinen Vorgängern und Zeitgenossen gegenüber denken wie man will[45] für seinen *maḏhab* implicite der Begründer der *ḥijal*-Literatur, wenn er diesem Gegenstand auch keine Schrift gewidmet hat.

Aber wir können die *ḥijal*, nicht als Thema eigener Werke, wohl aber als Gegenstand des Interesses und der Übung noch weiter hinauf verfolgen. Abū Ḥanīfas bedeutendster Lehrer und Vorläufer in der Anwendung des *ra'j* war Ḥammād ibn abī Sulaimān (st. 119 oder 120),[46] und er ist auch sein unmittelbarer Vorgänger im Isnād der eben erwähnten Tradition über Eidkniffe und tritt auch sonst noch als Überlieferer von *ḥijal*-Ḥadīṯen auf.[47] Eine Reihe von *ḥijal*-Traditionen, darunter auch derselbe Grundsatz für Eidkniffe, geht auf den berühmten kūfischen Theologen und Juristen Ibrāhīm an-Naḫaʿī (st. 95 oder 96) zurück.[48] Das ist kein Zufall. Hat doch die kūfische Theologenschule überhaupt sich bemüht, den Anforderungen des Lebens und der tatsächlichen Praxis möglichst Rechnung zu tragen.[49] Eine dieser Traditionen, wenn vielleicht auch nicht geradezu echt, so doch jedenfalls gut erfunden und durchaus bezeichnend, lautet folgendermassen: ʿUqba ibn abil-ʿIzār erzählt: wir pflegten Ibrāhīm zu besuchen, während er sich vor al-Ḥaǧǧāǧ ibn Jūsuf versteckt hielt; wenn wir ihn dann verliessen, sagte er uns gewöhnlich: wenn man euch nach mir fragt und ihr schwören müsst, dann schwört bei Allāh, ihr wisset nicht, wo ich sei, noch an welchem Orte ich mich befinde, und meint dabei, ihr wisset nicht, an welchem Orte (nämlich im Hause) ich gerade sitze oder stehe; dann habt ihr die Wahrheit gesagt.[50] Das ist ein ausgesprochener Eidkniff. Noch etwas älter ist der bekannte al-Muhallab (st. 82 oder 83) mit dem Beinamen al-Kaḏḏāb; er erscheint bei al-Mubarrad[51] als Verbreiter folgenden Ausspruchs des Propheten, der auch bei aš-Šaibānī und al-Ḫaṣṣāf[52] vorkommt (allerdings mit anderm Isnād): die Lüge ist in drei Fällen erlaubt: wenn jemand lügt, um unter zwei Leuten Frieden zu stiften, wenn jemand seiner Gattin gegenüber lügt, und die Lüge im Kriege, ein Grundsatz, der allerlei Kniffe rechtfertigen soll; al-Mubarrad hat der Schilderung seiner Listen einen längeren Abschnitt gewidmet. Ist es auch unmöglich, al-Muhallab in engere Verbindung mit Ibrāhīm zu setzen, so sei er doch als ältester mir bekannter bedeutsamer Vertreter der *ḥijal* im Islām erwähnt, denn ʿAlī, der in mehreren Traditionen[53] als der grosse Täuscher erscheint, darf natürlich hier keinen Platz finden, ebensowenig wie andere Autoritäten des ältesten Islām und Muḥammad selbst, die zweideutige Ausdrucksweisen angewendet, gebilligt und empfohlen haben sollen.[54]

Al-Muhallab ist aber nur der Exponent einer Auffassung, die das ganze vorislāmische Arabertum beherrscht und, wie wir sehen, sich auch im Islām fortsetzt.[55] In der Heidenzeit waren doppeldeutige Ausdrücke und besonders Eide allgemein bekannt, geübt und gebilligt. Noch zur Umaijadenzeit konnte Ǧarir sagen: «*walā* (scil. *ḫaira*) *fī jamīnin gaira ḏāti maḫārimī*»,[56] und in fein pointierter Weise sagt an-Nābiġa, um einen ganz festen Eid zu bezeichnen: «*ḥalaftu jamīnan gaira ḏī maṭnawījatin*».[57] Es liegt auf der Hand, dass die Eidkniffe und überhaupt «Redekniffe», die sich bei Ibrāhīm, Ḥammād, abū Ḥanīfa und andern finden, aus dieser Auffassung heraus zu verstehen sind. Andrerseits finden wir bei abū Ḥanīfa und in seinem *mādhab* die Réchtskniffe voll ausgebildet, von denen die Eídkniffe dan nur eine deutlich abgesonderte Unterabteilung darstellen.[58] Es erhebt sich also die Frage: wer hat den Begriff des Kniffes von den Eiden auf die andern Kapitel des Gesetzes übertragen? Diese Frage kann nicht glatt beantwortet werden; es wäre denkbar, dass abū Ḥānīfa selbst es gewesen ist; möglich ist auch, dass schon Ibrāhīm an-Naḫaʿī diesen wichtigen Schritt getan hat; er wäre also als Schöpfer der islāmischen Rechtskniffe anzusehen.[59]

8

Wir haben gesehen, wie die Rechtskniffliteratur bei den Ḥanafiten vom Beginn ihres *maḏhab* an heimisch ist, und haben auch ihr Entstehen aus einem schon vorislāmischen Gedankenkreis beobachten können. Als etwas in der Entwicklung ihres *maḏhab* ganz Neues treten uns aber die *ḥijal*-Bücher dreier Šāfiʿiten entgegen, nämlich das des abū Bakr Muḥammad ibn ʿAbdallāh, bekannt als ibn aṣ-Ṣairafī (st. 330), das des abul-Ḥasan Muḥammad ibn Jaḥjā ibn Surāqa al-ʿĀmirī (st. vor 410) und das des abū Ḥātim Maḥmūd ibn al-Ḥasan al-Qazwīnī (st. 440 oder nicht lange vor 460) – dies allein unter ihnen erhalten.[60] So etwas wäre in der ersten Zeit des šāfiʿitischen *maḏhab* ganz unmöglich; aš-Šafiʿī und anfänglich auch seine Schule waren Gegner der ḥanafitischen Rechtskniffe, und ihre Polemik ist es auch, die in der Stellung des Šāfiʿiten al-Buḫārī zu den *ḥijal* zum Ausdruck kommt.[61] Als dieser Kampf, der seinem Wesen nach nur eine Auswirkung des Streites um das *ra'j* zu sein scheint,[62] abgeebbt war, hatte abū Ḥanīfa in den Augen seiner Anhänger unsterblichen Ruhm als Spezialist für Eidkniffe gewonnen;[63] davon mussten auch die Šāfiʿiten Kenntnis nehmen, und sie fühlten sich bewogen, auch ihren Imām in der scharfsinnigen Lösung von Eidfragen sich betätigen zu lassen;[64] ebenso waren auch die ḥanafitischen *ḥijal*-Werke berühmt geworden; daher konnte man auch auf šāfiʿitischer Seite wagen, als Konkurrenzunternehmen entsprechende Schriften zu schaffen. Nur so lässt sich das ganz unvermittelte Auftreten der *ḥijal*-Bücher im šāfiʿitischen *maḏhab* erklären. Bei der ganzen Sachlage ist es selbstverständlich, dass sich, abgesehen von der formalen Anregung, nur sehr wenige nähere Berührungen zwischen der šāfiʿitischen und der ḥanafitischen *ḥijal*-Literatur finden.[65]

Mit dem Aufkommen der *ḥijal*-Schriften ist der wesentliche Umschwung in der šāfiʿitischen Lehre besiegelt; aš-Šāfiʿi hatte die *ḥijal* für *ḥarām* oder *makrūh* erklärt, wenngleich er ihre äussere Gültigkeit anerkennen musste;[66] nunmehr bleibt selbstverständlich ihre Gültigkeit unangetastet, und sie werden nach dem mit ihnen erstrebten Ziel und den bei ihnen gebrauchten Mitteln von Fall zu Fall in erlaubte (diese bilden die Hauptmasse), missbilligte und verbotene eingeteilt. Das ist der Standpunkt, den die Ḥanafiten schon immer einnahmen.

Frelich darf es uns nicht verwundern, dass sich noch längere Zeit Widerspruch gegen die zur Herrschaft gekommene Lehre hören liess, so bei al-Ġazālī (st. 505), von dem wir etwas anderes nicht erwarten,[67] und bei ʿAbdarraḥmān ibn Zijād, dem Muftī von Zabīd. Dieser erklärte die Kniffe im Widerspruch zur šafiʿitischen Lehre sogar für nichtig, wurde aber von ibn Ḥağar (st. 975) in mehreren Fetwās äusserst heftig bekämpft[68] und bei dem Ansehen, das ibn Ḥağar im šāfiʿitischen *mādhab* geniesst,[69] ist seine Ansicht die geltende geblieben.

9

Endlich sind hier noch zwei Ḥanbaliten zu erwähmen. Der berühmte ibn Taimīja beschäftigt sich in seinem *kitāb qijām addalīlʿalā buṭlān at-taḥlīl*[70] mit einer Spezialfrage, bei der sein ablehnender Standpunkt deutlich hervortritt.[71] Sein grosser

Schüler ibn Qaijim al-Ǧauzīja (st. 751) ist weder Vertreter noch Gegner der Rechtskniffe, sondern ihr kritischer Betrachter. In seinem *Kitāb iʿlām al-muwaqqiʿīn ʿan rabb al-ʿālamīn*[72] widmet er den *ḥijal* eine sehr ausführliche und gründliche Auseinandersetzung unter starker Benutzung der über diesen Gegenstand handelnden Werke. In seinen von hohem sittlichem Ernst getragenen Darlegungen teilt er die Kniffe ein in verbotene und erlaubte, d. h. solche, durch die ein erlaubtes Ziel mit erlaubten Mitteln erreicht werden soll; gegen die Anwendung dieser hat er nichts einzuwenden, während er jene zugleich für ungültig erklärt. Es ist besonders hervorzuheben, dass er beide Gattungen von seinem Standpunkt aus möglichst sachlich abzugrenzen bestrebt ist, also durchaus nicht als Gegner der *ḥijal* bezeichnet werden kann. Namentlich auf dem Gebiete des Handelsrechts lässt er trotz seines bekannten Eifers gegen alle «Missbräuche» viele Kniffe unbeanstandet passieren, ein Beweis dafür, dass er sich einen freien Blick für die Erfordernisse der Praxis bewahrt hat. Auch dort, wo er gegen die *ḥijal* polemisiert, ist seine Argumentation stets von beachtenswerter Tiefe.

10

Hiermit hätten wir die Übersicht über die uns bekannten Fiqh-Werke, die sich mit den *ḥijal* beschäftigen, abgeschlossen und wollen anhangsweise wenigstens einen Blick auf die Rolle der Kniffe in der nichtjuristischen Literatur werfen.[73]

Das weite Feld der doppeldeutigen Ausdrücke, die bei Eidkniffen eine grosse Rolle spielen, steht auch der grammatischen und lexikographischen Behandlung offen. So hat der grosse Gelehrte abū Bakr Muḥammad ibn al-Ḥasan ibn Duraid (st. 321) nach mehreren Vorgängern das noch erhaltene *Kitāb al-malāḥin* über zweideutige Worte beim Eide verfasst mit der ausgesprochenen Absicht, den zu Eiden Gezwungenen ihr Gewissen salvierende Mittel an die Hand zu geben;[74] von den zahlreichen Beispielen, die er bringt, findet sich aber in der juristischen *ḥijal*-Literatur nur eins, das auf dem Doppelsinn von جارية[75] beruht, während بيت الله[76], حر[77], اعترض[78], على[79], طالق[80], ما[81], نساء[82], نعم[83], وطئ[84] in entsprechender Weise zwar bei aš-Saibānī und al-Ḫaṣṣāf verwendet werden, bei ibn Duraid aber fehlen.[85]

Auf ein ganz anderes Gebiet führt uns al-Ǧaubarī (st. etwa 650); er widmet einen Abschnitt seiner «*aufgedeckten Geheimnisse*», die allerlei mechanische, physikalische und chemische Kniffe und Kunststücke enthalten,[86] zwei Urkundenkniffen, von denen der erste,[87] recht interessante bei al-Qazwīnī[88] ein Gegenstück hat; auch sonst berühren sich die Rechtskniffe bisweilen mit physikalischen *ḥijal*,[89] die ja bekanntlich eine eigene Literatur besitzen.

Ḥijal ist auch terminus technicus für Kriegslisten und kommt als solcher in Büchertiteln und auch sonst häufig vor (cf. z. B. *Fihrist* ed. Flügel 314, 23; ein *Kitāb al-ḥijal wal-ḥurūb* Leiden 499 und 92 [Katalog[I] 1414. 1415]; im zweiten Abschnitt des Schlusskapitels des *ǧihād*-Werkes von ad-Dimašqī [st. 814] Leiden 324 [Katalog[I] 1853] fol. 213 b ff. heissen die Kriegslisten *makā'id*, *ādāb* und *ḥijal*).

Aus der schönen Literatur sei ausser dem 61. Kapitel des *Mustaṭraf* von Muḥammad ibn Aḥmad al-Ibšaihī (st. 850; Brockelmann II 56) noch des ibn abid-Dunjā (st. 281; Brockelmann in EI II 377) wenigstens auszugsweise erhaltenes *Kitāb mudārāt an-nās* (Ahlwardt 5436, 2; 8458 fol. 155 b ff.) erwähnt, neben das eine Menge von zum Teil anonymen Erzählungen über das beliebte Thema von Kniffen, Listen und Ränken aller Art tritt;[90] ihnen schliessen sich manche Geschichten aus 1001 Nacht an, in denen bisweilen abū Jūsuf die Hauptrolle spielt.[91] Schon bei al-Ǧāḥiẓ (st. 255) tritt er als freilich nicht unübertroffenes Muster von Scharfsinn auch ausserhalb des eigentlich juristischen Gebietes auf;[92] so werden auch in der Kosmographie des al-Qazwīnī (st. 682) anlässlich seiner Erwähnung in dem über Baġdād handelnden Artikel drei Anekdoten von ihm mitgeteilt.[93] Dass die ganze spätere Literatur in abū Jūsuf den grossen Praktikenmann sieht[94] hat einige Berechtigung, insofern er der erste Verfasser eines *ḥijal*-Buches war, und diese seine Schrift hat sicher starken Eindruck gemacht (cf. al-Ǧāḥiẓ). Das genügt aber auch vollständig zur Erklärung seines Rufes, und man braucht ihn keineswegs für einen hervorragend spitzfindigen und scharfsinnigen Faqīh zu halten, um so weniger, als in Wirklichkeit eher abū Ḥanifa den Ruhm besonderen Scharfsinnes – auch hier cum grano salis – beanspruchen zu dürfen scheint.[95]

11

Nun kommen wir zum Inhalt der Rechtskniffbücher. Wir haben gesehen, dass die *ḥijal*-Literatur Theorie und Praxis versöhnen will, finden aber zahlreiche Kniffe, die diesem Ziel nicht dienen können, weil sie für die Praxis durchaus unbrauchbar sind. Zur Erklärung dieser schon angedeuteten[96] Tatsache muss festgehalten werden, dass sich der spekulative Scharfsinn und die Spitzfindigkeit aller Gebiete des Fiqh sehr bald im Übermass bemächtigt hat;[97] danach darf aber das Ganze nicht beurteilt werden. Der gesunde Sinn der Ḥanafiten zeigt sich gerade darin, dass solche Übertreibungen bei ihnen ganz zurücktreten, während sie bei al-Qazwīnī geradezu die Regel bilden – kein Wunder, denn die šafiʿitischen *ḥijal* sind eine späte, künstliche Schöpfung ohne wesentliche Bedeutung für die Praxis.

Auch in anderer Beziehung ist der Inhalt der *ḥijal*-Bücher recht bunt: neben die Eidkniffe, die bei den Ḥanafiten noch als selbständige Gruppe bestehen bleiben,[98] treten die *ḥijal* auf den andern Gebieten des Fiqh; bei al-Qazwīnī ist diese alte Ordnung schon gestört, indem beide Arten, die allerdings bisweilen ineinander übergehen, wirr durcheinanderstehen. Bei letzterer Art, die – abgesehen von den erwähnten Spitzfindigkeiten – auch in ihrer systematischen Ausbildung über das ihr eigentlich zustehende Gebiet, das wir anfangs[99] näher umschrieben haben, bisweilen, aber nicht oft, hinausgreift, kann es sich darum handeln, unerwünschte Folgen eines abgeschlossenen Rechtsgeschäftes zu verhindern oder ein Rechtsgeschäft so abzuschliessen, dass jene Folgen, zu denen auch die Nichtigkeit des ganzen Aktes oder die Ungültigkeit einzelner Bestimmungen gehören kann, überhaupt nicht eintreten. Eine überaus wichtige Rolle spielt hierbei der *Iqrār*, die Erklärung oder der Anerkennungsvertrag, der ein Universalmittel zur Herstellung von Rechtsfiktionen ist.[100] Entsprehend kann es sich bei Eiden darum handeln, unangenehme Folgen geleisteter Eide zu bannen oder Eide so zu leisten, dass keine solchen Folgen eintreten. Hier ist die reservatio mentalis ein sehr oft gebrauchtes Mittel.[101]

Nach der Art des angewendeten Verfahrens kann man zwei Gruppen unterscheiden, juristische im engeren Sinne und faktische, wie ich sie nennen möchte: jene sind Rechtsgeschäfte und haben unmittelbar juristische Bedeutung, diese sind Handlungen zunächst ohne juristischen Inhalt, die aber infolge der eigentümlichen Lage des Falles, in dem sie vorgenommen werden, die Anwendbarkeit irgendwelcher Rechtssatzungen irgendwie modifizieren,[102] den äussersten Flügel, auf dem man von «Umgehungen» garnicht und von «Rechtskniffen» nur mit Vorbehalt sprechen kann, bilden dann Fälle wie al-Ḫaṣṣāf 31, 15; 33, 5. aš-Šaibānī 11, 17, wo einer rechtlichen Zwangslage ganz unjuristische, menschlich aber desto wirksamere Mittel entgegengesetzt werden, und al-Ḫaṣṣāf 84, 13 f. aš-Šaibānī 11, 15 f. sowie al-Qazwīnī IV 4 u. ä., wo es sich um die scharfsinnige Interpretation einer anscheinend rettungslosen Lage handelt.

Viele Kniffe laufen auf die Herstellung der Billigkeit in den Beziehungen zweier Parteien zueinander und die Sicherung gegen Unredlichkeit der andern hinaus;[103] nicht wenige wollen aber auch nur der einen gewisse Vorteile zuwenden, und bisweilen wird dieselbe Frage von den entgegengesetzten Standpunkten beider aus behandelt (z. B. al-Ḫaṣṣāf 4, 13 f. 19 f. 34–37; 19, 1-4).

Dies sehr bunte und recht ausgedehnte Gebiet wird bei al-Qazwīnī noch bedeutend erweitert, aber so, dass wir hierin geradezu die Auflösung des Begriffes der *ḥīla* als Rechtskniff erblicken müssen: die faktischen Kniffe gehen bisweilen in rein physikalische über, die mit dem Fiqh nur durch ein ganz loses Band verknüpft sind, und noch weit über das, was wir eben bei al-Ḫaṣṣāf zu beobachten Gelegenheit hatten, hinaus werden die richtige Beantwortung irgendwelcher schwieriger Fragen, geradezu die Lösung von Rätseln (*algāz*), besonders aus dem Gebiet des Erbrechts, oder die richtige Vornahme von Rechtsgeschäften, bei denen ein Formfehler Unheil stiften kann, ohne weiteres als *ḥijal* bezeichnet;[104] etwas in dieser Richtung kaum zu Überbietendes steht V 92.[105]

Al-Qazwīnī hat eine Einteilung der Kniffe in verbotene, missbilligte und erlaubte, die er aber nicht einmal selbst konsequent durchführt (cf. unten Anm. 6), während die *ḥijal* bei den Ḥanafiten nach sachlich bedingten Kapiteln angeordnet sind.

12

Wenn wir zum Schluss noch zwei Worte über die Beurteilung der *ḥijal* im Islām und in der abendländischen Forschung sagen dürfen, so ist zunächst zu bemerken, dass es im Islām selbst Gegner der Rechtskniffe gegeben hat.[106] Es ist aber bezeichnend, dass ihre Polemik[107] sich gerade nicht gegen die Eidkniffe, die uns vielleicht am anstössigsten vorkommen mögen, richtete, weil diese nur die konsequente Auswirkung der gemeinislāmischen Anschauungen über den Eid überhaupt sind, die seiner Hochhaltung keineswegs föderlich sein konnten.[108] Bald aber sahen sich die Šāfi'iten, die die *ḥijal* bekämpft hatten, veranlasst, selbst eine *ḥijal*-Literatur zu schaffen, die sich – und das möchte ich mit besonderem Nachdruck betonen – vor der ḥanafitischen keineswegs durch grössere Moralität auszeichnet.[109] Auch den Ḥanafiten geht das Gefühl für den Unterschied zwischen erlaubten und verbotenen Kniffen nicht ab.[110] Wenn sie aber bei den *ḥijal* Gültigkeit und Erlaubtheit, forum externum und internum trennen,[111] so befinden sie sich in vollkommener Übereinstimmung mit einer bekannten Hauptnorm des Fiqh, dass der irdische Richter sich nur an die äusseren Handlungen zu halten habe, während die *nīja* des Menschen allein von Allāh beurteilt werden könne; dazu kommt noch die Unerforschlichkeit von Allāhs Willen und die Unbegreiflichkeit seiner Verordnungen.[112] Und wenn wir uns nun auf den selbstverständlich ebenfalls möglichen Standpunkt der Wertung der *nīja* stellen, so sagen zwar die Gegner der *ḥijal*, sie seien unerlaubt, weil mit ihnen die Erreichung von etwas Verbotenem beabsichtigt werde, ihre Vertreter behaupten aber mit demselben Recht ihre Erlaubtheit, weil sie zur Vermeidung des Verbotenen und Erreichung des Erlaubten geübt würden[113] (abgesehen natürlich von bestimmten Fällen); jene setzen die praktische Erfüllbarkeit der *šarīʿa* voraus, diese stellen sich mutig auf den Boden der Tatsachen. Die *ḥijal* haben also gesiegt, weil sie im Fiqh zweifellos historisch und systematisch berechtigt sind, mag auch die Absicht von Leuten wie aš-Šāfiʿī, al-Buḫārī und ibn Zijād ihnen alle Ehre machen.[114]

So hat auch die abendländlische Forschung die *ḥijal* bisweilen als ein Moment der Lüge und Unehrlichkeit im Islām bezeichnet. Wenn wir aber das eben Ausgeführte bedenken, dann können wir jenes Urteil nicht aufrecht erhalten. Die Rechtskniffe sind vielmehr genau so moralisch wie das ganze islāmische Gesetz; sie gehen ihrem Wesen und Ursprung nach nicht auf Kreise zurück, die sich offen über alle gesetzlichen Bestimmungen hinwegsetzten – diese waren im Islām keineswegs spärlich vertreten –, sondern auf solche, die auch unter ungünstigen äusseren Verhältnissen seine Vorschriften möglischst wenig zu verletzen sich bemühten; die Gegner der *ḥijal* waren jedenfalls gezwungen, das Gesetz auf Grund der Notwendigkeit zu übertreten, wo ihre Befürworter es wenigstens formell beobachten konnten.

NOTES

1 Der vorliegende Aufsatz gibt in erweiterter Form die Grundgedanken eines auf dem Münchener Orientalistentag 1924 gehaltenen Vortrages wieder (cf. *ZDMG* N. F. 3 LXXVI). Ausführliche Belege für einzelnes hier in den Resultaten Mitgeteilte gedenke ich an anderer Stelle zu bieten. Wie der Untertitel besagt, bilden die *ḥijal* im Fiqh das Thema, wenngleich es nicht verwehrt sein soll, auch auf andere damit zusammenhängende Anwendungsgebiete dieses Wortes einen kurzen Blick zu werfen.

2 Damit soll natürlich nicht etwa die Echtheit dieser Traditionen behauptet werden.

3 Bis hierher gebe ich Gedanken wieder, die Snouck Hurgronje (cf. *Verspreide Geschriften* II, besonders 300 ff. und 369 ff.) zuerst ausgesprochen hat, daher auch möglichst mit seinen eigenen Worten. Cf. auch C.H. Becker, *Islamstudien* I, namentlich 44 f. 56 f. 63 f. 218 f. 354 f. 358.

4 Becker l. c. 57. 64.

5 Goldziher, *Vorlesungen*[1] 59 ff., besonders 64–67. Auch in späterer Zeit üblich, «um der Gefahr des Sündigens zu entgehen»: Snouck Hurgronje l. c. 148. 155. Cf. Grasshoff, *Die suftaǧa und ḥawâla der Araber* (Diss. Königsberg 1899) 25 f.

6 Juynboli, *Handbuch des Islāmischen Gesetzes* 166 Anm. 2. Am bekanntesten sind wohl die Kniffe zur Umgehung des Zinsverbotes: ebd. 274 ff. Sachau, *Muhammedanisches Recht* 281, 19. al-Ḫaṣṣāf ed. Schacht S. 65, 1 ff. Weitere *ḥijal* z. B. Juynboll 266; Sachau 148, 21; 417, 3; 503, 5; 608, 25.

7 Beachtung verdient dabei, dass die *ʿbiādāt*-Kapitel nur einen äusserst geringen Bruchteil von Kniffen stellen: das gilt von aš-Šaibānī ebenso wie von al-Ḫaṣṣāf (auch in dem noch nicht edierten Rest seines ersten Kapitels werden nicht etwa viele Kniffe zur Umgehung der *zakāt*- und *ḥaǧǧ*-Pflicht geboten, sondern nur eine *ḥīla* wird zum Gegenstand langer Erörterungen gemacht). Etwas anders steht es mit al-Qazwīnī, wo die *ḥijal* aus dem Gebiete der *ʿibādāt* allerdings nicht ganz so spärlich vertreten sind; hier aber haben wir es mit im wesentlichen nicht praktischen Kniffen zu tun (cf. al-Qazwīnī ed. Schacht S. 6 und unten S. 229). Dazu ist mein Erklärungsversuch al-Ḫaṣṣāf S. 41, 8 ff. und Strothmanns Bemerkung *Islam* 14, 192 zu vergleichen. Aus dem Befunde von al-Ḫaṣṣāf Kap. 1 scheint mir also keine Schwierigkeit zu erwachsen.

8 Näheres unten S. 229. Eine ähnliche Rolle, sowohl in ihrer Wichtigkeit für die Erschliessung der Praxis wie auch in der Notwendigkeit einiger Skepsis bei ihrer Verwertung, spielen die Fetwās; cf. Snouck Hurgronje l. c. 421–423.

9 Goldziher hat im Abendland als erster auf die hier skizzierte Rolle der *ḥijal* und ihren Zusammenhang mit der Rechtspraxis hingewiesen: *Muhammedanische Studien* II 57; *Vorlesungen*[I] 68. Die Wichtigkeit der *ḥijal* für die Praxis ist schon al-Ḫaṣṣāf I, 19 ausgesprochen. Cf. auch ebd. 67, 23 = aš-Šaibānī ed. Schacht 6, 22. Zu der Rolle, die die *ḥijal* noch heute im Leben der Muslims spielen, cf.

Snouck Hurgronje l. c. II 263; IV 2, 255, speziell über Umgehungen des Zinsverbotes *Atjèhers* 193. 317; *Verspreide Geschriften* II 153. 239. 245; *Mekka* II 3.

10 Wie ja die *šurūt* überhaupt auf die Wirklichkeit meist in starkem Masse Rücksicht nehmen.

11 Die in Betracht kommenden Stellen finden sich in der jüngeren Rezension, stammen also spätestens aus dem 4. Jahrhundert (cf. unten S. 218); aus früherer Zeit ist auf ḥanafitischer Seite nur das *kitab aš-šurūt al-kabir* des aṭ-Ṭaḥāwī (st. 321 oder 322; Brockelmann I 174, 4) das ich bald zu edieren gedenke, zum Teil erhalten.

12 Cf. Goldziher, *ZDMG* 60, 213 (dazu Fischer ebd. 250). Horovitz *Islam* 3, 63. Natürlich differieren die einzelnen Sekten hierin; bei den Zaiditen z. B. ist die *taqīja*, wie ich einer freundlichen Mitteilung von Herrn Prof. Strothmann entnehme, auf das auch bei den Sunniten gestattete Mass, wie es in dem Kapitel vom *ikrāh* seinen Ausdruck gefunden hat, beschränkt.

13 Cf. unten S. 223 [414].

14 al-Ḫaṣṣāf 63. 3 = aš-Šaibānī 1, 30 = al-Buhārī, *adub* 116.

15 Strothmann, *Islam* 14, 192. Herr Prof. Strothmann hatte die Güte, mir reiches Material über die *taqīja* bei verschiedenen šīʿitischen Sekten zur Verfügung zu stellen, wofür ich ihm auch hier meinen ergebensten Dank ausspreche.

16 Themata, die allgemeineres Interesse beanspruchen und für alle *mādāhib* Bedeutung besitzen, sind davon natürlich ausgenommen, wenngleich die Entwicklung auch hier im wesentlichen gesondert verläuft.

17 Die andern *mādahib* haben, soviel ich sehe, nichts dieser Gruppe Entsprechendes.

18 Hier beschränken wir uns auf die *ḥijal*-Bücher unter Beiseitelassung der Kniffe, die vereinzelt in den verschiedenen Kapiteln des Fiqh erwähnt werden.

19 Erwähnt bei al-Ǧāḥiẓ, *Kitab al-ḥajawān* III 4, 2 (zitiert unten S. 228 [417] Anm. 3 [92]).

20 Kairo III 103 liegt vielmehr das *Kitab al-maḫārig fil-ḥijal* des aš-Šaibānī vor.

21 al-Ḫaṣṣāf 31, 18. Stark abhängig von abū Jūsuf ist aber das *ḥijal*-Werk des aš-Šaibānī und durch dessen Vermittlung das des al-Ḫaṣṣāf, die für die Rekonstruktion jener Schrift zunächst in Betracht kommen. Cf. aš-Šaibānī, Einleitung § 15.

22 III 103. Eine von mir besorgte Ausgabe dieser Schrift erscheint als Heft 7 der *Beiträge zur semitischen Philologie und Linguistik.*

23 Wiedergegeben in meiner Ausgabe des aš-Šaibānī.

24 Sein Tod wird auch auf 448, 449, 452 datiert.

25 Für alles Nähre cf. aš-Šaibānī, Einleitung § 3. 17.

26 Flügel, *Klassen der hanefitischen Rechtsgelehrten* (Abh. S. G. W. 1861) 287.

27 *Fihrist* ed. Flügel 206, 6; ibn Qutlūbugā ed. Flügel Nr. 227.

28 Cf. aš-Šaibānī, Einleitung § 3.

29 Hier zeigt sich dasselbe wie oft in der arabischen Literaturgeschichte: die älteren Werke sind durch die jüngere Darstellung, der durchaus

nicht soviel Originalität eignet wie jenen, verdrängt worden; das gilt selbst für das Verhältnis der beiden Rezensionen des al-Ḫaṣṣāf zueinander: die längere ist in späterer Zeit das ḥanafitische *ḥijal*-Buch und gilt als Originalwerk des al-Ḫaṣṣāf, während die kürzere fast ganz in Vergessenheit geraten ist.

30 Gleichwohl wird aš-Šaibānī in der kürzeren Rezension und, wie man mit Sicherheit annehmen kann, auch in dem Original des al-Ḫaṣṣāf kein einziges Mal genannt, wie überhaupt alles ängstlich getilgt ist, was an ihn erinnert; seine verhältnismässig auffallend wenigen Erwähnungen in der längeren Rezension sind erst durch den Redaktor hineingebracht. Hier liegt die auch sonst zu beobachtende Erscheinung vor, dass der Autor gerade seine aufs stärkste ausgenutzte Hauptquelle nicht nennt. Cf. aš-Šaibānī, Einleitung § 4.

31 Beide von mir herausgegeben in den *Beiträgen zur semitischen Philologie und Linguistik* Heft 4.

32 Ich kann also Heffening nicht folgen, wenn er *OLZ* 1924, 660 zur Erklärung der Unterschiede zwischen beiden Rezensionen vermutet, dass sie auf zwei verschiedene kollegs des al-Ḫaṣṣāf zurückgingen; das scheint mir schon durch die S. 30–33 meiner Ausgabe behandelten Tatsachen ausgeschlossen zu werden, zu denen noch Eingriffe von der S. 41, 17 angedeuteten Art kommen. Die von Heffening aufgezeigte Möglichkeit ist natürlich stets im Auge zu behalten, aber die wesentlichen Unterschiede zwischen den beiden Rezensionen vermag sie doch wohl nicht zu erklären.

33 as-Samʿānī 557 b 5.

34 Cf. Goldziher *ZDMG* 60, 223 Anm. 3.

35 Cf. Goldziher, *Muhammedanische Studien* II 234.

36 So in den Titeln der Kapitel 1. 3. 5. 6. 7. 8 (auch 9 in Verbindung mit dem Folgenden). 12. 13.

37 Al-Buḫārī und al-Qasṭallānī waren bekanntlich Šāfiʿiten, al-ʿAinī dagegen Ḥanafit: er lässt daher auch beide Parteien objektiv zu Worte kommen, schwächt bisweilen sogar al-Buḫārīs Polemik etwas ab.

38 Es ist zudem nicht ganz ausgeschlossen, dass wir von der einen oder andern derartigen Schrift überhaupt keine Kenntnis haben.

39 Cf. oben S. 213 [406] und Anm. 3 [6].

40 Über die Verwertung der *ḥijal*-Literatur bei ibn Qaijim al-Ǧanzīja cf. unten Seite 226 [416].

41 Goldziher, *Ẓâhiriten* 16 nach al-Ǧāḥiẓ, *Kitāb al-ḥajawān*. Der von den Gegnern des *raʾj* gegen abū Ḥanīfa und seine Schule ins Feld geführte Vorwurf, dass sie sich nicht mit der Praxis beschäftigten, sondern sich auf unfruchtbare kasuistische Spekulationen verlegten (*Ẓâhiriten* ebd.), beweist als Polemik von Gegnern nichts gegen den durchaus praktischen Charakter der *ḥijal*. Wir sehen ja auch bei Dāwūd aẓ-Ẓāhirī eine kasuistische Wortklauberei, die der sonst den Ḥanafiten zur Last gelegten nichts nachgibt (l. c. 40). Hier sei noch erwähnt, dass sich die Lehren der Ẓāhiriten nicht selten mit *ḥijal* berühren (l. c. 41 ff.): man sieht aber sogleich, dass die Ähnlichkeit rein äusserlich ist und beide Erscheimungen auf ganz verschiedene Gründe zurückgehen.

42 So bei Fahr ad-dīn ar-Rāzī (*Mafātih al-gaib* I 411); cf. Goldziher, *Vorlesungen*[1] 69. Cf. unten S. 229 [417] und Anm. I [95].
43 al-Ḫaṣṣāf 1, 8; 63. 10; 71, 23; 83, 12a. aš-Šaibānī, 1, 17; 13. 24; 23, 17; cf. auch I, 1. 4. 7. 16.
44 al-Ḫaṣṣāf 64, 28; 66, 1 u. ö. aš-Šaibānī 2, 30; 5, 1 u. ö.
45 Cf. Dimitroff *MSOS* A. 1908, 70–73.
46 Cf. Goldziher, *Ẓâhiriten* 13.
47 al-Ḫaṣṣāf 1, 3; 63, 5; 66, I; 69, 1. aš-Šaibānī 1, 7. 16. 23; 5, 1.
48 al-Ḫaṣṣāf 1, 3. 4. 7. 9. 10. 17; 61, 53; 63, 4. 5. 6. 9; 66, I; 67, 42; 69, I. aš-Šaibānī 1, 6. 7. 16. 23. 24. 28. 31. 32. 33. 37. 44; 5, 1; 6, 41.
49 Cf. oben S. 213 [406] und Anm. 2 [5].
50 al-Ḫaṣṣāf 1, 9; 61, 53. aš-Šaibānī 1, 31.
51 *Kāmil* 632, 5; cf. ibn Ḫallikān ed. Wüstenfeld Nr. 763 mit ausgiebiger Benutzung des *Kāmil*; Ḥāǧǧi Ḫalīfa II 522.
52 al-Ḫaṣṣāf I, 14. aš-Šaibānī I, 41. 43.
53 al-Ḫaṣṣāf I, 12. 13. 15. aš-Šaibānī I, 4. 38.
54 al-Ḫaṣṣāf I, 1. 2. 5. 6. 11. 14. 16. 18; 63, 1. 2. 3. 4. 7. 8. 11. aš-Šaibānī 1, 3. 4. 5. 8. 13. 14. 18. 19. 20. 21. 22. 25. 26. 29. 30. 34. 36. 39. 40. 41. 42. 43. Daneben steht al-Ḫaṣṣāf 1, 20 als das einzige derartige Ḥadīt, das einen Kniff billigt, der nicht auf dem Gebiete des Eides oder der Rede liegt (aus dem *Muwatta'* entlehnt), fällt also aus dem sonstigen Schema (cf. darüber unten S. 224 Anm. I) heraus und könnte gerade deshalb echt sein, zumal da man an ihm kaum eine Tendenz wahrnehmen kann. Übrigens lassen sich viele der erwähnten Traditionen auch in den bekannten Sammlungen nachweisen.
55 Vgl. oben S. 215 [407]. Für Einzelheiten hierzu und zum Folgenden cf. Pedersen. *Der Eid bei den Semiten*, besonders 191 ff., 217 ff., 228 f., aber auch al-Gazālī bei Bauer, *Islamische Ethik* I 79.
56 *Naqā'id* ed. Bevan 754–3.
57 Ahlwardt, *The Divans* 2, 5.
58 Auch in den Fiqh-Büchern geniessen sie eine Art Sonderstellung; cf. Juynboll., *Handbuch des islāmischen Gesetzes* 270.
59 Die Schwierigkeit der Eintscheidung liegt in Folgendem: sowhol Ḥammād (al-Ḫaṣṣāf 66, 1; 69, 1; aš-Šaibānī 5, 1) wie Ibrāhīm (al-Ḫaṣṣāf 66, 1; 67, 42; 69, 1; aš-Šaibānī 5, 1; 6, 41) kommen in Isnāden bei der Behandlung von Réchtskniffen vor; zwar wird in den Traditionen selbst kein Kniff gegeben, einen berechtigten Platz im Zusammenhange des Buches haben sie aber nur, wenn sie auf solche hinauslaufen. Andrerseits finden wir zwar viele auf den Propheten und die Ṣaḥāba zurück geführte Traditionen, die die Eīdkniffe rechtfertigen sollen, aber keine zugunsten der Réchtskniffe (mit Ausnahme von 1, 20; diese ist aber möglicherweise echt – cf. oben S. 223 [414] Anm. 2 [54] – und kommt jedenfalls in ihrer Vereinzelung und Tendenzlosigkeit hier nicht in Betracht), während doch zu erwarten wäre, dass auch sie sich auf eine Reihe von Ḥadīten stützen könnten, wenn sie zur Zeit der Traditionsbildung schon eine bedeutende Rolle gespielt hätten; daher Rönnte man Bedenken haben, sie bis auf den historischen Ibrāhīm zurückzuführen. Vielleicht wird man beiden Tatsachen gerecht durch die Annahme, dass sie damals zwar schon bestanden, zu grösserer Wichtigkeit aber erst bei abū Ḥanīfa gelangten. Wieweit ich

die im vorhergehenden verwerteten Ḥadīte für echt halte, geht aus der Behandlung selbst hervor.

60 Von mir herausgegeben in den *Beiträgen zur semitischen Philologie und Linguistik* Heft 5. Belege bietet die Einleitung § 5 und 6.

61 Material darüber ist bei al-ʿAinī und al-Qasṭallānī zu finden.

62 Cf. oben S. 221 [412].

63 Cf. ebd.

64 Leider steht eine derartige Entscheidung, die den Scharfsinn aš-Šāfiʿīs in helles Licht setzen soll (Wüstenfeld, *Der Imâm el-Schâfiʿi* II [Abh. G. W. G. 37] Nr. 71) bei aš-Šaibānī 21, 22 f. (cf. meine Anmerkung dazu), näher ausgeführt, unter ihresgleichen.

65 al-Qazwīnī S. 5 f.

66 Wegen der unten S. 232 erwähnten Hauptnorm des Fiqh, die gerade aš-Šāfiʿī ganz konsequent durchgeführt hat; cf. Mahmoud Fathy, *La doctrine musulmane de l'abus des droits* (1913) 178 ff.

67 Qaṣtallānī; ibn Ḥağar, *Fatāwā* III 19; cf. unten S. 231 [419] und Anm. 4 [107].

68 *Fatāwā* III 1–38. Cf. Snouck Hurgronje, *Verspreide Geschriften* II 423 ff.

69 Juynboll, *Handbuch des islamischen Gesetzes* 37; Snouck Hergronje l. c. 387 f.

70 In einer Notiz auf fol. 1 a der Leidener Handschrift 511 (Katalog[I] 1833) heisst es *Kitāb al-ḥijal wat-taḥlīl.*

71 Cf. Ahlwardt 4664 (lies الحيل) und 4665.

72 Kairo 1325 am Rande des *hād al-arwāḥ* III 103–109. 119–377 (!).

73 Hier seien zunächst fünf Werke angeführt, die weder mit den Rechtskniffen noch mit den *ḥijal* überhaupt etwas zu tun haben: das *Kitāb al-maḫāriğ* des abū Sahl Mūsā ibn Naṣīr ar-Rāzī (*min aṣḥāb Muḥammad ibn al-Ḥasan*) (ibn Qutlūbuġā ed. Flügel Nr. 225) behandelt die Erbanteile, wie Flügel *Klassen der hanefitischen Rechtsgelehrten* (Abh. S. G. W. 1861) 289 zutreffend bemerkt, und vier Schriften, die Ḥāğği Ḫalīfa III 120 unter حيل anordnet, handeln über Pferde, خيل, nämlich die des abū ʿAbdarraḥmān Muḥammad ibn ʿAbdallāh al-ʿUtbī (st. 228) (ibn Ḫallikān ed. Wüstenfeld Nr. 674), die des abū ʿAbdallāh Muḥammad ibn ʿAbbās al-Jazīdi (st. 310 oder 313) (Flügel, *Grammatische Schulen der Araber* 91) und eine grosse und eine kleine des im Text zu erwähnenden ibn (Ḥāğği Ḫalīfa: abū) Duraid (st. 321) (Wüstenfeld, *Der Imâm el-Schâfiʿi* II [Abh. G. W. G. 37] Nr. 92; Flügel, *Grammatische Schulen* 101 f. [sic]; Pedersen *EI* II 398).

74 Herausgegeben von Thornbecke Heidelberg 1882. Cf. Goldziher *ZDMG* 60, 224.

75 ibn Duraid 5, 4; al-Ḫaṣṣāf 61, 13; 84, 2. aš-Šaibānī 11, 2.

76 al-Ḫaṣṣāf 1, 3; 61, 14; 63, 5; 84, 11. aš-Šaibānī 1, 23; 11, 13.

77 al-Ḫaṣṣāf 61, 25.

78 al-Ḫaṣṣāf 1, 10. aš-Šaibānī 1, 32.

79 al-Ḫaṣṣāf 62, 1 f.; 84, 3 f. aš-Šaibānī 11, 3 f.

80 al-Ḫaṣṣāf 61, 26.

81 al-Ḫaṣṣāf 1, 7; 63, 9; 84, 17. aš-Šaibānī 1, 28; 11, 20.

82 al-Ḫaṣṣāf 61, 12. 21.

83 al-Ḫaṣṣāf 61, 20; 84, 1. aš-Šaibānī 11, 1.

84 al-Ḫaṣṣāf 62, 6. 9 f.; 84, 6 f. aš-Šaibānī 11, 6 f.

85 Etwas anderer Art sind die ادغامات al-Ḫaṣṣāf 31, 4; 52, 17. 19 f.; 61, 19: 62, 12, 14; 84, 8 f. aš-Šaibānī 11, 8. 11, zu denen sich bei Giese, *Tevāriḫ* ٦٣ , 22 ff. eine interessante Parallele findet.

86 Cf. de Goeje *ZDMG* 20, 485 ff., besonders 500; dazu Fleischer l. c. 21, 274 ff.

87 Nach dem Konstantinopler Druck des كتاب المختار فى كشف الأسرار للعلامة زين الدين عبد الرحيم بن عمر الدمشقى المعروف بالجوبرى S. 60 [die Abschrift des Abschnittes, die ich nach Ablieferung des Manuskripts nach der Leidener Handschrift 2101 (Landberg 385) genommen habe, ist mir bei der Korrektur leider nicht zugänglich]: الفصل الثانى والعشرون عندهم (so zu lesen)
بالأمور الشرعية وهم اشرّ الخلق فى كشف اسرار الكتاب وهم (so zu lesen) اصحاب الشروط (اعلم) انّ هذه الطائفة
اذا كتبوا ايع (so zu lesen) النواميس الساسانية من الدهاء والحيل والمكر ما لا يعلمه غيرهم، وهم اخبر العالم
ولهم اسرار لا يعلمها غيرهم وسأكشف لك اسرارهم (فمن ذلك) آنهم

حصّة شائعة فى ملك يقولون ووقفا على ذلك. فإذا ذكروا لفظ ذلك كان هذا البيع مفسوخًا، والدليل
عليه انّ الحصّة لا تكون معيّنة حتى يقفا عليها، بل هى شىء من شىء. فلا يقع ثمّ تعيين إلّا على
الأصل، ومنهم مَن لا يعلم هذه المسألة، ثمّ يبصرون مَن هو النادم مِن البائع او المشترى
فيقولون له كم تزن حتى تفسيخ هذا العقد بالشرع فيتّفقون معه على شىء. ثمّ يفسخ العقد بهذه
النكتة فى الشرع، لأنّ الكتاب اذا لم يقل وقفا على ما منه المبيع كان هذا العقد مفسوخًا، وإذا
قال ووقف المشترى على جميع الذى منه تلك الحصّة ولم يذكر الحصّة فإنّها غير معيّنة. فافهم.

Es folgt eine Schilderung der Urkundenfälschung mit verschiedenen Verfahren.

88 V 18.

89 al-Qazwīnī S. 7.

90 Z.B. Ahlwardt 8483, 11. 12; 8492; 8493; 8527, 2; 9074; 9075; 9104. Hier sei auch Nāṣir ad-dīn aṭ-Ṭūsī, *Aḫlāq i Nāsirī* II 3 (lith. Lucknow 1300) 307 f. erwähnt.

91 Chauvin, *Bibliographie* VI Nr. 185. 331–342 (cf. das Verzeichnis S. 172 Anm. 1); VII 383 f.(!); VIII passim, besonders 28; zum Teil sind die Stoffe auch sonst in der Märchenliteratur nachzuweisen. Cf. die Arbeiten von Rescher. Goldziher, *Vorlesungen*[I] 69; *Zâhiriten* 16 Anm. 4. Cf. oben S. 217 [409].

92 *Kitāb al-ḥajawān* III 4: وحدثنى محمد بن الصباح قال بينا ابو يوسف القاضى
يسير بظهر الكوفة وذلك بعد أن كتب كتاب الحيل اذ عرض له ممرور عندنا اطيب الخلق فقال
له يا ابا يوسف قد احسنت فى كتاب الحيل وقد بقيت عليك مسائل فى الفطن فإن اذنت لى
سألتك عنها. قال قد اذنت لك فسل. قال اخبرنى عن الحِرّ كافر هو او مؤمن. فقال ابو
يوسف دين الحرّ دين المرأة ودين صاحبة الحرّ، إن كانت كافرة فهو كافر وإن كانت مؤمنة
فهو مؤمن. قال ما صنعت شيئًا. قال فقل انت اذا لم ترض بقولى. فقال الحرّ كافر. قال وكيف
علمت ذلك. قال لأنّ المرأة اذا ركعت او سجدت استدبر الحرّ القبلة واستقبلت هى القبلة،
ولو كان دينه دين المرأة لصنع كما تصنع، هذه واحدة يا ابا يوسف. قال صدقت. قال
فتأذن لى فى اخرى. قال نعم. قال اخبرنى عنك اذا اتيت صحراء فهجمت على
بول وخراء كيف تعرف ابول امرأة هو ام بول رجل. قال والله ما ادرى. قال اجل والله
ما تدرى. قال فتعرف انت ذاك. قال نعم اذا رأيت البول قد سال على الخراء وبين يديه
فهو بول امرأة وخراء امرأة، وإذا رأيت البول بعيدًا من الخراء فهو بول رجل وخراء رجل.
قال صدقت. قال وحكى لى جواب مسائل فنسيت منها مسألة فعاودته فإذا هو لا يحفظها.

93 II 211 f. (Wüstenfeld).

94 Strothmann, *Islam* 14, 194.

95 Cf. al-Ḫaṣṣāf Kapitel 33; 80, 1; 86, 1. 2. aš-Šaibānī 10, 1; 11, 17; 12, 1 f. Abū Ḥanīfa war tatsächlich ein praktischer Kopf und bis zu einem

gewissen Grade ein Praktikenmann, zugleich aber haben schon seine Zeitgenossen diesen Zug übertrieben: cf. aš-Saibānī Anm. 3. Cf. oben S. 221 [412].

96 Cf. oben S. 214 [406] und Anm. 1 [8].

97 Zur gerechteren Würdigung dieser Erscheinung ist aber Snouck Hurgronje, *Verspreide Geschriften* II 82 zu vergleichen.

98 Mit Recht, wie wir oben S. 223 [414] und Anm. 6 [58] gesehen haben.

99 Cf. oben S. 213 [406].

100 Cf. al-Qazwīnī Anm. zu II 3; ein besonders bezeichnendes Beispiel al-Ḫaṣṣāf 19, 42.

101 Ihrem Wesen nach verschieden von der Anwendung doppeldeutiger Ausdrücke, über die oben S. 226 [416] f. gesprochen wurde. Ebesno wie der *Iqrār hat auch sie ihre Grenzen; cf. al-*Ḫaṣṣāf 1, 8; 63, 10. aš-Šaibānī 1, 17; ferner gilt die *nīja* nicht im forum externum bei dem vor Zeugen geleisteten Eid: al-Ḫaṣṣāf 62, 10 1 u. ö., auch bei aš-Šaibānī; eine weitere Einschränkung al-Ḫaṣṣāf 78, 10 f. aš-Šaibānī 21, 11. Cf. auch Goldziher, *Muhammedanische Studien* II 179 Anm. 3.

102 Näheres siehe al-Qazwīnī S. 7.

103 Cf. oben S. 213 [406]. Deshalb ist bei al-Ḫaṣṣāf (z. B. 3, 5; 4, 2. 4. 7. 13 f. 20. 21. 24. 26. 31 f.; 8, 1; 10, 1. 4. 5; 11, 13. 15. 20 f. ; 19, 35; 22, 14; 36, 2; 46, 8; 64, 1. 3. 14. 18. 31; 67, 10. 25. 29. 35; 68, 3. 4. 6. 7. 13. 18. 29. 38. 41. 45. 47; 69, 8; 70, 4. 6. 7. 10. 14. 21. 30. 38) und aš-Šaibānī (z. B. 2, 1. 3. 14. 18. 36; 6, 9. 24. 28; 7, 4. 6. 7. 13. 18. 29. 38. 42. 46. 48; 8, 4. 6. 7. 10. 14. 21. 30. 38) öfter von *aṭṭiqa* u. ä. die Rede, deshalb spielt hier auch das Institut der gemeinsamen Vertrauensleute (Notare) eine so bedeutsame Rolle (cf. z. B. al-Ḫaṣṣāf S. 75, 23 bis 76, 10). Bei al-Qazwīnī tritt dies für den praktischen Verkehr sehr wichtige Ziel wieder gegenüber al-Ḫaṣṣāf und aš-Šaibānī stark zurück.

104 Hier zeigt sich bei al-Qazwīnī der Einfluss der *furūq*-Literatur, die Fälle behandelt, deren äusserer Tatbestand anscheinend gleich, deren Beurteilung im Fiqh aber verschieden ist. Cf. meinen Aufsatz in *Islamica* 2.

105 «Der Kniff besteht darin, dass er keine neue mehr vornimmt»: dann ist vielmehr überhaupt kein Kniff notwendig. Man bemerke auch hier, wie wenig Sinn für die Praxis al-Qazwīnī im Verhältnis zu al-Ḫaṣṣāf und aš-Šaibānī zeigt (cf. die oben zitierten Stellen!).

106 Cf. oben S. 224–226 [414–416].

107 Auch die des ibn Qaijim al-Ǧauzīja; selbst al-Ġazālī billigt die Eidkniffe: Goldziher, *Streitschrift des Ġazālī gegen die Bāṭinijja-Sekte* 73–80. 102; noch im *ihjā'* empfiehlt er Reservationen: Bauer, *Islamische Ethik* I 80, wenngleich er die *ma'āriḍ* zurückdrängen möchte.

108 Cf. Pedersen, *Der Eid bei den Semiten*, besonders 217 ff. 228 f. Cf. auch Gottschalk, *Das Gelübde nach älterer arabischer Auffassung* (Diss. Berlin 1919) 73. 159 ff. Vergleiche oben S. 223 [414].

109 Man vergleiche nur al-Qazwīnī II 12 mit al-Ḫaṣṣāf 56, 17 f. Die Einteilung der Kniffe bei al-Qazwīnī (cf. oben) beweist nicht das Gegenteil; sein Kapitel V vereinigt ja auch Kniffe aus allen drei Gattungen; zudem ist das S. 7 Anm. I meiner Ausgabe Bemerkte zu beachten.

110 al-Ḫaṣṣāf 1, 18–20; (der noch nicht edierte Rest des ersten Kapitels); 58, 1; 67, 23. aš-Šaibānī 6, 22 sowie das von Strothmann, *Islam* 14, 194 Angeführte; öfter wird betont, dass alle Kniffe, die den Nächsten schädigen, verboten seien; ein وطء مكروه wird al-Ḫaṣṣāf 49, 2 nur verschleiert empfohlen.

111 Eine Unterscheidung, die sonst bekanntlich allgemein durchgeführt wird.

112 Cf. z. B. Snouck Hurgronje, *Verspreide Geschriften* II 142. 153. 239. 245; Goldziher, *Streitschrift* 72 f.

113 Dass die bekannte *nīja*-Tradition (Goldziher, *Muhammedanische Studien* II 178) von beiden Parteien für sich in Anspruch genommen wurde, sagen die Kommentare zu al-Buḫārī (Anfang des *kitāb al-ḥijal*).

114 Damit soll natürlich nicht im geringsten der Eindruck erweckt werden, als verkennte ich irgendwie die grossen Verdienste aš-Šafiʿīs (cf. Bergsträsser, *Islam* 14, 76).

14

ZUR SOZIOLOGISCHEN BETRACHTUNG DES ISLAMISCHEN RECHTS[1]

Joseph Schacht

1 EINLEITUNG

Max Weber in *Wirtschaft und Gesellschaft*, Kapitel VII[2] eine Rechtssoziologie geschaffen, deren Begriffssystem er vor allem der abendländischen Rechtsgeschichte abgelesen hat, wie er es in erster Linie auch auf sie anwendet. Dem islamischen Recht widmet er neben vereinzelten Hinweisen eine zusammenfassende Besprechung (S. 474 ff.), die aber mangels genügender unterlagen über dessen System und Geschichte unbefriedigend ausfallen musste. Der Versuch, eine ähnliche Betrachtungsweise in das Studium des islamischen Rechts einzuführen, wird nicht nur eine bisher fehlende Charakterisierung seiner inneren Struktur nachholen, sondern auch die Anwendbarkeit soziologischer Fragestellung auf die islamische Rechtsgeschichte[3] nachweisen können. Doch dürfen die Weber'schen Begriffe nicht ohne weiteres als auf das islamische Recht anwendbar vorausgesetzt werden; vielmehr ist dessen Geschichte ganz allgemein auf ihre soziologische Ausbeute hin zu untersuchen.[4] Dabei wird sich herausstellen, dass sich die verschiedenen Perioden der islamischen Rechtgeschichte auch soziologisch voneinander abheben und umgekehrt verschiedenartige Tatsachen in ein soziologisch bedingtes Verhältnis zueinander treten; wenn sich ausserdem viele der von Weber verwandten Begriffe auch auf dem Gebiet des islamischen Rechts als sinngemäss erweisen, so mag das sekundär zur Bestätigung der

Source: *Der Islam*, 1935, vol. 22, pp. 207–38.

beiderseitigen Ergebnisse dienen. Es bedarf wohl kaum der Hervorhebung, dass es sich hier ausschliesslich um die soziologische Einordnung des islamischen Rechts im technischen Sinne, und nicht um die Darlegung seiner Theorie und Praxis auf den Gebieten sozialen Lebens handelt.

2 DIE DIFFERENZIERUNG DER SACHLICHEN RECHTSGEBIETE

Die *Šarīʿa*, das islamische Gesetz, kennt keine prinzipielle Differenzierung der sachlichen Rechtsgebiete, die für sie unius generis sind. Nur sekundär stellt man diejenigen Rechtsgebiete, die für das Volksbewusstsein eine besondere enge Beziehung zur Religion haben und auf denen sich die *Šarīʿa* denn auch in der Praxis mehr oder weniger durchgesetzt hat, bisweilen den anderen gegenüber. Gelegentliche formale Einteilungsversuche[5] bleiben im Äusserlichen stecken. So ist der *Šarīʿa* auch die Scheidung zwischen ‚öffentlichem' und ‚Privatrecht' als solche fremd.[6] Der Bereich des Privatrechts in unserem Sinne ist sehr ausgebreitet, und die öffentlich-rechtlichen Zuständigkeiten erscheinen meist als subjektive Ansprüche bzw. Pflichten.[7] Das beruht vor allem auf der religiösen Fundierung des islamischen Gesetzes.[8] Unserer weiteren Scheidung zwischen Strafrecht und Zivilrecht entspricht in der *Šarīʿa*, historisch aufschlussreich, der Gegensatz von ‚Ansprüchen Allahs' und ‚Ansprüchen der Menschen', die durch den Koran (und die Tradition) festgesetzten *Ḥadd*-Strafen für Unzucht, Verleumdung wegen Unzucht, Weintrinken, Diebstahl und Strassenraub gehören prinzipiell[9] zur ersten Kategorie, und die zweite umfasst sowohl Zivil- wie Delikthaftung. Jenes Strafrecht hat sich als rein islamische (wenn auch zum Teil durch das Judentum angeregte) Neuerung auf religiöser Basis entwickelt; diesem religiösen Charakter entspricht einerseits der Ausschluss des Verzichts auf Bestrafung, andererseits die Berücksichtigung der ‚tätigen Reue'[10] und die Einschränkung der Anwendungsmöglichkeit des *Ḥadd* durch enge Fassung der Tatbestände, kurze Verjährungsfristen und Erschwerung des Beweises; entsprechend ist die ‚Verfolgung von Amts wegen' sehr schwach ausgebildet.[11] Die durch *Ḥadd* geahndeten Vergehen sind in rein äusserlicher Zusammenstellung jene, die im Koran (und in der Tradition) verboten und mit Strafe bedroht werden und dadurch sekundär zu Religionsverbrechen geworden sind

(Bergsträsser)[12] die eigentlichen Vergehen gegen die Religion werden mit Ausnahme der Apostasie[13] der Verantwortung im Jenseits überlassen. Im Gegensatz dazu fallen für die in die *Šarīʿa* übergegangene Schicht vorislamischen Gewohnheitsrechts Straf- und Zivilverfolgung als ‚Wiedergutmachung von Unrecht' unter Ausschaltung des ‚Schuld'-Begriffes zusammen (vgl. unten Abschnitt).[14] Das islamische Recht hat diese Vorstellung entschieden nach der zivilrechtlichen Seite hin entwickelt. Daher ist einerseits der Begriff der reinen Zivilobligation voll ausgebildet;[15] andererseits ist die ‚Rache' für Körperverletzungen durch Wiedervergeltung (*Qiṣāṣ*) oder Sühnegeld zwar streng geregelt, aber kaum in Ansätzen zu einem wirklichen Strafrecht entwickelt,[16] sondern dem Zivilrecht, das nur die einfache Restitution bei Unrecht mässigkeiten vorsieht, entsprechend behandelt. In der Sphäre des religiösen Strafrechts, bei den *Ḥadd*-Strafen, findet die Exekution ‚von Amts wegen' statt;[17] die Sphäre des ‚zivilen' Strafrechts kennt fast durchweg[18] nur die ‚Selbsthilfe' des obsiegenden Teiles, der infolgedessen auch zum Verzicht auf den *Qiṣāṣ* und auf das Sühnegeld berechtigt ist. Ihm wird die Person des Verurteilten zwecks Ausführung des *Qiṣāṣ* übergeben; die Obrigkeit überwacht lediglich das ‚Selbsthilfe'-Verfahren, schützt seine Durchführung und stellt gegebenenfalls ihren Apparat dafür zur Verfügung – prinzipiell ebenso wie bei der ‚zivilrechtlichen' Vollstreckung, die von der Selbsthilfe nicht scharf geschieden ist.[19] Diese beiden Sphären repräsentieren die Typen der ‚Ahndung von Religionsverbrechen' und der ‚privaten Rache', auf die man alles Strafrecht zurückführt, in grosser Reinheit. Auf beide Gebiete erstreckt sich der *Taʿzīr*, die diskretionäre Bestrafung durch den Kadi: er tritt einerseits als Ersatz für den *Ḥadd* in Fällen ein, in denen jener nicht voll verwirkt ist, auch verstärkend neben ihm, sowie bei nicht mit *Ḥadd* bedrohten religiösen Übertretungen; andererseits neben der ‚zivilen' Delikthaftung als eigentlich strafrechtliches Element. Von den theoretischen Vorschriften der *Šarīʿa* ist die islamische Rechtspraxis, gerade auch auf dem Gebiete des Strafrechts, erheblich abgewichen. Auf dem Grenzgebiet zwischen beiden bewegen sich die Funktionen des *Nāẓir al-Maẓālim* und des *Muḥtasib*.[20] Beide Ämter werden zwar auch von der *Šarīʿa* anerkannt, kommen in ihrer Auswirkung aber häufig mit ihr in Konflikt – auch dort, wo sie materielle Forderungen des Heiligen Rechts durchsetzen wollen, weil sie sich nicht an seine Verfahrensvorschriften halten können.[21] Jener tritt als ‚Prüfer von Gewaltakten' überall da ein, wo die Gerichtsbarkeit des Kadi sich nicht durchsetzen kann;[22] um selbst erfolgreich durchgreifen zu können, besitzt er weitgehende Vollmachten im Prozess- und Vollstreckungsverfahren; während ihm die Sphäre des religiösen Strafrechts entzogen ist, bringt er in die des ‚zivilen' ein starkes im technischen Sinne strafrechtliches Moment hinein. Dem *Muḥtasib*, dessen Hauptfunktionen die Strassen-, Markt- und Gewerbepolizei umfassen und der für diese Gebiete eine beschränkte richterliche Zuständigkeit besitzt, fällt zugleich die Verfolgung der Übertretungen des Gesetzes zu; in dieser Beziehung gilt sein Amt als behördliche Normierung der allgemeinen religiösen Pflicht des ‚Auf-forderns zum Guten und Verbietens des Schlechten', führt faktisch aber zu einer, ‚Verfolgung von Amts weben' in der Sphäre des religiösen Strafrechts. Die Entwicklung zeigt also eine gewisse Tendenz zur etwas stärkeren Betonung eigentlich strafrechtlicher Gesichtspunkte.

Das islamische Recht zeigt sowohl das Phänomen der Gewaltbegrenzung wie das der Gewaltenteilung in starkem Grade. Zwar erhebt die *Šarī'a* theoretisch den Anspruch, das gesamte Leben der Muslims ausnahmslos und ausschliesslich zu regeln; aber in der Rechtspraxis der islamischen Völker hat sie sich auf die Dauer nur auf den für das Volksbewusstsein mit der Religion enger zusammenhängenden Gebieten behaupten können, während auf den anderen das Gewohnheitsrecht, modifiziert durch die Obrigkeit, herrschte; dieser Sachverhalt hat neben der stillschweigenden Duldung der Religionsgelehrten ausserhalb der eigentlich theologischen Kreise selbst theoretische Anerkennung gefunden. Innerhalb der *Šarī'a* hinwiederum unterliegt die obrigkeitliche Gewalt weitgehender Beschränkung durch die stark ausgebildeten subjektiven Rechte der Untertanen.[23] Ferner ist nach islamischer Auffassung die Rechtsschöpfung der menschlichen Tätigkeit entzogen (vgl. aber unten, sowie Abschnitt 3 und 5); und selbst die Interpretation der Rechtsquellen liegt nicht in der Hand der Obrigkeit, sondern der durch den Konsensus als massgebend anerkannten Religionsgelehrten. Nur in die Rechtsfindung kann die Obrigkeit durch Beschränkung der Zuständigkeit der *Qāḍī's* nach Ort, Zeit und Materie und ihre Bindung an bestimmte Schulen bzw. Autoritäten in theoretisch peripherer, praktisch aber sehr tiefgehender Weise eingreifen, wodurch die materiellen Rechtsnormen nicht direkt aufgehoben, aber in ihrer Anwendbarkeit modifiziert werden (vgl. unten Abschnitt 4 und 6). Eine Trennung administrativer und richterlicher Funktionen ist dem islamischen Recht aber fremd: der *Qāḍī* und der *Muḥtasib* vereinigen beide. Der patrimoniale Charakter der Herrschaft im Islam äussert sich auch in dem Fehlen einer rationalen Gewaltenteilung auf dem der Obrigkeit überlassenen Gebiete, so dass die entsprechenden Partien des öffentlichen Rechts in der Theorie kaum und in der Praxis nur schwach ausgebildet sind, sowie darin, dass die ‚Regierung' vorwiegend als freie Verfügung von Fall zu Fall ohne generelle Regeln erscheint; ganz entsprechend ist es in der *Šarīʿa* nie zu einer rationalen Regelung des *Taʿzīr* gekommen.[24] Die materiellen Hauptmittel der Rechtsfindung, Zeugenbeweis und Eid, stammen aus dem vorislamischen Gewohnheitsrecht und sind in der *Šarīʿa*, trotz ihrer strengen technischen Normierung, stark irrational geblieben: der Zeugenbeweis ist streng formell gebunden und bietet für die freie Beweiswürdigung keinen Raum; der Eid, einer der beiden Parteien nach ebenso streng formalen Regeln auferlegt, ist beim Ausfall des Zeugenbeweises entscheidend; Indizien spielen als Beweismittel so gut wie überhaupt keine Rolle. Besonders stark irrational ist die *Qasāma*, der fünfzigfache Eid im Mordprozess gegen einen unbekannten Täter, ein von der *Šarīʿa* nur zögernd anerkanntes Stück altarabischen Beweisverfahren,[25] und der fünfmalige Eid beim *Liʿān*, der Klage des Gatten gegen die Gattin wegen Unzucht, eine echt islamische Neuerung; in beiden Fällen ist die magische Bedeutung des Eides noch ganz deutlich. Der Nachdruck der islamischen Prozessordnung liegt darauf, festzustellen, welche Partei als Kläger die Beweislast trägt und welche als Beklagter den Eid zu leisten hat, wenn kein Beweis erfolgt; da infolge der Natur des Zeugenbeweises der beweislose Prozess eine grosse Rolle spielt, erscheint die Pflicht oder eher das Recht zur Eidesleistung, das nach einem System von Präsumptionen festgestellt wird, fast als Teil des materiellen Rechtsanspruchs, so dass das ‚materielle' und das ‚Prozessrecht' bisweilen schwer zu scheiden sind. Besonders ist dies mit dem *Iqrār*, dem unwiderruflichen Anerkenntnis, der Fall,[26] der formell das dritte Mittel der Rechtsfindung darstellt, dessen sachliche Bedeutung aber weit darüber hinausgreift: da er den, der ihn abgelegt hat, ohne weiteres bindet, ist er das geeignetste Mittel zur Herbeiführung von Fiktionen geworden, die den Interessenten materiell sehr weitgehende Abweichungen von den Rechtsnormen ermöglichen;[27] schliesslich werden sogar einfache Rechtsgeschäfte aller Art in seine für das Prozessrecht besonders wirksame Form gekleidet.[28] Den Urkundenbeweis, der im vorislamischen Gewohnheitsrecht von Mekka eine Rolle spielte und den auch der

Koran in einem Einzelfalle ausdrücklich vorschreibt,[29] in einem anderen wenigstens vorausgesetzt,[30] erkennt die *Šarīʿa* nicht mehr an:[31] ein im islamischen Recht seltener Fall von rückläufiger Entwicklung. Ausserdem aber sind Rechtsschöpfung und Rechtsfindung im islamischen Recht in anderer Weise gegen einander abgegrenzt als dort, wo letztere sich als Anwendung von generell geschaffenen Normen auf einen konkreten Einzelfall darstellt; diese Auffassung und die mit ihr im Zusammenhang stehenden Postulate (Weber S. 396) sind der *Šarīʿa* fremd. Neben die Rechtsschöpfung, d. h. nach islamischer Auffassung die Setzung der Rechtsquellen, die, wie bereits hervorgehoben, der menschlichen Tätigkeit entzogen ist und die sich selbst grossenteils auf Einzelfälle bezieht, tritt die Interpretation der Rechtsquellen, d. h. in der Hauptsache die Beurteilung weiterer Einzelfälle. Diese Tätigkeit und die richterliche gelten in der *Šarīʿa* als gleichartig, mag es sich um ihre vollberechtigte Ausübung durch den *Muğtahid*, den zu selbständiger Rechtsforschung befugten Gelehrten, oder den Anschluss an die Meinung der massgebenden Autoritäten seitens des dazu verpflichteten *Muqallid* handeln. So erhebt die *Šarīʿa* zwar den Anspruch, die Elemente zur Beurteilung eines jeden auftauchenden Falles zu bieten, will aber kein alle denkbaren Fälle umfassendes, lückenloses System darstellen.

3 DER FORMCHARAKTER DES OBJEKTIVEN RECHTES

Die Systematik, die das islamische Recht aufzuweisen hat, beschränkt sich nicht auf ein äusseres (allerdings sehr mangelhaftes) Schema der Ordnung des Rechtsstoffes, sondern greift auch auf das ‚Inbeziehungsetzen' der einzelnen Rechtsverhältnisse (daher z. B. die gleichmässige Struktur eines grossen Teiles des Obligationenrechts), ihre Wertung nach einheitlichen religiösen Gesichtspunkten (z. B. durch das Verbot von Zins und Unsicherheitsfaktoren, *Ġarar*) und ihre ‚juristische Konstruktion' über. Diese Systematik hat die *Šarīʿa* nicht zusammen mit dem vorislamischen Rechtsmaterial übernommen, sondern im wesentlichen[32] erst selbst geschaffen. Die für das islamische Recht in weitestem Umfange typische Kasuistik hat nicht etwa zur Entwicklung von logisch hoch sublimierten Rechtssätzen vermittels der analytischen Methode geführt, sondern ist – soweit nicht reine Darstellungsform oder Konstruktion von komplizierten

Fällen – wesentlich ein parataktisches Assoziieren nach Analogie zur Erschöpfung aller Möglichkeiten in Fällen von Unfähigkeit generellbegrifflicher Verarbeitung. Irrational ist das islamische Recht nur in geringem Umfang: formell irrational war – abgesehen von den irrationalen Elementen magisch-vorislamischer Herkunft (magische Formeln, Beweismittel u.s.w.) – sowohl vom historischen wie vom islamisch-systematischen Standpunkt aus lediglich die durch den Propheten ergangene göttliche Gesetzgebung; materiell irrational ist es soweit, als konkrete religiös-ethische Wertungen des Einzelfalls in die Anwendung der generellen Normen eingreifen können.[33] Die Rationalität des islamischen Rechts ist sowohl formeller wie auch materieller Art. Seine formelle Rationalität zeigt sich in seinem Formalismus; dieser beruht aber mehr auf sinnlich-anschaulichen Merkmalen (daher auch das Vorwiegen der Kasuistik) und weniger auf logischer Sinndeutung (daher wenig Neigung zu abstrakten Regeln). Dieser schwachen Entwicklung des formal-juristischen Charakters entspricht die starke Ausbildung der ihm entgegengesetzten materiellen Rationalität, die für das islamische Recht in weitem Umfange bezeichnend ist; sie äussert sich darin, dass nicht ‚logische Generalisierungen von abstrakten Sinndeutungen', sondern Normen religiös-ethischen Charakters die Entscheidung von Rechtsproblemen bestimmen. Die Durchführung dieser materiellen Rationalisierung ist neben der Systembildung gerade der Hauptinhalt einer entscheidenden Periode der islamischen Rechtsgeschichte.[34] Dabei zeigt sich wieder ein Fall von rückläufiger Entwicklung, indem das Begriffspaar gültig-ungültig, das die *Šarīʿa* zusammen mit anderen formaljuristischen Elementen[35] aus dem vorislamischen Gewohnheitsrecht übernommen hat, durch das andere, echt islamische erlaubt-verboten überlagert und gestört ist. Mit dem magisch-irrationalen Charakter der Entscheidungsmittel hängt die formale Bindung des Beweisrechts unmittelbar zusammen (vgl. oben Abschnitt 2). Der formell irrationale Charakter der prophetisichen Gesetzgebung wirkt sich bis in den Einzelfall hinein aus: einzelne Offenbarungen im Koran und in der Tradition können durch andere abrogiert werden (*nāsiḫ* ‚abrogierend' und *mansūḫ* ‚abrogiert'), so dass selbst die generellen Anweisungen labil sind.[36] Faktisch bedeutete also die Existenz der irrationalen Offenbarung eine „weitgehende Beweglichkeit der Normen", während die spätere Herrschaft der ‚Tradition' zum Schluss zu einer „erhöhten Sterotypierung" führte (Weber S. 471). Die Zeit des Propheten ist die einziger, in der die islamische Rechtsgeschichte das Phänomen der spontan bewussten Rechtsschöpfung, und zwar auf dem Wege der Offenbarung, aufweist; dabei handelt es sich sowohl um die Regelung von Einzelfällen wie um die Aufstellung genereller Normen, ohne dass zwischen ihnen ein wesentlicher Unterschied besteht (beide beruhen in gleicher Weise auf der persönlichen Qualität des Propheten); den Anstoss zu diesen hat grossenteils das Auftreten von ‚bisher nicht geordneten Problemen' gegeben. In der auf die prophetische Zeit unmittelbar folgenden Entwicklungsperiode spielen die ‚Präjudizien' der ‚Richter', sowohl der Kalifen wie Stellvertreter, als primäre Quelle der Rechtsnormbildung eine besonders wichtige Rolle; die ältesten *Qāḍī*'s entschieden ebenso wie ihre Auftraggeber irrational, noch ohne jeden Gedanken an die ‚Anwendung' einer ‚Entscheidungs-norm', nach freiem Ermessen auf Grund des Gewohnheitsrechts des ihrer Jurisdiktion unterstehenden Gebietes oder auch ihrer Heimat mit einer je nach ihrer persönlichen Stellung mehr oder weniger starken Betonung der religiösen Richtlinien (Bergsträsser).[37] Alsbald aber „erscheint ... jede getroffene Entscheidung ... als Ausfluss ... der allein, also dauernd richtigen Tradition"; der „Glaube, nur schon geltende Normen anzuwenden", beherrscht die islamische Rechtsgeschichte jedenfalls seit dem Ende des Zeitalters der ersten Kalifen. Dieser Glaube wirkt sich in zweierlei Richtung aus. Einerseits entsteht eine gewaltige Masse von Traditionen (*Ḥadīt*), die vorgeben nicht nur für das Recht, sondern auch für viele andere Lebensgebiete autoritative Vorbilder in den Aussprüchen und Handlungen des Propheten und seiner Zeitgenossen zu enthalten, in Wirklichkeit aber lediglich eine Zurückprojizierung der Entwicklung in etwa den beiden ersten Jahrhunderten des Islam mit ihren verschiedenen, einander oft widerstreitenden Tendenzen[38] auf die Urzeit darstellen; in diese Masse sind auch die realtiv wenigen echten Berichte derart ein gegangen. Übrigens gelten nicht die Traditionen als solche ohne weiteres als autoritative Richtschnur, sondern die sich mit ihnen nurzum Teil deckende, zum Teil über sie hinausgreifende *Sunna*, d. h. das ‚Übliche', die – erst sekundär als mit der *Sunna* des Propheten identisch präsumierte – Übung der islamischen Gemeinde, also durch aus die ‚Tradition' im soziologischen Sinne. Prinzipiell dieselbe Einstellung zur ‚Tradition'[39] ist es auch, wenn sich die gesamte spätere Entwicklung als Interpretation der ein für allemal gesetzten Rechtsordnung göttlichen Ursprungs darstellt. Andererseits entwickelt sich der *Iǧmāʿ*, der Konsensus[40] der islamischen

Gemeinde, repräsentiert durch ihre anerkannten Religionsgelehrten, aus einer Ergänzung der im Koran und in der *Sunna* bzw. den Traditionen) niedergelegten Vorschriften[41] zu der eigentlich entscheidenden Instanz, die nicht nur die Authentizität jener beiden materiellen ‚Quellen' und ihre richtige Interpretation garantiert, sondern auch darüber hinaus für sich allein ein selbständiges Kriterium darstellt. Ihre formale Rechtfertigung erhält diese Rolle des Konsensus durch eine Tradition, nach der Muhammed erklärt haben soll, dass seine Gemeinde nie in einem Irrtum übereinstimmen werde. Der Konsensus wird also als eine Art von rechtsschöpferischem Prinzip über die Zeit des Propheten hinaus auch theoretisch anerkannt, aber nur im normativ den Irrtum abwehrenden, nicht im positiv produktiven Sinne (Bergsträsser). Historisch betrachtet, hat er sich zwar in der älteren Zeit, noch ohne theoretische Besinnung, sondern einfach als Ausdruck des religiösen Bewusstseins der Islamgemeinde, wierderholt selbst gegen den Wortlaut des Korans durchgesetzt und bildet für wichtige Teile der islamischen Lehre die einzige Grundlage, wirkt aber, je länger desto entschiedener, als immer wiederholte Bestandsaufnahme der Fragen, über die eine allgemeine Einstimmigkeit erreicht ist und die dadurch als ein für allemal entschieden gelten, als ein durchaus traditionell-konservatives Element. Dieser für ein ‚heiliges Recht' typische Traditionalismus äussert sich auch in dem primär mündlichen, durch Zeugenketten garantierten Charakter seiner Überlieferung; das gilt prinzipiell in der gleichen Weise sowohl vom Koran wie von den Traditionen wie von den Rechtsbüchern; die für den Koran sehr früh, für die Traditionen etwas später einsetzende und bei den – ohnehin nicht in die älteste Zeit zurückgehenden – Rechtsbüchern von Anfang an geübte schriftliche Aufzeichnung dient daneben im Prinzip nur als Gedächtnisstütze.[42]

Das „typische Problem des Ausgleichs zwischen einem, universale Geltung beanspruchenden, rationalen Recht und den vorgefundenen lokalen ... Rechten", wobei „das universale Recht als allein legitim auftrat", kommt in dem für die islamische Rechtsgeschichte (im weiteren Sinne) grundlegenden Verhältnis zwischen der nach der Theorie auf göttlicher Satzung beruhenden *Šarīʿa* und der *ʿĀda*, dem Gewohnheitsrecht, zum Ausdruck. Unter dieser ist die gesamte von der *Šarīʿa* abweichende (oder über sie hinausgehende) Rechtspraxis zu verstehen, welches auch ihr Ursprung sein mag. Ungeachtet der Tatsache, dass die *Šarīʿa* selbst, historisch gesehen, in weitem Umfange aus dem vorgefundenen

Gewohnheitsrecht hervorgegangen ist, erkennt sie der *'Āda* bindende Kraft nur insoweit zu, als sie ausdrücklich darauf verweist, was relativ selten der Fall ist.[43] Namentlich in der späteren Entwicklung der Lehre der mālikitischen Rechtsschule, wie sie im westlichen Islam herrschend geworden ist, ist die Grenze zwischen dem von der *Šarī'a* unter dem Zwange der Tatsachen still schweigend geduldeten, theoretisch aber ignorierten Gewohnheitsrecht und jenem, das von ihr assimilier worden ist und als Teil von ihr gelten kann, bisweilen fliessend.[44] Am intensivsten berühren sich die Theorie der *Šarī'a* und die Praxis des Gewohnheitsrechts in den Umgehungsgeschäften (*Ḥijal*).[45] Mit ihrer Hilfe gelangt man durch der *Šarī'a* formell entsprechende Rechtsgeschäfte auf Umwegen zu faktischen Ergebnissen, wie sie die Praxis verlangt, die Theorie aber, wenn man sie direkt danach befragte, nicht anerkennen könnte.[46] Sie beweisen einerseits das Bestreben der *Šarī'a*, sich die andersartige Praxis wenigstens formell zu assimilieren – die Verfasser der *Ḥijal*-Bücher sind gerade *Šarī'a*-Gelehrte –, andererseits die Geneigtheit der Praxis, sich einer solchen Legitimierung zu unterziehen – denn der praktische, nicht fingierte Charakter der *Ḥijal* ist in vielen Fällen evident. Die *Ḥijal*-Literatur stellt geradezu eine Hauptquelle für unsere Kenntnis der mittelalterlichen islamischen Rechtspraxis dar. In etwas anderem Sinne berühren sich Theorie und Praxis des islamischen Rechts in dem Urkundenwesen. Die Urkunden (*Šurūṭ*, *Wāṭā'iq*) entsprechen inhaltlich im allgemeinen[47] durchaus den Anforderungen der *Šarī'a* und sind gerade Belege für deren Anwendung in der Praxis; zugleich aber beweisen sie, dass das von der Theorie abgelehnte[48] Prinzip der schriftlichkeit in der Praxis gleichwohl eine äusserst wichtige Rolle spielte,[49] lange bevor sich der Urkundenbeweis in der letzten, ‚modernistischen' Entwicklungsperiode der *Šarī'a* seinen festen Platz eroberte.[50] Auch von dieser neben der Theorie der *Šarī'a* herlaufenden Praxis haben ihre Gelehrten Notiz genommen und eine umfangreiche Literatur von Formularsammlungen, z. T. mit eingegehender Kommentierung aller Einzelheiten, geschaffen. Beide Erscheinungen, *Ḥijal* wie *Šurūṭ*, lassen erkennen, wie wenig sich auch im Islam das Recht als solches nach ökonomischen Momenten gerichtet hat und wie zugleich „die Rechtstechnik ... ihre eigenen Wege gegangen" ist (Weber S. 395, 424). Der Ausgleich zwischen *Šarī'a* und *'Āda* hat zu einer im wesentlichen überall gleichmässigen Abgrenzung der beiderseitigen Geltungsphären geführt, indem der *Šarī'a* die mit der Religion mehr oder weniger eng zusammenhängenden

Rechtsgebiete (Kultus, Ehe und Familie, Erbrecht, Stiftungen)[51] zufielen, während der Staat einen Teil der Rechtspflege, besonders das Strafrecht, in die eigene Hand nahm,[52] das eigentliche Verkehrsrecht aber immer unter der Herrschaft des Gewohnheitsrechts blieb; dies stand übrigens in keinem direkten Gegensatz zur *Šarīʿa*, sondern zeichnete sich in der Hauptsache durch eine grössere, den Verkehrsbedürfnissen angepasste Beweglichkeit aus (Bergsträsser).[53] Dieses Gewohnheitsrecht lässt besonders in den *Ḥijal* die (neben den ‚Präjudizien der Richter') zweite primäre Quelle der Rechtsnormbildung, nämlich das ‚Gemeinschaftshandeln der Interessenten', das zum ‚Typischwerden von Einverständnissen' führt, in ihrer Wirkung aufs deutlichste erkennen. Die Bemerkungen Webers (S. 400) über die Kalkulierung der ‚Chancen des Rechtszwanges' und die Anpassung des abzuschliessenden ‚Zweckkontraktes' an sie treffen durchaus auf die *Ḥijal* zu, die nichts anderes sind als eben solche der Forderung der formellen *Šarīʿa*-Gemässheit angepassten Zweckkontrakte. Soweit der staatliche Rechtszwang[54] nicht genügt – denn die meisten dieser Institutionen „bestanden praeter legem" (Weber S. 476) –, tritt an seine Stelle die Konvention; das prägt sich in der Erscheinung der Mittelsmänner aus, die für viele *Ḥijal* unentbehrlich sind und dafür zu sorgen haben, dass die Parteien von ihren der *Šarīʿa* formell entsprechenden Rechtsgeschäften nur den Gebrauch machen, der dem zwischen ihnen herbeizuführenden faktischen Verhältnis entspricht. Es versteht sich von selbst, dass die Interessenten an diesem Verkehrsrecht der Mitwirkung ‚berufsmässig' arbeitender Berater bedurften, und diese sind, wie wir sowohl bei den *Ḥijal* wie bei den *Šurūṭ* gesehen haben, in der Hauptsache gerade unter den *Šarīʿa*-Gelehrten zu suchen. Ihre Tätigkeit besteht vor allem in dem ‚cavere' – ein der Sache nach und auch als Terminus (*Iḥtijāṭ*) in der *Ḥijal*- und *Šurūṭ*-Literatur immer wiederkehrender Zug – und geht in die Erfindung neuer Kontraktschemata – eben der *Ḥijal* – über. Dadurch wird auch das gewohnheitsmässige Verkehrsrecht als ein ‚Juristenrecht' charakterisiert, das sich dank der „Erfindungsgabe der Kautelarjuristen", die ein „selbständiges Element der Rechtsneubildung durch private Initiative" darstellt, aus dem vorgefundenen Gewohnheitsrecht durch Anpassung an den Rechtszwang der *Šarīʿa* entwickelt hat. Umgekehrt zeigen die gewohnheitsrechtlichen Ordnungen, die sich bei verschiedenen islamischen Völkern selbst im Familien- und Erbrecht im Widerspruch zur *Šarīʿa* erhalten haben, wie „derartige einmal eingelebte Formen des

Einverständnishandelns ohne alle Rücksicht auf staatlichen Rechtszwang jahrhundertelang fortexistieren können".

4 DIE RATIONALISIERUNG DES RECHTS DURCH DIE ‚RECHTSHONORATIOREN': RECHTSLEHRE UND RECHTSPRECHUNG

Der Vorgang der materieilen Rationalisierung, dessen treibende Kräfte nicht von fachlich-rechtlichen, sondern von heterogen-materialen Grundlagen ausgehen (vgl. oben Abschnitt 3), hat in der *Šarīʿa* gerade nicht in der Richtung der Entfaltung ihrer ‚juristischen' Qualitäten gewirkt; das ist in erster Linie durch die Eigenart der ‚Rechtshonoratioren' bzw. ‚Rechtspraktiker'[55] bedingt, d. h. des Personenkreises, der auf die Rechtsgestaltung ‚berufsmässig' Einfluss zu nehmen in der Lage war (Weber S. 412). Den Anstoss zu dieser Rationalisierung hat im islamischen Recht nicht die „steigende Bedeutung des Güterverkehrs", sondern das Bedürfnis eines bestimmten Kreises von Frommen nach religiöser Wertung aller Lebensverhältnisse gegeben. So erfolgte die Entwicklung der *Šarīʿa* in einer entscheidenden Periode ihrer Geschichte nicht ‚empirisch-handwerksmässig' im Zusammenhang mit der Praxis, sondern ‚theoretisch-rational', aber doch nicht ‚juristisch-formal'. Denn nicht die formal juristisch präziseste, sondern die den religiösen und ethischen Anforderungen der Frommen entsprechendste Ausprägung wird erstrebt; eine Sonderung des ‚Rechts' von der ‚Ethik', dem Ritual und der Anstandslehre ist garnicht beabsichtigt (Weber S. 461, 468). Dadurch ist die *Šarīʿa* zu einem typischen ‚heiligen Recht' geworden, und die Art ihrer Lehre entspricht der von Weber (S. 459) als den ‚Priesterschulen'[56] eigentümlich charakterisierten. Von hier aus erklären sich die Rolle der ‚Tradition', die Art der dem islamischen Recht eigenen Kasuistik, die Eigenart seiner Begriffe, die zwar abstrakt, aber zu allgemein generalisierend und daher leer, farblos und unanschaulich sind (Bergsträsser), die Erscheinum der formalistischen Umgehungen (*Ḥijal*) der feststehenden Normenim Interesse der Rechtsinteressenten, die Aufstellung „idealer, religiös-ethischer Forderungen an die Menschen oder die Rechtsordnung", im Gegensatz zur logischen Bearbeitung einer empirisch geltenden Ordnung – Erscheinungen, die zum Teil schon oben zur Sprache gekommen sind. Aus dem Charakter der *Šarīʿa* als ‚heiliges Recht' ergeben sich Beschränkungen ihres Geltungsbereichs. Beschränkt ist er einerseits durch ihre selbstgesetzten Grenzen: sie verpflichtet nur den Muslim, und auch diesen nur zum Teil im Islamland, den Nichtmuslim nur beschränkt im Islamland – also eine Mischung des personalen und des territorialen Prinzips (Bergsträsser); andererseits durch das Bewusstsein von ihrem eigenen idealen Charakter, die Rücksichtnahme auf die Verderbnis der Zeit und die menschliche Schwäche. Daher verlangt das Gesetz vom Muslim zwar bedingungslose theoretische Anerkennung (Leugnung seiner Verbindlichkeit ist Unglaube), betrachtet aber den Zwang der Umstände als Entschuldigung für seine faktische Nichtbefolgung und lässt dem Gläubigen bei Verletzung religiöser Pflichten die Möglichkeit der ‚Reue' (*Tauba*). Dass man die Nichtmuslims nicht dem islamischen Recht unterworften, sondern ihre Rechtsverhältnisse unangetastet hat weiterbestehen lassen, ist ein Ausfluss nicht des Personalitätsprinzips, sondern des Charakters der *Šarīʿa* als religiöser Pflichtenlehre (vgl. unten Abschnitt 6) zwangsweise greift das islamiches Recht nur insoweit ein, als Muslims direkt oder indirekt mitbetroffen sind; das sich dabei ergebende Minderrecht der Nichtmuslims ist im wesentlichen religiöser und staatsrechtlicher Art (Bergsträsser). Als ‚heiliges Recht' ist die *Šarīʿa* in weitem Umfange[57] heteronom; daher gelten ihre Regeln autoritativ kraft ihres blossen Vorhandenseins, nicht vermöge ihrer eigenen Sinnhaftigkeit; die Unentwegtheit im Ziehen von Konsequenzen bis zum Widersinn ist die eine Folge, die Wahrung des Buchstabens unter Nichtachtung des Sinnes die andere[58] (Bergsträsser). In ihrer endgültigen Gestalt, vor allem in ihrer Systematik, ist die *Šarīʿa* ein „Produkt der Schullehre";[59] daher wird „eine Fulle von Kasuistik längst veralteter Institute" mitgeschleppt; daher gelten die späteren Juristen nicht zur selbständigen Tätigkeit (*Iǧithād*) in der Interpretation der Rechtsquellen befugt, sondern sind zum Anschluss (*Taqlīd*) an ihre Vorgänger verpflichtet;[60] daher sind die massgebenden Texte der späteren Zeit nicht etwa der Koran oder die Sammlungen von Traditionen, sondern die durch den Konsensus anerkannten ‚Rechtsbücher', d. h. Privatarbeiten von Rechtsgelehrten; daher ist nicht der Anschluss an eine beliebige Autorität gestattet, sondern nur die Wahl zwischen vier sich gegenseitig als *Sunna*-gemäss anerkennenden Rechtsschulen (*Maḏhab*'s) freigestellt.[61] Von diesen Bindungen versucht sich erst in der Gegenwart der aus der Auseinandersetzung mit den europäischen Ideen erwachsene Modernismus freizumachen;[62] es bleibt abzuwarten, ob sich etwa neben der traditionellen Form der *Šarīʿa* eine modernistische entwickeln wird,[63] die – wenn auch unter gewandelten Voraussetzungen – an dem Punkte wieder anknüpft, an dem jene die lebendige Berührung mit der Praxis verloren hat (vgl. den historischen Überlick unten Abschnitt 5).

Der erörterte schulmässig-technische Charakter der *Šarīʿa* bringtes mit sich, dass der einzelne Interessent zur Feststellung ihrer Lehre über eine bestimmte Frage kaum imstande ist; vielmehr bedarf er dazu der Auskunft (*Fatwā*) eines Fachmannes, der danach *Muftī* heisst und staatlich angestellt sein kann; seine Tätigkeit beschränkt sich auf die (oft ohne Begründung erfolgende) Mitteilung der geltenden Lehre und trägt zur Weiterentwicklung des Rechts nur bei neu auftauchenden Fragen bei, hat sich dann aber innerhalb der Lehrent wicklung seiner Schule zu bewähren; irrational und unkontrollierbar (Weber S. 475) ist sie also nicht und weist auch mit der des respondierenden römischen Juristen (Weber S. 466) trotz äusserer Ähnlichkeit kaum eine tiefere Verwandtschaft auf.[64] In diesem Zusammenhang ist auch der von Weber öfter (besonders S. 477, 486) verwandte Begriff der ‚Kadijustiz' richtig zu stellen: der ihm von Weber gegebene Inhalt trifft in keiner Weise auf die Rechtsprechung des nach der *Šarīʿa* entscheidenden *Qāḍī* zu, sondern vielmehr auf die im Gegensatz zu jener stehende ‚weltliche' Rechtsprechung der politischen Gewalten; jene ist, um Webers Terminologie (S. 486) zu gebrauchen ‚theokratisch', diese ‚patriarchal'. Dagegen liegt ein irrationales Element der Rechtsprechung nach der *Šarīʿa* in der Inappellierbarkeit der vom *Qāḍī* als Einzelrichter gefällten Urteile[65] sowie in dem häufigen Nebeneinanderstehen von mehreren *Qāḍī*'s (auch solchen verschiedener Schulen) zur Auswahl der Partei;[66] diese Verhältnisse sind im vorigen und im gegenwärtigen Jahrhundert in verschiedenen islamischen Staaten nach europäischem Vorbild durch eine feste richterliche Organisation mit Richterkollegien und Appellationsmöglichkeit ersetzt worden, für deren Einführung die *Šarīʿa* selbst den politischen Gewalten die Möglichkeit bietet. Von Anfang an betrachtet die Theorie nämlich die Gültigkeit des Richteramts als unabhängig von der Rechtmässigkeit der einsetzenden Obrigkeit und anerkennt dementsprechend die von der Obrigkeit verfügten Einschränkungen der Zuständigkeit des *Qāḍī*'s als bindend (vgl. oben Abschnitt 2). Hier hat sich also (ebenso wie auf dem Gebiete des Strafrechts, vgl. unten) die *Šarīʿa* selbst ausser Kraft gesetzt. Die *Qāḍī*'s rekrutieren sich faktisch aus den in den „zünftigen Theologenschulen" herangebildeten Anwärtern;[67] die Theorie fordert lediglich den Besitz bestimmter Kenntnisse und Charaktereigenschaften; wer von der Obrigkeit ernannt worden ist, ohne diesen Anforderungen zu genügen, ist gleichwohl rechtmässiger *Qāḍī*.

Wie sich aus dem historischen Überblick (unten Abschnitt 5) ergeben wird, ist die entscheidende Tatsache in der Geschichte der *Šarīʿa* nicht die, dass die „Lösung der heiligen Gebote vom weltlichen Recht" ausblieb das ist allerdings auch der Fall gewesen), sondern umgekehrt dass die religiöse Pflichtenlehre des vorhandene und einer selbständigen Weiterentwicklung fähige ‚weltliche' Recht durchdrang. Das Ergebnis war das gleiche: es entstand ein spezifisch unformales Recht. Dass eine solche Durchdringung erfolgte, der sich das profane Recht nicht entziehen (und von der es sich bis zur Gegenwart nicht mehr freimachen) konnte, liegt an der Eigenart und dem gegenseitigen Verhältnis von Religion und Staat, Frommen und Herrschern (vgl. ebenfalls Abschnitt 5). In der Praxis konnte sich das heilige Recht zwar nur auf gewissen Rechtsgebieten durchsetzen (vgl. oben Abschnitt 3) – eben jenen, für die sich die heiligen Rechte überhaupt in erster Linie interessieren[68] –, aber es hat doch der ungestörten Entwicklung profanen Rechts auf sämtlichen Rechtsgebieten den Weg versperrt. Selbst die weltliche Gerichtsbarkeit, die die meisten islamischen Staaten neben den stets aufrechterhaltenen *Šarīʿa*-Tribunalen eingerichtet haben, befand sich, was das Verkehrsrecht anlangt,[69] jenen gegenüber immer in einer prekären Lage, da sich die Rechtsuchenden zwar in der grossen Mehrzahl der Fälle an sie wandten, der Rekurs zu den *Šarīʿa*-Tribunalen aber nie prinzipiell ausgeschlossen werden konnte. Aus dem gleichen Grunde der Monopolisierung der vollberechtigten Rechtspflege durch die *Šarīʿa* musste die weltliche Gesetzgebung und Rechtsprechung grossenteils den Charakter der ‚Verwaltung' annehmen (vgl. oben Abschnitt 3). Diese Verhältnisse bestehen heute noch selbst in einem unter europäischem Protektorat stehenden Staat wie Marokko weiter.[70] Andererseits hat es, unter der Einwirkung europäischer, vor allem politischer Ideen, gerade Ägypten als unabhängiger islamischer Staat vermocht, die Zuständigkeit der *Šarīʿa*-Tribunale gesetzlich auf bestimmte, möglichst eng abgegrenzte Rechtsgebiete zu beschränken und im übrigen eine moderne Gesetzgebung einzuführen, ja sogar in die *Šarīʿa* selbst auf den ihr überlassenen Gebieten durch starke gesetzgeberische Änderungen erheblich einzugreifen.[71] Das unterscheidet sich wesentlich von den früheren Gesetzgebungen islamischer Obrigkeiten, deren bekanntestes

Beispiel in den osmanischen *Qānūnnāme*'s vorleigt; diese konnten in der Hauptsache nur Ergänzungen oder Ausführungs bestimmungen zur *Šarīʿa* innerhalb der von der Theorie gesetzten Grenzen sein oder zu sein prätendieren, wenngleich sie auf dem Gebiete des Strafrechts (vgl. oben) zu einem wirklichen Ersatz der unanwendbaren *Šarīʿa* durch eine weltliche Gesetzgebung geführt haben. Wenn aber die moderne Türkei noch vor der Loslösung des Staates vom Islam die *Šarīʿa* überhaupt abgeschafft hat, „so ist damit das innere Problem des Islam nicht gelöst, sondern beiseite geschoben" (Bergsträsser).

5 HISTORISCHER ÜBERBLICK: DIE ROLLE DES ‚IMPERIUMS'

Damit sind wir beim Gegenstand des historischen Überblicks angelangt, der die wichtigsten bisher betrachteten Eigentümlichkeiten des islamischen Rechts in ihrem Entstehen aufzeigen soll.[72] Zur Zeit Muhammeds herrschte in Arabien die altererbte Stammesorganisation; allein die Stammeszugehörigkeit verlieh Rechtsschutz für ‚Besitz und Leben'; die wichtigste Garantie war die Blutrache unter solidarischer Haftung des Stammes mit der Möglichkeit der Ablösung durch das Blutgeld in leichteren Fällen; durch die Stammes organisation war zugleich das Personen-, Familien- und Erbrecht-bedingt. Die übrigen Rechtsgebiete wurden durch ein bei den Beduinen primitives, in den Städten (vor allem Mekka und Medina) entwickelteres Gewohnheitsrecht beherrscht, das auch schon Elemente fremder (wohl römisch-provinzialrechtlicher und vielleicht auch babylonischer)[73] Herkunft enthielt; in diesem fortgeschritteneren Recht, das im wesentlichen das Verkehrs- und Vermögensrecht umfasste, kann man den Anteil der Handelsstadt Mekka und der Datteloase Medina unterscheiden. In diese Verhältnisse trat als religiöser Erwecker Muhammed, der mit seiner Übersiedelung von Mekka nach Medina auch zur Schlichtung von Stammesstreitigkeiten und zur Rechtsprechung berufen war und damit zu einem ‚Rechts propheten' wurde. Er fand also bereits ein geltendes Recht und damit den Gedanken vor, dass die Maxime der Einzelentscheidung auf künftige gleiche Fälle anzuwenden sei. An sich hatte er keinen Anlass, das geltende Recht zu ändern; sein Ziel war, die Menschen zu lehren, was sie tun müssen, um dem drohenden Gericht zu entgehen und sich das Paradies zu sichern, also eine religiöse Pflichtenlehre zu verkünden. Aber auch diese greift in das Rechtsleben erheblich ein; ihrerseits sind die auf das Rechtsleben bezüglichen Vorschriften des Korans durchaus ethisch gehalten, d. h. von dem Geiste des Tunsollens und Nichttundürfens bestimmt, im Gegensatz zur Verknüpfung bestimmter Rechtsfolgen mit bestimmten Handlungen. In diesem Sinne werden vor allem das Familienrecht, das Erbrecht und das Kriegsrecht geregelt; den Anlass dazu gab das Bedürfnis einerseits nach stärkerem Schutz des Schwachen, andererseits nach der Ausfüllung von Lücken im geltenden Recht, das den neuen Verhältnissen nicht mehr genügte; auch die strafrechtlichen Vorschriften, bei denen der Bruch mit dem Alten besonders deutlich ist, sind durchaus normativ-ethisch gemeint. Die ersten Kalifen übernahmen Muhammeds, auch im Koran ausdrücklich verankerte, Richterstellung; seine Rechtsprophetenstellung konnten sie nicht übernehmen; der Gedanke der Vererbung des Charisma auf sie ist im orthodoxen (sunnitischen) Islam nicht gefasst worden. Vorhanden ist er bei den Schiiten: sie kennen die Vererbung zwar nicht der Prophetie, aber des göttlichen ‚Lichtes' in der Familie des Propheten auf die unfehlbaren *Imāme* (Leiter der Gemeinde), deren letzter nach der Lehre der verbreitetsten, in Persien herrschenden Richtung seit dem Jahre 878 unsichtbar ist. Diese Lehre ist aber auf dem Gebiet des Rechts fast nur Theorie geblieben;[74] die tatsächliche Rechtsentwicklung war von der sunnitischen abhängig, und die schiitischen Lehren gehen fast stets mit wenigstens einer der sunnitschen Rechtsschulen zusammen. Die ersten Kalifen und ihre Stellvertreter haben bei ihren richterlichen Entscheidungen noch nicht die Vorstellung gehabt, nach ‚islamischem Recht' zu richten; die Vorschriften des Koran wurden natürlich beachtet, und auch sonst erfolgte die Rechtsprechung im Geist des Propheten; da das Rechtsleben aber noch grossenteils religiös indifferent war, konnte das geltende Recht in weitem Umfange beibehalten bzw. in den neu eroberten Provinzen fremdes Recht unbedenklich rezipiert werden. Die Fortdauer dieses Zustandes hätte zu einem stellenweise von der religiösen Pflichtenlehre beeinflussten, aber im Ganzen aus der Praxis erwachsenen und in ihr tatsächlich geltenden Recht führen können (Bergsträsser). Gestört wurde diese Entwicklung durch die politischen Verhältnisse: der engste Kreis von Muhammeds Gefährten vermochte die Macht nicht festzuhalten, die an das altmekkanische Adelsgeschlecht der Umaijaden überging. So entstand der Gegensatz zwischen den umaijadischen Kalifen von

Damaskus und dem Kreise der Frommen von Medina. Diese widmeten sich der Reinerhaltung und dem Ausbau der Pflichtenlehre und unterwarfen auch das gesamte Rechtsleben einer konsequenten religiös-ethischen Beurteilung. Die Tendenz dieser Kanonisierung des Rechts richtete sich gegen die Weltlichkeit der Umaijaden und die tatsächlichen Verhältnisse, war also rigoristisch und wirklichkeitsfremd. Aus dieser Periode, der Zeit der ‚7 Juristen von Medina', stammt die Hauptmasse der Traditionen, der Begriff der *Sunna* und auch schon die praktische Anwendung des Prinzips des Konsensus und des Analogieschlusses.[75] Ein nochmaliger Wandel erfolgte mit der Übernahme der Macht durch die abbasidischen Kalifen. Hochgekommen durch die Agitation gegen die weltlichen Umaijaden, zeigten sie sich betont religiös und prätendierten, das Gottesreich auf Erden durchzuführen. Sie versuchten, die Kluft zwischen dem heiligen Recht und dem Leben zu überbrücken, holten Rechtsgutachten sogar über Fragen des Staatsrechts und der Verwaltung ein und beriefen Religionsgelehrte in hohe Richterstellen. Aber es war zu einer wirklichen Durchführung der *Šarīʿa* zu spät, bald schwand auch der Wille und dann die Macht dazu. Als Ergebnis bleibt die Verknüpfung des Richteramts mit dem heiligen Recht (Bergsträsser): seit den Abbasiden ist der *Qāḍī* ein Religionsgelehrter.[76] Zwar blieb er, auch in seinen Entscheidungen, abhängig von der Regierung, die ihn ein- und absetzt und ihm die Machtmittel zur Vollstreckung gewährt oder versagt; aber man hat doch immer *Qāḍī*'s eingesetzt und sie im Prinzip mit den nötigen Vollzugsorganen versehen. Daneben jedoch setzte nunmehr die verwaltungsmässige Entscheidung von Rechtsfragen ein. Die produktive Periode der Rechtswissenschaft, die religiöse Durchdringung des Rechtslebens, ist in frühabbasidischer Zeit zu Ende, es erfolgt die Konsolidierung und die Systematisierung des Rechts in verschiedenen, zum Teil ältere Richtungen fortsetzenden Rechtsschulen, die sich nach anfänglich heftigen Kämpften allmählich gegenseitig anerkennen und von denen vier dauernd überleben (vgl. oben Abschnitt 4). Der Gründer einer von ihnen, aš-Šāfiʿī (st. 820), hat das juristische Denken zum Bewusstsein seiner selbst erhoben und ist dadurch zum Begründer der Rechtswissenschaft im Islam geworden (Bergsträsser). Alsbald tritt eine Verengerung und Erstarrung ein, da das Prinzip des Konsensus die weitere Diskussion über einmal entschiedene Fragen unmöglich macht. Das führt schon am Ende des 9. Jahrhunderts zu der Auffassung, dass für weiteren *Iǧtihād* kein Raum sei, dass es sich nur noch um Anwendung und Interpretation der überlieferten Lehre handeln könne; in Wirklichkeit war auch diese spätere Tätigkeit noch (in unserem Sinne) rechtsschöpferisch, insofern sie sich der Erfassung neuer Sachverhalte widmete, die ihr vor allem im Zusammenhang mit den *Fatwā*'s zuströmten (Bergsträsser). Jene Erstarrung bot andererseits eine bei dem Fehlen einer stützenden staatlichen Autorität in der Verfallszeit besonders wertvolle Gewähr der Stabilität, durch die sich das islamische Recht über jene Periode des Niederganges hinweggerettet hat. Eine neue Periode in der Geschichte der *Šarīʿa* eröffnete das Eintreten der osmanischen Türken in den Islam. Unbelastet von historischen Voraussetzungen nahmen sie das islamische Recht besonders ernst und verhalfen ihm in seiner hanafitischen Gestalt zu der grössten Geltung, die es seit der ältesten Zeit je besessen hat. Die *Šarīʿa*-Rechtsprechung und der *Qāḍī*-Stand werden staatlicherseits gefördert; daneben wird mit den *Qānūnnāme*'s eine eigene Gesetzgebung geschaffen in dem guten Glauben, der *Šarīʿa* nicht zu widersprechen, sondern ihr zur Durchführung zu ver helfen bzw. ihre Lücken auszufüllen; dabei stehen das Polizei-, Strafund Liegenschaftsrecht, auch das Kriegsrecht und das Recht der nichtmuhammedanischen Untertanen im Vordergrund. Mit dem Niedergang der Türkei ging auch diese Nachblüte des islamischen Rechts zu Ende, und die Reformbewegungen des 19. Jahrhunderts drängten seine Geltung, speziell durch die Einführung von Gesetzbüchern nach europäischem Muster, immer weiter zurück. Freilich wurde es zunächst noch nicht völlig aufgegeben: das Obligationen- und Sachenrecht wurde 1869–77 in der *Meǧelle* kodifiziert, die materiell im wesentlichen islamisches Recht enthält, obgleich der Gedanke der Kodifikation dem Charakter der *Šarīʿa* durchaus widerspricht.[77] Parellel zu der Entwicklung in der Türkei vollzog sich das Eindringen europäischen Rechts in anderen islamischen Ländern, verschieden schnell und tiefgreifend je nach der Art des politischen Eingreifens europäischer Mächte. Die restlose Europäisierung des Staates und damit auch des Rechtslebens in der neuen Türkei bedeutete hier das Ende der Geschichte der *Šarīʿa*; umgekehrt könnte die Modifizierung ihrer traditionellen Form durch den Modernismus, deren erste Anfänge oben in Abschnitt 4 zur Sprache gekommen sind, zum Ausgangspunkt einer neuen Entwicklung werden.

Dieser historische Überblick hat zugleich die verschiedenen Phasen des Verhältnisses zwischen ‚Imperium' und ‚Tradition' ‚bzw': ‚gemeinem Recht' in der islamischen Rechtsgeschichte aufgezeigt. Speziell in dem oben weiderholt besprochene Verfahren, „entweder den entscheidenden Richter bindend zu instruieren ... oder die Prozesse freiwillig oder zwangsweise an sich selbst oder an ein besonderes Gericht zu ziehen", wodurch „im Effekt das geltende gemeine Recht [hier die *Šarīʿa*] weitgehend ausser Geltung" gesetzt wird (Weber S. 483f.), äussert sich eine typische Einstellung des ‚fürstlichen' zum dem ‚gemeinen' Recht, mit dem sich jenes mangels eines religiösen Charakters nicht auf die gleiche Stufe stellen konnte. Als ‚Amtsrecht kraft [des] Imperiums' (Weber S. 433) erscheint die häufig geübte, von der *Šarīʿa* selbst anerkannte Bindung der *Qāḍī*'s an bestimmte Schulen bzw. Autoritäten (vgl. oben Abschnitt 2). Besondere Erwähnung verdienen noch zwei Eigentümlichkeiten der osmanischen Entwicklungsperiode; es ist vielleicht kein Zufall, dass auch sie der von Weber (S. 483, 488, 490) für das Eingreifen des Imperiums in das gemeine Recht gegebenen Charakterisierung entsprechen. Das zeigt sich einmal in dem Interesse der osmanischen *Qānūnnāme*'s für das Strafrecht. Der Gedanke einer Tarifierung des Wergeldes stammt allerdings schon aus dem altarabischen Stammesrecht, und in der schöpferischen Periode der *Šarīʿa* ist er zu einem das Gesamt-gebiet der Körperverletzungen einschliessenden System von Sühnegeldern, das ergänzend neben die Talio tritt, ausgearbeitet worden;[78] aber das viel umfassendere und sich auch auf die *Ḥadd*-Strafen und den *Taʿzīr* erstreckende System von nach den Vermögensverhältnissen des Täters abgestuften Geldstrafen in den *Qānūnnāmme*'s ist eine ausgesprochen ‚fürstliche' Schöpfung. Sodann äussert sich in der Tatsache des Auftretens der *Qānūnnāme*'s als solcher das typische Streben des Imperiums, und zwar besonders einer starken politischen Neuschöpfung, nach Kodifikation[79] im Interesse der Rechtseinheit.[80]

6 ZU EINZELNEN RECHTSGEBIETEN

Als religiöse Pflichtenlehre weist das islamische Recht folgende Skala der religiösen Wertung der Handlungen auf: Pflicht (*Farḍ, wāǧib*), empfehlenswert (*Sunna*,[81] *mustaḥabb*), indifferent (*mubāḥ*), verwerflich (*makrūh*), verboten (*ḥarām*); *mubāḥ*, d. h. weder geboten noch verboten, ist verschieden von *ǧāʾiz*, d. h. zulässig, erlaubt, unbedenklich, sowie von *ḥalāl*, d. h. alles, was nicht *ḥarām* ist. Daneben besteht eine Skala der Rechtmässigkeit mit den beiden Plen rechtsgültig (*ṣaḥīḥ*) und nichtig (*bāṭil*); dazwischen liegen die nicht von allen Schulen gleichmässig anerkannten, am deutlichsten noch von den Ḥanafiten geschiedenen Stufen verwerflich (*makrūh*) und unvollkommen (*fāsid*); jenes ist ebenfalls rechtswirksam, dies berührt sich mit dem Anfechtbaren. Dass beide Reihen nicht zwei getrennte Sphären repräsentieren, zeigt schon die Gemeinsamkeit von *makrūh* und noch mehr die Bedeutung von *ǧā'iz*; es ist geradezu synonym mit *ṣaḥīḥ* und bezeichnet die Handlungen als zulässig im moralisch-religiösen und zugleich rechtlichen Sinne und daher als rechtsgültig, rechtswirksam. In dieser Bezeichnung liegt die religiöse Wertung des Rechtsstoffes am deutlichsten zutage; sie umfasst alles, was ohne weiteres passieren konnte.[82]

Damit erhebt sich die Frage nach dem Umfange der von dem islamischen Recht dem Einzelnen gewährten Vertragsfreiheit. Diese ist gegenüber den neuzeitlichen Begriffen vor allem im Verkehrsrecht erheblich beschränkt; das geschieht zum Teil durch direkte Verbote, wie das Verbot ungerechtfertigter Bereicherung (auch von Zins und anderen Wuchergeschäften) und das Verbot des Risikos (und überhaupt von Unsicherheitsfaktoren), oder die ausdrückliche Ablehnung gewisser altarabischer Rechtsgeschäfte, zum Teil aber auch einfach dadurch, dass das Recht keine Vertragsschemata zur Verfügung stellt und die Rechtsfolgen der normierten Tatbestände so gestaltet, dass sie mit den abgelehnten Vertragsabreden unvereinbar sind; ein Grossteil der *Ḥijal* ist eben dazu bestimmt, diese dem Verkehrsgebrauch gesetzten Grenzen zu erweitern. Da die Folgen der Rechtsgeschäfte bis in die Einzelheiten geregelt sind, findet sich innerhalb der zugelassenen Sphäre von Vertragsfreiheit relativ wenig ‚dispositives Recht', das dann gilt, wenn die Parteien nichts anderes vereinbaren; es beschränkt sich im wesentlichen auf die Festsetzung der ‚angemessenen Brautgabe' beim Ehevertrag und ähnliche Ergänzungen unvollständiger Vertragsabschlüsse. Auffällig weit geht die Handlungsfreiheit in einem Falle, der durch das ihm innewohnende ‚Sonderrecht' (vgl. unten) die Interessen Dritter in tiefgreifender Weise berührt, nämlich bei der Stiftung (*Waqf*); hier sind die Verfügungen des Stifters über die Nutzniessung und Verwaltung seiner Stiftung in weitestem Umfange rechtlich garantiert. Die allgemeine Einschränkung der Vertragsfreiheit kommt auf dem Gebiete des Verkehrsrechts den wirtschaftlich Schwachen zugute, die dadurch gegen die Ausnützung der wirtschaftlichen Überlegenheit durch die Markmächtigen geschützt werden. Überhaupt ist die Begrenzung der Vertragsfreiheit im islamischen Recht vor allem religiös-ethisch bedingt. Die das Verkehrsrecht beherrschenden beiden ausdrücklichen Verbote, die auf den Koran selbst zurückgehen, sind bereits erwähnt; im mekkanischen Handelsrecht hatten Zins und Spekulation eine wichtige Rolle gespielt.[83] Auf dem Gebiete der Sexualkontrakte wird der Frauentausch (*šigār*)[84] nebst einigen anderen altarabischen Formen der Eheschliessung abgelehnt, neben der vollwertigen Ehe das Konkubinat des Mannes mit seinen eigenen Sklavinnen sowie – bei den Schiiten, die hierin den ältesten, bereits vom Kalifen Omar (st. 644) abgeschafften Zustand erhalten haben – die Zeitehe anerkannt, jede andere Art von Geschlechtsverkehr und damit auch die Prostitution als Unzucht verboten. Ehe und Konkubinat spiegeln noch in wesentlichen Zügen die zur Zeit Muhammeds erreichte Entwicklungsstufe des altarabischen Rechts wider: die normale Eheform war der Frauenkauf, wenngleich das Brautgeld in der Regel schon der Frau selbst und nicht mehr ihrem Vormund zukam;[85] die Stellung der Frau ist durch den Koran und die anschliessende islamische Entwicklung bedeutend verbessert worden. Gegenüber den Einschränkungen bei der Eheschliessung geht die Scheidungsfreiheit, bei der der Mann vor der Frau bedeutend bevorzugt ist, überraschend weit.[86] Dadurch, „in Verbindung mit ökonomisch sehr freier und gesicherter Stellung [der Frau] im Ehegüterrecht", ist ein der sexuellen Vertragsfreiheit ähnlicher Zustand herbeigeführt worden (Weber S. 429). Das Erbrecht weist ein System fester Quoten vor der Agnaternerbfolge auf; diese ist altarabischen Ursprungs, jenes ist in den Grundzügen durch den Koran zum Ausgleich von Härten eingeführt worden; die Testierfreheit ist auf ein Drittel des Netto-Nachlasses beschränkt und gilt nicht zugunsten der Erben; das hat auf die Dauer die Zersplitterung selbst der grossten Vermögen zur Folge; daher hat man vielfach in der Errichtung von Stiftungen einen Ausweg gesucht oder das Erbrecht trotz seines religiösen Charakters bei Immobilien durch gewohnheitsrechtliche Regelungen ersetzt. Die Sklaverei wird geduldet, aber mit der Tendenz zu ihrer Einschränkung: Sklave wird man nur durch Geburt oder (als Nichtmuslim) durch Kriegsgefangenschaft, vertragsmässige Ergebung in die Sklaverei ist ausgeschlossen; die Freilassung wird religiös empfohlen, tritt in manchen Fällen gesetzlich ein und geniesst rechtliche Vorzugsbehandlung. Infolge des patriarchalen Charakters und der ethischen Ausgestaltung des Sklavenverhältnisses, die zu starken gesetzlichen[87] und darüber noch hinausgehenden konventionellen Sicherungen des Sklaven geführt haven, ist dessen Lage sehr erträglich; neben den zur Familie gehörenden Haussklaven gibt es als zinstragende Vermögensanlage gewerbliche und kaufmännische Handelssklaven mit grosser Bewegungsfreiheit, und die zeitweise erhebliche militärische Bedeutung der Sklaverei bot den Soldaten-Sklaven und Freigelassenen die Möglichkeit zu hohem sozialen Aufstieg; landwirtschaftlich-industrielle Arbeitssklaven zur wirtschaftlichen Ausbeutung hat es im Islam[88] kaum je gegeben. Der freigelassene Sklave bleibt zu seinem ehemaligen Herrn (Patron) in einem Klientelverhältnis mit familienrechtlichen Wirkungen. Ein entsprechendes Verhaltnies entsteht durch den Klientelvertrag eines Nichtarabers mit einem Araber; ursprünglich war jeder zum Islam übertretende Nichtaraber verpflichtet, sich durch einen solchen ‚Statuskontrakt' einem arabischen Stamm anzuschliessen, doch wurde das mit der zunehmenden Bedeutung der nichtarabischen Muslims bald obsolet.[89] Neben den ‚Statuskontrakten' Ehe und Klientelvertrag hat die *Šarīʿa* auch die ‚Zweckkontrakte' bereits fertig ausgebildet aus dem vorislamischen Gewohnheitsrecht übernommen; über ihre Vorgeschichte lässt sich nur aussagen, dass gerade auf dem Gebiete des Verkehrsrechts, dem die Zweckkontrakte eigentümlich sind, fremde Einflüsse gewirkt haben (vgl. oben Abschnitt 5); daher sei auf Einzelheiten, zu denen die von Weber (S. 416 ff.) entwickelte Theorie ihrer Entstehung gut stimmen würde, nur mit dem Vorbehalt eines ausserarabischen Ursprungs Bezug genommen.[90] Über die Zweckkontrakte hinaus verlangt ein entwickelter Geschäftsverkehr noch die Stellvertretung und die Übertragbarkeit der Forderungsrechte (Weber S. 423); beide (*Wakāla* bzw. *Ḥawāla*) liegen, wohl sicher ebenfalls auf Grund vorislamischer Institute, in der *Šarīʿa* ausgebildet vor; dagegen hat diese das bereits dem Gewohnheitsrecht von Mekka bekannte Prinzip der Schriftlichkeit wieder aufgegeben, so dass die historisch wichtige Kommerzialisierung des Urkundenwesens auf die Rechtspraxis beschränkt blieb (vgl. oben Abschnitt 2 und 3).

Die Sonderrechte, die die *Šarīʿa* vorschreibt oder anerkennt, sind vorwiegend religiös-ethisch bedingt; die Form ‚gewillkürten' Rechts und der Grundsatz der Rechtspersonalität spielen dabei nur eine untergeordnete Rolle.[91] Die nebeneinander bestehenden Rechtsschulen sind überhaupt keine Sonderrechte, deren Anwendung der Einzelne oder eine Personengruppe als Privileg für sich beanspruchen könnte, sondern verschiedene Auffassungen der einen *Šarīʿa*, die der Einzelne seinem Verhalten und der *Qāḍī* (vorbehaltlich einer bindenden Anweisung durch die Obrigkeit, aber ohne Rücksicht auf den *Maḏhab* der Rechtsuchenden) seinem Urteil zugrundelegt. Die religiöse und politische Bedingtheit des Sonderrechts der Nichtmuslims ist bereits oben (Abschnitt 4) hervorgehoben; selbst ihre ausserhalb der islamischen Rechtsgeschichte stehenden autonomen Rechtsordnungen können von der *Šarīʿa* aus nur mit Vorbehalt als ‚gewillkürtes' Recht bezeichnet werden,[92] und das von der *Šarīʿa* für die Nichtmuslims positiv vorgeschriebene Minderrecht trägt überhaupt nicht jenen Charakter.[93] Die Ansätze zu weiteren Sonderrechten, vor allem der Armen und der Nachkommen des Propheten, tragen ebenfalls religiösethischen Charakter. Politischer und steurrechtlicher Art sind die von der *Šarīʿa* vorgesehenen Differenzierungen des Immobilienrechts und die im Anschluss daran von weltlichen Autoritäten eingeführten sonderrechtlichen Regelungen des Grundsteuer- und Lehenswesens, aber selbst hier handelt es sich nicht um den Gegensatz zwischen ‚Wilkür' und ‚Landrecht'.

Der Begriff der juristischen Person, der aus dem Problem der Verbände entsteht (Weber S. 439), ist dem islamischen Recht ebenso wie die korporative Organisation und der Anstaltsbegriff unbekannt. Die einzige von der *Šarīʿa* anerkannte ‚Korporation' ist der aus der altarabischen Stammesorganisation übernommene blutrechtliche Sippenverband (*ʿĀqila*), dem in den meisten Fällen die Zahlung des Blutgeldes obliegt. Die *ʿĀqila* besteht zunächst aus den Stammesangehörigen, für den Freigelassenen und den Klienten aus seinem Patron und dessen *ʿĀqila*;[94] islamisch ist die Übertragung des *ʿĀqila*-Begriffes auf die Soldempfanger (die Leute des *Dīwān*), wenn der Täter zu ihnen gehört, sowie auf die Gewerbegenossen bzw. Nachbarn (nach ḥanafitischer Lehre); doch ist diese Anpassung an städtische Verhältnisse unzureichend (Bergsträsser), und die ganze Institution ist früh abgestorben. Daneben sieht die *Šarīʿa* lediglich bestimmte Typen der Erwerbsgesellschaft vor, für die der Rechtspersönlichkeitsbegriff überhaupt inadäquat ist (Weber S. 440f); vielmehr sind es ziemlich variierte, rationale Ausbildungen des Prinzips der ‚Gesamthand' unter „Behandlung der Gesamtheit als eines gesonderten Rechtssubjektes und ... Sonderung des gemeinsam besessenen Vermögens.[95] Ignoriert werden vom islamischen Recht die eigentlichen, als Verbrüderungen und Kultgenossenschaften organisierten Korporationen der Berufsverbände; vorislamisch-antike Traditionen fortsetzend, kennen sie gemeinsame Kassen und Kultmahle, schliessen Kriminalund- und Zivilklagen zwischen ihren Mitgliedern aus und beanspruchen Autonomie für ihre gewillkürten Satzungen; deshalb und wegen religiös-islamischer Einwände gegen manche ihrer Gebräuche sind sie von den *Šarīʿa*-Gelehrten sogar wiederholt positiv abgelehnt worden. Nur die Rechtspraxis kennt, vornehmlich in der älteren Zeit, die leiturgische Kollektivhaftung von Zwangsgenossenschaften, vor allem von Dorfgemeinden. Der Staat wird weder als ‚Anstalt' noch überhaupt als Rechtspersönlichkeit im Vollsinn aufgefasst; die Rechtssphäre der Mitglieder ist von der des Verbandes faktisch zwar in weitgehendem Masse, prinzipiell aber nur unvollkommen geschieden;[96] die Staatskasse ist zwar privatrechtlich erwerbs-, aber nicht prozessfähig.[97] Auch die Stiftungen besitzen keine Rechtspersönlichkeit;[98] sowohl in ihrer ursprünglichen religiösen Zweckbestimmung wie in ihrer Übertragung auf weltliche Verhältnisse sind sie von der *Šarīʿa* wohl zweifellos aus dem Recht der eroberten Gebiete übernommen worden[99] und haben dann im Islam eine ausserordentlich wichtige Rolle gespielt; zur Entwicklung eines Anstalts- und Korporationsbegriffes haben sie aber nicht beigetragen.

Wiederholt ist aus dem Vorhergehenden deutlich geworden, wie die *Šarīʿa*, so wichtige Teile des altarabischen Gewohnheitsrechts in ihr auch fortleben, gerade die jenen Rechtsverhältnissen zugrundeliegende Stammesorgansation mit ihrem zivil- und strafrechtlichen Solidarismus zurückgedrängt hat; das ist die Wirkung des für den Islam charakteristischen, auf Muhammed selbst zurückgehenden Ersatzes des Stammes durch die Gemeinde unter Betonung der persönlichen Verantwortlichkeit. Das hat im Zusammenhang mit dem Fehlen der dinggenossenschaftlichen Form der Justiz wohl schon bei den vorislamischen Arabern und dem mit den Abbasiden endgültig ein ziehenden patriarchalen Charakter des politischen Patrimonialismus gegen die korporative Organisation gewirkt. Nach den vorstehenden Ausführengen wird man nicht erwarten, die *Šarīʿa* als Ganzes oder für einzelne Teilgebiete durch ein einziges Schlagwort inhaltlich charakterisiert zu finden; ihre formell hervorstechendste Eigenschaft aber, die auch auf ihren Inhalt entscheidend zurückgewirkt hat, ist ihr Charakter als religiöse Pflichtenlehre, als heiliges Recht.

NOTES

1 Bei den folgenden Ausführungen, von denen einige Grundgedanken auf dem 7. Holländischen Orientalistenkongress in Leiden (vgl. *Oostersch Genootschap in Nederland. Verslag von het zevende Congres*, Leiden 1933, S. 36f.) und auf dem 7. Deutschen Orientalistentag in Bonn (vgl. *ZDMG*, N. F. Bd. 13, S. * 13 *) vorgetragen worden sind, liess es sich nicht vermeiden, mancherlei dem Islamisten Selbstverständliches mit anzuführen. Mit dem Namen Bergsträsser wird auf seine im Druck befindlichen *Grundzüge des islamischen Rechts*, bearbeitet und herausgegeben von J. Schacht, verwiesen.

2 *Grundriss der Sozialökonomik*, III. Abteilung, 2. Aufl. 1925, S. 387ff.

3 Dieser Begriff ist hier in seinem weitesten Umfange genommen, sodass er die vorislamisch-arabische periode einerseits, die neben der Theorie herlaufende Rechtspraxis der islamischen Völker andererseits mit umfasst; im Mittelpunkt der Betrachtung steht das islamische Recht im engeren Sinne.

4 Der Übersichtlichkeit halber bin ich in der Einteilung des Stoffes im wesentlichen Weber gefolgt; es entsprechen Abschnitt 2–6 den Paragraphen 1, 2, 4/5, 5/6, 3 bei Weber.

5 Etwa bei den Zwölfer-Schiiten: *'Ibādāt* gottesdienstliche Pflichten), *'Uqūd* (Verträge), *Īqā'āt* (einseitige Rechtsgeschäfte), *Aḥkām* (sonstige ‚Vorschriften', darunter das Strafrecht und Erbrecht).

6 Nicht einmal die alte Kapiteleinteilung des *Fiqh*, der Rechtswissenschaft, hat die ‚öffentlich-rechtlichen' Normen irgendwie konsequent materiell zusammenzufassen gesucht, eben weil der Sinn für diese Unterscheidung vollkommen fehlte; jene finden sich vielmehr in der Hauptsache unter folgende Kapitel verstreut: Ritualgebet (Erwähnung des *Imām*, des Leiters der islamischen Germeinde, in der Freitagspredigt als Zeichen der Souveränität), Almosensteuer, *Ḥadd*-Strafen, Religionskrieg und Beziehungen zu den Ungläubigen, *Imāmat*, Rechtspflege; viele stehen in engstem sachlichen Zusammenhang mit ‚privatrechtlichen' Vorschriften. Dem widerspricht nicht die Tatsache mongraphischer Behandlung von ‚öffentlich-rechtlichen' Materien, wie des Finanzrechts durch Abū Jūsuf, Jaḥjā ibn Ādam, Abū'Ubaid und Qudāma ibn Ǧa'far, des Staatsrechts durch al-Māwardī und Ibn Ǧamā'a.

7 z. B. im Kriegsrecht die Zuständigkeit zur Erteilung des *Amān*, der Gewährung von Sicherheit für einen Ungläubigen, in der Almosensteuer-Gesetzgebung die Verpflichtung zur Zahlung der *Zakāt*.

8 Zusammenhänge mit dem im Islam zeimlich ausgeprägten ‚patrimonialen' Charakter der Herrschaft (Weber S. 388) sind dagegen nicht er-kennbar.

9 Mit gewissen durch die Art des Delikts bedingten Einschränkungen beim *Ḥadd* für Diebstahl und für Verleumdung wegen Unzucht; aber selbst bei Diebstahl schliesst der *Ḥadd* nach der Lehre der Ḥanafiten (und der Mālikiten dann, wenn der Dieb arm ist) die vermögensrechtliche Haftung aus.

10 Bei Diebstahl und Strassenraub führt die tätige Reue vor der Ergriefung den Wegfall des *Ḥadd* herbei, und die begangenen Delikte haben nur ‚Ansprüche von Menschen' zur Folge.

11 Verleumdung wegen Unzucht und Diebstahl sind Antragsdelikte; bei der Unzucht spielen die Zeugen eine ähnliche Rolle wie sonst der Antragsteller; wohl aber kann man beim Strassenraub von einer ‚Verfolgung von Amts wegen' reden, z. T. auch beim Amte des *Muḥtasib* (vgl. unten).

12 So steht auf dem – im Koran ebenso wie das Weintrinken verbotenen – Genuss von Schweinefleisch kein *Ḥadd*; er kann höchstens durch *Ta'zir* (vgl. unten) bestraft werden.

13 Aber selbst die Tötung des Apostaten gilt vorwiegend nicht als *Ḥadd*.

14 Daher kann der Herr seinen Sklaven für ein von diesem begangenes Delikt abtreten, wenn er die vermögensrechtliche Haftung dafür nicht übernehmen will, und umgekehrt den mit seiner Person verfallenen Sklaven unter Umständen loskaufen.

15 Ist etwa der Satz, dass die Schulden des Erblassers nicht auf den Erben übergehen, noch als Folge des ursprünglichen Zustandes (Weber S. 392) zu betrachten?

16 Solche Ansätze liegen in der religiösen Busse der *Kaffāra*, die als ‚Anspruch Allahs' gilt, und der unter Umständen neben dem Sühnegeld eintretenden diskretionären Bestrafung durch den Kadi, dem *Ta'zīr*; vgl. auch die übernächste Anm.

17 Desgleichen bei dem sich auf beide Sphären erstreckenden *Ta'zīr*.

18 Eine vereinzelte Ausnahme liegt in der mālikitischen Ansicht vor, dass im Falle von Mord, unter erschwerenden Umständen an einem Deszendenten begangen, der *Qiṣāṣ* von Amts wegen ausgeführt wird, also auch ein eventueller Verzicht des Bluträchers keine Wirkung hat.

19 Das Erscheinen des Beklagten kann im Strafprozess ganz ebenso den Gegenstand einer „Bürgschaft für die Person" (*kafāla bin-nafs*) bilden wie im Zivilprozess (vgl. Weber S. 321).

20 Vgl. Amedroz, *JRAS* 1911, S. 635 ff.; 1916, S. 77ff., 287ff.

21 Ähnliche Verhältnisse bestehen im Verkehrsrecht; vgl. unten-Abschnitt 3 zur *'Āda*.

22 Dieses Amt setzt schon an sich ein gewisses Versagen der Kadi-Rechtsprechung voraus und ist denn auch der ältesten Zeit unbekannt.

23 Bezeichnend sind die bereits oben in anderem Zusammenhang angeführten Beispiele der Erteilung des *Amān* im Kriegsrecht und der Zahlung der *Zakāt* im Steuerrecht.

24 Der einzige bekannte Versuch derart seitens der Obrigkeit, die dazu gemäss den Normen der *Šarī'a* befugt gewesen wäre (vermittels der oben erwähnten Zuständigkeitsbeschränkung), in dem afghanischen Strafgesetzbuch von 1924 (vgl. S. Beck, *Die Welt des Islam* 1928, S. 67ff.) ist an dem Widerstand der Stämme gescheitert.

25 Vgl. Goldziher, *Z. vgl. Rechtswiss.* 1889, S. 406ff.

26 Vgl. z. B. Vesey-Fitzgerald, *Muhammadan Law*, S. 28, 91.

27 Diese Funktion macht den *Iqrār*, auch in doppelseitiger Anwendung, zum Hauptbestandteil zahlreicher *Ḥijal* (Umgehungsgeschäfte), die die andersartige Rechtspraxis mit der Theorie in Einklang brigen sollen.

28 So in einem schon früh verbreiteten Urkundenschema.
29 Sure 2, 282.
30 Sure 24, 33.
31 Ihr sind die Urkunden lediglich Hilfsmittel für den Zeugenbeweis.
32 Zu einer Ausnahme vgl. die drittnächste Anmerkung.
33 Ein Beispiel bei Bergsträsser, *Islamica* Bd. 4, S. 289f. Bisweilen-erscheinen solche Durchbrechungen der generellen Normen als *Istiḥsān* (‚Gutdünken') oder *Istiṣlāḥ* (‚Berücksichtigung des allgemeinen Interesses'), beides Abweichungen von der Analogie (*Qijās*). Im allgemeinen aber stellen die für die *Šarīʿa* charakteristischen religiös-ethischen Gesichtspunkte gerade generelle Normen dar.
34 Vgl. Bergsträsser, *Islam* Bd. 14, S. 80 sowie unten Abschnitt 4.
35 Dazu gehören Angebot (*Īǧāb*) und Annahme (*Qabūl*) als konstitutive Elemente der Verträge (vgl. *OLZ* 1927, Sp. 664ff.); der erste Terminus (‚bindend machen'; zur Bedeutung vgl. Ausdrücke wie *waǧabat lahu l-'ǧanna* ‚ihm ist das Paradies zugefallen, er hat sich das Paradies erworben') kann keine primäre Bezeichnung für ein ‚Angebot' sein (dabei sei nicht einmal besonderer Wert darauf gelegt, dass das Angebot nach der Lehre des *Fiqh* vor bzw. selbst nach der Annahme zurückgezogen werden kann), sondern setzt wohl eine noch ältere Auffassung voraus, die das konstitutive Element in der Rechtshandlung des einen Kontrahenten (und zwar beim Kaufvertrage vermutlich des Käufers) erblickte, von der aber im altarabischen Gewohnheitsrecht keine weiteren Spuren nachweisbar sind.
36 Das Beispiel schon bei Weber S. 401.
37 Die ‚kriegerischen Umwälzungen' (Weber S. 409) dagegen, d. h. die militärische Expansion des Islam unter dem Propheten in Arabien und besonders unter den frühen Kalifen in den umliegenden Ländern, sind für die rechtssoziologische Betrachtung von keiner besonderen Bedeutung; sie hatten – ganz allgemein gesprochen – in Bezug auf das Gefangenen-, Beute- und Bodenrecht zunächst das Fortleben der altarabischen bzw. der in den eroberten Ländern vorgefundenen Zustände zur Folge; und die diesbezüglichen Verfügungen des Propheten und der Kalifen unterscheiden sich qualitativ nicht von ihrer sonstigen Rechtsschöpfung bzw. Rechtsprechung; daher erhebt sich hier auch nicht das Problem des Ausgleichs zwischen ‚imperium' und ‚Tradition'.
38 Darin liegt der dokumentarische Wert der Traditionen.
39 Im soziologischen, nicht im islamwissenschaftlichen Sinne.
40 Ursprünglich nur die Feststellung der Mehrheit (vgl. Nöldeke-Bergsträsser, *Geschichte des Qorāns*, 2. Aufl., 3. Teil, S. 130 Anm. 8.
41 So noch bei aš-Šāfiʿī (st. 820); vgl. die Übersetzung des diesbezüglichen Abschnitts seiner *Risāla* bei Schacht, *Der Islam* (Religionsgeschichtliches Lesebuch, 2. Aufl., H. 16), S. 25 f.
42 Webers Bemerkungen über den Koran (S. 459) sind durchaus unzutreffend; auch die von ihm als typisch angeführte Motivierung der Schriftlichkeit (S. 460) trifft für das islamische Recht nicht zu.
43 Gewisse Vertragstypen sind zugelassen, soweit sie in der Praxis üblich sind (aber selbst das ist in erster Linie einschränkend, nicht erweiternd gemeint [Bergsträsser]); bisweilen gilt das Gewohnheitsrecht als

Interpretations prinzip für Erklärungen; und anderes derart.

44 Zu diesen und anderen Berührungspunkten zwischen *Šarī'a* und *'Ada* vgl. *Islam* Bd. 20, S. 209 ff. sowie oben Anschnitt 2 zum *Nāẓir al-Maẓālim*, zum *Muḥtasib* und zur *Qasāma*.

45 Vgl. *Islam* Bd. 15, S. 211 ff.

46 *Islam* Bd. 20, S. 210.

47 Ausnahmen bilden einerseits die für gewisse *Ḥijal* benötigten *Muwāḍa'a* Urkunden (vgl. Schacht, *Das kitāb al-ḥijal wal-māḫāriğ des al-Ḫaṣṣāf*, S. 75f.), andererseits die späteren mālikitischen Urkunden des Westens, die stärkere Einflüsse des Gewohnheitsrechts aufweisen (vgl. oben).

48 Vgl. oben Abschnitt 2.

49 Diese islamische Urkundenpraxis hat die Entwicklung des europäischen Wertpapierwesens im Mittelalter „zum erheblichen Teil" beeinflusst (Weber S. 424).

50 Vgl. *Islam* Bd. 20, S. 213, 223, 232; *REI* 1931, S. 512 ff.

51 Und daher z. T. das Immobilienrecht; vgl. die übernächste Anm.

52 Das geschieht vorwiegend in der Form der *Maẓālim-* und *Muḥtasib-*Gerichtsbarkeit (vgl. oben Abschnitt 2), also durch polizeiliche ‚Verwaltung' (Weber S. 389; vgl. unten Abschnitt 4). Dabei versucht man, den materiellen Forderungen der *Šarī'a* nach Möglichkeit nachzukommen (Abschneiden der Hand des in flagranti ertappten Diebes, Prügelung des Weintrinkers [dies noch bei den Osmanen], u.s.w.), ohne zu beachten, dass jene ein ganz bestimmtes Verfahren vorschreibt.

53 Das in der *Šarī'a* wenig ausführlich behandelte Immobilienrecht ist auf den von ihr dargebotenen Grundlagen in nach Ländern und Zeiten verschiedener Weise geregelt worden; natürlich kann die Auswirkung einer solchen Ergänzung mit der *Šarī'a* in Konflikt kommen (Bergstrasser). Die von Weber (S. 477) für einen Einzelfall hervorgehobene Rechtsunsicherheit (ganz ähnlich wie in Tunesien liegen die Verhältnisse in den meisten islamischen Ländern) ist nicht durch Eigentümlichkeiten der Rechtspflege der *Šarī'a* (vgl. unten Abschnitt 4 zur ‚Kadijustiz'), sondern durch die mangelnde Sicherung gegen falschen Zeugenbeweis und – in der Praxis – falsche Urkunden bedingt; die Eigenart des islamischen Beweisrechts spielt erst sekundär, und zwar nicht wegen irgendeiner ‚Unberechenbarkeit', sondern gerade wegen seiner formalen Bindung mit hinein. Das Staats- und Kriegsrecht der *Šarī'a* ist reine Fiktion und hat so überhaupt nie existiert.

54 Webers Bemerkungen (S. 400) über die Wirkung des staatlichen. Rechtszwanges auf die Geschichte der islamischen Rechtsschulen sind zwar im Tatsächlichen ungenau und unvollständig (vor allem durfte das Osmanische Reich nicht mit der ganzen Welt des Islam gleichgesetzt werden), in der Beurteilung der Erscheinung aber im wesentlichen zutreffend; freilich ist der politische Faktor nicht der einzige, der die Verbreitung der Rechtsschulen bestimmt hat.

55 Über das Verhältnis des von ihnen geschaffenen Rechts zur Praxis soll damit nichts ausgesagt sein; vgl. im Gegenteil weiter unten.

56 Der Gebrauch dieses Terminus soll nicht implizieren, dass es im Islam

‚Priester' gegeben habe oder dass die Überlieferung des religiösen Gesetzes in jener Periode in ‚Schulen' erfolgt sei. Übrigens ist im Islam die Art der Rechtslehre, d. h. die Schulung der ‚berufsmässig' *Šarīʿa*-Kundigen, nicht erst für die Art des Rechtsdenkens bestimmend gewesen (so allgemein Weber S. 412, 456), sondern ihrerseits durch die im Text angeführten Verhältnisse bedingt worden. Auch was Weber (S. 466) über die Bildung der späteren islamischen Juristen ausführt, ist grossenteils unzutreffend (vgl. den historischen Überblick unten Abschnitt 5).

57 Ein autonomes Element liegt im Konsensus vor.

58 Hier liegt der systematische Ansatzpunkt für die *Ḥijal*, die also nicht das Ergebnis einer laxen Einstellung zur *Šarīʿa* sind; die Richtung der Ẓāhiriten die sich unter Ablehnung des Analogieschlusses nach dem Wortlaut von Koran und Tradition zu richten bestrebte und die man sicher nicht als lax bezeichnen kann, ist in der Pflege des Buchstabengeistes am weitesten gegangen.

59 Nach Weber (S. 461) ist das mit allen typischen ‚heiligen' Rechte der Fall. Im Islam ist der Charakter der *Šarīʿa* als ‚stereotypiertes Juristen recht' (Weber S. 475) besonders stark ausgeprägt, weil das ‚unfehlbare Lehramt' allein durch die massgebenden Juristen verkörpert wird.

60 Diese Ablehnung des *Iǧtihād* ist erst nachträglich formuliert worden, nachdem durch die stetig wachsende Bedeutung des Konsensus (vgl. oben Abschnitt 3) eine fast völlige Stabilisierung der *Šarīʿa* herbeigeführt worden war; in Wirklichkeit ist der Übergang seit den ersten Generationen von Rechtsgelehrten durchaus graduell. Ebensowenig besagt die nachträglich aufgestellte Theorie von den vier ‚Quellen' (*Uṣūl*) des islamischen Rechts (Koran, *Sunna*, Konsensus und die Methode der Analogie [*Qijās*]) etwas über den wirklichen Vorgang seiner Entstehung; die Analogie verdankt ihre Aufnahme unter die ‚Quellen' der Tatsache, dass zwar nicht ihre praktische Anwendung, wohl aber ihre theoretische Anerkennung heftig umstritten war; dagegen ist es zu einer entsprechenden Anerkennung der Gewohnheit (*ʿUrf*) durch die Gesetzesgelehrten trotz verschiedener Versuche nicht mehr gekommen.

61 Vgl. unten Abschnitt 5. Zwischen den vier Rechtsschulen (Ḥanafiten, Mālikiten, Šafiʿiten, Ḥanbaliten) bestehen keine prinzipiellen Verschiedenheiten; die Art ihres Rechtsdenkens ist die gleiche, und die Abweichungen in Einzelheiten sind relativ gering. Die Angaben Webers (S. 474 f.) über ihr gegenseitiges Verhältnis sind durchas unzutreffend, brauchen hier aber, da für die soziologische Beurteilung des islamischen Rechts ohne Belang, nicht richtiggestellt zu werden.

62 Aus dem entgegengesetzten Grunde, nämlich dem strengsten Traditionalismus heraus, verwirft die aus der ḥanbalitischen Rechtsschule hervorgegangene Richtung der Wahhābiten den *Taqlīd* und anerkennt als Konsensus nur den der Genossen des Propheten; das hat zwar für das Dogma und gewisse Formen der Frömmigkeit erhebliche Konsquenzen, für das Recht aber wird das ḥanbalitische System einfach beibehalten.

63 Zu einer Äusserung dieser Bestrebungen in Ägypten vgl. weiter unten.

64 Ein wesentlicher Unterschied liegt darin, dass das *Fatwā* im Gegensatz zum Responsum des römischen Juristen für den Richter nicht bindend ist. Was seine angebliche Irrationalität anlangt, so darf aus den zweifellos mit *Fatwā*'s getriebenen Missbräuchen nicht auf den Charakter der Institution im ganzen geschlossen werden. – Dagegen ist die von Weber (S. 475) hervorgehobene Ähnlichkeit zwischen islamischem und römischem Recht in Bezug auf die Stellung der Juristen als solcher zweifellos vorhanden.

65 Die von irgendeinem *Qāḍī* gefällten Urteile hat jeder andere *Qāḍī* auch dann anzuerkennen, wenn er selbst einer anderen Schule angehört oder wenner – im theoretischen Falle – durch *Iǧtihād* zu einem anderen Ergebnis kommt; das wurde von der Rechtspraxis bei den *Ḥijal* ausgenutzt. Die Lehre der *Šarīʿa* kennt nur ganz wenige Möglichkeiten, das einmal ergangene Urteil aufzuheben, die Praxis besass in dem Übergang zur *Maẓālim*-Gerichtsbarkeit die Möglichkeit der Appellation.

66 Dieser Zustand findet sich z. B. noch in Marokko, vgl. *REI* 1933, S. 380.

67 Nicht nur in Persien, wie Weber (S. 476) voraussetzt; auch die Zurückziehung der *Šarīʿa* aus der Sphäre des ökonomisch Relevanten (Weber S. 477) ist eine ganz allgemeine Erscheinung; umgekehrt übt gerade in Persien der Stand der „theologischen Juristen" noch in der Gegenwart einen starken politischen Einfluss aus.

68 Die von Weber S. 472 angeführten Anlässe für dieses Interesse treffen allerdings für das islamische Recht nur zum geringen Teil zu.

69 Im Strafrecht (vgl. oben Abschnitt 3) lagen die Verhältnisse anders, da sich hier die *Šarīʿa* durch die an den Zeugenbeweis gestellten Ansprüche praktisch selbst ausser Kraft setzte. Überhaupt ist von einem „spezifischen Interesse des heiligen Rechts an allen Straf- und Sühneproblemen" (Weber S. 472) in der *Šarīʿa* wenig zu bemerken (vgl. oben Abschnitt 2 sowie unten Abschnitt 5).

70 Vgl. *REI* 1931, S. 383 ff.

71 Zu diesem ‚legislativen Modernismus' vgl. *Islam*, Bd. 20, S. 214ff.

72 Die Formulierungen zum Teil in Anschluss an Bergsträsser.

73 Vgl. *OLZ* 1927, Sp. 664ff.

74 Selbst die Theorie der Rechtsquellen läuft bei den Schiiten im wesentlichen auf dasselbe Ergebnis hinaus wie bei den Sunniten (vgl. oben Abschnitt 4); sie anerkennen als solche nämlich zwei primäre, den Koran und die *Sunna*, und zwei sekundäre, den Konsensus und die Vernunft. Das beherrschende Element, an Wichtigkeit der Rolle des Konsensus bei den Sunniten vergleichbar, ist die *Sunna*, d. h. hier die *Sunna* des Propheten und der *Imāme*, auf deren Autorität alle Lehren durch Traditionen zurückgeführt werden, von denen Entsprechendes gilt wie von den sunnitschen (vgl. oben Abschnitt 3). Seit dem Verschwinden des letzten *Imām* ist massgebend der Konsensus der zum *Iǧtihād* befugten Gelehrten; da dem *Iǧtihād* (im Gegensatz zur herrschenden Lehre der Sunniten) keine untere zeitliche Grenze gesetzt wird, entsprechen diese schiitischen *Muǧtahid*'s sachlich auch den späteren Trägern des Konsensus auf sunnitischer Seite. Der von den *Muǧtahid*'s zur Ableitung von Gesetzesvorschriften aus Koran

und Sunna geübte Vernunftschluss ist nichts anderes als die sunnitische Methode der Analogie. Danach sind die Ausführungen bei Weber S. 476 f. zu berichtigen.

75 Die theoretische Lehre von den Rechtsquellen ist aber späteren Datums.

76 Zu dem früheren Zustand vgl. oben Abschnitt 3.

77 Zur Charakterisierung der *Meğelle* vgl. *Islam*, Bd. 20, S. 213.

78 Der von Weber hervorgehobene Einfluss religiöser Instanzen auf die Entwicklung des Strafrechts macht sich vor allem in der Zurückdrängung der Talio geltend; diese Tendenz wirkt sich schon im Koran aus und ist dann im System der *Šarī'a* weiter (allerdings nicht bis zu ihrer völligen Abschaffung) durchgeführt worden.

79 In den anderen islamischen Staaten ist dieses Bestreben, im Zusammenhang mit der ‚patriarchalen' Form der Herrschaft, auffallend gering gewesen; die Kodifikationen der Neuzeit, auch soweit sie (wie die *Meğelle* und der ägyptische ‚Kodex' Qadrī Pascha über das Ehe- und Familienrecht) inhaltlich islamisches Recht enthalten, stehen unter europäischem Einfluss; zu dem afghanischen Strafgesetzbuch von 1924 vgl. oben Abschnitt 2.

80 Demselben Interesse entspringen auf dem Gebiet der *Šarī'a* die gerade in osmanischer Zeit häufigen Bindungen der *Qāḍī*'s an bestimmte Schulmeinungen innerhalb der ḥanafitischen *Maḏhab*.

81 Dieser Befriff ist von *Sunna* im Sinne des ‚Üblichen' streng zu scheiden.

82 Diese Formulierungen im Anschluss an Bergsträsser.

83 Die zinslosigkeit des Darlehens nach islamischem Recht ist also kein Überrest des ursprünglichen Zustandes (Weber S. 420).

84 Nach Weber (S. 428) ‚der älteste Sexualkontrakt'.

85 Der patriarchale Charakter der Ehe, die Rücksichtnahme auf die Sippe der Frau, das Streben vornehmer Frauen nach Freiheit von der patriarchalen Mannesgewalt sowie die wesentlichen Merkmale der vollwertigen Ehe finden sich auch hier, jedoch fehlt die Einrichtung der Mitgift. Die stellung der Kinder aus dem Konkubinat hing vom Belieben des Vaters ab; erst das islamische Recht hat sie den aus der vollwertigen Ehe stammenden gleichgestellt, andererseits die Anerkennung illegitimer Kinder ausgeschlossen. Vgl. zu alledem Weber S. 428.

86 Unter den zur Verfügung gestellten Scheidungsformen leben altarabische irrationale Reste weiter.

87 Daher ist der Sklave dem Herrn gegenüber weitgehend prozessfähig.

88 Mit Ausnahme der umaijadischen Domänen in Arabien.

89 Zwei andere Statuskontrakte sind schon durch den Koran abgeschafft worden: die bei den vorislamischen Arabern übliche Adoption durch Sure 33, 4. 5. 37 und der selbst erst vom Koran (Sure 8, 72; ausführlicher in der Tradition) eingeführte Verbrüderungsvertrag zwischen den mekkanischen und den medinischen Gläubigen durch Sure 33, 6.

90 Dahin gehören (in den Einzelheiten nach ḥanafitischer Lehre) vor allem die Form des Prozessbeginns mit Selbsthilfe: „der Kläger schleppt den Verklagten vor Gericht und lässt ihn nur los, nachdem Sicherheit gegeben ist, dass er sich der Sühne, wenn der Richter ihn

schuldig findet, nicht entziehen werde"; die Rolle der ,Bürgschaft für das Erscheinen' mit Gefangensetzung des Bürgen bei Nichterfüllung bzw. des Beklagten durch den Bürgen zwecks Sicherstellung; die Haftung des Schuldners nicht direkt mit seinem Vermögen, sondern mit seiner physischen Person: daher gibt es keine gerichtliche Pfändung, sondern der Schuldner wird gefangen gesetzt, bis er zahlt oder sich seine Zahlungsunfähigkeit herausstellt; das Zusammenfallen von Zivil- und Deliktobligation (vgl. oben Abschnitt 2). Alle diese Züge des islamischen Rechts können mit ziemlicher Sicherheit auf die vorislamische Schicht zurückgeführt werden. Umgekehrt sind direkt mit der altarabischen Stammesorganisation zusammenhängende Eigentümlichkeiten wie die solidarische Delikthaftung der Sippe und das Fehlen eines eigentlichen Rechtsganges zwischen Sippengenossen von der *Šarīʿa* aufgegeben worden.

91 Hierbei handelt es sich um die Sonderrechte des älteren Typus, nicht um Sonderrechtsinstitute auf Grund allgemeiner Ermächtigung wie die Stiftung; vgl. Weber S. 431f.

92 Es fehlt ihre Auffassung als ,Privileg' und der Gedanke, dass ,Willkür Landrecht bricht'; im Gegenteil steht es jedem Nichtmuslim frei, den *Qāḍī* anzurufen, und dann gilt allein die *Šarīʿa*; diese ignoriert die Rechtsverhältnisse der Nichtmuslims mehr als dass sie sie anerkennt.

93 Das altarabische Minderrecht der Klienten, von dem eine Nachwirkung im Klientelvertrage (vgl. oben) fortlebt, ist im Islam aus religiösen Gründen bis auf wenige Spuren unterdrückt worden.

94 Hierin liegt die Hauptbedeutung der Klientel bzw. des Klientelvertrages.

95 Daneben steht noch die Verwendung von Handelssklaven „als Erwerbsinstrumenten mit unbeschränkter Berechtigung und beschränkter Haftung des Herrn für ihre Kontrakte und mit einer begrenzten Behandlung des peculium nach Art einer Sondervermögensmasse".

96 Der einzelne Muslim kann die Gesamtheit verpflichten, z. B. beim *Amān* (vgl. oben Abschnitt 2), desgleichen eine Gruppe von Einzelnen die Gesamtheit bei der Anerkennung eines neuen Gemeindeleiters (Kalifen, *Imām*); die Theorie der Verbandsorgane ist nur schwach ausgebildet; als Eigentümer der Staatskasse (*Bait al-Māl*) gilt die Gesamtheit der Muslims (daher: *Bait Māl al-Muslimīn*); die Grenze zwischen diesem Verbandsvermögen und dem Vermögen der Einzelnen ist zum mindesten bei der Behandlung der eroberten Ländereien und der Ablösung ihrer Verteilung durch Stipendienzahlungen fliessend gewesen, wird im ausgebildeten System der *Šarīʿa* aber deutlich aufrechterhalten; auch das Privatvermögen des Imām ist hier von der hauptsächlich religiös-politischen Zwecken dienenden Staatskasse streng getrennt (in der Praxis war der Zustand freilich oft der entgegengesetzte).

97 Wohl aber der *Imām* als Privatmann.

98 Die Frage nach dem Eigentümer der Stiftung ist im islamischen Recht nie klar entschieden worden (erwähnt sei der Lösungsversuch, der sie als Eigentum Allahs betrachtet).

99 Ihre genauere Herkunft ist noch nicht erforscht.

15

LES RÉVOLTES POPULAIRES EN ÉGYPTE A L'ÉPOQUE DES MAMELOUKS ET LEURS CAUSES ÉCONOMIQUES

A.N. Poliak

I

Parmi les desiderata si nombreux de l'orientalisme modern, la nécessité d'une histoire des explosions sociales qui ont secoué le monde musulman aux temps divers est indiscutable. Même la grande crise de l'époque ḳarmate n'est pas encore explorée d'une façon satisfaisante, malgré l'intérêt que lui ont témoigné De Gœje ou Massignon. Quant aux mouvements qui ont eu lieu aux pays arabes à la fin du Moyen Age et sous la domination ottomane, je ne connais aucun ouvrage qui leur soit consacré. La principale cause de ce phénoméne est sans doute l'isolement de ces révoltes l'une de l'autre, l'isolement aussi bien social que géographique et chronologique. Nous ne trouvons pas ici un courant révolutionnaire qui vent organiser et unir dans son sein, comme les Ḳarmaṭes de jadis, tous les mécontents contre le régime social existant: les paysans, les Bédouins, les esclaves, les artisans, les petits commerçants. Cette différence est causée par le changement des relations sociales et économiques. Si les révoltes des Zanj et des Karmates avaient été préparées par «la concentration de capitaux, grâce à la formation d'une caste de banquiers arbitragistes opérant de Bagdad comme centre avec des succursales au loin, ravitaillant l'État en métal monnaye», rendues possibles par la «concentration

Source: Revue des Études Islamiques, III, 1934, pp. 251–73.

de main'dœuvre, grâce aux razzias d'esclaves, raids coloniaux précisément subventionnés par ces mêmes banquiers sous prétexte de «guerre sainte», afin d'assurer le fonctionnement permanent d'ateliers dans les villes et de chantiers sur les plantations»[1] – ni la concentration de capitaux ni celle de main-d'œuvre ne subsistaient à l'époque dont nous allons parler. Tandis qu'à l'époque des révoltes ḳarmaṭes les relations monétaires se répandaient de plus en plus (comme l'a démontré A. Mez dans *Die Renaissance des Islāms*), la caractéristique de l'époque mamelouke, c'est l'extension des paiements en nature. Le tribut des petits États voisins était payé en majorité en nature;[2] de même les fermages (ḫarāj) en Haute-Égypte[3] et, semble-t-il, dans les villages syriens qui s'occupaient principalement de la culture des céréales.[4] Même les impôts et les allocations payés en argent étaient souvent accompagnés par des paiements complémentaires en nature. Par conséquent l'État qui, en outre, monopolisait l'importation des métaux nécessaires pour frapper la monnaie, n'avait pas besoin de l'imprunter des banquiers. Quand le trésor était vide, le sultan préférait obtenir les sommes nécessaires pour les paiements immédiats tout simplement en les percevant grâce aux fonctionnaires indigènes (al-mubāširūn),[5] par l'émission de pièces de mauvaise qualité ou par la confiscation des biens d'un riche personnage. Les rares cas d'emprunts pécuniaires ne sont que des exceptions qui confirment la règle.[6] Cette politique financière, combinée avec la confiscation habituelle d'une grande partie des biens transmis en héritage par le dīwān al-mawārīt («le bureau des héritages» du sultan), poussait les riches émirs et bourgeois à thésauriser des pièces d'or et d'argent, les enterrant dans la terre ou les cachant chez leurs hommes de confiance au lieu de les placer dans le commerce, l'industrie ou l'agriculture.[7] D'ailleurs, les possibilités de ce placement diminuaient toujours, grâce au système de monopoles sultaniens, ce moyen complémentaire de l'expropriation du revenu national par la classe dominante des «Turcs»: les revenus de monopoles servaient non seulement à agrandir la fortune d'un sultan électif et à équilibrer le budget, mais comme toutes les autres recettes du trésor fournissaient les moyens pour les donations extraordinaires (nafaḳāt), souvent exigées sous menace de soulèvement, aux émirs et aux Mamelouks. L'industrie prevée ne pouvait pas concurrencer l'industrie monopolisée, qui disposait de matières premiéres gratuites (les produits de domaines agraires due sultan), était exempte d'impôts, influençait sans doute le barème officiel des prix de marché (tasʿīr) et pouvait même recourir à la fermeture forcée des entreprises privées.[8] Mais le sultan lui-même, toujours menacé d'un coup d'État latent, envisageait ces entreprises seulement comme une source de revenus et non pas comme un lieu de placement de capitaux, même pour remplacer les ateliers privés ruinés par des ateliers sultaniens nouveaux. Nous ne citerons qu'un exemple: des 58 usines, privées, de sucre à al-Fusṭāṭ dont fait mention Ibn Duḳmāḳ (IV, p. 41–46), seulement 19 fonctionnaient encore au moment de la composition de son ouvrage. Des 39 autres, 5 s'occupaient de quelque autre production; 17 servaient de maisons d'habitation, boutiques, dépôts de charbon et de sel, hôtels et caravansérails; 5 étaient fermées ou démolies, et le destin de 12 n'était pas connu à l'auteur. Toutes les sept usines sultaniennes fonctionnaient (le sultan Ḥasan transféra trois usines à ses fils, «les rois du sucre» des campagnes égyptiennes).[9] Les grands marchands et industriels bourgeois devenaient soit des agents des monopoles sultaniens (tujjār as-sulṭān, wukalā' as-sulṭān),[10] soit, délaissant les branches plus productives de la vie économique des spéculateurs sur les cours toujours variables des trois ou quatre monnaies nationales (le dinar d'or, le dirhem d'argent, les fulūs de cuivre, et la plus récente «niṣf al-fiḍḍa» d'argent). Ces spéculateurs se créaient parfois des fortunes énormes, mais le sultan les ruinait bientôt.[11] Les émirs et les fils des sultans s'emparaient d'une grande portion des entreprises dépendantes de l'agriculture (particulièrement du commerce du blé et du transport aquatique; Ibn Duḳmāḳ mentionne 23 usines du sucre à al-Fusṭāṭ comme appartenant, en des époques diverses, à de grands émirs). Toutefois une concentration héréditaire de capitaux ne pouvait pas se développer même dans ce milieu: premièrement, car les émirs souffraient aussi, comme les bourgeois, des contributions et confiscations soudaines et de la politique fiscale du dīwān al-mawārīṯ; secondement, car le système agraire mamelouk, basé sur l'éviction permanente de la postérité arabisée des émirs (awlād an-nās, abnā'an-nās) par les Mamelouks nouvellement venus (al-julbān, al-ajlāb), ne favorisait pas la transformation des premiers en aristocratie foncière héréditaire. Et même si un émir admettait que ses enfants ne reçoivent tout au plus qu'une portion de ses fiefs, il y avait encore deux motifs qui l'empèchaient d'y établier des formes plus intensives de l'agriculture: sa translation fréquente d'un fief à un autre selon les événements de sa carrière militaire, et le fait que le montant du revenu annuel qu'un feudataire pouvait retirer de son fief ne devait pas l'également dépasser une certaine limite, correspondante à son rang militaire.[12] Par conséquent, il se contentait généralement de percevoir les redevances des fellāḥs, les laissant cultiver la terre selon leur usage. Il n'y avait pas de grands domaines cultivés par les esclaves, comme ceux de l'Irāk méridional au temps de la révolte des Zanj. Les esclaves noirs (al-ʿabīd), importés de la Nubie et du Mağrib,[13] comme indigènes (al-ğilmān) remplissaient en général le rôle de domestiques et d'ouvriers dans les maisons des riches citadins.

Après l'isolement social (pas de révoltes communes de cultivateurs et de travailleurs citadins) et géographique (même les révoltes d'un seul groupe social ne se répandent jamais sur toutes les parties du sultanat à la fois), le signe le plus caractéristique des révoltes populaires de lépoque mamelouke, c'est l'absence de toute idéologie religieuse. La principale cause de ce phénomène, c'est probablement la position sociale réactionnaire des théologiens musulmans de tous les courants à cette époque-là. Même pour le plus indépendant d'eux, Ibn Taymiya, «un indigent orgueilleux» (ʿāʾil mutakabbir) est une image aussi insultante qu'«un roi menteur» ou «un cheikh adultère».[14] Il n'y eut que trois exceptions: la révolte des esclaves au Caire en 1260 sous la conduite de l'acète chiite al-Kūrānī,[15] la révolte mahdiste des cultivateurs Nuṣayrīs sous le sultan Muḥammad ben Ḳalāun[16] et celle du «fils du fellah» aš-Šiʿšaʿ ou al-Mušaʿšiʿ, qui se déclara aussi le Mahdī et abolit certaines défenses religieuses. Commencée dans la région de Wadī-t-Taym en Syrie, la révolte du «fils du fellāḥ» atteignit son apogée en dehors de la frontière du sultanat mamelouke, en ʿIrāḳ, où les rebelles purent interrompre entre 1453–7 (857–61 de l'hégire) le pèlerinage à la Mecque, et se créèrent même une flotte considérable et un refuge maritime sur des îles du Golfe Persique.[17] Les épithètes décernées à ce Mahdī dans les sources mameloukes (ḫārijī, rāfiḍī, zindīḳ) indiquent seulement qu'il était un hérétique du point de vue de l'Islām sunnite; il était peut-être influencé par les croyances druses (Wādī-t-Taym) et, même ismaʿīlites (si relation il y a entre son mystérieux refuge maritime et la colonie ismaʿīlite d'al-Baḥrayn). Les rebelles étaient probablement des fellāḥs et des Bédouins des confins du désert, auxquels la guerre sainte déclarée par «le fils du fellāḥ» contre les Sunnites donnait une occasion de se révolter contre les féodaux.

L'isolement des révoltes et la clarté de leurs causes nous permettent de les classer en trois catégories distinctes: *a*) les révoltes agraires des cultivateurs bédouins et des fellāḥs (généralement désignées en Égypte comme «fasād al-ʿUrbān», les désordres des Bédouins); *b*) les soulèvements de la population pauvre des villes (al-ʿawāmm); *c*) les révoltes des esclaves au Caire.

II

La transformation lente des Bédouins de la vallée du Nil en population agricole sédentaire, qui n'atteignit sa fin qu'au XVIIIe siècle,[18] était à l'époque mamelouke encore à mi-chemin. Les Bédouins s'occupaient déjà de l'agriculture, mais en conservant une position sociale plus haute que celle des fellāḥs, grâce à leur participation à l'armée: en cas de guerre ils envoyaient une cavalerie auxiliaire,[19] et des cheikhs bédouins (arbāb al-idrāk) étaient responsables pour le maintien de l'ordre dans les campagnes.[20] Leur part dans la production agricole totale du pays était déjà assez grande: en Šawāl 809 de l'hégire, l'émir Jakam minʿAwaḍ, qui se proclama sultan à Alep, adressa des proclamations «aux Bédouins et aux fellāḥs de l'Égypte» (plaçant les Bédouins au premier lieu!), dans lesquelles il les excitait à cessor les paiements du ḫarāj[21] au sultan Faraj et à ses émirs et soldats.[22] Si Baybars I força en 1264 (661 de l'hégire) les représentants de deux tribus, Hawāra et Salīm, à signer l'obligation de cultiver leurs terres, cela ne veut pas dire qu'elles ne s'occupaient de l'agriculture que sous la pression du gouvernement: le sultanat mamelouk imposait à *tous* les détenteurs de terres l'obligation de veiller à ce que la superficie des terres cultivées ne diminue pas.[23] D'autre part, les fermages et la fixation arbitraire des rix du blé et de l'orge par les hauts émirs pouvaient parfois rendre l'élevage du bétail plus rémunérateur que la culture de céréales; c'est évidemment le sens d'un passage des ḥawādīt (pl. 458, 1. 17–20), où Ibn Taġrī Birdī déplore le fait que les Bédouins ont occupé la plupart des terres du sultan et des feudataires en Haute-Égypte, mais n'y sèment de blé que la quantité minima nécessaire pour payer les fermages. Il semble que, pour éviter leur assimilation aux fellāḥs, les cultivateurs bédouins habitaient soit des tentes, soit de petits hameaux particuliers (kufūr) près de grands villages anciens des fellāḥs (bilād, ḳurā).[24] Seuls, des cheikhs et des émirs pouvaient habiter les villages et les villes sans craindre de porter atteinte à leur propre position social.[25] Sur les terres salines de la province d'aš-Šarḳīya les Bédouins bâtirent des hameaux qui n'étaient pas enregistés dans les bureaux du gouvernement et, par conséquent, étaient exempts de fermages et d'impôts.[26] Ceux qui habitaient les tentes ne nomadisaient pas sur des espaces très vastes, car, quoique les Bédoins dussent fournir en cas de guerre une cavalerie, les relations sur leurs révoltes nous montrent que la plupart des rebelles étaient des piétons.[27] La participation des tribus nomades du Désert Arabe à l'est de la vallée du Nil dans ces révoltes ne semble pas avoir été considérable; du moins, les sources mameloukes n'en racontent rien. De l'ouest, la seule tribu nomade désertique qui fit des irruptions périodiques sur le territoire de l'Égypte (la province d'al-Buḥayra), pour y paître ses troupeaux pendant la sécheresse et échanger ses produits contre les marchandises dont elle avait besoin, était celle de Labīd. Sur les pourparlers de ses chefs avec les pouvoirs mamelouks et les tribus indigènes et sur les incidents de frontière causés par ces irruptions nous trouvons dans les sources une information opulente.[28] Ces nomades étrangers ne prenaient jamais part aux révoltes des Bédouins égyptiens, qui au contraire trouvaient chez les fellāḥs un appui assez naturel. Dans la relation sur la grande révolte en Haute-Égypte en 1353 (754 de l'hégire) sous la conduite d'Ibn al-Aḥdab, cheikh de la tribu d' ʿArak, Ibn Iyās use des mots «Bédouins (ʿurbān)» et «fellāḥs» comme s'ils étaient des synonymes.[29] L'effervescence des fellāḥs égyptiens pendant cette révolte poussa le sultan aṣ-Ṣāliḥ Ṣalāḥ ad-dīn à défendre, après son retour au Caire, à tous les fellāḥs de monter des chevaux et de porter des armes.

Selon *at-Taʿrīf* (p. 188, 1. 6–12), Ḥiṣn addīn ben Taʿlab établir un État indépendant en Haute-Égypte, et Baybars I réussit à s'emparer de lui seulement au moyen d'une ruse. Il semble, par conséquent que la narration d'Al-Maḳrīzī sur la répression complète de cette révolte par Aybak est une falsification, dont le but fut la glorification des «Turcs».

La seule révolte générale des Bédouins de l'Égypte éclata en 1253 (651 de l'hégire) sous la conduite du chérif Ḥiṣn ad-dīn ben Taʿlab, pendu sous Baybars I.[30] La répression brutale de cette tentative d'établir un sultanat bédouin n'empêcha que la crainte d'un nouveau soulèvement général continuât à terroriser les Mamelouks jusqu'à la chute de leur État, devint leur véritable *memento mori*. Cette crainte et la nécessité de parer au danger latent par la dictature d'un homme de fer furent les motifs officiels de l'élection de Baybars II, de Barḳūḳ et d'al-Muʾayyad Šayḫ au sultanat.[31] Cette crainte retenait aussi les émirs Mamelouks d'user des troupes bédouines dans leurs guerres civiles.[32] Très probablement c'est elle qui les poussait à rajeunir constamment la classe dirigeante par l'importation des nouveaux Mamelouks, à fermer de plus en plus les hauts postes militaires à la postérité arabisée des émirs (awlād an-nās), et à conserver l'isolement culturel de la classe dirigeante en maintenant la position privilégiée de l'idiome turc (même sous les sultans de l'origine circassienne). Pendant les guerres contre les Ottomans en 1488 et en 1516 (893 et 922 de l'hégire), la garnison du Caire faisait des démonstrations militaires particulières pour retenir les fellāḥs et les Bédouins d'utiliser cette opportunité pour attaquer la capitale;[33] et les défaites des Mamelouks pendant la guerre contre le roi turcoman Šāh Siwār (872–877 de l'hégire) faillirent entraîner une révolution paysanne.[34]

Cette crainte d'une révolte générale était alimentée par d'incessantes révoltes partielles, dont le caractère agraire est indiscutable. La concentration de la féodalité mamelouke dans les villes empêchait ces révoltes de prendre la forme d'attaques sur les châteaux des féodaux à l'instar des Jacqueries occidentales. Ici c'était une lutte autour des récoltes: en Haute-Égypte les seigneurs en recevaient une grande partie en nature, en Basse-Égypte la perception des fermages en argent forçait les paysans à vendre leur blé selon les prix déterminés par les seigneurs (qui contrôlaient le marché dublé). Il est vrai que les taux du ḫarāj en Basse-Égypte étaient aussi déterminés d'après ces prix; mais, vu les grands et brusques changements d'ordre spéculatif qui avaient lieu dans ces prix, cela fournissait seulement aux seigneurs une occasion supplémentaire d'exploiter leurs serfs. Ce qui donnait aux seigneurs la possibilité de contrôler les prix des denrées, c'était l'accaparement des grains (transportées de la Haute-Égypte sur le Nil) dans leurs grands greniers de «la rive des grains» (sāḥil al-Ğalla) à Būlāḳ près du Caire.[35] C'était un affamement méthodique des campagnes: les fellāḥs devaient parfois aller à la ville pour y acheter du pain,[36] et en cas de famine des paysans émigraient en masse au Caire, jamais des citadins aux villages.[37] Par conséquent, les revoltes paysannes étaient causées généralement par le désir de saisir le blé destiné aux seigneurs (dans les aires, les greniers locaux ou sur les bateaux), de piller ce que l'on pouvait prendre avec soi et cacher, de brûler le reste pour contraindre les seigneurs à se résigner à la perte irréparable de leur ḫarāj ou à sa diminution considérable. Une fois nous trouvons même un clair vouloir d'affamer la capitale pour se venger en représailles d'une expédition punitive mamelouke.[38] Les principales offensives de ces saisies du blé eurent lieu en 699 de l'hégire dans la province d'al-Buḥayra; en 701 et en 753 en Haute-Égypte; en 783, en 804 et en 872 dans al-Buḥayra; en 902 dans toutes les régions de l'Égypte; en 904 dans al-Buḥayra et al-Ǧarbīya; en 908 dans aš-Šarḳīya, al-Ǧarbīya et en Haute-Égypte; en 912–913 dans aš-Šarḳīya et al-Ǧarbīya; au Muḥarram 918 dans al-Buḥayra.[39] Cette liste est loin d'être complète: car premièrement, les sources mameloukes souvent mentionnent «des désordres des Bédouins» sans nous faire connaître les formes concrètes de ces désordres; secondement, parce que leur information est plus opulente pour la dernière période du sultanat mamelouk (XVe–XVIe siècles) que pour son commencement. Pendant les troubles, les tribus ennemies utilisaient, naturellement, cette opportunité pour régler leurs comptes, et la partie la plus faible de la population agricole, les fellāḥs, souffraient souvent des actes de pillage et de meurtre de la part des Bédouins.[40] Les rebelles attaquaient les voyageurs sur la grand'route,[41] ce dont les bandits s'occupaient professionnellement en temps normal, souvent avec la complicité des pouvoirs.[42] Les rencontres des rebelles avec la cavalerie mamelouke se terminaient ordinairement par un désastre pour eux, car les Bédouins ne possédaient pas la faculté particulière des «Turcs» à tirer leurs flèches en galopant sur leurs chevaux.[43] La faiblesse militaire des rebelles les empêchait d'attaquer les villes; une exception fut la prise de Damanhūr, chef-lieu d'al-Buḥayra en 781 de l'hégire.[44] Parfois de petits groupes de cavaliers bédouins pénétraient dans la banlieue du Caire pour piller les passants.[45] Il est à remarquer que dans les sources mameloukes nous ne trouvons pas de relations sur les «brutalités» commises par les rebelles. Dans une certaine mesure cela s'explique par la concentration de la féodalité mamelouke dans les villes, qui rendait les rencontres des rebelles avec des seigneurs non entourés d'une suite armée très rares. Néanmoins, même ceux qui réussissaient à s'emparer de voyageurs «turcs» sur la grand'route se contentaient généralement de les dépouiller de leurs bagages et habits (témoignage de Mešullam de Volterra).

Ce phénomène est d'autant plus frappant que les représailles des émirs mamelouks étaient suivies par des actes dignes de l'imagination maladive d'un de Sade. On ne peut pas les justifier en disant qu'ils correspondaient au système usuel de châtiments et de tortures de ce temps-là. Certainement, le système en usage au Caire n'était rien moins que clément envers le torturés: nous ne ferons rappel que du «tawsīṭ», du «tasmīr», des «maʿaṣīr», etc.

Néanmoins on n'y enterrait pas les victimes vivantes, on ne les rôtissait pas sur le feu, on ne les sciait pas du haut en bas, on ne leur enlevait pas le peau en commençant par la tête.[46] Un record effrayant fut atteint pendant la répression de la tribu d'ᶜAzāla en 904 de l'hégire: pendant l'entrée triomphale de l'émir Ṭūmān bay addawādār au Caire, les têtes des Bédouins tués étaient suspendues aux cous de leurs femmes, qui marchaient avec les enfants liés par des cordes; ensuite les hommes pris vivants furent cloués sur des chameaux, promenés dans les rues du Caire, et enfin pendus par les pieds sur les portes de la ville, où les passants devaient les lapider jusqu'à la mort.[47] Et il y avait au Caire des cheikhs indigènes prêts à composer des odes sur les «triomphes des Turcs sur les Bédouins (al-ᶜarab)» de cette espèce.[48]

Ces représailles n'étaient pas causées par la cruauté individuelle d'un tel ou autre sultan ou émir, mais étaient le résultat d'un froid calcul, formulé par Ibn Taǧrī Birdī,[49] selon lequel il valait mieux terroriser les paysans par le supplice monstrueux des prisonniers que par la destruction des villages, entrainant la diminution des revenus des seigneurs.[50] C'était la terreur politique dans sa forme la plus pure, le système de gouvernement d'une féodalité étrangère au pays et qui se sentait toujours menacée. Il semble qu'en raison du même calcul on ne réduisait pas les rebelles faits prisonniers à l'esclavage; ce n'était pas en effet raisonnable, à une époque à laquelle les féodaux s'efforçaient vainement d'enrayer la fuite des fellāḥs vers les villes.[51] Une fois seulement, le sultan Muḥammad ben Ḳalāūn employa des captifs dans la construction des digues d'irrigation;[52] peut-être leur caractère semblait-il trop indépendant pour les travaux de corvée. Les femmes et les enfants des rebelles étaient parfois détenus dans les prisons du Caire pour garantir la soumission de leurs maris et pères, et il y avait des cas, quoique rares, où on les vendait en esclavage.[53] Habituellement, on confisquait le bétail des Bédouins rebelles, leur principal bien mobilier; il est possible qu'on les voulait forcer de cette manière à s'occuper uniquement de la culture des céréales, ce qui les assimilait aux fellāḥs et augmentait les revenus des seigneurs.[54]

Les principaux bénéficiaires de ces révoltes étaient les féodaux bédouins (les šayḫ al-ᶜarab et les émirs). Ils habitaient parfois les villes, portaient souvent des noms turcs pour plaire aux pouvoirs mamelouks,[55] allaient jusqu'à se créer une garde mamelouke.[56] Néanmoins les membres de leurs tribus les envisageaient comme leurs chefs naturels en cas de révolte, ne connaissant aucune forme d'organisation hors de la tribu. Après la répression d'une révolte le gouvernement, la plupart du temps, s'efforçait de se concilier les cheiks et les émirs, leur concédant de nouveaux fiefs. La grande augmentation des terres des chefs bédouins en Égypte à l'époque mamelouke par la raison de cette politique du gouvernement est un sujet trop vaste our faire une partie de cet article (je m'en occupe dans l'ouvrage sus-mentionné sur les relations agraires).

L'information que les sources mameloukes nous donnent sur l'état de choses en Syrie est insuffisante pour former un tableau lucide. Il semble que les mêmes forces qu'en Égypte y étaient en jeu. Les grandes tribus agricoles de la Syrie et de la Palestine sont désignées dans les sources mameloukes par la dénomination d' «al-ʿašīr» (ou «al-ʿašaīr», «al-ʿUšrān»),[57] mais une partie (principalement les habitants des montagnes de Nāblus) conservait en même temps l'appellation d' «al-ʿUrbān» (Bédouins). Chez les Bédouins égyptiens le terme d' «al-ʿašīr» ne se trouve que pendant la dernière période du sultanat mamelouk.[58] Les troupes auxiliaires d'al-ʿašīr syro-palestiniennes en cas de guerre étaient composées pour la plupart d'infanterie (al-mušāt, ar-rajjāla) armée d'arcs et de pierres.[59] Les révoltes de ces tribūs parfois atteignaient des proportions considérables: par exemple, en 1280 (679 de l'hégire) les rebelles prirent Gaza;[60] en 1281 Nāblus;[61] en 848 de l'hégire, le gouverneur de Gaza Tūh al-Muʾayyadī,[62] fut tué dans une bataille. La région montagneuse de Kasrawān au Liban septentrional ne fut subjuguée par les Mamelouks qu'en 1300 (699 de l'hégire).[63]

Selon la version libanaise (Ṣāliḥ Ibn Yaḥyā, 2e éd., p. 31, l. 19; p. 32, l. 1; p. 100, 1. 4), la conquête de Kasrawān n'eut lieu qu'en 1305 (705), mais comme châtiment pour les attaques commises en 1300 (699). Quoique Ṣāliḥ appuie sa relation par l'autorité d'an-Nuwayrī et de Ṣalāḫ ad-dīn al-Kutūbī, il me semble que, vu l'intervalle trop long entre le crime et le châtiment, la narration chez Zetterstéen (composée par un contemporain de Muḥammad ben Ḳalāūn!) est plus exacte.

III

L'époque mamelouke fut pour la bourgeoisie citadine une période de décadence économique et d'impuissance politique. Les grandes villes (en Égypte, le Caire avec al-Fusṭāṭ; en Syrie, Damas, Alep et les autres centres de provinces: Tripoli, Ḥamā, Ṣafad, Gaza, al-Karak, Malaṭiya et Alexandrette) étaient de grands cantonnements militaires, où les habitants civils n'étaient que des citoyens de deuxième ordre, qui fournissaient tout le nécessaire à un nombre énorme de militaires et de leurs esclaves. Quand, après la conquête ottomane, fut créé au Caire le poste de maire (Šayḫ al-balad), ce fut une haute dignité *militaire*. Les autres villes (et les centres des provinces égyptiennes) étaient du point de vue administratif de grands villages, qui payaient le ḫarāj et les autres impôts à leurs seigneurs, et quoique possédant comme chaque village des maires civils[64] ne jouissaient pas d'autonomie, fiscale, policière ou judiciaire. Les révoltes dans les villes n'étaient pas l'expression de la lutte des commerçants ou des artisans pour le pouvoir municipal, mais les soulèvements des pauvres qui voulaient soit la réduction du prix du pain, soit la démission d'un fonctionnaire haï. La fuite des fellāḥs vers les villes et le chômage dans l'industrie maintenaient dans les villes une multitude de chômeurs permanents. Ces «ḥārāfīs»[65] parcouraient les rues en cherchant un gagne-pain provisoire, en mendiant et en utilisant les occasions de voler quelque chose (particulièrement du pain). Ceux d'entre eux pour lesquels, le brigandage devint une habitude («az-zuʿr» des sources mameloukes) étaient l'élément le plus actif pendant les émeutes; d'autre part, le gouvernement mamelouk lui-même utilisait parfois leurs penchants guerriers.[66] En cas de révolte, autour de ces gens qui n'avaient rien à perdre, se rassemblaient des esclaves (dont le mot «az-zuʿr» désigne aussi les plus turbulents), des ouvriers, des artisans et des petits commerçants. Les rebelles, armés habituellement de frondes et de pierres, ne pouvaient pas aspirer à s'emparer du Caire, où se concentraient les meilleures forces de l'armée mamelouke. Ils y prenaient part à la lutte d'un groupement mamelouk contre un autre, plus haï, ou bien cherchaient à exercer pression sur le gouvernement, afin qu'il tienne compte de leurs demandes. A la première catégorie se rapportent les cas suivants: la participation dans la répression d'une révolte des émirs en Rajab 768 de l'hégire;[67] dans la répression de la révolte du général en chef en 770;[68] dans la révolte des Mamelouks de l'émir Inbak al-Badrī en 779;[69] aux côtés de l'émir Timurbuġa Minṭāš contre le général en chef Yalbuġa an-Nāṣirī en Šaʿbān 791.[70] Pendant la dernière période du sultanat mamelouk, les Mamelouks ne permirent plus cette intervention des indigènes dans leurs luttes intérieures, probablement en conséquence de leur crainte d'une révolution bédouine. Le groupe mamelouk vainqueur excitait souvent le peuple à piller les maisons de ses rivaux, ce que la foule parfois s'empressait de faire même sans invitation.[71]

Quant à la deuxième catégorie, elle contient les soulèvements comme celui de 771 de l'hégire, quand les rebelles obtinrent le changement du chef de la police militaire (al-wālī) du Caire;[72] les émeutes de famine en 853–854 de l'hégire, quand le peuple enragé pilla les boutiques du pain, voulut lapider l'inspecteur des marchés (al-muḥtasib) ʿAli ben Iskandar (qui fut ensuite relevé de sa charge), et blessa le ḳāḍī Abū l-ḫayr ben an-Naḥḥās pour avoir dit au sultan que «les gens qui ont de l'or pour acheter du hachich et des sucreries, en auront pour acheter due pain» même au prix maximum;[73] une émeute en Šaʿbān 885 de l'hégire contre l'inspecteur des biens du sultan (nāẓir al-ḫāṣṣ), attaqué au milieu d'al-Madrasa aṣ-Ṣāliḥīya pour avoir proposé que la valeur des nouvelles pièces de cuivre (fulūs) soit plus grande que celle des anciennes;[74] les tumultes en Rabīʿ II 804 de l'hégire contre le cheikh Šihāb ad-dīn Aḥmad aš-Šīšī, qui donna au sultan l'autorisation légale de s'emparer de la rente bi-mensuelle des propriétés foncières et bâties (amlāk) pour payer une allocation (nafaḳa) à l'armée;[75] une émeute au commencement du règne de Ḳānṣūh al-Ǧaurī, causée par la perception des loyers des propriétés bâties (ainsi que des biens de mainmorte) au Caire pour onze mois d'avance, afin de donner l'llocation traditionnelle aux Mamelouks à l'occasion de l'avènement du sultan (nafaḳat al-bayʿa). La même perception causa une émeute à Damas, où les habitants chassérent le gouverneur de la ville (Ibn Iyās, IV, p. 23, l. 10–15).[76] Le gouvernement donnait usuellement aux rebelles une satisfaction partielle[77] pour ne pas mener les choses à l'extrème, sans changer pour cela sa politique générale. Une arme de lutte particulière aux arisans et aux commerçants était la fermeture des boutiques jusqu'à l'acceptation de leurs demandes.[78]

Des révoltes beaucoup plus considérables eurent lieu dans les villes syriennes, principalement à Damas. Ici encore il n'y avait pas tentatives d'établir un gouvernement municipal ni de recevoir des privilèges permanents; au moins les révoltés se sentaient ici assez forts pour chasser de la ville les forces d'un groupement mamelouk haï et mener des pourparlers officiels avec ses rivaux. Quand Barḳūḳ entra à Damas en 791 de l'hégire, un cas de pillage de la part d'un Mamelouk de son armée poussa les habitants à se révolter et à le chasser de la ville.[79] Même après la conquête de l'Égypte par Barḳūḳ «le bas peuple» de Damas et des autres villes syriennes continua à aider son rival, Timurbuġa Minṭāš, en combattant pour lui contre les forces de Barḳūḳ et en lui ouvrant les portes des villes.[80] Ce fut la population de Damas (ahl Dimašk) qui combattit Tamerlan pour défendre la ville et traita ensuite avec lui. Les ravages de son armée, peut-être un peu exagérés par les écrivains mamelouks, n'empêchèrent pas les habitants de se révolter l'année suivante contre le gouverneur mamelouk Tağrī Birdī, de le chasser de la ville et d'obtenir son remplacement par un autre.[81] Ibn Tağri Birdī, ne voulant pas admettre que son père eût été chassé d'une façon tellement ignominieuse, nous raconte d'une manière confuse qu'il quitta la ville à cause des intrigues de quelques émirs.[82] Deux émeutes moins considérables eurent lieu à Damas sous Ḳāibāy et al-Ğaurī.[83]

Dans les autres villes syriennes nous ne connaissons que des soulèvements isolés: à Ḥamā en 882 de l'hègire, à al-Karak sous al-Ğaūrī.[84] Après la bataille de Marj Dābeḳ en 1516 (922 de l'hégire), les habitants d'Alep ne laissèrent pas l'armée mamelouke entrer dans leur ville et la combattirent farouchement, pour venger les ravages des Mamelouks sultaniens sous al-Ğāurī.[85]

Il n'y a presque pas eu d'émeute contre les minorités nationales ou religieuses, ce qui s'explique par la composition internationale de la classe dominante des «Turcs» (ainsi nommée d'après sa «lingua franca»); par l'absence d'un sentiment national, au sens moderne, chez les indigènes (le terme «al-ʿarab» référait seulement aux Bédouins), et par l'antagonisme entre la classe dominante et les indigènes, plus fort que celui entre les Musulmans et les non-Musulmans.[86] Les persécutions des minorités étaient des actes administratifs du gouvernement, don't les plus usuels peuvent être classés en trois catégories: *a*) les ordres qui leur imposent les turbans d'une couleur particulière (aux chrétiens bleu, aux juifs jaune) et faits de pièces d'étoffe ne dépassant pas 7 ou 10 coudées, en 700, 754, 822, 857 et 867 de l'hégire; *b*) les ordres qui défendent de les employer dans les bureaux du sultan et des émirs, en 689, 700, 754, 825 et 867 de l'hégire; *c*) la perception de contributions pécuniaires extraordinaires sur les chrétiens et juifs simultanément ou d'une communauté à la suite de l'autre, sous Baybars I, Ḳāītbāy, Muḥammad ben Ḳāībāy, Jān Bulāṭ et al-Ğaūrī.[87] Les émeutes contre les chrétiens (accusés de sentiments pro-mongols) à Damas en 1260 et, plus faibles, contre les juifs (accusés de sentiments pro-ottomans) au Caire et à Ṣafad en 1516, étaient organisées avec la complicité du gouvernement.[88] Seulement deux fois les émeutes contre les non-Musulmans furent préparées par une longue effervescence d'une partie des

Musulmans indigènes: *a*) les excès qui suivirent les ordres de 1301 (700 de l'hégire), causés principalement par la haine des fonctionnaires et marchands musulmans contre leurs confrères coptes, chrétiens et islamisés (dont la position ressemblait à celle des Marranes dans la presqu'ile Ibérique);[89] *b*) Les émeutes à Damas en 1516 (avant l'entrée des Ottomans) contre la communauté samaritaine, composée des riches fonctionnaires, changeurs des monnaies et propriétaires fonciers,[90] mais aussi contre les marchands européens et les notables musulmans.[91]

IV

Tandis que le nombre des ouvriers libres diminuait probablement de plus en plus, celui des esclaves restait assez considérable, particulièrement au Caire.[92] La différence de condition entre les esclaves indigènes (al-ǧilmān) et les noirs (al-ʿabīd) n'était probablement pas très grande, car parfois (quoique rarement) les deux mots sont pris dans les sources comme synonymes.[93] *Al-ǧilmān* possédés par les Mamelouks en recevaient une solde mensuelle (ǧāmakīya);[94] nous ne saurions dire si les noirs en jouissaient aussi. Des esclaves des deux catégories allaient avec leurs seigneurs à la guerre, où beaucoup d'entre eux trouvaient la mort. Les ouvriers de l'Hôtel de la monnaie, ceux des Écuries sultaniennes et des divers magasins (buyūtāt de la Cour, les artilleurs (an-nafṭīya)) étaient aussi des esclaves. Il est probable que des ḥarāfīš cherchaient à devenir de bon gré des ǧilmān (le premier terme embrasse parfois le second), de même qu'encore au XVIIIe siècle, des étrangers se vendaient eux-mêmes aux marchands pour être reçus dans l'armée mamelouke.[95]

Nous avons déjà mentionné la révolte de 1260, dont le chef promettait à ses adhérents de leur donner des fonds de terre. Une autre offensive des émeutes d'esclaves se rencontre au XVe siècle. Au commencement de Rajab 841 de l'hégire eurent lieu des chocs sanglants entre les esclaves et les jeunes Mamelouks;[96] en Dū l-ḥijja 849 de l'hégire, le soulèvement de plus de 500 esclaves qui gardaient les chevaux de leurs maitres sur les pâturages d'al-Jīzīya et de Manbāba. Les rebelles élurent un «sultan» (bientôt tué par un autre prétendant) et l'entourèrent de la suite et de l'étiquette habituelles à la Cour mamelouke (le trône, le drapeau jaune, le vizir, le général en chef, l'émir-dawādār, et même les gouverneurs de Damas et d'Alep). Ils pillaient les caravanes de grains sans oser attaquer la capitale. Après la répression de leur révolte le sultan acheta tous les esclaves âgés du Caire et les envoya à l'État Ottoman pour les vendre.[97] Peut-être les rebelles avaient-ils l'espérance mystique de s'emparer du sultanat mamelouk, excités par des derviches semblables à ce Saʿdān (arrêté en 854 de l'hégire), qui jouissait d'une si grande influence même sur des émirs mamelouks.[98] Après cette révolte nous ne trouvons plus de tentatives de coup d'État, mais seulement de petites émeutes et des séries d'actes de pillage et de meurtre, avec la participation d'az-zuʿr,[99] d'al-julbān,[100] et même sur l'ordre de leurs maîtres, de Mamelouks.[101] Un wālī du Caire tua plus de 700 esclaves turbulents[102] et sous al-Ǧāurī chaque cas de désordres au Caire était suivi par une proclamation du sultan qui défendait aux esclaves, comme aux Mamelouks, de sortir la nuit des maisons.[103]

NOTES

1 Louis Massignon, L'influence de l'Islam au Moyen Age sur la fondation et l'essor des banques juives (Institut Français de Damas. *Bulletin d'études orientales*, t. l, 1931, p. 3).

2 Ibn Duḳmāḳ, V. p. 15, t. 5: *Sulūk* de Marḳrīzī-Quatremère, I, 11, p. 128–130; Ibn Iyās, I, p. 157, I. 26; *Ḥawādīt* d'Ibn Taǧri Birdi, éd. Popper, p. 481, l. 18.

3 Ḳalḳašandī, *Subḥ*, III, p. 453, 1. 18-p. 454, l. 3.

4 K.V. Zetterstéen, *Beiträge zur Geschichte der Mamlūkensultane* (Leyde, 1919), p. 82, l. 21–23.

5 Ibn Iyās, 1, p. 143, l. 27–30; 11, p. 41, l. 6; p. 43, l. 29; p. 93, l. 16.

6 Ibn Iyās, 1. p. 302, l. 10–12; *Nujūm* d'lbn Taǧrī Birdī (éd. Popper), VI, p. 122, l. 1–3. On peut difficilement classer dans cette catégorie l'emprunt de contrainte (en argent et en marchandises) pour la guerre contre Tamerlan (Ibn Iyās, I, p. 330, 1. 20–24; *Nujūm*, VI, p. 69, 1. 12–16).

7 Dans les listes des biens et héritages confisqués nous trouvons toujours en tête ces trésors cachés et de grandes quantitiés de pierres précieuses, de vêtements et d'étoffes (aussi une forme de thésaurisation, développée surtout depuis l'apparition des habits de fête militaires, *aš-šāš wa-l-ḳumāš*, sous Muḥammad ben Ḳalāūn: Ibn Iyās, 1, p. 173, l. 15). La propriété industrielle et agricole n'est mentionnée que passagèrement: *Sulūk*, II, 1, p. 114–115; Ibn Iyās, I, p. 155, l. 27; p. 156, l. 23; p. 162; l. 20; p. 172, l. 7–14; p. 197, l. 19-p. 198, l. 14; p. 304, l. 21-p. 305, l. 30; IV, p. 405.

8 M. Sobernheim, Das Zuckermonopol unter Sultan Barsbāī, *Zeitschrift für Assyriologie und verwandie Gebiele*, XXVII, 1912, p. 75–84.

9 Ibn Duḳmāḳ, V. p. 22, 1. 9; p. 24, 1. 8; p. 25, 1. 2.

10 *Ḥawādiṯ*, p. 97, 1. 15; p. 507, 1. 15; Ibn Iyās, I, p. 326, 1. 7; II, p. 162, 1. 17; p. 181, 1. 27.

11 La fortune du changeur de monnaies juif Samuel, confisquée par Ḳānṣūh al-Gaūrī, dépassait 500.000 dinars (Ibn Iyās, IV, p. 235, 1. 2–6). Le taux de change normal était 3 0/0 (*Nujūm*, VI, p. 69, 1. 17).

12 Je traite avec plus de détail de ce phénomène et de ses causes dans mon ouvrage sur l'histoire des relations agraires en Égypte, en Syrie et en Palestine sous les Mamelouks et les Ottomans (maintenant en préparation).

13 *Sulūk*, I, II, p. 131; II, l, pp. 90–98; Ibn Iyās I, p. 109, l. 16; p. 119, l. 2; p. 157, l. 26: *Ḥawādīt*, p. 214, l. 11.

14 *Majmūʿ ar-rasaʾil al-kubrā*, éd. 1323 de l'hégire, p. 103 Le caractére concret de ces trois exemples parallèles ne permet pas d'interpréter le mot «'āʾil» dans le seus de «celui qui s'écarlo de la justice». Ibn Taymiya demanda le massacre de tous les Nuṣayris révoltés.

15 *Salūk*, I, I. p. 122–8.

16 *Voyages d'Ibn Batoulah, éd. Société Asiatique* (3ᵉ tir.), I, p. 179.

17 *Ḥawādiṯ*, p. 199, l. 13–15; p. 249, l. 22-p. 250, l. 6; p. 305, l. 18-p. 306, l. 16 Ibn Iyās, II, p. 45, l. 11–12; p. 54, l. 6; p. 60, l. 11–13

18 E.W. Lane trouva encore vivante la tradition affirmant l'origine bédouine d'une grande partie des paysans de la Haute-Égypte; et pendant le XIXᵉ siécle beaucoup de fellāḥs égyptiens étaient encore affiliés aux tribus. G. F. Volney nous informe qu'en 1783 les Bédouins de l'Égypte étaient déjà «tellement dispersés et désunis qu'on les y traite comme des voleurs et des vagabonds», beaucoup d'entre eux étaient «dispersés par familles», et les tribus qui étaient stables en Égypte «y loueat des terres, qu'elles ensemencent et changent annuellement» (*Voyage en Syrie et en Égypte*, Iʳᵉ édition, I, p. 70–72). Il est possible que la tradition sur l'émigration des fellāḥs égyptiens au Ḥijāz septentrional au XVIIIᵉ siécle et la création de la tribu mélangée de Ḥuwayṭāt (Richard F. Burton, *The Goldmines of Midian*, London, 1878) se réfère aussi à cette dernière étape de la décomposition des tribus bédouines de l'Égypte.

Selon at-Tārīḫ d'al-ʿUmar, p. 76, l. 10 (cité dans *Subḫ*, VI, p. 160, 1. 7), les Bédouins égyptiens étaient «ahl ḥāḍira wu-zarʿ». La seule exception était les tribus d'al-Buḥayra, mais au temps d'al-Ḳalḳašandī elles étaient déjà semblables aux autres (*Ṣubḫ*, VII, p. 161, 1. 1). La population bédouine moderne des *contrées désertiques* de l'Égypte est composée principalement de tribus venues d'Al-Maġrib (et dans une certaine partie de l'Arabie) pendant les trois dernier siècles. Ou peut fixer quelques étapes de cette immigration d'aprés l'information que nous donne al-Jabartī; comp. aussi: P. et H., *Égypte sous la domination de Méhémet Aly* (L'Univers: Égypte moderne, Paris 1848), pp. 108–110 l'infomration sur Hawāra est inexacte!).

19 Ibn Iyān, I, p. 331, l. 7–9; II, p. 252, l. 11; p. 262, l. 14–15; V (éd. Kahlo), p. 21, l. 12–14, etc.

20 *Subḫ* III, p. 458, 1. 3. *Nujūm*, VI, p. 481, 1. 8; p. 829, 1. 10. La même expression désignait une espèce des agents de ville au Caire (Ibn Iyās), V, p. 52, 1. 17, etc. Aujourd'hui dans le langage des journaix arabes «ad-darak» = gendarmerie.

21 Son caractère primitif d'un impôt payé par les cultivateurs non musulmans au Trésor de l'État était complètement oublié, et il était envisagé à cette époque-là simplement comme les fermages des terres cultivées (*Subḥ*, III, p. 452, l. 14; *Nujūm*, VI, p. 69, l. 9–10).
22 *Nujūm*, VI, p. 183, l. 20.
23 *Sulūk*, I, I, p. 246. Pour les fondataires mamelouks comparer: *Ḥawādit̲*, p. 105, l. 3–10; Ibn Iyās, IV, p. 104, l. 17–18.
24 Ibn Iyās, II, p. 67, l. 20. Sur la signification du mot «kufūr» comp. Ibn al-Ji'ān p. 9, l. 4; p. 15, l. 22, 27; p. 20, l. 3, 6; p. 21, l. 1; p. 22, l, 18; p. 24, l. 21; p. 25, l. 7; p. 26, l. 21, etc. Ibn Taġri Birdī appelle les fellāḥs «fallāḥū-l-Ḳura», pour les distinguer des cultivateurs Bédouins (*Hawādit̲*, p. 692, 1. 11, 16–17). Comp. l'expression «villagers and tribesmen» dans les documents de l'administration anglaise en Palestine de nos jours, où aussi presque tous les Bédouins s'occupent de l'agriculture (*Census of Palestine*, 1931, I, p. 334–5).
25 *Ḥawādit̲*, p. 721, l. 21–23; *Subḥ*, IV, p. 71, sur la famille de Banū Yūsuf.
26 Ẓāhirī, *Zubdat kahšf al-mamālik*, p. 34, l. 9.
27 *Sulūk*, I, 1, p. 40–42. *Ḥawādīt*, p. 362, l. 4.
28 *Nujūm*, VI, p. 728, l. 18; p. 729, l. 1–5; VII, p. 9, l. 4; p. 570, l. 25; p. 654, l. 3; p. 711, l. 4. *Hawādit*, p. 1901, 1–5; p. 209, l. 1; p. 210, l. 1–4; p. 211, l. 12–18; p. 213, l. 1–3, 13–14, 18–21, p. 500. l. 1. Ibn Iyās, II. p. 67, l. 28; p. 122, l. 1–2. L'indication de Maḳrīzī que cette tribu habitait entre Alexandrie et 'Akaba («*al-Bayān wa-l-'a'rāb*', éd. Wüstenfeld, p. 42, citée par W. Popper dans une note à *Nujūm*, VI, p. 728) se relate évidemment soit à un temps antérieur, soit à l'espace maximum sur lequel Labīd pouvait nomadiser à l'intérieur de l'Égypte, soit à une autre tribu homonyme.
29 Ibn Iyās, I, p. 200, l. 12–14.
30 *Salūk*, I, I, p. 40–42; *Subḥ*, IV, p. 68, l. 1–9.
31 Ibn Iyās, I, p. 149, l. 9; p. 257, l. 12; p. 358,l. 19.
32 Ibn Iyās, II p. 38, l. 3–5; p. 379, l. 29. *Ḥawādīt*, p. 632, l. 13.
33 Ibn Iyās, II, p. 252, l. 3–7; V, p. 53, l. 21; p. 54, l. 2.
34 Ibn Iyās, II, p. 139, l. 5–6.
35 *Ḫiṭaṭ*, I. pp. 88, l. 37. *Ḥawādit̲*, p. 89, l. 7; p. 256, l. 13–17. Ibn Iyās, II, p. 49, l. 14; p. 149, l. 13–14; IV, p. 241, l. 11; p. 369, l. 16.
36 Ibn Iyās, II, p. 170, l. 20–29.
37 *Ḥawādit̲*, p. 109, l. 1–3; p. 110, l. 21.
38 *Ḥawādit̲*, p. 696, l. 1–3.
39 Ibn Iyās, I, p. 142, l. 20–27; p. 196, l. 10–11; p. 256, l. 19–22; p. 348, l. 1–2; II. p. 96, l. 9; p. 320, l. 21; p. 327, l. 15–16; p. 346, ll. 8–12; IV, p. 51, l. 19–21; p. 52, l. 14–19; p. 96, l. 12; p. 99, l. 12; p. 104, l. 19–20; p. 115, l. 20; p. 116, l. 8; p. 256; l. 12–23. Zetterstéen, p. 107, l. 10. *Ḥawādit̲*, p. 652, l. 3.
40 Ibn Iyās, I, p. 348, l. 1–2; II, p. 346, l. 8–12. *Ḥawādit̲*, p. 458, l. 21.
41 *Nujūm*, VII, p. 483, l. 18; p. 492, l. 18. Ibn Iyās 11, p. 134, l. 16; V, p. 80, 2–12.
42 *Ḥawādit̲*, p. 692, l. 3–4. Les bandits non protégés sortaient probablement du milieu des rebelles exaspérés.
43 Voir la relation du voyageur juif-italien Mešullam de Volterra, qui

visita l'Égypte et la Palestine en 1481 (en hébreu): J. D. Eisenstein, *Ozar Massaoth*, New-York, 1926, p. 97. Déjà au IX's., al-Jāḥiẓ signala cette supériorité des cavaliers turcs sur les Bédouins (*Mājmū'at rasā'il*, Ire édition, p. 28, l. 2).
44 Ibn Iyās, I, p. 249, l. 8; p. 250, l. 2.
45 Ibn Iyās, II, p. 58, l. 22–25; p. 135, l. 1–6; p. 154, l. 25. *Nujūm*, VII, p. 484, l. 1.
46 Ibn Iyās, II, p. 116, l. 12–15; p. 243, l. 23; IV, p. 52, l. 14; p. 451, l. 20–23.
47 Ibn Iyās, II, p. 357, l. 20; p. 358, l. 4.
48 Ibn Iyās, I, p. 250–252; II, p. 358, l. 5–18.
49 *Ḥawādiṯ*, p. 696, l. 5–7.
50 Pour cette considération économique Muḥammad ben Ḳalāun ne massacra pas tous les hérétiques Nuṣayris après la répression de leur révolte mahdiste.
51 Ibn Iyās, IV, p. 104, l. 18; p. 262, l. 15; p. 428, l. 4; V, p. 40, l. 7–8.
52 Ibn Iyās, I, p. 159, l. 1–2.
53 Ibn Iyās, I, p. 142, l. 20–27; p. 249, l. 8–29; II, p. 243, l. 23.
54 Zettersteen, p. 107, l. 8–20; Ibn Iyās, I, p. 142, l. 20–27; p. 249, l. 8–29; p. 256, l. 22; 11, p. 353, l. 18.
55 *Ḥawādiṯ*, p. 18. l. 5; p. 60, l. 16; *Sulūk*, II, I, p. 106. Le chef des Bédouins d'aš-Šarḳiya sous al-Ğaūrī se nommait Baybars ben Baḳar (Ibn Iyās, IV, p. 66, 72, 93, 270).
56 *Subḥ*, IV, p. 70, l. 10–12.
57 E. Quatremère supposa premièrement que cette dénomination se relate aux «Arabes» (Bédouins) ou aux Kurdes (*Sulūk*, I, I, p. 186–7, n. 65), ensuite qu'elle désigne spécialement les Druses (*Sulūk*, I, II, p. 273–4). En fait, elle est commune à tous les cultivateurs qui conservaient l'organisation tribale: les Druses, les Kurdes, les «ʿUrbān jabal Nāblus» (Ibn Iyās, II, p. 250. l. 20, lire «al-ʿUšrān» au lieu de «al-ʿasarāwāt»; p. 252, l. 17), les habitants de la province de Gaza (*Subḥ*, IV, p. 99, l. 1]).

Sur la dénomination d'«Al-ʿqšīr» par rapport aux «ʿUrbān jabal Nāblus» voir aussi: Ibn Iyās, II, p. 109, l. 18; p. 123, l. 27.
58 Ibn Iyās, II, p. 257, l. 11; IV, p. 51, l. 19–21; p. 52, l. 17; V, p. 21, l. 13.
59 *Sulūk*, I, II, p. 37, n. 44; p. 115; *Ḥawādiṯ*, p. 701, l. 7; p. 709, l. 8; Ibn Iyās, I, p. 329, l. 3; V. p. 8, l. 3; p. 88, l. 13–14; Gaudefroy-Demombynes, *La Syrie à l'époque des Mamelouks* (Paris, 1923), p. 111–12, n. 2,
60 *Sulūk*, II, I, p. 33.
61 *Sulūk*, II, I, p. 43.
62 *Nujūm*, VII, p. 142, l. 7; p. 296, l. 16.
63 Zettersteen, *Beiträge*, p. 81, l. 1–4. Comparer la version libanaise, citée par H. Lammens, dans *La Syrie* (Beyrouth, 1921).
64 Ibn Iyās, I, p. 169, l. 21; II, p. 157, l. 16.
65 *Sulūk*, I, II, p. 195–107. Ibn Iyās, I, p. 92, l. 11; p. 99, l. 20; p. 103, l. 15–19; p. 104, l. 3; II, p. 262, l. 3. Zettersteen, p. 44, l. 11. *Nujūm*, VI, p. 763, l. 11.
66 Au Jumādā II 891 de l'hégire, Ḳāītbāy voulut les employer dans la guerre contre les Ottomans, payant 30 dinars à chacun (Ibn Iyās, II,

p. 237, l. 9). Le 11 Dūl-ḳaʿda 922 de l'hégire, Ṭūmān bāy les amnistia et leur promit des soldes et des montures en cas de leur participation dans la défense de l'Égypte (Ibn Iyās, V, p. 117, l. 18–22).

67 Ibn Iyās, I, p. 220, l. 21.

68 Ibn Iyās, I, p. 223, l. 4, 8, 15.

69 Ibn Iyās, I, p. 240, l, 3.

70 Ibn Iyās, I, p. 278, l. 14–15.

71 Ibn Iyās, I, p. 224, l. 3; p. 246, l. 19; p. 311, l. 12; p. 320, l. 12–21. *Nujūm*, VII, p. 845, l. 7–14. Ibn Iyās fait appel au «fait étrange» que les az-zuʿr qui dominaient les rues de la capitale les jours du coup d'État des adhérents de Barḳūḳ, au commencement de Ṣafar 791, se contentérent de piller les maisons de émirs vaincus, sans attaquer aucun homme civil et sans voler même un dirhem de la population civile (I, p. 286, l. 8–15).

72 Ibn Iyās, I, p. 226, l. 3–13.

73 Ibn Iyās, II, p. 31, l. 28; p. 32, l. 3. *Najūm*, VII, p. 175, l. 3; p. 179, l. 6; p. 195, l. 15–17. *Ḥawādīt*, p. 47, l. 21; p. 88, l. 19.

74 Ibn Iyās, II, p. 210, l. 19.

75 Ibn Iyās, II, p. 258, l. 10–14. Les rebelles étaient sans doute, comme sous al-Ǧaūrī, des Locataires, desquels les propriétaires demandaient le paiement des loyers d'avance pour deux mois.

76 Ibn Iyās, IV, p. 18.

77 Les biens du ḳāḍī Abū l-ḫayr ben an-Naḥḥās furent confisqués par le sultan, et lui-même exilé; uš-Šīšī se vit obligé à se cacher et quitta ensuite le Caire pour la Mecque; al-Ǧaūrī se contenta des loyers pour sept mois.

78 Par exemple Ibn Iyās, IV, p. 305; IV, p. 16, l. 16–17; p. 327, l. 3–4; p. 430, l. 6–7.

79 Ibn Iyās, I, p. 282, l. 25; p. 283, l. 2.

80 Ibn Iyās, I, p. 287, l. 26; p. 292, l. 27; p. 293, l. 3; p. 294, l. 18–19, 21.

81 Ibn Iyās, I, p. 341, l. 3–4.

82 *Nujūm*, VI, p. 92, l. 19–22.

83 Ibn Iyās, II, p. 160, l. 16, IV, p. 88.

84 Ibn Iyās, II, p. 174, l. 6; IV, p. 94.

85 Ibn Iyās, V, p. 71, l. 23; p. 72, l. 5.

86 Le 7 Rajab 856 de l'hégire le sultan ordonna d'arrêter le Ḳāḍī mālikite (indigène) al-Walawi pour avoir condamné un marchand juif-circassien (c'est-à-dire natif de la patrie de la souche mamelouke la plus aristocratique) à la flagellation et à la prison (*Ḥawādiṯ*, p. 129, l. 19; p. 130, l. 8). Selon Ḳalkašandi (t. IV) la majorité des Circassiens à cette époque étaient des chrétiens (comparer *Ḥawādiṯ*, p. 601, l. 18).

87 *Nujūm*, VI, p. 400, l. 19–21; p. 559, l. 14; VII, p. 186, l. 9–10; p. 721, l. 7; p. 722, l. 12; *Sulūk*, I, II, p. 16, 154. Zetterstéen, p. 84, l. 21; p. 88, l. 2. Ibn Iyās, I, p. 104, l. 5–10; p. 143, l. 13–23; p. 201, l. 2–5; II, p. 249, l. 5; p. 302, l. 7; IV, p. 244, l. 12–18; p. 297. Voir aussi: *ṣubḥ*. XIII, pp. 377–387 (sur les ordres de 1301); Ibn Iyās, IV, p. 16 (sur une imposition au commencement du règne d'al-Ǧaūri).

88 *Sulūk*, I, I, 106–8; S. Rosanes, *Histoire des Israélites de Turquie* (en hébreu), I, éd. Tel Aviv, 1930, p. 177, 179.

89 Zettersteen, p. 81–92. La relation de l'historiographe juif du XVIIe siècle Šambarī (Ad. Neubauer, *Mediaeval Jewish Chronicles*, I, p. 135–7) contient beaucoup d'exagérations et d'inexactitudes: par exemple il y mentionne la destruction de l'église copte de Šubrā, qui n'eut lieu qu'en 759 de l'hégire (Ibn Iyās, I, p. 206–7). Sur la position des Coptes islamisés voir aussi *Nujūm* VI, pp. 398–400.

90 Zetterstéen, p. 83, l. 9–10. *Sulūk* II, I, p. 89. *Nujūm*, VI, p. 804, l. 16–20. Selon l'auteur juif ʻObadya di Bertinoro, la communauté samaritaine du Caire, affiliée à la Juive, était la partie la plus riche de la dernière. Sous al-Gaūrī le changeur des monnaies samaritain Yaʻḳūb al-Yahūdi était le directeur de l'Hôtel de la monnaie (Ibn Iyās, IV, p. 244. l. 12–18; p. 283; V, p. 78, l. 14. Voir aussi *ṣuhḥ*, XII, p. 403 (des formules spéciales pour les ordres de nomination des fonctionnaires samaritains à Damas). Quoique Yaʻḳūb al-Yahūdi ne soit pas signalé par Ibn Iyās comme Samaritain, un passage relatif à lui (IV, p. 214, l. 12–18), combiné avec le fait que malgré le témoignage d'ʻObadya di Bertinoro sur la richesse des Samaritains du Caire Ibn Iyās ne donne à aucun riche de son temps l'appellation d' «as-Sāmiri», rend l'origine samaritaine de Yaʻḳūb assez probable.

91 Ibn Iyās, V, p. 82, l. 9–10; p. 104, l. 19–22.

92 Selon Sambari, Ṭūmān bāy arma en 1516 12.000 esclaves au Caire (Rosanes, p. 178).

93 Par exemple *Ḥawādiṯ*, p. 19, l. 12.

94 Ibn Iyās, IV, p. 369, l. 17.

95 Volney, II, p. 50, sur la carrière d'Aḥmad-pacha al-Jazzār.

96 *Nujūm*, VI, p. 757, l. 9–21.

97 *Ḥawādiṯ*, p. 19, l. 11; p. 20, l. 6. Selon Ibn Iyās, II, p. 28, l. 19–29, cette révolte ent lieu en 846 de l'hégire.

98 *Ḥawādiṯ*, p. 63.

99 Ibn Iyās, II, p. 220, l. 28–30.

100 Ibn Iyās, II, p. 230, l. 6.

101 Ibn Iyās, II, p. 54, l. 10–13.

102 Ibn Iyās, II, p. 158, l. 11–13.

103 Ibn Iyās, IV, p. 178, 313, 416. Voir aussi: Ibn Iyās, p. 363, l. 10, p. 415, l. 22–23; p. 444, l. 8.

16

LE CARACTÈRE COLONIAL DE L'ÉTAT MAMELOUK DANS SES RAPPORTS AVEC LA HORDE D'OR

A.N. Poliak

I

La Mort Noire, quis selon l'avis du continuateur du *«ta'rīḫ d'Abū l-fidā'»* Ibn al-Wardī, commença à dévaster l'Extrême-Orient vers 734 de l'hégire (1334), après avoir passé par la Chine et l'Inde parvint en 747 au «pays d'Uzbek».[1] Dans la même année elle passa en Crimée, et des marchands alépins, venus de là, racontèrent à Ibn al-Wardī que le nombre des morts identifiés s'y était élevé selon le recensement officiel à 85,000. De la Crimée l'épidémie se tourna vers le Sud, et après avoir dévasté les stations de la voie maritime (l'Asie Mineure, l'Archipel et l'île de Chypre) parvint à l'Égypte en 749 (1348), y faisant un carnage énorme (selon Ibn Iyās, deux mois apportèrent plus de 900,000 morts), l'épidémie ne tarda point à s'abattre sur La Mecque d'un côté, sur Gaza de l'autre. De Gaza elle monta vers le Nord, s'avançant par le littoral (Acre, Saïda) jusqu'à Beyrouth, et par les voies de l'intérieur à Jérusalem, à Damas, à Baalbek, à Homs, à Ma'arrat an-Nu'mān et à Antioche. En Rajab de la même année Ibn al-Wardī priait Dieu de la défendre, contre la peste arrivée à Alep. Il avait encore le temps de consacrer un nécrologe à Šihāb ad-dīn al-'Umarī, l'auteur d' «at-ta'rīf» et de «masālik al-abṣār», qui succomba à Damas en du l-ḥijja.[2]

Source: *Revue des Études Islamiques*, 1935, vol. 22, pp. 231–48.

L'itinéraire de la Mort Noire en 747–9 de l'hégire nous permet de rétablir la carte des principales voies de commerce du Proche-Orient au XIVe siècle, après les changements causés par les invasions mongoles. Quoique la conquête mongole n'ait pas entraîné immédiatement une décadence complète de Bagdad,[3] sa position de centre du commerce oriental fut gravement atteinte par la création d'un nouvel intermédiaire entre l'Asie Centrale et les contrées méditerranéennes, la *Horde d'Or.* C'est par cette nouvelle route que l'État Mamelouk reçut la majorité de sa classe dominante. Selon al-Ḳalḳašandī[4] sous les premiers sultans mamelouks les membres de cette classe provenaient en majorité d'al-Ḳabjāḳ) (Ḳipčāḳ), terme sous lequel il désigne la Horde d'Or; selon al-Māḳrīzī[5] ils venaient particulièrement du Turkestan.[6] Les deux textes sont conciliables si, premièrement, nous remarquons que la Horde d'Or tenait une partie du Turkestan (le Khuwarezm septentrional et les steppes du Nord) sous sa domination, – et que pour cette cause elle est désignée par al-Ḳalḳašandī aussi sous le nom de «mamlakat Tūrān-Ḫuwārazm wa-l-Ḳabjāḳ», – et si deuxièmement, nous admettons que les Mamelouks d'origine turkestanienne étaient recrutés pour l'Égypte non pas dans leur patrie lointaine mais dans les villes de la Horde d'Or sur le bas Volga. La dépendance de l'État Mamelouk de l'importation régulière des Mamelouks de la Horde d'Or était tellement grande qu'elle entraîna une vassalité politique officielle: selon al-Makrīzī[7] le nom d'un souverain de la Horde d'Or Berke-Ḫān ben Jučī, était mentionné dans le sermon de vendredi (ḫuṭba) dans tous les domaines des Mamelouks. On doit envisager les hostilités entre Baybars I et les Mongols iraniens comme les épisodes de la lutte menée contre ces derniers, par Berke[8] et les militaires venus de la Horde d'Or à l'Égypte sous Baybars I et acceptés dans l'armée mamelouke (al-wāfidīya) – comme des renforts fournis par Berke à son vassal. Leur nombre était assez grand: 200 cavaliers en 1262,[9] 1300 en 1263,[10] des renforts additionnés en 1264.[11] Les Turcomans de la province d'Alep se vantaient encore au XVe siècle d'être «de la pure origine ḳipčaḳienne».[12] Cependant dans leur grande majorité les «Turcs» venaient à l'État Mamelouk non pas comme des militaires libres mais comme des esclaves achetés (probablement très souvent de leur bon gré) dans les domaines de la Horde d'Or et transportés des ports de la Crimée à l'Égypte, y achetés par le sultan ou par des émirs, chez lesquels ils recevaient pendant quelques années l'instruction militaire et ensuite, ayant reçu les chevaux, les habits militaires et les armes (ḫayl wa-ḳumāš wa-silāḥ), restaient au service de leurs maitres à titre de leurs affranchis (maʿātīḳ).[13] Je crois que leurs vendeurs étaient assez souvent leurs propres pères ou chefs de famille: il y a des documents sur des ventes semblables dans le Turkestan de l'Est au XIIIe siècle;[14] et encore le premier gouverneur de l'Égypte sous la domination ottomane, Ḫayr bēk, fut donné par son père au sultan mamelouk Ḳāīt bāy comme un présent.[15] Il est difficile de dire dans quelle proportion les divers peuples qui habitent maintenant les parties méridionales de l'U. R. S. S. participaient à cette migration pendant la première période de l'État Mamelouk. Les Russes y étaient représentés aussi.[16] Il semble que deux appellations topographiques dans les environs de Caïffa, Wādī 't-Tatar et Nabʿat al-Ḳazaḳ, ne peuvent dater que de l'époque mamelouke.[17] La deuxième nous fait penser à ces aventuriers et vagabonds tatares et slaves qui erraient alors dans les steppes au Nord de la Mer Noire et dont le nom passa aux Cosaques postérieurs. Ces aventuriers participaient sans doute dans une certaine mesure à l'émigration à l'État Mamelouk qui, jusqu'aux jours de Barḳūḳ pouvait leur promettre les plus hautes destinées.[18] Les éléments mongols s'infiltraient dans cet État aussi de la frontière Est, grâce aux captifs de guerre[19] et aux émirs qui passaient du service du sultan mongol de l'Iran à celui du sultan mamelouk.[20] Le plus grand événement de ce genre fut la venue d'une tribu de Kalmouks, composée de 10,000 hommes, en 1296.[21] Les notables (dont le nombre s'éleva à 113 selon une version, à 300 selon l'autre) reçurent des grades militaires et des fiefs en Égypte, et se fixèrent dans le quartier d'al-Ḥusaynīya au Caire; les autres reçurent 1000 petits fiefs dans la province de Damas et continuèrent à nomadiser sur le littoral palestinien et dans al-Biḳāʿ. Diminués par une émigration additionnelle en Égypte, ils finirent probablement par l'assimilation avec leurs voisins Arabes et Turcomans.

L'étude de tous les résultats de l'influence de la Horde d'Or et du Turkestan sur la vie sociale et culturelle de l'État Mamelouk nous amènerait trop loin, et nous n'en résumerons ici que les principaux:

a) La loi séculaire de l'État Mamelouk, as-siyāsa (selon al-Maḳrīzī une forme altérée du mot mongol yāsa au yasaḳ), basée sur les lois de Čingiz-Ḫān.[22] Cette loi réglait les relations intérieures des membres de la classe dominante des Turcs, tandis que la loi musulmane (aš-šarāʿa) réglait la vie des indigènes, des citoyens du deuxième ordre. Même les marchands étrangers favorisés jouissaient du droit de ne pas être jugés selon la loi musulmane: en 753 de l'hègire ce droit fut accordé aux marchands persans,[23] et sous les sultans Circassiens même les marchands juifs (et sans doute leurs confrères chrétiens (nàtifs de la Circassie) ne devaient pas être jugés selon la loi musulmane dans leurs contestations avec les indigènes musulmans).[24] Les juges séculiers, al-ḥujjāb ou ḥukkām aš-šurṭa,[25] étaient critiques, quand ils se permettaient de rendre des jugements selon les termes de la loi musulmane.[26] Le côté curieux de cet état de choses était que le sultan mamelouk selon la théorie officielle n'était rien moins que le chef suprême des Musulmans; auquel un khalife fantôme – dont les titres généalogiques n'étaient peut-être pas plus véridiques que ceux des Fāṭimites[27] – déléguait toutes ses fonctions.[28]

b) Le dialecte turc des Mamelouks (al-luġa(t)at-Turkīya des sources arabes). Il était la langue officielle des conseils des émirs[29] et le parler commun pour les Mamelouks d'origine diverse, qui habituellement prenaient aussi des noms turcs. Un fonctionnaire en quête d'honneurs devait aussi savoir la langue des maîtres,[30] tandis que savoir lire et écrire en arabe n'était pas indispensable pour un vizir indigène.[31] Des sultans «détestaient ceux qui portent les noms des prophètes et des amis de Mahomet, et leur préféraient ceux qui portent les noms des Mamelouks»;[32] par conséquent un émir bédouin, un chérif de la Mecque ou un autre chef indigène qui voulait plaire à ses maîtres portait un nom turc.[33] Un «Turc» moyen pouvait ne pas savoir l'arabe du tout,[34] et les sultans le savaient parfois fort peu,[35] malgré leur séjour prolongé en Égypte. Ce dialecte turc et sa littérature[36] mériteraient d'être l'object d'études spéciales, et nous nous contentons ici de remarquer que: 1e: il était profondément imbu d'éléments persans. La plupart des termes techniques étrangers (par rapport aux hauts emplois de l'État, aux habits, aux sports) acceptés à cette époque dans la langue arabe littéraire de l'Égypte sont des mots persans. Dans la langue parlée le nombre des mots persans devait être encore plus grand, vu que nous trouvons dans les sources des mots persans isolés non accompagnés d'explication.[37] L'intermédiaire entre le persan et l'arabe était le «turc»; 2e: vraisemblablement ce dialecte était au commencement une branche de la langue des Turcomans (Guzz) de l'Asie Centrale, qui était, à la veille de la conquête mongole, le parler dominant du Khuwarezm.[38] Al-Maḳrīzī distingue entre al-luġa(t) at-Turkīya et la langue de Ḳipčaḳ.[39] Les fugitifs Khuwarezmiens, – qui, en Égypte participaient, dans le corps des Baḥrites qui devint le noyau de l'armée mamelouke,[40] et en Syrie formaient entre 634–644 de l'hégire un corps séparé de mercenaires et ensuite passèrent individuellement au service des princes locaux,[41] – consolidèrent la position dominante de leur dialecte, raffermie ensuite par l'immigration des Mamelouks turkestaniens de la Horde d'Or. Sous les sultans Circassiens ce dialecte put subir une évolution particulière à lui: Ibn Iyās, qui continue après la conquête ottomane à n'user de l'appellation de «Turcs» que par rapport à l'ancienne classe dominante de l'Égypte, parfois désigne les conquérants sous celle de «Turcomans», ce qui peut signifier que leur langue parlée, étant plus purement turque que celle des Mamelouks, semblait à ces derniers plus archaïque.

c) Les principes fondamentaux de la féodalité mamelouke. Le signe extérieur de l'influence mongole était le fait que les contestations relatives aux fiefs (iḳṭā'āl) étaient portées devant les juges séculiers[42] et non pas devant les Ḳāḍīs, c'est-à-dire décidées selon *as-siyāsa* et non pas selon *aš-šari'q*. Toutes les sources mameloukes publiées jusqu'à maintenant sont en arabe et non en «turc», et par conséquent il est difficile à dire si les termes techniques que nous y trouvons étaient usités dans la langue des maitres ou seulement dans celle des indigènes, si la différence entre leur signification sous les Khalifes et à l'époque mamelouke est due à une évolution locale, ou s'ils étaient usités chez les écrivains de cette époque simplement comme des traductions plus ou moins exactes des termes turco-mongols.[43] En tout cas le ḫarāj mamelouk correspond plutôt au «kalan», les fermages des terres cultivées qui étaient payés aux féodaux dans tous les Etats mongols de l'Asie Antérieure,[44] qu'à son ancien homonyme.[45] Les relations agraires dans la Horde d'Or ne sont pas encore suffisamment explorées, mais celles qui existaient dans son autre État feudataire (et ensuite héritier), la Moskovie, accusent de remarquables rapprochements avec celles de l'État Mamelouk. Nous y retrouvons l'institution des fiefs viagers,[46] dont la mesure dépend du grade militaire des feudataires; l'accompagnement de ces fiefs par la solde pécuniaire; l'obligation des feudataires à veiller à la culture des terres; les fiefs concédés aux gouverneurs locaux pour le temps de leur service.[47] Il semble que l'idée de la répartition périodique des terres cultivées entre le sultan et les féodaux (rawk) fut aussi importée dans l'État Mamelouk par la Horde d'Or. Les détails de cette répartition, comme l'indique déjà son appellation,[48] étaient copiés des usages de la répartition des terres communes entre les fellāḥs dans les villages locaux:[49]

a) Les terres sont premièrement mesurées et évaluées de nouveau, et divisées en portions, dont les possesseurs ne sont pas encore fixés.

b) Ensuite vient la loterie publique de ces portions: les lots (sur lesquels elles sont désignées) sont tirés du sac par une personne dont la probité est indubitable (dans les villages par de petits enfants, en cas du rawk par le Sultan – ou par son représentant – qui tend le lot à l'un des feudataires sans le lire.[50] Le receveur n'a pas de droit de se plaindre de «ce que Dieu lui alloua» ni de demander une rectification.[51]

c) Si dans un village cohabitent plusieurs grandes familles (ḥamūlāt), chacune est autorisée d'avance à une partie fixée de la superficie totale, souvent exprimée par un nombre de ḳīrāṭs (ḳīrāṭ = 1/24); de même pour un rawk, le nombre des ḳīrāṭs alloués au Sultan, aux émirs et aux membres d'al-ḥalḳa était fixé d'avance.[52]

d) Dans les villages la portion reçue par chaque fellāḥ est répartie dans plusieurs lieux afin qu'elle contienne toutes les espèces de terres locales; de même le fief d'un militaire égyptien était réparti dans plusieurs villages situés dans les provinces diverses de l'Égypte, et celui d'un Syrien dans les parties diverses de sa province (mamlaka).[53] Mais si les *détails* du rawk étaient copiés par les fonctionnaires indigènes des usages de la communauté villageoise locale, et si les sultans l'utilisaient comme une arme de lutte contre les féodaux, néanmoins le simple fait que nous ne retrouvons pas le rawk des fiefs dans l'histoire antérieure de l'Égypte (quand la classe dominante n'était pas si isolée des indigènes comme à l'époque mamelouke) semble indiquer que l'*idée* de la répartition périodique les fiefs fut amenée par les «Turcs» de dehors. Ici encore nous trouvons en Moskovie une chose pareille, justement pendant les premières années après l'annexion des pays tatars sur le Volga, accompagnée par l'acceptation d'une partie considérable des féodaux locaux dans la noblesse moskovite. Vers 1556, les fiefs militaires furent réorganisés pour adapter la mesure de chacun au grade militaire de feudataire et au nombre des soldats fournis par lui en cas de guerre.[54] En 1564, le czar divisa l'État en deux parties: les terres de l'une[55] il les assigna à l'entretien de sa Cour et aux fiefs de ses courtisans, et les terres de l'autre furent réparties de nouveau entre les militaires.[56] On peut espérer que les recherches sur les relations agraires dans l'Empire Mongol permettront un jour d'éclairer complètement ces problèmes.

II

Il semble presque certain que l'exécution des éléments turcs dans l'État Mamelouk à la fin du XIVe siècle fut causé par les guerres de Tamerlan contre la Horde d'Or, qui entraînèrent la décadence de la route commerciale allant du Turkestan à la Horde d'Or. Peut-être que déjà pendant le déclin des villes de la Horde d'Or dans la deuxième moitié de ce siècle, causé par les guerres des féodaux[57] et par les effets de la Mort Noire,[58] les marchands avaient commencé de parer à la diminution des Mamelouks turkestaniens par les achats de Circassiens et d'autres habitants du Caucase occidental.[59] Ce changement fut d'autant plus facile qu'encore al-Ḳalḳašandī[60] considéra la Circassie comme une province de la Horde d'Or, et que cette province était plus proche des ports de la Crimée que la capitale. La cessation complète (ou presque complète) de l'importation des Mamelouks turkestaniens depuis les guerres de Tamerlan entraîna un changement non seulement dans la composition ethnique des «Turcs» égypto-syriens mais encore dans leur régime social et politique. «Barḳūḳ et ses successeurs jusqu'à nos jours ont complètement renversé le régime de l'État, en préférant leurs compatriotes aux autres, en concédant les grands fiefs à leurs parents, des jeunes hommes nouvellement venus, et en nommant ceux-ci aux hauts emplois. C'est la cause prinipale du déclin de l'État et le contraire de l'usage des rois antérieurs, qui ne faisaient pas attention à la question de nationalité, mais avançaient et honoraient celui qui se distinguait par de nobles qualités ou par le courage.»[61] Si pendant la première période de l'État Mamelouk théoriquement chaque Mamelouk pouvait devenir le sultan, maintenant les principaux emplois et fiefs étaient généralement tenus par un petit cercle, dont les membres étaient unis par les liens nationaux et familiaux et par la qualification religieuse commune de renégat, tel est le sens de l'indication des voyageurs européens que seul un ex-chrétien pouvait devenir le sultan.[62] Les sultans mamelouks souvent envoyaient des ambassades spéciales à la Circassie pour en amener leurs parents, et à leur arrivée leur facilitaient une élévation rapide.[63] Particulièrement le sultan Ḳāītbāy était entouré d'émirs liés à lui par des liens familiaux qui remontaient au Caucase.[64] Vu que les sultans et les émirs Mamelouks se liaient par des mariages aux familles principales de la Circassie,[65] et sans doute aidaient à leurs parents restés dans la patrie, on peut croire que pratiquement en Circassie et dans l'État Mamelouk le pouvoir était entre les mains du même groupe. Ce groupe est désigné dans les sources mameloukes sous le nom d'al-ḳarānīṣ ou d'al-ḳarāniṣa, au singulier ḳirnāṣ.[66] Al-ḳarānīṣ étaient représentés dans les degrés variés de la hiérarchie militaire, mais partout ils jouissaient d'une considération plus grande que leurs camarades et même supérieurs, et étaient les premiers candidats pour un avancement. Par exemple, le sultan futur Ṭaṭar fut recommandé par un émir au sultan comme un ḳirnāṣ quand il était encore un Mamelouk non affranchi.[67] Il y avaient aussi des ḳarānīṣ parmi al-mamālik as-sulṭanīya, c'est-à-dire les Mamelouks affranchis qui étaient au service du saltan.[68] Un petit corps particulier formait «al-ajnād al-ḳarānīṣ», candidats à l'émirat[69] et possesseurs de fiefs (arzāḳ) considérables, dont le rang social était semblable à celui des «émirs de cinq».[70] Ce Corps était composé des gens qui s'étaient fixés dans l'État Mamelouk depuis longtemps, mais naturellement ils y avaient des ḳarānīṣ aussi parmi al-julbān, les Mamelouks nouvellement venus.[71] Il va sans dire qu'ils étaient représentés parmi les émirs, et ici encore c'était l'appartenance à cette noblesse qui, plus que le grade militaire, déterminait le position sociale d'un émir: le gouverneur de Jérusalem Ḫušḳadam as-sayfī (mourut en 853 de l'hég.) malgré son courage «n'appartenait pas aux notables et à ceux qui sont les chefs de ses compatriotes»,[72] tandis qu'un simple militaire (jundī), Lājīn (mourut en 804 de l'hég.) était considéré par les Circassiens (même les émirs) comme un candidat certain au sultanat.[73] Pour jouir d'une haute considération un ḳirnāṣ n'était pas obligé à porter des beaux habits et à monter des belles montures, et beaucoup d'entre eux mettaient un point d'honneur à se distinguer par des habits sales et usés.[74] Je ne connais aucun cas où un créole (ibin an-nās) soit cité comme ḳirnāṣ. Il est intéressant à noter qu'encore chex al-Jabartī, très influencé par le langage des sources mameloukes, nous trouvons le mot al-ḳarāniṣa dans le sens de «hauts émirs».[75] De même qu'ils formaient l'aristocratie des Circassiens, les Circassiens formaient l'aristocratie des «Turcs» parmi lesquels le pourcentage d'autres peuples était considérable.[76]

On peut envisager l'État Mamelouk comme l'empire colonial des féodaux et des marchands des pays au Nord de la mer Noire, dans le sens dans lequel on peut envisager les États Francs en

Syrie comme un empire colonial des féodaux et des marchands de l'Europe occidentale, c'est-à-dire sans cette dépendance administrative directe qui caractérise les empires coloniaux de nos jours. Pendant la première période, les féodaux et les marchands du métropole étaient organisés dans un État uni, la Horde d'Or. Pendant la deuxième période, à la tête de l'élément féodal étaient al-ḳarānīṣ Circassiens, et à la tête de l'élément mercantile les marchands de la Crimée. Les deux éléments étaient parfois liés par des liens familiaux.[77] Dans leur empire colonial commun, le lot des féodaux était: *a)* les fermages des fellāḥs; *b)* les impôts et les revenus des monopoles sultaniens, répartis entre les «Turcs» sous la forme de la solde pécuniaire (jāmakīya) et des payements extraordinaires (nafaḳa); *c)* le commerce de céréales à l'intérieur de l'Égypte et leur exportation en Syrie[78] et au Hedjaz;[79] *d)* d'autres branches du commerce et de l'industrie, liées le plus étroitement à l'agriculture; *e)* seulement à la fin de l'époque mamelouke, l'importation des Mamelouks.[80] La sphère d'influence des marchands, défendus contre la concurrence des indigènes par un régime de capitulations (basé sur «as-siyāsa»), était le commerce extérieur de l'État Mamelouk. Ce commerce devait généralement se balancer avec un déficit énorme pour l'État Mamelouk et un excédent correspondant pour la métropole. Vis-à-vis des sommes énormes dépensées annuellement pour les achats des Mamelouks, des fourrures (sous les sultans circassiens un élément presque indispensable des habits de fête, même en été), et même de la production industrielle de la métropole (encore sous al-Ġawrī nous trouvons souvent l'épithète «kafawī», de Caffa, par rapport aux vêtements), l'État Mamelouk n'avait aucun objet d'exportation propre à les contre-balancer. On peut douter si le commerce entre l'Inde et l'Europe servait d'antidote contre cet épuisement: 1e Une partie considérable des marchandises indiennes était consommée par l'État Mamelouk lui-même et non pas réexportée en Égypte; 2e Ibn Iyās, un écrivain qui nous fait connaitre les pensées des Cairotes de fortune moyenne, ne perçut aucune conséquence négative de la découverte de la voie maritime de l'Europe à l'Inde en dehors de la disparition des habits féminins (ʿuzur) et des turbans (šāšāt) de provenance indienne.[81] Et même cette conséquence unique était due plutôt à la rigidité des douaniers mamelouks à Djedda[82] qu'aux attaques des corsaires portugais contre les navires de commerce musulmans. Par conséquent, on ne doit pas exagérer le rôle du commerce indien dans la vie économique de l'Égypte; 3e Les grands marchands «kāremites» réalisaient sans doute des profits considérables, même après l'établissement de l'hégémonie portugaise dans l'Océan Indien;[83] mais c'est une autre question, celle de savoir dans quelle mesure les indigènes participaient à ce commerce et dans quelle mesure ses profits restaient dans l'État Mamelouk.

Il est difficile de douter que cet état de choses fût la cause principale de la grande crise économique des années 790–810 de l'hégire, dont le motif immédiat fut la disparition du métal d'argent nécessaire pour frapper les dirhems. Al-Ḳalḳašandī[84] explique cette disparition par la cessation de l'importation de l'argent de l'Europe et par sa consommation intensive par les artisans. A ce dernier motif, on peut ajouter la thésaurisation de grandes quantités des dirhems par les riches; mais enfin le Sultan, de son côté, confisquait sans cesse les argenteries et les trésors cachés par les riches et les envoyait de nouveau au Trésor et à l'Hôtel de la monnaie. On ne pouvait trouver un remède plus efficace contre l'exportation des pièces d'argent non compensée par leur importation, c'est-à-dire contre la passivité du commerce extérieur.[85] Les symptômes principaux de cette grande crise furent la hausse des prix de la production agricole de 300–400 0/0,[86] la hausse des fermages des terres cultivées (ḫarāj) en Basse-Égypte de 1,000–1,250 0/0,[87] et la dévaluation métallique du dirhem, qui à la fin de l'époque mamelouke n'était plus qu'une monnaie de cuivre.[88]

Dans l'administration intérieure de l'État Mamelouk son caractère colonial, souligné encore par la crainte constante d'une révolution bédouine se faisait sentire principalement par un renforcement sévère de la supériorité des «Turcs» sur les indigènes. Dans «l'armée victorieuse» (al-jayš al-manṣūr) des «Turcs», les émirs d'origine arabe n'étaient que de rares exceptions. Les chefs des tribus kurdes et turcomanes en Syrie pouvaient obtenir tout au plus le grade d' «émir aṭ-ṭablaḫāna»,[89] mais sans être égaux aux émirs «Turcs» des même grades, ce qui était souligné même par la forme extérieure de leurs diplômes féodaux (manāšīr).[90] C'était aussi le cas des chefs des tribus agricoles ('ašīr) syro-palestiniennes: le représentant le plus considérable de la famille de Ṣaliḥ Ibn Yaḥyā, Nāṣir Yaḥya-ad-dīn «al-kabīr», n'était qu' «émir de vingt»,[91] et Ṣāliḫ décerne l'épithète d' «émir» à tous ses proches qui n'étaient que des ajnad al-ḥalḳa.[92] Seulement un membre de cette famille fut émir aṭ-ṭablaḫāna, pendant une année.[93] Le plus grand féodal libanais au moment d'arrawk an-nāṣirī, ʿAlī Ibn Ṣubḥ, était émir aṭ-ṭablaḫāna.[94] En Égypte, les simples cheikhs bédouins étaient des membres d'al-ḥalḳa;[95] sur les grades des émirs bédouins de l'Éypte nous ne sommes pas informés. Généralement, on peut dire que le plus haut grade militaire, celui d' «émir de cent (Mamelouks) et commandant de mille (chevaliers d'al-ḥalḳa)», restait inaccessible pour les indigènes et difficile d'accès pour les créoles, et que les chefs des troupes auxiliaires indigènes pouvaient aspirer tout au plus à celui d'émir aṭ-ṭablaḫāna (normalement = de 40 Mamelouks).

NOTES

1 Bilād Uzbek = la Horde d'Or (du nom d'Uzbek-Khan, dont le règne fut l'apogée de sa prospérité).

2 Abū l-Fidāʿ, *Taʾrīh*, éd. 1286 de l'hég., IV, p. 150, l. 15–20; p. 156, l. 13, p. 158, l. 9; p. 159, l. 26–30. *Subḫ al-aʿšā*, XIII, p. 79, 1. 3–5. Ibn Iyās, I, pp. 191–2, Ṣāliḥ Ibn Yaḥyā, 2ᵉ éd., p. 137, l. 16–17.

3 Ibn Tağrī Birdī attribue cette décadence à la domination des rois turcomans au xvᵉ siècle (*Nujūm*, VI, p. 416, l. 1–4). Généralement l'effet destructif des invasions étrangères sur les grandes villes orientales à cette époque fut exagéré de beaucoup par des écrivains tendancieux ou postérieurs. Damas se révolta contre le gouverneur mamelouk une année après son occupation par Tamerlan. L'affirmation d'al-Jabartī (I. p. 20, l. 32–33) que Sélim I causa la cessation de plus de 50 métiers au Caire par l'exil des artisans à Istanbul est due à un malentendu: le texte correspondant d'Ibn Iyās (V, p. 203, l. 16) relate une interruption passagère pendant les jours troublés du séjour de Sélim I au Caire. Après la mort de Sélim I tous les Égyptiens exilés (hormis les militaires) durent retourner dans leur patrie sous peine de mort (Ibn Iyās, V, p. 389, l. 19; p. 393, l. 1–2).

4 *Ṣubḫ*, IV, p. 458, l. 5.

5 *Ḫiṭaṭ*, I, p. 95, l. 4.

6 Bilād at-Turk. La désignation officielle de l'État Mamelouk était ad-dawla at-Turkiya ou dawlat al-Atrāk («l'État des Turcs»). L'Asie Mineure fut désignée par Ibn Tağrī Birdī sous le nom d 'at-Turkiya, par les autres auteurs mamelouks sous celui d'ar-Rūm.

7 *Ḫiṭaṭ*, II, p. 221, l. 17–18. Probablement le nom d'un fils de Baybars I, Baraka (= Berke) Ḫān, lui fut donné comme un hommage au suzerain mongol.

Selon le manuscrit d'al-Kutubī cité par Barthold (*12 Vorlesungen über die Geschichte der Türken Mittelasiens*, p. 176), parmi al-wāfidiya venus à l'Égypte se trouvait le fils de Berke, Muḥammad, oncle maternel de Berke-Ḫān égyptien. L'absence du nom de Berke b. Jūči sur les pièces monétaires frappées par Báybars I s'explique par le fait que Berke lui-même frappait la monnaie non pas avec son nom mais avec celui de l'empereur mongol, et n'était pas soucieux d'agrandir la zone d'influence de celui-ci (d'ailleurs les noms des khans mongols devaient être écrits en lettres ouïgoures, inconnues dans l'Hôtel de la monnaie au Caire).

8 Voir l'article sur Berke dans l'*Encylopédie de l'slam.*

9 *Sulūk de Makrīzī-Quatremère*, I, I, p. 180.

10 *Sulūk*, I, I, p. 221–222.

11 *Sulūk*, I, I, p. 241. Comp. *Sulūk*, I, II, p. 23; *Ḫiṭaṭ*, II, p. 221, l. 17; Zetterstéen, *Beiträge zur Geschichte der Mamlūken sultane*, p. 29, l. 15–19.

12 *Ṣubḥ*, XIII, p. 37, l. 7.

13 En cas de Mamelouks du sultan, ceux qui recevaient encore l'instruction dans les casernes ṭibāḳ, sing. ṭabaḳa) de la citadelle du Caire étaient appelés al-mamālīk al-kitābiya, une promotion ḫarj, les affranchis simplement al-mamālīk as-sulṭāniya.

14 Voir l'article (en russe) de S. E. Malov, *Ouïgourskié roukopisnié dokoumenti (Zapiski institouta vostokoviedeniya Akademii Naouk*, 1, p. 132–133).

15 Voir sa biographie: Ibn Iyās, V, p. 199, l. 18; p. 200, l. 8; p. 478, l. 18; p. 479, l. 6.

16 *Ṣubḥ*, IV, p. 182, l, 11; p. 216, l. 14. Comp. le nom de l'émir mamelouk Baybuğā Rūs ou Baybuğā Urūs (tué en 1353; les données biographiques sur lui ont été collectées par L.A. Mayer, *Saracenic heraldry*, Oxford, 1933, p. 111).

17 *Zeitschrift des deutschen Palāstina-Vereins*, 1908, pp. 14, 20. La conservation des noms topographiques nombreux dans cette région depuis l'époque mamelouke est prouvée par la comparaison de la liste dans *Ṣubḥ*, XIV, p. 55, l. 18; p. 56, l. 1 avec la carte dans *ZDPV*., 1980, p. 258, où nous retrouvons ad-Dāliya, al-Karak, ad-Damūn (*sic*, lire ainsi au lieu d'ar-Rāmūn dans le texte arabe), Lūbiya, Ḫirbat Yūnus, Rušmiya, aṭ-Ṭira (*Ṣubḥ*, XIV, p. 55, l. 12–14), al-Manṣūra et al-Harāmīs (*Sulūk*, II, 1. p. 181).

18 Les Cosaques sont désignés dans les sources russes anciennes aussi sous le nom de Čerkasi, ce qui nous fait penser soit au nom ethnique des Circassiens en cas où il était une désignation générale des Mamelouks (chez Ibn Iyās, après la conquête ottomane), soit au mot jārkas ou jarkas, utilisé par les Mamelouks comme un nom personnel, dont le sens fut selon *al-Manhal aṣ-sāfī* d'Ibn Tagri Birdī, II (Ms. de Paris 2069), feuille 173, p. 1, «[l'homme qui possède] quatre âmes» = un brave.

19 Le sultan Katbuğā était un prisonnier de guerre tatar. Comp. *Ḫiṭaṭ*, II, p. 221, l. 16, sur la bataille d'ʿAyn Jālūt.

20 Zetterstéen, p. 128, l. 20–24; p. 132, l. 6–12; p. 195, l. 17; p. 196, l. 6; p. 197, l. 6. Il y avait aussi une migration contraire.

21 *Ḫiṭaṭ*, II, p. 22, l. 14; p. 23, l. 13. Abū-l-fidā, *Taʾriḫ*, IV, p. 34, l. 23; p. 35, l. 1. Zetterstéen p. 38, l. 15; p. 39, l. 1; p. 58, l. 2–4. *al-Manhal aṣ-ṣāfī* III (Ms. de Paris 2070), f. 182, p. 2, l. 21–22 f. 189, p. 1. l. 5. Le nom que les sources leur donnent, al-Uwayrātīya (vocalisation d'après Zetterstéen), écrit avec un ʾalif (*Ḫiṭaṭ, al-Manhal aṣ-ṣāfī*) ou un ʿayn (Abū l-fidāʾ, Zetterstéen) au commencement, = «les Oīrates», l'ancienne appellation des Kalmouks, maintenant prise par les tribus

turques d'Altaï pour elles-mèmes. Leur chef était marié à une petite-fille de Hūlāgu.

22 *Ḫiṭaṭ*, II, p. 219, l. 28; p. 222, l. 10.

23 *Ḫiṭaṭ*, II, p. 222, l. 4–10.

24 Ibn Taǧrī Birdī, *Hawādit* (éd. Popper), p. 129, l. 19; p. 130, l. 8.

25 Cette fonction était tantôt déléguée à un émir spécial, tantôt remplie par le gouverneur local. La fonction du juge séculier suprème (ḥājib al-hujbāb) fut séparée de celle du vice-sultan de l'Égypte en 746 de l'hégire (*Ḥiṭaṭ*, II, p. 221, l. 37. A Jérusalem jusqu'en 860 de l'hég.; c'était un ḥajib particulier; depuis cette année ses fonctions furent rattachées à celles du gouverneur (*Majīr ad-dīn*, p. 616, l. 5–15.

26 Abū l-fidā' IV, p. 105, l. 28–29.

27 Abū l-fidā' III, p. 224, l. 13. Un «Abbasside» si douteux était absolument entre les mains de son maitre le sultan.

28 Par conséquent le sultan mamelouk était «sulṭan al-lslām» et juridiquement, le seul prince autorisé à s'appeler sultan (*aẓ-Ẓāhirī*, p. 89, l. 13). Depuis l'avènement d'al-Mu'ayyad Šayḫ le nom du khalife n'était plus mentionné dans le sermon de vendredi, et l'on faisait seulement une allusion brève au «Khalife» ou au «Khalifat abbasside» sans la préciser (*al-Manhal aṣ-Ṣāfi*, IV (Ms. de Paris 2071), f. 14, l. 18–22). Au même temps le sultan mamelouk était considéré comme le chef religieux suprême par les Isma'ilites syriens, en sa qualité d'héritier des Fāṭimites (*Ṣubh*, XIII, p. 245, l. 18–21). Le drapeau jaune des sultans, c'est peut-être le symbole officiel des Isma'ilites (*Ṣubḥ*, XIII, p. 247, l. 5; p. 248, l. 1–2), accepté par Saladin pour se concilier les adhérents des Fāṭimites. Dans les documents du gouvernement mamelouk, les Isma'ilites syriens portent l'appellation de «combattants de la guerre sainte», al-mujāhidūn (*Ṣubḥ*, VII, p. 228, l. 16–18).

Il semble que l'autorite du Khalife égyptien ne fut jamais reconnue par les Ottomans; au moins je ne connais aucun cas d'investiture (taḳlid) d'un sultan ottoman par ce Khalife, tandis qu'il y eut des cas de ce genre par rapport aux princes indiens. Le titre de «Sulṭān al-Islām», fut porté par les Sultans ottomans déjà avant la conquête de l'Égypte (L. Forrer, *Die osmanische Chronik des Rustem pascha*, Leipzig, 1923), et nous voyons de la relation d'Ibn Iyās qu'après la conquête Sélīm I, tout en tolérant le Khalife comme une institution locale des Musulmans syro-égyptiens, ne demanda de lui aucune investiture, ni par rapport aux pays nouvellement conquis ni par rapport à domaines anciens.

29 Sulūk, I, I, p. 73. *Aẓ-Ẓāhirī*, p. 99, l. 20; p. 100. l. 1.

30 *Ḥawādiṭ*, p. 387, l. 18. Ibn Iyās, IV, p. 348, 374, 481.

31 Ibn Iyās, II, p. 78, l. 7.

32 *Ḥawādiṭ*, p. 616, l. 5–8.

33 *Nujūm*, VI, p. 662, l. 14. *Hawādiṭ*, p. 18, l. 5; p. 25, l. 2. Ibn Iyās, IV, p. 72, l. 22; p. 270, 19, 22.

34 I.D. Eisenstein, *Ozar massaoth*, New York, 1926, p. 96 (dans la relation de Mešullam de Volterra, en 1481, en hébreu). Il est à remarquer que les sources arabes de l'êpoque mamelouke, habituées à citer les paroles dans le dialecte vulgaire de l'Égypte, la metient aussi dans la bouche d'un «Turc» (Ibn Iyās, I, p. 246, l. 29; II, p. 170, l. 21), et

même dans celle d'un ḳāḍī ottoman dans sa conversation avec le gouverneur de l'Égypte, Ḫāyr bēk (V. p. 229, l. 8) ! Évidemment, ce ne sont pas des citations, mais simplement un moyen littéraire pour faire la narration plus vivante.

35 Par exemple Ḳalāūn (*Sulūk*, II, I, p. 111, *aẓ-Ẓāhir Ḳānṣūh* Ibān Iyās, II, p. 369, l. 8). Encore plus significatif est le fait que les historiographes mamelouks rapportent chaque cas d'un bon savoir de l'arabe: par un sultan, comme *Ḫušḳadam* (Ibn Iyās, II, p. 82, 1. 15) ou Ḳāitbāy (*Ḥawādiṯ* p. 648, l. 24), et même par un émir influent (*Ḥawādiṯ*, p. 579, l. 4; Ibn Iyās, II, p. 77, l. 15; p. 213, l. 20).

36 Par exemple, Maḥmūd al-ʿAynī composa des livres en «turc» comme en arabe (*Sulūk*, I, II, p. 222–225).

37 Merdād = hommes (Zetterstéen, p. 102, l. 15); ruḫ = face (Ibn Iyās, II, p. 190, l. 3).

38 Encore sous la domination ottomane les Mamelouks (alors, pour la plupart, des Caucasiens étaient appelés al-Ǧuzz (al-Jabartī, use souvent de cette appellation, et elle est mentionnée aussi par E.W. Lane, *The Manners and customs of the modern Egyptians*, ed. Everyman's Library, 1917, p. 113).

39 *Salūk*, II, I, p. 111.

40 La légende rattache les sultans mamelouks Ḳuṭuz et Baybars I à la famille royale du Khuwarezm (sur Ḳuṭuz: *Sulūk*, I, I, p. 113; sur Baybars I: «*Sirat aẓ-Ẓāhir*», citée par Lane, p. 407). Le corps des Beḥrites fut composé: *a)* de ces fugitifs (*Sulūk*, I, I, p. 101); *b)* de captifs vendus par les Mongols *Ḫiṭaṭ*, II, p. 22), l. 13–15.

41 *Abū l-fidā*, III, p. 167, 5–12; p. 183, l. 19.

42 *Ḫiṭaṭ*, II, p. 219, l. 33.

43 Seulement par rapport aux pâturages communs des Mamelouks près du Caire nous connaissons et la traduction arabe (ar-rabīʿ) et le terme turc («iṭlāḳ» = otlaḳ): *Sulūk*, I, I, p. 16–17, n. 16; Ibn Iyās, I, p. 242, l. 26; II, p. 54, l. 14–15; p. 79, l. 23–25; p. 180, l. 20; 247, l. 28–29; p. 313, l. 28; p. 314, l. 6; p. 318, l. 4; IV, p. 283, l. 2–9; V, p. 266, l. 19; p. 267, l. 2; *Ṣubḥ*, III, p. 456, l. 3–4; *Nujūm*, VI, p. 251, l. 20; p. 253, l. 16; *Hawādiṯ*, p. 19, l. 12; p. 251, l. 14–18; p. 462, l. 8; p. 466, l. 16; p. 537, l. 11–15. La dérivation du terme iṭlāḳ du verbe arabe qui signifie «mettre des troupeaux en liberté» est impossible, vu qu'ici les montures devaient paitre «ʿalā l-marābit», liées aux pots de bois. Sur l'altération des mots et des noms étrangers par les Égyptiens, comp. *al-Manhal aṣ-ṣāfi*, IV (Ms. de Paris, 2071), f. 3, p. 1, et les mots comme as-siyāsa ou ṭawāšt (Mamelouk d'un émir, ṭābūsī).

44 A. Yakoubovsky, *La Société féodale de l'Asie Centrale et son commerce avec l'Europe Orientale aux* xᵉ–xvᵉ *siècles* (en russe, dans le recucil «Le commerce avec la Moskovie et la position internationale de l'Asie Centrale aux xviᵉ–xviiᵉ siècles», *L'Académie des Sciences de l'U. R. S. S.*, 1933), p. 48–49.

45 Il suffit à dire que sous les Mamelouks les fermages des terres privées (mulk) se nommaient aussi ḫarāj: Ibn Yaḥyā, p. 102, l. 13; p. 103, l. 1.

46 Pomiestyé, étymologiquement un équivalent du synonyme persan d' «iḳṭāʿ», jāgir: miesto = jā = lieu (sur jāgīr comp. *Journal Asiatique*, 1843, p. 143–164).

47 Les fermages payés au gouverneur par les habitants du fief proprement dit («les terres noires») et les impôts (plus modérés) payés à lui par les paysans des autres domaines et fiefs de sa région étaient désignés sous le nom de korme, étymologiquement un équivalent des termes mamelouks arabes ḫubz (= un fief, particulièrement un fief d'al-ḥalḳa; le revenu du fief de ce genre) et riẓk (= un fief d'al-ḥalḳa, un fief de pension; le revenu du fief de ce genre). Le terme russe et les deux arabes peuvent être des traductions du terme turc dīrlik, que nous retrouvons sous les Ottomans (P.A. v. Tischendorf, *Das Lehnswesen in den Moslemischen Staaten*. s. 95, 117). Sur les fiefs de gouverneurs chez les Mamelouks, comp. Ibn aš-Šiḥna, p. 261, l. 3; *Mujīr ad-dīn*. p. 423, l. 6–7, et de nombreuses indications chez Ibn al-Ji'ān.

48 Comp. Dozy, *Supplément aux dictionnaires arabes*, I, p. 573.

49 Les matériaux les plus opulents sur ces usages ont été collectés par rapport à la Palestine (en Égypte la communauté des terres commença de disparaître beaucoup plus tôt, et déjà au temps de la conquéte française n'existait qu'en Haute-Égypte). Voir, par exemple: S. Berghbim, *Land tenure in Palestine (Pal. Explor. Fund quarterly statements*, 1894), p. 191–195; J.H. Simpson, *Report on immigration, land settlement and development*, 1930, p. 31; H.C. Luke and E. Keith-Rooch, *The handbook of Palestine and Trans-Jordan* (3e éd., 1934), p. 261.

50 *Ḫiṭaṭ*, I, p. 90, l. 18–24. Ibn Yahyā, p. 95, l. 12–19.

51 *Ḫiṭaṭ*, I, p. 90, l. 24–27. Ibn Yahyā, p. 95, l. 19; p. 96, l. 2.

52 En Égypte, le Sultan possédait au commencement de l'État Mamelouk 4 Ḳirāṭs, les émirs 10, ajnād [al-ḥalḳa] 10. La proportion fixée pour ar-rawk al-ḥusāmī, en 1208, fut: le sultan 13 (dont pour ses Mamelouks), les autres II; pour ar-rawk an-nāṣirī en 1315: le sultan (pour lui-même) 10, les autres 14. Voir *Ḥiṭaṭ*, I, p. 87, l. 3–5; p. 88, l. 11–13; p. 90, l. 5–6.

53 Des féodaux et des fonctionnaires musulmans accusaient les fonctionnaires coptes de désirer d'affaiblir par cela l'armée musulmane: *Ḥiṭaṭ*, I, p. 90, l. 6–8; *al-Manhal aṣ-ṣāfi*. V (Ms. de Paris, 2072), f. 96, p. 1, l. 16–21. En fait, cela raffermit la position du Sultan vis-à-vis les féodaux.

54 Comp. sur ar-rawk ar-nāṣirī en Syrie et en Palestine on 1313: Ibn Yaḥyā, p. 90, l. 1–2. 20; p. 91, l. 2.

55 Oprienina. Ce mot équivaut (étymologiquement et par son usage) au terme mamelouk, arabe al-ḫāṣṣ; en russe il existait déjà avant celle répartition, mais avait une autre signification.

56 Eu tête de cette partie furent placés, l'un après l'autre, deux khans tatares.

57 Yakoubovsky, p. 54.

58 *Abū l-fidā'*, IV, p. 150, l. 15.

59 Les Circassiens recrutés par Kalāūn, qui ne formaient qu'une partie du corps d'al-Burjiya (lui aussi seulement la moitié des Mamelouks de Ḳalāūn, *Suluk*, II, I, p. 111), n'étaient qu'un phénomène isolé (*Ḥiṭaṭ*, I, p. 95, l. 4–8, ne les mentionne guère).

60 *Ṣubḥ*, p. 462, l. 1–2. *Ṣubḥ* fut achevé le 28 Šawāl 814 de l'hégire = 1412 (XIV, p. 404. l. 1–2).

61 *Al-Manchal as-Ṣāfi*, III (Ms. de Paris 2070), f. 186, p. 1, l. 17–23.

62 La plupart des Circassiens étaient alors des chrétiens (*Ṣubḥ*, IV, p. 462, l. 5.

63 Voir sur Barḳūḳ: *Nujūm*, VI, p. 149, l. 22; p. 150, l. 1. Sur Barsbāy: *Nujūm*, VI, p. 571, l. 7–9; *Hawādit*, p. 594, l. 14. Sur Ḳāītbāy: Ibn Iyās, II, p. 190, l. 24. Sur Ḳānṣūh al-Ġawrī: Ibn Iyās, p. 433, l. 15–19; p. 437, l. 6–8; p. 470, l. 22; p. 471, l. 2.

64 Ibn Iyās, II, p. 158, l. 5; p. 168, l. 29; p. 187, l. 19; p. 188, l. 22; p. 190, l. 15, 26; p. 194, l. 9; p. 199, l. 2; p. 201, l. 9; p. 202, l. 12; p. 207, l. 10; p. 211, l. 14; p. 226, l. 4; p. 230, l. 14; p. 232, l. 19; p. 280, l. 26; p. 308, l. 15; p. 309, l. 6; p. 330, l. 2.

65 Voir *Ḳawādit*, p. 55, l. 11–14, sur le mariage du sultan Jaḳmaḳ avec la fille de l' «émir de la Circassie», arrivé depuis peu au Caire.

66 Hammer-Purgstall (*Geschichte des Osmanischen Reiches*, 2e éd., 1, p. 757) confusa ce mot avec Ḳurṣān = corsaires (comp. sur la même page une confusion semblable par rapport au mot julbān). Popper (*Nujūm*, VI, p. LI) supposa que c'était un grade militaire, celui des Émirs de cinq», ce qu'est contrarié par l'auteur même qu'il cite, aẓ-Ẓāhirī lequel nous informe que le nombre d'alajnād al-ḳarānis était «jadis 100 et maintenant moins», et celui des émirs de cinq-30 (p. 115, l. 20; p. 113, l. 8). M. Mostafa (*Zeitschrift der Deutschen Morgenlandischen Gesellschaft*, 1935, p. 221) nous fait connaître que les ḳurḍān (*sic!*) étaient «les vieux Mamelouks, transmis au sultan ses prédécesseurs et par des émirs morts» – une définition exacte, non pas des ḳarānīs, mais de deux catégories d'al-mamālik as-sulṭanīya: as-sulṭāniya et as-sayfīya (aẓ-Ẓāhirī, p. 116, l. 13–14).

67 *Nujūm*, VI, p. 510, l. 3.

68 *Nujūm*, VI, p. 16, l. 11.

69 Ils partageaient ce droit avec al-ḫāṣṣkiya, les Mamelouks qui servaient le sultan hors de céremonies officielles: aẓ-Ẓāhirī, p. 115, l. 22.

70 Aẓ-Ẓāhirī, p. 115, l. 17–20. C'est là la cause de l'erreur de Popper; mais al-ajnād al-ḳarānīṣ non seulement n'étaient pas identiques avec les émirs de cinz, mais encore ne contenaient pas tous les ḳarānis. Je ne saurai pas dire si l'appellation d'ulūğalar (aẓ-Ẓāhirī, p. 115, l. 20), identifiée par P. Ravaisse comme le mot tatar uluğlar = les grands, se réfère à tous ḳarānis ou seulement à ce petit corps.

71 *Ḥawādit*, p. 250, l. 21. Comp. *Nujūm*, VI, p. 511, l. 2: «ḳarāniṣ wa-akābir wa-ḳudamā' al-hijra».

72 *Al-Manhal aṣ-ṣāfī*, III (Ms. de Paris 2070), f. 48, p. 2, l. 10.

73 *Nujūm*, VI, p. 155, l. 3–17; *al-Manhal aṣ-ṣāfī*, V (Ms. de Paris 2072). f. 56, p. 2. Le but de son programme (abolir les waḳfs, brûler les livres de la loi musulmane, persécuter les docteurs de cette loi, nommer un «Turc» à l'emploi du ḳādi suprême) fut la création d'une grande réserve territoriale pour fournir des fiefs aux nouveaux immigrants Circassiens, par le moyen d'abolition des biens pieux variés (awḳāf, aḥbās, ar-rizaḳ al-aḥbāsīya), administrés et protégés par les juristes indignènes. Ibn Tagrī Birdī, un porte-parole des créoles (awlād an-nās), demandait au contraire la cessation de l'importation des nouveaux Mamelouks (*Mawādit*, p. 534, l. 11–17).

74 *Al-Manhal aṣ-ṣāfī*, III (Ms. de Paris 2070), f. 136, p. 1, l. 9–10.

75 I, p. 417, l. 31; II, p. 150, l. 30.

76 *Hawādit*, p. 525, l. 14–16.

77 L'épouse du sultan Barsbāy, Fāṭima, était fille d'un des principaux marchands de la Crimée: *Nujūm*, VI, p. 784, l. 8; p. 812, l. 6 («awlād tujjār al-Ḳirim» étaient évidemment une souche influente en Égypte). Nous trouvons en Égypte aussi des «tujjār al-Jārkas», mais il est difficile d'imaginer la Circassie comme un centre indépendant du commerce mondial.

78 Ibn Yahyā, p. 183, l. 3, *Ṣubḥ*, VII, p. 201, l. 1–6.

79 *Ṣubḥ*, III, p. 469, l. 12–15.

80 Déjà le futur Sultan Yalbāy fut amené en Égypte non pas par un «ḫawājā» (marchand) mais par un émir (Ibn Iyās, II, p. 84, l. 8; comp. sur les autres Sultans: I, p. 259, l. 25; II, p. 3, l. 1; p. 15, l. 27; p. 24. l. 18; p. 39, l. 18; p. 70, l. 5; p. 90, l. 7). Depuis 891 de l'hégire a «tājir al-mamālīk» était un fonctionnaire de l'État (II, p. 293, l. 14) et sous al-Ğawrī un émir.

81 IV, p. 109, l. 10.

82 V, p. 88, l. 15–18. Nous retrouvons, en effet, les étoffes de l'Inde parmi les objets d'importation au xviiie siècle (al-Jabartī, I, p. 31, l. 13–15; p. 32, l. 15–16).

83 L'expansion de l'usage du café suivit de si près cet événement que la possibilité que les Kāramites le lancèrent pour s'en compenser ne doit pas être négligée.

84 *Ṣubḥ*, III, p. 467, l. 7–14.

85 Le fait que la disparition du métal argent ne fut pas suivie par la disparition de l'or indique aussi que sa cause était la passivité étranger: dans tous les États mongols de l'Asie antérieure le dinar était comme le dirhem, une pièce d'argent et non pas d'or, et par conséquent tous les payements aux marchands de ces États devaient être faits en argent.

86 *Ṣubḥ*, III, p. 448, l. 1–8.

87 *Ṣubḥ*, III, 454, l. 7–13. Nous voyons que la crise fut pleinement exploitée par les féodaux. La hausse des fermages et les guerres des féodaux entrainèrent une décadence considérable de l'agriculture égyptienne (*Ḥiṭaṭ*, I, p. 91, l. 13–15; Ibn al-Jiʿān, p. 3, l. 9; *Najūm*, VI, p. 773, l. 19–21).

88 La fin de cette crise fut marquée par la création d'une nouvelle monnaie d'argent (niṣf al-fiḍḍa) par al-Muʿayyad Šayḫ.

89 *Ṣubḥ*, VI, p. 190, l. 6–7, 17.

90 *Ṣubḥ*, XIII, p. 158, l. 19.

91 Ibn Yaḥyā, p. 93, l. 1.

92 Comp. p. 189, l. 21 et p. 190, l. 8. Ṣāliḥ évidemment exploita le fait que *chaque militaire* était appelé «émir» dans les lettres de gouvernement adressées à lui: *Ṣubḥ*, VII, p. 159, l. 16–17; XII, p. 286, l. 20; p. 287, l. 4, 7, 9. La définition d'al-ḥalḳa donnée par Quatremère – «un corps de troupes qui entourait le prince et composait sa garde» (*Sulūk*, I, II, pp. 200–202) – ne réfère qu'à l'origine étymologique de ce mot; en fait, c'était le corps des chevaliers qui ne dépendaient pas personnellement (comme les esclaves ou les affranchis) du sultan, dont certains avaient à leur service 1–4 Mamelouks (Ibn Yaḥyā,

p. 89, l. 6–11; p. 94, l. 3–9; p. 200, l. 14, comp. l. 22), et qui à la fin de l'époque Mameloukе étaient pour la plupart des créoles exempts du service militaire actif (par exemple Ibn Iyās, IV, p. 150, l. 13; V, p. 147, l. 7–9; p. 148, l. 5–6.

93 Ibn Yaḥyā, p. 84, l. 8; p. 85, 1. 4.

94 Ibn Yaḥyā, p. 84, l. 7–9. Il est à remarquer que la famille d'ar-Ramlūni (Ibn Yaḥyā, p. 158, l. 5; p. 165, l. 17) n'est pas autre que la dynastic future des Ma'nides. Quoique l'appellation d' «Ibu Ma'n» se trouve déjà dans ce texte (p. 149, l. 8), l'identification ne fut faite ni par Cheikho ni par Lammens, probablement influencés par le style dédaigneux de Ṣaliḥ, qui nous informe que les ar-Ramṭūnī n'étaient d'origine que des simples fellāḥs et que le premier d'entre eux à devenir un «émir de cinq» ('Alam ad-din Sulaymān) reçut ce grade grâce à Nāḍir ad-din «al-Kabir». Mais *al-Manhal aṣ-ṣāfi* (III, f. 8, p. 1) présente le fils de ce Sulaymān, Jawād, comme «ibn amir al-'arab» et comme un descendant des rois d'al-Ḥira (la même généalogie que Ṣāliḥ attribue à sa propre famille). Une remarque postérieure sur les marges du manuscrit atteste que l' «émir Faḫr ad-din (II?) se disait descendu de cet émir Jawād». La famille de Ṣaliḥ lui-même n'est pas mentionée par les sources égyptiennes, même passagèrement.

95 *Ṣubh*, III, p. 458, l. 3.

17

THE ISLAMIC GUILDS

Bernard Lewis

The craft-guilds are one of the most interesting and characteristic phenomena of medieval Muslim civilisation. In the Islamic lands, one finds hardly a trace of what might be called a civic spirit, a municipal life. The Muslim cities of the Middle Ages were for the most part ephemeral, enjoying a commercial and intellectual efflorescence for a century or so, and then dwindling or disappearing. There have thus rarely been any clearly defined municipal institutions, or any crystallised and permanent urban entities. All that spirit of local solidarity and organisation, that is so important in medieval Europe, was excluded by the permanently unsettled state of Muslim political conditions from expression in the political field, and was driven to seek an outlet in economic life. Thus, in the craft-guilds and confraternities of Islam, we find the equivalent, not merely of the European guilds, but also of that intense local life that is one of the most significant aspects of medieval European history.

So important was the guild in Muslim life, that in many cases the very topography of the Muslim city, which was built essentially on the idea of a market, was determined by the needs of the guildsmen. From Morocco to Java, with surprising uniformity, the Muslim city rose round three or four central points, always the same. The first fixed point is the exchange – always an important centre in a bimetallist economy such as that of medieval Islam. Around it are the toll-gatherer, the local mint (where there is one), the auction market, and the Muhtasib, or inspector of markets. Here, too, are stationed the porters. The second centre is the Qaisaria, a strong, closed-in building where foreign goods and valuables are stored. The name is probably of Byzantine origin.

Source: *Economic History Review*, 1937, vol. 8 (1), pp. 20–37.

The third is the thread-market (Suq al Ghazl), where the women come to sell their own handiwork. And here, too, are stationed the dealers in such commodities as women are likely to buy – butchers, bakers, market gardeners, etc. The fourth centre is the university, usually attached to a mosque. In it, teachers and students form a genuine guild organisation.[1] Around these four centres are distributed the guildsmen; each guild in its own market. As will readily be seen, granted the fixity of these four points, the topographic distribution of the guilds in different towns will likewise tend to be fixed.

Let us now consider the problem of the origins and early history of the guilds – one in which the generally undeveloped state of the subject is specially noticeable. A fairly obvious suggestion is that they are a continuation of their Byzantine predecessors. We know that until the seventh century AD, on the very eve of the Arab conquest, there were numerous guilds in the Byzantine provinces of Syria and Egypt,[2] and it is rather improbable that these guilds were destroyed by the conquerors, whose policy, as we know, was to leave more or less intact the administrative and economic machinery left to them by the Byzantines. Yet it is not until the tenth century, 300 years later, that we find any definite indication of the existence of Muslim guilds, and then they are of a type entirely different from the pre-Islamic ones. For the whole of the intervening period we possess few notices, and those of a brief and fragmentary character. The first is a sentence in the historian Ibn-ul-'Idhari, who tells us that in the year AD 770 the Arab governor of Qairouan, in Tunisia, "regulated the markets and allotted to each craft its place."[3] Although the text in which this statement is made is itself of the tenth century, there is every reason to believe it genuine. The information is interesting, as it shows that the governor brought the artisans and markets of Qairouan, a new city built by the Arab conquerors, under the same form of public control and supervision as was exercised by the eparch in the Byzantine cities around. To deduce from this, however, as do von Kremer[4] and Atger,[5] the existence of Arab *guilds* in Qairouan seems to me unjustified by the evidence available.

By the end of the ninth century, we have a fair number of sources indicating the existence of some form of corporative organisation of merchants and craftsmen. These guilds are not yet of the characteristic Islamic type, and are rather a public regulation and control of markets and crafts, of the kind described in contemporary Byzantine sources.[6] From these indications it would seem permissible to deduce the retention by the Muslim rulers of the forms of public control of the crafts employed in the Byzantine administration, at least in dealing with non-Arab and non-Muslim artisans, and perhaps even its extension to the Muslims themselves. It is not, however, until the following century that we find any considerable development of what may be called Islamic guilds, and then they are of a type which cannot be explained by Byzantine influence or heritage.

Beside the Byzantine theory, however, there is another theory, the examination of which will necessitate a brief excursus on a subject with which non-orientalists will probably be unfamiliar.

During recent years, orientalists have begun to realise more and more that Sunni (orthodox) Islam, during the epoch of the Caliphate, was never the true religion of the masses. The more one studies the Islamic literature of the Middle Ages, the more one sees that Sunnism was regarded everywhere as the religion of a dominant caste, the religion of the State, the distinctive mark of the conquering Arab aristocracy.[7] In the earlier stages, this was the attitude even of the conquerors themselves. For many centuries after the Muslim conquest, the vast majority of the Caliph's subjects were not Sunni, and hated Sunnism as the emblem of an oppressive regime and of a foreign, privileged ruling class.[8]

Nevertheless, the religious sentiment was present and powerful among the masses. It found its expression in a whole series of mystical, heretical sects, running from the eighth century AD until the Mongol conquest. These sects were almost all characterised by a syncretistic philosophy, containing elements borrowed from pre-Islamic systems, especially Neoplatonism, Manichæism and Mazdakism,[9] by a revolutionary and equalitarian social philosophy, and by a secret, quasi-masonic organisation, usually interconfessional, with graduated ranks of initiation. An interesting modern parallel to the success of these movements and the failure of Sunnism is to be found in the situation in Dutch Indonesia and French West Africa, where, despite vastly superior resources, the Christian missions make far less progress among the native population than does the propaganda of Islam. Here, again, it is because Christianity is associated in the mind of the Malay or the Negro with the foreign rule, and he chooses to be a first-rank Muslim rather than a second-rank Christian.

In the tenth and eleventh centuries these movements were at their height. It was a period of industrial development and urban agglomeration. The rise of an elaborate system of banking, with headquarters at Baghdad and branches all over the empire, served to keep the state well supplied with coined money and to maintain generally a monetary economy. Reacting on the growing industrialisation, it resulted in a concentration of both capital and labour.[10] As was to be expected, the rapid growth of large-scale capitalism provoked grave social crises. In Baghdad, we read, there were a series of dangerous outbreaks,[11] in Mesopotamia, already in the ninth century, a revolt of Negro slaves,[12] and everywhere continual risings of the sects. During this period the Muslim world was shaken to its foundations by a movement of revolt, at once intellectual, political and economic, which threw off as a by-product the Fatimid anti-Caliphate of Cairo, and which, in its final failure, dragged down the whole of medieval Islamic civilisation with it. The Qarmati ("Carmathian") movement, as we may call it, after the name of its most active and most important section,[13] was characterised by an extraordinary liberalism. It appealed to all the innumerable religions and sects of the Muslim world – Sunnis, Shiis, Christians, Jews, Zoroastrians alike, in the name of intellectual liberty and social justice. Its exact philosophy is difficult to determine, our sources being mainly either Sunni, and thus violently antagonistic and prone to misrepresent, or Isma'illi, belonging to a later epoch, when the doctrines had suffered considerable modification. It seems clear, however, that it was a form of rational idealism, recognising the relativity of all religions, rejecting the formal law of Islam, and basing itself on a system of justice, toleration and complete equality.[14] By an ingenious system of interpretation, known as Ta'wil, these doctrines were read into the text of the Quran and Muslim holy writings. Jewish and Christian scriptures, too, were treated in the same way.[15] The Qarmati 'Ubaidullah is unmerciful in his exposure of the social basis of orthodox Islam: "The true aspect of this is simply that their master (Muhammad) forbade to them the enjoyment of the good and inspired their hearts with fear of a hidden Being who cannot be apprehended. This is the God in whose existence they believe. He related traditions to them about the existence of what they will never witness, such as resurrection from the graves, retribution, paradise and hell. Thus he soon subjugated them and reduced them to slavery to himself during his lifetime and to his offspring after his death. In this way he arrogated to himself the right to enjoy their wealth, for he says: "I ask you no reward for it except friendliness to my relatives" (*Quran*, lxii, 23). His dealings with them were on a cash basis, but their dealings with him were on credit.[16] He required of them an immediate exchange of their lives and property for a future promise which would never be realised. "Is paradise aught save this world and its enjoyment? Or are hell and its torture anything but the state to which the observers of the Law are reduced, namely, weariness and exertion. . . ."[17] This extract is cited by a Sunni author who died in AD 1037, as an example of the iniquities of the Qarmatis, and its authenticity is doubted by some scholars. Yet, though it is somewhat crude in form, there is nothing in it apart from the personal depreciation of Muhammad that cannot be corroborated by quotations from the few Qarmati or neo-Qarmati sources that we possess.

The movement was also a great educative force, distinguishing itself by the foundation of schools and universities of which the most famous, that of Al-Azhar in Cairo, converted to orthodoxy, still exists, and by the compilation of a great encyclopædia which reminds us of the French Encyclopædist movement of the eighteenth century. In this encyclopædia, the *Rasā'il Ikhwān as-Safā* (Epistles of the Pure Brethren), we find almost all the progressive ideas of the epoch, and a few valuable hints on forms of organisation. From it we learn of the existence of societies of "pure brethren" all over the empire, working for the dissemination of their ideas among all classes of the population and especially among the artisans.[18]

It is the theory of Prof. Massignon that it was the Qarmati movement which created the Islamic guilds and gave them their distinctive character, which they have retained till today. The Islamic guild, he says, was essentially a weapon forged by the Qarmati propagandists in the struggle to weld the labouring classes of the Islamic world into a force capable of overthrowing the Caliphate and all that it represented. It was to reach the artisanate that they created and dominated the guilds, which thus came to have a double character, being at once professional guilds and Qarmati fraternities.[19]

Let us examine the evidence in favour of this hypothesis. In the first place, we must note the great interest in the artisan classes displayed by the Qarmatis. A whole epistle of the *Rasā'il Ikhwān as-Safā* is devoted to a consideration of the manual crafts, their classification, and their essential nobility.[20] A second factor is the difference in the situation of the guilds under the Fatimids and under Sunni states. Under Sunni rule, the guilds were persecuted, submitted to a thousand restrictions, deprived of any legal rights. There was a legal functionary, the Muhtasib, whose main duty was to supervise the guilds and to nip in the bud any attempt at independent action. We possess an interesting anti-guild literature, demonstrating the distrust felt by the Sunni state for the guilds.[21]

Quite different was the position of the guilds under the Fatimids, where they enjoyed great prosperity. Recognised by the State, they seem to have possessed considerable privileges, and to have played an important part in the commercial revival that took place under Fatimid rule. It was under the Fatimids that was founded the guild of teachers and students which formed the great university of Al-Azhar, of which we have already spoken. In 1171 the Fatimid anti-Caliphate was destroyed by Saladin, and Egypt recovered for orthodoxy. Immediately the guilds were deprived of most of their rights and privileges, and submitted to a very strict control.

A third factor in favour of this hypothesis is the strong trace of Qarmati influence left in the guilds long after the disappearance of Quarmatism. In thirteenth-century Anatolia, Köprülü tells us, the guilds still had a graded system of initiation closely resembling that of the Qarmatis,[22] and studies of different guilds in different parts of the Islamic world have revealed similar traces.[23] An Egyptian guild-tract of the sixteenth century, studied by Thorning and Goldziher,[24] reveals a fierce hatred of the Ottoman rule and a social messianism closely resembling that of the Qarmatis. Most significant of all is the interconfessionalism of the guilds, which distinguishes them sharply from their European counterparts. Muslim, Christian and Jew are admitted on equal terms, some guilds being even predominantly non-Muslim (as those of doctors, dealers in precious metals, etc.). This connects the guilds very closely with Qarmati doctrine.

From all this it is clear that Qarmatism has played a great rôle in the development of the Islamic guilds, and has left a deep and lasting imprint in their inner life – though, it seems to me, there is not yet sufficient evidence to show that it actually *created* them.[25] What seems more likely is that the Qarmatis gave a new *élan* and a new meaning to forms of organisation already existing. Whether these forms were of Byzantine origin, or were imitations of contemporary Byzantine institutions beyond the frontier it is impossible to say. Such an interpretation is supported by the traces of craft organisation in the pre-Qarmati period, and by the considerable Hellenistic element in Qarmati thought. The Islamic guilds would thus be a synthesis of a material framework of organisation inherited or imitated from the Græco-Roman world, and a system of ideas coming essentially from Syro-Persian civilisation, giving as result a movement at once Islamic, Hellenistic, interconfessional, philosophic and corporatist.

In the middle of the thirteenth century took place the great disaster of the Mongol conquest. This conquest, which destroyed the Caliphate and submitted Sunni and heretic alike to the domination of a foreign and infidel race, tended to obliterate the distinctions between the two, and facilitated the more or less general conversion of the masses to Sunni Islam. With the almost complete disappearance of Qarmatism, the guilds, too, began to acquire a certain precarious status in Sunni society. Nevertheless, difficulties remained. The guildsmen, still suspicious of the religion of the ruling classes and of the State, linked themselves with a religious tendency which, though not actually heretical, was not always above suspicion, namely Sufism. Into relatively recent times periodic denunciations have been hurled against the guilds by Sunni jurists. Note for example the edicts issued against the guilds by the great Syrian jurist Ibn Taymiyya (*d.* 1327), or by the Ottoman Sheikh Müniri Belĝradi, in the seventeenth century.

In spite of this hostility, however, the position of the guilds in the post-Mongol period was fairly stable; and remained so until the Turkish reform movement of the nineteenth century began a process which has resulted in their general decline. It is from the post-Mongol period that most of our documents come, and all the information that we possess regarding the interior organisation of the guilds.

Before passing on to consider this organisation, however, it is worth while to examine a problem of considerable interest in Islamic guild history. At about the same time as the guilds begin to merge with the Sufi or Dervish brotherhoods, we find them coming into ever-closer association with yet another form of organisation – the Futuwwa. The origins of the Futuwwa movement are extremely obscure, and this is not the place to consider them. Suffice it to say that in the twelfth and thirteenth centuries Futuwwa associations spring up all over the Islamic lands. The Futuwwa is a group of young men, bound together by an ethical and religious code of duties and an elaborate ceremonial. They are under obligation to practise certain virtues and usually to render military service to the cause of Islam. The Futuwwa, as will thus be seen, constitutes in a certain sense a Muslim parallel to the European conception of chivalry, and von Hammer indeed has gone so far as to ascribe a Muslim origin to the latter.[26]

In the period immediately following the Mongol conquest, the Futuwwa tends to identify itself more and more with the Sufi brotherhood and, through the bonds of a common membership, with the craft-guilds. The process, starting in Anatolia, spread rapidly all over the Muslim world, and before long Futuwwa and guild became synonymous terms. How exactly this fusion took place, and what was the precise relationship between the different organisations, is an obscure question which has not yet been sufficiently elucidated.[27] Tæschner[28] distinguishes three stages in the history of the Futuwwa – three stages of progressive social decline. Starting as an aristocratic, chivalrous order, they suffered, he says, a "Verbürgerlichung," a transformation into a bourgeois movement, in the thirteenth century, and finally, in the fifteenth century, sunk still lower by becoming proletarianised and thus identifying themselves with the craft-guilds. Thorning,[29] on the other hand, maintains that the guilds and Sufis did not absorb but imitated the Futuwwa orders, adopting their ceremonial, their ideals and finally their name. Most convincing, however, is the explanation of Gordlevsky,[30] who, with Köprülü,[31] places the fusion of guild and Futuwwa in thirteenth-century Anatolia, and connects it with the highly important organisation of the "Akhiyan-i-Rum" (Akhis[32] of Anatolia). The Akhis first appear in Anatolia in the years immediately following the Mongol conquest. The period was one of general anarchy and disorder. The Mongols, who had destroyed the Saljuk State, failed to provide any effective alternative, and the administration crumbled away. During this period of crisis, the Akhis appeared as a strong widespread organisation, willing and able to control. With "solidarity and hospitality" as its code, the artisan class as its social basis and "the slaying of tyrants and their satellites" as its task, the Akhi movement spread rapidly in town and countryside. It was a movement at once social, political, religious and military. At an early stage a visitor noticed that all the members of a given lodge were of the same craft. The complete identification of the Akhi orders with the craft-guilds must have taken place at a very early date – perhaps even at the very inception of the movement. But the Akhis were not merely a professional organisation. They adopted as their duties the maintenance of justice, the prevention and punishment of tyranny, the observance of a moral and religious code, and the fulfilment of military obligations if necessary in defence of their rights. Membership was not reserved to Muslims, and at a later stage Christians appeared to have been very numerous.

In the Akhi movement is thus realised for the first time the union of guild, Futuwwa and religious brotherhood. Interesting corroborative evidence of Qarmati influence in the guilds is provided by Gordlevsky,[33] who discerns strong heretical influences in the Akhis and connects their origin with the Ikhwan as-Safa, already cited. Köprülü[34] goes even further, and asserts that the Akhis were actually heretics, of the same type as the Qarmatis themselves.

An interesting description of the Akhis of Anatolia has come down to us in the record of the travels of Ibn Battuta, a native of Tangier who visited Anatolia in the middle of the fifteenth century.[35]

With the rise and consolidation of the Ottoman Sultanate, the Akhis inevitably lost much of their power and influence, and after a tenacious but unsuccessful resistance, were compelled to renounce their political and military activities. Never, however, did they sink to the rank of a purely professional organisation. The spirit of the earlier period survived, and right on into the twentieth century[36] the guilds have retained an inner, spiritual life and a moral code.

From Anatolia, the interpenetration of guild, Futuwwa and fraternity spread rapidly, and by the fifteenth century the process was complete in all the central lands of Islam.

It is from these Futuwwa guilds that most of our documents on interior organisation have come. Every guild had a code of rules, customs and ceremonial, usually orally transmitted. This code was known as the Dustur (a Persian word meaning "permission," later "constitution"). In some cases, the codes have been committed to writing, and a large number of such tracts, dating from the fourteenth century onwards, have come down to us. Kitab-al-Futuwwa, or Fütüvvet-Name, as these guild-tracts are termed, constitute, together with a number of touristic and geographical works, our principal sources of information.[37]

From them it is possible to some extent to reconstruct the hierarchy of the guild. In doing so, however, it is wise to bear in mind that our documents come from a field extending in time from the fourteenth to the twentieth century, and in space over the whole of Islam. Although there has been very little change through the centuries, there is considerable local diversity. We shall attempt, therefore, to present a composite picture, while noting the chief divergences according to place and period.

At the head of the guild is the Sheikh.[38] He is elected by the master craftsmen, and, once elected, is unchallenged ruler of the guild, combining the functions of head, treasurer and scribe. After him come the Ikhtiyariyya, or elders among the master craftsmen, who co-operate generally with him in the administration of the guild. Next come the master craftsmen (Usta, sometimes Mu'allim), the main body of the guild. The journeyman (Sani') does not play a great part in the Islamic guild, and is usually missing altogether, the transition being direct from apprentice to master. In some there is an intermediary stage, during which the artisan is called Khalifa, or Khalfa (companion, adjunct). This stage, however, is merely temporary.

The apprentice (Mubtadi)[39] completes the series. In the majority of cases no time of apprenticeship is fixed, nor is any masterpiece in the European sense required. The time of study and of acceptance are fixed by the master with whom the apprentice works. Discipline is exercised either by the Sheikh alone, or by the Sheikh and Ikhtiyariyya together, according to different texts.

A somewhat different form of organisation is found in the later Anatolian guilds described by Gordlevsky.[40] Here an apprenticeship of one thousand and one days is demanded. During this period the apprentice receives no salary, but is entitled to tips and to a banquet on initiation. He receives at the same time his craft training from the master and moral instruction at the Zawiya. At the end of his apprenticeship he is required to present a masterpiece, and is formally initiated at a public ceremony by the Esnaf Başi and the Yiĝit Başlari (elders). He then becomes Khalfa, adjunct. He must remain a Khalfa for at least six months, after which he may establish himself as a master craftsman.[41] In this he is usually aided financially by his teacher and the other masters.

The guild is headed by a committee (lonca heyeti) composed of the elders.[42] The final decision remains with the chief, who is usually chosen for his piety. The council meets fortnightly. The orders and punishments resolved upon are executed by the Çauş, or the Iş-başi. The council jealously guarded the quality of production, the penalty for bad craftsmanship being temporary exclusion from the guild. Raw materials were purchased under the supervision of the Sheikh, the poorer craftsmen taking precedence of the rich. A general meeting was held once yearly.

We may note in passing the important part played in guild life by ceremonial garb. The outer characteristic of the early Futuwwa was the Sirwal, or ceremonial trousers, and Arab writers often speak of putting on the Sirwal as a way of saying "joining the Futuwwa." This custom passed into guild usage, and until quite recently the ceremony of initiation took the form of putting on certain garments – the Sirwal, or trousers, the Shadd, or girdle, and the Pishtimal or apron being the chief.[43]

We possess two detailed descriptions of the Islamic guilds, which it is worth while to examine individually. The first of these is contained in the book of travels of a Turkish traveller, Evliya Çelebi, who in the early seventeenth century, at the request of the Sultan, compiled a detailed list of the guilds and corporations of Constantinople. In this work we find for the first time a full description of the guild organisation of a Muslim city.[44]

Evliya Çelebi prefixes to his description of the guilds a Fütüvvet-Name, which is apparently reproduced textually, and which contains the usual legends and catechisms, and also a description of the ceremony of initiation. The hierarchy here described consists of the Sheikh (head), the Naqib (vice-head), the Çauş (usher), the Usta (master) and the Şagird (= çîrak, apprentice). The journeyman, it will be noticed, is not mentioned at all.

He then proceeds to an enumeration "of all the guilds and professions existing in the jurisdiction of the four Mullas of Constantinople, with the number of their shops, their men, their Sheiks, and their Pirs." They are divided into fifty-seven sections, containing in all one thousand and one guilds.[45]

Space does not permit us to follow Evliya in his description of all the fifty-seven sections. Let us just note as general principle that each section is under the headship of a single person, usually the head of the principal guild within the section, who holds the higher office *ex officio* as it were. The few sections that are headed by official personages like the Su-Başi are exceptions, the reason being the official or semi-official character of the professions themselves.

Once a year the guilds held a public procession, and great importance was apparently attached to the order of precedence. Evliya gives an amusing description of a dispute of this kind between the butchers and the Egyptian merchants, in which the final decision is given by the Sultan in favour of the merchants.

Our second source comes from the second half of the nineteenth century. In 1884, Elia Qoudsi, a Syrian Christian, presented to the International Congress of Orientalists the results of an *enquête* on the guilds of Damascus conducted by him in the previous year.[46] Although relatively recent, this study may be regarded as a historical source, for most of what it describes has since disappeared, without having been studied again.

At the head of all the guilds of the town, he tells us, was the Sheikh ul-Mashaikh, the Sheikh of Sheikhs. This post was hereditary in a certain family. He could not be elected, deposed, or replaced, and was removable only by his own death or resignation (occasionally, however, by the Sultan). In earlier times he was supreme judge in all guild affairs. Tradition said that in days gone by his powers had been very wide, extending even to the right to inflict death penalties. He had long retained, however, the right to imprison, chain and whip the guildsmen. He lived on his hereditary Waqfs (i.e. lands in mort-main, the revenues of which always belonged to the incumbent Sheikh ul-Mashaikh). After the Tanzimat (nineteenth-century Ottoman reforms) his powers were considerably diminished, and the post became almost purely honorific. The incumbent at the time of Qoudsi's *enquête* was a great scholar, but entirely ignorant of all crafts. His sole function was to ratify the investiture of guild heads by the masters.

The post of Sheikh ul-Mashaikh, it may be noted in passing, would appear to be purely Damascene, as no trace of it can be found in any other city.

Since the Sheikh ul-Mashaikh could not personally attend all guild-meetings, whenever a meeting was held for the initiation of journeymen or masters, or any other matter of general interest, the Sheikh ul-Mashaikh sent a functionary called the Naqib. When the office of Sheikh ul-Mashaikh was an important and influential one, they used to be many Naqibs. At the time of his *enquête*, however, Qoudsi found only one, who possessed the knowledge of craft and guild affairs which the Sheikh lacked.

Next was the Sheikh ul-Hirfa (Sheikh of the guild), elected by the eldest workers from among the best craftsmen and guildsmen. No rule of priority, whether of age or length of membership, was observed. The Sheikh might be and often was a very young man. He was required to be of good character, a skilful craftsman, respected by the guildsmen and capable of representing them before the authorities. In some guilds the Sheikhship was hereditary, but always subject to the ratification of the electorate. The Sheikh was appointed for life, but could be replaced if found remiss. His duties were as follows – to summon and preside at meetings, to watch over the maintenance of the standard of the craft, to punish those who violated the rules of the craft, to regulate the conditions of labour (this was delegated to the masters); to initiate new journeymen and masters, to be the responsible head of the guild in all dealings with the government. As regards the election of the Sheikh, Qoudsi notes that he was not elected by a majority vote. On the vacation of the post, the senior masters assembled and discussed eligible candidates. If in discussion they failed to reach an agreement, a Sheikh was appointed by the Sheikh ul-Mashaikh, who in any case confirmed the new Sheikh in his office at a special ceremony.

As assistant to the Sheikh, there was the Shawish (an Arabicised form of Çauş), who stood in the same relation to him as the Naqib to the Sheikh ul-Mashaikh, with the important difference that whereas the Naqib was nominated by the Sheikh ul-Mashaikh, the Shawish could only be appointed with the approval of the electors. The Shawish had no powers of his own – he was merely the representative and executive officer of the Sheikh ul-Hirfa. The office, Qoudsi tells us, "is very ancient, but the name is recent."

The apprentice (Mubtadi) worked without pay for a number of years until he reached manhood and the mastery of the craft (sometimes, however, he received a small weekly wage according to merit). He then became a journeyman (Sani'). If he did not achieve mastery, his wages remained low, and he was not allowed to open on his own account.

The journeyman, in Qoudsi's time, formed the backbone of every guild, and were in a large majority. Through them, he tells us, the compactness of the craft was preserved and the secrets of craftsmanship were transmitted.

Qoudsi then goes on to describe in detail the ceremonies of initiation, the oaths of secrecy and good craftsmanship involved, the elaborate set of rules (Rusum) regulating every aspect of the guildsmen's lives and the signs and gestures of recognition. In conclusion, he points to the resemblance between their movement and European freemasonry, and asks whether there may not be some relation between the two.[47]

Some notes on the Egyptian guilds at about the same time show some divergence. The Sheikh ul-Mashaikh is here unknown, the guilds being under the general control of the chief of police. The guild head (here called Sheikh ut-Taifa) had the power to supervise the workers, to adjudge professional conflicts, to punish faults. In case of necessity he convoked a council of Mukhtars (vice guild-heads), which formed a sort of corporative court of justice. The grade of journeyman did not exist, the apprentice, on initiation, becoming at once Usta, or master. A masterpiece was required.[48] Of particular interest is the information that the Cairo guilds possessed a form of unemployment and sickness insurance, in which all members participated.[49]

All these organisations, which have survived almost without change into the nineteenth and sometimes even the twentieth century, have not been able to resist the shock of the European invasion. Everywhere in the Muslim lands the old forms of production are giving way to new ones, and inevitably the old guilds are falling to pieces. Often they are transformed into trade unions (Naqabat) of the European type. Those of Tunisia, Syria and Dutch Indonesia have affiliated themselves to the Communist Trade Union International. Others are still in a state of transition.

There remains[50] to be mentioned one very curious phenomenon in Muslim guild life – that of what are known as the immoral guilds. From the earliest times[51] we find, in Muslim lands, organised guilds, complete with ceremonial, code and rites, of such "professions" as thief, brigand and bandit. The Banu Sasan, or organised bandits of Cairo, long exercised considerable power, and during the period of disorders under the Abbasid Caliph al-Muqtafi (1136–60), the thieves' guilds of Baghdad seem to have dominated the town.[52] These organisations, which, needless to say, had no real contact with the true artisans' guilds, nevertheless served to bring the latter into disrepute, and were often used by anti-guild polemists as a means of attack.[53]

What are the general conclusions to be drawn from this survey of the Islamic guilds? It seems to me that we can point to four distinctive qualities, marking off the guild organisations of Islam from those that have grown up in Europe, as follows.

Unlike the European guild, which was basically a public service, recognised, privileged and administered by public authorities, seigneurial, municipal or royal, the Islamic guild was a spontaneous development from below, created, not in response to a State need, but to the social requirements of the labouring masses themselves. Save for one brief period, the Islamic guilds have maintained either an open hostility to the State, or an attitude of sullen mistrust, which the public authorities, political and ecclesiastical, have always returned. How deep is this anti-authoritarian feeling is shown by its sudden revival in the twentieth century, exemplified in the important part played by the guilds in the

Persian revolution, by the startling development of the Islamic guilds into a mass revolutionary organisation in Indonesia, by the close connection established by some of the guilds with European Socialism and Communism.[54] The fact that occasionally Sunni sovereigns accorded some limited status to the Islamic guilds, in the hope of winning their support, does not invalidate this conclusion, any more than do the occasional disagreements between European sovereigns and guilds disprove the essentially public nature of the latter.

It is partly from this, and partly from the unchanging character of the forms of production in the Islamic lands from the twelfth to the nineteenth centuries, that springs the second distinctive characteristic of Muslim guild life. There is nothing in the history of the Islamic guilds to parallel the great efflorescence of the European guilds in the fifteenth and sixteenth centuries, culminating as it did in the crystallisation of masters and journeymen into two distinct and hostile classes; in a great commercial and political rise of the masters, and in the constitution of separate journeymen's guilds as a weapon in the acute struggle of classes that developed.[55] In Islam, master, journeyman and apprentice remain essentially of the same class, in close personal contact. The rank of journeyman, always of an occasional and transitory character, often entirely missing,[56] never developed into a permanent social group without hope of ever attaining mastership. Free from the inner social differentiation[57] that split the European guild, the Islamic guild thus retained the popular and equalitarian character imprinted upon it in the tenth and eleventh centuries, when it came into existence in its typical form as an artisan revolt against the rising commercial and financial capitalism of the day.

The third distinctive mark of the Islamic guilds is their interconfessionalism. Whereas the European guilds excluded even heretical Christians, the Islamic guilds were open to Jew, Christian and Muslim alike, some guilds, as we have already mentioned, being even predominantly non-Muslim.

Finally, we must notice the significance of the inner spiritual life of the Islamic guilds. Unlike the European, the Islamic guild was never a purely professional organisation. From the days when the guilds formed a part of the masonic system of the Qarmatis, until the present day, they have always had a deep-rooted ideology, a moral and ethical code, which was taught to all novices at the same time as the craft itself.

NOTES

1 I am indebted for this classification to the valuable study of L. Massignon, "Le corps de métier et la cité musulmane," *Revue Internationale de Sociologie*, v. 28, 1920, p. 473 ff. See also J. Sauvaget, "Esquisse d'une Histoire de la ville de Damas," *Revue des Études Islamiques*, 1934, p. 450 ff.
2 See Stöckle, *Spätrömische und Byzantinische Zünfte*, Leipzig, 1911.
3 Ibn-ul-'Idhari, ed. R. Dozy, Leyden 1851, p. 68.
4 von Kremer, *Kulturgeschichte des Orients*, Vienna, 1877, vol. ii, p. 187.
5 Atger, *Les corporations tunisiennes*, Paris, 1909.
6 See von Kremer, *op. cit.*, and Mez, *Die Renaissance des Islams*, Heidelberg, 1922, chap. 26.
7 See van Vloten, *Recherches sur la domination arabe*, etc., Amsterdam, 1894. Also Becker, *Islamstudien*, Leipzig, 1924, vol. I, and Barthold, *Mussulman culture*, Calcutta, 1934, pp. 72–7 and 100–2. It is interesting to note, however, that the division between Sunnis and heretics does not correspond exactly with that between Arabs and non-Arabs. The Persian ruling classes of the old Sassanid Empire were soon incorporated into the social structure of the Caliphate and also into the Sunni faith. The poorer Arab populations of Syria and Iraq, on the other hand, came under the influence of Manichæn and other heresies.
8 See *Streitschrift des Ghazzali gegen die Batinijjesekte*, Goldziher, Leyden, 1916.
9 A religio-communist movement which in the sixth century AD had seriously shaken the Sassanid empire in Persia. Browne, *A Literary History of Persia*, 1906, vol. 1, and Christensen, *L'Iran sous les Sassanides*, Copenhagen, 1937.
10 See Mez, *Die Renaissance des Islams*, Fischel, "The origin of banking in mediæval Islam," *Journal of the Royal Asiatic Society*, 1933, pp. 339 and 569, and *Jews in the social and economic life of mediæval Islam*, London, 1937. Massignon, "L'influence de l'Islam au Moyen Age sur la fondation et l'essor des banques juives" *Bulletin d'Etudes Orientales de l'Institut Français de Damas*, vol. 1.
11 Hamza Isfahani *Annales*, Petropoli, 1844–8, vol. 1, p. 201, vol. 2, p. 155.
12 See Nöldeke, *Sketches from Eastern history*, Edinburgh, 1892.
13 Other names are Batiniyya, Ta'limiyya, Isma'iliyya.
14 Even today the Ahl-i-Hakk, a fossilised remnant of one of these sects, inhabiting a few villages in N.W. Persia, retain something of this character. One of their eschatological poems, for example, contains the promise that "the Sultans will be punished." See Minorski, "Notes sur les Ahl-i-Hakk," *Revue du Monde Musulman*, vol. xl, 1920, pp. 20–97 and *Encylopædia of Islam* supp. Ahl-i-Hakk. Minorski notes particularly the popular character of the religion which is, he says, "professed particularly by the lower classes, nomads, villagers, inhabitants of the poorer quarters, dervishes, etc."
15 See Kraus, "Hebräische und Syrische Zitat", *Der Islam*, vol. 19.
16 The same sentiment and metaphor will be found in the quatrains of 'Umar Khayyam.

17 Baghdadi, *Al-Farq bain al-Firaq*, Cairo, 1910, pp. 281 and 282. Eng. translation by Halkin, Tel-Aviv, 1935, p. 137.
18 *Rasā'il*, Cairo edition, vol. iv, p. 214.
19 Unfortunately Massignon has not yet fully worked out his theory. As he himself says, "les matériaux sont encore à réunir." In the following, general suggestions will be found in support of this hypothesis. "Le corps de Métier," *op. cit. Enc. of Isl.*, articles Sinf and Shadd. *Enc. of Soc. Sci.*, article Guilds (Islamic). *La Passion d'al-Hallaj*, Paris, 1922, vol. i, pp. 83, 399, 410.
20 *Rasā'il*, vol. i, pp. 210 *ff.* As late as the seventeenth century, a Persian Isma'ili religious poet devotes a whole passage to a discussion of craft guilds (*Divan i Khaki Khorasani*, Bombay, 1933, ll. 771 *ff.*).
21 See Bernhauer, "Les Institutions de police chez les Arabes," *Journal Asiatique*, 1860 et 1861, and Colin et Lévi-Provençale, *Manuel Hispanique de Hisba*, Paris, 1931. Bouvat notes the strict control to which the guilds of Transoxania were submitted during the Timūrid period ("Essai sur la Civilisation Timouride," *Journal Asiatique*, 1926 (avril–juin), pp. 273–5).
22 Köprülü, *Origines de l'Empire Ottoman*, Paris, 1935, p. 111.
23 See "Enquêtes sur les corporations due Maroc," *Revue du Monde Musulman*, vol. lviii, and also Gavrilov, "Les corps de métier de l'Asie centrale," *Revue des Études Islamiques*, 1928, p. 209.
24 The MS. is in Gotha. See Goldziher, *Abhandlungen zur Arabischen Philologie* II, Leyden, 1899, pp. lxxvi *ff.* and Thorning, *Beiträge zur Kenntnis des Islamischen Vereinswesens*, Berlin, 1913, pp. 41 *ff.*
25 To this extent, the theory of Massignon is accepted by Gordlevsky, Köprülü and other authorities. Tæschner, however, reserves judgment, "diese Frage ist noch im einzelnen genauer zu untersuchen." (*Zeitschrift der Deutschen Morgenländischen Gesellschaft*, 1933, p. 31.)
26 Von Hammer, "Sur la chevalerie des Arabes," *Journal Asiatique*, 1849, pp. 5 *ff.*
27 An interesting study on the relations of guild and fraternity in Europe will be found in Billioud, *De la Confrérie à la Corporation; les classes industrielles en Provence aux XIVme, Xvme, et XVIme siècles*, Mémoires de l'Institut Historique de Provence, t. IV, Marseille, 1929.
28 Tæschner, *Die Islamische Futuwwabünde. Z.D.M.G.*, 1933, pp. 6 *ff.*
29 Thorning, *Beiträge, op. cit.*
30 Gordlevsky, *Iz Žizni Tsekhov v. Turtsii*, Zapiski Kollegii Vostokovedov, vol. ii, p. 235. A very brief French summary is given by G. Vajda in *Revue des Études Islamiques*," 1934, pp. 79–80.
31 Köprülü, *Les Origines, op. cit.*, pp. 76–8 and 100–12.
32 The etymology and meaning of the word Akhi are uncertain. Gordlevsky derives it from the Arabic "Akh," a brother, and connects the Akhis with the Pure Brethren (Ikhwan as-Safa). Deny on the hand derives the word from an east-Turkish root "aqi," meaning chivalrous, generous (*Journal Asiatique*, 1920, part ii, p. 183). In a recent lecture, unfortunately not printed, of which he has been kind enough to lend me the MS., Deny has developed his theory further and, I think, proved it beyond question.
33 Gordlevsky, *Iz Žizni Tsekhov, op. cit.*, p. 247–8.

34 Köprülü, *Les Origines du Biktachisme, Essai sur le Développement Historique de l'Hétérodoxie Musulmane en Asie Mineure*, Paris, 1926.
It should be noted however that Tæschner denies any Isma'ili or Qarmati traces in the Akhi movement, and regards them as basically Sunni (*Beiträge zur Geschichte der Akhis in Anatolien*, Islamica IV, 1931, p. 17 *ff.*)

35 Ibn Battuta, Paris 1854, vol. II, p. 260 *ff.* For an examination of other sources on the Akhis, see Tæschner (*Beiträge op cit.*), who examines a very interesting Akhi manuscript of the 14th cent., attributed to Yahya ibn Halil. In this tract, three grades are distinguished – Yiĝit (= fata in Turkish), Akhi and Sheikh – the last being rather theoretical than real. The Akhi had the duty of summoning and presiding at the weekly meetings, and instructing and initiating novices (terbiyyet). The Yiĝitler (plural of Yiĝit) were divided into two classes, Qavli and Saifi, the latter being those from whom new Akhis were appointed when vacancies occurred. As permanent functionary, there was the Naqib, or Master of Ceremonies.

36 Gordlevsky, *Iz Žizni Tsekbov, op. cit.*

37 With two or three exceptions, these tracts are all still in manuscript, and are scattered all over Europe and Asia in public libraries and private collections. For a survey and classification see Thorning, *Beiträge*, p. 15–54 and Tæschner, *Futuwwa-Studien*, Islamica V, 1932.

38 The Sheikh is also known as Amin, 'Arif, and sometimes as Naqib, the Naqib as separate rank disappearing. In Turkey the Sheikh is called Sheikh-Usta or Esnaf Başi, and in Central Asia Aqsaqal.

39 Also Muta'allim, and in Turkish 'çĭrak'.

40 Gordlevsky, *Izvestia Akademii Nauk S.S.S.R.*, 1927, p. 1171 (= *Revue des Etudes Islamiques*, 1934, pp. 81 *ff.*).

41 Gordlevsky says that owing to lack of capital the period during which the artisan was Khalfa often extended beyond the minimum.

42 Sometimes of the Sheikh, the Kiaya (vice-head) and two masters.

43 See further *Enc. of Is.* Article "Shadd."

44 Evliya Çelebi *Siyahat-Name*, Istanbul, 1314, vol. I, pp. 473 *ff.* An English translation, unfortunately inaccurate and incomplete, will be found in *Narrative of Travels in Europe, Asia and Africa by Evliya Efendi*, translated by J. von Hammer, London, 1846, vol. I part II pp. 90 *ff.*

45 Note that the number is the same as that fixed for the days of apprenticeship in Anatolia.

46 Elia Qoudsi, *Notice sur les corporations de Damas.* (In Arabic) Travaux de la VI-e Session du Congrès International des Orientalistes, Leyden, 1884, pp. 3 *ff.*

47 With reference to this, it may not be out of place to mention a curious connection between freemasonary and the Islamic guilds. At the beginning of the nineteenth century some French travellers in Syria claim to have discovered a close resemblance between the secret signs of the freemasons and those of the Druzes, a heretical sect inhabiting the Lebanon. As the Druzes are more or less identical with the Qarmatis, whose great influence on the Islamic guilds we have already mentioned, the connection is interesting. Von Hammer regards the

whole European guild system as being derived from that of Islam. (*Constantinopolis und der Bosporos*, Pesth, 1822, p. 395.)

48 Another observer of the Cairo guilds denies this. See Martin, *Les Bazars du Caire*, Paris, 1910.

49 M. Sedky, "La Corporation des Cordonniers ... du Caire," *Revue Egyptienne*, 1912, no. 4.

50 Our survey of the Islamic guilds has of necessity been mainly confined to those of the Central lands of Islam, viz. Egypt and S.W. Asia. There remain, however, the very interesting guilds of the peripheral lands, especially of Indonesia, Asiatic Russia and Morocco, which possess special characteristics of their own and which it is impossible to consider here. For further details see Gavrilov, R.E., I, 1928 *op. cit.*; Schuyler, *Turkestan*, London, 1876, vol. i, and *Enquête sur les Corps. du Maroc*, *op. cit.*, and Atger, *Les corporations tunisiennes*, Paris, 1909.

51 E.g. Mas'udi (*d.* AD 956) notes the existence of a thieves-guild in Baghdad (*Les Prairies d'Or*, Paris, 1861, viii, p. 189).

52 Ibn Khaldun, Paris, III, p. 513. See also Ibn Jawzi, *Talbis Iblis*, Cairo, 1340, pp. 415 *ff.*

53 Prof. Coornaert tells me that such organisations are not special to Islam, as similar guilds are to be found in the later Middle Ages in France.

54 See *Revue du Monde Musulman*, vols li, lii, lviii. Even in twentieth-century Fez, Massignon notes that the guilds preserve "un esprit de frondeur très particulier contre le Souverain" (*Le Corps de métier*, *op. cit.*).

55 An apparent exception to this statement is to be found in thirteenth- and fourteenth-century Anatolia. Here a section of the master craftsmen of the Akhi associations, as Tæschner (*Beiträge*) and Köprülü (*Origines*) have observed, seem to have evolved into a sort of urban bourgeoisie – a "Bürgerliches Patriziat" in Tæschner's phrase – enjoying considerable economic as well as social power. This tendency thus provides some parallel to the communal and municipal movement in Europe. It is however strictly limited in scope, and never developed far enough for any conflict of interests between masters and journeymen to arise. It is exclusive to Anatolia, where the strength of Byzantine influences and the recent immigration of the Turks created special circumstances, and even there it was suppressed as soon as the Ottoman dynasty succeeded in establishing itself. This temporary and local divergence does not therefore invalidate our general principle. Tæschner, it may be mentioned, regards these Akhis as an essentially bourgeois movement rather than a bourgeois outgrowth of the guilds, and places actual identification of Futuwwa and guild a couple of centuries later.

56 Although Qoudsi says that the journeymen form the main part of the guild, it should be remembered that Qoudsi is a late testimony, given when much had already changed. Evliya and Sedky on the other hand do not mention the rank.

57 See Billioud (*op. cit.*, pp. 22 and 23), on the monopolistic and feudal character of the French "Corporations." The masters, he notes, form

a "caste féodale héréditaire," and are "par avance hostiles à de futurs concurrents, c'est-à-dire à tous les éléments nouveaux, étrangers à leur caste." Compare with this the attitude of Masters towards candidates for mastership in the Islamic guilds.

18

AN EPISTLE ON MANUAL CRAFTS

Bernard Lewis

The eighth epistle of the first series of the *Rasā'il Ikhwān aṣ-Ṣafā* is devoted to the consideration of the practical crafts. This is the earliest record we possess containing a classified survey of the trades and crafts of mediæval Islam, and is, despite its somewhat abstract and philosophic treatment, a most valuable document for the economic history of the Islamic lands. Classical Arabic literature is in the main the product of a leisured class, the so-called Khawāss, which considered such matters beneath their attention, and only by the laborious collection of odd references in various works it is possible to reconstruct a picture of the life and development of the unprivileged classes in Islamic society. Only in the *Ḥisba* literature, intended to aid market-inspectors in controlling the wayward tendencies of the market folk, is any consideration of artisans and tradesmen to be found. It is thus of some significance that the Pure Brethren should have seen fit to devote one of their epistles to this subject, and to include it in the same series as geometry, astrology, music, psychology and other subjects more within the range of contemporary learning.[1] This interest in artisans and craftsmen tallies well with the popular tendency attributed to the Ismā'īlī movement, of which the *Rasā'il* are a product, and with the strong Ismā'īlī strain discernible in the ideology and structure of the Islamic guilds.[2]

After this epistle, we must wait until the development of the *Ḥisba* literature, the earliest extant specimen of which dates from the 12th century, before we find any detailed account of the organisation and distribution of the people of the markets.[3] Among

Source: *Islamic Culture*, 1943, vol. 17, pp. 142–51.

other sources we may note a brief classification of crafts by the 13th century geographer Qazwīnī,[4] and a second abstract consideration by the historian ibn-Khaldūn,[5] in the 14th century. The treatment of ibn-Khaldūn clearly owes much to that of the *Rasā'il* but, as may be expected, it is sociological in its conception, dealing with the place of the artisan in civilised society.

The *Risāla* opens with a series of general philosophic statements and abstract definitions of a type well-known from the remainder of the work. Crafts, we are told, are of two kinds, intellectual and practical. The latter form the subject of the *Risāla*, which will deal with "their matter, their essences, their quantities and their qualities, and the quality of the manifestation of their craftsmanship on the materials allotted to them." Manual labour consists of the impression by the craftsman on his material of the form which he has in his mind, and the product is thus a sum of form and matter. Products are of four kinds – human, natural, spiritual, and divine. "Human products are those which craftsmen make by shaping, painting, and dyeing natural bodies in the city market-places. . . ." Natural products are the phenomena of the animal, vegetable, and mineral kingdoms; spiritual products are the four elements – earth, fire, air, and water – and the astral bodies. Divine products are the abstract forms of created matter, emanating from God.

The next passage contains a discussion of form, matter, and implement. The same body can sometimes be matter (*hayūla*), sometimes material, (*mawḍū'*), sometimes form (*ṣūra*), sometimes product (*maṣnū'*), sometimes instrument (*āla*), and sometimes implement (*adāt*). Thus iron as such is matter. When used by a blacksmith it is material. When made into a knife it is a product. When used as a knife by a butcher it is an implement.

The materials used by craftsmen fall into two categories, simple and complex. The former consists of the four elements, the latter of the animal, vegetable, and mineral kingdoms. The craftsman needs both instruments, which are defined as being parts of the body, and implements, which are external aids "such as the axe of the carpenter, the hammer of the smith, the needle of the tailor, the pen of the scribe, and the awl of the cobbler." A classification of seven movements, one circular and six straight, follows – *e.g.*, the axe goes from above downwards, the saw goes backwards and forwards, the gimlet moves in a circle. The next passage, dealing with material gives us our first classification of crafts according to the material used. These may most conveniently be set out in tabular form.

1. Simple material.

(*a*) WATER

sailor:[6] ملاح
water-carrier:[7] سقاء
those who sell water from skins:[8] رواء
maker or seller of syrup:[9] شراب
swimmers: سباح

(*b*) EARTH

diggers of wells
miners
diggers of rivers[10]
grave-diggers[11]
diggers of canals

(*c*) FIRE

naphtha-extractor:[12] نفاط
torch-bearer:[13] مشعل
stoker: وقاد

(*d*) AIR

piper: زمار
trumpeter: بواق

(*e*) WATER AND EARTH

potter: فخارى
earthenware-pot seller:[14] قدورى
porcelain-maker:[15] غضار
milk-beater: ضراب اللبن

2. Complex materials.

(*a*) MINERAL

smith:[16] حداد
glazier:[18] زجاج
coppersmith:[17] قار
goldsmith:[19] صواغ
lead-worker: رصاص

(*b*) VEGETABLE

(*i*) *Basic vegetable material*

carpenter: نجار
reed-mat seller:[20] حصرى
palm-leaf seller: خواص
basket-maker: القاصى
rush-mat seller: بوار

(*ii*) *Bark, etc.*

flax-spinner:[21] كتان
paper-worker:[22] من يعمل الكاغد
hemp-worker: من يعمل القنب

(iii) Secondary vegetable material (leaves, flowers, fruit, seed, etc.)

flour-dealer:[23] دقاق

pressers:[24] عصار — seed-dealer: بزار

rice-dealer:[25] رزاز — sesame-dealer[26] شيرجي

(*c*) ANIMAL

(i) Animals

hunter: صياد — grooms:[27] ساسة الدواب

shepherds and cowherds: دعاة الغنم والبقر — farrier: بيطار

bird-keepers:[28] اصحاب الطيور

(ii) Animal bodies

butcher:[29] قصاب — cobbler: خرّاز

roaster:[30] شواء — leather-worker:[34] سيوري

cook:[31] طباخ — (?) leather-bottle maker: دنان

tanner:[32] دباغ

shoemaker:[33] اسكاف — (?) sandal-maker: حذاء

(iii) Quantities of bodies

weigher:[35] وزان — money-changer:[36] صيرف

measurer: كيال — market-crier:[37] دلال

cubit-measurer: ذراع — evaluator: مقوم

(iv) Human bodies

physician: طبيب — barber: مزين

This concludes the first classification, according to material, and brings us to the second, according to tools and implements.

1. Those who use only their own limbs, and no implements.

(*a*) THE TONGUE

preacher[38] — judge

poet — reader

(*b*) THE EYES

sentinel:[39] ناطور — watchman:[40] ديدبان

(*c*) HAND AND TONGUE

weaver: حاكي — wailing-woman: نائحه

(*d*) WHOLE BODY

dancer:[41] رقاص — swimmer: سابح

2. Those who use tools.

(*a*) ONE TOOL

trumpeter — drummer: دفاف
piper

(*b*) TWO TOOLS

tailor: خياط (using needle and scissors)
scribe: كاتب (using pen and ink)

Incorporated in this section we find a secondary classification according to movement and posture.

(*a*) PERMANENT MOVEMENT

messenger:[42] ساعى — surveyor: ماسح

(*b*) PERMANENTLY SEATED

garment-mender: دفاء — carder: نداف

(*c*) PERMANENTLY STANDING

carder:[43] حلاج — rice-grinder: دقاق الرز

"he who works the water-wheel with his feet."[44]

After a digression on the usefulness of fire in the practice of crafts and trades, the *Risāla* goes on to its third classification, according to "ranks." This is the only one that is based on economic principles, and is by far the most practical and realistic. It is followed in its main lines by ibn-Khaldūn.[45]

Crafts are divided into three main groups: (a) primary, i.e., those called forth by necessity, (b) ancillary, i.e., accessory and finishing trades to the foregoing,[46] (c) luxury, "those which beautify and adorn." The three main sub-divisions of the first class are weaving, agriculture, and building, which satisfy the three basic needs for clothing, food, and shelter. Each of them has a group of secondary trades belonging to the second class.

(*a*) WEAVING

spinning[47] غزل — the craft of fuller: قصارة
carding[48] — mending: رفو
tailoring[49] — embroidering: طرز

(*b*) AGRICULTURE

irrigation — milling:[51] طحن
canal-digging — pressing:[52] عصر

carpentry[50]	baking:[53] خبز
smiths	cooking
mining	

(*c*) BUILDING[54]

carpentry	smiths

The luxury trades, in conclusion, deal with commodities such as brocade, silk, and perfume.

After another digression on the philosophic principles of the Pure Brethren, we come to the last main classification, according to "nobility," that is, according to the titles of the crafts to merit and distinction.

Crafts may derive their nobility from their indispensability, such as the three primary crafts mentioned above; or from the precious nature of their material, as is the case with jewellers, perfumers, and mint-workers; or from their skilled workmanship, as astronomical instrument-makers. "For a piece of copper, worth 5 dirhams, when wrought into an astrolabe is worth 100 dirhams, and this price is not for the matter but for the form that has been impressed upon it;" or from the fact that the exercise of their crafts benefits the community as a whole, without distinction, as bath-attendants, scavengers and barbers – "For the use of the bath is for small and great, noble and humble citizen and foreigner, near and far, all of them equal and without privilege in its use. In most crafts there is inequality among their users, and they differ as to their food, drink, dwellings, and other products of the craftsman. The state of the rich differs from that of the poor, except in the case of the bath-attendant, the barber, and their like. As for the trade scavenger, the harm resulting from their abandoning it is grievous and universal to the people of the city. Thus, if the perfumers, the material of whose craft is the opposite of that of the scavengers, were to close their shops and markets for one month, the harm which would befall the people of the city would be less than that which would result if the scavengers were to cease their work for one week, for the city would be filled with refuse and ordure and filth and carrion, and with that which would plague the life of its people."

I have quoted this passage at some length, as the conception of social functions contained in it is of no small interest. The equalitarian ideas implicit in it go beyond the routine expressions of the poetists, and illustrate once again the social tendencies of the Ismāʿīlī movement.[55]

The classification by title to merit concludes with those whose nobility lies in the craft itself, as jugglers, painters, and musicians. The discussion of the last two is of some interest, but falls beyond the scope of this analysis.

Having completed their classification of the crafts, the Pure Brethren turn to the factors determining the choice of a craft. As one might expect, astrology plays a large part, and the practices of the ancient Greeks are quoted in support. A passage of some interest gives the astrological causes of the existence of four classes who do not take to crafts at all – those who do not learn a craft "because of pride, as the sons of kings . . . because of asceticism and piety and contentment with little of the things of this world and preoccupation with the seeking of the next, as prophets and those who emulate them . . . because of laziness and clumsiness, and contentment with humiliation and contempt in the seeking of a livelihood, as labourers and beggars . . . because of their contemptibility, weakness of nature and littleness of understanding, as women and those who resemble them among men."

The transmission of a craft from father to son is also commended, and the Sāsānid king Ardashīr, son of Bābakān[56] is quoted with approval as having made this compulsory: "And know, O, brother, that all this is a protection for kingship, so that those who are not of it should not seek for it. . . ."

The remainder of the epistle consists of pious and philosophic generalisations, and only the following passage is of any interest: "And know, O, brother, that every human craftsman requires a teacher (*Ustādh*) from whom he learns his craft or his science, and that his teacher in turn requires a teacher before him, and so on until one is reached whose knowledge does not derive from any human being. And this can be in one of two ways – we can say, as do the philosophers, that he invented it himself by the powers of his own soul, thought, vision, and effort, or we can say, as do the prophets, that he inherited it from one who was not human.

Despite the general terms in which it is couched, this passage may conceivably be connected with the hierarchy and legends of the Islamic guilds, which are known to us from the documents of later centuries. The guild-tracts,[57] surviving specimens of which date from the 14th century onwards, are almost all constructed on the same plan, in three parts. The first part consists of legends concerning the origins of the craft, the adventures of the traditional founder, etc. It usually gives a chain of initiations – e.g., God initiated Gabriel, Gabriel initiated Muḥammad, Muḥammad initiated ʿAlī, ʿAlī initiated Salmān Fārsī, Salmān initiated the *Pīrs*,[58] the traditional patrons of the guilds, the *Pīrs* initiated the *Furūʿ*, the secondary patrons of the sub-guilds, and these initiated the ordinary guild chiefs. These legends usually show strong Ismāʿīlī and Ṣūfī influence. The second part contains the list of *Pīrs* and *Furūʿ* of the different crafts. These are usually figures drawn from the Old Testament, the Qur'ān, or from Muslim history and hagiology. Thus, Adam is the patron of peasants and bakers, Seth of weavers and stitchers, Noah of carpenters, Idrīs (Enoch) of tailors, David of smiths, Abraham of cooks, and Ismael of armourers. The third section consists of a catechism for the initiation of an apprentice (*Mubtadi or Mutaʿallim*). The master-craftsmen were known as *Muʿallim*, or more frequently as *Ustādh* or *Usta*. This use of the word in this context by the Pure Brethren is to be noted.

Such then is the contribution of the Pure Brethren to the history of the Islamic crafts. Its defects are great and obvious. It is throughout abstract and theoretical in its approach. Except for one brief and problematic reference, it tells us nothing of the organisation and ideology of the guilds, though these were undoubtedly in existence at the time. Nor does it offer any information about the conditions and methods of work of the type found in the *Ḥisba* writings. Its value is none the less great, and lies in three things: in its enumeration and classification, to some extent on economic lines, of the chief crafts practised at the time; in the evidence it offers of Ismāʿīlī contacts with the artisan community; and, finally, in its pioneer statement of the nobility of labour, anticipating and perhaps influencing the documents later produced by the guildsmen themselves for the glorification and honour of their own callings.

NOTES

1 See also Vol. IV, p. 214.

2 Cf. B. Lewis, '*The Islamic Guilds*', *Economic History Review*, VIII, London, 1937.

3 The most readily accessible *Ḥisba* texts are: ibn al-Ukhuwwa, *Maʿālim al-Qurba fī Aḥkām al-Ḥisba*, ed. R. Levy, London, 1938, and As-Saqaṭī, *Manuel Hispanique de Ḥisba*, ed. G.S. Colin and E. Lévi-Provencal, Paris, 1931. A survey of *Ḥisba* literature will be found in the introductions to both editions.

4 J. Ruska, *Kazwinistudien*, Der Islam, IV, p. 244.

5 The *Muqaddima*, ed. de Slane, II, pp. 306–328. There are also other late sources, e.g., the *Irshād al-Qāsid* of al-Akfānī and later encyclopædias. A detailed survey of the guilds of 17th century Istanbul will be found in Evliya Celebi, *Siyahat-Name*, Istanbul, 1314. I, p. 687 ff. Partial English translation by J. von Hammer, London, 1846, I, ii, p. 90 ff. On the guilds of modern Morocco see *Enquête sur les Corporations Musulmanes du Maroc, R.M.M.*, Vol. 58.

6 Ma'ālim, p. 222, where rules against overloading vessels are given.

7 Ibid., p. 239 ff.

8 *Ma'ālim* where they are referred to as اصحاب الزوارق or ارباب الزوارق.

9 Ibid., p. 155 where a list of the kinds of syrup made is given. Their inclusion in this category seems to cast a serious light on the profession, which is perhaps explained by the remarks in the *Ma'ālim*; "The frauds in this class are numerous . . . it is the duty of a Muḥtasib to frighten them and warn them of divine retribution and earthly penalties."

10 The Arab geographers give detailed accounts of the digging and opening of canals in Iraq, Egypt, and elsewhere. Large canals are often described as *Nahr*, river. See Hitti, *History of the Arabs*, London, 1937, p. 349, and references there quoted.

11 Saqaṭī, p. 68 gives some rules of the practice of this profession.

12 See E. Wiedemann, *Beiträge zur Geschichte der Naturwissenschaften* (S. N. Phys. Med. Soz., Erlangen), VI, p. 39, on the extraction of naphtha and the processes used.

13 Cf. Evliya, p. 544, Tr. 127, on the *Mes'aleci*.

14 *Ma'ālim*, p. 222, as sellers of قدور.

15 Ibid., p. 223–4 on potters (فاخران) and porcelain-makers.

16 *Ma'ālim*, p. 148; Saqaṭī p. 65.

17 *Ma'ālim*, p. 147, on the نخاس.

18 Saqaṭī, p. 67.

19 *Ma'ālim*, 144, where elaborate rules are given, containing the sad reflection: "In sum, the frauds and deceptions of the goldsmiths are secret, and can hardly be recognised. Nothing can keep them from this but their honesty and their religion."

20 *Ma'ālim*, p. 232, discusses the choice of reeds, the process of manufacture, and the trade regulations. Cf. Evliya, p. 554. Tr. 201, on the *hasīrcī*, or mat-maker.

21 *Ma'ālim*, p. 143, with the note; "No one may be allowed to trade in flax until his loyalty, chastity, and virtue have been established in the *Muḥtasib's* court, for their dealing is with women."

22 On the introduction of paper to the Arab world, see Hitti, p. 414. The first paper-mill in Baghdad was established by the Barmecide Faḍdl b. Yaḥya.

23 Saqaṭī, p. 20 ff, where the making and marketing of flour is discussed at some length.

24 *Ma'ālim*, p. 238; "The rice-dealers are greatly addicted to fraud. A reliable man should be appointed over them to prevent their mixing salt with the rice and selling it to the Muslims as good rice, for this is forbidden."

25 I.e., those who press fruit, olives, etc. See Saqaṭī, p. 68; *Ma'ālim*, p. 227–8.

26 *Ma'ālim*, p. 227–8.
27 *Ma'ālim*, p. 150, for a detailed statement.
28 Evliya, p. 583, Tr. 197 enumerates the bird-catchers, fowlers, bird-dealers, poulterers, sparrow-merchants and nightingale-merchants.
29 *Ma'ālim*, 99.
30 I.e., sellers of cooked meats. See *Ma'ālim*, p. 92; Saqaṭī, p. 40.
31 Saqaṭī, p. 35; *Ma'ālim*, p. 106, where they are accused of giving much fat and little meat, and deluding people into thinking that there is much meat.
32 *Ma'ālim*, p. 239; Saqaṭī, p. 63.
33 *Ma'ālim*, p. 149. The difference in meaning between the اسكاف , the خراز and the حذاء is not quite clear. On the word *Iskāf* see Lammens, *Les mots francais dérivés de l'arabe*, Beirut 1890, p. 107.
34 The دن is a vessel for water or wine. The *Vocabulista* (Schiapazzel, Florence, 1871) has "indria" (?) (Idria ?). The context indicates a leather or skin vessel instead of the more usual meaning of wood or earthen ware. Cf. Aramaic *Udnā*, a leathern bottle.
35 The *wazzān* and the *kayyāl*, are considered at some length in Saqaṭī, chapters 2 and 3, pp. 11–20. The former dealt with weights, the latter with measures of capacity, more particularly of grain. The *kayl* is often mentioned as a specific measure, e.g., Saqaṭī, p. 31, "half a *kayl* of flour." The ذراع is not mentioned as such, but Saqaṭī (p. 69) speaks of ذرع as a cloth measurer. The *Ma'ālim* deals with weights (p. 83), capacity measures (p. 85) and measures of length (p. 87) in chapter 10.
36 *Ma'ālim*, p. 143.
37 A kind of commission agent or broker. See *Ma'ālim*, p. 135, where some sound economic principles are given. It is forbidden to act both as agent and as principal in a transaction. The *dallāl* is mentioned both by the *Enquête* and by Evliya.
38 Evliya, p. 522, Tr. 111, includes these along with other learned professions.
39 Two imported words – *Nāṭūr* from Aramaic *Nāṭōrā*, etymologically equivalent to Arabic *Nāẓir*. *Dīdbān* is of course Persian. In later times the word was used to describe a customs-inspector. See Dozy, *Supplément*, I, 481 and II, 683.
40 According to *Ma'ālim*, 51, and other juristic works, this profession is illegal. The legal regulations of Sa'ūdī Arabia at the present day expressly forbid it.
41 This may refer to the class of building workers mentioned in *Ma'ālim*, 234–9.
42 Cf. Evliya, p. 521, Tr. 110.
43 See Lane and Dozy for the two different processes described by ندف and حلج. The *Vocabulista* translates both as "*carminare*."
44 On the water-wheel see Wiedemann, VI, p. 30.
45 *Muq*. II, p. 316 ff. ibn-Kh. divides crafts into two classes, useful and noble. The first is sub-divided into agriculture, building, and weaving, with an argumentation similar to that of the *Risāla*. The noble include writers, physicians, librarians, etc.
46 It is interesting to note that according to Evliya this principle was

generally adopted in the classification of the guilds of Istanbul. Thus, the salt-makers (p. 537, Tr. 121) and water-carriers (p. 539, Tr. 123) were ancillary (*yamak*) to the bakers, as water and salt are necessary in the making of bread. "*Ekmek tuzsuz olmaz.*" The hemp-merchants are likewise ancillary to the boatmen (Tr. 130, missing in printed text).

47 *Ma'ālim*, 136.

48 The thread-market (*Sūq al-Ghazl*) was a focal point in the mediæval Muslim city. V. Massignon, "Le corps de Métier et la Cité Musulmane," *Rèvue Internationale de Sociologie*, v., 28, 1920, p. 473 ff., and Lewis, *Guilds*, p. 20.

49 See *Ma'ālim*, p. 137, on tailors, menders, and fullers. Also Saqaṭī, p. 62–3, where a rather more detailed enumeration of clothing trades is given.

50 The carpenter, blacksmith, and miner are included here as producers of agricultural implements and their raw materials.

51 *Ma'ālim*, p. 89; Saqaṭī, p. 21. "Their deception is that they mix the bad with the good, . . . and their work is hidden."

52 V. Supra.

53 Saqaṭī, p. 20; *Ma'ālim*, p. 81. For kneading, bakers may not use their feet, knees, or elbows, as this involves disrespect for the bread, and also the danger that drops of sweat may fall into it.

54 On the building trades in general see *Ma'ālim*, pp. 234 ff.

55 Among the Sunni polemicists both Ghazālī (*Streitschrift gegen die Batinijjasekte*, ed. Goldziher, Leyden, 1916, Extracts 2, 14, 15, 16) and ibn al-Jauzi (*Talbis Iblīs*, Cairo, 1926, pp. 111, 113, 116) mentions the special concern of the Ism'īlīs for the *'awāmm*, the common people, and are quite frank in considering it a social as much as a theological danger to the established order. On this subject, and on the alleged communism of the Isma'īlīs see further Lewis, *The Origin of Ismā'ilism*, Cambridge, 1940, p. 90 ff.

56 The founder of the dynasty, in the 3rd century AD

57 Called *Kitāb al-Futuwwa* or *Futuwwat-Nāmā* in Arabic and Turkish respectively. With two or three exceptions scattered all over Europe and Asia in public and private collections. For a survey and classification see Thorning, *Beiträge zur Kenntnis des Islamischen Vereinswesens*, Berlin, 1913, pp. 15–54, and Tæschner, *Futuwwa Studien*, Islamica, V, 1932. Goldziher has analysed an Egyptian tract in his *Abhandlungen zur Arabischen Philologie*, II, Leyden, 1899, p. lxxvi. The full text of a Turkish guild tract will be found in Evliya Celebi, p. 489, Tr., p. 90 ff. On the *Futuwwa* in general see Taeschner, *Die Islamische Futuwwabūnde Z.D.M.G.*, 1933, p. 6 ff.

58 In the Arab lands *Bir*, plural *Abyār*.

19

THE ORGANIZATION OF THE FATIMID PROPAGANDA

V. Ivanov

1 THE DĀʿI AND THE CAUSES OF HIS SUCCESSES

The Bāṭinī (i.e. Ismaili) *dāʿī* already at an early date becomes a prominent figure in the annals of Islam.[1] As elusive and omnipresent as the 'Scarlet Pimpernel', as malicious, ruthlessly cruel, and unscrupulous in farfetched diabolical schemes as the leader of a criminal gang in any detective best seller, as superhumanly clever, brave, persevering, and daring as any detective hero of the best American cinema film, the *dāʿī* appears as the chief 'villain of the plot', responsible for many failures and defeats which the corrupt and incapable Abbasid administration had to suffer. He was at the bottom of every political murder, of every uprising, every manifestation of popular discontent, as seen through official eyes, discussed in bazar rumours, and recorded by the authors of many historical works, who surrounded him with a halo of mystery, romance, and, above all, of the fame of extraordinary organizing talent. And such is the power of 'wide publicity', of advertisement, that by the mere fact of the continuous repetition this obviously exaggerated and mythical figure has for ever acquired historic reality, completely obscuring the real Ismaili propagandist and teacher. Even now, with more developed sense of proportion and critical methods of research, this fictitious figure is often taken as true and real. Such eminent Orientalists as the late Prof. de Geoje and E.G. Browne may serve as good

Source: *Journal of the Royal Asiatic Society* (Bombay Branch), 1939, vol. 15, pp. 1–35.

examples: they apparently accepted the story, and unreservedly believed in it.[2]

The difficulty of verifying this traditional version arises from the complete absence of impartial records, and also the great scarcity of information coming from the sectarian sources which, although not impartial, can to some extent help us to check the facts. Such information is only available about very few *dā'īs*: the one who laid the foundation of the Fatimid empire, Abū 'Abdi'l-lāh ash-Shī'ī, about Rāshidu'd-din Sinān, and very little about the Manṣūru'l-Yaman, or Ḥasan b. aṣ-Ṣabbāḥ. These, of course, were extraordinary men, giants as compared with the ordinary, rank and file, *dā'ī*. They appear first of all as born leaders, talented generals, men of iron will, of unfliching devotion and high religious enthusiasm, and yet broadminded, with plenty of commonsense, and strong creative intellect. They apparently had nothing in common with the 'classic' figure of the *dā'ī*, as it appears in general literature[3]—a lurking preacher of sedition, atheism and looseness. We can firmly believe that these outstanding men did not represent a class entirely different from the ordinary *dā'ī*. It only was that their towering personalities presented on a gigantic scale the features which certainly existed, although on a much smaller scale, in the character of every one of their subordinates and less outstanding colleagues.

But if we disbelieve legend, and 'uncrown' the romantic figure of the *dā'ī*, we have to seek elsewhere for a reliable explanation for the indubitable historical fact of his extraordinary successes, almost bordering upon the miraculous. The immense success of the Ismaili propaganda, from the Atlantic to innermost Asia, is a fact which is beyond dispute. The solution of this problem obviously lies in the psychology of the masses under the Omayad, and later on the Abbasid rule. Continuous unrest, economical distress, and dissatisfaction with the conditions of life, laid enormous stress on the possibilities which in popular ideas would be offered by the theocratical organization of the state, on the lines of the Shi'ite ideal. This explains the astounding number of almost completely hopeless Shi'ite risings all over the Islamic world, which was full of Messianistic expectations, longing for the ruler, Imam, 'who will fill the earth with justice and equity just as much as it is filled with injustice and oppression of one by the other'.

It seems quite obvious therefore that the supernatural success of the *dā'īs* is nothing but illusion, the same aberration of the vision as the rapid movement of the landscape seen from the window of a rapidly moving train: not that the *dāʿīs* were seducing the masses, but the masses were waiting for someone to organize the movement which already was widespread and general, and only required co-ordination of effort and linking together of the isolated groups.

We know quite well the peculiar mentality of the decaying and no longer popular régimes everywhere: to the last moment, when they are overthrown, and even after this, their heads and supporters can never understand and realize their own failure. They would continually and blindly believe that their subjects love, even worship them; that they are only too willing to sacrifice everything to please them. That their administration, even if not perfect, nevertheless is all that is wanted. And that if there are signs of discontent and opposition, this is the work of the enemies of the state, spies, conspirators, of those who sow sedition and trouble, seducing the poor simple people who otherwise would never be able to feel discontent, or complain on anything, without the incitement of such villains. No, they would be only too glad to obey their government, and believe in God according to the rules prescribed by the religion, approved and recommended by the state. How many terrible catastrophes and explosions, accompanied by enormous sufferings of millions, would have been avoided in history by timely realization, and doing the needful, on the part of those concerned. But usually all their energies become devoted to the extermination of the 'mischief mongers', while very little is done to alter the conditions of the masses in such a way as to paralyse the effect of the mischief makers from inside.

The Abbasids were no exception to this rule—which perhaps is the only rule that knows no exceptions generally—and persecuted all sorts of sectarians, especially the Shiʿites, attributing to them all kinds of fantastic schemes to uproot Islam and turn the people to atheism, or to the ancient religion of the Persians.[4] But this only could drive the popular discontent under ground, making it still more dangerous and subversive, because it not only remains beyond the control, but also out of the vision of the officials, and thus may at any time strike an unexpected blow.

With the ground prepared in this way, the Fatimid propaganda was able to achieve its wonderful successes mainly through one of its most peculiar features—the complete decentralization of its agents. From the original Ismaili document, which is summarized in this paper, and which dates from the period at which the power of the Fatimids attained its culminating point, we can see how carefully the candidates for the post of *dāʿī* were selected, how high standard of ability was expected from them, and how difficult was it to satisfy the demands. The responsibilities of the *dāʿī* were tremendous, and the candidate had to possess exceptional talents to be fit for the duty. But once he was appointed, he was given full authority. It is really astonishing to see how independent was he expected to be in his work: the *dāʿī* was not encouraged to bother the Imam and the central government with trivial and routine matters. He had to use his own discretion, conforming with the general tendency and spirit of his mission. 'Just as when the husband deposits his sperm into the womb of his wife, and she conceives, he does not interfere with the development of the embryo, etc., but merely feeds and protects his wife, so the Imam, having sent his *dāʿī* to a certain community, does not interfere with his work, and only gives general directions and guidance to his people.' And the *dāʿī* takes the whole responsibility upon himself. 'If God asks the Imam to account for the welfare of the community the Imam refers Him to the *dāʿī* in charge, who takes upon himself the whole responsibility for this.'

The results of this policy we can see from history: decentralization, coupled with the selection of the right type of men—the virtue of princes, which the earlier Fatimids possessed, especially the great statesmen like Mahdī, Qā'im, and Muʿizz—helped to build a great empire. It seems that the increase of centralization always indicates a certain distrust of rulers in their subjects. It is a fact that the most unpopular or even hated régimes always are the most centralized—we have an ample opportunity to see this now for ourselves. And if the supreme ruler, especially semi-Divine, as the Ismaili Imam, instead of keeping himself far above the squabbles of his subjects, and the imperfect working of the administrative machine, himself takes up the drudgery of practical government, making himself directly responsible for all its wrongs —as the last Fatimid caliph-Imam al-Āmir bi'l-lāh did—then the play is finished, and the curtain falls. What invariably happens, is rapid decay, and final rot. This is why the Mastaʿlian community could survive the catastrophe only in remote Yaman, under the rule of an autonomous *dāʿī*.

Such were the two important causes which contributed to the success of the Fatimid propaganda, helping it to achieve its almost miraculous results. Instead of the ridiculous and childish pictures drawn by the authors of the anti-Ismaili camp, we can easily visualize a far more convincing state of affairs. Suffering population, longing for peace, a change towards more normal and human conditions, dreaming about the righteous ruler from the house of the Prophet, receives the *dāʿī*, a specially selected and trained man of outstanding abilities, strong character, an enthusiast in his devotion, ambitious, hard working, a man of wide education, of broad vision, acute and shrewd. It is difficult to believe the stories that such a man would drop from the sky. Surely, the ground was always prepared for him, in some way or other. And when he gets into a commanding position, and really knows his people, helping them, ruling them justly, etc., his success, and the success of his mission, are sure. This is apparently the typical course of the *dāʿī*'s career; from such individual local successes, under the able supervision of a born ruler, the Fatimid empire was built.

II THE DOGMA OF THE ḤUDŪDU'D-DĪN

As mentioned above, Ismaili literature contains very few materials which would permit us to form an idea about the organization of the propaganda under the Fatimids. This is particularly sad, because rarely any Ismaili dogmatical or esoteric work omits to deal with a peculiar abstract theory of priesthood and its hierarchy, *ḥudūdu'd-dīn*, which was evolved and emphasized by the doctrine of Ismailism.

As is known, the Sunnite majority in Islam has at a fairly early date adopted the belief that the Prophet left for the guidance of his newly founded religious community the Coran (which was at that time not yet collected and codified), and his own example (which was only known in full to very few among his closest associates). The Shiʿites (and especially, later on, the Ismailis), tried to preserve the original theocratical system of the Islam state, as it was under the Prophet himself. In his absence they accepted as the supreme secular and religious head of Islam his lineal descendant,[5] the Imam, who was believed to be the repository of special and higher religious knowledge, which was his exclusive hereditary property, bequeathed by the Prophet to his, the Imam's, progenitor, ʿAlī ibn Abī Ṭālib; the latter was the closest associate, cousin, and son-in-law of the Founder of Islam, who treated him as his brother. This knowledge, both exoteric and esoteric, made the Imam the only person fully competent to interpret, explain, and apply the doctrine of the Coran and religious institutions to the requirements of daily life, in a correct way.

Thus the Imam not only had to inherit the Prophet's secular functions, as the head of the state, but also his most important religious function, the preaching of the Divine Revelation. For this reason the idea of religious teaching and preaching always was so strong in Ismailism that it outweighed many other sides in its system. Before the political successes of Ismailism detracted the attention of its enemies from its religious doctrine, the Ismailis usually were referred to under the name of the *Ta'līmiyya*, i.e. 'the sect of teaching', *ta'līm*. And later on they themselves adopted the term *da'wat*, 'call', i.e. preaching, as the description of their religion.

The Imam, the theocratical ruler of Islam, and its Great Pontiff, supreme religious authority, as he should be, obviously could not impart his precious and all important knowledge to all his subjects personally. Therefore a new institution was brought into existence which was unknown to the earliest patriarchal phase of Islam—the institute of priests, as intermediaries between the Imam and his subjects, and his accredited agents.

It is quite possible that this new development (as it can be traced in the earliest available sources), started from the same idea as in all other Islamic schools, i.e. from the functions of a religious teacher, *'ālim*: he, being versed in the difficult knowledge of the prescriptions of the religion and law, acted as the leader of congregational prayers, a teacher, and a judge. With gradual differentiation of the society and the advance of civilization, obviously more complex system became necessary, with an elaborate hierarchy of ranks, special duties assigned to each, etc.

But the most important difference which was introduced by Ismailism, as compared with Sunnism, was the idea of the *priest*, in approximately the same sense as it is in Christianity and some other religions.[6] As is known, a Muslim *mulla* cannot be called a priest, in the real sense of the word, because he is not *ordained*. He acquires his position by virtue of his own learning, talents, piety, and by the consent of the congregation. This applies even to the great doctors, supreme authorities in legal matters, the *imāms* in the Sunnite sense. All of them are merely specialists or experts in religious matters, just as there are expert medical men, engineers, astronomers, etc.

The Ismaili *dā'ī*, i.e. accredited agent of the imam, *is ordained*. In addition to the position of ordinary Islamic *mulla*, he has spiritual authority, commission, received either directly from the source of the religious authority, the Imam, or indirectly, through those who themselves received it from him, together with the right of transferring it to others. The sacrament which he is commissioned to perform is not only teaching, i.e. distributing the sacred wisdom of the Imams, but also accepting, on their behalf, the oath of allegiance of the followers.

This is quite different from the state of things in Sunnism, although it cannot be regarded as a heretical practice, *bid'a*, for the simple reason that it is respected and sanctified by Sunnism in its Sufic form. As many other ideas and institutions, this one has a complete parallel in the Sufic theory of the 'chains' of permissions, by which accredited spiritual teachers, *murshids*, receive their authority ultimately from the Prophet himself, through a long succession of similar commissioned priests. Just as the Sufic *murshid* without a genuine *ijāza, khirqa*, or other certificate of his commission, is an impostor, however pious and learned he may really be,[7] so the *dā'ī* is a *dā'ī* only in so far as he is commissioned by the Imam, in whose name he accepts the oath of allegiance from his converts.

The importance of this institution was apparently appreciated from the outset, in the conditions which accompanied the earliest history of the Ismaili movement. Not only did it permit of the unification and standardization of the dogmatical and other sides of the religion, but also provided a kind of an automatically working mechanism of propaganda, which could function even in the absence of the visible head, the Imam, who often had to live in the strictest disguise, being known only to a few amongst the most trusted devotees. This is why no effort was spared by the Ismaili dogmatists to build a sound foundation for this new institution, both from the arguments derived from the *ẓāhir*, i.e. the Coran and tradition, by the selection of appropriate quotations, etc., and in the *bāṭin*, or the symbolical and abstract theory of the religion, by philosophical speculations. Everything was mobilized for this purpose, and the tradition was established of attaching enormous importance to the theory.

From what apparently was the earliest scheme: Imam, *dā'ī*—ordinary initiated follower—the theory grew into a complex, mystic and philosophic, symbolical system, based on the fundamental 'rhythm of the universe', observed in some coincidences of different numbers, their mystical values, etc. Childish as these speculations may appear to modern man, they appealed to the mentality of the time; profound mysteries were sincerely sought in them; and it is such material that constitutes the greatest secrets of the ancient Ismaili wisdom which was so zealously guarded from the profane eye.

There is, however, nothing original in these speculations, as all of them are derived from different mystical theories of Neo-Pythagoreans, from Neo-Platonism, and Plotinian philosophy, just as in the case of Sufic speculations, based on imperfect knowledge of the original systems, and their aribitrary amalgamation. As the matter of the most fundamental importance in the religious life, the hierarchy of the *ḥudūdu'd-dīn* had to be based on the same scheme as the physical universe, and the world of the spirit. The process of perfecting these parallels, and making them convincing to the student, chiefly occupied the philosophic thought of the sect ever since the philosophical interpretation of Islam was introduced.

The original simple and natural scheme was tremendously complicated. The hierarchy of the *ḥudūdu'd-dīn* had to comprise everything in the religious sphere. It begins with God, followed by the Prophet (*Nāṭiq*), *Asās* (or *Ṣāmit*, or *Waṣī*), *Imām*, and a large set of different ranks of *dā'īs*: *bāb*, *ḥujjat*,[8] three kinds of *dā'īs* in the narrower sense, two ranks of *ma'dhūn*, *mukāsir*, and *mustajīb*, each rank being treated as a 'cosmic category'—contrary to the practice, in which all these dignitaries more or less regularly were called *dā'īs*. Such an elaborate scheme was required to bring the hierarchy into agreement with the Ptolemian system of the universe which was universally accepted at the time. As is known, it taught that around the earth there are several concentric transparent spheres, each rotating under its own laws. The fixed stars, the sun and moon, and different planets were affixed to these, and moved together with the spheres. According to pre-Islamic speculations, the forces which produce the rotation of the spheres were associated with the different emanations of the Divine Source of Being. In these abstruse speculations the highest sphere was associated with God Himself, the next with the 'Logical Principle of the Universe', which is usually in a vague way called 'Universal Reason', and so on. Speculations with all these cosmic entities appeared as convincing and plausible to the people a thousand years ago as similar speculations about electrons, protons, neutrons, etc., appear to us now. Therefore it was 'quite scientifically' proved that the religious sphere, and its organization, fully coincides in its structure with the cosmos and the world of the Divine Spirit, *al-ḥudūdu's-samāwiyya* (or *aṭ-ṭabī'iyya*), and *al-ḥudūdu'l-'ulwiyya* (or *ar-rūḥāniyya*).

Such speculations again do not form an exclusive feature of Ismailism. Apparently there was a wide psychological demand for them, so that they even found their way, in a simplified form, into folklore, and became a part of the popular superstition of the Muslim masses, as the belief in *chihil-tan*, or the *rijālu'l-ghayb*, *abdāls*, etc. This theory of the invisible holy ascetics who tour the world, and guard its religious purity, is also built in the form of a hierarchy, which strikingly reminds the Ismaili scheme of the *ḥudūdu'd-dīn*.

Rarely a dogmatic or esoteric work in Ismailism omits this important subject. But apparently without a single exception these speculations are only speculations, abstruse and foggy, having not the slightest connection with real life and real organization of the priestly apparatus of the Fatimids. Therefore, although it is impossible to pass over in silence such important and fundamental doctrine, directly connected with the organization of the *dāʿīs* under the Fatimids, we are not in the least benefited by it in our efforts to reconstruct this detail of the history of Ismailism.

III THE EVOLUTION OF THE ORGANIZATION

For the reasons mentioned above nothing but rare allusions in different works can be used for forming an idea about the *dāʿī*. Fortunately, there are in Ismaili literature a few works which, dealing with the ideal virtues of the ideal *dāʿī*, permit us to read between the lines something about the real conditions.

One of the greatest difficulties of this difficult subject is the great confusion in terms, used both in Ismaili and non-Ismaili works. The term *dāʿī* apparently came into general use as late as about the end of the IIIrd/IXth century, the period of the great expansion of the Fatimid propaganda. It means 'one who calls' (to the true religion, or to the true sovereign of the Muslim state, etc.). Apparently before this, when the functions of the Ismaili priests were more those of teachers rather than propagandists, they most probably were known under the name of *'ālim*, teacher, also used in other sects of Islam. Such terms as *ḥijāb* (plural *ḥujub*), *naqīb*, etc., were also met with in the accounts of the real or supposed to be Quarmaṭians, and preserved at a much later period in the works of the Druzes, of Syrian Nizārīs, etc. The term *ḥijāb* most probably disappeared under the Fatimids when it was no longer required. At the earlier periods, the term was applied to a specially reliable and devoted head priest, directing propaganda in a certain province, who, for the purpose of 'screening' the Imam, who always lived under threat from the vigorously searching Abbasid agents, would assume the title of the Imam and his name, to receive, on the latter's behalf, the oath of allegiance of the followers, while the real Imam would live in strict disguise, known only to the trusted few. With the installation of the Fatimids on the throne of their empire such necessity disappeared.

It is possible that the *ḥijāb* roughly corresponded with the *bāb*, or the *dā'ī-in-chief* of the Fatimid period. But it is not quite clear who the *naqīb* was—was he the same as the *ḥujjat*, or the *bāb*? Or all three were the same?

In any case there is no doubt that the term *dā'ī* during the Fatimid period meant priests in general, particularly 'commissioned' ranks in the religious hierarchy.[9] The author of *al-Mūjizatu'l-Kāfiya* (see below) plainly says in his discussions of the duties of the *dā'ī* that these apply not only to the *dā'ī* in the narrower, technical sense, but also to every rank in the hierarchy, 'because every rank acts as a *dā'ī* with regard to the rank immediately below him'. In quotations from the books of different authors who are well-known as the possessors of high ranks, of *ḥujjat*, etc., they are very often referred to simply as *sayyid-nā ad-dā'ī qaddasa'l-lāh sirra-hu*. The term of *dā'ī* is applied to the religious heads of huge provinces—as the great Abū 'Abdi'l-lāh ash-Shī'ī, the founder of the Fatimid empire—as equally to quite petty priests.

It is difficult to follow the evolution of the hierarchy. It appears that such terms as *ḥujjat* and *bāb* were introduced only at a fairly late period. Was there only one *bāb*, a sort of 'minister for religion' at the court of the Fatimids, or were there several *bābs*? Anyhow, in the honorific titles of some saints there appears the expression *bābu'l-abwāb*; this, however, apparently was not an official title.

There is little doubt that the *ḥujjat* was the chief *dā'ī* in the province or district, a sort of archbishop.[10] But everything beyond this seems doubtful: at the period of great successes of the Fatimid propaganda there were 24 *ḥujjats*, twelve 'of the day', and twelve 'of the night'.[11] It is not at all clear what were the differences in their duties. Moreover, there is yet another question. The *ḥujjat* was supposed to be the spiritual head of a *jazīra*. This expression originally means an island, but it is also applied to large provinces.

The traditional geography mentions 'twelve' *jazīras* (although their names vary in different works). It appears that in the Ismaili sense of the Fatimid period this term was applied to what would better be described as 'religious colony', i.e. Ismaili community in a country which politically was not under the Fatimid sovereignty. Thus there were 12 *jazā'ir*; at the head of each stood a *ḥujjat*. But I so far have never been able to find the names of these *jazīras*. Apparently they did not coincide with the geographical *jazīras*, and all were lying outside of the political boundaries of the Fatimid empire. The only *jazīra* which is always mentioned by name in Ismaili literature, is the Yaman.[12] But, however strange, its head priest apparently is never called *ḥujjat*—from the time of the great founder of the Ismaili community there, in the end of the IIIrd/IXth c., the Manṣūru'l-Yaman, to the post-Fatimid time.

After the *ḥujjat* in the Fatimid hierarchy follows a set of three different *dā'īs*: the *dā'ī'l-balāgh*, *ad-dā'ī'l-muṭlaq*, *ad-dā'ī'l-maḥsūr*. It is not at all clear what the differences in their functions were. The second probably connoted what the *dā'ī* should be according to the earliest ideas—the head of a diocese. The third, obviously, was his deputy or assistant. But it is very difficult to find out what the first was: was he the priest specially in charge of the missionary activities, or had he some other functions?[13] It is also not clear whether all these ranks were functioning not only in the 'religious colonies', but also within the limits of the Fatimid state.

Again there not everything is clear about the lower ranks of the priesthood. Immediately below the *dā'ī* there were: two *ma'dhūns* and *mukāsir*. The *ma'dhūns* (i.e. the licenced ones), were the 'greater' (*akbar*), or *muṭṭlaq* (absolute), and 'smaller' (*aṣghar*), or *maḥṣūr* (limited.[14] They, as also *mukāsir* ('one who breaks the arguments of the opponents'—apparently in the disputes), were assistants of the *dā'ī*, in charge of different departments of his administrative machine. And it is interesting that in our principal source of information, *al-Mūjizatu'l-Kāfiya*, referred to above, the expression is often used: the *ma'dhūn* and *mu'min*. Thus obviously the term *mu'min* implies a separate rank of the priesthood. At a later date apparently the term *mu'min* was generally applied to Ismailis as opposed to all other *muslims*. But it is doubtful whether even *mustajīb*, i.e. initiated Ismaili, is here regarded as a *mu'min*.[15]

As mentioned above, Ismaili literature apparently has not preserved any works specially devoted to the technique of the organisation of the priesthood, and even incidental references seem to be exceedingly rare. Apparently nothing on this point can be found in the great religious encyclopædia of Abū Ḥātim ar-Rāzī, the exceptionally erudite theologian and philosopher of the beginning of the IVth/Xth century—his *Kitābu'z-Zīna*.[16] This work apparently was intended for the public at large, and not only for the Ismailis; therefore it avoids such technical matters.

The works of his contemporary, Abū Ya'qūb as-Sijzī (d. in 331/942) usually are intended for the initial education of the members of the community in religious matters, and do not apparently touch on the subject.

Very interesting theoretical speculations on the ideal virtues of the *dā'ī* are contained in the treatise by the famous *qāḍī*, Abū Ḥanīfa an-Nu'mān (d. 363/974),[17] the author of the great legal code of Ismailism, the *Da'ā'imu'l-Islām*. In his work *Kitābu'l-Himma fī ādāb ātbā'i'-A'imma*,[18] he deals, in the first half, with ethics in general, and especially the virtues which are expected from the Ismailis. In the second half of his book he explains the rules of conduct and etiquette prescribed to the followers of the Imams when they come in personal contact with their lords: how to stand before the Imam, how to sit in his presence, how to address him, etc. The last chapter of his book is devoted to the duties of the *dā'ī*: 'How the *dā'īs* of the Imams should act in their preaching in the Imams' favour.' It contains much interesting information, and a great portion of it is summed up further on.

An interesting document, although it does not deal with the organization of the *dā'īs*, may also be referred to in this connection, to serve as an excellent specimen of what was the doctrine preached by the *dā'īs* in reality. It is an epistle to the people of Ray (the ancient Rhagae, near Tehran), by a *dā'ī* Ḥasan, or Muḥsin, or Muḥassin b. Muḥammad al-Mahīdī (or Mahbudī, etc.),[19] written at the time of al-'Azīz bi'l-lāh. From the letter itself it appears that the author, coming to Ray for propaganda, was received as a heretic, and narrowly escaped death. His opuscule forms a really classic elementary exposition of Ismailism as it was preached in his time, written with extreme lucidity and conciseness. It is therefore included into his famous chrestomathy of standard Ismaili works, by Sayyid-nā Muḥammad b. Ṭāhir (d. 584/1188),[20] and later incorporated in the third volume of *al-Azhār*.[21]

The author who has left us the fullest information so far available, Sayyid-nā Aḥmad b. Ibrāhīm (or Muḥammad) an-Naysābūrī, apparently belongs to the first half of the Vth/XIth century. He composed the most interesting work, *ar-Risāla al-Mūjizatu'l-Kāfiya fi Shurūṭi'd-Da'wati'l-Hādiya.*[22] Only a portion of it, apparently the main part, is preserved, being incorporated into the much later work, by the third Yamanite *dā'ī*, Hātim b. Ibrāhīm (d. 596/1199), his *Tuḥfatu'l-qulūb wa farjatu'l-makrūb* (which is described further on). The work of an-Naysābūrī is somewhat chaotic in arrangement. Therefore, further on, its contents are summed up, as closely to the original text as possible, in a re-arranged and systematized form.

To the same author belongs another interesting work, of more or less historical contents, dealing with the events which accompanied al-Mahdī's escape from Syria, and the beginning of his adventures which ultimately brought him to the throne. This work contains some valuable allusions to the *dā'īs* of that early time. It is the *Istitāru'l-Imām*, which was edited by me in the *Bulletin of the Faculty of Arts of the Egyptian University*, Cairo (1936/1939, Vol. IV, pp. 89–133. I am also preparing an English translation of this work).

Most probably when Ismaili literature of the Fatimid time is properly studied, many interesting references will be found scattered in different early works. But it seems that as early as the period immediately following the fall of the Fatimid empire no other works on the subject were known, as may be seen from the statement of the author of the *Tuḥfatu'l-qulūb*, in the concluding passages of his work. This certainly means that no other such work was known in the Yaman. But as everywhere outside this province Ismaili literature has perished, we have to be content with this.

The next work, in chronological sequence, dealing with the subject, is the *Tuḥfatu'l-qulūb wa farjatu'l-makrūb*, referred to above. It belongs to the post-Fatimid period, and was compiled by the third Yamanite *dā'ī*, Sayyid-nā Ḥātim b. Ibrāhīm (d. 596/1199).[23]

The author's purpose, as explained in his preface, was to satisfy those of his friends who were interested to have reliable information about the history of the *dā'īs* in the Yaman. To this subject the author devoted only twenty pages out of 240.[24] His information, anyhow, is extremely valuable, and all later works on the history of Ismailism are based on it. He deals with the story of how the administrative centre of the Musta'lian branch of the Ismailis was after the assassination of al-Āmir transferred to the Yaman. His narrative is very concise, even meagre; but, in the absence of anything else, even this is precious.

All other 220 pages out of 240 are occupied with the 'allied subjects'. Although compiling a treatise on such a special subject, the learned Sayyid-nā cannot withstand the temptation of starting *ab ovo*, and giving a very simplified general account of Ismaili theology and theosophy. In the most boring way he starts with the doctrine of unity of God, creation, universe, prophets, Imamat, man and his soul, etc., etc. With all this, as he says himself, he had already dealt with in another work, *ar-Risāla al-Jawhara*, which apparently is not preserved. After this he continues his ruminations about the theory of the *ḥudūdu'd-dīn*, and ultimately inserts the text of *al-Mūjiza* of an-Naysābūrī. This, and the historical references about the *da'wat* in the Yaman, mentioned above, occupy roughly one-third of the work, and make it extremely valuable. There would be one more exceedingly valuable item in his book, namely his frequent controversial references to the '*ghulāt*', i.e. an extremist branch of the Ismailis, or generally Shi'ites. But in the most irritating manner of all the Ismaili controversialists, the author enlightens his reader about all sorts of nasty things attributed to these heretics, and their perversion of the original doctrine, but he deliberately remains silent on one point: the name of the sect. Who are they: Nizārīs? Druzes? Nuṣayrīs? or some other sect which exists no longer? Thus what would be priceless information, remains completely wasted.

Amongst the still later works, touching indirectly on the same matters, we may also mention the *Zahuru'l-ma'ānī* by Sayyid-nā Idrīs, the 19th Yamanite *dā'ī* (832–872/1428–1468).[25] In his 19th chapter he deals with the *ḥudūd*, and the guidance which they impart to the community. This is still more boring than the ruminations of the preceding author. The account is filled with superstitious speculations, fantastic parallels, theosophical deductions, etc., quite depressing reading which invariably raises the question whether this could be written by the same man who wrote the well-known historical work, the '*Uyūnu'l-akhbār*, and if he really did, what can be the value of such a history for research?

This is all that may be considered in this paper. But however little it is, we must be grateful to those ancient authors who recorded these ideas, and those people who preserved their works.

IV VIRTUES OF THE DĀʿI ACCORDING TO AL-HIMMA

What the *dāʿīs* of the Imams should do in their preaching?

The people who are the subject of this chapter first of all should take great care about the righteousness of their souls (*ṣalāḥ anfusi-him*), in the ways which we have already described in the preceding chapters. And not only this, but they must do this in all sincerity and without any reserve, abiding in such state of full self resignation, zealously guarding it. As the people whom they call to God and His Saints follow their example, and judge by what they see in the *dāʿīs* about their religion, they must be particularly punctilious in the cultivation of piety, righteousness, fear of God, chastity, doing good, and abstaining from doing bad. This chapter more particularly deals with the (initiated) devotees, *mu'mins*, just as the preceding chapters equally apply to Muslims in general.

(The author refers to the words of Imam Jaʿfar, who called his followers to be 'silent *dāʿīs*', i.e. the people whose example is a sufficiently eloquent advertisement of the superiority of their religion.) By acting righteously the *mu'min* increases the influence of his Imam. But every one must do the proper thing. He must do neither more nor less of what he is expected to do. The highest virtue of those who carry on propaganda in favour of the Saints of God (i.e. the Imams), their greatest work, and the highest attainment—is their own righteousness based on sincere devotion, self-control based on religious feeling, convincing preaching, soul healing admonitions.

The *dāʿī* must carefully study the ideas which he preaches, must personally know every member of his community, know their affairs, their aspirations. With this knowledge at his disposal he must gradually deliver his call to God and His Saints, in such a way as not to overtax the intelligence and the patience of his audience. When he has explained to his followers what he wanted to teach them, he must know how to handle them. He must learn to observe the people, recognize the state of their minds, their abilities, extent of their endurance. This is the most important knowledge needed by the *dāʿī* for the organization and training of his followers. Ignorance of such matters tremendously affects his work, and the community (*daʿwat*) suffers from this.

Calamities befall those *dāʿīs* who permit themselves to slacken their efforts in the discharge of their duties. The number of their defects grows as time goes on, and ultimately these become so numerous and far reaching that it would be too long to describe them.

The *dāʿī* must completely free himself from such defects; he must more than any one of his followers stick to the rules and principles which he preaches to others, strictly observing these under any circumstances. He must follow all such rules with perfect sincerity, always show unshakeable determination to abide by them. He must always be moderate in his needs, must possess an active mind, sincere faith, broad vision, must know how to control his temper, and always resolutely to go ahead with his duties, heedless of whether this brings him profit and respect of people, or not. He must persevere in his work both when this enhances his importance, his reputation in the eyes of everybody, or, on the contrary, leads to his humiliation. The position, of course, is different in case he specially needs (for the success of his mission) to acquire high regard amongst those in authority, whose ideas and opinions in such matters he must not disregard. In such cases his real merits are not affected by the (apparent) efforts at self aggrandizement—if he really needs to associate himself with such people, outwardly complying with the standards and ideals, accepted amongst them, of virtue and merit. This obviously cannot be regarded as his own and personal desire of seeking position and importance.

Association with the people in whose hands authority is concentrated in religious matters, and the respect which the *dāʿī* may acquire amongst them for his complying with their ideas of piety, etc., creates the atmosphere of friendliness and goodwill, which greatly facilitate the chances of this people's collaboration and of their becoming converted, when they see him making great progress in what they agreed with esteem and respect.

Human nature is inclined to jealousy, and the majority of those who desire to acquire learning or piety start being prompted by the feelings of jealousy, or rivalry with their friends and associates: their primary aim is to acquire high status. Only later on, when they get into the spirit of their work, those amongst them who pray God attain real success and genuine taste in their task. This is why some one rightly said: by God! at first we do not study for the acquisition of learning for the sake of God; but gradually knowledge which we acquire works upon us in such a way that we ultimately turn to Him.

The *dā'ī* must aspire respect of himself amongst his converts; they must feel fear before him. He must strictly observe his own actions so as not to give any reason to them to treat him lightly, or lose respect to his orders. The more respect he inspires in them, the more spiritual advantage they derive from his instruction, and the more virtuous they become. But his imposing manners should be accompanied by a real attitude of goodwill, quiet dignity, kindness to everyone, inviting address and pleasant companionship. There must be no sign of pressing his importance upon any one, of haughtiness in his treatment of others. No, modesty in appearance, combined with dignity of thought, should be his usual attitude.

Imam Ja'far said: study in order to acquire learning, and to adorn yourself with it; cultivate dignity and goodwill; treat with respect those who teach you, and those whom you teach. Do not make your learning oppressive to anyone, and do not permit your vanity to destroy the effects of what is really good in you.

The same Imam also said: those who acquire learning merely for the purpose of opposing the learned, or teaching fools, or attracting the attention of the public and of showing their own superiority over others, such people shall be punished after death, because religious leadership should belong only to those who really deserve it.

The *dā'ī* should inspire respect in others quite naturally, simply by his behaviour, without any special effort or attempts at pressing his own importance on others, without showing vanity. He must be sympathetic to the weak and those in inferior position, because by doing so he enhances his influence, makes his position firm, achieves his aims, and organizes his community, thus preparing his work to bear fruit. He must treat nicely those who do their best, giving them the position which they deserve according to their behaviour, never leaving them without his supervision. But he must punish those whose behaviour is not good, and of whose evil actions he comes to know.

Those *dā'īs* who have firmly established their authority, must train their followers in different disciplines. They must excommunicate the sinners, making all their followers to boycott them, speaking not a word to them, never approaching them, so that they should live in isolation amongst their own people, out of touch with them and their heads, until life becomes misery to them, and they would request the *dā'ī* to accept their repentance, and to re-admit them to their community after the necessary testing of their sincerity in whichever way he pleases. He may either punish or fine them in case he sees something wrong on their part in the course of time, after their re-admission.

The *dāʿī* tests some by giving them high posts, others by reverting them in their position. He may order some to be flayed alive, others to be executed in some other way for their mischief. He may test the loyalty of his nearest associates by ordering one to kill his own brother, or some other relative. Those who are sincerely devoted must do this, however hard such orders may be for those who receive such commands. And if they do not comply with the order, the *dāʿī* should excommunicate them. Those who sincerely obey such test orders, receive great blessing. The *dāʿī* should punish his followers for every error, leaving nothing neglected or overlooked. In this way he disciplines them. . . .

Dāʿīs and residents (*wulāt*) must make themselves acquainted with what is explained in this book. They should comply with these principles, and believe in them, not only ostensibly, in words, but sincerely, proving this by their acts, in their religious beliefs, and in their ideals. . . .

(Here follow different sayings attributed to ʿAlī b. Abī Ṭālib and some other Imams, chiefly dealing with the question of the capital punishments, *ḥadd*, prescribed in the *sharīʿat*).[26]

V THE DĀʿI AND HIS DUTIES ACCORDING TO AL-MŪJIZA

As mentioned above, *al-Mūjizatu'l-Kāfiya*, by Sayyid-nā Aḥmad an-Naysābūrī, is the most detailed work available in Fatimid literature on the subject of *dāʿī*. It was composed, most probably, early in the fifth/eleventh century, and is known only from the extract incorporated in the later work, the *Tuḥfatu'l-qulūb*, by Ḥātim b. Ibrāhīm, described above; from there it was repeated in the chrestomathy called *al-Azhār*. An abbreviated English translation of it was published about 1920 in a work devoted to the controversy between the progressive and the reactionary parties in the Indian Bohora community, supporting the views of the anti-Mullaji camp. Its title is: *Gluzare Daudi For The Bohras of India. A short note on the Bohras of India, their 21 Imams and 51 Dais, with their customs and tenets.* Compiled and Published by Mian Bhai Mulla Abdul Husain, BA, KHM, PCS, Burhanpur. Printed (500 copies) at the 'Amarsinhji' P. Press, Ahmedabad. (No date, apparently 1920.)

The book is out of print long since. It is one of the numerous outcomes of the present flood of litigation within the sect which seems to be the principal form of the activities of its headquarters. The purpose of the work is controversy; the author is technically helpless, and the monstrous misprints which adorn the book make its use for reference very difficult. In any case, the translation needs careful revision.

The language of *al-Mūjizatu'l-Kāfiya* shows that its author was in all probability a Persian, and this explains its business-like tone, and the simple and intelligent treatment of the subject. Arabs rarely can stand the temptation of sacrificing every thing to form: rhymed prose, stuffed with rare words, and stilted vague verbiage very often obscure what little originality is left in their ideas.

As it has already been mentioned above, the author uses the term *dā'ī* in a broad sense, as generally a member of the priestly hierarchy. As a proof of his having written his work under the Fatimids, he always refers to the Imam as *Amīru'l-mu'minīn*, the title which was only given to the caliphs. Great difficulty is presented to the translator by his rather confusing use of the terms *dīn* and *da'wat*. Sometimes they are obviously the same. Sometimes the first, *dīn*, means religion, piety, as it etymologically should; but occasionally it is difficult to translate it in any other way than the congregation, community, diocese, or even the religious interests and welfare of the Ismaili community. The term *da'wat* is used not only in the sense of preaching, religious instruction, but also in the sense of the *dā'ī-ship*, the profession of the *dā'ī*; sometimes, like *dīn*, it implies the Ismaili community in general, or a local 'diocese'.

The author describes the moral, religious, educational, personal, social, and other qualifications required from the ideal *dā'ī*, his duties towards the community, towards the Imam, his assistants; his methods of work, tactics with the outer world, etc. All this is arranged somewhat chaotically and contains many repetitions; there is no division into chapters. Therefore all his statements, except the numerous quotations from the Coran or of tradition, are here translated, either literally or freely, and re-arranged according to the subject with which they deal. Nothing is left out, except for the formula of the *'ahd*, or *mīthāq*, i.e. the oath of allegiance and a concise creed, which really belongs to the dogmatical side of the religion.[27]

1. *The meaning of the words dāʿī and daʿwat.* The *daʿwat* is God's own call of humanity to righteous ways of life as demonstrated by prophets, *Sunnatu'l-anbiyā'*. It is an explanation of the signs and indications of the will of God. Its aim is to call humanity to stick firmly to monotheism, and strive to enter the Abode of Salvation, *Dāru's-salām*, i.e. to build the ideal Divine theocratical state, the Church, which can never perish nor decay, which saves those who join and enter it, offering them shelter and protection from the injustice and oppression of the sinful world.

The title *dāʿī* is a great distinction. The Prophet himself applied this name to his own mission, and it can only be applied to 313 *rasūls*, or great Prophets, whom God has sent in the course of history to different nations to preach true religion. Ordinarily the *dāʿī* is the Ismaili priest, just as there are priests in Zoroastrianism, in Judaism, and in Christianity.[28]

The *daʿwat*, which the *dāʿī* is commissioned to carry on, is the guidance of mankind by the *ilhām*, or inspiration, and *tawfīq* or Divine guidance (by the Imam) which the *dāʿī* broadcasts by persuasion and instruction in his preaching. The *daʿwat* is concerned with and comprises all forms of religious life and thought. Therefore it is the most important thing in everyone's life, all other matters being only secondary.

2. *The position of the dāʿī in the community.* Just as man, cohabiting with his wife, deposits his sperm into her womb, and when she conceives, he does not in any way interfere with the development of the embryo, and the birth of the child, but only protects and feeds his wife, so the *dāʿī*, being commissioned by the Imam, is left to work autonomously in his diocese. The Imam only gives general guidance to his *dāʿīs* and the Ismaili community as a whole; he is not to be bothered by references in routine work. The *daʿwat*, as already Imam Jaʿafar expressed, is an extraordinarily difficult task, implying tremendous responsibilities which none can take but a great prophet, an angel of high rank, or a faithful whose heart and sincere devotion have been thoroughly tested.

(In view of such tremendous responsibilities only those candidates can be selected for this task who possess the necessary intellectual abilities, education, religious and moral qualities, political and social tact, and innate character and qualities of a leader.) This applies to all ranks of the hierarchy, from the *bāb* to the *mukāsir*, because every higher rank is the *dāʿī*, or teacher, of those below him.

For this reason the *dāʿī* must combine in himself all the ideal qualities and talents which may separately be found in the people of different professions and standing. He must posses the good qualities of an expert lawyer (*faqīh*), because he often has to act as a judge; he must possess tact (*ṣabr*), good theoretical education (*ʿilm*), intelligence, psychological insight, honesty, high moral character, sound judgement, etc. He must possess the virtues of leaders, such as strong will, generosity, administrative talent, tact, tolerance. He must be in possession of high qualities of the priest, because he has to lead the esoteric prayer of his followers. He must be reproachlessly honest and reliable, because the most precious thing, the salvation of the souls of many people, is entrusted to him. He should be a real *mujāhid*, a warrior for the religious cause, in his heart, ready to sacrifice his life and everything for the religion. He must have the virtue of the physician, who delicately and patiently treats the sick, because he himself has to heal sick souls. Similarly, he has to possess the virtues of an agriculturist, of a shepherd, of the captain of a ship, of a merchant, etc., developing in himself the good qualities required in different professions.

3. *The dāʿī's learning and education.* The *dāʿī* must be well-educated, so that he may carry the light of religious knowledge to his followers. With regard to the Ismaili religion he must be well conversant both with the *ẓāhir* and the *bāṭin* subjects. His learning must be sufficiently wide so that he could not be placed at an awkward position by any question put to him by his pupils.[29] The *ẓāhir* subjects are: *fiqh*, or jurisprudence; *ḥadīth*, *akhbār*, *riwāyat*, *isnāds*, i.e. all branches of tradition; the Coran, its *tafsīr*, or philological interpretation, and *ta'wīl*, or allegorical meaning; theory of preaching, arguing, religious stories; and the art of controversy and dialectics (*jadal* and *kalām*). He must be acquainted with the teachings of different sects, heretics, zindiqs, dahrites, etc.[30]

His equipment with regard to the *bāṭin* subjects must include the knowledge of everything that pertains to the physical (*maḥsūs*) world, i.e. cosmogony, physics, branches of natural history, etc. And also disciplines dealing with abstract matters, such as philosophy, logic, etc. To this must be added profound learning in *ta'wīl* matters, in *āfāq wa anfus* (i.e. parallelism of the universe with human organism), *al-ḥudūdu'l-ʿulwiyya*, or philosophy of emanations, and generally *alʿilmu'r-rūḥānī*, spiritual subjects, or religious philosophy.

He must also know the biographies of the Imams, and have some idea about the activities of the former (famous) *dāʿīs*.

Generally speaking, he must be encyclopædically educated, so as not to be lost on any question. He must be able to write well, and be able to operate correctly with abstractions. At the same time, he must have good knowledge of things belonging to secular education, *adab*, because only theological learning (*ʿilm*), not accompanied by *adab*, deprives the man of the necessary polish, *rawnaq*, which evokes admiration, and attracts people.

The *dāʿī* generally must be a man of high intellectual culture, capable of handling the subjects connected with spiritual life and experience. He must be a man fond of learning and learned conversation. He must associate himself with the people who can carry it on. He must patronise learning and students, always showing respect and courtesy to the learned, *ahlu'l-ʿilm*, even if they are poor, and shabbily dressed.

4. *Moral and religious virtues of the dāʿī.* The *dāʿī* must be a strict monotheist. This means that he should never attach so much importance to anything that it should interfere with his discharge of his duties to God. His faith must be unshakeable. He must be a man of sincere and profound devotion (*ʿābid*), offering his usual and esoteric (*ẓāhir* and *bāṭin*) prayers to God.[31] He must not be the man who only preaches religion, but also the man who sincerely follows the principles which he teaches. An ignorant, impious, or insincere man cannot be a *dāʿī*. He must firmly know what is right and what is wrong, and make his followers also to know this.

On no account should he make for himself exceptions from the rules which are laid by the Imams for ordinary followers of the religion. In his behaviour and religious life he must be an example to others, so that to him may be applied what Imam Jaʿfar said about 'silent *dāʿīs*', i.e. those people who by the mere behaviour in life make their religion so attractive to others that they begin to feel the desire to join it.

There are several religious virtues which the *dāʿī* should possess: *taqwā*, or fear of God, or conscience, honesty before one self. It should be the basic tone of the whole of his life and activity, religious and private, of his knowledge, faith, and actions; it should be inseparable from the fundamental commandments of the Coran. This sense must be cultivated by careful study of religion. But this should not remain as some sort of theoretical knowledge, because it is worthless if it is not always and systematically applied to life.

Self-discipline, *as-siyāsatu'l-khāṣṣa*, is also extremely important. Before educating and disciplining others, the *dā'ī* should himself possess the necessary mental and religious discipline, i.e. mastery over his own emotions and desires of doing what is condemned by religion, restraining himself from what is regarded as bad habits or actions, undesirable passions, or lust.[32] Restraining himself from these, he must, at the same time, cultivate positive or laudable qualities, such as punctiliousness in the obligatory forms of religious worship (*farā'iḍ*), mastering his evil passions. He must cultivate that spirit of gratitude to the Creator for the most precious gift granted by Him to man, life, and the possibility to behold His greatness. By sustained effort at self-training the *dā'ī* should develop that clean and balanced mentality which should by itself impress his subordinates and pupils, and make them to covet it, in the same way as the words of Imam Ja'far about 'silent *dā'īs*' imply. He must know it firmly that none can rule others (properly) who cannot rule himself, and that one must master himself before others will follow and obey him.

Self-discipline and conscience have the greatest importance in religious life, in the mastering of both the formal side of the religion, *ẓāhir*, and its spirit, inner meaning, *bāṭin*. They give man that fundamental sense of the idea of God being above all, all-important and overpowering everything else, making impossible *shirk*, i.e. regarding anything as of equal importance with it, or attributing disproportionate importance to some aspects of the idea of Deity, on the lines on which one thinks about His creations.

The same two qualities make one obey sincerely those in the religious organization, who are placed above him, or to be modest and friendly with those of equal standing.

Devotion, *dīn*, or sincere attachment to the religion which he preaches, unshakeable faith in its teaching, without any reserve or doubt, must be a fundamental quality of the *dā'ī*, just as sound learning, and punctiliousness in formal worship. But at the same time the *dā'ī* must be an intelligent and shrewd man of sound and critical reason, *'aqīl kāmilu'l-'aql*. Learning in a fool often becomes a dangerous and destructive thing.

In addition to the complying with the recognized expressions of piety, *wara'*, the *dā'ī* must be a man of strictly moral life (*'iffa*). He must be a man of sympathetic attitude to others (*shafqa*), merciful and condescending to human weaknesses. Man is normally inclined to mischief and disobedience, and God punishes him for this. But the *dā'ī* must not be rigidly formal and pitiless.

He must be friendly and helpful to his followers and subordinates. He must especially keep away from haughtiness, arrogance, swollen-headedness with those who are in his charge. He must be modest and accessible, must have the sense of shame (*ḥayā'*), which is one of the chief qualities of a religious man, keeping him away from committing unfair things, which offend religion, and ruin the congregation.

He must always be honest with his followers, as otherwise he would lose all credit in their eyes, and nobody would trust him. And he must be particular to keep sacredly his word. Piety is nothing without *wafā*, i.e. faithfulness to one's promise or oath. The community is ruined by nothing so much as by treachery and fraud.

Penny-wiseness and misery ruin the cause of the *da'wat*, because they encourage fraud and 'charging extra' (*infāq*) in the *dā'ī*'s subordinates, who have to resort to these to counteract their evil effects. Therefore the *dā'ī* should be generous, *sakhī*, and must possess *muruwwa*, i.e. unselfishness and broadmindedness.

The *dā'ī* must know how to keep secrets entrusted to him; if he does not possess the necessary ability of *kitmān*, i.e. preserving confidential matters unrevealed, he may cause grave calamity to his followers, and ruin the cause of the community.

He must possess *ra'y*, i.e. sense of discretion and clear thinking, tact, coupled with *ḥilm* and *ṣabr*, i.e. sympathetic attitude and patience. He has to deal with people of different status, education, intelligence, etc., who come to him with their needs and requests. If he treats them harshly, losing his temper and feeling irritated, he will soon become unpopular, and his mission will suffer. Therefore he must particularly cultivate a friendly manner in dealing with such people, necessary self-control and patience, being *ṭayyibu'l-kalām*, i.e. polite and friendly with everybody and his subordinates, never showing contempt of them, or humiliating them. He must preserve the best relations with the people amongst whom he lives and works, carrying on with them, whatever they may really be. As Imam Ja'far said: 'live (friendly) with people, even if they have bad manners, and do not tell them bluntly that they are pigs'. He must be polite with every one, although preserving his dignity, not talkative. If he speaks, he must touch only on serious matters, or learned subjects, as otherwise respect to him may be affected.

He must always keep up his spirits and cheer up his followers. In their bereavement, misfortune, sickness, he must show them his compassion and sympathy, visiting them, or sending someone to convey his kind word, offering a prayer for them. Similarly, on an auspicious occasion, or festivity, he must send to the people his congratulations and greetings, acting as a loving brother with his co-religionists.

The door of his house must be open to every member of the community, both to his supporters and to those who may oppose him. He should not keep aloof from his followers, so that an estrangement may not arise between him and them. He must not accustom himself to suspect them in evil things, or distrust them, because distrust and suspicion lead to fraud.

The *dāʿī* must possess a powerful personality (*waqār*), and inspire great respect (*hayba*) in his followers and subordinates. But he must not develop greed for authority and domination of others. He must realize the responsibility which authority implies, and must make himself worthy of it. If he only thinks of self-aggrandizement (being not worthy of his high position), this is nothing but false pretence, or lie, and lie is the source of all vices, of misery, hatred, and calumny, which ruin piety and righteousness.

The *dāʿī* must not be licentious or loose, sensuous or lustful, because this leads to his spiritual degradation and loss of respect in the eyes of his people.

He must especially avoid greed, *ṭamaʿ*, which leads to the practice of bribes, illegal gratification. This is contrary to the oath of allegiance (*ʿahd*) to which he is expected to be faithful. And if he violates it, it means that his religious sincerity (*dīn*) is gone; such a man is lost for the *daʿwat*. Even if he repents, and his oath is accepted again, he still remains a great offender, just as a man who has committed murder or rape.

The *dāʿī* must not develop the manner of turning everything into a joke, treating things lightly. This leads to the loss of respect for him, and even hostility and contempt for him on the part of his followers.

5. *Special qualifications of the dāʿī.* He must be a clever and intelligent man, learned, and a born orator and preacher. He must know the local language of the province in which he works, just as he must know the local religions, and be up to the standard of the local cultured society, so that he may have a common language when addressing them. But above all he must be a shrewd psychologist, possessing sufficient insight to recognize at once the real value of the man whom he meets, and anticipate the attitude of

the people with whom he deals. He must develop the understanding of human psychology, observe the words and the actions of his associates. He must correctly judge about their intelligence. An experienced *dāʿī* can at once see how far his pupil may be permitted to learn abstract doctrines without the danger of being left in confusion.

He must have the talent of an organizer, which is the chief virtue of a ruler. He must strengthen the organization of his community, both secular and religious (*bi-siyāsa milliyya wa sharʿiyya*) before he becomes their real spiritual head, who rules their souls by the authority of learning (*bi-riyāsa ʿilmiyya*), so that the purpose of his mission (*daʿwat*) can be attained.

6. *The mission of the dāʿī*. The *dāʿī* can only be made by *idhn*, i.e. permission, or commission (of the Imam, directly or indirectly, through intermediary authorities).[33] One who has not got such permission (but calls himself a *dāʿī*), is an impostor and traitor, messenger of evil. (The object of his mission, *daʿwat*, his learned and personal qualifications, are explained above.)

He brings (new) life into the souls of the initiated by imparting to them his knowledge and wisdom, delivering to them his spiritual knowledge (*alʿilmuʾr-rūḥānī*), revealing to those amongst them who have stood the test of their sincerity, the secret meaning of their religion. He teaches them both the formal side of the religion, *ẓāhir*, and its abstract, or hidden side, the *bāṭin*.

He also accepts, on behalf of the Imam, the oath of allegiance from them (*ʿahd*, or *mīthāq*). His mission has three main points: imparting the (true religious) knowledge, raising the spirit of fear of God, and organizing (*siyāsa*) the community.

7. *Management of the community*. The *dāʿī* must entirely devote himself to the affairs of his mission (*daʿwat*), and the community which he manages on behalf of the Imam, from whom he holds his commission. He must always attach the greatest importance to the interests of the mission, encouraging those who are loyal to it. He must never miss a chance for proving the greatness of the religion, and add to its respect in the eyes of his followers, or to denounce its enemies, exposing their weak points.

He must at every opportune moment impart instruction to his followers, teaching them to appreciate religious knowledge and learning, which should bring them many advantages. He must emphasize the spiritual reward which they may gain by this. All this helps the community to keep up their spirit at the time of difficulties. When he preaches, he is not compelled to answer every question put to him by his followers. He must first make sure whether the question is asked out of sincere desire for the guidance, or out of vain curiosity. It is, however, not advisable to refuse to reply in any case.

After he has finished his admonitions, he must leave the pupils alone to think over and to 'digest' his instruction.

He must keep himself well-informed, and must always look for fresh information (to keep himself up-to-date). He must not shun the discomforts and hardships of travelling for the inspection of his diocese, and acquiring first hand knowledge of the people, and their needs, or for preaching to them.

When a messenger, or a convert escaping from his original co-religionists (*muhājir*) arrives, the *dāʿī* must receive him as he should according to his position and status, giving him encouragement, and strengthening his heart. And if he himself sends a messenger to a town or province, he must select for this purpose a suitable, reliable, conscientious and honest man, because he will be questioned (in addition to the message which he conveys) by the people to whom he is sent. He must know how to answer their questions in a light favourable to the community, and not to harm its interests. He also should be able to tell honestly what he has seen and heard on his tour, when he comes back.

The *dāʿī* must dispense justice to his followers, satisfying their just demands, seeing to it that no one should be wronged. He must settle their disputes, if asked, and must collaborate with the secular authorities on the spot, helping them to maintain law and order, in so far as his collaboration in religious sphere may prove effective. If the dispute arises between different parties of the initiated, *mu'mins*, i.e. members of the sect, the *dāʿī* should persuade them to settle their dispute before him, without referring the case to secular authorities. They should not go before the *sulṭān*, or *qāḍī*, because their own *dāʿī* is their immediate authority. Those who disregard this principle, sin; those who deliberately oppose it, deserve condemnation; and those who (really?) do this, invoke the condemnation of all Saints of God (i.e. Imams). The disputing parties must come to a settlement (normally) only with his consent.

It is generally the duty of the *dāʿī* to preserve peace between his followers, and reconcile their disputes, leading them towards friendly co-operation, affectionate relations, and mutual help. He must dissuade them from envy, hatred, intrigues, enmity, concealment of truth, etc. One must not wish for others what he does not wish for himself.

If anyone starts oppressing his brother *mu'mins*, the *dāʿī* must take steps to put a stop to this, and punish him. If the offender persists, the *dāʿī* must make his offence public, and excommunicate him until he comes to his senses.

In case anything untoward happens in the community, corruption or offence against the spirit of religion, if cases of treachery occur, or renegacy spreads, or disconent or rebellion are started, the *dāʿī* must have information at once, and take necessary measures for putting things right. If he leaves the things to worsen, by neglect or deliberately, by an error, or out of laziness, or incapability, he becomes responsible for the crime, and must be punished. (The responsibility for the affairs of the community lies with him entirely.) If God asks the Imam to account for the condition of the community, its preservation or obedience, the Imam may lay responsibility for these on the shoulders of the *dāʿī*, who takes it upon himself, volunteering to guarantee the welfare of the congregation, and has to account for this. If he feels himself unfit to carry out his obligations, he must inform the Imam at once, and resign from office, so that another man, fit to fill the post, may be appointed instead of him.

In his instruction to the community the *dāʿī* must always urge his followers to be obedient to the Imam, and to be affectionately devoted to him, carrying out all his orders, and offering their own selves and their property to propitiate him, and to be ready even to sacrifice their lives if required. One pleases God by pleasing the Imam, and obeys God by obeying him. The *dāʿī* must make it clear to his followers that the Imam is not obliged to do anything for any one. And if he grants the wishes of his people, giving them things of this world, or learning, he does this not for necessity, but out of his generosity.

8. *The dāʿī and his assistants and immediate subordinates*. No *mu'min* deserves the name of *mu'min*, unless he prepares and educates another *mu'min* like himself.[34] It is therefore the duty of the *dāʿī* to train his subordinates in their work by teaching religious subjects, imparting to them general information, disciplining them, and testing their abilities. He must train them to carry out his instructions, and take into consideration the individual abilities of every one amongst them. He must train his *ma'dhūn* how to handle those who are in his charge. Similarly, he must give proper education to other ranks, in religious subjects and in the *technique* of their work, so that they may gradually rise to being eligible for the Imam's commission (*ḥaddu'l-idhn*).[35] Similarly, he

must educate the ordinary initiated (*mustajīb*), organizing them, and instructing them in all subjects that they should know, as far as they are capable of understanding them.

He also should not neglect the uninitiated (*ahlu'z-ẓāhir*), making them live in peace, conducting discussions with them on religious subjects. The low and noble, Muslims and non-Muslims, must equally receive his attention and thought, his instruction and his care about their safety, in the spirit of honesty, justice, and tolerance.

The *dāʿī* should not select his assistants (and candidates to priesthood) out of consideration of their material affluence, personal friendship with him, those who are under his protection,[36] or are subservient to him, etc., because such practices lead to the ruin of the community in the eyes of everybody, just as the messengers who cheat and betray their religion by praising those who bribe them, and reviling those who do not satisfy their greed.

The *dāʿī* must look after the *mu'mins* and *ma'dhūns*, and those who are appointed to teach them, making them observe the prescriptions of the *sharīʿa*, and understand the doctrine of *ta'wīl*, which they should learn consciously, sensibly, and seriously. He must give them necessary explanations (if they ask for these), test their intelligence in various ways, in the sphere of religion or in other matters, thus acquiring a complete idea of what they really are. When he finds them fit and suitable (for his work), he raises them to the position of *dāʿīs*. He tests them by giving them charge of the education of *mustajībs*, under his own supervision. If they pass the test, he promotes them further, and appoints them as (deputy) *dāʿīs* in some localities, controlling them closely in their work. Thereafter he promotes them further, until they reach the position of being in charge of a district, or even a province. He continues testing and trying them all the time until he knows them thoroughly.

If such candidate to *dāʿī*-ship shows great zeal, making great progress in his training, and the *dāʿī* sees that he will make a good assistant to himself, or will be fit to take over his own duties, he has no excuse for not making him a *dāʿī*, although the man may be only a *mu'min* by his rank.[37]

(But) the *dāʿī* should not trust any man who is not properly tried and tested by him, whose sincerity is not proved, and who does not comply with the regulations of the *daʿwat*. He can rely on him only after he has served for some time, proving his ability, and giving a satisfactory account of himself. If some people approve of him, but others object to him, the *dāʿī* should not employ him, because objection overrules the approval.[38] This is because those who trust in him, believe only in what is good and sensible in him that they have seen. But those who oppose had the chance to see in him what was not good. Even if a thousand people testify to his being eligible for the work, and only two oppose, pointing out some defects in his character, and four other men point out some other shortcomings, the *dāʿī* must accept the opinion of those who are against him. (Popular) accusations of *dāʿīs*, just as of witnesses, judges, or trustees, usually cannot be treated as seriously as real accusations in some offence, proved by reliable evidence. Many of such charges are based on hearsay, repetition of rumours, stories of 'trusted men'; but even if in case of the candidate to *dāʿī*-ship different allegations are not supported by proper evidence, and do not imply any serious offence (*ḥadd*), it would nevertheless be better to get rid of him, because later his position may become difficult.

But what to do in the event that all agree in trusting the man as good, and he proves to be a deceiver? And what to do with the man who is generally regarded as bad? In any case, if two respectable *muʾmins* swear and prove that so-and-so is unfit to be employed as a *dāʿī*, the *dāʿī* must not employ him in the *daʿwat* service. If notwithstanding this the *dāʿī* endangers the life and property of the faithful (by employing such a man?), he commits a crime, and it is treachery not only against the property, but also the existence of the congregation of his province, which may be ruined by dishonesty or lack of administrative talent on the part of the (new) *dāʿī*. This happens from time to time through greed of some *dāʿīs*, their impiety, ignorance, etc.

The *dāʿī* must manage his community with determination and energy, keeping himself well informed, especially in the provinces which are under the hand of tyrannical and hostile rulers. Therefore a man should not be appointed as a *dāʿī* (without proper qualifications) simply in the course of ordinary promotion, in fulfilment of a promise, out of favouritism, nepotism, friendly relations, protection, for consideration of some material interests, out of respect, or under a threat, etc. All such reasons are contrary to the spirit of religion, justice, trust, and word of God and His Prophet. A great deal of corruption may be introduced into the community by permitting such irregular practices.

If a *dāʿī* (satisfactorily), working for some time, does something that angers his superior, and is concerned with purely personal matters, such as not rendering a (personal) favour, etc., the superior *dāʿī* should not dismiss him from his post. He must do this (only) in case of his subordinate's treachery against religion. The *dāʿī* may employ one if he sees that the candidate has sufficient religious qualifications (*dīn*), even if he does not like him personally, or is personally against him. But if the subordinate *dāʿī* strays from the right path, or misappropriates religious funds, etc., he becomes a criminal, a trespasser of the law, and his oath of allegiance is annulled.

If the *dāʿī* notices that a *mu'min* or *ma'dhūn* commits treachery, or misbehaves himself, he must admonish him to repent. But if the sinner persists, despite his admonition, and if his actions affect the interests of the community, or create dissension in the people, the *dāʿī* must severely reprimand him, and even, if this does not suffice, he must make his offence known to the whole of the community, and dismiss him, sending some one to take over his post. In case, however, his mistakes do not seriously affect the community, and are merely the sins for which he is only responsible before God, then the *dāʿī* should not give the matters wide publicity.[39]

Whenever the behaviour of the subordinate *dāʿī* affects the interests of the community, the superior *dāʿī* must warn his followers against him, so that his example should not be followed, and there would be difference between those who act rightly, and those who act wrongly.

If the *mu'min* or *ma'dhūn* shows his righteousness, trustworthiness, loyalty, high moral standard, and learning, it is necessary that the superior *dāʿī* should encourage him, showing more confidence in him, raising his position above that of others, so that his enthusiasm may increase. Other subordinate *dāʿīs*, seeing his example, may desire to emulate it, bettering their work. If there should be no difference between good and bad, and a bad worker should not suffer disadvantage, then nothing would stop corruption and decay spreading in the community, and there would be no incitement to any one to do good. This would lead to the ruin of the people, increasing their deterioration and disorderliness.

The *dāʿī* must educate his *mu'mins*, improving their manners, so that they may become fit to appear before the Imam, and answer sensibly and politely his questions, without feeling confused; or ask him about necessary things in proper language and manner, at the proper time, what is really needed.

The *dāʿīs* must not enrich themselves with the Imam's money, or demand more than is really needed. And if they ask, and their request is not granted, they should not at once bear a grudge against the Imam, or let their devotion to him become undermined.

The *dāʿī* should not criticise or disagree with any act of the Imam; he must obey all his orders or restrictions, and rules laid by him. He must accustom his followers not to demur to anything coming from him, and to be certain that all the actions of the Imam are based on a higher wisdom, and special reasons (which remain unknown to them). If they do not know his motives at present, they perhaps will know them later.

If they recognize the Imam as the wisest man of the time (*ḥakīmu'z-zamān*), they must realize that all that he does is based on his supreme wisdom. If they fail to understand this, this is because they are incapable of understanding the superior substance of the Imam.

The *dāʿī* must properly train and curb his followers; and when he employs them in the *daʿwat* service, or sends them on any religious or political mission, he must properly instruct them as to their duty. He must carefully explain everything to them, what they are expected to do, warning them against dishonesty or deliberate attempts at wrecking the work, or neglect, or cowardice on their part. And if his agent commits one of such offences, he (the agent) becomes responsible for these before the religion, his allegiance is broken, and he becomes covered with eternal shame, in this world and in after life, so that he would deplore his behaviour, losing all his reward which was otherwise due to him.

If any of his assistants cheats or swindles him, the *dāʿī* must punish him severely, reduce him in rank, so that his case may serve as an example for others. On the contrary, seeing his devotion and enthusiasm, the *dāʿī* should reward him, and promote him to a higher position.

The *dāʿī* should properly instruct his assistants and followers that in case any one of them notices that some one is betraying the interests of the Imam, in the religious or secular sphere, or tampering with the administration of the community, he must at once interfere, suppressing the offender. And if he cannot do this, he must at once report the matter to the Imam (or his accredited representative), as otherwise great calamity may be caused to the community, leading God knows to what.

9. *The dāʿī and the mustajīb*. The *dāʿī* must select as his *mustajībs*, i.e. initiated followers, people of good appearance (i.e. physique), and sound faith. These indicate general soundness in

a man, and sound health indicates that he is living an orderly life, and has a good disposition. He must be free from bodily defects such as deafness, absence of one of his limbs, mangyness, lameness, etc. Similarly he must be free from blemish in his religious beliefs, e.g. from *ghuluww*, or Shi'ite extremism. The *dā'ī* must carefully study the candidate, detecting all his blemishes, and reject those who are unfit to be admitted. It sometimes happens that through the *dā'ī*'s neglect or carelessness unfit persons are permitted to join, and swear the oath of allegiance; but later on decay and corruption creep into the community through this.

The *dā'ī* is responsible for the proper choice of his *mustajībs*. When the man of the right type is selected, the *dā'ī* must make it certain whether he takes the oath of allegiance quite sincerely, and has no hidden motives, such as greed, coveting a position, or whatever it may be.

The *dā'ī* should not accept an initiate (*mustajīb*) for the consideration of money, or other interest, but only after ascertaining the candidate's sincere devotion. This can be done only gradually. If the candidate has some ulterior motive in his conversion, he must not be accepted. But if everything is all right with him, the *dā'ī* must dispell all his doubts as to his former religion being wrong, so that no prejudice against his new persuasion may be left in his mind. Then he takes from him the oath of allegiance (on behalf of the Imam); and he begins to teach him only after this the (Ismaili) doctrine, gradually, not revealing much at a time, in order not to make him confounded, as this may cause him much harm. This must be done by special lectures, for which the *dā'ī* should reserve specified hours, when his pupils can ask him different questions. Non-initiated should not be present at such conversations.

10. *The dā'ī and the religious funds*. The question of the control of religious funds, trusts, and property has not received much attention in *al-Mūjiza*. The *dā'ī* must not misappropriate the Imam's property (i.e. religious funds) when using these for the purposes sanctioned by his authority. The Imam needs money and property in order to increase the might of his community, and strengthen the foundations of the religion: money guards religion.

If, however, the *dā'ī* conceals for his own use something from the religious funds in his hands, this amounts to a very great sin against the *da'wat*, or religion. And if the *dā'ī* disregards the prescriptions of his religion, he must be punished even more severely than the ordinary man under similar circumstances.

In his routine *da'wat* expenses he must keep within the limits of what is sanctioned; but at the same time he must not bother the Imam with asking for special sanction for every trivial item, or delay payments, making his work suffer.

11. *The dāʿī and the policy towards the world outside the community.* The *dāʿī* should realize that *mulk*, state, is the guardian of religion and the people who profess it. The empire of the Imams is based on religion (*dīn*). The spread of the religion (*dīn*), and the success of the *da'wat* (Fatimid domination) strengthen the empire, removing obstacles and difficulties in the way of its progress. All the subjects of the Imam may then become his devotees, residing either within the limits of the empire (*fī ḥaḍrati-hi*), or in different *jazīras*, i.e. religious colonies, where they form his *jund*, vanguard, or his auxiliares, or supporters who should never betray the interests of the Imam, or revolt against him.

But everybody would become dissatisfied, and develop a hostile and disloyal attitude towards the Imam, if mistakes are perpetrated in the religious administration (*dīn*). If his *dāʿīs* are inefficient and worthless, incapable of carrying on the administrative work, ignorant and impious, the religious spirit of the masses is bound to deteriorate. (Losing interest and trust in it) they may begin to apostatize, returning to the fold of the religion which they professed before their conversion (to Ismailism); or many may become atheists (*dahriyya*), or join some heretical sectarian movement. They would resent the miserable state of things in their community (*dīn*), their souls would be affected with grief; discontent, rebellion, factional fights, splits would spread, dishonesty, violence, etc., would become common, and the community would become engaged in self-destruction.

This is the picture of what would happen if mistakes are permitted to accumulate in the religious management of the community. The unrest would necessarily spread to *jazīras*, or religious colonies, and this would be the end of the religion, as the people would be reduced to the state of wild beasts.

There are three principles on which the policy of the *da'wat* should be based, and they sum up everything: enlightenment (*ʿilm*), conscientious attitude towards one's duties (*taqwā*), and (sound) organization (*siyāsa*). The duty of the *dāʿī* (with regard to the population which is not yet converted) is to introduce good secular administration, based on strict observance of law (*siyāsa milliyya sharʿiyya*). He should dominate them by his enlightened intellectual superiority (*riyāsa ʿilmiyya*), and then he would succeed to dominate their souls, and thus complete the aim of the *daʿwat*, their conversion.

The true guidance of the people (*as-siyāsatu'l-ʿāmma*) in charge of the *dāʿī* means to educate them in strict respect for law, and social advancement (*ta'dīb millī*). The *dāʿī* should train them in obedience to law, discourage them from infringing its prescriptions, and introduce in them admiration for moral virtues (*faḍā'il*). Those who do not obey him, must receive appropriate punishment.

The *dāʿī* therefore should attach special importance (*himma*) to the correct discharge of his administrative duties, both religious and secular, because only such policy helps the Imams to acquire mastery over the world. The man who is unfit to control himself, his relatives and servants, cannot rule others, and therefore cannot be appointed as a *dāʿī*.

12. *The dāʿī and society.* Only men of good families should be appointed *dāʿīs*, because good birth (*nasab fī qawm*) gives good standing in society. The people would not so willingly associate themselves with the *dāʿī* who is of a low origin, or accept his tuition, treating him with contempt. I myself (says the author of *al-Mūjiza*) saw many people who did not like to join the religion only because the *dāʿī* (who wanted to convert them) was a man of low birth, or because he had been in jail, or suspected of something disreputable. For these reasons only people of good and respectable families should be appointed to commanding positions in the community, because noble origin adds respect in the eyes of one's subordinates.

The *dāʿī* must possess good bearing and manners, must dress properly. He must know how to treat people who come in contact with him. He must be circumspect, kind to everybody, but must not degrade himself by lengthy chats with the people undeserving this. Nor should he be abrupt and rude with any one. Mistakes in etiquette create ill feelings. In social functions every one should be given the place to which he is entitled, and every one must treat each other with respect and courtesy.

(In his private life) the *dāʿī* should prefer the company of learned people (as mentioned above). He must also treat with respect ascetics and devotees (of other religions). And he must keep away completely from the people of doubtful reputation and bad character.

13. *The dāʿī in his family life.* Orderliness in family life (*as-siyāsatu'l-ḫāmma*) must be strictly adhered to by the *dāʿī*. He must

make all his relatives observe discipline and decency, respect virtue, and avoid committing mischief. If they commit errors, he must punish them. Every man preserves in his family the spirit or tradition which he leaves as a legacy to his progeny. The *dāʿī* must make learning, high morals, and good manners a family tradition, so that his children, being brought up in this spirit, may acquire salvation. He must make a point of compelling every member of his family to be punctual in offering the prescribed prayers, paying *zakāt*, etc. If he is unable to keep his family life running in an orderly way, how can he be entrusted with the guidance of others in religious and general matters?

The *dāʿī* should not employ as servants young boys, or any one who may give food to suspicions as to his good morals. This would inevitably become the subject of talk everywhere, and the prestige of the *dāʿī* might be ruined. His servants must take special care about their own reputation, as its ruin may ruin that of their master's. The *dāʿī* should not tolerate any drunkard near himself, or a man suspected of something bad, as this endangers his own reputation. His domestic servants (*ḥāshiya*) must be initiated members of the religion (*mu'min*), modest men, devoted to the work of religion and their community. As in the house of the *dāʿī* discussions may often be carried on of different doctrinal and theological matters (which may be secret), such things must not reach the hearing of the uninitiated. Therefore the servants must be trusted and reliable. They must be of good character also because wives and children of the *dāʿī*'s followers often enter his house, and they should be safe from anything undesirable. The women whom he employs in his family, must be either relatives whom he cannot marry according to the rules of the *sharīʿa*, or his wives, or slave-wives.

In his private life the *dāʿī* must keep, as far as possible, indoors, discussing important questions with decent, respectable and learned people. They also may occupy themselves with recitations of the Coran, offering prayers at the prescribed times, etc. In such conversations with his personal friends the *dāʿī* should see that the people behave themselves decently, do not utter indecent jokes, or use obscene and rude language, as this may (become known, and) ruin his prestige.

14. *The personal staff of the dāʿī.* The secretary (*kātib*) of the *dāʿī* must be a modest and unpretentious man. By his profession he has to know his master's and the community's secrets and confidential matters; therefore only a *mu'min*, or initiated member of

the sect, may be employed for this work. It is said that the secretary is the trustee (*wakīl*) of his master's knowledge, or his mater's reasoning (*manṭiq*). Therefore it is absolutely impossible to tolerate having a man in such a position who may happen to be a bad character (*fāsiq*), dishonest, corrupt, or rapacious. Such man could cause incalculable damage to the *dā'ī*'s work.

Similarly, the *dā'ī*'s major-domo, or chamberlain, *ḥājib*, also should be an intelligent man, of good manners, polite, of good address, modest and not venal. Being in charge of the management of the house, he is in this respect the lieutenant of his master. It is known that by one's chamberlain one may judge what his master is, and what are his habits, just as by one's servant the people judge about his respectability. Nothing can ruin the prestige of a master so much as corruption shown by his servant.

The *dā'ī* must keep a reliable porter, *bawwāb*, a trusted man, belonging to his community. He should be polite and considerate to the people who call on his master. If they come at reception time he must admit them in a courteous manner. And if someone calls at an unusual time, the porter should politely ask him to wait, report to his master his arrival, and ask whether the guest should be admitted. As wives and children of the members of the community have often to call at the *dā'ī*'s house, the porter must be selected from amongst reliable men of irreproachable character.

NOTES

1 It would be interesting if students of the history of Islam coould definitely ascertain the first date at which this term is used. It would also be interesting to find out in how far the same term *dā'ī* was applied to the propagandists of other Shi'ite sects, especially the Ithna-'ashari. As is known, the Zaydīs freely used it. In the case of the Ismailis a great deal of confusion is inevitable due to their being always mixed up in the non-sectarian annals with the Qarmatians.

2 E.G. Browne's views are summed up in his well-known *Literary History of Persia* (Vol. I, pp. 391–415), where he endorses the similar views of de Goeje and Dozy (p. 394 sq.).

3 So E.G. Browne visualized him from his observations of the Bahā'ī missionaries whom he met with in Persia. Cf. his *Library History of Persia*, Vol. I, p. 410.

4 Tremendous amount of speculation is found in the different works of some Orientalists about the 'typically Persian' nature of Ismailism, of its 'Persian' mentality, dogmas, etc. All this completely defies my comprehension. The exoteric doctrine of Ismailism is the strictest form of Islam, while its esoteric system is entirely built up from *Greek*

elements. Surely, Islam itself, in its most orthodox form, contains many Christian, Jewish, Zoroastrian, and other elements; and they are not a wit more prominent in Ismailism, as it was under the Fatimids. The aberration of judgement is obviously based on the fact that before genuine Ismaili literature became accessible, the information offered by the anti-Ismaili authors was extremely misleading. It completely distorted the picture by withholding all mention of what Ismailism had in common with other Islamic schools, and by laying absurdly exaggerated stress on the few ill-understood, or deliberately perverted tenets calculated to serve as food for accusations.

5 Through his daughter Fāṭima, as is well-known. Although the Fatimids emphasized this point, many Shi'ite sects endowed 'Alī ibn Abī Ṭālib with much greater religious importance, so that they even followed the line of his descendants who were the children of 'Alī by his other wife, Ḥanafiyya.

6 The author of *al-Mūjizatu'l-Kāfiya*, as may be seen further on, plainly compares the Ismaili *dā'ī* with the priests in the three main religions known to him—Zoroastrian, Jewish, and Christian, although it is not clear to what extent he realizes the implications of such comparison.

7 Obvious autodidact and self-made *murshids* had to declare that they had received their *khirqa* either from Khiḍr, or from a certain famous saint during their sleep, in a dream. This sort of pious fraud was apparently condoned by the public at the period of the gradual decline of Sufism, but was impossible during its flourishing early phase.

8 I preserve this Persian way of pronunciation of this word, and *da'wat* instead of the Arabic *ḥujja* and *da'wa* which are somewhat unfamiliar to readers in India and in Persia.

9 As may be seen further on, from the summary of *al-Mūjizatu'l-Kāfiya*, the idea of the 'commission', in its real sense, could apply only to the *dā'īs* occupying an independent position, residents in different smaller or larger dioceses. The lower ranks were simply employees in the *da'wa* service; in case of dissatisfaction with their work they could be dismissed by the *dā'ī*.

10 It is really remarkable that in a work such as *al-Mūjizata'l-Kāfiya*, specially dealing with these matters, there is not a single allusion to the duties of the *ḥujjat*, or the *dā'ī's* being under his control. The title *da'ī'd-du'āt*, now and then met with in some works, apparently was not an official title, and it is difficult to determine whether it was applied to the *ḥujjat*, or the *bāb*. The latter seems more probable.

11 It is generally regarded by the Ismailis at present that the *ḥujjats* 'of the night' were superior to those 'of the day'. Personally I have not yet found anything about this in the works which I have had occasion to see, and no explanation of the implications of the title.

12 Utilizing historical information about the distribution of the Ismailis, it is possible to think that in addition to the Yaman there were *jazīras* in Khorasan, Mawaraannahr, Badakhshan, Ray (with Isfahan), Kerman, Khuzistan, 'Irāq, and India (Sind), i.e. nine altogether, excluding Syria, which for the most part was incorporated into the Fatimid empire. Nothing is known to me about the existence of similar *jazīras* in the Maghrib, or within the limits of the Byzantine empire.

13 It seems that this rank appears only at the latest Fatimid period, and probably was quite an artificial title bestowed upon the more distinguished *dāʿīs*.

14 This also seems to be a shadowy rank, most probably invented, as that of the *dāʿī'l-balāgh*, to bring the hierarchy to the required mystical number.

15 In this paper, I have deliberately avoided the question as to the 'degrees of initiation', so inevitably described in every work dealing with Ismailism. From what I have seen of the genuine Ismaili works, I believe that the idea is simply based on a misunderstanding of the hierarchy of the priests, and that there really never was anything as a division of the Ismailis into strictly defined groups of progressive 'initiation', similar to that of the masons, etc. In reality, most probably, there were groups with different educational qualifications, as in every religious community: uninitiated, initiated, but not learned, well-educated, and experts. Although there are no clear indications, it seems that the title *mu'min*, referred to here, had much to do with this, and perhaps was applied to a *well-educated* (in religious sense) Ismaili, who was not regularly employed in the *daʿwat* service, and had no official rank, although by his educational qualifications he was eligible for a fairly high post.

16 Cf. V. Ivanov, *Guide to Ismaili Literature*, No. 18. The fact that the work was known to Ibn Nadīm, and is mentioned in his *Fihrist*, may indicate that it was quite popular in his time, and was not, anyhow, kept secret.

17 On his biography and works cf. A.A.A. Fyzee's article in the *J.R.A.S.*, 1934, pp. 1–32.

18 Cf. V. Ivanov, *Guide*, No. 85. The original text of this work is being prepared for publication by Prof. M. Kāmil Ḥusayn of Cario. Therefore in the translation given further on the original text is not edited.

19 Cf. *Guide*, No. 110.

20 Cf. *Guide*, No. 195.

21 Cf. *Guide*, No. 275: *Kitābu'l-Azhār wa malmaʿu'l-anwār*, by Ḥasan b. Nūḥ b. Yūsuf al-Bharūchī (d. 939/1533). The work is in seven volumes; the last three are exceedingly scarce.

22 Cf. *Guide*, No. 113.

23 Cf. *Guide*, No. 207. The work mentioned under a slightly different title as No. 208 is the same as the preceding. The fault lies with the author himself, because he gives its title in two different forms at the beginning and the end of the work.

24 In my copy, of course. The number of pages is merely given for showing the proportions.

25 Cf. *Guide*, No. 260.

26 In his account of the *dāʿī*'s virtues and duties the author, Qāḍī Nuʿmān, as usual, carefully avoids touching on the matters connected with esoteric doctrine. This is the most prominent feature of all his works, and it is not yet clear what the reason was for this policy.

27 About this cf. V. Ivanov, *A Creed of the Fatimids* (Bombay, 1936), pp. 13–17.

28 As already mentioned above, it is doubtful whether the author takes into consideration all the implications of this parallel. Most probably his parallel does not go beyond the fact that the *dāʿīs* are the servants of religion in the same way as all other priests are servants of their respective religions. It is noteworthy, however, that he does not mention the Sunnite *mullas* in this connection.

29 As just mentioned above, the author refers to all ranks of the *dāʿīs*, i.e. religious functionaries, equally, 'from *bāb* to *mukāsir*'. Thus it is very interesting that he demands from the ideal *dāʿī* good knowledge of the *bāṭin*, making not the slightest allusion to the 'degrees of initiation', which should be the limits assigned to every rank.

30 This is exactly the scope of the religious encyclopædia of Abū Ḥātim ar-Rāzī, the *Kitābu'z-Zīna*, referred to above. For this reason it may well be regarded as a manual in the *ẓāhir* for the *dāʿīs*.

31 Apparently these 'exoteric and esoteric prayers' are what in other, especially later works, are styled *al-ʿibādatu'l-ʿamaliyya* and *al-ʿibādatu'l-ʿilmiyya*. These expressions, however, do not appear in this work at all.

32 As is known, Ismailism completely rejects ascetic practices, mortification of flesh, celibacy, and all other ideas. It professes that the body must be as sound as the soul: the former is the riding animal of the latter. If one weakens his *markab*, while travelling in this world, he would not be able to cross the desert of human life, and may perish before he reaches his destination. Therefore the self-discipline which is referred to here is simply what may be in a more modern term called 'building up character'.

33 In the work of the same author, the *Istitāru'l-Imām*, a special expression is used for the idea of commissioning a *dāʿī*, *akhadha ʿalay-hi*: he (the Imam) accepted from him the oath (*al-ʿahd*, which is here implied). As every initiated Ismaili had to swear allegiance to the Imam, and as obviously non-initiated would not be admitted into the secret propaganda service, it is clear that there was a special oath which the *dāʿīs* had to take to the Imam in addition to the usual initiation oath. In the *Sīra* of Jaʿfar al-Ḥājib (*Bulletin of the Faculty of Arts of the Egyptian University*, Vol. IV, p. 112) it is narrated how the Imam (al-Mahdī), being in a dangerous situation, at the mercy of his *dāʿī*, renews the latter's oath (*ʿahd*). It may be added that the term *idhn*, mentioned here, perhaps was only used at an earlier period. Anyhow, in the post-Fatimid period the term which is used is *naṣṣ*, which originally was only applied to the Imam's appointment to his position by his father.

34 These are supposed to be the words of al-Muʿizz bi'l-lāh himself.

35 Cf. note 38 on p. 571, in which the question of the selection of the candidates to the post of the *dāʿī* is discussed.

36 This apparently refers to 'clients', i.e. the people who for various reasons were associated with a tribe or family, although they did not belong to it originally.

37 This apparently implies the case in which the successful candidate does not possess the rank of the *ma'dhūn*. As already discussed above, it is not clear what really was the distinction between the *ma'dhūn*,

mukāsir, and *mustajīb* on the one side, and the *mu'min* on the other, in this sense. One may well think that he was a well-educated layman, privately employed by the *dā'ī*, not an official member of the *da'wat* service.

38 It is not quite clear what this and the following sentences really have in view: does this mean that ordinary members of the community also had the right to be consulted in the appointment of a new *dā'ī*? Or does it mean that those who were consulted, or had the right to dispute the nomination, were other *dā'īs*, of subordinate ranks? Anyhow, it appears that the *dā'ī*, i.e. in this case the *ḥujjat*, or some other kind of a chief *dā'ī*, had no right to appoint any one independently. As mentioned by the author, he had to prepare the candidate to be eligible for the post. And then the matter was not decided simply by the *dā'ī*'s (or the *ḥujjat*'s) recommendation to the Imam, but some additional procedure was to be followed, asking the consent either of the community, or of fellow-*dā'īs*, as it seems.

39 This again sounds as if implying the *dā'ī*'s consulting the community concerning the offence of his subordinate. And again it is dark whether only members of the service, or also laymen are consulted.

20

DAS ERBE DER ANTIKE IM ORIENT UND OKZIDENT

C. H. Becker

BEI historischen Betrachtungen ist die früher so beliebte Feststellung von Entlehnungen unmodern geworden. Es hat sich nämlich herausgestellt, daß mit dem Nachweis einzelner übernommener Ideen oder Formen weder für die Eigenart einer Persönlichkeit oder Institution noch für die Bedeutung eines Kunstwerks oder einer Gedankenschöpfung irgend etwas Wesentliches ausgesagt wird. Entscheidend ist immer nur, was das gestaltende Subjekt aus den übernommenen Ideen oder Formen gemacht oder nicht gemacht hat, und welche Schlüsse aus seinem Verhalten auf sein eigenes Wesen gezogen werden können.

Es kann deshalb auch nicht der Sinn des heutigen Vortrages sein, die zahllosen Entlehnungen aus der Antike – worunter hier nur die klassische, d. h. griechisch-römische Antike verstanden wird – im Orient und Okzident nachzuweisen und aufzuzählen. Vieles wäre ebenso uncharakteristisch wie die Tatsache, daß wir unseren Tag und unsere Stunden noch heute nach dem Duodezimalsystem der Babylonier einteilen. Geschichtlich wesentlich ist nur das Charakteristische, d. h. die Aktivität oder Passivität des beteiligten Individuums oder der Kulturschicht. Unsere Fragestellung lautet deshalb: Wie rezipieren Orient und Okzident das antike Erbe? Gleichartig oder verschieden? Und welche Gesichtspunkte ergeben sich daraus für die Wesensbestimmung beider Kulturkreise und ihrer führenden Individuen?

Aber was verstehen wir unter dem Erbe der Antike? In einem gedankenreichen Aufsatz „Der Orient und das griechische Erbe“ hat mein Freund und Kollege Hans Heinrich Schaeder die Einwirkungen des griechischen Geistes auf die Entwicklung der geistigen Kultur des Orients und die Wandlungen des griechischen Geistes unter dem Einfluß orientalischer Vorstellungen herausgearbeitet. Das Problem des Hellenismus, d. h. die Vermählung griechischen Denkens mit orientalischer Religiosität, ist wohl kaum je so tief erfaßt worden. Wenn Schaeder vom griechischen Erbe redet, so meint er zunächst den echt griechischen Geist, für die Spätzeit aber den vom Orient umgestalteten griechischen Geist des Hellenismus, der einer immer orientalischer, d. h. asiatischer werdenden Welt als griechischer Geist schlechthin erscheinen mußte. Unsere Aufgabe ist eine andere. Während Schaeders Begriffsbestimmung von Orient und Okzident aus dem Ringen zweier lebendiger Kulturwelten geschöpft ist, soll heute der Versuch gemacht werden, das Nachleben des antiken Erbes in der mittelalterlichen und modernen Welt des Ostens und Westens zu untersuchen. Von einem „Erbe" kann man doch wohl erst sprechen, wenn der Erblasser verstorben ist. Ideen wie Institutionen sind Ausdrucksformen lebendigen Lebens; sie haben aber auch ihr Sonderleben, unabhängig von ihren Erzeugern. Ebenso interessant wie das Problem des Hellenismus von Alexander bis zum Auftreten des Islam ist die Frage nach dem Fortleben der gesamten antiken Geisteskultur nach dem Untergang des alten Griechenland, der Diadochenstaaten und des Römerreiches, wobei es nicht von entscheidender Bedeutung ist, ob man die Antike mit Konstantin, Justinian oder mit Heraklius, d. h. mit der arabischen Völkerwanderung und dem Aufkommen des Islam enden läßt. Wenn wir uns heute, dem Beispiel des Gercke-Nordenschen Handbuches der Altertumswissenschaft folgend, der letzteren Datierung anschließen, so können wir unser Thema auch so formulieren: Welche Rolle spielt das antike Erbe in der Kulturgeschichte der islamischen und der gleichzeitigen europäischen Welt, und was lernen wir daraus für das Wesen beider Kulturkreise?

Orient und Okzident stehen im 7. Jahrhundert unserer Zeitrechnung der Antike als einer abgeschlossenen Periode gegenüber, deren Erbe in beiden Kulturkreisen literarisch und organisatorisch weiterlebt, und zwar praktisch, mehr als theoretisch bewußt, das Dasein des Alltags bestimmt. Ein erheblicher Unterschied zwischen beiden Kulturkreisen zeigt sich auf den ersten Blick. Im Abendland bleibt die gleiche Kultursprache, und wenn auch die Germanen mehr zerschlagen haben als im Osten die Araber, so führt dafür die christliche Kirche sprachlich wie institutionell die Traditionen der spät-antiken aber christianisierten Kultur fort und verbreitet sie weit über die Grenzen des römischen Imperiums hinaus. Im Orient hingegen wechseln Sprache und Religion. Das gewaltige Erbe der Antike muß zunächst einmal arabisiert und islamisiert werden. Hat im Abendland das antike Erbe, und zwar auf die Dauer immer stärker, neue Völker gewonnen und damit sich an neuen personellen Trägern erproben können, so hat im Orient die bisherige tragende Schicht der hellenistischen Bildung sich islamisieren müssen. Im Osten also Auseinandersetzung des antiken Erbes mit neuen Ideen, im Westen mit neuen Menschen.

Gewiß sind auch die Araber nur wenig hellenisiert gewesen, also insofern auch ein neues Volk, aber sie sind nicht die Träger der geistigen Auseinandersetzung; das war vielmehr die hellenistische Bevölkerung der von den Arabern eroberten Kulturländer. Aber wie sah nun dies antike Erbe aus? Dem Islam trat es als später Hellenismus entgegen, d. h. in der Gestalt des orientalischen Christentums, des nachbiblischen Judentums, des Manichäismus und des hellenisierten Zoroastriertums. Das antike Erbe war also bereits reichlich orientalisiert, jedenfalls viel orientalisierter als im Westen, obwohl auch das abendländische Christentum seine orientalische Herkunft nicht verleugnen konnte. Schaeder hat in dem zitierten Aufsatz Griechentum und Orient sehr fein durch die Begriffe Paideia und Soteria gegensätzlich zu charakterisieren versucht. Das griechische Bildungsideal der Paideia will das eigenste Wesen des Ich an den objektiven Werten und an der Gemeinschaft rational entwickeln, während die entscheidende Haltung des orientalischen Geistes das Heilsbedürfnis, die Soteria der Seele ist, die den Abgrund zwischen der Allmacht und Ferne Gottes und dem menschlichen Individuum zu überbrücken sucht. Ist der theoretische Gegensatz zwischen orientalischem und griechischem Geist dadurch auch gewiß richtig charakterisiert, so ist doch in der Praxis so früh eine wechselseitige Beeinflussung eingetreten, daß wir wirklich manchmal nicht wissen, ob der antike oder der orientalische Geist in der Mischung überwiegt. Man denke an die Orphiker, an Pythagoras, an die Stoa, an den ganzen Hellenismus. Ja es muß sogar die vielleicht ketzeriche Frage aufgeworfen werden, ob nicht Platos einzigartige Wirkung gerade daraus sich erklärt, daß sein Ingenium griechisches Denken und orientalische Religiosität miteinander zu verbinden wußte, weswegen er von einer späteren Zeit geradezu als Vorläufer des die gleiche Mischform aufweisenden Christentums empfunden werden konnte.

Jedenfalls nimmt der griechische Geist zu verschiedenen Zeiten seiner Entwicklung immer wieder neue orientalische Elemente in sich auf, am deutlichsten in der Epoche zwischen Alexander und dem Beginn unserer Zeitrechnung und dann erneut durch die Verschmelzung des in diesen Jahrhunderten entstehenden Hellenismus mit dem Christentum, dem Manichäismus und anderen orientalischen Religionen. Dieser stark orientalisierte Hellenismus findet schließlich sein Ende im Islam.

Der Kampf des Christentums um seine Selbständigkeit gegenüber dem griechisch-orientalischen Geist der Gnosis wiederholt sich unter anderem Namen im Islam der ersten Jahrhunderte. Wie das ursprüngliche Christentum ist auch der ursprüngliche Islam in der Hauptsache unhellenistisch. Gewiß steht Muhammed in seiner Predigt vom Gericht dem nestorianischen Christentum und vor allem der Gedankenwelt des christlichen Mönchtums nahe. Aber gerade diese Prägungen eines z. T. auch griechisch sprechenden Christentums sind orientalischer Herkunft. Das Charakteristische am Koran ist aber geradezu, daß er in einer so durch und durch hellenisierten Zeit ganz unhellenistisch wirkt. Mit dem Moment, da der Islam die Grenzen seines Heimatlandes überschritt, mußte die Auseinandersetzung beginnen. Früher hatte man geglaubt, daß diese sich in einem polemischen und apologetischen Ringen mit dem Christentum abgespielt hätte, da dessen Hauptproblemstellungen zwar nicht in der Lösung, aber in der Frage übernommen wurden. Heute ahnt man, daß Manichäismus und Zoroastriertum mindestens ebenso gefährliche Gegner waren, und daß namentlich die Gnosis des Manichäismus und verwandter Strömungen dem Islam direkt gefährlich wurden. So hat z. B. die erste dialektische Schule im Islam, die Muʿtazila, ihre Problemstellung zum Teil im Kampf gegen den Manichäismus gewonnen. In diesen Kämpfen bildet sich eine sonderbare Kampffront. Staat und Orthodoxie gehen wie überall auch hier zusammen; im Kampf gegen die alle Autorität auflösende Gnosis aber rufen sie den unverfälschten griechischen Geist zu Hilfe. Symbolisch zeigt sich dieser Gegensatz in dem berühmten Prozeß gegen den gnostisierenden Mystiker Halladj, der 922 in Bagdad hingerichtet wurde. Wenn auch nicht offiziell Gegenstand seines Prozesses, so ist doch am berühmtesten die Formel geworden, mit der er seine mystische Einswerdung, seine ekstatische Liebesvereinigung mit Gott proklamierte: „Ich bin Gott." Sein maßgebender Kritiker und Richter war Ibn Da'ud, ein orthodoxer Gläubiger und zugleich ein Kenner Platons, dessen „Buch des

Planeten Venus" die platonische Liebe beschreibt und dabei solche Vertrautheit mit dem Platonischen Schrifttum verrät, daß z. B. der berühmte Mythus vom gespaltenen Vollmenschen aus der Aristophanesrede des Symposion wörtlich zitiert wird. Es steht also hier der Platon des Gastmahls gegen den Platon der Gnosis, was in diesem Zusammenhang keine Wertung bedeutet.

Die Gnosis beherrscht eben die zunächst ketzerische und erst durch Ghazzali entgiftete und in die Orthodoxie rezipierte Mystik und das gesamte Sektenwesen des jungen Islam. Auch als der Islam schon ziemlich gefestigt ist, bedroht ihn immer aufs neue das antikorientalische Mischprodukt der Gnosis. Zwar ist noch nicht sicher, wie die Bewegung entstand, aber jedenfalls sind es gnostische Ideen, die der schiitischen und später der ismaelitischen Propaganda der Fatimiden ihre Stoßkraft verleihen. Ein junger Gelehrter, Paul Kraus, hat kürzlich das Corpus der Djabirschriften als ismaelitsch und als Vorläufer des Schriftenkreises der Lauteren Brüder von Basra erwiesen, welche noch heute von den Ismaeliten in Indien ihrer Lehre zugrunde gelegt werden. Religiös wie politisch bekämpft die Gnosis den Islam, der sich im Kampf gegen diesen Feind den griechischen Logos, d. h. die griechische Philosophie zu Hilfe holt und eine der abendländischen Scholastik nah verwandte dialektische Welt religiöser Wissenschaften entwickelt. Es sind also islamische Orthodoxie und griechischer Logos verbündet gegen die Logos und Soteria vermengende Gnosis. Aus dieser Situation heraus erklärt sich vielleicht auch der ganz unorientalische und schwer verständliche Eifer des Kalifen Ma'mun, möglichst viele griechische Philosophen ins Arabische übertragen zu lassen. Man hat das bisher meist als löblichen Bildungsdrang eines aufgeklärten Despoten interpretiert, aber wie sich nachweisen läßt, daß die Übersetzungen antiker Mediziner meist aus praktischen Bedürfnissen der großen Medizinschulen entsprangen, dürfte wohl auch die Übersetzung namentlich des Aristoteles aus praktischen Gründen erfolgt sein. Wenn es reiner Bildungseifer gewesen wäre, hätte man ja vielleicht auch Homer oder die Tragiker übersetzen können, aber dafür hatte man eben keine Verwendung und danach kein Bedürfnis.

Es wäre aber ein falsches historisches Bild, wenn man sich die islamische Orthodoxie als Sieger über die hellenistische Gnosis vorstellen wollte. Die islamische Religion wird durch ein in freier Diskussion entstandenes Lehrgebäude, nicht wie die christliche durch die hierarchisch geordnete Heilsanstalt der

Kirche repräsentiert. Der Unterschied zwischen griechisch-orientalischem und römisch-lateinischem Geist kommt darin deutlich zum Ausdruck. Der Variation ist im Islam ein viel größerer Spielraum gelassen. Es fehlt die letzthin entscheidende Instanz. Gewiß kommt der hellenistische Geist am stärksten in der islamischen Sektenbildung zum Ausdruck. Die Imamvorstellungen der Schiiten z. B. sind nachweislich aus der Gnosis entlehnt. Hier liegen Ansätze zu einer viel strafferen Autoritätsbindung, als sie die Orthodoxie entwickelt hat; ihr Sieg hätte den Islam in andere, vielleicht noch hellenistischere Bahnen gedrängt, ihn damit dem Anstaltscharakter der abendländischen Kirche aber nicht nähergebracht, sondern noch weiter von ihm entfernt. Die abendländische Kirche hat, wie gesagt, im Kampf gegen die Gnosis ihren Eigenwert, ihr wahres Wesen herausgearbeitet, während die islamische Orthodoxie zwar theoretisch die Gnosis bekämpft, sie aber in der Praxis des Alltags durch zahlreiche Hintertüren, namentlich auf dem Wege über die volkstümliche Frömmigkeit der breiten Massen wieder hineingelassen und nachträglich mit ihrem Lehrsystem harmonisiert hat. Wir stehen erst in den Anfängen der Erforschung der Geschichte der islamischen Frömmigkeit; aber eines steht bereits fest, daß der Einfluß der Gnosis das dem Urislam widersprechende Muhammedbild und den Muhammedkult des späteren Mittelalters und der Gegenwart geschaffen hat. Die Heiligen des Islam sind die Pneumatiker des Hellenismus. Muhammed, ihr Prototyp, wird schließlich unverhüllt zum präexistenten Nous, ja zum allmächtigen und barmherzigen Heiland, eine Lehre, durch die der Offenbarungsbegriff des alten Islam geradezu in sein Gegenteil verwandelt wird. Vor allem über die verschiedenen Formen der Mystik werden neuplatonische und neupythagoräische Ideen auch im Islam lebendig. Der Anthropos teleios wird zum „vollkommnen Menschen", dem Insān kāmil, die Isotheos Physis die gottgleiche Natur zur dhāt ḥaqqānijja. Man kann die ganze hellenistische Terminologie im Islam, und zwar auch bei orthodoxen Schriftstellern wiederfinden. In Werken wie den schon zitierten Schriftenkreisen des Djabir und der Lauteren Brüder lebt der ganze Plotin weiter, ohne den überhaupt die Geistesgeschichte des Islam nicht zu verstehen ist.

Man sollte meinen, daß es sich hier um letzte Wissenschaft der Eingeweihten handelte. Es war aber zum Teil eine Art von Popularphilosophie der Bildungsschicht, neben der für das Volk Theorie und Praxis des gemein-hellenistischen Zauber- und

Deutungswesens als eine religiöse Unterströmung einherlief. Dies unendlich differenzierte Zauberwesen, Astrologie, Sandzauber, Inkubation, Zahlenmystik, Liebesrezepte, Amulette aller Art, wurde äußerlich arabisiert und islamisiert; aber es war rein gnostisch zum Teil schon auf dem gleichen Wege in den Hellenismus eingedrungen. Man konnte seine Verbreitung nicht hemmen; es war eben lebendige Praxis der Massen. So wurde es durch den Namen Allahs legitimiert. Heute eilt z. B. in Afrika dies gleiche islamisierte Zauberwesen dem Islam voran und erobert heidnische Negergebiete, die dann später, oft viel später, aber wie selbstverständlich dem offiziellen Islam zufallen. Das Tertium Comparationis mit dem Eindringen des gnostischen Zauberwesens in den orthodoxen Islam als Vorbote seiner Hellenisierung ist die Ideenverbreitung durch Contagion. Nicht bewußter Wille, sondern lebendige Berührung des Zufalls und des Zwangs führt zur Ansteckung und damit zur Übertragung. Dieser Vorgang ist für unsere Fragestellung von großer Wichtigkeit. Antike Ideen und Formen werden nicht als solche bewußt ergriffen und zu ideellen Forderungen gemacht, sondern sie leben meist unbewußt – gelegentlich bekämpft, aber unüberwindbar – einfach weiter. Der Islam ist eben nichts anderes als weiterlebender, auf die Dauer sich aber immer mehr asiatisierender Hellenismus. Was hier beim Zauberwesen für die magischen Ideen und Formen gilt, das läßt sich auch bei den soziologischen Gebilden nachweisen, in deren Rahmen diese Zauberriten vornehmlich erscheinen. Die soziologische Form der Mystik war das Bruderschaftswesen, die Bünde und Orden der Derwische. Sie sind wesentlich nichts anderes als überlebende Formen der spätantiken kultischen Gemeinschaften. Jedenfalls erfüllen sie im heutigen Orient die soziologischen Zwecke unseres Vereinswesens. Daß dieser Prozeß nicht nur auf religiösem Gebiet gilt, beweist die Entstehung des islamischen Lehnswesen aus der spätantiken Steuerpacht und dem römischen Praktorenwesen.

Eigentlich ist dieser Vorgang ganz natürlich. Nur weil man den Islam für etwas ganz Neues hielt und Religion und Kultur identifizierte, konnte das Märchen von der Kultur der Araber entstehen, das den Blicken der Historiker das Naheliegendste verbarg: die Kontinuität der tragenden Menschenschicht und des Schauplatzes. Der Islam war der Fremdling, der die spätantike Welt erobern wollte, dann aber ihrer kulturellen Überlegenheit erlag und sie nur äußerlich arabisierte und islamisierte, sie allerdings gleichzeitig vom Abendland abschloß, das schon lange vor dem Auftauchen des Islam durch die Römerherrschaft zum eigentlichen Sitz des antiken Kulturgedankens geworden war. Ehe die politische Zerreißung erfolgte, bildete aber das Imperium Romanum bei aller lokalen Differenzierung eine kulturelle Einheit. Die endgültige Kodifikation des römischen Rechts fand ja nicht allzulange vor dem Auftreten des Propheten statt. Sein Einfluß ist dann auch im islamischen Recht überall greifbar. Fast für jeden seiner Grundsätze kann man die römisch-rechtliche Entsprechung aufführen, und doch ist das islamische Recht gar kein Recht im römischen Sinne, sondern als Ganzes wie im einzelnen etwas vollkommen anderes. Das islamische Recht ist vielleicht die selbständigste geistige Schöpfung des islamischen Kulturkreises. Das römische Recht ist in das islamische Recht hineingeflossen wie die Gnosis in die islamische Religion, nicht etwa nach Art des Ringens des römischen Rechts mit dem germanischen von seinen Anfängen bis zu den Kämpfen um unser deutsches bürgerliches Recht.

Daß auf den Gebieten der Staatsorganisation, der Kriegskunst, der Wirtschaft, der Wissenschaft, der Technik alles beim Alten blieb, versteht sich bei der kulturellen Überlegenheit der von den Arabern eroberten Kulturgebiete einfach von selbst. Man wundert sich immer über die gewaltige Übersetzungsliteratur und meint, daß damit neue Gedanken in die islamische Kulturschicht importiert worden seien. Diese Anschauung ist im Grunde falsch. Es blieb alles in der Praxis wie zuvor. Nur wie man die griechisch, persisch oder koptisch geführten Staats- und Verwaltungsakten nun arabisch abfaßte, ohne an der Verwaltung selbst etwas Wesentliches zu ändern, so mußte man auch die geltenden Lehrbücher aller Wissenschaften und die volkstümliche Literatur mit dem Überhandnehmen des Arabischen als Verkehrssprache der Gesellschaft in dieses neue Idiom übertragen. Eine wirkliche Auseinandersetzung mit neuen Ideen gab es nur auf dem Gebiet der Religion, und selbst hier siegte, wie wir sahen, die hellenistische Praxis. Daß Ptolemäus weiter das Weltbild bestimmte, war ebenso selbstverständlich wie die Vorherrschaft des Hippokrates und des Galen auf dem Gebiete der Medizin. Nur weil man nicht alle gebräuchlichsten antiken Schriftsteller von heute auf morgen übersetzen konnte, wirken die Nachrichten von ihrer Übertragung wie ein bewußter Wille zur Hellenisierung. Davon kann gar keine Rede sein. Man folgte praktischen Bedürfnissen des Augenblicks und mußte der Tatsache Rechnung tragen, daß die führenden Männer des Staates wenigstens in der ersten Zeit nur Arabisch verstanden. Der Nachweis, daß bei diesen Übersetzungen ein neuer Bildungswille akut wird, müßte erst noch geführt werden. Scheint diese Auffassung für die Staatsverwaltung, Wirtschaft, Wissenschaft und Technik auch ohne weiteres einleuchtend, so liegen die Dinge auf dem Gebiet der religiösen Wissenschaften und der schönen Literatur natürlich etwas anders. Von den Kämpfen um Religion und Recht wurde schon gesprochen. Die schöne Literatur mußte natürlich weitgehend von der herrschenden Sprache bestimmt werden, und neben Religion und Recht war die arabische Sprache das dritte selbständige Kulturgut, das die Eroberer neu importierten. Die arabische Poesie war der künstlerische Ausdruck der arabischen Seele schlechthin. Architektur, Plastik und Malerei brachten die Araber nicht mit. So wurde das ästhetische Ideal der Beduinenpoesie ein mitbestimmender Faktor in der nun entstehenden mehr oder weniger hellenistischen Literatur in arabischer Sprache. Die Forschung steht hier in ihren Anfängen, aber einzelne Beispiele legen den Gedanken nahe, daß antike Kunstformen wie Ideen und Stoffe besonders aus den Kreisen der Neupythagoräer und Kyniker bei der Bildung der islamischen Unterhaltungsliteratur eine entscheidende Rolle spielen. Die islamische Literatur wird noch einmal zur Ergänzung der spätantiken dienen können.

Im Orient tritt jedenfalls kein Bruch mit der spätantiken Überlieferung ein; sie wird einfach weitergelebt, wohl etwas modifiziert und in eine neue Sprache übertragen. Daß auf einzelnen Gebieten auch Fortschritte erarbeitet werden, so in der Mathematik und den Naturwissenschaften, vielleicht auch der Medizin, versteht sich von selbst. Dieser Tatbestand macht es erklärlich, daß der Orient in späteren Jahrhunderten zum Lehrmeister Europas werden konnte, wo eben keine so relativ ungestörte Weitertradition überkommenen Wissens statt hatte. Was Europa übernahm, war arabisierte und etwas weiterentwickelte hellenistische Wissenschaft und antike Originalwerke in arabischer Übersetzung, wie z. B. echte, nicht neuplatonisch entstellte Schriften des Aristoteles. Ihre Pflege war kein besonderes Verdienst der Araber; sie hatten nur konserviert und bearbeitet, was sie schon vorgefunden hatten. Daß damals auch literarische Einflüsse schöngeistiger Art über Spanien und durch die Kreuzfahrer nach Europa kamen, von praktischen Verbesserungen der Staatsverwaltung oder der Handelstechnik zu schweigen, sei hier nur gestreift, da nur schwer feststellbar ist, inwieweit der Islam auch hier nur als Vermittler antiken Erbgutes erscheint.

Das Gesagte hat hoffentlich genügt, ein ungefähres Bild davon zu geben, wie sich der Orient in nachantiker Zeit zum antiken Erbe gestellt hat. Er hat es weiter tradiert und modifiziert und tut es zum Teil noch heute. Der Islam hat dieses Erbgut als Teil seiner Bildung über die ganze islamische Welt verbreitet, und aristotelischer Dialektik und hellenistischem Zauber begegnet man heute in Indien wie am Tschadsee. Man hat die antiken Schriftsteller geschätzt und verwertet, aber sie niemals in den Mittelpunkt einer bewußten Bildungsbewegung gestellt, wie wir sie mit dem Ausdruck Humanismus bezeichnen. Das nichtliterarische Erbe der Antike hat der Islam niemals als solches erfaßt, da es zu seinen unbewußten Lebensformen gehörte. Die Pflege des antiken Erbes hat stets in direktem Verhältnis zur Blüte und zum Niedergang der islamischen Zivilisation gestanden. Die Renaissance des Orients in der Gegenwart, dessen Zeugen wir sind, knüpft nicht an die Antike, sondern an das moderne Europa an, und zwar an den realistischen Bildungswillen Europas und nicht an den humanistischen. Das antike Erbe war im Orient immer nur Material, nur Stoff. Die Antike ist dem Orient nie als Idee, als Prinzip, als höchstes Vorbild erschienen, an dem sich die eigene Schöpferkraft entzündete. Im Humanismus liegt der entscheidende Unterschied in der Wirkung des antiken Erbes im Orient und Okzident.

Nicht als ob der Okzident das antike Erbe nicht auch einfach weitergelebt hätte. Wenn man die äußeren Formen frühmittelalterlichen Lebens in Art und Wert miteinander vergleicht, wie ich es vor 25 Jahren in einem Büchlein „Christentum und Islam" unternommen habe, so gewinnt man den Eindruck, daß – abgesehen vom religiösen Bekenntnis – das übrigens ganz anders gemeinte Wort des Westöstlichen Divans Wirklichkeit geworden sei: „Orient und Okzident sind nicht mehr zu trennen." Die allgemeine Auffassung von Welt und Leben ist, da sie aus gemeinsamen Quellen gespeist wird, tatsächlich sehr ähnlich. Wenn wir aber, von unserer heutigen Fragestellung ausgehend, von der Verschiedenartigkeit der Rezeption des antiken Erbes zum Verständnis der Eigenart von Ost und West gelangen wollen, dann scheint diese Ähnlichkeit nur im äußeren Gewand zu bestehen. Eine andersartige, ethnische Zusammensetzung, ein anderes geographisches Milieu und eine selbständige Geschichte lassen das antike Erbe im Abendland eine von den bisher behandelten orientalischen Verhältnissen völlig abweichende Entwicklung durchmachen. Diese Entwicklung ist eines der

Hauptprobleme der abendländischen Geschichte, nicht nur der Geistesgeschichte. Es wäre deshalb Vermessenheit, in diesem Rahmen mehr geben zu wollen als ein paar herausgegriffene Belege zur Illustrierung unserer These.

Entscheidend war die Akzentverschiebung, die sich aus der Trennung in eine griechische und eine lateinische Welt ergab. Zwar wirkte das römische Recht, wie wir sahen, auch auf die östliche Umgestaltung. Aber die spezifischen Leistungen der römischen Kultur waren im Westen natürlich viel handgreiflicher und das ganze griechische Erbe erschien zunächst nahezu ausschließlich im lateinischen Gewande. Der Orient war schließlich römische Provinz gewesen, und selbst Justinian hatte trotz der gewaltigen Problematik des Ostens den Blick immer nach dem Westen gerichtet. Das Imperium Romanum war eben doch nur das ewige Rom, eine Vorstellung der Antike, die das ganze abendländische Mittelalter beherrscht hat, und die in den von den Arabern eroberten Provinzen des Ostens natürlich ohne Bedeutung war. An die Chosroen, nicht an die Cäsaren knüpfte die Staatsidee der Kalifenzeit an. Im Westen war die antike Imperiumidee auf die Kirche wie auf das westliche Kaisertum übergegangen. So war die große Problematik der mittelalterlichen Kämpfe zwischen Papsttum und Kaisertum ein dem Osten unbekanntes Erbteil der Antike.

Auf diesem großen politischen Hintergrunde spielt sich nun die geistesgeschichtliche Auseinandersetzung des Westens mit dem antiken Erbe ab. Die Problematik lag schon von Anbeginn deshalb anders als im Osten, weil das antike Erbe im Okzident durch das Humanitätserlebnis des Römertums hindurchgegangen war. Der Humanismus beginnt nicht erst in der historischen Mitte der Renaissancezeit, sondern die noch unsere heutige Bildungsproblematik bestimmende Humanitas ist nicht nur in ihrer lateinischen Wortform, sondern auch in ihrem Wesen und Sinn eine Prägung der Römer, denen die griechische Bildung als Idee ein ihre eigene Bildung schaffendes, ganz bewußtes Erlebnis geworden war. Humanismus ist, um mich der Worte Werner Jaegers zu bedienen, „der eigentümliche, auf dem Gedanken der reinen Menschenbildung beruhende Kulturbegriff, den die Griechen auf der Höhe ihrer Entwicklung ausgeprägt haben" und zugleich die Kultur- und Bildungssynthese bestimmter Völker mit dem Griechentum, „nicht also eine bloße historische oder kausale Abhängigkeit, sondern die bewußte Idee einer geistigen Durchdringung mit griechischer Kultur, wie sie von den Römern typisch zuerst verwirklicht worden ist".

Es ist wichtig, daß dieser Prozeß bei den Römern vollendet war, ehe die Orientalisierung des späteren Römerreichs einsetzte. Es war damit eine Gesinnung literarisch und lateinisch geworden, die einfach durch ihre literarische Existenz im lateinischen Schrifttum sich auch in der christlichen Zeit erhielt. Man denke nur an Augustin. Vorher und gleichzeitig war spätantikes Gut stark orientalischer Prägung auch in den Westen gedrungen. Charakteristisch für den Grad der Anpassung des Christentums an die antike Welt ist ein Urteil des berühmten Neuplatonikers Porphyrius über den gleichzeitigen, bedeutendsten christlichen Theologen Origenes: „In bezug auf die Ansichten von den Dingen und von der Gottheit dachte er wie ein Grieche." Daß daneben Gegensätze bestanden, wie schon gleich in der Frage nach der Ewigkeit oder dem Erschaffensein der Welt, versteht sich von selbst. Aber in Philosophie, Mythus, Kultus und Frömmigkeit der Christen etwa des 3. Jahrhunderts bestanden so große Ähnlichkeiten mit den spätantiken Vorstellungen und Praktiken, daß das Christentum die alte Welt ganz automatisch ablösen konnte. Damals wäre ein römischer Humanismus nicht mehr möglich gewesen, und dann auch vielleicht die abendländische Entwicklung anders verlaufen. In der Periode, die wir heute betrachten, gehörte die geschilderte Entwicklung zur Vorgeschichte. Wenn sie auch für lange Jahrhunderte nur unter der Decke oder in der Verkleidung der christlichen Gedankenwelt weiterleben konnte, die Idee des Humanismus war aber geboren und sollte zu gegebener Stunde wieder auferstehen.

Diese christliche Gedankenwelt des Mittelalters war nun aber der gleichzeitigen islamischen außerordentlich änlich. In beiden Lagern wurde mit den gleichen Mitteln der antiken, speziell griechischen Dialektik der grandiose Versuch unternommen, den Glauben mit der Vernunft zu bewältigen. Hier wie dort beherrschen Platon und Aristoteles die Diskussion, oft als Gegensätze, häufig völlig mißverstanden und verfälscht; aber der Einfluß der von ihnen angeregten Gedankenwelt ist unverkennbar. In beiden Kulturkreisen das Ringen der Scholastik gegen die Mystik, der kirchlich fixierten Lehre gegen die persönliche Frömmigkeit. Durch jüdische Vermittlungen und Übersetzungen aus dem Arabischen – man denke nur an Maimonides – sogar direkte Beeinflussung. In Ernst Kantorowiczs „Kaiser Friedrich II." findet sich eine sehr lebendige Schilderung dieser Verhältnisse. In dieser Periode zeigt sich das orientalische Produkt des antiken Erbes dem europäischen entschieden überlegen. Jedenfalls ist die ganze

Geisteswelt des Mittelalters ohne das antike Erbe völlig undenkbar. Gewiß läßt sich bei näherem Zusehen auch schon in dieser Periode eine Verschiedenartigkeit der Reaktion nachweisen, wenn wir z. B. Franz von Assisi oder Thomas von Aquin mit entsprechenden Geistesgrößen des Islam vergleichen, aber der sich hier manifestierende Unterschied ist doch nicht so groß wie in der Periode der Renaissance. Auch ist der Strom der antiken Einflüsse, der neben der Scholastik einherläuft, im Abendland erheblich breiter. Die historische Erinnerung an die großen Gestalten der römischen Antike sind hier natürlich ganz anders lebendig als im Osten, während dort vielleicht mehr griechische Profanwissenschaft weiter existierte. Dazu kam, daß das ganze heidnische Schrifttum in lateinischer Sprache ohne weiteres zugänglich war. Wie viel hiervon noch in gebildeten Kreisen lebendig war, zeigt das Nebeneinander christlicher und heidnischer Gestalten in der Divina Commedia, und daß es Virgil war, der zu Dantes Führer erkoren wurde. Das charakteristische der Situation war aber vielleicht doch das Zusammentreffen dieser literarischen Überlieferung mit der Barbarisierung Italiens und der Hinaustragung der christlichen Bildung in völlig jungfräuliches Land ohne Bildungstradition. Die ethnischen, wirtschaftlichen und politischen Grundlagen des Abendlandes standen in einem eklatanten Gegensatz zu der supranaturalistisch-asketischen Tendenz der christlichen Bildung. Geradezu klassisch ist die Schilderung, die Friedrich Paulsen von diesem latenten Spannungsgegensatz entwirft. „So nahmen die Franken und Sachsen die alten heiligen Formeln, die ihnen die Kirche vorsagte, als ihr Bekenntnis an, ohne daß ihre Lebensstimmung und ihr Wille in seiner Grundrichtung dadurch umgewendet worden wäre. Das Mittelalter gleicht einer in die Tracht des Alters gehüllten jugendlichen Gestalt. In der Renaissance kommt die Unangemessenheit zum Bewußtsein. Man entdeckt, daß die supranaturalistisch-asketische Religion des Christentums die eigene Lebensstimmung gar nicht ausdrückt. Und gleichzeitig entdeckt man, daß der Lehrmeister, das Altertum, einmal jung war und damals ganz anders empfand und dachte, als in seinem Greisenalter. Man hatte davon eine abstrakte Kenntnis freilich auch früher gehabt; aber jetzt erst ging das Verständnis dafür auf. Und nun entstand unter den abendländischen Völkern ein wetteiferndes Bemühen, die christlich-supranaturalistischen Formen, wie sie das Mittelalter in der Kunst, in der Literatur, in der Wissenschaft getragen hatte, abzutun und dafür die altklassischen anzulegen." Damit war die Renaissance geboren. Umsonst eifert Savanarola gegen Aristoteles, Plato, Virgil, Horaz und Cicero. Die ganze, in letzter Linie orientalische Heilsidee der Soteria flammt noch einmal auf. Am Schrifttum des römischen Humanismus hatte das Abendland sich selbst gefunden.

Es ist hier nicht der Ort, in die Diskussion über die Entstehung der Renaissance und des Humanismus einzugehen. Seit Jacob Burckhardt wissen wir, daß die Antike nur das Instrument ist, an dem sich der nationale Geist zunächst des italienischen Volkes entzündet. Mit der Besinnung auf sich selbst, mit der Entdeckung des abendländischen Ich fällt das kirchliche Mittelalter, und der Weg wird frei für das neue Europa. Im einzelnen war der Prozeß natürlich sehr kompliziert. Der Flammentod Savanarolas war nur ein Symbol und eine Episode. Die Anfänge liegen weiter zurück. Man hat von einer karolingischen und ottonischen Renaissance gesprochen und mit Recht die Renaissance mit Dantes Sprachschöpfung beginnen lassen. Für unseren Gedankengang ist die entscheidende Frage: Warum ist es nur im Abendland zu einer solchen Entwicklung gekommen?

Die Situation war nämlich im Osten und Westen ziemlich ähnlich. Fürstenhöfe nach Art der der Renaissance hat es im Orient auch gegeben. Die antike Wissenschaft wurde auch dort gepflegt. Lobredende Literaten nach Art der ersten Humanisten haben auch dort gegen Entgelt in prunkenden Reden ihre Brotherren gefeiert. Auch im Orient bestand die Spannung zwischen religiöser Forderung und leichtsinnigem Lebensgenuß. Der Absolutismus herrschte hier wie dort. Und trotzdem eine so ganz andersartige Entwicklung, ein lethargischer Auflösungsprozeß, Versandung, Entartung. Und doch gab es im Zeitalter der Renaissance vielleicht mehr Wissen von antiker Wissenschaft im Orient als im Okzident.

Nach einem Jahrhundert klassischer Philologie und humanistischen Gymnasiums sind wir nur zu geneigt, Humanismus mit Wissenschaft zu verwechseln. Sowohl bei den Römern wie in der Renaissance war der Humanismus aber alles andere als Wissenschaft. In der Römerzeit war er eine Frage der Persönlichkeitskultur und in der Renaissance ein literarisch-poetischer, d. h. ein ästhetischer Protest gegen die philosophisch-wissenschaftlich Schulmeisterei der Hochscholastik. „In diesem Sinne also," sagt Paulsen, „kann man den Humanismus als eine Evolution der ‚unwissenschaftlichen' Bildung des Geistes bezeichnen." Der Weg wurde frei für eine neue Wissenschaft, nachdem man die alten Autoritäten zerschlagen und damit die Herrschaft der Theologie über die Philosophie gebrochen hatte. „Ein zum Poetisch-Phantastischen neigender naturalistischer Pantheismus war die Philosophie der Renaissance.“ Man wurde platonisch statt aristotelisch. Man übernahm von den Arabern die hellenistische Mantik in der Form des Picatrix-Pseudo-Hippokrates bei Agrippa von Nettesheim. Aber das Entscheidende war, daß man sich von der herkömmlichen Meinung über die Dinge zu den Dingen selbst wendete, und daß man die Dinge mit eigenen Augen sah, dilettantisch, subjektiv, aber mit Einfühlungsvermögen und dem Willen zur Wahrheit. Adolf v. Harnack sagt einmal: „Daß Luther die Psalmen, den Apostel Paulus und den Augustin zu lesen vermochte, und daß er sie so gelesen hat, wie er sie las, nämlich ihre Erkenntnisse und ihre Lehren empfindungsvoll fortsetzend und steigernd – das verdankt er nicht nur seinem Genius, sondern auch seinem Zeitalter, nämlich dem Humanismus.“ Deutlicher kann man nicht aussprechen, aus welchen Tiefen der Humanismus emporstieg, und daß er auch Wissenschaft sein konnte, aber in erster Linie eine bewußte geistige Haltung war.

Die ersten Humanisten sind sich der Rolle, die sie in der Geistesgeschichte des Abendlandes spielten, nicht bewußt gewesen. Ihnen war Paideia oder Humanitas noch gleichbedeutend mit Eloquenz. Sie legten auf ihre antikisierende und ästhetisierende Populargelehrsamkeit einen größeren Wert als auf die innerliche Persönlichkeitsäußerung, auf Grund deren wir sie noch heute verehren. Petrarca zum Beispiel hatte kein Interesse für die Verbreitung seiner in der Sprache des Alltags verfaßten Sonette, während er sich als Propagandist antiker Überlieferungen, als Rhetor und Meister der Eloquenz selbst sehr hoch einschätzte. Das historisch Bedeutende des Sängers an Laura war nicht dieses gelehrte Literatentum, sondern die Herausstellung des Menschlich-Persönlichen auf einem anderen Gebiete als der mystischen Seelenkultur, in der sich bisher das Humane ausgelebt hatte. Das Individuum wurde in dem Momente frei, als es aus dem Typismus kirchlich approbierter oder doch geduldeter Gefühlsäußerung herauskam und ungescheut bekannte, was seine Seele erfüllte.

War es wirklich griechischer Geist, was hier durchbrach? Es ist bekannt, wie wenig das Griechische damals bekannt war. Petrarca konnte überhaupt kein Griechisch, aber er begeisterte sich an einem Homerexemplar, das er nicht lesen konnte. Er berichtet selbst, daß damals in Rom kein Mensch Griechisch konnte, in

Florenz drei oder vier und in Bologna einer. Deutschland nahm später den Humanismus sehr viel ernster und natürlich als gelehrte Angelegenheit. Gilt das schon für Erasmus, so besonders für die spätere Entwicklung der nachidealistischen Periode. Unser heutiger Humanismus ist fast rein griechisch eingestellt, und wir empfinden die lateinischen Nachahmungen durchaus als das, was sie sind. Hat der griechische Geist auch in der Verdünnung, in der allein er damals aktiv werden konnte, wirklich das Wunder des Humanismus gewirkt, und warum hat er nicht die gleiche Wirkung im Orient ausgelöst?

Es lag in der historischen, geographischen und ethnischen Situation des Orients, daß ihn von dem Inhalt der griechischen Schriften nur das interessieren konnte, was allgemeine Gültigkeit besaß und zugleich seiner Mentalität entsprach, so vor allem der dialektische Rationalismus. All das, was mehr der griechischen Seele als dem griechischen Intellekt entstammte, so vor allem die griechische Lyrik, die ganze dramatische Literatur, aber auch, was bodenständig griechisch war, die Götterwelt des Homer und die großen griechischen Historiker blieben dem Orient verschlossen, und wenn etwas davon z. B. in der Mantik oder in der Burleske sich in den Orient verirrte, so wurde es ebenso unbarmherzig orientalisiert wie im mittelalterlichen Europa die griechischen und römischen Göttergestalten christianisiert wurden. Aber es war doch ein Unterschied. In Italien blieb die Antike lebendig; gigantische Ruinen zeugten von der Größe der Vergangenheit, und an ihnen entzündet sich das nationale neben dem persönlichen Selbstbewußtsein. Es vollzog sich damals etwas Ähnliches wie heute in Ägypten, wo das erwachende Nationalgefühl der Niltalbewohner auch die Pyramiden und Tempel der Pharaonen gleichsam neu entdeckt. Hier wie dort sind aber die Reste der Vergangenheit nur die Instrumente und Symbole, deren sich der gewandelte Zeitgeist als Manifestation seiner neuen Selbstdarstellung bedient. Denkt man das zu Ende, so bekommt die Burdachsche Renaissancetheorie eine neue Stütze.

Das hellenistische Erbe hatte das ganze Mittelalter in Ost und West gebunden. Wenn die italienischen Humanisten es als Interregnum asiatischer und gotischer Roheit empfanden und unmittelbaren Anschluß an Cicero und Virgil suchten, so vergaßen sie dabei ganz, daß es hellenistischer, d. h. doch auch antiker Geist war, den sie in der mittelalterlichen Kirchlichkeit bekämpften. Der antike Geist hat nicht nur befreit, er hat auch gebunden. Ohne Aristoteles keine Scholastik. Auch das Dogma war doch vielleicht nur das christliche Kind des griechischen Nomos. Was aber jetzt namens der echten Antike gefordert wurde und eintrat, war der prinzipielle Bruch mit der Überlieferung, so sehr auch diese vom Geist der Antike genährt war. Sie mußte in Italien als Selbstbesinnung des italienschen Volkes an das vorchristliche Römertum anknüpfen, und der Feind schlechthin war der hellenistische Aristoteles der Scholastik. Scheinen so die Rollen auf den ersten Blick vertauscht, so war es doch der autonome Geist der echten Paideia, d. h. der griechischen Persönlichkeit, der im verwandten Volkstum sich wehrte gegen die Hypertrophie des in der Wurzel ebenfalls griechischen Rationalismus. Die Persönlichkeit zerbrach die Zwangsjacke einer übersteigerten Form. Und mit diesem Durchbruch der autonomen Persönlichkeit war der Geist geboren, der das moderne Europa aufbauen sollte. Der Orient hat keinen solchen Bruch erlebt. Noch heute kann man beobachten, daß selbst Journalisten mit Schriftbeweis und Vernunftbeweis operieren. Man hat nicht die Möglichkeit gehabt, auf ein ähnliches Schrifttum autonomen Menschentums zurückzugreifen, und man hat auch nicht das blutsmäßige Bedürfnis nach der Schaffung eines solchen verspürt.

Am deutlichsten wird uns der Unterschied zwischen Ost und West vielleicht an der Stellung zur bildenden Kunst. Kann man sich die Geburt des modernen Menschen vorstellen ohne die Kunst der Renaissance? Auch die christliche Kunst hatte schon den Menschen behandelt. Der Orientale hatte sein künstlerisches Bedürfnis in der Architektur und anderen unpersönlichen Künsten erschöpft. In Persien und Indien hat auch unter dem Islam eine feine Miniaturmalerei existiert, aber wie wenig bedeutet sie gegenüber den Schöpfungen eines Michelangelo, Rafael oder Tizian? Die Welt der Statuen bleibt für den Orient immer nur ein Ärgernis oder eine Torheit. Wäre in der orientalischen Seele das gleiche zwingende Bedürfnis wie in der griechischen und abendländischen gewesen, so wäre auch im Orient trotz aller religiösen Vorschriften eine bildende Kunst entstanden. So aber schied dies weite Gebiet völlig aus. Im Abendland wurde die Schönheit der antiken Formenwelt, namentlich auch das Bild des nackten Vollmenschen maßgebend als sinnfälliges und greifbares Vorbild des neu entstehenden Menschenbildes griechischer Herkunft, während im Orient die lebendige Sinnenwelt hinter blassen gedanklichen Abstraktionen zurücktrat oder sich in individuellen, manchmal höchst differenzierten Liebesbeziehungen hellenischer wie hellenistischer

Prägung auslebte. Dem Orient fehlt eben der Eros zur plastischen Darstellung seines Ich sowohl in der bildenden Kunst wie im Drama. Deshalb gibt es im Orient keine Parallele zu der Linie Phidias-Michelangelo-Rodin oder Klinger noch zu der ganz andersartigen von Mantegna bis zu Feuerbach oder der von Aischylos zu Shakespeare, Calderon, Corneille oder Goethe. Ebenso fehlt die Linie, die von Poggio und den Antikensammlungen der Renaissance über die Dilettanti und Winckelmann zur klassischen Archäologie der Gegenwart führt. Es fehlen die entsprechenden literarischen wie musikalischen Repräsentanten; es fehlt auch die Wiederentdeckung des Körpers vom Turnvater Jahn bis zum modernen Stadion. Dem gegenüber hat der Orient die mittelalterliche Geisteshaltung bis mitten in die Neuzeit hinein weiter bewahrt und steht nun vor der Frage, ob man die moderne Geisteswelt realiter übernehmen kann, ohne sie human innerlich zu bewältigen.

Im Abendland hat man – und das war das Verdienst der gelehrten Forschung – auf die Dauer immer deutlicher die griechische Bildungsidee von allen Verkleidungen und Schlacken der Römerzeit und des Mittelalters befreit und sich freudig zu ihrer Einmaligkeit oder doch Erstmaligkeit bekannt. Auch haben alte Kulturvölker Europas die Kultursynthese mit dem Griechentum oder der gesamten Antike vollzogen, wie sie Werner Jaeger formuliert hat. Daß diese Synthese bei den romanischen Völkern sich mehr an das Lateinische hielt, bei den germanischen aber auf die Dauer immer stärker an das Griechische anknüpfte, erklärt sich aus historischen Gegebenheiten oder Spannungen. Dabei war das Entscheidende nicht die gelehrte Tradition, sondern die menschliche Kongenialität der geistigen Führerpersönlichkeiten des Abendlandes mit den Begründern der griechischen Paideia und des römischen Staatsgedankens, der sich mit der griechischen Paideia auf die Dauer immer mehr verschwisterte. Gewiß ist Shakespeares Julius Cäsar nicht ohne Plutarchstudien entstanden und von einer humanistischen Bühnenkonvention beeinflußt; aber Shakespeares Wirkung stammt doch aus einer schöpferischen Persönlichkeit, die in die gleiche Ebene und damit in einen über allem Humanismus stehenden inneren Zusammenhang mit den großen Dramatikern Griechenlands gehört. In die gleiche Linie gehört Goethe, den seine mangelhafte Kenntnis des Griechischen nicht verhinderte, ein echter Grieche zu sein, nicht weil er in antiker Tradition gelebt hat, sondern weil auch er naturnotwendig die griechische Paideia verlebendigte.

Gewiß tat er es in anderer Weise als die großen Franzosen, die, ihrem Nationalcharakter entsprechend, mehr das Formale betonten. Und wenn Goethe auch sagt, daß eher ein Marquis den Alcibiades nachahmen könnte als Corneille den Sophokles, so kann doch nicht geleugnet werden, daß auch die Franzosen über die Antike den Weg zu sich selber gefunden haben.

Der Weg des Humanismus ist, wie schon der Name sagt, der Weg über das Menschliche, das Persönliche. In Deutschland haben gelehrter und intuitiver Humanismus einander abgewechselt. Aber in allen Krisenzeiten unserer Bildungsgeschichte haben wir uns am Altertum orientiert. Es hat Zeiten gegeben, in denen die klassische Philologie Gefahr lief, die Rolle der Scholastik gegenüber einem neu aufsteigenden Humanismus zu übernehmen. Der Humanismus darf auch nie zu einer rein gelehrten Angelegenheit werden; denn dann könnten höchste Menschheitswerte hinter dem Dorngestrüpp der Schulweisheit verloren gehen. Wenn manche Kreise unserer Tage glauben, daß die griechische Paideia als reine Menschenbildung ebenso gut ohne fremde Sprachkenntnisse geübt werden könne wie einst von den Griechen selbst, andere dagegen die Unerläßlichkeit einer exakten philologischen Schulung betonen, so steht hinter beiden gleichmäßig die humanistische Idee. Der Unterschied liegt darin, daß die einen die Segnungen des antiken Erbes auch für breiteste Kreise zugänglich machen wollen, während die anderen das notwendig Aristokratische der humanistischen Bildung erkennen und wollen. Gerade unsere heutige Betrachtung hat uns gelehrt, daß ganze Völker, wie z. B. die Orientalen nicht die Kraft zu haben scheinen, den Weg der Griechen zu wandeln. Sollten darum alle Angehörigen der begnadeten Völker geborene Griechen sein? wobei noch immer vergessen wird, daß auch in Griechenland die Paideia eine durchaus aristokratische Angelegenheit war. Aber soll man deshalb die Übermittlung an alle unversucht lassen? Jedenfalls ist die Paideia auch uns aufgegeben.

Deutschland hat in seiner Bildungsgeschichte bereits zweimal den Humanismus aus einer zu lebenden in eine gelehrte Angelegenheit verwandelt. Der vollmenschliche Typus des italienischen Humanismus ist in Deutschland unter dem Einfluß der religiösen Innerlichkeit des Protestantismus zu einem Problem der Studierstube geworden – für einen Holbein gab's in Deutschland keine Wirkungsmöglichkeit –, und der zweite Humanismus der Lessing, Goethe, Winckelmann und Humboldt ist mit dem Aufkommen des wirtschaftlichen Zeitalters und der

Industrialisierung zu einer Angelegenheit von Professoren und Oberlehrern geworden, während z. B. im doch gewiß nicht weltfremden England der Humanismus die geistige Atmosphäre der Aristokratie und der Staatsmänner war; Oxford und Cambridge haben bildungsgeschichtlich keine Parallele in Deutschland. Zum drittenmal wird uns in der Gegenwart eine Chance geboten. Eros, Kairos, Weihe und Schönheit sind wieder Brennpunkte der geistigen Bewegung unserer Zeit. Neben dem George-Kreis erscheint der mehr philologisch orientierte Mitarbeiterkreis der Zeitschrift „Die Antike". Wenn in der Gegenwart abermals ein Kampf um das Platonbild unserer Tage entbrannt ist, so geht es dabei um mehr als um die Deutung eines griechischen Philosophen. In einer Zeit, die Wirtschaft und Technik mit Recht bejaht, geht es hier um den Menschen. Der Mensch aber bleibt heute mehr als je das Maß aller Dinge. Auch der Realismus hat nur dann Bildungswert, wenn er humanistisch betrieben wird. Es ist nicht nur eine Erkenntnis, die sich als Resultat unserer heutigen Betrachtung ergibt, es ist auch eine Verantwortung, wie Goethe es in „Philostrats Gemälde" so unvergleichlich formuliert hat:

> Jeder sei auf seine Art ein Grieche,
> Aber er sei's.

Anmerkungen

Es ist unmöglich, alle die Werke aufzuzählen, deren Studium sich in den Ausführungen dieses Vortrages auswirkt. Ich beschränke mich deshalb auf den Nachweis direkter Zitate. Meine eigenen Vorarbeiten sind zusammengefaßt in meinen *Islamstudien* Bd. I Leipzig 1924; Bd. II ist nahezu fertig gedruckt und wird noch in diesem Jahre erscheinen. Die Grundthese dieses Vortrages habe ich in *Islamstudien* Bd. I S. 34 ausgesprochen; hier sollte sie ausführlicher begründet werden.

S. 572, Z. 26: *Die Antike*, Bd. IV S. 226 ff; vgl. auch SCHAEDERS ausgezeichnete Studie *Das Individuum im Islam* in BRUGSCH-LEWY, *Die Biologie der Person* S. 913 ff.

S. 575, Z. 29: H. S. NYBERG, *Zum Kampf zwischen Islam und Manichäismus. Orient. Lit. Zeitung* Bd. 32 (1929) Sp. 425 ff.

S. 575. Z. 35: LOUIS MASSIGNON, *La Passion d'al-Hosayn-ibn-Mansour al-Hallaj, martyre mystique de l'Islam*, Bd. I S. 177. Über das Verhältnis zwischen Gnosis und Islam vgl. TOR ANDRAE, *Die person Muhammeds in lehre und glauben seiner gemeinde* 1917 (*Archives d'Études Orientales* Bd. 16) und von dem gleichen Autor *Der Ursprung des Islams und das Christentum*, Uppsala 1926.

S. 576, Z. 15: PAUL KRAUS, *Der Zusammenbruch der Dschābir-Legende* im dritten Jahresbericht des Forschungs-Instituts für Geschichte der Naturwissenschaften in Berlin, 1930.
S. 577, Z. 22 ff: Nach TOR ANDRAE; daß bei Einführung der Maulidfeiern auch christliche Einflüsse mitgewirkt haben, scheint mir sicher.
S. 578, Z. 31: *Islamstudien*, Bd. I S. 234.
S. 579, Z. 8 ff: Ich begrüße freudig G. BERGSTRÄSSERS Ausführungen in seiner Besprechung von SANTILLANA's *Istituzioni di diritto malichita* in *Orient. Lit.-Zeitung* 1929, S. 277 ff.
S. 580, Z. 21: Ein Anfang in dieser Richtung MARTIN PLESSNER, *Des Oikonomikos des Neupythagoraers ‚Bryson'*, Heidelberg 1928 (*Orient und Antike* Bd. 5).
S. 581, Z. 9 ff: Der Orient kennt kein Humanitätserlebnis. Das muß ausdrücklich festgestellt werden gegenüber dem Mißbrauch des Begriffs Humanismus in dem sonst nicht unverdienstlichen Buche von Dr. M. KAMIL AYAD, *Die Geschichts-Gesellschaftslehre Ibn Haldūns* (BREYSIGS *Forschungen zur Geschichts- und Gesellschaftslehre*) 1930, S. 32. Auch der Titel des bis auf diesen Titel geradezu glänzenden Werkes von A. MEZ, *Die Renaissance des Islâms*, Heidelberg 1912, ist irreführend.
S. 581, Z. 27: Jetzt *Islamstudien* Bd. I S. 386.
S. 582, Z. 26 ff: Gedacht ist an die Arbeiten NORDENS und JAEGERS; vgl. z. B. WERNER JAEGER, *Antike und Humanismus*, S. 12 und *Der Humanismus als Tradition und Erlebnis* in *Vom Altertum zur Gegenwart*, Leipzig 1919.
S. 583, Z. 8: VON HARNACK, *Aus der Friedens- und Kriegsarbeit*, S. 49.
S. 584, Z. 25: *Geschichte des gelehrten Unterrichts*, 3. Aufl. Bd. I S. 9.
S. 585, Z. 40: Bd. I S. 75.
S. 586, Z. 6: HELLMUT RITTER, *Picatrix, ein arabisches Handbuch hellenistischer Magie*, Studien der Bibliothek Warburg, Bd. I S. 1 ff.
S. 586, Z. 11: *Erforschtes und Erlebtes*, S. 99.
S. 586, Z. 39: PAULSEN, Bd. I S. 70.
S. 587, Z. 33: Einen guten Überblick und Literaturnachweise gibt PROF. DR. BURDACH, *Deutsche Renaissance*, Berlin 1906 (Deutsche Abende im Zentral-Institut für Erziehung und Unterricht Nr. 4).
S. 589, Z. 33: GUNDOLF, *Caesar*, S. 175.
S. 590, Z. 3: *Zum Schäkespears Tag*, Jubil.-Ausg. Bd. 36 S. 4.
S. 591, Z. 7: GUNDOLF, *George*, S. 43.
S. 591, Z. 11: KURT HILDEBRANDT, *Das neue Platon-Bild* in *Blätter für deutsche Philosophie*, Bd. IV (1930) S. 190.
S. 591, Z. 19: Jubil.-Ausg. Bd. 35 S. 129.

For Product Safety Concerns and Information please contact our EU representative GPSR@taylorandfrancis.com
Taylor & Francis Verlag GmbH, Kaufingerstraße 24, 80331 München, Germany

www.ingramcontent.com/pod-product-compliance
Lightning Source LLC
Chambersburg PA
CBHW060546280326
41932CB00011B/1412
9780415510646